COCHITI

COCHITI

A NEW MEXICO PUEBLO,

PAST AND PRESENT

CHARLES H. LANGE

UNIVERSITY OF NEW MEXICO PRESS

Albuquerque

Library of Congress Cataloging-in-Publication Data

Lange, Charles H.
    Cochiti : a New Mexico Pueblo : past and present /
    Charles H. Lange.
        p.   cm.
    Originally published: 1959.
    Includes bibliographical references.
    ISBN 0–8263–1188–1
    1. Cochiti Indians—Social life and customs.
2. Cochiti Pueblo (N.M.)—Social life and customs.
3. New Mexico—Social life and customs.   I. Title.
E99.C84L3   1990   89–29200
978.9′004975—dc20   CIP

TABLE OF CONTENTS

CHAPTERS

Topography, 3
Geology, Terrain, and Soils, 4
Climate and Life Zones, 4

Prehistory, 7

History, 8
*Spanish Exploration Period, 1540–1598, 8; Spanish
Colonial Period: Seventeenth Century, 9; Spanish
Colonial Period: Eighteenth Century, 10; Mexican
Colonial Period: 1820–1846, 11; American Period:
1846——, 12*

Long-term Non-Indian Cultural Impacts, 13
*The Spanish-American Residents and Neighbors,
14; The Roman Catholic Church, 20; The United
States Government, 25; Other Neighbors, Friends,
Tourists, and Anthropologists, 33*

LIST OF FIGURES

MAP

LIST OF PLATES
(Following page 296)

PREFACE

The subtitle, "A New Mexico Pueblo, Past and Present," states the basic aim of this monograph which, in effect, is the combination of two fundamental approaches of anthropology to the study of culture. It portrays the way of life of present-day Cochití Indians in the kind of community study that is commonly used in social anthropology; data are discussed in the present tense (or in terms of "today," "present-day," etc.) for instances typical of the period of the study, 1946–1953, and which may be expected to carry on into the immediate future. Specific events within this period of field work have been dated more or less precisely. At the same time, the monograph reveals, wherever possible, antecedents for the present in the manner of historical ethnography.

Although these two approaches have frequently resulted in distinct reports, I believe that the optimum presentation for the ultimate understanding of a culture, such as that of Cochití Pueblo, can be achieved only by this merging of data. Although this leads to a more lengthy (and hence more costly) publication, the benefits from the more complete time perspective outweigh any other consideration.

In general, comparative data have been held to a minimum. However, an occasional attempt has been made to place the people of Cochití and their culture in the context of various Indian pueblos and non-Indian communities of the middle Rio Grande Valley of New Mexico.

Although a fairly complete and balanced coverage has been attempted, there are numerous phases that remain inadequately presented insofar as certain specialists are concerned. Other phases, beyond my present capacity, have been virtually ignored. These are the recognized handicaps of any investigator who works alone; however, for a number of reasons such an approach has thus far been most feasible. It is hoped that future research by collaborating or independent specialists and advanced students will expand the scope and enrich the present data.

Although many monographs consist largely of the author's original contribution, sometimes to the complete exclusion of the findings of earlier writers, this study includes considerable data from accounts published earlier in order to achieve greater depth in time perspective and wealth of detail. Also, certain points in the earlier accounts need correction, elaboration, or clarification if an accurate picture of Cochití culture is to be obtained. It would seem that any monograph such as this bears the responsibility of appraising preceding studies and bringing the total mass of data up to date whenever this is necessary or possible.

Use was made of Cochití monographs and papers by Father Noël Dumarest, Frederick Starr, Esther S. Goldfrank, Ruth Benedict, and the Cochití material included in Volume XVI of *The North American Indian*, edited by Edward S. Curtis. Of a less precise nature, but nevertheless of value, were descriptions from such earlier observers as Adolph F. Bandelier, John G. Bourke, Carl and Lillian Eickemeyer, and Charles F. Lummis. Important Keresan material for comparative purposes came from numerous papers of Leslie A. White, Elsie Clews Parsons, and others.

Unpublished material regarding social organization and the life cycle was obtained from records of the Franciscan Fathers at Peña Blanca. These data extended back to 1870, before the birth of any Cochití living in 1952. Modern economic, educational, and health data were obtained from the United Pueblos Agency, Albuquerque Regional Office, United States Indian Service. From collections of the School of American Research and the Museum of New Mexico, Santa Fe, came many photographs ranging in date from 1880 to 1920. These were of great assistance in refreshing the minds of informants regarding village layout, house construction, people, and events of this period. From the archives of the same institution, the unpublished journals of Adolph F. Bandelier for the years 1880–1892 provided valuable data of a specific nature often lacking in Bandelier's published works and were important in providing considerable time depth for modern phenomena. Unpublished material of Frederick Starr in the Newberry Library, Chicago, and in the archives, University of Chicago Library, was similarly important.

Further data were gleaned from a collection of Starr photographs of a half-century ago, now in the Museum of the American Indian, Heye Foundation, New York; from a number of Vroman and other photographs in the files of the Bureau of American Ethnology, Washington; and miscellaneous photographs in the Southwest Museum, Los Angeles. Data for the 1920's were obtained from manuscripts and notes of Franz Boas and notes and photographs of Elsie Clews Parsons, all now in the library of the American Philosophical Society, Philadelphia. Additional perspective was gained from the collections in the Denver Art Museum, Denver.

Despite the imposing body of new information compiled from the above-named sources, the greatest amount came directly from the Cochití themselves.

Field procedure is described below with several groups of readers in mind. One comprises those interested in evaluating personally the validity of new ethnographic data; another, those interested in benefiting from it in their own field experiences; and a third consists of readers from Cochití Pueblo, who will find their own culture recorded and analyzed.

A village of three or four hundred individuals is a relatively small community. In such a society, gossip, politics, and similar activities play important roles. Despite the impression often gained by a stranger, pueblos, like other communities, are commonly split into many factions, arising from the innumerable and often unpredictable events of daily life. (Bandelier, after a few weeks' residence at Cochití, recorded in his journal of November 21, 1880, "There is much jealousy about me in the pueblo.") The ethnographer must be aware of these factions and their implications. They provide data on the actual functioning and interplay of cultural patterns. If ignored or misjudged, an offended faction may easily cause the ousting of an ethnographer from the community, with potentially damaging repercussions to others of his profession, as the factions momentarily unite against the intruder.

Published accounts revealed society memberships, kinship groups, and other personnel data which, though incomplete and somewhat obsolete, provided insight regarding possible factions in the economic, social, ceremonial, and political life.

A major group at Cochití is called "Conservative," a term which refers to those who believe in the supernatural powers of the cacique, in the supernatural knowledge and powers of the medicine men, and in the authority of the war captains. This group is in contrast to the "Progressives," who obey only the governors, the *fiscales,* and the Council of *Principales,* except for certain matters assigned by the council to the jurisdiction of the war captains. Informants were selected partly at random, especially in earlier phases of the field work, and partly with the conscious intention of sampling as many Cochití viewpoints as possible. Members of one society have attitudes which differ from those of another society's members and from those of nonsociety members; those who have established residence away from the pueblo vary in views from those who have remained at home; ex-servicemen constitute another group, though not as distinctly demarcated at Cochití as was once anticipated; different viewpoints also occur between the sexes and within different age groups of each sex. During the course of field work, more than forty Cochití served as what might be termed "major" informants. In addition, all resident and some nonresident men became known by sight and name, as did most women. Not as wide an acquaintance was achieved among the children.

In time, informants were found who were both willing and able to help with the project. Contacts with others of less value as informants were maintained, partly to eliminate jealousies and other forms of antagonism. To reduce the possibility of revealing the identities of those who did serve as informants and to obscure the source of certain data so far as other Cochití were concerned, obvious relationships were fostered with several individuals despite their continued refusal to act as informants. In the course of even such superficial relationships, chance remarks, often miscellaneous but occasionally of real significance, were obtained. These same contacts may also bear fruit in the future as attitudes change regarding what information is esoteric when aliens are concerned.

The interpretation of esoteric, or "secret," ranged greatly from one person to another. Very little was obtained that the author considered in this category; much was obtained that would be so considered by at least some Cochití in reference to an outsider. It was revealing to learn that the concept of "secret" among the Cochití themselves ranged beyond the expected society and nonsociety lines. Such events as the Spring Dance used to be open to the public, but since 1947 they have been witnessed only by the so-called Conservatives—the Progressives being barred along with Spanish-Americans, Anglos, and non-Cochití Indians. Ka'tsína dances, in the kivas, certain large homes, or at secluded spots in the hills northwest of the pueblo or along the river, can be seen by Conservatives, whether they are from Cochití or another tribe, whereas all others are banned. Some Conservatives stated that this practice is not an actual ban on the attendance of the Progressives; if anything like that exists, it is self-imposed by the Progressives. Others insisted that the Progressives have forfeited any right to attend ka'tsína performances.

It is readily apparent that this monograph employs spellings which vary from those used in earlier publications relating to Cochití. This applies both to writings of others and to my own. In earlier papers, I tended to use spellings commonly employed in the literature. However, in this volume, intended as a relatively comprehensive summary of Cochití culture, a more precise recording of terms such as *Ku-sha'lī, Kwe'rana, ka'tsína,* and others, seemed preferable to perpetuating certain inaccuracies now in the literature. Although linguists may find still other terms that need correction, it is hoped that the great majority of those used here are accurate reproductions of present-day Cochití pronunciations.

In the recording of native terms, the following phonetic symbols have been employed:

Vowels:

a as in father	o as in note
e as in met	u as in hut
ē as in prey	ū as in rule
i as in pin	ai as in aisle
ī as in machine	au as in kraut

Consonants:

ñ as Spanish ñ

d and t vary in the same word spoken by different informants, with a tendency for either to be somewhat explosive.

r and l tend to be blended, with some speakers emphasizing one or the other value, whereas others actually used a fused r and l

Accent:

Slighted enunciation has been indicated by exponent position, e.g., pī'hī[a]. Accent, whether indicated by a stress mark or not, commonly falls on the first syllable.

At this point I wish to call attention to the fact that the key to phonetic symbols in Appendix 43, "Cochiti Choreographies and Songs," contributed by Dr. Gertrude P. Kurath, and the key in Appendix 44, "A Note on Cochiti Linguistics," contributed by Mr. J. R. Fox, differ from my own and from each other. The explanation for having three keys under one cover is that each author collected his data in the field with no thought of collaboration and each used what seemed most appropriate under the circumstances. It has seemed wisest to me to keep each system intact rather to risk certain inaccuracies that would almost inevitably result from change.

Generally information was recorded openly. Informants usually displayed an interest in having their material recorded accurately rather than showing any hesitancy when confronted by pen and paper. Resentment concerning prior publications appeared more often to be caused by inaccuracies than by the mere fact of publication. (In this respect, it is sincerely hoped that the errors inevitable in a monograph of this length will be few and of minor importance.)

During the months I lived in the pueblo—twelve weeks in the summer of 1947, five in the summer of 1948, and six in the summer of 1951—participating and nonparticipating techniques of observation were both employed. (As recently as 1942, White, in his report on Santa Ana Pueblo [1942: 9], noted the impossibility of living in most of the Eastern pueblo villages or conducting ethnographic investigations within the pueblo confines.) Questions regarding details were sometimes asked and answered on the spot. In other instances, points were clarified later in informal conversations or in regular interview sessions.

Identical items were checked with various informants in order to cover a full range of opinion and to obtain additional details. Identical items were also discussed with the same person on different occasions to check accuracy and to expand certain details which had been intentionally or unintentionally omitted or obscured. Discrepancies were closely analyzed for varying behavior patterns, or indications of misinformation. In these instances, actually quite rare, attempts were made to ascertain the motives involved.

Co-operation of individual informants varied. Several voiced their appreciation of having data recorded before they were forgotten. For some, this meant a willingness to help to the limit of their ability. Perhaps the outstanding example of this viewpoint was the voluntary offer to have the data on ka'tsīnas placed in a permanent record so that available details would be saved for future generations of Cochití. Such a view on this highly esoteric subject was held by not one but several. It is also of interest that this view was held by actual participants in the Ka'tsīna Cult and not, as might be expected, by those who no longer followed this pattern of belief. Others, while expressing an equal sympathy for the project, lacked precise information or were unwilling to risk collaboration. In this matter, the fear of collaboration was much less related to experiences with earlier ethnographers than it was to a suspicion that the writer might be doing "stories" like one published in *Family Circle* (October, 1947, by Mary Sutherland), which was strongly resented by some Cochití for certain statements that they considered untrue or that they believed placed the tribe in an unfavorable position.

Some information was obtained in the presence of family, or other, groups. However, most information came from private interviews, where the informant was encouraged to withhold an answer or explanation rather than improvise. This approach proved highly satisfactory and resulted in a minimum of prevarication. At their unanimous request, informants were guaranteed anonymity for their individual protection and, equally important, for their peace of mind. Payment was made to informants for the time they spent in helping, not, it was stressed, for the type of information derived from them. In this regard, an entry in Starr's diary for September 26, 1897, is of interest:

Juan now impressed upon me the danger he ran, begging me not to show anyone the pictures or to say that we saw any pinturas. He says that yesterday *Antonio* went to the cacique and told him that *he* was taking us to see sacred paintings and not only so but at half the price that we paid *him* for showing us only the old ruins. Juan said in case it was known he would be punished and his office taken away; he would be put out of the tribe and then he was "lost."

Informants' data should be taken as true for the period 1946–1952 unless specified otherwise. A brief visit in the summer of 1957 and a season of field work in the summer of 1958 revealed data that have particular relevance for some subjects discussed in this monograph. Although there has been no attempt to correlate all data obtained during this period with the entire study, several statements have been added when it seemed they would be valuable in rounding out the picture of culture change.

Where widespread agreement was found among the Cochití, no specific designation of informants has been indicated. Elsewhere, numbers within brackets represent specific informants who supplied the information. Although an appreciable portion of the phenomena herein described was personally observed, there were many details learned solely from informants. For the sake of brevity, comments to this effect have not always been included in the account.

While the reaction of the Cochití to the appearance of these data in printed form cannot be fully predicted, it is hoped that the prevailing opinion in the course of years will be sympathetic. If so, repeated visits to Cochití Pueblo may be anticipated. Thus, more complete data will be gathered, errors will be corrected, and additional views on controversial points will be gained; also, an accurate account of the nature and degree of both cultural change and stability can be recorded. Only by such continued research over a considerable span of time can our knowledge of specific cultures and cultural processes achieve the fullness required as reliable bases for comparative analyses.

ACKNOWLEDGMENTS

Sincere appreciation is expressed first to the numerous Cochití Indians whose co-operation and interest have made this study possible. For reasons understood best by those who have engaged in ethnographic work among the Pueblo Indians, these individuals are thanked collectively and without specific designation. In preparing the original body of data for use as a dissertation, I received valuable assistance from my committee: Dr. W. W. Hill, chairman, Dr. Edward F. Castetter, and Dr. France V. Scholes, University of New Mexico. After additional field work and further research, a later and more detailed manuscript was critically read by Dr. Hill, Dr. Fred Eggan, and Dr. Leslie A. White. Appreciation is expressed to each of these men for his willingness to accept a task of such proportions. Their commentaries and queries have made important contributions to the final manuscript. The interest and assistance of Dr. Esther S. Goldfrank have been both helpful and gratifying. The appendices contributed by Dr. Gertrude P. Kurath, "Cochiti Choreographies and Songs," and Mr. J. R. Fox, "Cochiti Linguistic Notes," respectively, have enabled me to present, under one cover, data that would otherwise have been omitted.

This research, extending over a considerable span of years, has involved the assistance of numerous other individuals in a variety of capacities. Sincere gratitude is expressed to each of the following: Miss Eleanor B. Adams, Dr. Arthur J. O. Anderson, Dr. Frank G. Anderson, Dr. Wilfrid C. Bailey, Dr. Donald D. Brand, Mr. Carroll A. Burroughs, Dr. Winfred Buskirk, Dr. Thomas N. Campbell, Mrs. Dorothy Batey Cassidy, Dr. Carlos E. Castañeda,* Mr. Kenneth M. Chapman, Father Angelico Chávez, O.F.M., Dr. Stephen E. Clabaugh, The Rt. Rev. John M. Cooper,* Dr. Herbert W. Dick, Mr. Dewey Dismuke, Dr. Howard J. Dittmer, Mr. John Dolzadelli, Dr. Frederic H. Douglas,* Dr. Edward Dozier, Dr. Bertha P. Dutton, Dr. Florence Hawley Ellis, Mr. Albert G. Ely, Dr. George C. M. Enger-

* Deceased.

rand, Miss Dorothy Field, T/Sgt. Claude E. Fullerton, Mrs. Lois Olivard Fussill, Father Titus Gehring, O.F.M., Dr. T. H. Goodspeed, Mr. Eric Hagberg, Father Julian Hartig, O.F.M., Father Gerónimo Hesse, O.F.M., Mr. Volney H. Jones, Dr. J. Charles Kelley, Dr. Alex D. Krieger, Mr. Peter Kunstadter, Father Anthony Kroger, O.F.M., Mr. Ralph Loken, Dr. J. Gilbert McAllister, Father Theodosius Meyer, O.F.M., Dr. W. W. Newcomb, Jr., Dr. Stanley Newman, Mr. Charles Payne, Dr. Paul Reiter,* Dr. Frank H. H. Roberts, Jr., Mr. William Rose, Dr. James S. Slotkin,* Dr. Leslie Spier, Mr. Hal Story, Mr. Stanley Stubbs,* Mrs. Nancy Patterson Troike, and Mr. James W. Young.

Grateful acknowledgment is expressed to the members of the Executive Committee of the Institute of Latin American Studies of the University of Texas and the directors, Dr. Charles W. Hackett* and Dr. Lewis U. Hanke, for grants-in-aid for field research in the summers of 1951 and 1952. This assistance made possible the gathering of additional data and permitted the clarification of certain points in the material included earlier in a doctoral dissertation, "An Evaluation of Economic Factors in Cochiti Pueblo Culture Change," unpublished manuscript placed in the Library of the University of New Mexico in December, 1950. I also wish to thank the University of Texas Research Institute for a grant which greatly facilitated the completion of the final manuscript during the 1953/54 academic year.

The assistance of all those mentioned above might well have fallen short of the final goal of publication had it not been for the generous support of the Bollingen Foundation.

Since joining the faculty of Southern Illinois University in September, 1955, it has been most gratifying to receive the wholehearted interest and support of the Research Council and various administrators in the completion of this book and in continuing research in other phases of Cochití culture history.

Finally, my deepest gratitude is expressed to my family for their continued interest and assistance through the years of this research. This is especially due my wife, Elizabeth March Lange; her collaboration in the field, in research, and throughout the preparation of the several drafts of this manuscript has contributed immeasurably.

                                                    CHARLES H. LANGE
Carbondale, Illinois

INTRODUCTION

Since the period of field research for this volume (1946–1953) and the subsequent published editions of this study (University of Texas Press [1959] and Southern Illinois University Press [1968], the Indians of Cochití Pueblo, New Mexico, have experienced numerous changes—some of rather far-reaching consequences.

My formal fieldwork among the Cochití people stopped after the 1953 season. However, numerous visits to the pueblo have taken place over the intervening thirty-five years; these contacts have made it possible to keep up-to-date to some degree at least. This has been particularly true in more recent years following my retirement from Northern Illinois University–DeKalb in 1980 and our subsequent move to Santa Fe in the late summer of that year.

Since then, being only thirty miles away, the more frequent visits have enabled me, and my family as well as friends, to renew and maintain earlier relationships. An unfailing cordial hospitality has been extended whenever I, alone, or with family or friends, visit the village and various homes. In the course of these visits, from both conversation and observation, a steady stream of changes in the Cochití way of life has been all too apparent. Some changes have come in past years with the ramifications and repercussions in the culture still being felt. Other changes have been of a far more subtle nature, at times barely perceptible, if at all, even to the Cochití people themselves.

As this new edition is being prepared, it seems appropriate that some of the more significant of such changes be noted in this Introduction. These developments have been, or still can be, seen by anyone who familiarizes himself with any of the present-day Pueblo Indian tribes. The Cochití Indians, like most Indians in the neighboring pueblos, are undergoing a process of acculturation which has tended to blur their "Indianness"; at the same time, there has been a surprising degree of retention and to some extent a revival of their cultural uniqueness—a distinctiveness in which the Cochití take considerable and increasing pride.

In the great majority of cases, it is difficult to assign primary and secondary roles to the changes; many occurred more or less simultaneously, with one pushing another along the way. It does seem safe to give a certain prominence to the impact of the World War II years upon Cochití culture. In the case of World War I, a number of the Cochití became involved, most commonly in war industries rather than military service or actual combat. In World War II, this situation changed quite dramatically. Cochití Indians were involved in various services and in theaters of operations virtually the world around. There were a number of fatalities; there are living in Cochití and participating in much of the culture today veterans of Bataan and Japanese prison camps, servicemen who saw action in North Africa, Europe, and flying the Hump in the Far East.

In the years immediately following the return of these individuals, there were problems in the community as they reentered their culture. Today, any number of these people have assumed leadership roles—both in the political structure of the tribe and in ceremonial functions, including membership in the secret, or medicine, societies. Several of the returning veterans took advantage of various GI training and educational programs, with a distinct benefit to themselves and to their community.

The same patterns have persisted through the Korean and Vietnam war years. With or without veterans benefits, more and more Cochití are taking advantage of post–high school training and also going to colleges or universities or professional/vocational schools and more and more of them are finishing their course programs. Having done this, however, it has become something of a problem to find employment reflecting such training, either in the pueblo or even in nearby communities.

When these young people are forced to leave the area, tribal affairs are affected adversely. The Cochití tribe needs as many of its members as possible in the community in order to carry out ceremonial roles, civic offices and responsibilities, and social functions. As the young people have left the village in increasing numbers in recent years, they make more and more contacts with outsiders that often lead to marriage. When this happens with someone from one of the nearby Keresan-speaking Pueblos, there is a better chance that they will retain contact with Cochití and also that when children enter the scene, there is a greater chance of their learning the native language. The native language is fundamental to the perpetuation of the rich tribal ceremonial lore. Without the native language, the rituals cannot be carried on. When the parents only share English as a language, the children rarely learn either of the parental tongues.

At present, there is a reasonably comfortable accommodation between the native rituals and ceremonialism and Roman Catholicism. In times past, by way of contrast, the interrelationship was often one of confrontation between the religious hierarchy and civic leaders and the priests.

Probably the event that has weighed most heavily upon Cochití culture was the agreement reached in the early 1960s by tribal leaders, the Indian Service, and outside land developers. This was the sequel of an earlier decision whereby the U.S. Army Corps of Engineers would construct a new and much larger dam across the Rio Grande a few miles north of the pueblo and on Cochití Reservation land. This was originally aimed at improving flood control and providing a more reliable supply of irrigation water for the Cochití agricultural fields, as well as fields of downstream Indian Pueblos and Hispanic communities. In rather short order, however, the project was expanded to include a new town, Cochití Lake, and recreational facilities such as a golf course, marinas, and picnic/campgrounds. These developments were to take place along the northern border of the Cochití Reservation, west of the river, on 7,500 acres leased to the developers for an initial period of ninety-nine years. The Cochití were to receive periodic payments from the lease, royalties on the concessions, and precedence over non-Cochití in employment opportunities.

In addition to the preparations for construction of the dam, preliminary surveys were conducted in the area and archaeological salvage excavations were made for several seasons within the general site of the new dam, the barrow pits, and other construction areas.

On December 12, 1965, at the Cochití Dam Lease Signing Ceremony, the Cochití Governor, Fred Cordero, included these remarks in his statement on that occasion:

We shall continue to grow our crops, to have our Sacred Ceremonials . . . but gradually change will come. Today we take a great step forward into an experience that is new and strange to us. We want it to be a benefit to others as well as ourselves.

Unfortunately, this expression of optimism was not to materialize. A year after the dam was completed in 1975, the Pueblo began to report damage from the rising water table. Experiencing a series of years of unusually heavy snows and rains, storage behind the dam steadily expanded. Despite complaints from the Cochití as the seepage increased, it was not until 1988, two years after the Pueblo of Cochití had filed a lawsuit and under some congressional pressure, did the engineers admit that the dam was causing a problem. As of 1988, engineering consultants for the tribe noted that 615 acres of farmland and 250 acres of the adjacent bosque were waterlogged and useless for traditional agricultural purposes. As of this time, a satisfactory settlement is still in the offing. In the meantime, farming—a fundamental ingredient in Cochití ceremonialism—has been virtually eliminated from the tribal economy.

Reflecting the optimism expressed initially, there was an upswing in various aspects of Cochití life. A HUD program resulted in a number of new homes constructed on the northern and western edges of the village. These were flat-roofed "Santa Fe style" in some cases, and pitch-roofed ranch style in others. All were equipped with modern kitchens and bathrooms made possible by the construction of a sewage system—a system that enabled the older houses in the middle of the pueblo to be modernized as well.

Along with these improvements, the Cochití people have enjoyed better health and health care—eyeglasses, hearing aids, dentures, and inoculations have all been used to a far greater degree than in earlier times.

As they have been forced to abandon their traditional agricultural pursuits, the Cochití have turned to wage-earning activities in the neighboring cities and have significantly expanded their participation in the making of various arts and crafts. Drums continue to be a major product, and the manufacture of pottery, especially the "Story-teller" figurines, initially begun by Helen Cordero but now made by many of the Cochití and also numerous potters in other pueblos, has been an important activity. Again, as a result of the decline in farming, quite a number of Cochití men have taken up pottery making.

Thus far, ceremonialism at Cochití, both esoteric and public, has continued with little apparent loss. By many, this component is considered an important index of the viability of a puebloan culture. However, a number of the more perceptive individuals express increasing concern over the loss of the native language—partly the result of extratribal marriages, partly a spin-off from the shift away from the agricultural base, and partly due to the widespread popularity of television programs, a true "Trojan horse" in the context of cultural continuity. Without it, changes would obviously occur; with it, the changes are simply amplified and greatly accelerated.

CHARLES H. LANGE
Santa Fe, N.M.
March, 1989

COCHITI

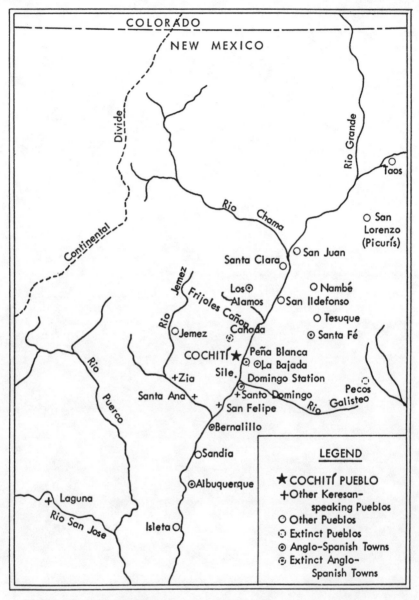

MAP 1: COCHITI AND VICINITY

Scale 1:1,267,200
1 inch = 20 miles

1 GEOGRAPHICAL BACKGROUND

Topography

COCHITÍ (Ko-tyīt') is the northernmost pueblo of the Keresan-speaking Pueblo tribes of New Mexico. It is situated on a low gravel terrace half a mile west of the Rio Grande some thirty miles southwest of Santa Fe. (See Plate 1.) The nearest neighbors are Santo Domingo (Gī'wa), ten miles south, which is commonly recognized as the most conservative of the Keresan towns, and San Felipe (Katch'tya), five miles below Santo Domingo, and almost as conservative. Across the mesa to the west are Santa Ana (Ta'mai-ya) and Zia (Tsī'ya), both Keresan in speech, and Jemez (Hē'mī-shet-ze), the sole-surviving Towa-speaking pueblo. To the north lie the various Tewa pueblos, with several of which, such as San Ildefonso (Pa'kwit) and Tesuque (Diū'so-kē), the Cochití maintain considerable contact despite the linguistic handicap. The degree to which these relationships antedate the use of Spanish as a lingua franca is difficult to ascertain.

Considerable contact has likewise been experienced with the neighboring Spanish-American settlements of Peña Blanca, Sile, La Bajada, Domingo Station (formerly Wallace), and the now extinct settlement at Cañada de Cochití. Through the years, contacts with Santa Fe and Albuquerque have been increasingly significant. (See Map 1.)

Geology, Terrain, and Soils

West of the Rio Grande, the Cochití country rises quite sharply in a series of mesas and canyons which, in turn, form the base of the Jemez Mountains. Evidences of past volcanic action are readily apparent; low-grade deposits of gold and silver supported limited mining a half-century ago. East of Cochití, approximately twenty miles, is the Cerrillos District, where veins of turquoise have been mined for centuries. (Ellis 1930: 85–87, 94)[1]

Probably the most influential element of the natural landscape surrounding Cochití is the Rio Grande. Situated at a point about six miles below White Rock Canyon, Cochití lies at the head of the long, narrow river basin known in recent years as "The Middle Rio Grande Conservancy District." (Harper, Cordova, and Oberg 1943)

The elevation of Cochití is approximately 5,200 feet, with the Jemez Range reaching heights of more than 11,000 feet. To the northeast and farther away the southern peaks of the Sangre de Cristo Range exceed 13,000 feet, and to the south lie the Sandia Mountains, rising to 10,692 feet.

Soils of the area can be divided into two categories: (1) A very permeable soil, ranging from grayish- or light-brown to reddish brown, lies on the mesa slopes where it has been washed from higher altitudes. It sometimes forms alluvial fans on the valley floor. (2) A sedimentary soil brought down by the Rio Grande and its tributaries, comprised of sands, gravels, and clays ranging from a dark- to a grayish-brown, often with a reddish tint, covers the valley floor. This, along with the alluvial fans, is the soil that the Cochití cultivate. (Bloodgood 1930: 8–9)[2]

Climate and Life Zones

No official weather data are available for Cochití or the immediate vicinity. With allowances for elevation differences, certain relatively accurate estimates can be made from the data in Appendix 1. Average temperatures for January and July are about 32° and 70°, respectively. Annual maximum and minimum temperatures range from about 98° to −12°. (Bandelier, in his journal of October 27, 1880, noted that Padre Ribera gave extremes for the past seven years of

[1] Additional data may be found in Northrup 1944.
[2] See also United States Department of Agriculture 1938: 1089–1090, 1125, 1135.

95° and 0°, with the comment that both were rare. Later, in his entries for mid-July, 1885, Bandelier recorded a reading of 102°.) Farmers can expect a growing season of approximately 180 days, roughly between April 23 and October 20. Annual precipitation amounts to 12 inches, or less, of which two-thirds normally occur between April and September. Actually, the greatest portion falls from mid-July to mid-September. These summer storms often are quite violent and are accompanied by thunder, lightning, and hail, with considerable damage from the hail and flash floods frequently resulting. Such storms in the Cochití area were typical as long ago as 1782, as described by Father Morfi. (Thomas 1932: 99)[3]

As analyzed by Bailey (1913: 27–28, 41–46, 46–49)[4], almost the entire Cochití Reservation falls within the Upper Sonoran zone. The extreme northwestern corner of the reservation is included within the Transition zone. Briefly summarized, the Upper Sonoran has a sparse vegetation in which desert shrubs, cacti, yucca, and short grasses dominate. Where somewhat greater moisture prevails, there is a scattered growth of junipers and piñons, and the grass is better.

Agriculture, without irrigation, is rarely present in the Upper Sonoran zone, according to Bailey. However, for the period just preceding Bailey's field studies, comments of several Cochití indicated that a different situation prevailed. Until the turn of the century, dry farming was practiced with some success by the Cochití. Interesting time perspective is provided by an entry of Bandelier in his journal of November 15, 1880, which suggests that this desiccation had begun some years before the turn of the century:

> It is the same story; formerly there was more rain. Juan José recollects that within his time there were very rainy years, while the last years were even exceptionally dry. He also adds that originally they raised only maize, for which, he says, irrigation is not indispensable. He affirms to have seen crops of maize gathered in places where there was no irrigation, which exceeded those from the acequias.

Such statements undoubtedly indicate not so much an era of appreciably greater rainfall as simply a better balance among precipitation, water table, and vegetation. This has been corroborated by studies

---

[3] It seems quite likely that this account was based upon an earlier account of the Cochití area by Friar Antonio Cavallero in 1779. (Biblioteca Nacional Archives, *Legajo X*: Document 59)

[4] See also Florence Bailey 1928 and Merriam 1898.

of Bryan (1925, 1929, 1941) and others in connection with climatic cycles in the Southwest.[5]

Immediately northwest of the Cochití Reservation in the higher altitudes of the Jemez Mountains are the Transition and Canadian zones. Both play important roles in Cochití culture because of the flora and fauna which are utilized. For brevity, only the more important members of the biota of these zones are listed here. (Bailey 1913: 43–46, 47–49)[6] Various species of pine, spruce, and fir dominate the higher regions, while junipers and piñons are found on the mesas. Along the Rio Grande and in the mountain canyons several species of cottonwood are common. Common animals include deer, wildcat, bear, badger, coyote, wolf, fox, rabbit, skunk, and squirrel. Antelope and mountain lion, formerly quite common, are rarely seen now. Elk and mountain sheep were formerly present but never in important numbers. Bison were seldom seen west of the Pecos Valley. Principal birds include eagle, various hawks, owl, turkey, ducks, road runner, quail, and dove. The bull snake, king snake, and rattlesnake, as well as numerous small lizards, toads, and turtles, are native to the area.

[5] Additional papers on this topic include Bailey, R. W., 1935; Hack 1942; and Schulman 1938.

[6] Other sources are Bailey, F., 1928; Benson and Darrow 1944; and Wooton and Standley 1915.

2 PREHISTORY AND HISTORY

Prehistory

THE PREHISTORY of Cochití, as of neighboring pueblos, is relatively little known owing to the lack of thorough archaeological research within the pueblo and its vicinity. Preliminary reconnaissance already accomplished gives indications of what may be found when such investigations are made.

As revealed in Benedict's collection of Cochití origin tales (1931: 1–18), the Cochití begin their accounts of tribal existence on earth in the mythological past when their ancestors were living at White House, following their emergence from "Shī'pap." More concretely, some claim to have lived next at Frijoles Cañon "along with all the other Pueblo Indians." [3, 42, 62][1] Although this latter claim is overly inclusive in light of present anthropological research, there does appear to be a general inclination to agree that the Cochití and probably other Keresans (perhaps other linguistic groups as well?) occupied Frijoles until a few centuries before the advent of the Spanish in 1540. Douglas (1932: 179) has gone to the extent of designating Cochití as "half a tribe," the other half being San Felipe.

[1] Attention is again called to the practice (see the Preface, p. xii) of enclosing in brackets the designations of informants who held a particular point of view on subjects about which there was not complete unanimity of opinion among all the informants.

Starr (Scrapbook) made repeated reference to "the seven migrations of the Cochiti" but failed to document or elaborate on these
movements. As of the moment, no scientific evidence can be offered
in support of this reference.

In the vicinity of the reservation and within the pueblo itself pot-
sherd collections show a sequence extending from the present back
to Glaze 1 red and yellow wares, with dates as early as A.D. 1225.
Other sites, such as Pueblito, west of Cochití in the Santa Fe National
Forest, show pottery types of the period 1050–1250.[2] The Cochití,
however, claim no direct association with the majority of these ruins
other than those in and adjacent to Frijoles Cañon, including those
in association with the well-known Stone Lions of Cochití[3] (Plate 3),
and those above and in Cañada de Cochití. Stubbs (1950: 63, 121–
122) states that the present site of the pueblo has been occupied for
at least seven hundred years, thereby placing the tribe at this location when the first Spanish explorers arrived.[4]

History

Historical references to Cochití are disappointing in their brevity and
generalities. Many travelers, because of Cochití's position across the
Rio Grande from the principal routes, completely ignored the village
in their notes. If mentioned at all, it was merely located on their
sketch maps or simply described as generally similar to those pueblos
previously described.

Spanish Exploration Period, 1540–1598. Although Castañeda, the
chronicler of the Coronado expedition, failed to name individual

[2] Chronology of pottery wares is based on personal conversations with Paul
Reiter and Stanley Stubbs during the summer of 1951. General agreement was
found except for a few wares which Stubbs dated about twenty-five years later
than Reiter.

[3] These figures are described and illustrated by Bandelier (1892: 152–156,
161–163) (See Plate 3). When I inquired about the second pair of stone lions
on the Potrero de los Idolos in 1947, I was surprised to learn that no Cochití knew
of their existence. After the surviving member of the pair had been found again
in 1952 by one of the Cochití and myself, the incident proved to be of practical
aid in demonstrating the value of recording other aspects of Cochití culture (see
Plate 4). In his journal of December 6, 1880, Bandelier noted that two men had
told him that they could not recall the time when the second lion had not been
mutilated, thus indicating some antiquity for this vandalism.

[4] This occupation was continuous with the exception of several years during
the Pueblo Indian Revolt, 1680–1692, when the Cochití and others occupied
Potrero Viejo, above Cañada. For details, see Hackett 1942 and Espinosa 1940.

Keresan pueblos (Winship 1896: 503, 519, 524–525), Bandelier (1893: 216) stated that Cochití was one of eight pueblos mentioned by Castañeda.

Because of discouraging reports of the Coronado venture, the region remained undisturbed by the Spaniards for almost forty years. In 1581, the Rodríguez-Chamuscado expedition entered the Pueblo area. According to the Gallegos account (Hammond and Rey 1927: 8, 48), Cochití was visited in the fall of 1581. The pueblo was described as having 230 houses of two and three stories, and it was named "Medina de la Torre."

In 1582, the Espejo expedition visited Cochití, which was briefly noted as follows by Luxán (Hammond and Rey 1929: 82): "This pueblo was called Cachiti [Cochiti: Hammond and Rey]. The people are very peaceful. They gave us maize, tortillas, turkeys, and pinole. We bartered very fine buffaloskins for sleigh bells and small iron articles." Upon the return of the Espejo party to Chihuahua in September, 1583, interest in the northern frontier—"New Mexico"— greatly increased. (Hammond and Rey 1938: 23–24).

Spanish Colonial Period: Seventeenth Century. Although Cochití received more frequent mention during this period, ethnographic data were rarely noted. With the settlement of colonists under Don Juan de Oñate in 1598, contacts with Spanish culture were begun and continued with almost unbroken sequence until the Mexican government assumed control early in the nineteenth century. Several tribes submitted to Oñate at Santo Domingo in July, 1598, after which he established headquarters farther north at San Juan. Rods of office were given tribal chieftains, and missionaries were assigned parishes among the pueblos. Father Rosas went to the parish which included Cochití (Bolton 1916: 202–203). By 1599, permanent Spanish colonies had been established, European fruits and vegetables had been introduced, and herds of livestock were being cared for and expanded (Bolton 1916: 216–217).

Several seventeenth-century sources list Cochití as a *visita* of Santo Domingo: 1614 (Scholes and Bloom 1944: 333, 335), 1626 and 1667 (Scholes 1929: 47, 54–55; Scholes, personal interview, December, 1946), though in 1637 a resident friar was noted at Cochití (Scholes and Bloom 1945:66). The 1667 reference is noteworthy as the first reference to the Cochití mission as "San Buenaventura," its present designation.

Occasional mention of Cochití was made during the mid-seventeenth century as its people became enmeshed in the struggle for supremacy between Church and State.[5] In 1680, the Cochití joined with other Pueblo tribes in their revolt against the Spaniards; as mentioned already (n. 4), during the years between 1680 and the reconquest in 1692–1693, the Cochití and their comrades left the home village and lived in the pueblo on Potrero Viejo, above Cañada.[6]

After a brief period of calm, open revolt came again on June 4, 1696, in the northern pueblos with which the Cochití joined. Five missionaries were killed, and the whole region was terrorized. Father Fray Alonzo de Cisneros, stationed at Cochití, managed to escape death by fleeing to the still loyal Indians of San Felipe. (Bancroft 1889: 216–217) It is interesting that this incident is still familiar to many Cochití and is one of the favorite tales of "the old days."

Spanish Colonial Period: Eighteenth Century. The first mention of Cochití in the documents of the eighteenth century appears in a list of military outposts established by Governor ad interim Don Francisco Cuervo y Valdés, 1705–1707 (Bancroft 1889: 228). Early in 1706, an appeal was made to keep Governor–Captain-General Cuervo in office. Representatives from Santo Domingo, Jemez, Pecos, Cochití, and other pueblos spoke, in that order. The governor of Santo Domingo, Don Cristóbal Coriz, was mentioned as the "principal war chief of the Queres nation."[7] The governor of the Pueblo of San Buenaventura de Cochití, Don Luís Romero, was noted as speaking Castilian (Hackett 1937: 369), apparently not a frequent accomplishment at that time.

In 1706, Fray Juan Olvarez made the following declaration regarding Cochití, then under the charge of Fray Miguel Muñiz (Hackett 1937: 375):

This mission has a broken bell without a clapper. (The Indians took all the clappers away, to make lances and knives.) There is one of the ornaments which his Majesty gave. The vials are a silver one, a glass one, and another of tin plate. The church is being built. This mission has about five hundred and twenty Indians. . . . It is called San Buenaventura de Cochití.

---

[5] For details of this struggle, see Scholes 1937 and Scholes 1942.

[6] In addition to citation in n. 4, see Leonard 1932.

[7] This reference to a governor of a pueblo as a war chief for several villages is interesting in view of the usual separation of the two offices and also because of the tendency of the pueblo tribes to remain unaffiliated. It would be interesting to know whether the title reflected the critical times during which the Keres had recognized a common leader or whether it was simply a nonliteral generalization by the Spaniards in referring to a reputable warrior.

According to Hackett (1937: 404), Fray Miguel de Menchero in 1744 described Cochití as a village of more than eighty Indian families, some ranches, and with a resident friar in the mission.

One of the most detailed descriptions of Cochití, though emphasis was placed on the mission, was the report of the *Visitador*, Fray Francisco Atanacio Domínguez, who arrived in New Mexico in March, 1776. The following excerpt was taken from his report, as translated and edited by Adams and Chavez (1956: 159).

PUEBLO

Having considered this location, it remains to be said that the pueblo itself is toward the north in relation to the church, planned and arranged of adobe houses which form two small plazas with all their four blocks separate from one another. One is east of the others, and another to the west, with a tenement, or building, in between that faces south. The arrangement of doors, adornment, and alignment as in the other pueblos via ladders and *cois* [roof entrance].

Its Lands and Fruits: All the important farmlands which this pueblo owns lie on the east side of the river, downstream along the river, extending the breadth of the plain and down to join those of the pueblo of Santo Domingo. There are some milpas on the bank on which the pueblo stands, and very few up to the north on both banks. All take the water of the said river for irrigation through deep wide ditches. They yield very abundant crops of everything sown in them. There is an occasional peach tree.

The natives of this pueblo are Queres, whose native tongue they speak, and also Spanish, but brokenly. With regard to their particular customs, the same as those of Santo Domingo, and here is the

CENSUS

116 families with 486 persons[8]

Early in the nineteenth century, 1817 and 1818, reports showed Cochití as a mission; in both years, Father Fray Juan Caballero Foril was listed as the resident friar (Biblioteca Nacional, *Legajo X*: Documents 79, 80).

Mexican Colonial Period: 1820–1846. In 1821, Cochití was noted

[8] This is one of the first reports showing Santo Domingo as a larger pueblo than Cochití. Cochití had a larger population during the initial Spanish contacts and probably continued to be larger until the time of the Revolt of 1680. Through Cochití losses during the Revolt, a Tano influx into Santo Domingo about that time, localized epidemics, or other causes, Santo Domingo became the larger and has remained so to the present.

as having a resident friar (Bloom 1913: 28). In his journal of March 21, 1882, Bandelier recorded a certificate of Juan Estévan Aragon, alcalde of Peña Blanca, March 26, 1831, to the effect that Fray Manuel Bellido was the priest at Cochití from January 1, 1820, to July, 1823.

In reports of 1822 and 1832, Cochití was listed among those communities having a judge and attorney (Bloom 1913: 146; Bloom 1928: 44). During this period, in August, 1837, the Mexican governor, Colonel Albino Pérez, was assassinated. As an insight into the fidelity with which such documented events are passed down in an essentially nonliterate culture such as that of the Cochití, it is interesting that Bandelier noted in his journal of November 18, 1880, that a Cochití was pointed out to him as the grandson of the Manuelito who killed Pérez.

American Period: 1846——. Along similar lines, in the same entry Bandelier wrote that he was told that during the Taos rebellion, 1846/47, the Cochití had been called upon to assist. However, they had held back, expecting an attack upon themselves at any moment.

Among the papers of James S. Calhoun, Indian agent, the entry for October 15, 1849, disclosed that Indians from Cochití had come in to inform Governor Washington that they had killed three Apaches who had attempted to drive off some Cochití sheep. Other Apache raiders were continually attempting to drive off stock, kill the men, and capture the women and children. "This Indian, in behalf of the people of Cochití, asked for Munitions of War." (Abel 1915: 50)

In 1851, Calhoun reported a meeting of Pueblo Indians at the agency for several days. Twelve tribes, including the Cochití, expressed their desire to maintain the old customs and usages (Abel 1915: 368–371): ". . . these people must be treated with the utmost delicacy, or bloody scenes will be witnessed in this Territory. A delicate induction will bring these people to any point you may desire, but it must be delicate, and protection must be afforded them." In September of that same year, Calhoun notified his successor, Major E. H. Wingfield, of Navaho depredations near Cochití (Abel 1915: 426).

After Calhoun's records, there is a gap of almost three decades before the journal of Lieutenant John G. Bourke furnishes a valuable, and entertaining, description of various pueblos in 1881. Bourke and his small party visited Cochití on November 6, 1881. He described the party's visit to the governor of the pueblo; details of the interior of several houses; the appearance of the pueblo, including the church; various activities of the people; and other ethnographic details. (Bloom 1938: 234–237)

Beginning with 1880 and continuing sporadically through 1892, the unpublished journals of Bandelier provide much additional detail. Since many of his publications presented a blend of data from various unspecified pueblos, they have been of dubious value in precise ethnographic research. However, the original journals contain observations and comments made by Bandelier during several periods of residence at Cochití and are important both in presenting details and in extending time perspective. Although some comments readily reveal his lack of training, and his failure to capitalize on certain opportunities reflects his greater interest in archaeology, the data in these journals have been of great value in the present study.

Other historic and ethnographic accounts, from such writers as the Eickemeyers and Starr, are cited repeatedly in subsequent chapters and further mention here is omitted.

Throughout the historic periods there has been sporadic recording of census data. Although the categories often do not permit exact comparisons, Appendix 2 presents a summary of the usable census data for Cochití. Rather abrupt fluctuations within brief periods may be explained by the varying degree of thoroughness of the census-takers, the occasional inclusion of non-Cochití in church census data, and the sudden losses suffered from epidemics.

Long-term Non-Indian Cultural Impacts

Any discussion of prehistoric and historic material relating to the Cochití must consider several non-Indian influences that have contributed to the form and content of Cochití culture through several historical periods: Spanish-American residents and neighbors, the Roman Catholic Church, the United States government, and other non-Indian neighbors, friends, tourists, and anthropologists. Such influences have been cumulative and, to some degree and at various times, interrelated. For these reasons, they are discussed here from a topical viewpoint rather than chronologically. In a certain sense, the material in this section might equally well comprise the concluding unit of this study, being a summary of so-called acculturative influences or primary contributors to culture change. However, it is presented at this point to provide better perspective with which to approach the various components of Cochití culture—economics, politics, religion, and social organization.

The Spanish-American Residents and Neighbors. Perhaps one of the more distinctive features of Cochití Pueblo has been the long-standing presence of Spanish residents within the village itself. While all the Rio Grande Pueblo tribes have lived for several centuries in close proximity to Spanish settlements and have experienced contacts with them during this time, few tribes have had these Europeans as actual neighbors within the pueblo confines. In certain aspects, the cultural effects of this situation at Cochití have been even more deep-seated than with other Pueblo tribes. Bandelier (October 21, 1880) commented: "There is evident feeling of distrust and jealousy existing between the Indians and the Mexicans. Thus, Pacífico is not looked upon with kindness. He, however, speaks with praise of the women of the Pueblos and says they are chaste and virtuous—more so than the Mexican women." On the other hand, present-day Cochití voiced the opinion that relations with the Spanish residents had been more pleasant in earlier times—"There was more co-operation then." Undoubtedly, such opinions, largely individual and reflecting the nature of over-all personal and family contacts, vary considerably from person to person and from time to time.

These Spanish families have held homes and the lots on which these buildings have stood; in addition they have held agricultural tracts. Poore (1894: 429), the Indian agent, in describing the pueblo as of 1890, noted: "Eight Mexican families dwell here and fraternize with the Indians. As long ago as 1820 the Mexicans acquired land here. They are regarded as under the jurisdiction of the pueblo, and perform communal work upon irrigation ditches and roads by command of the governor of the tribe."

Bandelier's journal, October 24, 1880, mentions approximately the same date:

He knew all about the destruction of the idols, but says that at that time (1819) there were two parties in the pueblo. One of them, infected by the uprising of the Mexicans against Spain, sought the rights of citizenship, and sold many of their lands to Mexicans; therefore the Mexican population of Cochití. Three years previous, the first fever epidemic occurred, and there was great strife in the pueblo. Both parties sent delegates to Guadalajara, where the matter was settled. . . . In the year after 1819, the second fever broke out. These two epidemics destroyed the pueblo.

In view of historical documents already cited, however, there is a suggestion that Mexican residents may have been there earlier than Poore and Bandelier stated, their residence dating perhaps from the late seventeenth century. These Spanish holdings have gradually been purchased for the tribe; at present there is little land or property held by these non-Cochití. There has been a long-standing dispute over the actual status of such property. The Cochití believe that it was originally loaned to those Spaniards who would live among them and join in mutual assistance against Navaho and Apache aggressions. In an entry of March 29, 1882, Bandelier cited a petition signed in Peña Blanca on April 9, 1835, by former residents of the Cañada de Cochití who, seeking relief, had fled to the pueblo of Cochití in February, 1835, because of Navaho attacks.

The Spanish descendants insist that the land and rights were outright gifts in exchange for this armed assistance. So long as the crises persisted, questions of ownership and rights remained dormant; once the danger had vanished, it became a continual point of contention. The remaining Spanish families, including the only two storekeepers (Luciano Gallegos and Leopoldo Rael) in the village, maintain that they are rightfully in the pueblo and do not care to leave (a stand which places them in the most advantageous bargaining position in any eventual confiscation-compensation proceedings). The Cochití feel the Spanish-Americans have long since served their purpose in being there, and they are eager to have these lands and buildings restored to the pueblo.

In 1947, negotiations were begun by the Cochití to exchange land along the road near the southern periphery of the village for house lots which had been purchased by Rael from other Spanish families. Rael wished to keep his present home and store but was willing to trade his other lots and corrals for greater acreage. The Cochití officers were anxious to regain the various lots, primarily those in the vicinity of the Turquoise Kiva, but they did not want Rael to keep his house and store, nor did they want to meet his demands of acreage in exchange. [21, 45] No agreement had been reached as of 1952. About 1950, Clofe Arquero, a Cochití, bought a house at the northeast corner of the pueblo from the heirs of the Segura estate, thereby eliminating another Spanish-American holding. Little information is in the literature regarding such homes. A few notes were made by the Eickemeyers (1895: 91–92) on a Spanish home they had visited during their stay in Cochití in 1894:

This Mexican room was very different from those in the Indian houses, resembling one that might be seen in the poorer quarters of any town. There was a rag carpet on the floor (the rooms in the Indian houses were not even boarded), and, besides several chairs and a table, there was a bedstead with a gaudy blanket of Mexican manufacture for a covering. The walls were covered with a cheap paper, and what struck us as being very peculiar were two frames, the faces of which were turned to the wall. They were looking-glasses, which in the case of a death in a family are always turned toward the wall for one year.

The first mention of Spanish trading posts or stores in Cochití Pueblo is also found in the Eickemeyers' observations (1895: 95): "There are two of these stores in the pueblo, both kept by Mexicans, who supply the villagers with groceries, canned goods, cheap calico, harness, and other articles, which are always bought in small quantities, for no one, Indian, or Mexican, has much money with which to purchase these luxuries, as they are considered."

In recent years there have been two stores also, both operated by Spanish-Americans. While dates for their establishment are not known exactly, it is probable that the two stores mentioned by the Eickemeyers in 1895 are operated by the same families today.

Luciano Gallegos has operated a store at Cochití continuously since 1893 except for a few years early in this century when he worked for the railroad. His store is in the same location today that it has occupied from its beginning.

From about 1895 to 1916, a store (Plate 12a) was operated by Juan José Romero, the grandfather of Leopoldo Rael, in the block south of the church near Joe Melchior's present home. From 1900 to 1923, José A. Rivera had a store in the present location of the Rael store. In 1923, Leopoldo Rael married Rivera's daughter and at the same time took over the operation of the store. Since 1923, the store building (and home) has been rebuilt once, with an addition in 1947/48 of homemade pumice-cement blocks.[9] [45, 65] (See Plate 12b.)

[9] In the winter of 1954, fire destroyed Rael's store and home. The family moved to the home of Juan José Trujillo (whose family moved across the river to their "ranchito") where they lived and also continued their business during the rebuilding of their own home and store. Although this arrangement had its economic aspects, it also demonstrated that this opportunity for "freezing out" this non-Cochití trader was not exploited and that friendship and neighborliness were influential.

The principal change in the storekeeping business during the recent decades has been a shift from an almost exclusive barter system (primarily of corn and wheat for sugar, flour, yard goods, etc.) to one of cash sales, though some credit is extended, with or without pawn. There is no special government-control of prices; they depend upon wholesale prices, transportation costs, and "what the traffic will bear." County and state licenses are required for these trading posts, as for any similar store off the reservation. The people used to be far more dependent upon the local stores than they are now. With motor transportation increasingly available, periodic trips into town provide ample opportunities to trade outside the pueblo. Local storekeepers maintain that these changes have actually not hurt their businesses as much as one might expect, that trading with stores outside the pueblo is concentrated on various "luxury" items not handled by the Cochití stores. Essential commodities, such as sugar, salt, coffee, flour, and other foodstuffs, are still purchased locally. This may be true to some extent, but personal observations indicate otherwise. The Cochití regularly bring large boxes, cartons, and sacks of groceries, including staples and other supplies, into their homes from outside. In a year's aggregate, the effect of these purchases cannot help but be felt upon the trade of local storekeepers.

At present, only four Spanish families live at Cochití—Gallegos, Lucero, Rael, and Tafoya, all descendants of families of long residence in the pueblo. Other Spanish families formerly in the village are the following: Hernández, Herrera, Hurtado, Lucero, País, Rivera, Romero, Salas, and Segura. They moved ten or fifteen years ago either to Peña Blanca or Cuba, New Mexico, leaving subsequent to the settlement of various land cases. [65] The homes of the Lucero, Tafoya, and Gallegos families are on the eastern periphery of the village; the Rael home, adjoining their store, is more prominent because of its central location and its two stories.

In spite of their relatively small number, Spanish-American families are quite conspicuous in present-day Cochití life since two of them operate the only stores in the pueblo. The Rael store is located on the only road passing through the pueblo, a good location for attracting trade. Another advantage enjoyed by this store is its use as a distribution and collection point for the mail, though it is not an official post office, being served on a Star Route out of Peña Blanca. It carries a fairly wide range of groceries (including some perishables since the recent installation of an electric refrigerator-display case), some dry goods, and a limited supply of cosmetics.

The store of Luciano Gallegos, located near the eastern edge of the pueblo, is somewhat less conspicuous to the nonresident. However, it is almost equally well patronized by the Cochití. It had the only gasoline pump in the village in 1952. As would be expected, families shift from one store to the other as stocks and brands fluctuate, as credits are extended or revoked, and as personal relationships vacillate.

Noneconomic relationships between the Cochití and the resident Spanish-Americans have varied through the years according to specific events and associated emotions and depending upon the individuals. There have been, and still are, Cochití who are consistently antagonistic; they alternate between ignoring the presence of these outsiders and actively pressing for their ouster from the community. In mentioning ka'tsīna dances, Bandelier on November 28, 1880, noted that "the Mexicans are strictly forbidden to see them. They are held in the timber. A few years ago, Telisfero Lucero was nearly killed by the Indians of Cochití on that account." From such instances of idle curiosity, it is easy to see some grounds for resentment. Other Cochití have shared sincere friendships (see n. 9) with these outsiders. Bandelier, April 4, 1882, in mentioning the cacique, said, "He is the medicine-man of the pueblo; even for the Mexicans . . . [who] consult him frequently."

Friendships have, in some cases, resulted in marriage between Cochití and Spanish-Americans. In most instances, the Spanish-Americans who have married Cochití have been women, and the great majority of these have not been residents of the village. As noted in later chapters, these marriages have commonly led to residence away from the pueblo and generally mean that the Cochití involved cease to participate in tribal matters. Bandelier noted, October 18, 1880, that "Juan José is (in writing) invited to a Mexican wedding to be celebrated in the pueblo today. They will have a dance, possibly in his own house, as they have asked for it."

In a few cases, Spanish-American wives have lived in the pueblo, and, especially in former times, they have actually joined in the Indian culture, being adopted into clan and kiva organizations and in other ways accepting the Indian way of life. Goldfrank (1927: 11, 16–17) cites examples of women who have thus entered into clan and other phases of Cochití life. She also noted the intimate nature of these alien influences and the often disintegrating effect they had had on the native customs. These points will be elaborated upon later.

At one time, children of the Spanish families attended the day school in the pueblo. However, the antagonism of a few Cochití families resulted in their withdrawal, and since then all the pupils have been Cochití Indians. [27, 45, 48, 65, 70] In play, however, the Spanish children do associate with many of the Cochití, with no unusual incidents. This relationship is carried on into adolescence and youth, the Cochití learning some Spanish (though not as much nor as well as did their parents and especially their grandparents) and the Spanish-American children learning Cochití.

Something of the close tie existing between certain individuals is revealed in an incident of the Reyes (Kings') Day celebration of January 6, 1947. In the evening of this celebration, it is customary for groups of young dancers to perform in the homes of the newly appointed officers, sometimes in the homes of the retiring officers, and in the home of a Rey or Reyes. In 1947, there was, among others, a group of three older girls dressed as eagle dancers (actually, the true eagle dancers are always males) and accompanied on the drum by a Cochití man, a council member. Two of the girls were daughters of the storekeeper Rael. It was pointed out by several Cochití, with obvious pride, that these girls spoke Cochití better than some of their own young people. Unanimous approval of the performances of these dancers was also expressed.

Through the years the baseball teams of the pueblo have included Spanish-American players who have participated as their skills have warranted, with apparently no discrimination to attempt to keep the team strictly Indian. (Plate 23b)

During the Second World War, three Spanish-Americans of Cochití—Eloy Gallegos, Ramón Lucero, and Polito Rael—were in service. This experience, shared with more than thirty of their Indian contemporaries, formed another tangible link between these individuals.

Certain Spanish-Americans who have attained some facility in English have been consulted through the years by Cochití who need assistance in reading, writing letters, and filling out various government, and other, forms. This practice has come about partly from a pueblo tendency to keep confidential matters from other Indians and partly to take advantage of the Spanish-Americans' real or imagined broader acquaintance with modern American ways.

Another bond between the resident Spanish-Americans and the Cochití, especially those of the Progressive faction—though not exclusively so—has been the Catholic religion. In 1952, the Rosary was regularly led by Oliver Rael, son of the storekeeper.

The Roman Catholic Church. Cochití, like other Rio Grande pueblos, has been strongly influenced by Catholicism. During the three and a half centuries of almost continuous contact, these influences have been sometimes relatively superficial and sometimes far more profound.

In this section Catholicism is discussed; the physical church and its furnishings are described in Chapter 3 under "Property and Ownership within the Village." As noted there, the Cochití have the feeling that the building (and its activities) belongs to them. If necessary, they could bar the padre from the church, but he could never keep them out of "their" church.

In his journal of November 23, 1880, Bandelier mentioned that he had "met on the road August Wilcken, Mormon elder, with whom José Hilario had stayed three years ago when he went to California. He was going to Cochití to preach and convert." Apparently, this effort, and any subsequent ones by this denomination or any other except the Catholic, failed to meet with any success among the Cochití. While there has been an occasional Protestant entry into the vicinity, none has ever gained a foothold in the pueblo, and no Cochití, so far as can be learned, has ever become affiliated with a Protestant group. The greater pageantry and numerous items of tangible paraphernalia of the Catholic church have undoubtedly contributed to this preference by the Cochití.

The superficial nature of much of Catholicism and the simultaneous decline of native religion were noted among the Zia in 1890 by Stevenson (1894: 15):

Thus the railroad, the merchant, and the cowboy, without this purpose in view, are effecting a change which is slowly closing, leaf by leaf, the record of the religious beliefs and practices of the pueblo Indians. With the Sia this record book is being more rapidly closed, but from a different cause. It is not due to the Christianizing of these Indians, for they have nothing of Protestantism among them, although professedly Catholic, they await only the departure of the priest to return to their sacred ceremonials.

The Catholic priest baptizes the infant, but the child has previously received the baptismal rite of its ancestors. The Catholic priest marries the betrothed, but they have been previously united according to their ancestral rites. The Romish priest holds mass that the dead may enter heaven, but prayers have already been offered that the soul may be received by Sus-sis-tin-na-ko (their creator) into the lower world whence it came. As an entirety these people are devotees to their religion and its observances, and yet with but few exceptions, they go through their rituals having but vague understanding of their origin or meaning. Each shadow on the dial brings nearer to a close the lives of those upon whose minds are graven the traditions, mythology, and folklore as indelibly as are the pictographs and monochromes upon the rocky walls.

As at Zia and other pueblos since Stevenson's time, Catholicism at Cochití has grown stronger as the native religion has weakened. The more profound influence of the Catholic church was probably first felt when it attempted to suppress native ceremonials (see accounts of the return of De Vargas and the post-1692 period), particularly those in which the masked supernaturals, or ka'tsīnas, appeared. The result was that the Ka'tsīna Cult and other aspects of native religion were driven underground, but definitely not out of existence. An already well-developed faculty for keeping rituals secret even from their own people who did not belong to a particular society was readily transferred to their concealment from Europeans, who attacked them as being both pagan and immoral.

A combining of various native celebrations with the calendar of the Catholic church accompanied this suppression, or attempted suppression, of native rites. Ceremonies described as part of the ceremonial calendar (Chapter 9) exemplify this merger. Although there has been a tendency for ethnographers to stress winter ceremonials because they are generally of a purer native ceremonial nature, the series of summer celebrations associated with the Catholic feast days are also important to the Cochití.

In addition to these local observances of church ceremonial events, the Cochití participate, generally only as spectators, in the feast days of other tribes as well. The Taos celebration in September, Laguna in September, Jemez in November, San Felipe in May, Santa Ana in July, Santo Domingo in August, and Zia in August are all well known to the Cochití and are well attended. Essentially Catholic dates, the celebrations involve considerable mixture with Indian patterns. In their visits to other pueblos on various feast days, the Cochití seldom enter the churches, though they sometimes march in the procession that escorts the image of the saint to and from the shelter in the plaza where the dancing occurs.

At Cochití, most Conservatives attend Mass, participate in the procession to and from the church as the saint's image is moved, and take part in the dancing which follows; the Progressives attend Mass, march, and then become only spectators in the remainder of the ceremonies. Conservatives and Progressives alike join in rooster pulls, foot races, and present-throwing. Spanish-Americans of the village and the vicinity play in the rooster pulls and in the present-throwing, but they do not run in the races nor join in the dancing. Despite such limited participation and the form of dancing already described on the evening of January 6, 1947, a Catholic feast day, the Spanish-Americans do not participate in ceremonial events such as the *Tablita* dances, hunting dances, and similar rites which occur on other Catholic occasions. This is most probably a ban self-imposed by the Spanish. The few instances of these people entering into Cochití life, as has been noted, involve individuals who have completely forsworn their previous life. If they abandon it, which is possible, they *are* Cochití; if they retain their Spanish cultural heritage, they are not Cochití and do not become involved in these "Indian" ways.

An interesting account of church services, in Bandelier's journal of December 14, 1880, is included in his description of the celebration of Guadalupe Day (this festival actually falls on December 12, but at Cochití it has traditionally been observed on December 13 because the priests are at Peña Blanca on the twelfth):

After two early Masses, service, High Mass was performed at 10 A.M. I went behind the altar to sing with Hayoua and Zashua. Padre Acorsini led us, and afterwards the vicar-general himself came to assist us. The voices of the boys were uncultivated, therefore rather raw, and they sing Dumont's masses, etc. more from memory and faultier "drill" than anything else. Still, there is something like correct hearing, for they stop whenever they find out they are wrong. Padre Gromm sang the office with a very good voice, and Padre Truchard preached on the apparition of Nuestra Señora de Guadalupe. He has the voice of a stentor and once had certainly a handsome baritone. After the service, a procession was formed. The church was full, and one-third more outside. Nearly all the people of Cochití had turned out—men and women, girls and boys, in their best apparel. Many of Santo Domingo also came, and some of San Felipe; also Mariano from Cia. . . . No Indians took part in the procession.

At present, attendance at Mass is quite general among the Cochití, the worshipers being segregated according to sex, as is customary in missions of the Southwest and many other places. Women and small children sit on the floor along the north wall, and men and older boys sit along the south wall or stand across the back of the church under the choir loft. People come and go with little apparent respect for the progress of the Mass.

The present choir at Cochití is well thought of by the people, the priests, and most visitors. It is trained by Juan Estévan Chávez, a Cochití, who for a time studied for the priesthood but was forced to give it up because of poor health. Both Indians and Spanish-Americans sing in the choir. In addition to the Spanish-Americans and Progressives, many Conservatives are very regular in their attendance at Mass and other rites of the church.

According to one Franciscan father, fees are set throughout the diocese by the archbishop in Santa Fe,[10] and the people at Cochití

[10] This uniform character of Catholic laws and regulations within a certain area, such as an archdiocese, is emphasized in the following excerpts from a letter (March 5, 1954) from Father Angelico Chávez, O.F.M., to me in answer to an inquiry about the law of abstinence as it applied to the Pueblo Indians: ". . . First of all, the Catholic Pueblo Indians have been bound by all the laws of the Church as stipulated for a territory without regard to race or nationality in that area.

"The law of abstinence, that is, of abstaining from meat on Friday and certain days in Lent, is an ancient practice by which the Church as a corporate whole does penance in honor of Christ's offering of His Flesh on the Cross. The law simply forbids the partaking of meat or its derivatives on that day. *It does not prescribe fish at any time.* Hence there is no question of substituting fish for flesh at any time. (Because fish is generally taken in Europe and other 'fishy' parts of the globe when flesh-meat is not to be had, the fish has become a symbol of abstinence days on the calendars.) But the main point, that the eating of fish is never prescribed, must be kept in mind. This will take care of any taboos among indigenous peoples concerning fish—they can take it or leave it.

"Up to five or more years ago, the eating of meat on Fridays was allowed in New Mexico and the rest of Latin America. This was not an Indian privilege, nor one granted to this specific territory 'because fish was scarce,' as many suppose. It was a hangover from the 'Crusade' privilege granted by the Pope to Spain and all her possessions as a reward for Spain's saving of Europe from Saracenic conquest. So up to a few years ago any Catholic in New Mexico, Indian, Spanish, Anglo, etc., could eat meat on Friday. Even a visiting Catholic from other parts could do so as the privilege was territorial and not personal. Hence any New Mexican Catholic outside of New Mexico had to abstain. To make observances universal once more, and so abolish a source of much confusion in the Southwest, the Holy See instructed the bishops to withdraw the his-

are expected to pay the same fees as all others in the diocese. "This is a policy aimed at preparing the Indians to become full citizens with the same privileges and obligations other people have." For baptisms, marriages, and deaths the people make an offering of whatever they can afford, usually fifty cents or a dollar. If the family cannot pay anything, the service is performed by the priest anyway. One dollar is charged for a regular Mass; two dollars for a special Mass; and five dollars for High Mass. Banns are announced three times prior to marriage, though dispensations can be obtained for one, two, and five dollars, respectively (the last, only with permission of the archbishop). [37] White (1942: 64) was told the following at Santa Ana:

The Catholic priest charges a fee for performing the ritual of baptism: fifty cents for an adult, twenty-five cents for a baby. He also charges for performing a marriage ceremony, the maximum charge being about $3.00. Priests do not always charge fees for these services; "If one doesn't want to, he doesn't." But if he does wish to receive money for a service he does not hesitate to ask for it.

Offerings at the usual church service at Cochití average about three dollars, consisting largely of nickels and dimes and a few quarters. Half-dollars or larger denominations are extremely rare. [37]

A minor, yet significant, facet of Catholicism in Cochití Pueblo has been a group of Penitentes, or *Flagelantes*. That this movement is of considerable antiquity in the locality is shown by an entry of April 7, 1882 (Good Friday) in Bandelier's journal:

At 9 P.M. there was a horrible noise at the church, shouting, beating, etc. etc. The "flagellants" were there performing. The church closed and the lights put out. In the dark night it was lugubrious to listen to the dismal sounds. The flagellants are from the Cañada mostly, all Mexicans, and the superstition is connected with the performance, that it makes the clouds form and thus brings Rain. It is falling into disuse now.

A middle-aged informant stated that the Penitentes, though no longer so active as formerly, still use the *Morada*, located near the southern edge of the pueblo (see Chapter 3), but that the rites now performed on Good Friday night consist simply of prayers. Whip-

toric privilege of the Crusades, and so now all Catholics in New Mexico must abstain from flesh-meat on Fridays and other prescribed days with the rest of the world. But fish does not have to be eaten, unless one has it and likes it." [In a letter of March 15, 1954, Father Chávez stated that the privilege was withdrawn in the Archdiocese of Santa Fe in October, 1951.]

ping is no longer practiced; he himself had never seen it, though an older brother had. [42]

The local branch belongs to what is known as the "Brothers of Light" sect. They lead in the Rosary for the Dead and special services on Christmas Eve. *Velodia* (a local form of *velada*, meaning "watch" or "wake"?), or Rosary Services, were said for the servicemen before they left and after their safe return. Rosaries may be said at any home; if possible, they should be led by a Penitente. If none is present, the Sacristán ordinarily takes the lead. [92] (The final statement of the preceding section [page 20] should be noted here; Oliver, as of 1952, so far as known, is neither a Penitente nor sacristán.)

No Cochití is currently a member, and, from all information, it seems that José Antonio Montoya was the only Cochití who ever joined this group. His case is all the more interesting in that this man withdrew from membership in the Kusha'lī Society in order to join the Penitentes. Typical was the comment, "It strikes me as funny how a man can go from one extreme to the other." [55]

The United States Government. Analysis of the years of interrelationships between the Cochití, through their officers, and the supervising agency for the United States government involves an account so lengthy and complex that it can be only summarized here. Cochití, like other tribes (see Dale 1951, for general survey), has been administered by some understanding and capable officials and by some who were not.

Following passage of the Indian Reorganization Act in 1934, the federal government set up the United Pueblos Agency in Albuquerque in 1935 (Aberle 1948: 54–60). In 1950, the agency was absorbed by the Albuquerque Regional Office of the Bureau of Indian Affairs. Before 1935, Cochití had been shifted from the control of the Northern Agency in Santa Fe to the Southern Agency in Albuquerque and back again. Since 1935, Cochití has had more stable administration and less interference in internal tribal affairs than previously. Part of this change is attributable to the more enlightened policies that accompanied the change in administrative organization.

Aberle (1948: 57) listed four objectives of the Pueblos Agency: (1) to assist the Indians in becoming self-supporting tribes; (2) to give the Indians the opportunity for better education; (3) to assist interested Indians or co-operatives in establishing businesses; (4) to vest a recognized power in the governors and councils of the tribes so that they could conduct their businesses with the same legality

as could any other municipality. Aberle also said that in the execution of these objectives, goals had had to be interpreted in terms of
the dominant Anglo culture. Hence, monetary considerations had
displaced communal co-operative values. Incentives for group action
had disappeared when individuals and smaller groups began to accumulate private savings, thus causing certain vested interests to
form that were alien to traditional cultural patterns. "Recognition of
the person as primarily an individual rather than primarily a member
of the community, which had for long been creeping into Pueblo
thinking, was accelerated by the program of the Federal Government."

Since 1935, the United Pueblos Agency has created several divisions: Education, Health, Construction (which included Irrigation,
Civilian Conservation Crops of the Indian Bureau, and Roads),
Forestry, Range, Law Enforcement, and Land Use (Aberle 1948:
57). The basic objectives listed by Aberle and the divisions created
within the Agency, which have been continued in approximately the
same form up to the present time, illustrate the emphasis the federal
government places upon economic improvements. Objectives and
divisions, in almost every case, have been directly or indirectly concerned with advancing the economic status of the Indians. In each
pueblo, government officials have worked through the secular officers.

The economic, and other, advantages of the government services
are steadily becoming more obvious to the Cochití. In general, these
people have taken quite readily to many of these services, though
they cannot yet claim to be the most progressive among the various
Pueblo tribes in this respect. Several brief mentions of educational
matters will help illustrate the development at Cochití. Bandelier's
entry of April 7, 1882, for example, includes some interesting data
obtained from Juan José Montoya:

He says that, previous to the years 1845 and '46, there were schools at
the Pueblos, under the direction of the church, that 5 or 6 Indians of
Cochití could, then, read and write, but that paper, books and Ink, were
extremely scarce, so scarce that the writing material was mostly sheepskin on tablets of wood. To write their "letras" upon it, they made a pencil
by flattening and sharpening a ball of lead, with this they drew lines, and
then with a quill they wrote. When the tablet was full, they washed it off,
and dried it again for future use. The Ink they made of charcoal pulverized,
mixed with water, saliva, or "slime" to bind it. Their inkstands were deer-
prongs cut off and one end stopped with a wooden prop. Still they wrote

and learnt to write. The first teacher at Cochití which he went to was Meregildo Lucero. After the American Invasion the schools were gradually abandoned.

In his journal of October 4, 1880, Bandelier reported having been told that there were several in the pueblo who could read and write, one of whom was Juan José Montoya, a brother of José Hilario, who was one of Bandelier's closest friends there. Two days later he was told that Juan José was "self-instructed" (a contradiction of the statement of April 7, 1882). In an entry of October 7, Bandelier stated there had been a school at Cochití four or five years earlier. The people had set everything against it, however, and the teacher had left in disgust. The agent had then refused to give more funds for schooling. This may well have served as a lesson to the Cochití, for in all comments found for subsequent dates, the people are consistently praised as being highly appreciative of the advantages of education. Examples of such appraisements include remarks by Pedro Sánchez, Indian agent, in 1883 (1895: 414), observations of the Eickemeyers in 1894 (1895: 76–89), and Agent Walpole's report for 1899 (1899: 247).

As is true of most Pueblo Indian tribes, virtually all Cochití families send their children to the day school from the preschool year through the sixth grade. An occasional child has attended the parochial school in Peña Blanca. After completion of the sixth grade, Cochití children generally attend the government boarding school in Santa Fe. A few go to St. Catherine's in Santa Fe, and occasionally, depending upon family circumstances, a boy or girl will attend the Albuquerque government school, or a parochial school in Santa Fe, Albuquerque, Bernalillo, or some more distant community. Since this calls for extra financial expenditures for tuition in addition to the greater inconvenience and isolation from the family, the most common practice is to attend the Santa Fe government boarding school.

Various sources have been unanimously agreed that Cochití has been fortunate in the caliber of teachers who have taught there, and, in turn, the Cochití have been named as among the most co-operative tribes in the educational program. At present, the Cochití day school is handled by two teachers. These women are important not only in their classroom work but in their extracurricular contacts with the adults of the pueblo.

As representatives of the Indian Service, the teachers, through the pueblo governor, arrange evening meetings in the school, sometimes with films and sometimes with speakers on farming methods and machinery, food-preserving methods, and other modern techniques, usually aimed at improving the economic condition or health of the people. They show the women how to preserve fruits and vegetables with pressure cookers and other improved methods, assisting when needed. School kitchens are used for much of this, and school shower rooms are available to the people on certain days each week.

According to educational testing data obtained from the Albuquerque Regional Office, results of the Gates Reading Test showed the Cochití Second Grade with an average of 3.18, compared with an area average of 2.95, and a national average of 2.80. The same test for the Cochití Third Grade gave figures of 3.60 against 3.70 and 3.80 for the area and the nation, respectively. Other data for the 1950/51 school year were obtained from the California Progressive Tests, based upon a five-year plan in which the Albuquerque Regional schools are in the second year. Totals from reading, arithmetic, and language sections for the fourth grade gave Cochití 5.20; the area, 4.6; and the nation, 4.8. For the fifth grade, totals gave Cochití 5.6; the area, 5.3; and the nation, 5.8. For the sixth grade, the totals were: Cochití, 6.5; the area, 6.2; and the nation, 6.8.

From these data, it can be seen that the Cochití averages were above those for the area in which Cochití is included but fall somewhat below the national average in most grades. Agency supervisors stated that, in general, the Indian school system of the Region compares favorably with the national averages by the fourth grade; this ranking is held until the seventh grade, where the Indian averages dip slightly but improve at the ninth grade, after which there is a general lag. With this generally satisfactory showing of Cochití school children, it was interesting to hear one father reiterate the oft-made evaluation of modern school systems: "Schools now are nowhere near as strict as when I went; boys wouldn't talk back and get away with it then. They were more courteous to their family, and they learned more in those days." [29] Similar comments were that the boys learned more about farming from their families than they do at boarding school. "Practice is the best teacher." However, in general, Cochití parents encourage their children at least to finish high school, an attitude which can be taken as implicit endorsement of the advantages derived therefrom.

The great adjustment problems associated with the change from day schools to the boarding schools and again to the high schools were cited as specific handicaps which must be overcome in the general program of expanding and improving Indian educational facilities and standards. The Cochití day school was also cited as one of the very few in which an experimental program in the teaching of Spanish was being tried, apparently with very satisfactory results. In regard to the teaching of Spanish, it was revealed that a teacher in the Cochití school was chosen as one of the teachers and was transferred to another pueblo for the experiment. The Cochití officers, however, came to the Agency to protest the loss of this teacher. Upon learning the reason for her transfer, they insisted that she remain at Cochití and the Spanish program be brought to their pueblo. This was done.

Co-ordinated with the day-school program are the periodic visits of the government nurse, doctor, and dentist, who examine school children, preschool children, and adults. Spanish-Americans in the pueblo can take advantage of this health service, though, as previously stated, their children have had to attend school elsewhere since the protests some years ago of several Cochití women over their attendance at the Cochití school.

Welfare services are provided for widows, the physically handicapped, and others unable to support themselves and their dependents. The pueblo governor is frequently the go-between in arranging for this extra care. In less serious and short-term cases, relief may still be provided locally, the traditional method of handling such matters. To an increasing extent, however, the people are taking advantage of the facilities and services available from the federal government. [62]

The present system of having Extension Service field representatives visit the pueblo each week has effected a great improvement, both in operation and personnel. Primarily agricultural consultants, they assist in procuring better seed and better breeding stock and help with the aquisition, use, and maintenance of agricultural, and other, machinery. The Cochití are much more satisfied with this service than with that of the former resident "government farmer." Too often, this official was a political appointee deficient in technical training; several Cochití claimed they had taught the "farmer" more than they had learned from him. In discussing this technician at Acoma, White (1932a: 53) noted: "This 'farmer' does almost everything but farm. He is really the executor of all orders from the office of the superintendent at Albuquerque regarding Acoma."

Other technical experts are sent by the Indian Service to assist the pueblo officials. The water system, with its covered wells, windmills, and gasoline pump, is supervised and regularly tested by these men and laboratory technicians. [20, 44, 45, 62]

In the long-standing problem of disputes over land ownership with the Spanish-Americans, the federal government has been actively helping the Indians regain clear titles. In the summer of 1947, a party of Agency engineers surveyed various house lots in the pueblo as a preparatory step in the proposed trade of land between the pueblo and Leopoldo Rael (p. 15). The trade was still pending as of 1952, amid rumors that Rael was selling out his present holdings and leaving the community. The fact that the trade was still pending also indicates the current Indian Service policy of giving technical assistance when asked, but allowing the Cochití, through their officers, to reach their own decisions. (See Myer, 1951, for a statement of current policy.) Road-building and maintenance have improved in recent years, particularly in the years immediately following the Second World War when El Pueblo Bus Line began operation. (Plate 24d)

Aside from periodic maladministration, Cochití was most seriously disturbed by governmental interference in internal affairs during the first quarter of the century. Beginning as a dispute over the jurisdiction of secular officers, the ramifications of this intrapueblo conflict spread to all phases of Cochití culture. Thus it is essential to know the major features of this controversy if one is to understand the last few decades, the present, and the future of this pueblo.

Toward the end of the last century, three Cochití went to Carlisle, the Indian school in Pennsylvania, the first of their tribe to receive such education. [16] Two of them—Juan de Jesús Pancho and Santiago Quintana—returned to the pueblo with the adopted names of John Dixon and Cyrus Dixon, respectively, though they were not closely related. [3, 15, 48, 49, 53] Bandelier, in his journal of November 28, 1882, noted that Hayoua (John Dixon) was away "at school in Carlisle, Pa."

With Juan Pedro Melchior, a Shrū'tzī member, these two men became leaders of the "Progressive" faction. The third student, Isidro Cordero, has remained a "Conservative," holding active membership in the Ku-sha'lī as one manifestation of this attitude. The Progressives believed that traditional Indian ways, best exemplified by the native religion led by the cacique, medicine men, and war captains, were detrimental to the future welfare of all. They advocated acceptance of the white man's culture in every feasible manner. They wanted to abolish the existing pueblo officers and replace them with judges, sheriffs, and other officials found in Anglo government. They likewise insisted upon a strict interpretation of Catholicism whereby native ceremonies would no longer be tolerated. In this, they received encouragement from Father Gerónimo (Jerome) Hesse, the Franciscan then serving Cochití. Father Jerome left Cochití soon after the bitterest portion of this controversy, having been strongly identified with the Progressives. (It was with somewhat mixed feelings that the Cochití learned that he had been transferred back to Peña Blanca in the summer of 1948 to take charge of the parish, though not to work with the Cochití directly.) In dealing with the Cochití, the common attitude of the Franciscans was that the people had been told the proper behavior for members of the Catholic faith. Since they were informed, compliance rested strictly with the Indians, not with the priests. [37]

The first Progressives were joined by the four Chávez brothers— Cipriano, Francisco, Juan Estévan, and Natividad—José Melchior, Rosendo Trujillo, Abenicio Trujillo, Juan Pancho, and others, almost all of whom happened to be members of the Pumpkin Kiva. [15, 48, 70] Refusing to recognize the authority of the regular pueblo officials, John Dixon became "judge" about 1921. This encroachment on the governor's power was resisted by the Conservatives, among whom Marcial Quintana was a leader. Much tension arose between the factions in their struggle for supremacy. Alcario Montoya and Juan José Trujillo of Cochití, along with representatives from other pueblos, went to Washington to have John Dixon removed as "judge." Washington officials, however, took the side of their local representatives, who supported Dixon in an effort to break the power of the traditional secular and religious leaders. It was rumored that John Dixon was on the government payroll especially for this purpose. The Conservatives fought back with what means they had, one of the most effective being the economic weapon of confiscating the agricultural lands of the Progressives. The fact that some of these lands had been "homesteaded" and, as such, according to pueblo custom, could not be reclaimed by the community, did not deter the Conservatives from attempting to do so.

During the 1920's, the overt antagonisms slowly subsided. The "judgeships" were abolished by the government in 1923, and early in 1925, the most vigorous of the Progressives, John Dixon, died. Within the next decade, Cyrus Dixon and Juan Pedro Melchior also died. Other Progressives continued, for the most part, to live in the pueblo. While there are still some deep-seated resentments on both sides, these feelings are seldom openly expressed now. Progressives today recognize the authority of the governor, the *fiscale,* and the strictly secular officers. They do not recognize the authority of the war captain, nor the powers of the cacique, the medicine men, the ka'tsīnas, and other supernatural manifestations of the native religion.

At present, members of both factions co-operate in performing agricultural community work except for work on the cacique's fields or crops; both help maintain the church, build roads, and join in other activities of this nature. Members of both factions play together on the pueblo baseball teams, and the two groups have been further merged through several intermarriages. It was interesting to learn in the summer of 1951 that several young women from Progressive families who had married Conservative husbands had participated in several of the recent dances, such as the Feast Day *Tablita* Dance. [3, 44] At the 1952 Feast Day, following the suggestion of the Conservative governor, several Progressives assisted in policing the crowd of spectators throughout the day. Thus, though not actually dancing, they were contributing to the smooth functioning and general success of the day's activities.

One of the more recent causes of internal strife at Cochití arose from acquiring the right to vote in national and state elections. From erroneous impressions obtained from poor advisors—some intentionally deceiving the Indians—tribal leaders have feared that by exercising this right to vote, the Indians will expose themselves to property tax and other forms of taxation. The Cochití Council of *Principales* was sufficiently convinced of this to specifically instruct their people not to vote. This directive had been followed except by a few of the Progressives, primarily nonresidents. According to rumor, one older man who had recently been at odds with tribal authority had registered at Peña Blanca, thereby displaying his independence. However, he was ill on election day, and, as of 1952, no resident Cochití had actually voted. [42, 55, 70, 88]

Having developed this tolerance of the other's stand, the people of Cochití have become better able to co-operate in taking advantage of what they desire from the services offered by the currently more enlightened administration of the Indian Service.

Other Neighbors, Friends, Tourists, and Anthropologists. So obviously conglomerate a grouping is rarely discussed in such a tribal account as this. However, the cumulative effect of these outsiders through many decades has had profound influence upon the Cochití and their way of life. Specific instances, though difficult to relate in accurate and full detail, are numerous and varied in nature. Some have been sporadic and of brief duration; others have existed more or less continuously through the years. The experiences range from pleasant associations to instances of bitter disillusionment, frustration, and resentment. All have had repercussions in Cochití life. (Lange, 1952a, 1953).

Certain relevant data have already been discussed under the section "The Spanish-American Residents and Neighbors." Additional data appear at the end of Chapter 6 in the sections "Wage-earning within the Pueblo" and "Wage-earning away from the Pueblo." Contacts with neighbors, friends, and tourists have resulted in developments and changes in the economic phases of Cochití culture. In pre-European times, the Cochití made whatever items they needed, or obtained them through trade with other tribes. After the arrival of the Spaniards and others in the Southwest this pattern continued without extensive change. As already mentioned, local stores provided what were considered until recently essentially luxury items, and the Cochití remained on a barter economy for the most part.

In recent years, most discernible in perhaps the last generation, there has been an increased interest in money. Cash income has enabled the Cochití to buy ready-made items and in many cases items of materials superior to those to which they had access, or were capable of handling, at home.

Cash income, however, has not resulted in the disappearance of handicraft; there has been a continuation of these industries, though with some modification in materials and forms. This continuation and, in some cases, amplification reflect the steady rise of the tourist business in New Mexico and the entire Southwest. United Pueblos Agency figures for 1942 (Payne 1942: 11) indicated income at Cochití from arts and crafts as $2,563, a fourth-place ranking behind stock-raising, agriculture, and labor, in ascending order.

Despite the direct and deep significance of economic influences and changes, other influences have been important too. Friendships with non-Indians have paved the way for new perspectives in viewing the world and its events. In a few cases, this has amounted to an intentional infiltration and revamping of the Cochití traditional way; in most instances, it has resulted simply from an unconscious exchange and sharing of new ideas and values. Much of this has led inevitably to a breaking down of Cochití custom, though in some degree the Indian's awareness of his own culture and his pride in it have been reinforced.

A number of enlightened leaders of the Conservative faction have made tourist contacts that have developed into firm friendships. One outcome of these has led to the children's being assisted to advanced education, often away from Cochití and even out of the Southwest. In some cases the result has been that the individual left the culture; in other cases he has returned to the culture but invariably with interest in activities other than those traditionally followed.

I shall make no attempt to appraise the impact of my own presence in Cochití, but it appears worth while to consider the rather impressive list of my predecessors and their impacts. Beginning with the earlier investigators, such as Bandelier, Bourke, and Lummis, continuing on with Dumarest, the Eickemeyers, and Starr, and a generation later, Goldfrank, Benedict, and Boas, and those who gathered material for E. S. Curtis, it is apparent that Cochití has been steadily exposed to the probing and inquisitiveness of these individuals and undoubtedly innumerable others whose efforts were more superficial or at least have not appeared in print.

There is no doubt that the presence of these investigators, the interests they have manifested, and the discussions they have shared, both with friends and those who sought to oppose them, have exerted considerable influence on Cochití thought and attitudes. Certain subject matter written about the Cochití has obviously evoked great amusement, even ridicule among them. Attempts to investigate esoteric facets have met with open antagonism or the more diplomatic silence of feigned ignorance. Throughout Bandelier's journal, Starr's diary, and similar sources, there are continual references to the clandestine sale of images and idols, as well as to the open sale of various objects of interest to museums.

In practically any topic, however, the Cochití have shown interest. For some, their interest amounts to self-inspection engendered from the outside; for others, it takes the form of an awakening, or renewal, of regard for the old ways, whether or not they are followers of these ways. Some have viewed the probings of these investigators with a sense of history, a willingness to help compile and record data before they disappear along with the old people. For yet others, it is simply an opportunity to earn "easy" money. But whatever the nature of the relationship between Indian and investigator, the cumulative impact upon the Cochití has been considerable; its full extent and quality will probably never be fully realized.

3 RESOURCES, PROPERTY, AND OWNERSHIP

Pueblo Lands

ABERLE (1948: 5) HAS COMMENTED in regard to land among the Pueblo tribes of New Mexico: "Land being the basis of Pueblo economy, to understand the Indian's relation to his soil is vital. The years of contention over boundaries, titles to grants, and legislation influence the Indian's habit of thought as well as his laws. Land in the eyes of the Indian is his most precious possession."

Extent and Utilization. At present, the Cochití Reservation comprises the original Spanish grant, subsequently confirmed by the Mexican and the United States governments, totaling 22,763.31 acres (Aberle 1948: 84).[1] In addition, the Cochití lease 3,728.30 acres of land: 640 from the State of New Mexico and 3,088.30 from the Public Domain Grazing Service. Thus, the total land controlled by the Cochití amounts to 26,491.61 acres.

[1] Details of title history can be found in Brayer (1939) and in Twitchell (1914, I: 425–453, 469–471, 479). The latter source (p. 479) states: "The Spanish document, dated in 1689, is not genuine. The property was surveyed in 1859 for a fraction over 24,256 acres and was patented in 1864." Present Agency notes indicate the official survey shows 23,218.22 acres less 451.61 acres of non-Indian private claims plus 3.30 acres for the Government School site. Not included are 149.88 acres in dispute with the Pueblo of Santo Domingo. Bandelier, in his journal of October 15, 1885, noted that trouble was brewing over the Sile overlap with Santo Domingo.

Of this total, 24,624.61 acres are nonirrigated range land of which a considerable portion consists of relatively barren hills cut by many sandy arroyos. Irrigation ditches serve 1,867 acres, of which only 630 are cultivated, the remainder being used as pasturage.

The importance attached by the Cochití to these lands is indicated by a note in Bandelier's journal of April 12, 1882: ". . . seems that the Rio Grande is gradually eating its left bank. He [Juan José Montoya] made the very significant remark that it would be much better if the River would eat the pueblo than to have it eat up its lands. The pueblo would soon be rebuilt, elsewhere!"

Range Lands. Of the 26,491.61 acres used by the Cochití, 25,861.61 acres are devoted to grazing, all nonirrigated range lands except for 1,237 acres. Cochití has three windmills with storage tanks: one near the northwest corner of the reservation, another at the western edge of the reservation near the road leading to Peralta Canyon and over the Jemez Mountains, and a third in the northeast corner of the reservation. Stock on the open range can get water at any of these locations or from the canals or river, though fences bar access at some places. The outer perimeter of Cochití Reservation has been fenced since 1930. [21] The project was sponsored by the Indian Service, and the Indians were paid for their labor [62]. There are no other fences except those immediately enclosing and subdividing the cultivated acreage.

A report of the Extension agent for the United Pueblos Agency (Payne 1946: 4) describes the Cochití range as generally sandy, with small areas of alkali. Wind erosion is estimated as slight. Water erosion in areas with some grass is rated light to moderate, while in the more barren, higher altitudes, it is considered moderate to severe, reaching badland stages in small areas in the northwest corner of the reservation.

Poisonous weeds, primarily locoweed (*Astragalus mollissimus*), are described in Payne's report as a medium infection, causing moderate losses. Friar Antonio Cavallero reported in 1779 that the meadows south of Cochití were little used because of the damage to the animals that grazed on the plants there (Biblioteca Nacional, *Legajo X*: Document 59).

Rodents, mainly kangaroo rats (*Dipodomys* sp.), are noted as a medium to heavy infection in the lighter soils, with moderate damage resulting. Predatory animals on the range consist of a few coyotes (Canis sp.) which cause slight damage. (Payne 1946: 9) Unmentioned in Payne's report are bears and mountain lions; these larger animals have seldom, if ever, been seen on the reservation in recent years. A few remain in the mountains.

According to Agency data, a total of 484 animals (354 cattle and 130 horses) were on the range in 1943. This was noted as 100 per cent use of the range capacity (Payne 1943: 9). In 1950, there were 192 cattle, 191 horses and mules, 18 sheep, and no goats on the range (Nations 1950: 2). Although conservation recommendations have been made to these people since the early 1930's (Aberle 1948: 19–20), there still appear to be no actual tribal mechanisms for rigidly preventing overgrazing of the range. [20, 45]

Range land is owned in common and is available to any tribesman for such uses as cutting firewood, collecting wild-plant products, obtaining adobe and rock for building, and similar purposes. Grazing rights are theoretically limited by the governor, but lack of enforcement makes the restriction actually ineffectual. [1, 15, 44, 45]

Cultivated Lands. Cultivated lands are completely under irrigation, as described in the following chapter. Plots for dry farming and flood-water farming, in common use up to twenty years ago, are available, but no one has wanted them since the irrigation canals and dam of the Middle Rio Grande Conservancy District were constructed in the early 1930's. Cultivated tracts are owned in part by individuals and in part by the community. [3, 45, 53]

It is interesting that the Domínguez report of 1776 noted that there were no individual landholders (". . . y al mismo tpō no sean los individuos haciendados" [Biblioteca Nacional, *Legajo X*: Document 43]). A literal interpretation of this statement could indicate that the "homesteading" described in the following section was a Spanish, or later, introduction. On the other hand, the statement may only reflect oversimplification of the situation at the time of the Domínguez visit.

Ownership of Agricultural Land

Communal Ownership. Communally owned irrigated land falls into several categories. First are those fields reserved by the tribe for the cacique, their religious leader. Though referred to as "the fields of the cacique," they actually belong to the community. [3, 44, 45, 50, 88] Formerly more extensive, this tract consists of about two acres at present. Its location may be shifted at the discretion of the war captains. This is seldom done, however, but nutriment from the irrigation waters seems to revitalize the field sufficiently to keep it producing, despite the fact that it is planted solely in blue corn. [42, 92]

When the pueblo had a resident priest in the mission, land was set aside for his support. This land reverted to the pueblo many years ago. The extent of these tracts is difficult to ascertain. In 1754, Father Trigo described the church lands as several *fanegas*[2] of wheat and one *cuartilla* of maize, "whereby the father is assured he will not have to go with a sack on his shoulder." (Hackett 1937: 451)

In the Domínguez manuscript of 1776 these fields were described as four fine *milpas* of great fertility and supplied with water from an irrigation system. In addition, there was a small plot at the edge of the pueblo, near the *convento*, where garden produce was grown. The yield of the four *milpas* was described as eighty, or more, *fanegas* of wheat, and seventy, or more, of maize. (Biblioteca Nacional, *Legajo X*: Document 43) Here the use of the term *fanega* is identical with the Cochití present-day use of "anega." By current standards of production of these pueblo farmers, this means the fields were divided into about eight acres of maize and perhaps ten of wheat, with about an acre devoted to garden vegetables for the padre.

In 1817, the land which the pueblo furnished the resident priest comprised four *suertes*, with a fifth *suerte* used as a garden plot. (Stephens Collection: Document 2) The author of this document advocated one *suerte* for actual maintenance of the church building and its repairs instead of the priest's keeping all produce for himself. As illustrated by this document, the amount of land devoted to the maintenance of the church and the labor the Indians expended upon this acreage resulted in many controversies between the priests and the Indians.

Another type of community land consists of acreage recently purchased by the government from non-Indians who held land on the reservation, especially in the vicinity of Peña Blanca. A portion of this land is used as community pasture and is fenced and irrigated. [3, 13, 45, 49, 50, 53] The remaining few acres are planted with fruit trees issued by the government about 1937, or earlier. [40]

---

[2] Land set aside for the support of the church and priests characterized the seventeenth century as well. (Scholes 1942: 11–17, 25–26, *passim*.) I noted during the field work of 1951 that the Cochití spoke of "anegas" of wheat, units somewhat comparable to a bushel, an interesting derivation from the *fanega* as a unit of land.

The legal status of this orchard is somewhat confused. The land belongs to the pueblo, and the orchard is communally trimmed and irrigated. The trees, however, though originally issued to the tribe, were distributed to individual families, whose control is rather haphazard because of the distance of the orchard from the pueblo. Fruit is frequently claimed by the first discoverers, or raiders from Peña Blanca (often synonymous with "first"), or birds. Since owners get little, if any, there is a growing tendency to neglect these trees. Families that do value fruit find this orchard too inconvenient to use and too difficult to protect; consequently, they have planted other trees nearer their fields. The Peña Blanca orchard was intended as a replacement of the one torn up during construction of the western canal of the Conservancy District in the early 1930's. Damages were paid the pueblo, and these funds were used to begin the new orchard. [1, 3, 45, 70]

Individual Ownership. Private ownership of agricultural land can be acquired in four ways.

First, land can be inherited from parents or siblings. Normally, land is divided equally, regardless of age or sex of the heirs. [1, 3, 15, 70] Occasionally, a single tract is apportioned among heirs on the basis of so many furrows to each. [70] Stepchildren seldom share in inheritance since they have already received a portion of the estate of their own parent. [44] Adopted children share as fully qualified heirs. [15]

Second, land can be acquired through trade or purchase. No official permission is required for such transactions, which are limited by federal law to members of the tribe. [45, 53] Goldfrank's data (1927: 30) confirm this practice, noting that when leaving the pueblo for a long time, or marrying and moving out of the village, it is customary for a man to sell, give, or trade his property.

A third means of acquiring land is by "homesteading." Once cleared, such land remains in the possession of the man and his heirs until they choose to dispose of it. Permission to clear a tract of land is obtained from the governor and council, and this was done quite frequently prior to the Conservancy District construction. It also appears to have been more common when dry farming was less of a climatic risk. At present, there is essentially no land suitable for homesteading under the canals and ditches. [40, 44, 45, 50, 53] As a result, all cultivated land is individually owned or belongs to the community. Communal holdings are administered by the Council of *Principales* through the governor and other officers.

The fourth means of acquiring land is to petition the governor for an idle plot, or to ask for any plot of a certain size. The plot is given to the petitioner, assuming his need is justified, and remains in his, or in his heirs', possession so long as it is used. "Used" normally means cultivating the land annually, though it is possible for title to be retained if the plot lies fallow for several years. Apparently, this period is flexible and is determined by the current demand for land. At present there is a surplus of good agricultural land, especially east of the river. Hence plots may lie idle for periods longer than a few years without claims being made upon them. [3, 40, 45, 50] When assigned land is no longer used, it reverts to the tribe for reassignment, differing, in this respect, from land originally cleared, or homesteaded, by individuals.

Current features of landholding agree generally with observations for the early 1920's. Goldfrank's impressions (1927: 10–11, 27–30) of property concepts pointed to older patterns in which clan holdings were more important. Clan holdings actually consisted of the extension of family property through marriage, with no clan ever holding a particular plot of land. Evidence of this pattern was seen in the fact that after a man's death his property reverted to his mother and sisters if he had no direct heirs. However, the practice of allowing the widow to inherit property was becoming more prevalent. Goldfrank attributed this development to increasing contacts with Americans, to more frequent construction of houses by the men for themselves, and to the long-standing relations and intermarriages with Spanish-Americans. It appears doubtful that this development was recent, even at the time of Goldfrank's field studies in 1923. Bandelier recorded the following data regarding inheritance in his journal of October 7, 1880:

> If the wife had any land at the time of her marriage, it is set apart for her. The balance of lands are divided equally among her and the children, each child receiving an equal share. The "cosecha" (harvest) is hers. . . . The dying person can make a will, preferring child or grandchild, and it is respected. His [the informant's] mother preferred two grandchildren.

It is apparent that this emphasis upon the family, at the expense of the clan, has continued to the present day.

A 1940 analysis of landholdings showed twenty-nine heads of families holding more than 10 acres, three holding more than 40 acres, and fourteen families holding no land (*United Pueblos Quarterly Bulletin* 1939–40: 17). The 1944 Extension Service Report (Payne 1944: 8) indicated an estimated 22.6 acres of irrigated land as necessary for the support of a family of five. Individuals checked in 1947, 1948, and 1951 had tracts ranging from 9 to 30 acres. (See Appendix 6.)

In regard to farm-property ownership, one of the most obvious changes apparent to the Cochití themselves has been the great decrease in small ranch houses, "ranchitos," on the farms (Plate 11b). A generation ago and earlier, almost every family occupied a ranchito for extended periods, if not for the entire growing season. Poore (1894: 429) in his account as of 1890 noted, "Adobe houses of a single room are found where land is farmed at a distance from the pueblo." At present, some women have sets of metates and bins at the ranch rather than in the pueblo. Also, special subterranean roasting ovens for green corn are located at the ranchitos but not in the pueblo. In 1948, ranchitos were used by only ten families, and there were three or four other buildings standing but not used. In 1951, fourteen families regularly stayed at their ranchitos.[3]

As noted, this situation is in contrast to the "old days" (ha'ma hai'ko) when most families left the pueblo either in early spring or just after the July 14 Saint's Day celebration. They remained at their ranches until after harvest time except for occasional trips home for additional supplies or for the celebration of various feast days. In his entry for April 17, 1882, Bandelier noted in his journal that the village was virtually depopulated in the summer, nearly everyone going to ranchos where they lived until September or October. "Few remain in the Pueblo; even the Cacique leaves for his 'huerta.'"

Today many, having allowed their ranch houses to fall into ruin, make a daily trek to and from the fields. A few keep their houses as crude shelters while doing night irrigating and similar special work. If not traveling by wagon, the people walk, "hitchhike" on a neigh-

---

[3] In 1948, families using ranchitos included: Clofe Arquero, Ignacia Arquero, Juan Estévan Chalan, Joe Melchior (occupied by a renter), Epifanio Pecos, Damasio Quintana, José Domingo Quintana, José Hilario Quintana, Joe Trujillo, and Juan Velasquez. In 1951, others were using their ranchitos: Philip Cooka, Santiago Cordero, Francisco Herrera, Agrapina Quintana, Cipriano Quintana, and Delphine Quintana; the following had ranchitos but seldom stayed there: Estephanita Herrera, Carolyn Melchior Pecos, Juan José Suina, Juan Pancho, Ramón Herrera, Eleuterio Suina, Cresencio Pecos, and Diego Romero.

bor's wagon, or in a few cases ride horses. From 1945 to 1948—when the El Pueblo Bus Line (Plate 24*d*) operated on a daily schedule between the pueblo and Santa Fe or Albuquerque—there were some who "commuted" between their homes and fields. As transportation facilities have improved, many prefer to be in the pueblo as much as possible to take advantage of opportunities to attend various pueblo feast-day activities or to go to town for various reasons. Those who maintain their ranchitos feel they are more convenient to the farm work, their principal occupation, and they also like the greater coolness and quiet as contrasted with the "hot, noisy, crowded pueblo." [45, 49]

Fruit trees, normally located along the irrigation ditches on the edge of cultivated fields, are owned and inherited or transferred either together with, or independently of, the fields. In cases of joint inheritance, individual heirs often acquire title to specific limbs and their fruit. [53]

Water Rights

Nothing was found in historical documents or published literature regarding water rights at Cochití.

The total water supply for irrigation is regulated by the Middle Rio Grande Conservancy District. The pueblo is the first community below Cochití Dam, built in the early 1930's by the District. With allotments controlled by the District, this position is not so advantageous as it might appear. There have been times, however, when Cochití has benefited from its position. When water is turned into the Cochití ditches from either the eastern or western canal, rights to it are determined largely on the basis of "First come, first served." This means that a field located at the upper, or northern, end of a ditch (ko'pash-ti[awa]) or a field located immediately "under a ditch, or lateral" (u'sht[io]-wisht, or *sangría*) is most desirable. [3, 15, 49, 92]

Owners of fields at the bottom of the ditches, or farthest from the ditches laterally, are forced, when the water supply is low, to irrigate at night or at other times when the other farmers are not using water. When difficulties arise, through either undue monopoly of the supply or carelessness in maintaining gates or dikes, complaints are made to the governor. In such disputes or shortages, the governor, as "water boss," can theoretically ration and allot the water. In practice, this has rarely occurred. In comparison, White (1942: 105–106) found the position of "water boss" at Santa Ana to be a separate and important civil and sacerdotal office.

Although disputes over water rights are ordinarily settled by the governor, his decision can be appealed to the Council of *Principales*. Lack of formal regulation of water rights was found to be typical of other Southwestern tribes, such as the Havasupai (Spier 1928: 102) and Navaho (Hill 1938: 23). For San Ildefonso, Whitman (1947: 18) reported that the governor "arbitrates questions concerning land and water rights—the most fertile source of quarrels at San Ildefonso." Cushing (1920: 266–267) indicated more organized regulation of water use at Zuñi:

So limited is the supply of water during the dry months, that every householder keeps an account-stick hanging somewhere near the sky-hole. Every time he waters a set of his "earth-bins," he has to cut a notch in this account-stick; and as the latter is liable to inspection by the sub-chiefs any morning, he dares not, or rather does not, use more than his proper allowance of the water.

In all probability, the "First come, first served" policy was the rule during earlier times at Cochití. Before the 1930 dam and canal construction, which resulted in a more reliable supply of water, it is likely that this policy caused more frequent and bitter disputes than have ordinarily occurred in recent years. It should be noted that prior to the 1930 construction, and as far back as the Cochití could remember, there was less acreage irrigated from the Rio Grande. Many cultivated tracts depended upon arroyo flood waters, ground seepage, or precipitation. These aspects of water utilization are discussed in the next chapter.

Fields west of the river are preferred because they are more accessible. Bandelier noted in an entry of October 17, 1880, that soil was worth from one to three dollars per *vara*, depending on the length of the strip. He added that it was "not cheap." Such a vacillating evaluation also characterizes modern land values. It is virtually impossible to get a cash-value quotation on any tract, partly because the Indian thinks in terms of traditional barter instead of cash, and partly because of a reluctance to make a concrete statement that might prove a handicap in any future negotiations with a fellow tribesman.

The most highly valued tracts are those directly below the canals, as previously noted. Owing to a declining interest in agriculture among the young men, there has been for some years considerable unused acreage under the Cochití ditches. There has also been some hesitancy on the part of those who do farm to ask for additional acreage in view of the continued threat of water shortage. Others feel that farming is more difficult and tedious than other forms of labor and that the water shortage, though a factor, is not the dominant one contributing to the decline of farming.

Today, within the pueblo proper, there is a water system designed to furnish an adequate supply of pure water for drinking and general household use. Three wells, each with a windmill, and one of which has a gasoline pump, supply water to several outdoor hydrants and to several troughs for stock. The government school has its own windmill and tank. Anyone noticing that the water pressure is low is supposed to turn on a mill; if he sees a tank overflowing, he is expected to turn off the mill. [3, 45, 49, 70] A few families have water piped into their homes, and the number is steadily increasing as washing machines become more numerous. Several others have hydrants in their yards or have the pipes and fittings ready for installation as soon as they have modern kitchens. [16, 53]

For the most part, this water system is adequate for the needs of the village. Again, this water is used on an unregulated basis of "First come, first served," with no meters to measure consumption. Invariably, in the period immediately preceding the annual Feast Day, when preparations place an unusually heavy demand on the supply, it fails, partly because of the unusual demand and partly because the small capacity of the storage tanks prevents any advance storing. Also it is said there is relatively less wind in mid-July. The gasoline engine and pump were installed in 1945 to alleviate this condition. For the first time, the water supply did not fail in 1951, one of the driest years on record. This was attributed to the conscientious effort of two men and demonstrated that the system is adequate if proper care is exercised in handling it. [3, 15, 20, 27]

Major overhauls of the water system are supervised by engineers of the United Pueblos Agency, and this office collects periodic water samples for laboratory analysis. The Cochití pride themselves on their sanitary water-system as contrasted with the open wells still used in other pueblos. "We can dance and do other things just as well [i.e., adhere to the old way of life] even if we have these things." [15, 16, 44, 53]

Property and Ownership within the Village

The Site and Town Plan. As already stated, Cochití has occupied its present site for at least seven hundred years, the only interruption being the years of the Pueblo Revolt, 1680–1696. The first detailed account of the pueblo was that of the Domínguez party, in which Cochití was described as in the middle of the Río Grande Valley, elevated in respect to the river, and surrounded by broad, fertile plains. (Biblioteca Nacional, *Legajo X*: Documents 43, 59) When Bourke and Strout (Bloom 1938: 234–237) visited the pueblo in 1881, it was described by Strout as "built in a hollow in a rambling scattering kind of way, divided into four distinct villages, each with its own plaza. . . . Some of the houses are falling down and the pueblo has but little to say in its favor."

Bourke's notes (Bloom 1938: 235) differed from Strout's in recording two plazas rather than four, though they agreed upon four divisions of the pueblo. They also noted that houses were one- and two-storied, the lower portions being of basalt blocks laid in mud, and the upper, of adobes. Entrance was both by ladders to the roof entrances and by ground-floor doors (Plate 24a). Windows were of selenite (Plate 17a). They observed ovens of stone and mud both on roofs and on the ground, and house chimneys were constructed of adobe and pottery. (This reference is undoubtedly to the practice, still prevalent at Cochití and other pueblos, of placing one or more pots, with the bottoms knocked out, as an element of the chimney. As the encasing adobe weathers away, the pottery, of course, becomes exposed to view.) In addition, numerous corrals were noted, as well as two *estufas*, or kivas. The church (Plate 5a) was described as "very old and dilapidated; . . . The cross had fallen off from front of the Church and its whole appearance is strongly suggestive of decrepitude and ruin."

Details for 1890 were noted by Poore (1894: 429) as follows:

Cochiti has an extremely favorable site. It faces the river at a height of 25 feet and is surrounded on 3 sides by tillable plains. The buildings in town, 50 in number, are generally separated, not more than three dwellings being contiguous. The larger portion are of 1 story.

. . . .

The houses of the town are better built and more healthful than in many pueblos. Paneled doors, window sashes, and glass are generally used. Open antichambers for sleeping are noted. This is the most northern pueblo in which are to be seen inclosures, or yards, in front of houses. These are called corrals, and are used as such for horses in waiting for one or two hours. The fences are formed of cedar trunks driven in the earth at close intervals and bound together with telegraph wire, thongs of leather, and horsehair. The plaza is unusually large and the streets wide. The Catholic church is in good repair, the Mexican contingent taking a greater interest than the Indians in its ceremonials.

Additional details on the appearance of Cochití toward the end of the last century can be obtained from photographs in this volume. Obvious changes are seen, both in the mission, with the change from the typical mission façade with its flat roof to the gabled sheet-iron roof with first a tall steeple and later the present-day shorter one, and in the present absence of multiple-storied buildings in the pueblo. Today, the sole two-storied building is the home and store of Leopoldo Rael, the Spanish-American storekeeper. The front-yard corrals have disappeared, but the domination of single-storied, separate houses prevails.

Apparently no further data regarding the site and town plan were recorded until Goldfrank's work. In her opening paragraph (1927: 7) she states, "On first entering the village one is impressed with its modernity, the new one-story buildings, the tin roofs, . . ."

These past descriptions of Cochití fit the 1952 situation with but one major exception: it is difficult to understand Strout's statement that Cochití was "built in a hollow," unless he meant in relation to the rather distant landscape with its various mountain ranges.

In the account by Poore (1894: 429) there is a statement that "Cochití has no orchards, and no trees are to be seen here save the cottonwoods and willows on the sandy island of the river." Trees now growing in the plaza and elsewhere in the village were there as early as 1912, but at Poore's time apparently were not there or were too small to be noted. (Compare the various plates in this volume.)

At present, as in the past, the life of the Cochití centers about the plaza (ka'katch^e). (Plates 2, 19, and 20) The series of houses surrounding the plaza on four sides, the two kivas, north and northeast of the plaza, and the church off the southeastern corner of the plaza constitute the heart, literally and figuratively, of the village. Additional plazas and house groupings, mentioned in early accounts, are difficult to identify because of confusion in the use of the terms *plaza, street,* and *open area.* Present-day Cochití designate but one plaza and recall no other. Bourke's additional divisions and plazas probably

included such groupings as the northeastern sector of the village and
the several blocks south and west of the church. In 1947, the officers
placed large posts several feet apart to prevent any vehicles entering
the plaza. This was done to keep the mobile concession stands, and
some spectators, from parking so close to the plaza that they interfered with the progress of the dancing. In 1952 these posts were still
in place and appeared to be permanent fixtures. A result of this has
been that the rooster-pulls, or *gallos,* have been moved to the open
space south of the church, for the posts interfere with the horsemen
riding in and out of the plaza and the officers fear that someone will
be injured because of them. [21, 44, 45, 49]

Modern Cochití, in the minds of the Indians, is divided into
six sectors, whose boundaries are shown on Map 2. The principal
function of these sectors is to delimit the territory which each of the
six *fiscalitos* and six *alguacilitos,* assistants to the major officers, must
cover in making official announcements to every household. Although
the number of these sectors coincides with the ceremonial number—
six—of the Cochití and may have originally come from this fact (as
may have come also the custom of designating six of each type of
minor officer), no correlation with the ceremonial directions and the
associated colors, plants, and animals is found aside from the east,
north, west, and south sectors. (No sector is associated with either
the zenith or nadir.) The six sectors are: East Group (Ha′ñī-sat-yu),
North Group (Gī′tī-sat-yu), West Group (Po′ñī-sat-yu), South
Group (Kwī′sat-yu), Round Mesa (Ko′lash-kū[le]), and Plaza Group
(Ka′kat[che]). [44, 62, 70]

Minor designations, and currently nonfunctional (formerly also?),
are three subdivisions of the South Group: the Southwest Group
(Kwī′poñī-sat-yu), the Southeast Group (Kwī′hañī-sat-yu), and the
Butterfly Group (Po[r]′la-ga). [44, 70]

On the eastern periphery, the village is restricted by the Conservancy District canal and cultivated fields. To the north and west, however, there has been considerable expansion, beginning about 1912.
Building dates noted on Map 2 show this development.

Aside from the expansion, another obvious shift has been that away
from multiple-storied dwellings. Although the Rodríguez-Chamuscado expedition (Hammond and Rey 1927: 8, 48) of 1581 reported
two- and three-storied houses, no one today can recall a house of
more than two stories at Cochití and none exists at present. Photo-

graphs in this volume show numerous two-storied homes at the turn of the century, and Map 2 indicates the locations of these as recalled by informants. As shown, most of these structures bordered on, or were near, the plaza. Older informants say that multiple stories made the lower floors cooler in summer and warmer in winter. "They look nice, too." [25]

Fairly common in the photographs of fifty years ago are windows of selenite mosaics (Plate 17a); no example remained as of 1952, though numerous informants recalled them and some had helped make or repair them. A special white clay was used to caulk the segments of the selenite. [88] In his journal of November 9, 1880, Bandelier stated that according to José Hilario, the Mexicans burned lime which the Indians bought, as they did not know how to burn it. He also said that, according to Zashua, when the Cochití wanted to prepare "the gypsum plates for their windows, they boil them in hot water, so as to further the cleavage."

Since multiple-storied houses have disappeared, there are no longer any ovens on the roofs, though almost every family has one or more in the yard. Other current architectural features fall within the normal pueblo pattern, with perhaps a slightly abnormal number of gabled roofs of galvanized iron, as noted by Goldfrank.

Perhaps the most drastic innovation of recent years in the outward appearance of the pueblo has been the electric wires and poles installed in 1950. As in other pueblos, even greater change in the lives of the people has come with modern appliances and other uses of electric power; these ramifications are elaborated upon later in this chapter.

Despite these changes, most new houses at Cochití are still blessed by the medicine men. No particular society is preferred for this task. When the family first moves into the house, there is a feast, and the house is dedicated by the medicine men in the presence of the assemblage. [50, 53] Another informant stated that prayer sticks (still another said "prayer feathers" [42]) are placed in the four walls of the house interior, just above the level of the floor. [44] In houses with adobe floors, they are often placed under the floor, which practice may have been the older one, antedating the use of wooden floors. This procedure, according to these two informants, is carried out by the medicine men, unwitnessed by the family or anyone else.

Community-owned Real Property. In this category are the two kivas; community houses associated with them; society houses; a house built for the "government farmer," who formerly resided in the pueblo; a community corral; and the water system.

The eastern kiva (Plate 9) belongs to the Turquoise people, or moiety, and is called Ha'nūnu, or Sho'ame, Chīk'ya (East, or Tur-

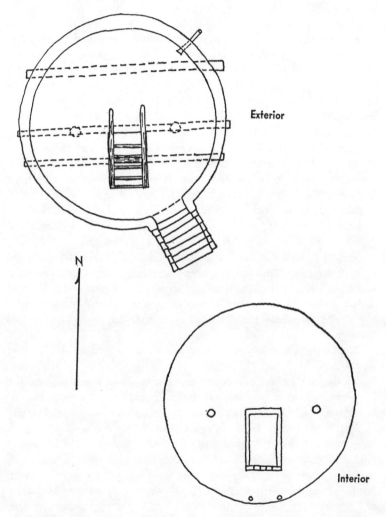

Fig. 1.—KIVA GROUND PLAN. (Plan essentially the same for both the Turquoise and the Pumpkin kivas.)

quoise, Kiva). That of the Pumpkin people, to the west, is called Po'nūnu, or Dañī, Chīk'ya (West, or Pumpkin, Kiva). In the old days, a kiva was sometimes called "shī'pap," reflecting the tribal place of emergence on to this earth, according to tradition. [92] The present kivas have remained unchanged, except for minor repairs, for as long as informants could remember; they were not familiar with a statement by Bandelier, in his journal of April 18, 1882, which noted that the kivas were always repaired unless they were fully destroyed —in which case they were rebuilt in another place.

Bandelier, in his journal of October 22, 1880, observed that the Cochití kivas were perfectly plain inside, with a hearth on the south side below the roof opening. Two large posts supported the roof; attached to the posts were simple board shelves on which to place candles. The wall was plain except for wooden pegs on which to hang scalps and to support the long pole on which the scalps were carried.

Bourke's notes, as of 1881 (Bloom 1938: 235), are also of comparative interest:

Two Estufas. 1st 12 paces in D. Circular, overground 8' deep, approached by a staircase of ten steps of undressed wood. Lower courses are stone—upper of adobe; plastered within and without; whitewashed within. Roof supported by a horizontal pine beam, squared, 2' thick, under which are vertical struts of pine. — No hole in wall, no windows & no air Except down through ladder-hole. Green corn painted on walls. Ground very damp. Second Estufa—identical with first. Cross on wall.

The features described by Bandelier and Bourke are very similar to present ones. The outside stairway (wī'yanī) remains a feature found in other eastern Keresan villages and stands in contrast to such pueblos as Jemez and Tesuque, where there are ladders both inside and outside. The Cochití kiva entrance is oriented toward the plaza, apparently for no reason other than convenience. The ladder (wa'kos —the term applied to any ladder [70]) of each kiva projects well above the roof, 10 feet or more; the Turquoise Kiva ladder has a decorative cap at the top; the Pumpkin does not.[4] The ladder enters

―――――――――

[4] In 1947, about three weeks before the July 14 Feast Day, the head men of the Pumpkin Kiva built and installed a new ladder. The practical way in which this was done and the almost complete absence of associated ritual were somewhat unexpected. The two pine poles measured about twenty-one feet in length, and there were eleven rungs of juniper spaced over the lower two-thirds of the ladder. The width of the ladder was the exact measurement of the roof entrance,

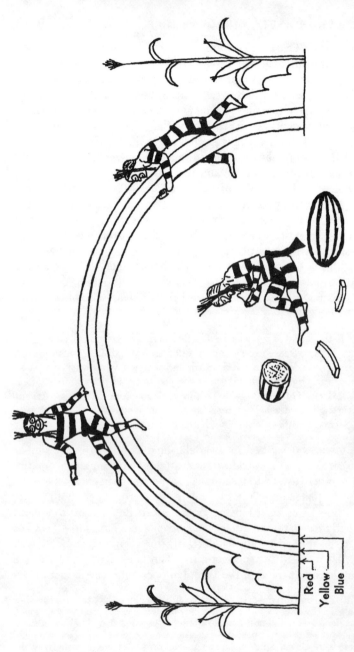

Red
Yellow
Blue

Fig. 2.—Turquoise Kiva Mural. (Based upon descriptions of informants.)

the kiva through a rectangular roof-opening, approximately 3 feet by 6, oriented with its long axis on a north-south line. The protruding ladder points northward. Unlike those of Santo Domingo, Jemez, and other pueblos, the Cochití kivas have no wall openings. The roof supports and struts mentioned in earlier accounts appear today as three heavy vigas with two vertical struts, or pillars, under the middle beam. (Fig. 1) Informants stated that there had been no murals in the Pumpkin Kiva for many years. The Turquoise Kiva, on the other hand, has various rainbow and lightning designs as well as a few simple Ku-sha'lī figures on the walls, painted several years ago by José Hilario Herrera, one of the younger artists in the pueblo and a kiva member. (Fig. 2) Although the walls have since been replastered, the murals were copied through the thin coating, thus retaining their general outline despite changes in detail. [55, 70] Tonita Peña, mother of José Hilario Herrera and a well-known artist in her own right, was also said to have done murals for the Turquoise Kiva. [15, 16, 23]

For the July 14 Feast Day in 1947 and again in 1948 both kivas were replastered and whitewashed inside and out. It was claimed that this was the traditional treatment of kivas for this occasion, though in 1951 only the stairways of the kivas had been whitewashed in addition to the general replastering. In 1952, no exterior whitewashing was done. The gypsum for the whitewash is gathered by the war captains near old La Bajada and baked in an outdoor oven for twenty-four hours or more. It is then ground into a fine powder by the *alguacilitos*, and each kiva group is given enough to decorate its kiva inside and out. [15, 16, 20, 21] This is usually done about a week before Feast Day, and the whitewash stays on until the first heavy rain.

---

just less than three feet. The rungs and poles were peeled and smoothed. The ends of the rungs were shaped to fit tightly into rectangular slots in the poles. This elongated socket prevented the rung from rotating when stepped upon. In tearing out the old ladder and placing the new one in the kiva, an ax was used to trim the entrance way, and the seatings for the ladder ends were rapidly dug into the floor with a spade. The two pits were leveled with a large pebble that a young boy was sent to pick up nearby. The installation was completed, everyone tested the ladder, and the party disbanded, with the only semblance of any ritual being a short concluding speech by the assistant war captain of that year, Santiago Arquero, a Pumpkin Kiva member. After that, the tools were collected, the old ladder was dragged away to be chopped up for firewood, and everyone went home. Later, several people complained that no decorative cap had been placed at the top.

Neither kiva has a bench or seats of any kind about the wall. No informant could recall any, nor does the literature mention one. Informants also said consistently that they had no knowledge of a floor or wall opening ("sī'papu") in their kivas or in those elsewhere. One informant volunteered that the entire kiva is still at times referred to as sī'papu, or more precisely, shī'pap. [44]

No informant recalled that weaving or similar handicraft had ever been done in either kiva or that either had ever been used as a general men's club, as described in early pueblo accounts. Council meetings were likewise said never to have taken place in kivas. "Kivas are like churches; there shouldn't be any fights or bad feelings in them." [44] In seeming contradiction of this statement, there was one account of a whipping being administered by officials in one of the kivas for transgressions against pueblo customs. [81] There is a chance in this case that the informant may have been confusing the kiva with a society house, or perhaps a community house.

Interior kiva walls are white, with no other marking except a reddish-brown wainscoting two or three feet high (and the already mentioned Turquoise Kiva murals). On either side of the ladder, the wainscoting changes to a small "stepped," or "cloud," pattern (ai'tshī, a term also used for a ceremonial altar).

The firebox, or pit (mo'katch, or mountain lion) of both kivas is entirely above the floor level. The term *mo'katch* was explained as a symbolic reference to the location of the firebox—"guarding the entrance and ladder." A note in Boas' field notes (MS 37: 29) mentions the use of the term *Ko'hai-o* (bear) for the firebox. The firebox is about a foot high in front and 3 feet high at the back (south end), where the edge is "stepped." It is approximately 3 feet wide and 6 feet long, duplicating the dimensions of the roof entrance. Its adobe-plastered walls are about 6 inches thick. The firebox is directly under the hatchway; hence in climbing the ladder, one passes over the fire. Both men and women must face the ladder as they climb up or down it; anyone climbing in any other fashion is halted and sent back to do it properly. [55, 92] Fires are made in these boxes only during the winter months, being used essentially for heat rather than ritualism. Firewood is kept in a pile close to a nearby corral and is transferred to the roof when needed.

The community houses are extensively used. The Pumpkin house was built in 1923, and the Turquoise house about 1938. Prior to their construction, large private homes were utilized for meetings, dance rehearsals, and similar occasions (sometimes serving as sites for ka'tsīna ceremonials as well). [2, 3, 15, 49] The Turquoise house is the larger and is normally used when the whole pueblo, or all the adult males, are called together, as, for example, when the medicine men announce the officers of the coming year on the night of December 29. The Turquoise house is approximately 20 feet wide and 60 feet long. Each house consists of two rooms, with a fireplace in the room that has no door opening to the outside. This fireplace is used for warmth and also for heating (i.e., tightening) the drums before dances. The interior walls are plain white with the usual red-brown wainscoting. Furniture is limited to a row of wooden benches around the walls. [44, 45, 55, 70] In outward appearance, these buildings look like ordinary residences.

Society houses constitute another form of community-owned real property. Actual ownership of the Kwe'rana–Shī'kame and Shrū'tzī houses is private. Since this is true, their inclusion here should be explained. These buildings have been loaned to the community by the owners until such time as the society decides that the community should build a house for it. As long as a society uses the house, its upkeep is the responsibility of the community. At any time the society should present a request to the war captains, the community would have to provide a special house for its use. "One of these days we will have to do that." [15]

The house shared by the Kwe'rana and Shī'kame societies is a loan from Eleuterio Suina, stepfather of Eufrasio Suina, Head Shī'kame (and only member) and also a Kwe'rana. The Shrū'tzī house has been loaned by Estephanita Herrera, a woman who is important in the Ku-sha'lī and general native ceremonial life. The Kwe'rana–Shī'kame house is on the east side of the plaza; the Shrū'tzī house is at the southern end of the pueblo, some distance from the plaza, a location providing somewhat greater privacy for ka'tsīna preparations.

The Giant house is on the north side of the plaza behind another house which is directly on the plaza. Two informants [55, 92] stated that the house belongs to the society; another [53] was of the opinion that it actually belongs to Cipriano Quintana, the Head Giant and only member as of 1952.

The Ku-sha'lī house, shared with the Flint society (Fig. 3), is located just beyond the southeast corner of the plaza at the rear of the church. This belongs to the societies, built for them by the commu-

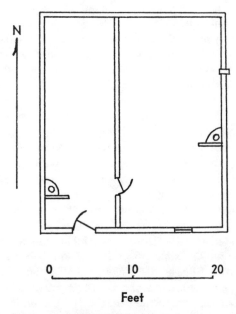

N

0   10   20

Feet

Fig. 3.—Flint–Ku-sha'lī House Ground Plan.

nity on the site of the former two-storied Ku-sha'lī house. The present
house was built about 1915, when Victoriano Cordero became cacique. It was built for the use of all subsequent caciques as their "office." (Fig. 3) A distinguishing feature of this otherwise ordinary-ap-
pearing house is the screened opening at the top and middle of the
east wall. (Plate 8b) Through this the rays of the rising sun enter the
inner room. Informants claimed to know nothing more than the fact
that "this has to do with the cacique's work of watching the sun." [44,
70, 88, 92]

The former Kwe'rana–Shī'kame house was a two-storied building
at the southwestern corner of the plaza. It was abandoned because of
its old age and dangerous condition, and about 1933 the societies
moved to their new location. [55]

The "house of the government farmer," a designation by which it
is still known, is at the edge of the canal in front of the church. It has
two rooms and is covered with a gabled corrugated-iron roof. Since
the position of government farmer was discontinued by the Indian
Service, the house has been appropriated for other community pur-

poses, primarily the storage of seed, tractor fuel and oil, spare parts for machinery, and similar community property.

A community corral is located northeast of the plaza. It is approximately 100 feet square, with a gate in the middle of the west side. It is made of vertical juniper stakes standing about 5 feet above the ground, and it is kept in good repair though rarely used. Formerly, the burro herd was brought in each night and placed there by community herders. [49] Plate 2 shows it as it appeared in 1947, unchanged in location and appearance through many decades. The only attention paid to the corral during my residence in Cochití was the brief ceremony there in 1948 during the celebration of Santiago's Day (Santiago is patron saint of the horses).

Another form of community property, no longer present but much in evidence several decades ago, comprises the various bridges (bridge, tse'sht[ia]-wa-tsech [92]) constructed across the Rio Grande. A bridge sketched and described by Bandelier (September 29, 1880) while at Santo Domingo was typical of the Cochití ones as well. (Fig. 4) On November 19, 1880, Bandelier noted that the Cochití bridge was broken, beavers having eaten the beams. "They [the beavers] are very frequent in the river, and large." On December 8 he commented that the bridge was intact, the beavers "have not attacked it." Further data on the bridges appeared in his journal of October 4, 1885:

Walked over to the Pueblo, the bridge is very good now, they have actually sunk "caissons" in the River. They are from 8 to 10 feet in diameter, and a basket of branches solidly interwoven and filled with rocks. These pillars can, of course, not be touched by beavers, unless they eat the tree-branches, and if the river rises, it can only float off the big hewn timbers which form the bridge as usual. It is far more solid than the other bridge & more pleasant to walk.

An interesting account of the construction of such a bridge was found in Starr's diary of September 24 and 25, 1897. Since this has not previously appeared in print, it is quoted here in its entirety:

We then went down to the river to see them working at the bridge. It was an interesting sight. A dozen or more men and large boys were stripped from below, wearing only shirts and breech-clouts. The governor was there inspecting but not greatly interfering. The "helpers" stood back a little way from the stream. There were six men and a boy in front: Each wore a tuft of feathers [?] like in his hair; some wore a second one also of different kind simply bunched. Each bore in his right hand a branch or bunch of long twigs with which he beat time. Behind them were four

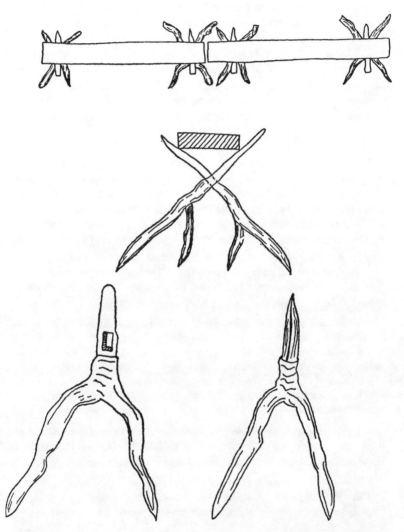

Fig. 4.—Bridges: Structural Details. (Based on sketches by Bandelier, journal entry of September 27–29, 1880.)

women, bare legged, blanketed and masked with leather masks, white with
eye and mouth markings on them in red. They wore short close fitting
drawers or trousers from waist to hip & mantas. Unfortunately, expecting
to have ample opportunity to look at them, I did not closely examine what
they carried. These eleven would wave their wands, sing and mildly dance
whenever the active workers were specially engaged. As for these, they
had already put one beam from shore to crib & were ready to place the
second from first to second crib. These cribs were round or elliptical baskets of large size which had been sunk & pegged into place and loaded with
stones. The second great timber was brought by perhaps fourteen to twenty
workers in pairs on poles transversely placed. The one end was rested on
the near crib. The men then supported it and wading into the river swung
it around until the free end was near the second crib. Then with a great
and united effort they raised the great timber onto the crib. Two or three
men particularly climbed up onto the sides of this & with their shoulders
under the timber directed and largely assisted in this heaving into position.
It was beautiful to watch. Then men with single stones or trays of stones
carried by two men went out and packed the crib full and firmly fixed the
end in place. These trays were made of several pieces of poles set lengthwise and wickered together. They were either carried by two men over the
newly constructed bridgeway or were more commonly carried in the water
just resting at its surface where the benefit of the buoyant water was
gained. The disadvantage of the *high* lift at the end would probably make
up for much of the advantage gained. We were wonderfully interested in
all and planned to watch it long but it rained hard. After some time in
shelter & around fire, & eating, the work in the cold river water was given
up and they adjourned to build a second smaller bridge over the stream
nearer town. They proceeded to weave a basketwork crib first. Marking out
a circle in the sand they drove a number of stakes into the ground at
fairly regular intervals. Between them they wove branches in & out regularly around & around—no branch of course anywhere near making a circuit. Every now and then a man with a heavy branch club would beat
down the wicker as compactly as possible. Meantime, others were dumping
stones on the one bank and building horizontal brush into a support in the
other. Here again the rain interfered & we had to go home—as they did.
Driven indoors we worked until near sunset when we saw the singing
men—most of them at the river [?] & more—marching and singing out the
orders for tomorrow. Perhaps eight in number they had their feather tufts,
their branches, etc., & marched abreast. Their song was "may there be
rain." But there was no need of singing that; we had already had more than
enough for their own & our pleasure.

.   .   .   .

25th. . . . We went down to watch the bridge builders work. [See Plate 10*a, b.*] They first finished up the little bridge across the nearer creek. We saw them roll down a crib, load it up with stone and then place the two timbers in place. From there they went to the river proper and continued the bridge building. We saw them carry out two cribs and place them. It is great work when they are squarely placed & before they are loaded. It takes the push of many to hold it against the current. The officiales were slow about beginning their work. When they did, they were neither so impressive nor curious as yesterday. The masks were gone & the men wore the blankets of yesterday over ordinary clothing. What I failed to note yesterday was that the men in the front line wore black or dark blue male blankets or ponchos. All stood today in one line.

Former means of crossing the river included various ferryboats owned by the tribe and operated by the men according to a rotating duty roster. Such a ferry was described by Bandelier in his journal of April 23, 1882:

. . . Examining the canoe. Bottom . . . are three trunks of trees joined together on the inside. To make it impermeable, they "cook" turpentine and when boiling, throw into it bark of the Sabino (Qui-pa) and anoint the trees and fill the joints with it. On top of these trees they fasten planks and thus form a rim. The whole is a clumsy rectangular machine. As the wood grows old, it becomes very heavy, and moisture begins to penetrate through it. At the time of high water 3 to 4 men are delegated every morning to attend to the ferrying across. They charge as they please, about 25 cents per person.

Present-day Cochití recall the ferry as sufficiently large to transport a team and wagon. Sometimes the owners preferred to unhitch and drive the team through the river while the wagon was being ferried across. The ferry operated until late spring, when the river was down and fording was easier. [40, 50, 53, 59] Bandelier had also noted earlier (October 8, 1880) that "when they crossed the river, it was on large 'Huaquis,' ollas, fastened to their girdles, and thus swimming." Perhaps this was a local solution to the problem of crossing high water when the bridges and the ferry were not in operation.

The Mission Church. Since the arrival of the Franciscan Fathers at the beginning of Spanish explorations and colonization, Cochití has had only the one church, the mission of San Buenaventura de Cochití. The building and its equipment are generally considered by the Indians as their property; the priest who says Mass and performs other duties, as well as the Spanish-American families who join in the wor-

ship, are present at the pleasure of the tribe. [17, 55, 92] This feeling
of complete possession has been noted in other pueblos; for instance,
White (1942: 61) reported of Santa Ana Pueblo, "But their Catholic
church, *i.e.*, the one in their pueblo, belongs to them."[5]

The church is the largest building in Cochití and is located off the
southeastern corner of the plaza. Its 3-foot thick adobe walls stand
about 35 feet high, and the over-all length of the building is about
130 feet. Kubler (1940: 61) described it as a continuous-nave church,
as contrasted to the cruciform, with the sanctuary narrower than the
nave. He cited (p. 56) Cochití as one of several atypical façades
found among Southwestern missions: "At Cochiti, a narthex, added
after 1880, presents a triple arcade to the courtyard." In Poore's account (1894: 429), as of 1890, the church was described as in good
repair, with credit for this being given primarily to the "Mexican contingent." Kubler (1940: 45) noted that the outer walls of the sanctuary were reinforced by a low bench which protected the bases
from eroding, undercutting, and collapse.

Another change occurred in 1912 when extensive remodeling and
repairs were made. The gabled galvanized-iron roof and tall cupola
were added. (Plate 7*b*) The tall cupola proved unsatisfactory, for the
force of the wind upon it began to crack the walls. Shortly thereafter,
it was replaced with a much shorter cupola, which was still in use in
1952. (Plate 8*a*) In recent years there has been some talk of tearing
down the cupola and gabled roof entirely, thus restoring the former
mission façade. About 1948, an extra bench was added on the north
(shady) side of the sanctuary simply to provide a comfortable place
for the choral group of one kiva to practice while members of the

[5] In a footnote to this statement, White (1942: 61) added the following comments: "The Indians claim that the church buildings, church lands, and church
paraphernalia, *as property,* belong to them. A former Superintendent of Pueblos,
Leo Crane, declares that the church at Acoma is the property of the Catholic
church, 'the title resting in the Archbishop of the diocese,' *Desert Drums,* p. 130.
The archbishop of Santa Fe is of the opinion that church buildings and the lands
upon which they rest in the pueblos belong to the Catholic church (letter from
Supt. S. D. Aberle, United Pueblos Agency, to the present writer, under date of
Nov. 22, 1938). The writer has gone to some pains to discover who really does
own the churches and lands in the pueblos, but with little success. But the fact
remains that the Indians believe and insist that it is they who own them. As
Crane put it, 'The Acomas retain very peculiar ideas concerning their mission
church,'—that is, they think they own it whereas Crane declares they do not (*loc.
cit.*). There is nothing 'very peculiar' about the ideas of the Acomas on this subject; they are held by all of the Keresan pueblos and in all probability by other
pueblos as well."

other kiva were dancing in the plaza. Plates 5 and 6 show the exterior and interior of the mission at the end of the last century or earlier. [22, 44, 45, 62] Photographs of more recent date than these fail to show murals on the front of the church.

In an account by Forrest (1929: 116–119), details of the church interior are given:

. . . The walls are decorated with the stations of the cross, and the old tin candlesticks were brought up from Chihuahua before the American occupation.

San Buenaventura, the patron saint of the Cochití, must have been a man of many personalities; for none of the three statues of this "santo" in his mission bear the slightest resemblance to each other. Because it has represented their patron saint for many generations, the oldest is held in great veneration and love by all of the indians, in spite of the black beard and hard, almost sinister expression of the face. The figure is only about eighteen inches high, and is adorned with the usual robe and several strings of beads around the neck. Another of the statues was carved from wood many years ago by an indian from old Mexico. The smooth, oval face has a pleasant expression, while a halo around the head adds to the saintly appearance. The most modern and the largest of the three was made in France and presented to the mission in 1901 by the Sisters of Mercy at Santa Fé. It is a fine piece of French workmanship. With its smooth, thoughtful face it is a marked contrast to the other two.

A large painting of San Buenaventura adorns the center of the wall above the altar, while the Nativity, the Transfiguration, the Last Supper, and three scenes of the Crucifixon form the reredos. All are ancient, cracked with age, and covered with the dust of years. The ceiling of the chancel is decorated with moons, horses, and other figures, in red, yellow, and black, the work of indian artists.

The description of these details is largely applicable at present; there are no benches or seats, other than a low adobe bench along the north and south walls. In winter there are two stoves. The altar, at the west end of the nave, is separated from the remainder of the church by a low wooden railing, and the altar is raised in respect to the main floor. (See Plate 6.) The choir loft, equipped with an organ, is in a balcony, over the entrance at the east end. Two rooms south of the nave are used by the priest for changing vestments and storing equipment. The third and easternmost room has been adapted by the pueblo as a storage spot for community property, including the threshing machine. The people, under the supervision of the *fiscales* and their helpers, the *fiscalitos*, furnish firewood for the church. [2, 3, 15, 20]

The *Campo Santo*, or churchyard and cemetery, was the only burial ground until about 1910. Since then, as this area had become so crowded, most burials have been in a newly consecrated *Campo Santo* a half-mile west of the pueblo, just north of the Peralta Canyon road. Burial is still possible in the churchyard if it is strongly desired, but this happens rarely. [42, 45, 70]

The Penitente Morada. Another building, associated with the Catholic Church, is the *morada* of the Penitentes (see Chap. 2, pp. 24–25). This one-roomed house, windowless, is on the south side of the pueblo's southernmost block. For many years, no Cochití has been a member, and with most Spanish families moving out of the pueblo, the Cochití *morada* has been little used in recent years, though it was renovated as recently as August, 1947. [3] Active participants normally join with their comrades in Peña Blanca. Wooden crosses which mark the "stations" of the Penitente ritual can still be seen on several knolls south of the pueblo. [16, 44, 45, 70]

The Government Day School. Descriptions of school buildings or school activities are conspicuously absent in most sources. An exception is the detailed account of the school and its activities as directed by the teacher, Mrs. Grozier, in the Eickemeyers' account of 1894 (1895: 76–90). The same building described in their account is the earliest school remembered by present-day informants. Today this building includes the home of Damasio Quintana and that of Alvin and Nestor Arquero, whose grandfather, Juan Arquero, built it near the end of the last century.

In 1912 a day school was built by the federal government at the western end of a tract of a little more than three acres, located in the southwestern section of the village. In the 1920's a second unit was built, which includes the shower rooms already mentioned as available to the people of the pueblo on certain days throughout the year. Facilities include residence quarters for the two teachers and classrooms and playground for a preschool year and the first six grades. The school has its own windmill and storage tank and a telephone. The buildings are used as a base for the visiting government doctors, dentists, and nurses who examine the children and adults periodically. They also provide facilities for night meetings and motion pic-

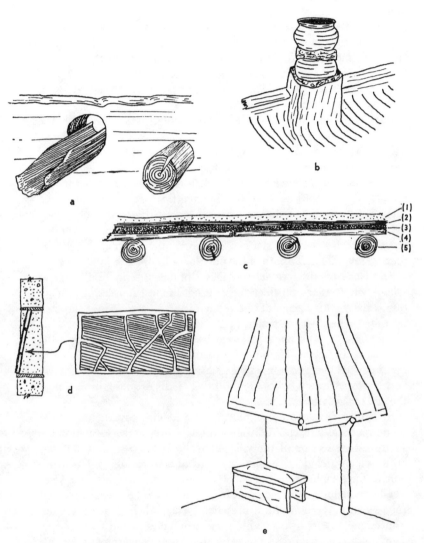

Fig. 5.—Early Architectural Features. *a*. wooden drainpipe; *b*. *olla* chimney; *c*. (1) adobe, (2) grass, (3) rods, (4) poles, and (5) vigas; *d*. selenite window, with cross section; *e*. comal and oven hood.

tures sponsored by the Indian Service Extension Division in adult-education programs of general information, with emphasis on health, home economics, and agricultural methods.

Privately Owned Real Property. This category includes houses, house lots, barns and sheds, corrals, a gristmill, outdoor ovens, and outdoor toilets. These are owned, exchanged through gift, trade, or purchase, and inherited as are the agricultural lands.

Joint ownership, particularly of houses, results usually from inheritance. Division may be made among multiple heirs on a basis of rooms. Since there are commonly more heirs than rooms, the division has frequently been made on the basis of so many vigas, or roof beams, per heir. Often one heir makes arrangements to buy or trade for additional shares. Today, inheritance on the basis of vigas has largely been discontinued because it often gave rise to conflicting claims. It is becoming more common for the heirs, or the owner in announcing his will, to divide the estate by balancing an entire room, or house, against other items, such as acreage. There is a growing tendency to keep the components of an estate in practical, usable units. [20, 53, 62, 70]

Families often live in the mother's house, especially when there is a stepfather. Other families live in houses owned by children of one of the couple, or by children of close kin. (Appendix 3 shows house ownership and occupancy as of July 14, 1952.)

The typical house (ka^j'rū-tē; older form, ai'ehē) has its foundation and lower courses of basalt and the upper courses of adobes, with the entire wall plastered with adobe inside and out, as noted by Bourke and Strout. The inner walls are much smoother than the outer, and they are whitewashed with a special preparation of ground gypsum gathered in a canyon north of the pueblo. The lower quarter of interior walls is usually finished with the reddish-brown wash made from ground stone found near the mouth of Cañada de Cochití. Roofs are supported by peeled pine logs, or vigas. Boards rest on the vigas and are covered, in turn, with tar paper and adobe. Roof tops are carefully hollowed, and in the center there are one or more pipes which drain the basin, generally protruding several feet beyond the outer wall to prevent excessive washing of the outer plaster. Leaky roofs are repaired with a few shovelfuls of fresh adobe, by raking the contours, and by cleaning the drainage pipes.

The roof and ceiling at present show little change from those in aboriginal times except for the use of metal drain pipes, tar paper,

Fig. 6.—Interior Corner Fireplace.

and boards. In earlier times, these functions were performed by wooden troughs and by layers of hewn wood, brush, and grass. (Fig. 5) A few houses still exhibit the old ceilings, though these are normally covered by cloth sheeting tacked across the vigas to prevent the dust from drifting down.

Almost every home in Cochití has one or more corner fireplaces, usually near the door. A low adobe wall protrudes three or four feet into the room to protect the fire from drafts. (Fig. 6) The corner fireplace—with the beehive oven shape—is Spanish in origin. While corner fireplaces have generally been considered post-Spanish, the excavation of a small Santa Fe Black-on-white site on the Cochití Reservation during the summer of 1958 revealed a corner fireplace (c. 1300), though there was no top structure indicated. Many homes also have wood-burning ranges, used both for cooking and heating. Since the recent installation of electricity, hot plates are being used to supplement the cooking facilities, especially during the summer. (The convenience of these appliances makes them very popular except when the utility bills arrive.) In his entry for October 7, 1880,

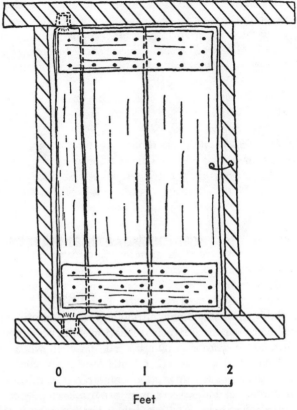

Feet

Fig. 7.—Door of Native Construction.

Bandelier provides an interesting account of the construction of a corner fireplace as well as details concerning the room in which he was then living.

While door and window frames continue to be made of regular lumber, an increasing number of them are being purchased from commercial mills. A few homemade products can be found in the pueblo, though there are none of the older form of door in which the parts were joined by wooden pegs and the door turned on a top and bottom rounded tongue, no hinge being used. [1] (Fig. 7) Modern homes are characterized by larger, movable, and more numerous windows. Screening on windows and doors is becoming more common but is still, for the most part, poorly kept up.

Floors vary between wood planking on joists and packed adobe. In either case, they are normally surfaced, more or less completely, with sheets of linoleum, frequently of differing patterns and vintages. Preferences range between wood, which is easier to clean, and adobe, which is less apt to become infested with mice, bedbugs, and the like. The practice of rubbing fresh blood over the adobe to make a smooth and hard surface, noted by Bandelier in his journal of October 24, 1880, is still followed by Cochití women whenever they can get sufficient quantities of beef blood. [92]

In the summer, a great deal of time is spent in the yards, especially by those who have shade trees. Others often construct *ramadas*, or sunshades, fashioned from pole frames covered liberally with cottonwood boughs. Many construct adobe windbreaks under such *ramadas*, and much cooking on open fires or wood ranges is done there.

Roughly half of the homes have single metates, ordinarily used for grinding chili, and a series of grinding bins for maize and wheat. Special ovens and equipment for making the traditional "paper bread" (ma'tzīn) are gradually disappearing, with only a dozen women, or fewer, still using them. [16, 17, 23, 27, 28]

Barns, sheds, and storerooms relieve the congestion of the houses, providing storage space for items seldom used. Several such structures are made of discarded railroad ties, obtained when the spur from Domingo Station to the Rio Grande north of Cochití was torn up about 1930. In the storerooms are kept large pottery storage jars, provisions, untanned hides, sections of tree trunks to be worked into drums, and similar items. Saddles, bridles, and harnesses are often hung in such places, especially if the rooms can be padlocked.

Many men have shelters in the corrals, under which they keep wagons and machinery. A common type is a platform of logs elevated eight or ten feet from the ground and covered with hay. This serves to protect the equipment and animals from the weather as well as to keep the hay out of reach of these animals. It also makes the hay convenient for feeding. A few corrals are made of rough planking, but the majority are a combination of barbed wire and juniper posts.

Some houses still have enclosed yards in front, as described by Poore and pictured in plates in this volume, but they are no longer used as temporary corrals. As a result of health education, there seems to be a conscious effort to keep stock away from the immediate vicinity of the houses. If a young boy leaves a horse standing near a house, he is reprimanded and told to tie it some distance away.

Almost every family possesses one, or more, outdoor ovens for daily and feast-day baking. Most breadstuffs are still made in these domed, "beehive," ovens, which range up to 5 feet in height and about the same in base diameter. They are made of a special tuff collected in the mountains northwest of the pueblo. When men go into the hills for firewood, their wives often go along to gather this volcanic rock. When a new oven is to be made, the old one is torn down, the tuff being salvaged and added to the new blocks if a larger oven is planned. The oven floor is of packed adobe; the walls, about 6 inches thick, are plastered inside and out. A small opening, about 2 inches in diameter, is left near the top for ventilation, and a main opening about 18 inches high and wide is formed at the base, the orientation varying. Usually, the oven has a platform, about 20 by 20 inches, in front of this opening. During baking, the small vent is closed with a corncob and wet rag; the main opening is closed by a metal sheet covered with a dampened sack. Wood and, even more commonly, corncobs are used for fuel.

As of 1952, Cochití had only one gristmill, an engine-powered mill owned by Frank Chávez. Because of the high operating costs and fee and a feeling that the flour absorbed the taste of gasoline, this mill was not patronized as much as water mills at Jemez and Nambé. [45] A second mill, a water mill, was sold to a Santo Domingo Indian in the winter of 1950/51 by its owner, Cipriano Quintana, who could no longer operate it because of old age and blindness. While in operation, this mill was well patronized by the Cochití, though no local person cared to continue its operation. Bandelier, in his journal of November 20, 1880, noted that Juan de Jesús Pancho had spent nearly a week in Santa Fe having his wheat ground at a water mill. For six *fanegas* he had paid three dollars.

Another form of personal property formerly at Cochití, but gone now for many years, was a ferryboat operated by Juan de Jesús Pancho (John Dixon) after his return from Carlisle. This served traffic between Peña Blanca and the mountain area west of Cochití. [3, 70]

Outdoor toilets are scattered throughout the pueblo, commonly located away from the dwellings and near the corrals. These structures were built according to Indian Service specifications, and, hence, are quite uniform. The floors are of concrete, the covered seats and side walls of wood, and the roofs of corrugated-iron sheeting. For the most part, they are kept in good repair by the owners, many of whom keep them padlocked for private use. As of 1952, there were no inside, water, or chemical, toilets in the village.

Personal Property

Furnishings and Equipment. Detailed descriptions of household furnishings are seldom encountered in the literature. Bandelier's journal contained numerous observations, and Bourke (Bloom 1938: 234) made the following notes on the governor's house or a room of it in which he stayed:

> Entered through the roof by ladder—room 30′ long × 15′ broad, 7′ high, lighted by two selenite windows. . . . Wooden images of Saints, abalone shells, ristras of chile—corn in ear or shelled—Batons of Office—young girl grinding wheat or corn-meal in metates.
>
> .   .   .   .
>
> Our room was 59′ l. 20′ w. 8′ high—Walls, adobe whitewashed, brown floor band 18″ in height—Floor, packed clay. Ceiling, round peeled pine rafters, 6″ thick, one ft. apart, covered with successive layers of twigs, hay, and clay. Three selenite windows on one side 2′ square set on outside of wall, the 12 in. thickness of which made a niche. Two fireplaces. One door to enter 4′ h. and 20″ w. of pine plank *nailed* together. No lock. Door held to by buckskin string.
>
> In room, plenty of corn in ear, piled on floor, chile and pumpkins, crosses and Saint's pictures in tin frames, Onions, Gourd & Tortoise rattles.

The Eickemeyers (1895: 97–98) described an Indian home as follows:

> In a house not far from the school were two squaws seated on the floor. . . . The room itself had a very neat appearance. The mattresses and blankets which had been used to sleep on, the night before, had been rolled up against a side wall and were being used as a settee. In front of this were several old buffalo skins with a very little fur left on the surface, showing they had been trampled upon for many years. In the centre of the room, from the roof timbers, was suspended, by a raw-hide rope, a papoose cradle, in which was a sleeping baby. . . .
>
> On the walls of the room were bows and arrows, some in course of construction, while others looked as if they had been used in killing birds and rabbits, a sport of which the Indian boy is very fond. They all handle the bow and arrow with great skill. The familiar Winchester and a belt of

cartridges, together with little trinkets, such as beadwork necklaces, medicine bags and eagle feathers, hung on wooden pegs on the wall. Along one
side of the room a long pole was suspended from the ceiling by a rope at
each end, and over it hung the bright-colored, zigzag-designed blankets
which are obtained by trading shell bead-work to the Navajoes. The black
squaw dresses, also of Navajo manufacture, and buckskin leggings, and
moccasins covered with beadwork and colored ochre, were hung over one
end of this pole. From the ceiling were suspended ten or twelve drums,
which the Indian considers sacred.

The foregoing description applies, in many respects, to modern
Cochití homes, particularly until about 1940; since that time there
has been an increasing tendency toward adopting furniture from
American culture. In 1951, this trend was augmented by the inception of a Veterans' Training Program at Peña Blanca, where boys
from Cochití, Santo Domingo, and Peña Blanca were taught to make
furniture, concentrating on Spanish colonial styles with considerable carving in which Indian designs were dominant.

Many homes are furnished with one or two double beds, perhaps
a cot or porch swing which can be used as a cot, a small table or two,
a dining table, several straight chairs, and a few stools or benches.
Occasionally, there is a rocking chair. Many have dressers or ward-
robes for storing clothing and other articles. One or more steamer
trunks provide additional storage space. Mirrors are hung on the
wall, attached to dressers, or are sometimes plastered into the wall
surface. These, framed religious pictures, and other framed pictures
are commonly bordered with a miscellaneous collection of family
photographs. Current favorites include pictures of local servicemen
and their units in the Second World War and the Korean fighting.
While the Cochití are fond of snapshots and some own cameras, they
are seldom seen taking pictures.

Most houses still have the long pole noted by the Eickemeyers.
This is of peeled pine and extends almost the entire length of the
average room. It is usually suspended from the vigas by baling wire,
which has replaced the rawhide of former times, and hangs at about
head height. Extra bedding, Navaho blankets, *mantas,* sashes, and
similar items hang from it.

Singer sewing machines are in almost every home. Dry goods are
a favorite item of trade, and materials are made into clothing of
all sorts by the women. Since the installation of electric power, many
homes have radios, replacing the battery sets which a few had owned

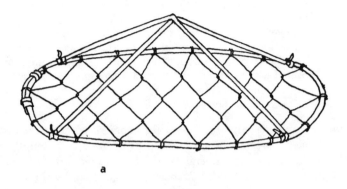

a

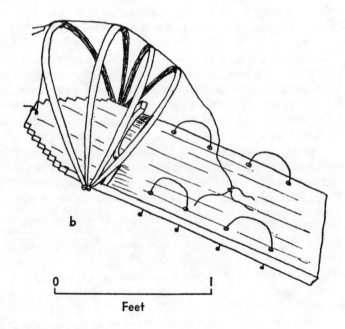

b

0   I

Feet

Fig. 8.—Cradle Types.

earlier. Radio programs of a wide variety are followed with considerable enthusiasm by all ages. (A brief visit to Cochití in the late summer of 1957 revealed as many as perhaps a third of the homes with television. The visual impact of these appliances—their programs as well as the advertising—added to the audio impact of earlier radios can hardly be overestimated as an effective vehicle of acculturation among the Cochití.)

Lighting, formerly by candles and kerosene or gasoline lamps, is by electricity except in a very few homes in the pueblo. A few have not yet put it in because they plan to build a new home in the near future. Initially, it was feared that electricity would be too costly, but the utility bills have, for the most part, been less than the cost of lamps, fuel, and parts. The service is far more satisfactory, and the desire to have electricity in the home is virtually unanimous. Consumption varies between those whose meters actually record considerably less than the minimum charge ($1.27 per month in 1951) and those who have hot plates, washing machines, refrigerators, radios, and other appliances. The increase in the use of appliances has been cumulative and has, undoubtedly, not yet reached its peak. Appendix 4 records Cochití use of electricity from October, 1950, through May, 1952. Appendix 5 shows appliances used in various households as of the summer of 1952.

Laundry equipment and facilities have changed from the time when washing was done along the river banks or irrigation ditches. With hydrants scattered through the village, many put their washboards and tubs in the yard and wash there; a few patronize "Serve yourself" laundries in Bernalillo, Santa Fe, or Albuquerque; an increasing number are acquiring electric washing machines. [13, 16, 18, 24, 92]

Electric irons have largely displaced the old-fashioned ones that were heated on the stove. However, some of the older women do not trust electric power (and each account of someone's receiving a shock due to wet hands or similar oversights strengthens this conviction) and still use the old irons and other nonelectrical devices.

Babies are still cradled in the manner described by the Eickemeyers. The cradle is formed by a sturdy hoop, generally of oak, with the inside of the loop filled with interlaced rawhide. (Fig. 8a) The baby is wrapped in blankets and placed on the cradle. The entire bundle is then lashed to the cradle which is given a gentle push from time to time by any passers-by.

Actual cradleboards, made of a flat board with three or four semi-circular splints to form a flexible canopy (Fig. 8b), are still used, though not so universally as formerly. There is also a tendency to take the child out of the cradle at an earlier age. [55]

In contrast to these survivals are "strollers," which are used by some families to transport their babies about the pueblo despite a general lack of firm ground to support the small wheels. The most common method of carrying a small child continues to be that of holding him high on the shoulder by means of a blanket, the method used by adults of both sexes as well as older children, especially girls.

Teams of horses and wagons are still used for transportation between the pueblo and the fields, mountains, neighboring pueblos, and nearby towns. A few wagons are but a year or two old; most are older and weather-beaten, with boards chipped, split, chewed, and worn from usage. Wagon repairs, for the most part, are done at home, discarded parts being utilized. Some metal work is done, but most of this is done in town at a blacksmith or welding shop.

Most harnesses are several years old and have been repaired with rawhide or baling wire. Saddles range from a few new ones to those showing many years of wear. They, like the harnesses, are kept in sheds (especially if rather new), hung from trees, or merely laid on the ground.

During the Second World War and the years immediately following, there were no passenger cars and very few trucks at Cochití, though there had been several before the war. With the service of the El Pueblo Bus Line and, since 1947, the acquisition of a community truck, there was little need for other facilities. However, with the discontinuance of the bus line in 1950, a number of Cochití, especially the younger men, in most cases veterans, have bought passenger cars and additional pick-up trucks. About 1950, the community truck was traded in on a newer model. [20, 42, 44, 45, 70, 92]

In former times, as recorded by Bandelier in his journal of November 28, 1880, farm produce belonged to the man until he had harvested and brought it in from the fields. Upon entering the house or storeroom, it became the property of the woman. Its subsequent use or disposal was her decision. While this practice is still true in some households, it is increasingly common for produce to remain the actual property of the man who raised it. [50, 92]

Children are recognized as sole owners of property, real estate, livestock, and other items, at early ages, depending upon circumstances of inheritance and individual family attitudes. Many families believe that the actual assignment of property, despite the possibility of its eventual loss or mismanagement, teaches valuable lessons in responsibility and judgment. [1, 3, 15, 20, 45] The ownership of other personal property, such as agricultural implements, utensils used in food preparation, arts and crafts products, ceremonial paraphernalia, and similar items, is discussed in subsequent chapters.

Clothing. This section considers only the usual dress worn by the Cochití in ordinary daily routine and on Sunday or other holiday occasions. Ceremonial costume is reserved until the ceremonial calendar is discussed.

Bandelier on April 23, 1882, noted: "Juan José recollects the time when the people, old men, in place of the maxtlatl [breeches] wore about the loins a piece of blue cloth, pushing it between the legs while eating. He also knew 2 Mexicans who still wore pig-tails. Up to the time of General Vizcarra [1822/23] the Mexicans wore their hair like the Indians." I have found no other specific details on Cochití clothing of prehistoric and early historic times, but the general Southwestern Puebloan costume of *mantas* and belts for the women and breechcloths and kilts for the men may be safely assumed. Both sexes used robes, woven of vegetable fibers, fur strips, or whole animal hides, and footgear of woven vegetable fibers or moccasins. Children lived in various states of nakedness, depending on the weather, gradually assuming adult garb as maturity approached.

Photographs of Cochití and neighboring Pueblo Indians taken fifty to eighty years ago surpass, of course, the memory of living informants so far as precise detail is concerned. These pictures show that European clothing had already achieved considerable popularity, especially among the men. Shirts, trousers, suit coats, vests, hats, hard-soled shoes and boots were worn by many. Headbands and blankets appear to be the major items distinguishing the Cochití men from other rural inhabitants of the area. Women's dress reveals less change during this period, though dresses and other apparel made of commercial yard goods were becoming more prevalent in combinations with the *manta,* belt, wrapped leggings and moccasins, necklaces, and headcloth, which are survivals. (See various plates for clothing and changes.) On August 6, 1947, just after the Santo Domingo Feast Day, three Hopi men stopped at our house in Cochití. They had women's belts and *mantas* for sale and were asking fifteen and eighty-five dollars for them, respectively.

Since the Second World War, Cochití dress has undergone no sharp break with the past, but shows simply a continuation of already existing trends. Work clothes of the men are standard work clothes— blue jeans, or Levi's, sun tans or khakis, Army fatigues, and such apparel. Army shoes and other heavy work shoes, cowboy boots, and moccasins are all used. Handkerchiefs and scarfs, worn either as bands or as complete head coverings, and felt and straw hats are commonly worn, regardless of whether the man has retained the older style of long hair with various styles of bangs. As of 1952, there was no man younger than forty-eight years of age with long hair; of the men over this age, somewhat more than half wore their hair long, either shoulder length or with the back hair longer and worn in a *chongo*. (See various plates for illustrations.)

For the women, *mantas* are virtually gone from ordinary wear, being kept for ceremonial occasions when the wearer is either a participant or a spectator. Full-cut cotton dresses, worn with the typical woven belt, several necklaces, and an apron, and hard-soled shoes, with or without coarse stockings, constitute the daily dress of the older women. The younger women wear either homemade or commercially made dresses. Both young and old habitually wear a head scarf flowing over their shoulders when out of the house. Almost every woman over fifty years old wears her hair in the typical *chongo* or down the back in a single braid which can be quickly tied in a *chongo* if she leaves home. The younger women either follow this older style, wear their hair shoulder length, or have permanent waves.

School-age children normally wear clothing typical of their age group elsewhere in rural America. Among preschool children, the same is true, though there are some survivals of the older pattern of a simple long shirtlike garment sufficing for either sex.

4 AGRICULTURAL ECONOMY

Farming Techniques

Dry Farming. Payne (1944: 8) spoke of dry farming as negligible. Most of the specific data gained from informants indicate that "negligible" actually has meant no dry farming since the early 1930's. Several, however, pointed out tracts used for dry farming during the last century, and it seems a safe hypothesis that this method was practiced in earlier centuries during periods in which precipitation, the water table, and vegetation were more favorably balanced (see p. 5) than at present. Of great importance also, of course, in terminating dry-farming practices was the construction of improved irrigation facilities by the Conservancy District in the early 1930's. Were it not for such facilities, some dry farming would undoubtedly be practiced at present, for it is well within the bounds of possibility, as indicated by Evans (1945: 5–6) and Linney, Garcia, and Hollinger (1930: 53–54).

No reference to dry farming was found in the historical data. In 1782, Father Morfi (Thomas 1932: 99) stated that no irrigation was practiced at Cañada, eight miles northwest of Cochití and at a higher elevation. He further commented that the settlers there were exposed to "frequent famines." These notes of Father Morfi appear to have been based upon the Domínguez report of 1776 (Biblioteca Nacional, *Legajo X*: Document 43); if so, they contained a misstatement. Domínguez noted that Cañada had a very limited stream that generally failed, making scanty harvests regular occurrences. Nevertheless there was ditch irrigation so long as the stream flowed, and it is significant that rainfall alone seldom permitted dry farming at Cañada.

At Cochití, intermittent dry periods would make dry farming hazardous at best. Maize, beans, pumpkins, and watermelons are said to have been the principal dry-farm crops. [49, 50, 88] Interestingly, Bandelier reported in his journal of November 15, 1880, that gradual or sporadic desiccation, according to one of his informants, had been a factor in the various Pueblo people's forsaking the higher mesa and mountain country, where, for maize, "irrigation is not indispensable," in favor of the valleys and irrigation water.

Floodwater Farming. Floodwater farming was appreciably more important at Cochití than dry farming, but even floodwater techniques had been largely abandoned by the end of the last century. A few continued the practice until about 1930. [49, 50, 53, 88] Several factors led to the abandonment of these fields. One was a damaging flood which washed many of them out and made their repair too costly. [50] Attempts to date this flood proved futile, but it may well have coincided with the construction of the dam and canal in the early 1930's.

Floodwater practices described for the Hopi (Hack 1942: 26–31), the Zuñi (Roberts 1939: 14, 172; Cushing 1920: 160–166), the Navaho (Hill 1938: 20, 24–25), and the Pima-Papago (Castetter and Bell 1942: see Index) testify to the former widespread practice of this method. (Also see Bryan 1929.) Unpublished studies of the Rio Grande Valley above the confluence of the Rio Conchos revealed similar floodwater practices during prehistoric and historic times. The inhabitants were finally forced to abandon the area when precipitation fell below the necessary minimum. (J. Charles Kelley, personal interview, October, 1948) Specific data for the upper Rio Grande are inadequate, but evidence compiled by Bryan for the entire Southwest suggests there was formerly floodwater farming in that area.

Informants indicated specific tracts once farmed in this way, locating them at arroyo mouths, primarily west of the pueblo. Diversion structures of logs, rocks, and brush (Plate 11*a*) were used to spread the water. Some of the best fields were at the mouth of the

"Long Arroyo," northwest of the village (Plate 11*b*), and at "Watermelon Farm," southwest of the pueblo. [49] As in dry farming, the principal crops were maize, beans, pumpkins, and watermelons. [40, 44, 49, 50]

Strout, who accompanied Bourke in 1881, noted, without specifying irrigation or the absence of it, "Their fields are on the E. side of the Rio Grande" (Bloom 1938: 237). This appears to be an outright error in view of previously cited documentary sources and the repeated statements of informants. Strout's statement may have been an inaccuracy due to oversimplification of possibly the result of his route having circumvented fields west of the river, though that is extremely improbable.

Although historical sources do refer to irrigated fields, no specific data on floodwater methods were found; it is likely, however, that a rather high proportion of "irrigated fields" actually did receive their water from floodwaters rather than from ditches. Documents mention ditch systems and the frequent failure of the water supply. Such references may be interpreted as meaning either floodwater or ditch supply. The Rio Grande did normally flow, but it is likely that during certain periods the water level dropped to a point where it was difficult to transfer water into a ditch system.

Goldfrank's notes (1927: 92) record that "in former times" planting was done "at the foot of the mountains so that the crops might get as much moisture as possible. Digging sticks made out of oak and a wood called *d^{y}ap^{uc}* were used. Corn, melons, pumpkins, and beans were grown."

In 1890, Poore (1894: 429) observed that "small patches of 1.5 to 2 acres are planted in corn" on an island in the river a little below the pueblo. There is a strong probability that the water table in such fields was sufficiently high that, with the periodic inundations of the island, no ditch irrigation was necessary. Bandelier made several journal entries which would tend to support this view. On July 15, 1885, he noted three currents in the Rio Grande and constant encroachment "on the right hand side." A year earlier, July 9–12, 1885, he had observed that "the poor people are in a bad plight, the River is encroaching on the East side, and washing away or cutting up their fields." On December 3, 1882, he recorded that at Sile, opposite Peña Blanca, the Rio Grande was divided into five narrow and swift-running branches, "Brazos." Again, July 13, 1882, he noted that "the Rio

Grande is very treacherous. We had to cross it [from Peña Blanca to
Cochití] five times and always with difficulty. It changes its bed almost daily."

Irrigation Farming. This section is concerned with the use of the
actual ditch systems. Although technically floodwater methods can
be considered irrigation, it will facilitate the analysis if they are discussed separately.

No archaeological evidence of ditch irrigation has been reported
for the Cochití area. Benedict (1931: 5) recorded a Cochití myth
relating to ancient times when the Pueblos were coming up from
Shī'pap: "In those days they treated one another as brothers, all the
Indians of all the Pueblos. They planted corn with the digging stick
and they were never tired; they dug trenches to irrigate their fields.
The corn ripened in one day." And another interesting tale from the
past was recorded by Bandelier in his journal of October 8, 1880:

Juan José Montoya was very talkative. He says that "in 1853 and 1854,
an old man named Antonio told me at night, in his rancho across the river,
that in his time (about 1800), the corn and all fruit was much better and
earlier, and that melons ripened on the 5th of July." He also told him that
the old men (principales) prophesied that a time would come when the
crops would be bad, and the corn not ripen any more. Also that if, in times
to come, a nation should come from the east, white, with good, four-
wheeled carts drawn by mules, then the world would last long and have
good times. They also said that these latter people would introduce a cart
which would run very swiftly. Juan José attributes this prophesy of the
old men to astrological knowledge.

The Domínguez report of 1776 and the report of Friar Antonio
Cavallero, 1779 (Biblioteca Nacional, *Legajo X*: Documents 43 and
59), mentioned fields irrigated by deep and wide ditches west of the
river, above and below the pueblo. In his annual report for 1899,
N. S. Walpole, Indian agent (1899: 246), described the irrigation
system of Cochití as equal to that of its neighbors.

Informants agreed that as a result of the construction of the dam
and canals in the early 1930's the total acreage of irrigated land (630
acres) has been appreciably increased. Two canals, one on each side
of the river, lead from Cochití Dam, some three miles north of the
village. These canals also supply the fields of Peña Blanca, Sile, Santo
Domingo Pueblo, San Felipe Pueblo, and some fields north of Algodones. From these canals, Cochití community ditches bring water

to the various laterals supplying individual fields. Above the head of the western Cochití ditch and below the dam, water is taken directly from the canal for a limited acreage. [49, 53, 65, 88]

In recent years irrigation has been hampered by the water shortage in the upper Rio Grande watershed. The District allows Cochití, and other communities, the use of water on certain days of the week only. In 1951, as a consequence of unfavorable forecasts of available water, there was a considerably reduced acreage planted. One well-informed person estimated that perhaps only 50 per cent of the total irrigated acreage was being farmed. [44]

Irrigation methods vary with the crops grown. Informants thought that if furrows were made closer together and deeper, with planting on each flank of the furrow, irrigation would be more effectual than it is under current methods. Sheet flooding of many crops is practiced, and in almost all cases fields are flooded before the initial spring plowing—a practice noted by Bandelier in his journal of October 17, 1880. His added notation that fields were kept small to facilitate equal distribution of the water is less applicable to the situation today when the use of heavy equipment so improves grading that larger units can be cultivated.

For a number of years, all crops have been planted in irrigated fields with the exception of a very few vegetables grown in small gardens around the houses. These are watered from the drinking-water system, a practice which causes considerable ill feeling, especially during periods of water shortage. [3, 15, 17]

Community Farm Labor. Since the cultivated land is dependent upon the irrigation system, each farmer is subject to duty in the annual ditch-cleaning and repair. Modern procedure is essentially unchanged from that of earlier times. Cochití, unlike Santo Domingo (White 1935: 45) and Santa Ana (White 1942: 105–106), has no regular ditch boss, or *mayordomo*. Each year the governor, usually in late February or early March or after frost is out of the ground, names a temporary ditch boss. [2, 3, 45] Under his direction, and with authority delegated by the governor, the community ditches are repaired and cleaned. The day for this work is selected by the governor and his officers; the *fiscalitos*, or governor's helpers, inform all farmers of the time and place to report for work. Bandelier, November 10, 1880, noted "in March or April, it takes three or four days to clean up each acequia, the eastern one often five days." Today, since the Middle Rio Grande Conservancy District construction, it takes a day and a half on the west ditch and two days on the eastern ditch. [42] In a journal entry of April 15, 1882, Bandelier noted:

Everyone at work on the acequia. They are very backward with their work this year and this they attribute to their governor. Other governors, they say, direct sowing of wheat sometimes at the close of February or even January, ordaining that those who do not sow then would have to wait until after work is done on the acequias. The governor has direction of these affairs, and unless he directs it, no work can be done previous to the cleaning, etc. of the acequia.

At present, the men start at the head of the eastern ditch, working as far south as the community pasture near Peña Blanca. Then the western ditch is cleaned, the men working from the head to the site of the former water mill just below the pueblo. One informant, a past governor, stated that work on the east ditch is supervised by the governor and his lieutenant and that on the west ditch, by the *fiscale* and his lieutenant [44], implying that two crews work simultaneously, if I interpreted him correctly. But another informant, a past *fiscale*, stated that both ditches were cleaned under the charge of the *fiscales*. A *mayordomo* is chosen who works on both sides. All the officers help. [42] The discrepancies here, coming from statements of reliable informants, seem to represent some deviation in work procedures.

The canals are maintained by the Conservancy District, not the pueblo. The ditch boss decides when the ditches have been sufficiently cleaned and also has authority to send the *fiscalitos* to bring any absentees to the job. Anyone not excused by the governor has to work or pay the pueblo. For many years, the payment has been one dollar, or the obligation may be met by furnishing a substitute. Owing to rising prices and wages, it is almost impossible to find substitutes to work for this amount, and the payment of a dollar is easier than working. Gradually, the ditch work is actually being done by an ever shrinking nucleus of the faithful, public-spirited citizens. [2, 15, 44, 62]

The increasing awareness of monetary values among the Cochití is further illustrated by an incident regarding community ditch labor. In the spring of 1948, all men living in Santa Fe were called home by the officers for a meeting concerned with water rights, as was a similar meeting held in 1946. The 1948 meeting was attended by only the officers of 1946, 1947, and 1948, not the entire council membership. The Santa Fe men were notified that they should pay eight dollars for the ditch cleaning or do the work themselves. Some agreed to pay it; others refused. Those who agreed did so chiefly to keep peace in the pueblo. The others felt that so long as their lands were lying unused, there should be no assessment. They also stated that if anyone wanted to use these lands, they would be willing to have them do so. For this use they asked no rent, but the tenant would be expected to perform the ditch work, or pay for it. They themselves, however, refused to pay or to work.

The 1948 governor threatened to confiscate these tracts for the pueblo. The Santa Fe men insisted that would be illegal because the tracts were privately owned and were not "on loan" from the tribe. This opinion prevailed, and the matter was dropped, though some feeling remained because the entire council had not been called. [48, 53, 70]

Such problems are becoming more frequent and serious with each passing year. As more men cease farming, ditch maintenance is falling to the lot of a smaller and smaller percentage of the adult males. Although the actual numbers living in the pueblo have not appreciably declined, the fact that there are so many nonparticipants in this work emphasizes the breakdown of the older pattern of community co-operation.

Another development, rising partly from this shift from farming and partly from the hesitancy of farmers to expand their acreages in view of threatened water shortage, is the unused surplus of irrigated land. Some honestly doubt that the water is sufficient to permit full use of this acreage, but others believe that it is more a matter of the younger men's being too lazy to work the land. It is easier to find employment for wages, even if it means leaving the reservation to do so.

Additional communal labor is expected at unpredictable intervals throughout the agricultural season whenever sudden rains damage the ditch system. Again, all adult males are expected to join in this work, but there is an increasing tendency for many to be "busy" with other tasks. [3, 42, 45]

Care of the cacique's field (ho'cha-ñī ka'ash) is also community work. Since the cacique is considered to be too occupied with his religious duties in behalf of the people to attend to these fields, the men of the pueblo do his plowing, planting, cultivating, irrigating, and harvesting. "If the people can't help with this work, they should

go pretty soon for a load of wood for him." [2] This work is conducted under the supervision of the war captains since, being intimately associated with the cacique, it has religious aspects. These
two men decide upon the time for work, and they excuse those whose
personal affairs prevent their helping. Public crying of such announcements as these work details is made three times: once in the
plaza, once in the area near the Turquoise Kiva, and once southwest
of the church. This is done on the evening preceding the work, and
then the *alguacilitos* are sent to individual households with the announcement. [3, 45, 49, 70] The Eickemeyers (1895: 76) mentioned
public crying by the governor, who was assigning work details at
sunrise, June 25, 1894.

In his journal of April 4, 1882, Bandelier noted that the cacique
fasted in seclusion on the day his field was planted and again the day
it was harvested. At present, the cacique is joined in these fasts by
the Giant head and the Shī'kame head. If any seed is left over after
the planting, it is distributed to the people, who mix these kernels
among their own seeds for extra insurance of a successful crop. [92]
Dumarest (1919: 202) stated that such communal work was under
the direction of the "head *alguazil*," who obeyed both the governor
and the war captains. According to my informants, this is simply a
misunderstanding of terms, officials, and functions; one title of the
war captain (now obsolete) was *alguazil* and the *alguacilitos* have
never been ranked in any way. [44, 88, 92]

The acreage set aside for the cacique used to be more extensive
than it now is and furnished his complete support. Planted entirely
in blue maize, the crop is repeated each year with no rotation or
special fertilization. The acreage may be moved if the war captains
decide that this should be done. The blue corn is used by the cacique
for prayer meal, paper bread, and for other more or less sacred purposes. Sometimes it is used to care for needy families of the pueblo,
"children of the cacique." An interesting interpretation of "need" was
given by one informant—the idea being that the cacique's store of
corn constitutes a seed reserve in case of failure elsewhere in the
pueblo. [1, 2, 3, 15] In 1946, the cacique's field yielded six wagonloads of blue maize. [2]

The practice of the present cacique (Marcelo Quintana, a relatively young man who became cacique in December, 1946, at the age
of forty-two) of working his own fields for the support of his family
and having only his official needs cared for by the community is a

recent development. Dumarest stated that hunts for the benefit of the cacique were organized, "and lands are cultivated for his maintenance" (1919: 197). The implication is that these lands, with the hunts, constituted his entire maintenance, personal and ceremonial. Goldfrank (1927: 93) merely stated, "Only blue corn is planted for the cacique."

White's data for Santo Domingo (1935: 35) and Santa Ana (1942: 97–98) further indicate that the old Keresan pattern was one of complete community support for their religious leader. This has also been well expressed by White regarding San Felipe (1932: 14): "The fields of the cacique are planted, tended, and harvested by the people of the pueblo under the direction of the Tsi'yak'i'ya [the war captain]." White added, "This does not mean that the cacique is treated like a king. Indeed, he lives like any other man, except that he does not work his fields."

That the incumbent Cochití cacique raised an appreciable portion of his own family's food is but one of several indications, to be elaborated upon later, that the cacique's concentration upon religious affairs is diminishing. Furthermore, the declining interest of the people in the native religion has tolerated this shift, or at least they appear powerless to combat it if they would.

A related but distinct form of community labor was reported by Bandelier in his journal of November 18, 1880: "It appears that about 15 years ago there was at Cochití a special tract of land whose crops were gathered separate and kept by the *governador* for the relief of needy members of the pueblo only. This tract was, however, sold. The tract of the cacique only remains, and this is never attended to first, but neither last." As suggested in Bandelier's notation, no present informant had any knowledge of such a tract; relief measures have come completely from the produce of the cacique's field for as far back as they could recall.

Another phase of community farm work disappeared with the discontinuance of a resident priest. An effort to date and identify the last resident priest has been unsuccessful. In the Preface to Dumarest's "Notes on Cochiti" (1919: 139), the editor mentioned a collection of objects "which Father Dumarest had secured during his residence in Cochiti." This may well have been a slight inaccuracy, with Dumarest actually having his residence at Peña Blanca but having close contact with Cochití Pueblo, especially during the several epidemics of the late 1890's. This seems probable, for no one among the Cochití could recall a resident priest in Cochití, though several individuals did recall Father Dumarest. [17, 50, 70] Bandelier, in his journal of November 8, 1880, stated he was told by the padre that about 1852 there was a resident priest at Cochití. This man then moved to Peña Blanca where the church, begun in 1867, was consecrated December 12, 1869.

When Cochití had a resident priest, land was set aside for his support. This was worked by the people in the same manner as that set aside for the cacique, with the exception that this work was supervised by the two *fiscales*. [3, 42, 53] In three documents dated 1817 (Stephens Collection: Folder 1904), considerable tension was revealed regarding acreage furnished to the church and the labor expended upon it. Complaint was also made regarding the number of household servants demanded by the padres as well as the manner in which they were treated. The names of the *fiscales*—Lázaro Coris and Joaquín—appeared several times. These two officials were caught between the displeasure of their own people and the demands of their positions to properly maintain the church property and provide for the priests residing there.

In a letter from Father Trigo, addressed to the Very Reverend Father Procurador General Fray José Miguel de los Ríos and dated July 23, 1754, was the following notation regarding Cochití (Hackett 1937: 451):

Crossing the river at the foregoing mission [Santo Domingo] and travelling to the west, one soon arrives at this one, for the journey is not quite four leagues. On the banks of the river it has fine melon patches, and its Indians are good workers. They (sow several) *fanegas* of wheat and one *cuartilla* of corn, whereby the Father is assured that he will not have to go with a sack on his shoulder. They pay no obventions, but they give to the convent two servants for the cell, a bell-ringer, a porter, a cook, the necessary wood which they bring in carts, and two women to grind the wheat.

Still another form of community farm labor is co-operative assistance rendered by relatives. Their only compensation is food while working and the reassuring knowledge that the relative aided can be called upon for reciprocal services. In Goldfrank's discussion of clan data, she (1927: 9) discussed this:

The clans are again important when they are called upon as a whole by an individual to assist in his planting, harvesting, plastering, house building, grinding. He visits the oldest member of his own clan, or he may appeal to one of greater or lesser strength depending upon the work to be done. He approaches the oldest member with cornmeal in a husk, a regular pattern of invitation. This is distributed to the other clan members when asking their aid. In return for the help given, the clan members receive their food, during the work time, from the person who has asked for their assistance. Individuals, societies, and estufas, not only clans, may be asked by an individual to aid him in his work, and in all cases, the pay remains the same.

At present, reciprocal labor among relatives (clan members) still exists, though changes in protocol are apparent. The ceremony of bringing cornmeal when making the request for services has almost completely disappeared. Similarly, the feeling, as noted by Goldfrank, that one is entitled to call upon any member of the clan has diminished. Among the children and younger generation of parents, it is noticeably lacking. In general, this request is made in a matter-of-fact way and is directed to all relatives bilaterally reckoned—brothers, sons, sons-in-law, fathers, grandfathers, grandchildren, and uncles. In other words, any or all close male relatives in the Anglo-American sense are called upon. Normally, they serve cheerfully, knowing their labor is good insurance against the time they may need similar help. Friends may be called upon, but ordinarily there are enough relatives available.

Agricultural Implements and Machinery. Such well-known agricultural implements as digging sticks, or dibbles, and wooden hoes and shovels are known to modern Cochití only through hearsay. Goldfrank (1927: 92) stated, "Digging sticks made out of oak and a wood called $d^{y}ap^{uc}$ were used." Though Goldfrank dated this practice only as "in former times," it is possible that a generation ago she was successful in finding individuals who had had firsthand experience with such implements. Several of my informants, about sixty years old, believed that their fathers had used such implements. They appear to have been of both the pointed type and the paddle type. (Fig. 9) This paddle form may well have been used more generally as a hoe than as a dibble. [1] (See Castetter and Bell 1942: 135–136.)

Bandelier, in his journal of November 22, 1880, stated that wooden hoes (*cavadores*) were formerly used, and later, on April 14, 1882, he noted that a wooden shovel was used to clean grain. This was of fir or spruce and was called "u-ia-shte-q'ume." A wooden fork, "zash-tiome," of oak was also used. In his journal of November 5, 1880,

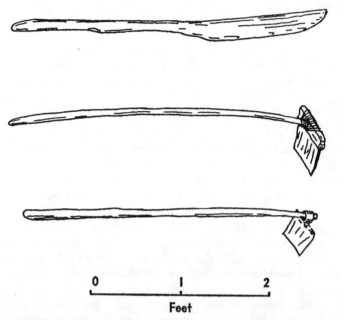

0   1   2
Feet

Fig. 9.—Hoes.

Bandelier noted that shovels or hoes, "of iron now," were used. He also stated there were thirty or forty plows in the pueblo, three or four Indian-owned. These were borrowed from one another. The plowshare was of oak, occasionally tipped with an iron point. (Fig. 10) [2] One man [52], born in the early 1880's, remembered seeing in his youth the use of oxen and the old Spanish wooden plow, assembled with wooden pegs and rawhide lashings. Bourke (Bloom 1938: 300) noted such plows on his visit in 1881: "The agricultural implements—the plows and harrows—were of the most ridiculously primitive description and the simple fact that they were in use spoke of the fertility of the soil." Another informant, born about the time of Bourke's visit, remembered his father's using oxen and a wooden plow but had only heard him tell of digging sticks. [50] None of my informants could recall wooden-wheeled carts, or *carretas*; they insisted that iron-rimmed, wooden-spoked wheels were all they could personally remember. (Plate 12a) However, Bourke (Bloom 1938: 234–237) noted "old & new carts," and Strout, who accompanied

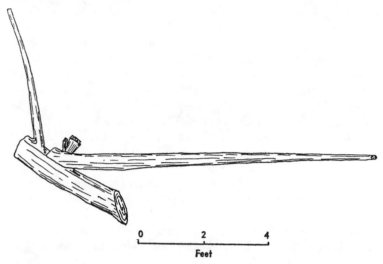

Fig. 10.—EARLY PLOW.

Bourke (Bloom 1938: 237), also recorded "Old & new style carts."
It would seem that these carts, as distinguished from wagons also
mentioned by Bourke, either had all but disappeared from Cochití
culture as it was in 1881, or the memories of the Cochití fall short in
this respect.

In contrast to this was the fact that many informants had had first-
hand experience with Spanish threshing methods. Most Cochití born
as recently as the early 1900's can relate personal experiences in
threshing with livestock on packed adobe floors. Several stated that
this was a principal reason for keeping as many horses as they formerly did. The animals were kept on the range until after the July 14
Feast Day, when herders brought them in to thresh wheat and other
grains. Adobe and water were carried to a flat and windy spot. A
hard-packed oval floor about thirty feet in diameter was prepared,
and a fence was erected around it. Formerly, this consisted of a few
stakes between which a single strand of rawhide or rope was strung.
(Plate 13) Blankets were hung over this, forming an enclosure. In
later years, enclosures were made of stakes and wire. Sheaves of grain
were piled on the floor to be trampled by animals, most commonly
horses but sometimes burros, as they were driven around and around.
The grain was winnowed by throwing it into the air. Goats were

usually used to pack the floor but not to do the actual threshing. [2, 15, 38, 49]

Bandelier (1890: 208) evaluated the Spanish introduction of the wooden plow, two-wheeled cart, clumsy iron ax, imperfect saw, and others with the comment that though these were poor in comparison with those of Europe "we are liable to forget . . . that the adoption of even these imperfect implements was a gigantic stride for the Indian at whose disposal they were placed gratuitously."

In reporting on Cochití in 1899, the agent Walpole (1899: 246) commented that farming methods were "of the crudest, having been in vogue for the past two hundred years. While the Indians are ready to make use of modern improvements when the same are offered them, they are not sufficiently cognizant of the advantages offered thereby to provide themselves with them." In the half-century since Walpole wrote, the Cochití have progressed to the point of not only appreciating agricultural machinery but taking an active part in securing at least some machines for their use. This is particularly true of community-owned equipment but it also applies to privately owned items.

Up to 1916, when the first threshing machine was bought by the pueblo, and in a few cases after that important event, livestock was used for threshing. This machine was used until 1934, at which time the tribe bought a second thresher, selling the first one to Frank Chávez, who still used it occasionally up to about 1950. In 1947, a combine harvester was purchased by the tribe. (Plate 14a) The old thresher was kept because some men thought the combine "wasted" much grain, missing some heads entirely and knocking kernels out of others before the blades reached them. The combine was also more expensive to use. Many did not have their fields or approaches leveled or regular enough to enable the tractor and combine to work. In 1947, three or four old men used the old thresher, but since 1948 essentially everyone has used the combine. "The combine is faster, easier, and just better all the way 'round." As of 1952, there was considerable talk of selling the threshing machine and buying a second combine to enable more fields to be cut at the optimum stage of ripening. Appendix 6 lists what the community collected for the use of the combine harvester in 1948 and 1951.

The foregoing discussion illustrates what Holmes (1932: 22) had reference to when he wrote, "The Cochiti Indians, well known to New Mexicans for their . . . thrift, industry and use of modern machinery. . . ." Walpole's remarks suggest that this favorable attitude toward machinery has existed at Cochití for a considerable time; it is also a quality that distinguishes Cochití from some neighboring pueblos. Densmore (1938: 119) was told at Santo Domingo that "all the Indian needs is the wind to blow away the chaff." Threshing machines were no good, for they wasted the wheat, and "they might forget something." In 1948, Santo Domingo finally yielded to the advantages of a threshing machine, and by 1951 there was mounting support for purchasing a combine harvester. Similar reluctance to accept agricultural machinery has been reported for Jemez (Parsons 1925: 15, 63), Taos (Parsons 1936: 18), and Zuñi (Parsons 1939: 19). Comparison was noted as early as Bandelier's time as indicated by his journal entry of October 5, 1880, in which he mentioned Padre Ribera's comments that "the Santo Domingo Indians worked with hoes and shovels, and had but oxen for their carts, whereas those of Cochití used horses and mules for draught. 'Son muy más castillanos, más ladinos. . . .' "

Common in the pueblo is the reaction of one informant to the failure of the older boys who have received mechanical-arts training at government schools to help operate the machinery: "All these boys go off to school, learn about tractors and other machines, and when the council says, 'O.K., you run it for us,' the boys all get scared and won't do it. What good is all this training?" [71]

This attitude overlooks the probable reason for such reluctance. Each year the council, just before the harvest begins, informs everyone that the combine crew will begin at the southern edge of the reservation. It will work northward, cross the river, and complete the harvest at the southern edge of the reservation on that side. Each wheat farmer must be ready for his turn or be bypassed. At the end of the first circuit, the crew retraces its route and harvests the remaining fields. Discontent inevitably arises over the sequence of the moves, and the crew members are subjected to considerable criticism. In actual practice the council tries to alternate the beginning between the east and west sides, thereby playing no favorites. This has, however, resulted only in antagonizing almost all farmers sooner or later. No one has as yet suggested announcing the season's plan of harvesting early in the spring so that planting schedules might be calculated to dovetail better with the harvest schedule. [3, 15, 20, 38, 49] Undoubtedly, the boys are not so much unwilling to share their mechanical talents as they are unwilling to subject themselves to the constant bickering of the older farmers. Even the older men who do run the combine find these incessant arguments and accusations unpleasant. [15, 20, 29 59]

The old harvesting implement, the hand sickle, is still used to clean corners and other areas missed by the combine harvester. The hand-fuls of grain are tossed onto the feeder belt as the machine circles the field. This cleanup work provides an opportunity for the older men to tell the younger ones of the hard times of their youth and how easy life has become. "Long ago we cut all day with the sickle; at night we crawled home on our hands and knees." [6, 38, 49, 62]

The Cochití are aware that despite their use of modern machinery, they are still poor farmers. They realize that their fields are irregular in shape, inadequately leveled, and that fallow field corners and borders between holdings increase weed growth. They also know that failure to plow after harvesting allows many weeds to mature and spread. Yet, few take positive steps to remedy these shortcom-ings. [6, 38, 49]

At present, the pueblo owns a thresher, a combine harvester, a hay-baler, two tractors, and a two-and-a-half ton stake-body Chevro-let truck, which aids in transporting produce from the fields and into town.

Surveys of pueblo property are subject to considerable suspicion because of evasive answers by the Indians, duplication in reporting, joint ownerships, and shifts in ownership; nevertheless, the following estimates are cited to afford some idea of the amount of agricultural machinery owned and used. According to the census of 1940, there were 89 family heads with estimated property as follows: 50 persons owned 85 plows; 12 had harrows; 50 men owned sets of harness, a few owning 2 sets; 45 had wagons; 15 had mowing machines; and 8 owned hay rakes. By reciprocal loans between siblings and other close relatives, this equipment quite adequately served the pueblo. (United Pueblos Agency, *Quarterly Bulletin*, I: 4: p. 17) Data for 1952 are not as completely recorded, but with some decrease from wear and breakage and also normal increase during the same inter-val, it was undoubtedly much the same. The growing interests in, and acquisition of, machinery were proportionate only, for during this same period there was an actual diminution in the number of Cochití actually engaged in farming.

Agricultural Produce

Crops. From the historical point of view, two classifications of crops are grown at Cochití: the aboriginal ones and those of Spanish or European origin. Some of those in the second category are quite recent, but most of them date back to the early seventeenth century. (For further data, see Brand 1939: 109–117; Castetter and Bell 1942: 28–121; Hill 1938: 48–51; and Whiting 1939.)

In pre-Spanish times, the basic agricultural crops were maize, or corn (*Zea mays*), pumpkins (*Cucurbita moschata* and, possibly, *C. pepo*), gourds (*Lagenaria siceraria*), beans (*Phaseolus vulgaris*), and cotton (*Gossypium hopi Lewton*). Of these, maize has retained its position of long standing as the most important crop, both from the standpoint of acreage and from yield. As suggested by Appendix 7, wherein crop acreages and yields are listed, the high rate of yield per acre is a primary factor in the continued prominence of maize, not only at Cochití but among other farmers as well.

The types of maize grown include yellow, blue, white, red, and variegated, yellow corn being by far the most common. Some popcorn (*Zea mays euerta*) is also grown, but it is generally easier to buy this from neighboring Spanish-Americans or from stores. A few farmers have tried hybrid corn, obtaining seed from Iowa and Illinois. It has proved quite satisfactory, but the annual renewal and high cost of the seed tend to reduce its popular appeal. There is also some feeling that seed from the Midwest is not suited to the local conditions at Cochití. About 1940, one of the more progressive farmers succeeded in raising a good crop (having failed the previous year). His success brought numerous requests for seed from various neighbors who did not understand the nature of hybrid corn. This placed him in the uncomfortable position of being disliked for withholding seed or being accused of witchcraft when the seed failed to produce a fine crop. He decided to keep the corn, and the following year, after he himself had ostensibly not used this for his seed, his actions were vindicated, though even yet not too well understood. [82]

Bandelier, in his journal of April 25, 1882, described still another type of corn which was not favored because of its association with witchcraft. "The way we came to talk about it [witchcraft] was by talking about corn. He told me the various names for various Grades of corn, and among others spoke of a certain brown or grey corn which was shunned by the people on account of its being 'maíz de brujerías.'" Bandelier made several references in his journal to the growing of corn. One, October 17, 1880, noted that the field was irrigated before the plowing; after planting, it was irrigated again; before the corn matured it was irrigated once or twice more. He also noted that before the field was planted, the clods left from plowing were broken up with hoes.

Further ethnographic material on crops and their handling is limited. Dumarest (1919: 146) merely commented that early in life the men assumed heavy labors in the fields, in which work they were unrivaled. Women did the grinding and cooking. Goldfrank (1927: 92–94) added some details: In regular planting, done ordinarily by the men, small mounds were made in the fields and seeds placed in them. (Bandelier, November 5, 1880, stated that the corn was "covered with the plough again." While this is apparently no longer done with corn, one informant [2], in speaking of wheat, remembered that "Indians like to plow the seeds under.") Planting was begun on the edge of the field, and the planter worked in a spiral, finishing at the center. Goldfrank did not state whether movement was clockwise or counterclockwise, but it was probably the latter. She stated that men worked in the fields. Wittfogel and Goldfrank (1943: 26–27) commented upon the dominance of the males in Rio Grande Pueblo agriculture, attributing this situation to the presence of irrigation. A generation later, her comments are applicable with but few exceptions. Corn is now planted in rows without prepared mounds.

Pumpkins of several types are grown. These are usually planted in hills scattered through the cornfields. [3] The most common type is the large, dark- and light-green striped form, already identified as to species. [15, 53] Bourke (Bloom 1938: 234–236) noted pumpkins only, while in the notes of his companion Strout both pumpkins and squashes were mentioned. True squashes (C. maxima) were unknown to aboriginal Southwestern tribes; they are rather recent introductions (Brand 1939: 116; Castetter and Bell 1942: 102).

Like the pumpkins, gourds are grown in hills scattered through the cornfields. They are not eaten but are utilized for dance rattles, pottery scrapers, ladles, and dippers, though metal containers have largely replaced gourd ladles and dippers. Gourds are also used to make animal or birdlike snouts or bills on ceremonial masks. [44, 70]

Beans, almost all of the kidney or pinto type, are raised by nearly every farmer. They are the crop second in importance, as indicated in Appendix 7. "Bean patches" in a few cases amount to as much as two-acre fields; most are much smaller, and in a few instances beans are planted with other crops.

Present-day Cochití say they have never seen cotton grown at the pueblo, though it is common knowledge that it was formerly grown there. One man, about fifty-five, thought that cotton had been grown in his father's time on a very limited scale. [44] Another, about sixty-five years old, said his grandfather had grown cotton. [2] Douglas (1939: 163) stated that cotton was grown at Cochití "until about 1900."

Cotton was used for making string to tie prayer sticks, in making ka'tsīna masks, and for other ceremonial purposes. Commercial string and absorbent cotton have been used for such purposes in recent years. [44, 70] Bandelier, in his journal of November 5, 1880, observed that Santo Domingo, but not Cochití, raised cotton at that time. Later, Bandelier (1890: 157) published his opinion that in the colder sections of the Southwest cotton had been displaced by sheep in post-Spanish times. Aside from a limited continued use in cere-monial paraphernalia, where changes would have been most strenu-ously resisted, wool quite rapidly supplanted native cotton.

Cochití is near the northernmost limit of possible cotton cultiva-tion. Bandelier (1890: 345) indicated this, and a more recent survey of the literature by Jones (1936: 51) confirms it. While the historical accounts comment frequently on clothing and presents of cotton *mantas*, they are not explicit about who grew the cotton. One source (Biblioteca Nacional, *Legajo X*: Document 70) to state definitely that the Cochití raised cotton was a letter from Fray Cayetano Fore, custodian, dated September 1, 1794. In it he described how limited quantities of cotton were planted each spring. He noted that planting was common in most of the pueblos of the Keres. He further stated that *mantas* and jackets of cotton and wool were woven for their own clothing and for trade with the Spaniards and neighboring Indians.

Another agricultural plant grown by the Cochití is tobacco. Castet-ter (1943: 320–321) has pointed out, however, that there is no con-clusive evidence that tobacco (*Nicotiana* spp.) was grown by any Southwestern tribe aboriginally. As of 1951, tobacco, or ha'mē, was grown by the families of the following men: Cresencio Pecos, Cipri-ano Quintana, Damasio Quintana, Marcelo Quintana, Diego Romero,

Vicente Romero, José Rey Suina, and Juan José Trujillo. [3, 15, 33, 49, 54] (A specimen was identified as *Nicotiana* sp. by Dr. Edward F. Castetter and Dr. Howard J. Dittmer, University of New Mexico, in December, 1949; a second specimen was similarly identified by Dr. Dittmer in September, 1951. Seed from this second specimen was grown in Austin, Texas, in the summer of 1953, and from these plants, an identification of *Nicotiana rustica* was made by Dr. T. H. Goodspeed, University of California, and also by Dr. Castetter.)[1]

These plants are normally a part of the family garden plot and, as such, are usually cared for by the women. These families have had their seed for "a long time—many, many years," or can recall obtaining it from one of the other families named. Thus, the source of all the seed seems quite certainly established, for, inevitably, it can be traced ultimately to Marcial Lucero, a Spanish-American formerly living at Cochití. In 1951, Marcial, eighty-six years old, was living in Peña Blanca. He had formerly lived at Cochití and, before that, at Cañada de Cochití, where he was the final resident, leaving about the turn of the century. Marcial said the seed had been brought from Mexico many years before by his father and grandfather. He had tended these plants in fields at Cañada "all my life." Whether these seeds actually had been brought from Mexico or had been gathered from the adjacent mountains and brought into cultivation remains an open question.

No Cochití was found who knew of *Nicotiana attenuata* growing wild. However, in checking on this point, Castetter reported collecting it on the Fenton Ranch, thirty air-line miles northwest of Cochití and on the far side of the Valle Grande from Cochití. (Personal correspondence, April 14, 1953.) Volney Jones also reported its presence in Jemez Canyon north of Jemez Pueblo. He also expressed the opinion that it was apparently never abundant nor so widespread as some statements in the literature might imply. (Personal correspondence, March 19, 1953.) While both of these areas are within range of Cochití travels, it is significant that they make no effort to gather it; in fact, the Cochití do not seem to know of its existence in these locations. Instead, their tobacco is grown in the fields and, without

---

[1] The matter of associating the term *punche* with the proper species of *Nicotiana* must await further field work. A considerable bibliography exists on this topic, and I formerly believed that an explanation could be made on the basis of the specimens at hand. However, due to the poor condition of earlier specimens, more definitive work must be delayed until new collections are made and examined both botanically and ethnographically.

exception, by families who are important in the native ceremonial life of the tribe. This tobacco is known as "punche." Although the Cochití do not gather wild *Nicotiana,* they do gather other wild plants (some of these also designated as "punche") for smoking. These are discussed in connection with the gathering of other wild-plant products in Chapter 6.

Tobacco, or punche, is used for council meetings and other cere-monial occasions, as it is in other pueblos. It is also used for gifts, for trading and selling (in 1951, a one-pound coffee can, level but not packed, sold for twenty-five cents), and occasionally for ordinary smoking. This last use is especially characteristic of older men who prefer it, generally blended with other wild plants, to commercial tobaccos. In recent years, commercial tobaccos have been smoked in council meetings, but they are still barred from the more sacred events. [3, 15, 44, 49, 70]

Tobacco, or punche, grown in the fields, comes up each year from seeds which dropped from the previous season's crop. (See Bande-lier's notes, Appendix 8, which suggest that seed was actually saved and sown the following season.) When five or six inches high, "so that it has good roots," it is transplanted, usually to the other side of the garden plot, where it is arranged in rows that can be cultivated and irrigated. Through the summer, small sucker stems and leaves are plucked in order to obtain the maximum growth of the main leaves. In late summer, as the leaves attain the desired size (com-monly indicated as the palms of two hands side by side), they are pulled off. The remainder of the plant is allowed to continue its growth. Stems may be left on these leaves or removed, depending on the individual's choice. It takes additional time to remove these stems, but the leaves without stems need to be "sweated" only four days as compared with about a week if the stems remain attached.

"Sweating" is done to make the tobacco sweet, i.e., less strong. It is done by laying the leaves flat between several thicknesses of paper. The paper and leaves are placed in a box and weighted down, the whole box being covered with sacks or cloth. The leaves are "sweated" in this press until they have turned yellow. Then they are taken out and spread on a cloth or canvas to dry in the sun. Care is taken that the wind does not blow the leaves away, and they are taken indoors if there is danger of rain. The sun-drying continues for about a week, after which the leaves are crumbled in the hands and placed in a gunnysack. Next, the sack is shaken to sift out the dust that may have blown on the leaves during the drying. They are then stored in a heavy paper sack or similar air-tight container, ready to be used. Most Cochití cure their tobacco in this manner, feeling that the sweating produces a milder, sweeter smoke. Those who only dry it in the sun have a much stronger and more bitter product. Leaves that begin to dry on the plant later in the autumn also tend to be more bitter than those picked green and cured by sweating. [16, 33, 34, 44, 45, 88]

Wheat (trigo, a'sha) is the most popular crop introduced by the Spaniards. Of the food crops, wheat acreage is second only to that of maize. This is almost entirely spring wheat. In planting, the seed is broadcast, "just covering the field with no particular plan to it." Wheat is harvested immediately after the July 14 Feast Day. [1, 2, 3, 44]

Bandelier, in his journal of October 17, 1880, stated that the wheat was irrigated when it sprouts, when it gets into ears, and when it blossoms. Some irrigated eight or ten times. In another entry on April 8, 1882, he wrote: "Sowing wheat today. They say wheat grows without previous irrigation, and that it rises unequally. It keeps without water for two months, but as soon as the lowest leaves begin to turn yellow, it must be irrigated again as it is a sign that the ground is drying again." A present-day wheat farmer stated that wheat is irrigated three times: usually when it is six inches high, again when it begins to put out heads, and finally just before it is ripe. If the season is unusually dry, the wheat might be irrigated as often as every eight or ten days. [42] And another informant stated that present practice is to irrigate when the wheat is about six inches high and then two or three times after it has reached full height. With normal rainfall, wheat is irrigated three or four times. [92]

For the use of the combine in 1948 each farmer paid every sixth sack of wheat (100 pounds) to the community. This was calculated by whole and half-sacks. The community's share in 1948 was about 128 sacks, valued at $256, an indicated yield of 768 sacks for the entire pueblo. In 1951, with the threat of a severe water shortage, only fifteen farmers, as compared with thirty in 1948, planted wheat. In 1951 the community took 2 sacks from each 11, the capacity of the harvester tank. The community collected 75.25 sacks, valued at $148.50, from a total crop of 408 sacks. In both years, the yield represented a return of between 3 and 4 sacks for each sack planted; this was considered a normal and fair return. In years past, when a threshing machine was used, the community collected every sixteenth bushel from each farmer. [40]

With the recent succession of dry years, alfalfa (*Medicago sativa*), because of its extraordinarily deep root system, has become increasingly important, claiming second place in the entire acreage planted. It supplements the inadequate open range, and it is also valuable as a cash crop. The planting of alfalfa as purely an income-producing crop is another departure from earlier subsistence-farming practices. Alfalfa fields are also used as autumn pasturage following the final (usually the third but occasionally the fourth) cutting. Bandelier recorded, October 5, 1880, that the Cochití were making the second cut of hay on the following day for the padre; the first cutting had occurred about the end of June. Modern Cochití are also well aware of the value of this legume as a soil-builder. [45, 53]

Oats, "kafir corn," and other crops introduced by the Europeans are grown occasionally but never extensively. [15, 20]

Garden plots, ranging up to an acre, are located in corners of the irrigated fields. Almost every family has a garden, normally tended by the women and children, which is planted primarily with European introductions: chili, watermelons, muskmelons, onions, cabbages, beets, string beans, peas, *havas, garbanzas,* and similar vegetables. There are a few instances of tobacco, as mentioned; particularly in former times, amaranth and similar native plants were cultivated. [1, 2, 3, 33, 34]

Chili patches have been common in the gardens for many years. Bandelier, in an entry of October 25, 1880, stated that three bundles of broom grass were worth a string (*ristra*) of green chili two meters long and that one string of green chili was equal to one-half string of the red. Green chili is no longer strung at Cochití. [92] In recent years, there has been considerable difficulty with the plants rotting and drying up. In 1951 this was explained as caused by faulty irrigating practices; water came so close to the plants that during the heat of the day the steam vapor and sun damaged them. This was said to be the report from the New Mexico Agricultural and Mechanical Arts College, and it somewhat puzzled the Cochití, for they had been using the same methods for many years without any difficulties. [3, 44]

Fruit trees are popular and are highly valued by the Cochití in spite of their apparent neglect of them. Peaches and apples are most common, with plums, apricots, and cherries less numerous. There are some grapevines, but their yield is of relatively small value. Many fruit trees are located along the ditches, and in spite of their private ownership, numerous passers-by, mostly children but also adults, help themselves freely. Apparently this lack of regard for private ownership of fruit trees is no great change from the attitude of a half-century ago. The Eickemeyers, in 1894, passed by the community orchard (the one destroyed during the construction of the Conservancy District canal in 1932), and they (1895: 59) noted shelters elevated on poles in the orchard corners. It was explained that the owners occupied these shelters during the fruit season to protect their produce from both birds and human beings.

Harvesting and Storage. One of the earliest discussions of Cochití harvesting was that by Walpole (1899: 246):

> It is in harvesting and threshing their grain that the most antiquated methods prevail, wheat and oats being harvested with the old reaping hook, which has been in use for thousands of years. Thrashing is done on a thrashing floor [see Plate 13], in precisely the same manner as among the peoples of three thousand years ago, viz, by driving animals over it until the grain is tramped out of the straw. In the process, it becomes mixed with all manner of foreign substances, which have to be picked out with the fingers or washed in water from a ditch.

Walpole concluded by pointing out that grain harvested in this manner did not command a high price on the market and recommended machines for Cochití and several other pueblos.

Despite the recent practice of using a combine harvester, already noted in the discussion of agricultural machinery, modern handling of the grain after threshing shows little change. It is emptied from the harvester tank, sacked in wagons, and brought into the pueblo, where it is placed in a shed or the house, being either left in the sacks or dumped upon the floor or a canvas. Within a few days, the grain is carried into the open by the women and is placed upon a packed, clean ground-surface, or a tarpaulin. Next, a woman takes a large Apache basket or a washbowl, fills it with grain, and, holding it over her head, allows the kernels to fall slowly to the ground. (Plate 14 *b*) The wind blows away the chaff. This process is repeated until the grain is free from foreign particles. Then the grain is washed. Formerly this was done in the river or irrigation ditches, but it is now done in large tubs of clean water drawn from the water system. Grain to be washed is still put in large, loosely woven yucca baskets of local manufacture. After being washed and dried, the grain is re-sacked or placed in storage bins until it is needed. [3, 16, 17, 27, 37]

In his journal of October 18, 1891, Bandelier noted that "every-body is gathering corn now. The Indians are working mostly at night while the leaves and stalks are moist and pliable." Goldfrank (1927: 92) noted that harvesting was normally men's work and drying and storing was women's work, with both sexes helping with the husking. While the corn was being picked in the fields, husking was being done in the pueblo. Four ears, known as "mothers," were left with the husks on and were placed at the corners of the pile in the store-room.

Today the men, sometimes assisted by the women, still pick corn by hand before the stalks are cut. Ears are thrown into wagons and brought to the pueblo for husking. The corn is generally shelled by rubbing one ear against another, though a few families use a small metal hand mill, which appreciably speeds up this process. This work is done by women, old men, and children. [16]

Much of the superstition noted by Goldfrank (1927: 93–94)—such as the danger of storing yucca near corn or wheat and entering the storeroom with shoes on—has lapsed. Similar shifts are evident in the modern practice of topping corn for fodder. I was told that this had been possible only since about 1925, for before then the council had forbidden this practice because the old people had objected to such tampering with the natural growth cycle of the sacred corn plants. The old practice of waiting until autumn, when the corn had dried, meant that the green stalks and fresher tassels, which were most valuable as fodder, were lost. [49] After the harvest, stock is regu-larly turned into the fields to graze.

Bandelier described in his journal of October 6, 1880, the process of harvesting beans. The plants were pulled up and piled in heaps. When dry, they were beaten with poles on the threshing floors used for wheat. Much the same process is used at present except that the beans are beaten on a smooth, hard area on the ground or on a can-vas, the regular threshing floors having vanished long ago.

In an entry for April 5, 1882, Bandelier stated that if watermelons were picked while the seeds still clung to the flesh, they would keep until the following March. He was told of one instance in which the watermelons had been left in the fields through the winter and were found to be good eating the next spring. Today there is an increasing tendency to eat the watermelons fresh; muskmelons are cut into

strips and dried for later use. The increasing use of home- and com-
mercially-canned vegetables and fruits is undoubtedly a factor in
reducing the amount of home-drying of melons and similar items.
[92] Despite a reduction in the quantity of fruit available, the practice of drying it is carried on by many families; a considerable amount
is canned. Much fresh fruit is consumed, and still more simply rots
on the ground. [3, 45, 49]

In Starr's diary of September 21, 1897, a description of the harvest
season's activities provided many details which can be duplicated at
the present time:

After dinner we took a long walk down through the fields to see the summer huts and the crop. They lie along the river for a long distance. The
houses are little single-room affairs, mostly of adobe or of brush. Some
have a little shelter of boughs in front: one or two have little dome or
arched brush huts erected on the flat roof of the hut proper. Everywhere
they were happy and drying corn, melons cut into strips, peaches cut in
two, etc. At one house where we took shelter from a sudden rain they had
great bunches of large green leaves [tobacco]. At the last one we visited
they had quantities of red peppers and in the well-kept fields in front
were pepper plants in bloom. . . . At one house we were welcomed with
a large well-flavored muskmelon and a bucket full of peaches: elsewhere
also we had peaches offered us.

In concluding this section on agricultural produce, the difficulty of
obtaining reliable statistics should be emphasized. Concurrence with
this view was well expessed by White (1942: 46) in relation to his
work at Santa Ana:

We have some figures on amount of land cultivated and quantity of
crops grown at Santa Ana. We do not believe that they are very accurate,
however. It is very difficult to collect statistics among the pueblos. As agent
John Ward observed in 1864: "It is impossible to arrive at anything like
a correct estimate of the quantity [of crops grown]. The utmost these
farmers can do is tell the number of *carrita* (cart) loads which they have
gathered from the field, and *carritas* being, as you are aware, of different
dimensions, and quite a variety of shapes. No one ever thinks about measuring his crops." (*Report of the Commissioner of Indian Affairs for 1864*,
p. 193) The same sort of situation prevails today. Nevertheless, we present
the following data for what they may be worth.

Paralleling White's observation is the fact that the Cochití themselves have never been interested in records of accurately measured

field production. Tracts are generally irregular in outline, and acreages are rough approximations, though Indian Service personnel have developed reasonably accurate estimates of acreages. Yields are vaguely stated, intentionally or otherwise. Such figures as those on the grain harvest are reasonably accurate, for these data are kept by the threshing crew, and standard units of measure are used. The other crops, such as maize, alfalfa (except when baled), pumpkins, beans, and the like, are measured, if at all, in terms of wagonloads, filled to varying degrees. "Boxfuls," "basketfuls," and other such fluctuating units are also quoted. "Loads" as often as not indicate trips from field to storeroom, an estimate that also includes variables. Again, storerooms and bins are of varying capacities.

To attempt to increase the accuracy of these statistics would undoubtedly necessitate such a prolonged and intensive study that the principal result would be to arouse the antagonism of most families. Cash sales of standard quantities and the increased use of hay balers and combines will facilitate the accurate gathering of such data. However, as long as the agricultural economy remains so dominantly one of subsistence and barter, production statistics will remain inaccurate. Nevertheless, the Agency figures presented in Appendix 7 are believed to have some value in indicating the relative importance of crops. As shown there, maize, alfalfa, and wheat acreage comprised 526 of a total of 601 cultivated acres in 1945. About 29 acres were fallow or unfarmed. Although the Cochití sometimes allow land to rest in this way, it is more common to plant alfalfa and leave this for several years. The unfarmed land generally belongs to the pueblo and is claimed by no individual.

This surplus of cultivated land at Cochití is interesting in the light of a statement by Aberle (1948: 22):

In a few villages there is a small amount of unassigned farming land which can be given to landless families, but this is not the rule. When new farming land is made available by the Federal Government, the land is turned over to the Governor and the Council to distribute. Since the demand for land far exceeds the amount to be distributed, the Governor usually turns to the Federal Government for some plan to insure a fair distribution. The old custom of distribution on the basis of need or request is inadequate to meet the pressure of the new situation.

In 1951/52, Cochití opinion was quite unanimous that somewhere between a third and a half of the tillable acreage (630 acres) was not being farmed. While this had in part resulted from the unusually pessimistic forecasts of water shortages since early in the spring of 1951, it also reflects the steady shift away from agriculture in favor of other economic pursuits by a number of Cochití, especially the younger men.

Stock-Raising

Livestock-raising is not so universally practiced as is farming, but the aggregate income from it compares favorably with that from farming. According to the United Pueblos Agency data for 1942, total Cochití income from stock-raising was $6,069 as compared with $8,060 for crop agriculture (Payne 1943: 11). In 1950, with improved control of reporting and also inflated prices, these figures were $13,-660 for stock-raising and $35,998 for crop agriculture (Nations 1950: 1–2). These figures were for sales and did not include home consumption. These statistics are subject, of course, to the same suspicion and criticism as those mentioned earlier, but they do suggest the relative importance of these two economic pursuits.

Cattle and Oxen. Cochití uses a community brand 人 for its cattle (and also horses). Individual ownership is indicated by supplementary brands or, more commonly, by earmarks. In recent years, Joe Melchior has been the largest cattle-owner in the pueblo and has served as brand inspector for the community at cattle sales. He spends most of his time on the range rather than in the fields. Other owners, such as Lorenzo Suina and his son, Ted, alternate in helping Melchior move cattle from one portion of the range to another. Normally, individual owners and as many relatives as are needed search for their particular animals and drive them into the corrals when they are wanted. [1, 44, 45, 49, 53, 70]

Individual handling of cattle stands in contrast to the community herding of horses and may have arisen from the fact that a relatively small proportion of the pueblo have ever been cattle-owners. This difference, however, already existed at the turn of the century, when there were more cattle and cattle-owners in Cochití than at present. Even then, the individual owners divided herding duties, usually rotating on a weekly basis as did the herdsmen of horses and burros. There was, however, one significant difference between these herding duties: only cattle-owners shared the work of herding, but for the horse and burro herds, all the older boys and men were called upon.

Before the reservation was fenced (1930), cattle were driven into the pueblo and placed in corrals every night. [49, 53]

The pueblo customarily keeps about five quality breeding bulls that run with the herd, which is handled as a unit though individual animals belong to various owners. The herd averages about 300 animals and ranges between 250 and 350 head, depending upon the season. [1, 44, 45]

Cattle are primarily a source of cash income, though some animals are butchered for domestic use, for feast days, weddings, and similar occasions. Electric refrigeration has made it easier to preserve large amounts of fresh meat in the warm months; but as there are only a few families with refrigerators, most prefer to sell the animals and use the income to buy meat as it is needed. Hides are valued for moccasins, especially with the decline in the number of deer killed each year, and for drumheads. Since drum-making is an important economic pursuit at Cochití, the local supply of hides is inadequate. Drum-makers go to other pueblos and to towns and ranches to purchase them, normally paying about two dollars per hide. [3, 15, 42, 62, 70]

Milk cows are not so common as they once were. This decrease is said to be due to lack of feed. [1] In Bourke's journal (Bloom 1938: 234), he mentioned buying two gallons of milk, "very pure rich stuff —the old woman asked 45¢, a very reasonable price." At present, fewer than a half-dozen cows are milked regularly. The owners use this milk raw or sell it to neighbors. No effort is made to feed the cows specially, however, and milk is not greatly valued by most Cochití. Canned milk seems to satisfy what little desire most of them have. The cows are tested by the government and seem to be of fair quality.

Perhaps one of the greatest shifts from the past, so far as cattle-raising is concerned, is the complete disappearance of oxen. Bourke and Strout made note of them (Bloom 1938: 236) and several informants, about sixty years old, have personally worked with oxen in the fields. [50, 52] Men in their fifties clearly remember them in the pueblo and saw oxen used in the field, but they were too young to have worked them themselves. [15, 44, 49, 53] No explanation was given for the complete shift to horses, but it was apparently related to—or at least was contemporaneous with—the replacement of Spanish plows by American plows, and the adoption of harrows, farm wagons, and similar equipment. Oxen disappeared from neighboring villages also at about this time. Whether this can be explained as a disappearing market, or supply, or the reverse, as a disappearing demand, could not be ascertained.

Horses and Mules. Although horses are less numerous than cattle, totaling fewer than two hundred head, they appear to be more highly regarded by most Cochití. Very few families are without at least one team. Most horses are of a light draft type, and also serve as riding horses. While there are not many exceptionally fine horses in the pueblo, neither are there many that are particularly old, worn out, or disabled. The relatively recent soil conservation and range policy of limiting the number of stock that should be put out to graze has undoubtedly effected a reduction in the number of horses at Cochití.

On days of chicken pulls (*gallos*), Santiago's Day, community hunts, and similar occasions, the young men turn out with their saddle horses. Some boys expend considerable energy on their horses; most simply saddle up what is at hand and join the crowd. In general, it seems that the tradition of being a "foot people" still holds. In this respect, an entry from Bandelier's journal, October 24, 1880, is of interest though of questionable validity: "From 1873 on, horses were kept; before that time there had been but one horse in the entire pueblo." The significance of the year 1873 as one of demarcation could not be ascertained, but the designation of these Indians as "foot people" appears justified. Horses are used in field work, and by a few of the more elderly men to travel to and from the fields, and are valued for these purposes. However, only a few individuals exhibit obvious pride in their animals.

From an economic viewpoint, horses are easier to obtain than to keep. Pasturage is limited but sufficient in summer. In winter, however, horses often have to be fed hay, and it is this cost, except for those who raise enough alfalfa, which causes hardship. Often a younger man depends upon his parents' teams, or on those of his wife's parents.

Most Cochití break their own horses to harness and to the saddle, accomplishing this by considerable handling of the animal for varying periods before the actual breaking, which is usually done when the horse is three years old. However, "sometimes a man gets busy and forgets—then with these older horses, he has a tough time."[3] After the horse becomes accustomed to being handled by people and to wearing portions of harness—halters, bridles, saddles, dragging ropes, and the like—for several days, the step to actual use is not difficult. A few animals that prove difficult to handle are given to a younger man recognized as a skilled rider or handler. Horses that cannot be broken are normally killed, for enough gentle horses are readily available. As most of the ground traveled is soft, most horses are unshod. When shoes are temporarily needed, they are put on by the owner. They are generally put on cold, with the hoof trimmed and filed to fit properly. [44, 45]

Old horses and wild ones are killed, usually by cutting the throat. They are carefully skinned, as the hides are valuable for drumheads. (Plate 16b) In the summer of 1948, a horse died from a neck injury. The owner offered the hide to Marcelo Quintana, the cacique, if he would skin it. With the aid of several young boys who gathered around, the skinning was completed. The carcass was then dragged by a team to a nearby arroyo, where it was left for "the dogs and the coyotes." One boy cut some steaks to feed his dog, and the remainder of the carcass was left untouched. No attempt was made to salvage the tail for use in ceremonial costumes. From a remark made at the time, it seemed probable that a few choice cuts might have been taken home for the Indians' own use had it not been for the pathologic growth at the animal's neck.

Mules have not been popular at Cochití, and there have never been more than a few teams in use at any time. In 1948, only one man had a mule team; in 1951, there was none. [3, 45]

Another change in recent years has been the shift from communal herding of the horses to private pasturage or individual responsibility for the welfare of these animals on the open range. Formerly, a herd of more than three hundred horses was guarded by the young men and older boys of the pueblo. [49, 50, 65] Herding was done on a rotating plan, under supervision of the war captains and *alguacilitos*. The war captains chose the weekly shifts of personnel who served under the *alguacilitos,* who also rotated. Selection was made in order of residence, with no consideration of kiva or clan affiliations. The herd remained on the range throughout most of the year, favorite pastures being near Bear Head Peak, Cañada, and Frijoles Cañon, all north and west of the pueblo. Late in June, the horses were brought to the community pasture near Peña Blanca, where they were kept until after the threshing. The war captain issued the call to drive in the horses, and many people participated in the roundup. Herders did their best to guard all the animals, but there were no damages paid when one was lost. [3, 49, 50, 65]

Attempts to date the cessation of community horse-herding at Cochití were unsuccessful. Bandelier, November 27, 1880, made reference to the communal horse herd, the "caballada," and on December
2, 1880, noted a fair amount of grass for grazing, despite snow on top
of the pasture ground at Cuesta Colorado. In an entry of October 21,
1880, he stated that four stallions were communally owned and kept
with the herd. Each week the war captain picked four herders to
take charge.

Dumarest and Goldfrank did not mention this work in their discussions of officers and their duties. Some of my informants, about
sixty years of age, had herded as very young boys before the turn of
the century. They could not fix a definite date on the discontinuance
of herding, though it appears to have ceased early in this century. At
the same time they stated that, as of 1948, the war captains and their
helpers still supervise communal horse-herding at Santo Domingo.
[44, 49, 50, 88] White (1935: 41) reported this, as of 1933, for Santo
Domingo, and in his report on Santa Ana, he (1942: 105) reported
the practice in the present tense at that pueblo.

One of the favorite Cochití "true stories" of earlier times involves
a trip to California near the end of the last century. It was made by
Santiago Quintana ("Old Man Guerro"), his father-in-law, Juan José
Garcia, and a third man, Ha'ro. This trip took a month with horses
and burros. They remained on the West Coast for a year or more,
earning good money at herding, cooking, and other jobs. When they
returned, they brought fine saddles, silver-studded bridles, and good
horses—racers, "the best around the pueblo for a long time." These
were the favorite horses in rooster-pulls, races, and other events.
[45, 49, 70] Possibly related to these events, it is interesting that in
Bandelier's journal of October 16, 1880, he mentioned meeting Pedro,
a boy who "has just returned from the Sierra with two fine horses,
white, a horse and a mare, both of which Adelaido and José Hilario
brought from California."

As of about 1895, the Eickemeyers (1895: 96–97) commented on
Cochití horses as follows:

The Pueblos get most of their horses from the Navajoes, who make a
special business of horse-raising and travel from village to village with
droves of Indian ponies or cayuses, which they trade for beads that the
Pueblo Indians make in great quantities. Four of these strings of beads
will buy a horse. Five dollars will also buy a horse; but strange to say, five
dollars will not buy the beads.

In recent years the value of horses, as with other goods, has greatly increased. Good draft and saddle horses cost more than $100, and young and unbroken, or older, animals range from $50 to $75. "Horses for less than $35 probably aren't worth much unless it's a young colt." [20, 44, 45, 62] In recent years, a community stud was kept by Clofe Arquero, who was privileged to work the animal in return for feeding and caring for him. However, no stud fee could be charged anyone in the pueblo. This animal died sometime before 1951 and, as of 1952, had not been replaced. [42, 44, 92]

Burros. One of the outstanding, and somewhat surprising, aspects of stock-raising is the complete absence of burros in present-day Cochití. Repeatedly in their accounts of earlier herding days, trading trips, wood-gathering, and other activities of their youth, informants spoke of the great numbers of burros. Bourke (Bloom 1938: 235) noted horses "in abundance" and burros, which may give some indication of their relative importance as of 1880/81, or may simply indicate what happened to be visible at the time. A decade later the Eickemeyers (1895: 96) wrote:

> . . . there came toward us into the pueblo a large bunch of burros driven by two Indians, who were bringing the animals into the village corral for the night. Raising burros is one of the principal occupations of the Indians of Cochiti. The animals are herded together, and each person owning any in the bunch has a special day assigned on which it is his duty to care for the lot. The horses are cared for in the same way.

In his diary for September 19, 1897, Starr noted that, as it was Sunday, the burro herd was late in going out from the pueblo, and that the boys had played with them in the corral.

According to one informant, there were more than 200 burros, more than 300 horses, and even more cattle at Cochití about 1910. Contrary to the Eickemeyers' statement on herding duties—which held true for cattle only—every man, whether or not he owned burros, helped in their herding just as he did in the herding of horses. Every night they were driven into the pueblo corral, located at the same spot where it now stands. [42, 49, 65, 70, 88] While herding burros, the boys had great fun riding them, playing *gallo* and other games. Their job was to keep the burros fom straying and from getting into the fields of the Spaniards in Peña Blanca.

Burros were preferred to horses for long trips despite the fact that a particular trip was described to the Eickemeyers (1895: 54) as "three days with burros and one day with a horse." Burros could be ridden, or used as pack animals. Best of all, they needed little care. The Indians did not mind walking, and horses were too difficult to care for on a long trip to the Estancia Valley salt lakes or to the Zuñi, Hopi, and Navaho reservations. [15, 25, 50]

Informants were unable to date the disappearance of burros from the pueblo. Presumably it was twenty years ago, or more. No single cause for their disappearance could be determined; it is probably the combination of the reduction in range forage, the steady increase in the use of draft horses on the farms and in transportation, and the discontinuance of trips by foot and burro for salt-gathering, trading, and wood-gathering. Horse-drawn wagons and, in more recent years, automobiles, trucks, and bus service have become the normal modes of transportation.

Sheep and Goats. The Pueblo peoples adopted sheep-raising and the use of wool from the Spaniards. The men—the traditional Pueblo weavers—shifted their medium from cotton, and perhaps other plant fibers, to wool and continued their work. In early Spanish accounts, weaving, especially of *mantas,* and general sheep-raising were mentioned as prominent in Pueblo industry. Bourke (Bloom 1938: 235) noted both sheep and goats on his Cochití visit, but Strout (Bloom 1938: 236), who accompanied him, noted "no sheep or goats." The Eickemeyers (1895: 102) saw both sheep and goats in 1894.

Some of my first informants (1946/47) stated there were neither sheep nor goats raised at Cochití. Later, I found at least two owners, each of whom had about a dozen sheep and were expanding their flocks. The sheep were penned each night to protect them from coyotes, and they were kept in fenced pastures rather than on the open range. These men thought sheep-raising was worth while from the standpoint of both wool and meat. However, they felt that they did not have sufficient private pasturage for sheep; they did not want to let them roam the open range untended; they could not afford to hire herders; and they did not want their children or other family members to spend their time in this way.

In the papers of Indian Agent Calhoun (Abel 1915: 50), an entry dated October 15, 1849, mentioned that the Cochití had killed three Apaches of a band that had raided the sheepherders in the mountains beyond Cochití. Cochití men have worked for some time for various owners of large herds of sheep in that section of New Mexico. One, Isidro Cordero, was the oldest person at Cochití in 1951. He had spent so much time away from the pueblo in his youth and later years herding sheep in the Estancia Valley and Pecos River country that several persons felt he was poorly informed on Cochití life. Despite his age and activities in the Ku-sha'lī Society and in native ceremonials, they claimed he spoke Spanish better than Keresan [3, 15, 18, 49, 70]

Each winter during the agricultural off season, others, such as Juan Estévan Chalan, had gone as far as Bakersfield, California, to herd sheep. This practice may have resulted from the trip made by Santiago Quintana and others (p. 108), who stayed several months herding and cooking on California sheep ranches. [49] Juan continued to go to Bakersfield as late as 1947, at which time his son-in-law gave up his nonlucrative welding and machine business in the pueblo to take Juan's place in California. [3, 6, 15]

Bandelier noted in his entry of October 10, 1880, that Juan José Montoya's son, Adelaido, was leaving the next day for Bernalillo, from whence he would go to the Navaho country and herd sheep for Mariano Otero until the following February.

Pigs. Pigs were mentioned by Bourke and Strout in 1881 (Bloom 1938: 235–236). Agency figures gave between 75 and 100 pigs at Cochití in 1945 (Payne 1945: 4), and between 150 and 200 in 1950, with an additional 244 sold during the year, bringing the highest total income for any one kind of animal. Of the 85 families, 47 had no pigs; 27 had from 1 to 5; 11 families had from 6 to 10. (Nations 1950: 1–2)

Pigs are kept in small pens around the perimeter of the pueblo, usually in or near the owner's corral. They are fed table scraps, wormy or bruised fruit, and tall grass cut fresh along the irrigation ditches. There is plenty of food for these animals, and their hides, meat, and especially the lard are greatly valued. Sometimes one family helps feed another's sow in return for one or more of the shoats. In this way, more and more people are acquiring pigs. [1, 2, 3, 15, 22, 38]

Rabbits. Some older boys have raised rabbits for meat and pelts, but the pens are generally inadequate, and the rabbits commonly burrow under and escape. Also, coyotes and dogs occasionally break in and kill the rabbits. Thus far, this potentially profitable enterprise has not been successfully exploited. In the summer of 1951, there were no rabbits kept in the pueblo. [16, 44, 53]

Poultry. Poultry is raised in a rather haphazard manner. Bourke noted that chickens were raised and Strout mentioned both chickens and turkeys (Bloom 1938: 235–236). At present, chickens are the most common fowl, though a few turkeys are also raised.

Hatching chickens is generally the responsibility of the hens, who hide their nests in or near the corral sheds and ranch houses. Some families send away to hatcheries for young chicks and raise them in improvised incubators. They are kept in wire enclosures, heated at night by kerosene lamps and similar devices. Considerable interest is shown in the chicks. As they mature, however, and their appetites increase, they are turned out to forage for themselves. As their range expands, they are rounded up with increasing carelessness until they are almost completely ignored. It is at this point that coyotes, "both two-legged and four-," enter, terminating the chicken business until another year.[2]

In addition to losses from coyotes and other mishaps, another aspect of Cochití life, the chicken pulls, or *gallos*—depletes the supply of roosters. *Gallos* occur on several Catholic feast day celebrations, each taking from 2 to 6 roosters.

There are very few turkeys. In 1946, informants stated there were no turkeys in the pueblo. [1, 44] In 1947 and 1948, one family had a few birds which were allowed to roam freely among the corrals, roosting each night in a corral near the owner's house. In 1951, these were gone but another family had about a dozen birds which were kept rather closely penned.

Feathers that fall from these birds are picked up by whoever finds them and saved for use on dance costumes. Most feathers for such purposes, however, are obtained from wild turkeys, turkey farms, outside friends, and similar sources. Turkeys, wild and domesticated, are, and have been for as long as any Cochití has any knowledge, eaten by both the men and the women, as well as the children.[3] Since

[2] In 1947, we moved our flock of about a dozen hens to our home in Cochití and later succeeded in having one setting of eggs hatch out. The birds were kept strictly enclosed and were fed laying mash, corn purchased locally, and table scraps. Several women came regularly to buy eggs, and even young children came, apparently of their own initiative. It was quite obvious that with proper care and feeding, a small flock of chickens would have been a remunerative business in the pueblo. When such a plan was suggested, the inevitable reply was that coyotes were bad or that there were other difficulties. When we left at the end of the summer, our chickens were eagerly sought by several families. Upon our return the following Christmas, most of the chickens had already disappeared.

[3] Data on this general topic have been recently summarized for the Southwestern area in two papers: Lange 1950a and Reed 1951.

turkeys are of much greater value, especially for their feathers for rituals, it is much more usual to eat chickens. [3, 50, 52, 62, 70] Agency figures reported a total of more than 100 turkeys, but in three summers of residence and in frequent visits to Cochití, I have seen no more than 12 or 15 at any time.

To provide a more vivid picture of what individual Cochití farms are like, as of 1948–51, Appendix 9 presents a series of selected farms in some detail. Appendix 8, already cited, is comprised entirely of an excerpt from Bandelier's journal of November 5, 1880, in which he describes the occupations of the people for the first nine months of the year; this further emphasizes the traditional importance of agriculture.

5 PREPARATION OF FOOD AND DIET

Preparation of Food. Paralleling the way in which aboriginal and European forms of produce and farming methods have been combined is the blending of old and new procedures in preparing foods.

Corn either is ground or is used in whole-kernel form. From cornmeal a wide variety of breadstuff is made, including the tortilla, normally cooked now on the top of a wood-burning range, but formerly cooked on a heated flat stone. Probably the major changes in preparing the tortilla have been in the method of cooking and the increased use of wheat in place of corn.

Cornmeal is still the basic ingredient for the famous *guayave*, or "paper bread" (mat'sīn), the Cochití "newspaper," or "Indian newspaper." In his journal of April 5, 1882, Bandelier provided the following account of this process:

José Hilario called me out to see how white Guayaves were made. They are not the Milk-Guayave but the Atolle-Guayave, "Matzinyi-q'ashia," or Matzinyi-chamutz. Corn is roasted, pounded, then boiled with Atolle, and when cooled off, a fire is made under the stone which they call Comal, and the solution rapidly spread over it. As soon as it begins to dry, another Guayave is laid over it and the upper end of the mass on the stone begins to curl up. It is then seized and pealed off and laid on the others. I timed the whole operation and found it to last from 20 to 30 seconds. The Comal [Yo'asha] itself is a flat rectangular slab, (it is about an inch thick) which is prepared as follows: It is first well polished with a stone, then watermelon-seed is crushed, boiled in water, and the upper-surface of the block well covered with it. Afterwards a coat of fat and turpentine is spread over, and the stone is heated from below until the turpentine has evaporated, leaving a glossy, black surface, very similar to the painted pottery.

At present, most paper bread is made of a mixture of blue corn and water. This is lightly smeared over the special stone, which has been heated to a high temperature and greased with a cloth rubbed in animal brains, or fat (usually from cattle or goats), before the dough is spread over it. The use of sunflower-seed oil for this purpose appears to be unknown [3, 23, 30], and the practice of using watermelon-seed oil is no longer followed. Brains are again rubbed over the stone after the cooking has been completed. [92] "Lots of young girls won't make this anymore. They don't know how very good, and they burn their hands. But they all like to eat it." [17]

Another favorite form of paper bread is made from red corn and milk. This mixture results in a somewhat thicker, reddish-buff bread, not as crisp as that made from blue corn and water. This reddish type appears to be the "wyavi de leche" [guayave de leche] described by Bourke (Bloom 1938: 234–235). Not many women have the equipment to make paper bread, and some who do have it have not used it for many years. Perhaps a dozen women, or fewer, continue to furnish this bread—usually the blue form—for various celebrations. They take great pride in the fact that others expect them to furnish this traditional breadstuff on festive occasions.

In his entry of October 8, 1880, Bandelier mentioned a "kind of corn steamed in the shuck and in their ovens. They are put in at night, fire being made, the oven closed, and then water poured in from above, the whole being allowed to steam until morning." This and similar preparations are only memories, and not very prevalent ones, at Cochití today. Bandelier's journal of April 7, 1882, recorded still another way of preparing corn that modern Cochití appear to have no knowledge of: [42, 92]

In September, they make of green maize a food called "o'ya-tshape-ritz." Green corn is boiled, then grains are carefully cut off with a knife, ground, and mixed with salt. They build a large fire in the hearth until it is thoroughly heated. They clear away embers and ashes, place on the hot base plate a layer of green maize leaves, bending the outer ones upwards. On this they put 3″ of dough, bending over the leaves, and covering the top with others. They set a comal on top, build a fire on it, and thus bake the mass to a kind of maize cheese. Juan José says it is very good.

With the greater use of prepared wheat flour, the women are making more elaborate breads, cakes, and dried-fruit pies, or tarts, though these are normally made for feast days and similar occasions. Tortillas are the usual everyday breadstuff to accompany chili stew.

Maize and chili are still prepared in the traditional manner, being ground with the mano, usually the two-handed type, and the flat metate. Many chili metates have three legs, in the Mexican fashion; others are detached flat slabs, generally of basalt. Corn metates, in contrast, are more commonly of sandstone and are arranged in a series of fixed floor bins. Bin walls are formed of about two-by-ten-inch planks, and individual bins are about two feet long and a foot and a half wide. Bins are placed directly against a house wall, or far enough from it that the women can brace their feet against it as they kneel to grind. The series is arranged with the metates side by side and sloping away from the grinder's position.

Modern Cochití recognize three grades of metate (ya'nī), called, from the roughest to the smoothest, osh'kolīna, po'trañī, and o'pañī-wan. Two-handed manos, which are by far the most usual type, are called ya'gat. Bandelier, October 20, 1880, recorded there were two, or more commonly three, grades of mano used. One, of black lava, was used to break the corn; another, of gneiss and equally large, was used to crush the corn; a third, smaller and triangular in cross section, was used to pulverize it, and was much smoother than the other two. Flint hammerstones were used to roughen the surfaces.

Grinding is currently considered hard work, though the women are happy to own a set of metates. Frequently a young married woman has to go to the home of her mother, her husband's mother, or her aunt to do her grinding. Often several close relatives join in a "grinding bee," with the women assisting one another and enjoying the comradeship during their work.

Frequently before feast days, young children are seen carrying, or pulling in coaster wagons, baskets of corn to be ground at a rela-tive's house where a feast is to be celebrated. More often the children bring meal already ground and present it to the woman of the house, who passes it on to a relative or bakes it herself.

Large bread jars and *ollas*, many of old Cochití manufacture but some also from the Zia and other pueblos, are treasured possessions of the women. Certain ones are considered particularly good for making bread rise. [23, 27, 28] After a large quantity of dough has risen, it is kneaded, made into loaves, and carried outside to the domed oven. Some ovens are no longer used except for emergencies; if possible, the women like to go to certain houses to use an oven of greater capacity or which heats better, that is, one whose fire draws well and whose walls retain heat longer and more evenly than their own. [16, 17, 23, 27, 28] Ovens are fired with wood and, more often, corncobs. When the oven is properly heated, the stone slab, section of iron roofing, or flattened washtub which covers the doorway is removed. Embers are raked out with brooms of stout twigs, or a similar implement. Next, the floor of the oven is swabbed out with a wet rag attached to the end of a pole, and the temperature is tested with a sprinkling of bran. If the bran quickly becomes charred, the oven is overheated and must cool down; if the bran darkens gradually, the temperature is proper. [55] Then the bread is placed in the oven by means of a long, flat-bladed wooden paddle, used also to remove the loaves after baking. When the oven is filled the door is blocked, often with the aid of a dampened gunny-sack.

These ovens appeared early in Spanish times and have been a part of the Pueblo landscape ever since. Despite their simple construction and basic similarity, each pueblo—Santo Domingo, San Felipe, Jemez, Zuñi, and others—has its distinctive form. On one the dome is more pointed; another, rounded; doorways differ in outline; the number and placing of the vents vary; and there are other slight, yet culturally significant, distinctions.

Several observations regarding manos and metates, made during my residence in the pueblo, are of archaeological interest. It appears that a woman normally has about six manos for each metate. Also, an explanation was found for the innumerable "hammerstones" of a miscellaneous, but obviously worked, nature that characterize most Pueblo archaeological sites. Hammerstones are still used at Cochití, not for chipping or flaking stone artifacts, as anthropologists often state, but for "sharpening up" the grinding stones, especially the manos, as noted by Bandelier. Grinding sessions before feast day and similar events are inevitably preceded by "sharpening" or roughing the grinding surfaces of the implements.

Bandelier, in his journal of October 8, 1880, stated that the Mexi-

cans ransacked the ruins for metates; today, the Cochití are still engaged in this activity—preferring to find these articles rather than
to make them.

In another entry (October 9, 1880), Bandelier commented upon
the fact that "every morning before breakfast, the girls grind the
corn for the tortillas. Therefore, the early singing." In his journal of
April 7, 1882, he stated that corn was sieved after the second grinding, but at the time of the Conquest they did not separate the bran
from the meal.

In preparing daily food, modern wood-ranges are commonly used.
In winter, they serve as cook stoves and also supplement the corner
fireplaces in heating the homes. Some families have no cooking facilities other than the corner fireplace, where cooking is done on rock
or iron supports, as in campfire cooking. In warm months, cook stoves
are moved outdoors under a porch or *ramada*. Sometimes small wind·
breaks of adobe are built to protect these outdoor fires. Ranges are
used for top-of-the-stove cooking and for warming canned goods.
Fried bread, made of wheat flour, is common, and is cooked in kettles
of grease over open fires or on the ranges. Range ovens are used to
bake cakes, pies, and other items which have been added to the
aboriginal diet. These ovens are also used by some women for the
preliminary drying, or baking, of pottery pieces. Although the breadstuff acquired from European culture is generally reserved for special
occasions, young girls sometimes like to exhibit skills learned in
boarding school home-economics classes.

Since the installation of electricity there has been considerable use
of electric hot plates, especially for warm-weather cooking. Even
before electricity and refrigeration came to the Cochití, warm
weather did not prevent their use of such popular innovations as
Jello and comparable products. Bowls of such food were placed in
the "wells" of the water system overnight; in the morning, it was
firm. One young veteran announced that he was buying a refrigerator
for his wife so he could "have Jello every day."

The flesh of cattle, sheep, or deer is "jerked," or sun-dried, in the
same way that meat has been cured by generations of ancestors.
Swarms of flies around the meat appear to be of little more concern
today than in the past. Much of the freshly butchered meat, animal
as well as fowl, goes immediately into stews, especially at the time
of the numerous feast days and other celebrations.

Aside from the increasing popularity of wheat flour, the greatest changes in preparing food are seen in the increasing reliance on a wide range of commercially prepared foods. Much of the wheat flour used at present is bought in fifty- or one-hundred-pound sacks in the stores. Bakery products are also becoming more common. Participants in tribal ceremonies, traditionally rewarded with native breadstuff, are given presents of Uneeda Biscuits, Nabisco wafers, or other packaged brands. According to informants, these intrusive items still are not recognized as proper gifts in return for the services of the medicine men. [44, 88]

Home canning, frequently done with the aid of the teachers in the government-school kitchen, accounts for as many as three thousand quarts of fruits and vegetables per year. There is a growing dependence upon these canned goods as well as upon the still greater variety of canned goods available in the stores.

Diet. A consideration of diet reveals several things. First is the relative deficiency of detailed information specifically on Cochití diet, or on the diet of most other pueblos. Generalized statements for the Pueblos exist in the literature, and it is felt that for the particular topic of diet these statements are applicable to Cochití.

The paucity of information can probably be blamed upon lack of interest. Perhaps some of it has been due to the unwillingness of the Indians to bother, or to permit others to bother, with precise measurements and weights of the foodstuffs consumed over a span of years, or months. In examining various comments on diet, several complete and yet compact statements were found. Poore's summary (1894: 437) as of 1890, was one of the best:

The diet of these Indians is largely vegetable, fresh meat being regarded as a great luxury, and eaten perhaps on an average of once in 3 weeks. Strips of dried flesh appear more frequently in stew of beans and red peppers. Goat flesh, beef, and mutton are easily cured, and after slight drying in the sun may be kept for an indefinite period. Peaches and apples are dried and stored for winter use. Muskmelons are peeled, cleaned, and hung upon the branches of young cottonwood trees which the owners of all melon patches cut in groves to surround their summer lodges. All branches unable to support the weight of a melon are removed, and on the dry racks thus formed the surplus of this much prized fruit is preserved. Corn is converted into meal or roasted green and eaten as a vegetable. Tortillas are made of flour partially leavened with sour dough, a heavy flapjack cooked with copper plates. Beans and stews are eaten with scoops; scoop and frijoles disappear together. The scoop is an article called guayave, made of thin corn meal, cooked upon hot rocks, resembling brown paper, and plastic enough to be rolled up and used as a scoop; an advance upon fingers, but a degree below pewter. Coffee is universally used and seldom without sugar. Wine is made at Jemez, Santa Ana, Sandia, and Isleta. No statistics of quantity could be obtained. With fruit in its season, the above is the bill of fare to be found in the pueblos.

Foods listed by Poore are still characteristic of Cochití diet. However, deviations are apparent. The shifts primarily involve those things which have been available in recent years in trading posts and stores as commercially prepared commodities. Numerous items noted throughout Bandelier's journal have all but disappeared from modern Cochití diet. In this respect, it is interesting that Bandelier, October 27, 1880, happily recorded that "Juan José promises me that he will show me and let me taste all of the original dishes of the Pueblos, before they changed their mode of life." He added, "This indicates that, previous to the advent of the Spaniards, they lived differently from now, that is, ate other food."

In the daily diet throughout the year, families eat a constant menu of chili stews, tortillas, and coffee. Stews are composed primarily of corn, beans, onions, potatoes, and other vegetables. Very little meat is used, though bones are cooked with the stew for additional flavor. Chili, generally red but also green, is the standard flavoring, and certain wild plants are also used for this purpose. (See the following chapter, under "Gathering.") Stews, regardless of their content, are commonly referred to as "chili." Although the most common use of fresh vegetables is in stew, they are occasionally served as individual dishes, especially green corn on the cob. Gruels, generally referred to as *pozole*, are also made of corn and other ingredients. Bandelier mentioned that guayaves were broken up and powdered for use in such mixtures. Today, guayaves are prepared so seldom that there are never any left to be used in this way. Peas are often served raw and in their pods; individuals help themselves and shell their own, much as one might eat nuts. Coffee is still the most common beverage, being present at virtually every meal.

Fruits are eaten both fresh and preserved. Watermelons, muskmelons, pumpkins, and squashes are eaten fresh or stored for winter. Sun-dried muskmelons are considered as candy. Chili is likewise used both fresh and dried. Beans, fresh or dried, are used primarily in stews.

Dietary changes are most evident in meals served on feast days and other celebrations. While traditional foods, such as paper bread, tortillas, and the inevitable chili stews, are on the tables along with coffee, they are currently all but overshadowed by an imposing array of cakes, cookies, puddings, Jello, various bottled drinks such as Coca-Cola, fruit and potato salads, occasionally fried chicken, and varieties of hard candy. For the late arrivals to these meals, it is the everyday chili stew—often minus the pieces of meat once present— tortillas, and coffee that are left.

Cochití families have eaten three meals a day for as long as they can remember. The schedule is quite flexible, considerable fluctuation being allowed for the activities of family members. Morning and evening meals are normally eaten with all members of the household together. Those with personal business elsewhere eat alone, before or after the others. Lunch is the lightest meal of the day, often consisting of coffee, bread or tortillas, and perhaps stew. Lunch in the fields consists of bread or tortillas, fresh fruit in season from nearby trees, and water carried in a glass vinegar jug wrapped in wet burlap to keep it cool. Individuals feel quite free to pause at mealtime with relatives or friends; there is always enough for another person.

Parsons' comments (1939: 23) are of interest here: "Pueblos are light eaters. A tortilla or fragments of wafer-bread, or a little wheat bread, sometimes with a meat stew with hominy, beans, and coffee, make a meal, and formerly there were only two meals a day, a late breakfast after several hours of work and an early supper." Meals for children are the same as for adults except for smaller portions. Eating between meals is common, with crackers, store cookies, paper bread, candy, and fresh fruit frequently in evidence.

Visitors are generally offered a cup of coffee, with canned milk and sugar, and a plate of tortillas or fried bread. If it is close to mealtime, they are urged to remain and eat with the family. On such occasions, a can of fruit, or some similar extra dish, is often opened. While Parsons' statement that these people are light eaters is generally valid, it must be remembered that many individuals visit homes of relatives on various errands of the day, and at each home they are usually urged to eat.

As mentioned, meat is generally lacking in the daily diet. Eggan (personal correspondence, March, 1952) recalled that James Watson pointed out in a Master's thesis (University of Chicago) that meat is used by the Hopi as a flavoring, not as a basic food, such as corn and beans. Other proteins, such as eggs, are likewise little used by the Cochití. However, high-protein beans comprise a considerable portion of the diet. Vitamins come from fresh fruits and vegetables, but the greatest portion of the diet is composed of starches—breadstuffs and corn, supplemented with potatoes and rice.

Modern Cochití depend little upon the aboriginal pursuit of hunting, fishing, and gathering, facets of their culture discussed in detail in the following chapter. Recently more non-Indians than Indians have hunted deer and turkey in the Jemez Mountains. Antelope and buffalo ranges have been supplanted by cattle and sheep ranches, and wild game has essentially disappeared from the diet.

Boys, a few men, and occasionally a few women do a little fishing, but the total effort expended and the total catch is negligible in the total Cochití economy and diet. (See also Chap. 2, n. 10.)

The gathering of wild-plant products has also diminished. Some families, especially those residing on ranchitos during the summer, still gather wild plants for teas, table greens, and similar purposes. A good piñon crop is always welcomed, but there have been few of these in the recent years of unusually scanty rainfall. Indicative of the gradual shift in diet away from the old pattern, the following quotation from Bandelier's journal of April 4, 1882, is offered for its applicability to the present situation as well as to that of his time:

Juan José further spoke of the fruits which they formerly ate, and still ate. He says that the fruit of the Palmillo ancho, the Latir or "hush-q'añi," was about foremost, but that of late, while it grows in spring, it mostly rots now or is eaten up by worms. This fruit the women went to gather in September and October, baking it until the skin could be taken off and the seed and fibres removed, then threw it into *Caxetes* and mixed it thoroughly, boiling it alternately, until it came down to a firm Jelly or paste. It was then spread into large cakes, about 1 inch thick and left to dry on hanging scaffolds, changing it and turning it over from time to time until perfectly dry. Then cut into squares, or rolled into loaves (Acoma and Laguna) and preserved. In spring it was eaten in various ways, as paste, dissolved in water and drank, or tortillas, guayaves, etc. dipped into the solution, thus using it like molasses or syrup. Among other plants which were used in former times he mentions the Guaco "Uaq'," the *quelite* "shq'oa," the verdolaga "q'a-aeshye," the "shi-pa" (possibly cress?), the "shir-ta-yaya," the "shti-tshu." The gauco was baked and made into loaves, the *quelite* also and preserved on strings. At new-years day they made sometimes a mess of all these ingredients together, boiling them in one Kettle as a "soup à la bataille." But their object in gathering these herbs and fruits was, to have it in the spring, when the crops gave out, and previous to the coming in of new crops. Now, he says, they have become less provident, or more indifferent to such means of subsistence. This is the natural effect of the approach of civilization.

6 NONAGRICULTURAL ECONOMY

WHILE AGRICULTURE has been the basis of Cochití economy, various nonagricultural activities have also been important. In this heterogeneous grouping, basic changes have occurred in the relative emphasis placed on each specific pursuit. Mentioned earlier is the almost complete disappearance of hunting, fishing, and gathering, which formerly were important supplements to agriculture in the subsistence economy. Other pursuits, many associated with the cash economy of Anglo-American culture, have become increasingly popular in recent decades.

Hunting

Hunting has traditionally been among the more popular aspects of American Indian life. In general, Southwestern Pueblo tribes have been pictured as primarily farming peoples. Considering their present economy, this exclusion, or at least minimizing, of hunting might be warranted; considering Pueblo economy in past centuries, however, one gains the impression that the importance of agriculture in relation to hunting has been overemphasized. From literature on Cochití and other Pueblo tribes and from opinions of Cochití informants, it seems probable that a half-century ago there would have been an important hunting complex at Cochití. A century or more ago there might have been a hunting complex that was a strong competitor of agriculture for man-hours and efforts expended. Goldfrank (1927: 85) noted, "Now very few people hunt at all, but formerly the animals were a much desired food, and there was an elaborate ritual."

In discussing hunting activities, it seemed advantageous to make a division between communal and individual hunting. This distinction again emphasizes the change from the former prevalence of communal effort to the present-day trend toward individual effort.

Communal Hunting. One of the earliest accounts of communal hunting found was an unpublished description in Bandelier's journal of November 6, 1880:

Everybody preparing for the rabbit hunt. Public crying early. . . . Finally, about 11 A.M., the horses were brought in. The public crier started accompanied by six men carrying rattles, the faces painted white, and on the head, leaning forward, a tuft of split corn leaves. [These were Kusha'li members; the Kwe'rana members at Cochití do not use paint. (92)] They, marching (or rather, tramped) through the whole place singing; came back across the plaza in the middle of which two of them left; then the other four tramped to the northeast corner of the plaza, when they slowly tramped out. Soon after, these four again started from the cross in the middle of the plaza, singing in a slow, measured tone, and again went around town. The boys, in their best clothes and on horseback, finally gathered about one quarter of a mile from the pueblo on the *lomas,* with some of the old men along with them. A fire was built, and when the girls began to arrive, mostly on foot, some of the old men gathered around the fire and one of them spoke for a long while in their tongue. It was done and listened to in an attitude of prayer. At the close of it, a short dialogue ensued between the man praying and the teniente of the war captain. (The captain is sick.) Then they presented themselves in rows of two, three, four, and five to the speaker, with arms upheld, and he switched them all right and left. [This is still done. (92)] Thereupon, they mounted their horses and dispersed over the *bosque,* etc., the women and girls following them on foot, and I soon heard their shouts scouring the fields. But few rabbits appeared. . . . They were partly in the *bosque* near the river and partly above. The sight of their galloping to and fro in their gaudy dresses was very fine. Shouts and yelling, howling like wolves, was heard. All at once the horsemen broke from the grove, a hare having been chased towards that way. The whole band chased around, clear around the pueblo, and it was only on the other side in the *bosque* that Adelaido Montoya killed the hare by his club.

.   .   .   .

About 4 P.M. the horsemen assembled in the plain northwest of the pueblo, and soon came galloping back, many of them having a girl or a woman sitting up behind "sidlings." I met Agustín, . . . He was very much excited. It appears that some of the boys had gone to the pueblo to drink water, and that there several men (young and old) chased them back, beating them with rods. Adelaido was beaten, and when Juan José [his father] interfered, to stop them, the son-in-law of Agustín turned upon him, striking him in the face and neck rather severely. Juan José then struck him with his hunting club, inflicting a rather painful though not a dangerous wound on the left side of the skull.

About two weeks later, there was another rabbit hunt, concerning which Bandelier noted the following in his journal of the seventeenth:

Further details in regard to the rabbit hunt. The speech is no prayer, but instruction. If a boy and a girl run for the same rabbit, and the girl is first, then they change garments, the girl rides, and the boy in woman's dress goes on foot until he kills a rabbit, when he pays it to the woman for his clothes; or, if he fails to kill one, then, after sunset he takes a load of wood and fetches it to the girl. Feast on fourth day, after which the boys present the girls with a *jícara* of flour. Should the hunt be impossible on account of bad weather, then the women have the right, all winter, as often as the men go hunting, to take the game from them, but must invite them on the fourth day. Each girl invites the man whose rabbit or game she took away.

In discussing hunting as of about 1920, Curtis (1926: 74) commented, "Hunting was usually a communal undertaking, and the rabbit-drive may still be observed."

Two communal rabbit hunts (*caza de liebre*) for the cacique are still held, and usually two others which are not for him. Those for the cacique are announced by the war captains, who decide upon the time. One comes in the spring, immediately before the planting of the cacique's fields, and the other, in the fall, just before the harvesting of his tract.

On June 25, 1947, we could hear singing in the pueblo from approximately midnight to dawn. There was then a summons called out by the war captain, after which the men left on horseback and were

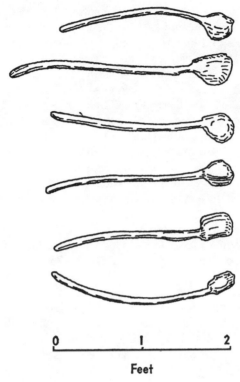

0   1   2

Feet

Fig. 11.—Rabbit Sticks.

gone until sundown. Some fifteen or twenty men went out and got four or five rabbits apiece. These were given to the cacique. [3]

On these hunts, the war captains are assisted by members of the Ku-sha'lī and Kwe'rana societies, depending upon whose year of control it is. The war captains also receive help from the Shī'kame Head, whose position has absorbed the functions of the Shai'yak, or Hunting, Society. Only men participate in hunts for the cacique, and all game, usually about twenty-five or thirty cottontails and jack rabbits, is given to the cacique at the end of the hunt. Since he does not accompany the hunters, the game is brought to his house and presented to him by the war captains. Rabbits either are shot or clubbed with oak sticks. The more popular type has a bulbous knot on one end (Fig. 11), but there are also some sticks which are flat and longer. On the day following the spring hunt, the women come to the cacique's home and prepare the rabbits to feed the men who plant his fields that day. In the fall, the same procedure is followed except there is a one-day interval between the hunt for the cacique and the harvesting. [2, 15, 42, 44, 49, 53]

Following the hunt for the cacique each spring and fall, there are hunts in which the women and children participate. These are also directed by the war captains. After the converging drive reduces the area, the rabbits are clubbed or shot. Women run after the game, and the first to reach the animal gets it, regardless of who actually killed it. Each woman keeps what she collects, perhaps four or five animals. Clothing may be exchanged with the men in the manner described by Bandelier. Four days later, she gives a present, generally of flour, to the man who killed each animal. [3, 42, 70] If two women reach an animal simultaneously and argue over it, a third can take it simply by crying out like a wolf, fox, or mountain lion. [92] (Further hunt details can be found in Curtis [1926: 74–76] and in Goldfrank [1927: 84–91].)

Game is not as abundant as formerly, especially south of the pueblo in the area adjacent to the Santo Domingo Grant. The Santo Domingo appear to have been more enthusiastic in their hunting and have no qualms about coming on Cochití land if they find no game on their own reservation. The Cochití seem powerless to do more than complain. [3, 70]

Rabbits are used only as meat except for a limited use of the fur in decorating ceremonial items, such as some ka'tsína masks and the bandoliers worn by the Ku-sha'lí members. Present practice is in sharp contrast to former times when not only the meat was used but also the pelts, which were cut into strips and woven into blankets, as described by the early Spanish explorers.

Until the disappearance of big game and until firearms became more common (about the end of the last century), communal hunts were the normal way of hunting deer, antelope, buffalo, elk, and mountain sheep. Occasionally in these drives, or surrounds, a bear or mountain lion would be included in the catch. [2, 3, 53] In his journal of October 24, 1880, Bandelier noted that on the Chapero, a rather high and prominent mesa in the mountains northwest of Cochití, the Indians surrounded game, driving it upward and killing any animal that failed to break through the cordon of hunters.

Announcement of the communal hunts was made four days in advance, and all hunters turned out for it. Bows and arrows, iron-tipped spears, and, in later years, firearms were used. Although the war captains directed these hunts—i.e., determined the day and selected the place—the actual success of the hunt depended upon the hunt chief, the Head (na'wai-ya) of the Hunting Society (Shai'yak). According to Curtis (1926: 74), this man was also known as "Cougar Man" (Múkats^a-hátstse). The Hunting Society had ceremonial control over game and hunting.

Parsons (in Dumarest 1919: 206) observed parts of a communal hunt and made the following comments:

> In October, 1913, I happened to be passing through Cochiti the day of a hunt, and, at a distance, I saw the start and the gay homecoming. Riding into town about 9 A.M. we passed about an eighth of a mile to the northeast of the town an elderly man sitting at prayer before a small fire. An hour or so later, in this locality, the hunters, men and women, gathered together and I heard singing. At sunset they returned. About an eighth of a mile to the northwest of the town, a group of men gathered together for a few minutes. The women in two's and three's came in on foot, laughing and talking and carrying the game—rabbits, small rodents, and quail. I was told that the woman first to reach a hunter after he has made a kill becomes the recipient.

In a footnote to the above comments, Parsons added:

> I was not allowed to join the hunt. "They would only let you go," said my guide from Santa Clara, "if you told them you were the daughter of the Cacique of Santa Clara." Seeing me look interested, he straightway repented of even that slight reference to custom or local joke, and withheld explanation.
> A like practice is or was followed at Laguna, I infer from an account of a communal hunt recorded by Dr. Boas. " 'When somebody kills a rabbit for you women, you will have to run for it.' Thus says the head war captain" before the hunters start out.

Even in Curtis' time, the Hunting Society had disappeared from Cochití, and its functions had been taken over by the Shī'kame Society, with the Head Shī'kame serving as Cougar Man. Goldfrank's data (1927: 46–47), of about the same period as those of Curtis, read as follows:

> Lastly, there is the Hunting Society whose membership in Cochiti is identical with that of the Cikame society. The officers of the Cikame so-

ciety are called by the same name as the supernaturals in charge of the hunt *(caiak, djaikatse, dreikatse)*. . . .

Just how the Hunting Society became identical with the Cikame I did not learn. I believe that, as in the other villages, the Hunting society was originally independent. Today practically no one hunts, although my informant was able to give me many details of former days, and with the lessening of interest and falling off of membership, perhaps the functions and ritual were assumed by the Cikame.

It would seem more accurate to state that when the last Shai'yak died, Shai'yak Society functions were simply assumed by the Shī'-kame Society, with no idea of duplicating memberships. [15, 44, 49, 50, 70] For several years now, Eufrasio Suina has been the Head and sole member of the Shī'kame Society; by at least some Cochití, he is occasionally still referred to as Shai'yak Head. [42]

In Goldfrank's material and in data from my informants, there is no precise designation of the Shī'kame Head as "Cougar Man" for communal hunts. Curtis (1926: 74, 76) stated that the headman, or another Shī'kame shaman, took the part of Cougar Man on communal hunts for big game as well as for rabbits. This is interesting in light of Dumarest's (1919: 189) comment that "for *shikarne chaiani,* rabbit meat is also a poison." This implies a ceremonial food taboo; present-day Cochití appear to know nothing of it.

On communal hunts, men were stationed at intervals, and at a given signal, they converged. Just above Cochití Dam is a box canyon which opens into the Rio Grande Valley from the east. This was formerly used as a trap for antelope and deer, which were impounded and slaughtered. Pit traps for game can still be seen in a narrow trail on a promontory (Bandelier's "Chapero"?) east of Bland, above Cañada de Cochití. The pits were located where the mesa top reduced to a narrow trail, with very high and steep walls on either side. Traps in the trail were covered with grass matting and dust, and hunters drove the deer and sheep onto the mesa and into the pits. Pits were never equipped with sharp stakes in the bottom; hunters shot the animals that fell into them. [44, 49]

The Cochití formerly went into the Pecos drainage to hunt buffalo. Occasionally buffalo were found in the Estancia Valley. On hunts held east of the Pecos, the Cochití usually joined hunters from Santo Domingo and the Tewa Pueblos. The chronology here is vague. Active hunters appear to be no more recent than the greatgrandfathers of today's generation. This would place these expeditions no later

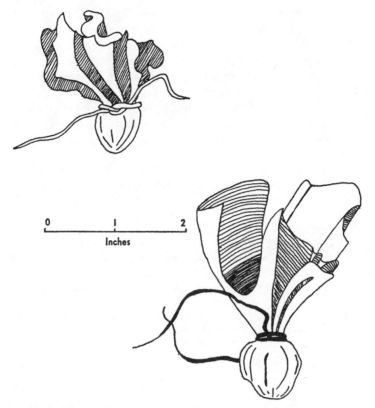

Fig. 12.–ALMAGRE BAGS.

than 1880. Henderson and Harrington (1914: 13–14) stated that even their older Tewa informants knew of buffalo and the hunting of buffalo almost entirely from hearsay. The joint expeditions were for mutual protection against the Comanche, Jicarilla, and Mescalero. Trips were made on horseback. The weapons used were bows and arrows, iron spears, and rifles, though there were few rifles. [44, 49]

At present, there is an occasional communal hunt for deer for the cacique. These are called at the discretion of the war captain, the frequency depending upon the conscience and energy of the individual holding the position. Announcement of the hunt is made in the usual manner; the first night in camp, the hunters are gathered by the helpers of the war captains (go'atchīnī) for a meeting. At this time the war captain explains that they are hunting for the cacique and, thus, for the good of all. It has been customary that the direction the hunt is to take from camp be announced also, but often this part is currently omitted, and the hunters merely disperse in whatever direction they feel will be lucky. Some older hunters take the extra precaution of passing by the shrine of the Stone Lions, Potrero de las Vacas (Plate 3, *a* and *b*), now in Bandelier National Monument, where they sprinkle red ochre (*almagre*, or ya'katshe) on the eyes of the lions, thereby increasing their own visual powers and general good luck. (At present, a special red ochre is obtained from the Hopi at a dollar per teaspoonful. [92]) Bandelier, October 26, 1880, mentioned this practice while visiting the shrine on the Potrero de los Idolos. (See Chap. 2, n. 3; also Plate 4, *a* and *b*.)

The puma was, at the toes and in the face (head), painted with streaks of red. This is done yet by the hunters, to propitiate the idol, to favor them while hunting. The same was seen at the Potrero de las Vacas. Juan José says that, as the puma is the best hunter of the animal kingdom in the Sierra, they still make these offerings to it, annointing the eyes to secure good eyesight, and the claws and feet for strength and agility. Juan José annointed his own eyes with *almagre* in my presence, stating that it improved his vision for shooting. The *almagre* is oxide of iron, and still contains, though pulverized, speculas of crystals of hematite. It is carried in a little leather bag, tied up with a leather string. [See Fig. 12.]

When a deer is killed, the hunter returns to camp for a go'atchīnī, who brings the carcass into camp, and the hunter then rejoins the hunt. If a bear or turkey should be encountered on such a hunt, it would be killed also.

On any group hunt under the war captain's leadership, whether or not it is for the cacique, it is necessary that the Shai'yak, who for some years has been the Shī'kame headman, accompany the group to assist with various rituals. Before the hunters depart, certain rules are agreed upon. For example, the group may agree that the person who shoots the deer gets it, or a major part of it, unless it is to be given to the cacique. However, it may be agreed that if someone else is "strong"—i.e., touches it first—he gets it. Another rule often followed is that if the deer does not fall but escapes from view, then it belongs to the next hunter who actually kills it or comes upon it. During a recent season, a Cochití hunter and another from Santo Domingo became involved in an argument over possession of a deer; another

Cochití came upon the two, perceived the situation, and, howling like a wolf, successfully claimed the deer. [92]

A custom continuing up until recent times dictated that visitors to a hunter's home would be given presents of the deer, antelope, or other meat for the first four days after the kill. After that time, the hunter could gracefully keep what remained. [92] These animals also provide hides, which are used for cloaks or blankets, for leggings and shirts of the kind commonly found among Plains tribes (these were actually worn in earlier times but now are used only for ceremonial costumes), and for moccasins and drum heads. Hoofs are used for rattles; horns, for implements and ceremonial paraphernalia. [3, 15, 25, 49]

While most older informants are aware of the methods used by the Hopi and Jemez Indians for catching eagles, they are unanimous in their statements that the Cochití have seldom followed these methods. Dumarest (1919: 193–194) gave a detailed account of the Jemez procedure but made no mention of Cochití, from which it may be inferred that the Cochití rarely indulged in this dangerous enterprise. Bandelier gave a similar account of Pecos eagle hunting in his journal of November 10, 1882, but gave no indication that the Cochití also did this.

However, present-day informants believe that a few Cochití have successfully trapped eagles in this way: A small, deep pit is made in which the hunter conceals himself under a cover of reed matting. A live, or freshly killed, small-game animal is fastened to the cover, or a captive eagle is tied to a nearby bush. As the eagle descends, the hunter seizes its feet, ties them, and pulls the bird into the pit with him. The diameter of the pit is small enough to prevent the eagle from getting full use of its wings. "This is very dangerous business." At Cochití, eagles are usually killed at present with firearms, caught in a steel trap, or are taken from the nest as young birds and raised in log cages. They are prized for their feathers. [15, 42, 44, 49, 50, 70] Most informants cannot remember a captive eagle in the pueblo, but one believed that the last head of the Warriors Society had a log cage of eagles on his roof a half-century or more ago. [44]

In discussing wild animals and hunting, the Cochití frequently mention the damage done by coyotes on the ranchitos and even around corrals bordering the pueblo. Informants were asked if there were ever any communal hunts to get rid of these coyotes. Apparently, either the idea had never occurred to them, or there was an undisclosed reason why this had not been done, for the reply was always that when someone lost enough to these raiders, he took it upon himself to keep an armed watch for a few days until he killed them or frightened them away. [3, 15, 49, 53]

In former times, the killing of a bear, mountain lion, or eagle at Cochití was considered essentially the same as the killing of an enemy, such as a Navaho. Until the Warriors Society (Ompī) died out near the close of the last century, a man became eligible for membership in it after killing either an enemy or one of these three animals of prey. Informants believed that the acceptance of animal-killers into Ompī, while undifferentiated from the acceptance of man-killers, had reached that high status only as the region became less subject to raids and general intertribal warfare. Whether this represented a complete substitution aimed at perpetuating the Ompī or whether it was simply an amalgamation of two distinct societies or of two grades within the Ompī never became clear. White (1942: 132) found both forms of Ompī (Opi) at Santa Ana, the man-killers being extinct but the animal-killers with four members in 1935.

At present, with the Ompī no longer in existence, those men who succeeded in killing a bear, lion, or eagle still enter into a "brother" relationship for the remainder of their lives. This status includes all the terminology, privileges, and obligations of sibship insofar as the two men are concerned; their families are not involved in the use of kinship terms or in any other way.

The actual killing of one of these three animals is accredited by the Cochití to the man who first touches it with his hand, gun, or a stick—not to the person who fired the shot or set the trap. The "brother" is the second man to touch the animal. Thus, it is conceivable that the man who fired the shot would be entirely excluded from the ritual and "brother" status resulting from it. [42, 44, 62]

Hunting is seldom done alone, but if the hunter is alone at the time of the killing, he goes to the village either before or after skinning the carcass. About half a mile away, he fires one shot and gives a war whoop, followed by others as he advances on the village. The first man to reach him congratulates him, shaking his hand. Thereby, without actually touching the animal, this man becomes the "brother." In this case, the two continue toward the village until they meet the war captain, who upon hearing the signal has come to meet them and learn the details. If the kill is made by a party, the second man, or brother, is sent to tell the news to the war captain, proceeding in the same manner as described.

While the war captain announces the news to the village, the killer builds a fire near the skin of the eagle or lion, or the skin and carcass of the bear at a spot about a half-mile north of the pueblo or at another site an equal distance west of the village. Marked by the smoke, the location is then "attacked" by the men of the pueblo with clubs, bows and arrows, and firearms, sneaking from bush to bush and uttering war cries as they go. On reaching the animal, each man strikes it or shoots it [42, 44, 62, 70]

Following the mock attack, the entire party, singing war songs, proceeds to the village. Three songs are always sung before the group leaves the camp, and a fourth is sung on the return journey. [42] The skin is carried by the killer; by this time the paws and forelegs, if the trophy is a bear, have been removed and given to the medicine men in the order of their arrival. Since the bear is believed to be "left-handed," the left paw and forearm are given to the first man, for they are believed the most potent; second choice is the right front paw and forearm; third, the left rear; and fourth, the right rear. These become the personal property of each medicine man, not the property of the society he represents. Arriving in the village at the Pumpkin Kiva (northwest corner), the group, still singing, proceeds to move counterclockwise through the streets.

The traditional procedure has been to move southward to the arroyo, eastward to the church, around it and northward to the Turquoise Kiva, from whence the procession moves westward returning to the Pumpkin Kiva. Then the group moves south to the Turquoise community house, where they turn and move eastward behind the row of houses in front of which they first passed. Going back of the church this time, the group comes to a halt in front of the Flint–Kusha'lī house [ho'chanī-īt'sa, or "capitol"], the "office" of the cacique, the head medicine man. Here another song is sung, and then the group enters the plaza, which is circled counterclockwise four times. As the group sings its way through the streets and plaza, it is stopped at intervals by women, carrying manos or wooden sticks for stirring corn mush, who throw prayer meal upon the skin. The skin is placed on the ground and the women beat it, all the time uttering coyote-like cries. [92]

After circling the plaza four times, the killer, his brother, and their close relatives go to the killer's home, where a feast is prepared and the "brother" relationship thereby becomes established. No particular attention is paid the skin at this time except that no person, other than the brothers, may touch it. [42, 44]

Occasionally, in more recent years, the above procedure is somewhat abbreviated. From the Pumpkin Kiva, the group may proceed directly to the Flint–Ku-sha'lī house, without stopping there, move along to the killer's home, where most of the women wait to strike at the skin. [42]

Next, the killer chooses one of the three medicine societies to wash and properly "care for the skin." The society makes its preparations for two or three days, and then makes it known that it is ready. The skin is brought to the society house and presented to the medicine men. A large bowl will have been filled with water and the mashed roots of the "Shiwanna bush" (a plant found near the Turquoise Trading Post along U.S. Highway 85). A hollow cane reed is used to blow bubbles until the bowl is filled. The skin is then washed in these suds by the medicine men and returned to the killer.

Following this ceremony, the owner may dispose of the skin in any way he chooses. Also, it may now be touched by anyone. After the ceremony, the killer's family bring presents of foods to the officiating medicine society; as mentioned earlier, these gifts must be something native, since nothing bought from a store is a fitting gift for a medicine man. [42, 44]

If it is a bear that was killed, everyone who goes to meet the hunter is given a portion of the meat. At the close of the procession bringing the skin into the village, each person takes his meat home to be cooked immediately, by roasting, frying, or in any way he chooses. After eating, the person draws a black mark on each cheek just below the eyes with charcoal—a sign that he has eaten bear meat—and the marks are left on until after the medicine society has washed the pelt. [42, 44]

Lion and eagle meat are never eaten, and nothing except their skins are brought back to the pueblo. After the bear meat has been eaten, the bones cannot be thrown into the yard or corrals as is done with cattle or sheep bones. Bear bones, carefully gathered, either are thrown into the river or are taken to certain shrines north or west of the pueblo.

The bear skulls, as well as the skulls of both lions and eagles, are taken and buried under rocks as offerings. [3, 44] One instance of an eagle killing was related in which the "brothers'" heads were washed by the Giant Society, after which the eagle skin and head were also washed. The society took the down and leading wing-feathers in return for this service. (The interest in these portions of the eagle by this particular society may well have stemmed from the fact that Ma'sha-wa, the Turkey Buzzard Ka'tsīna, is associated with the Giant Society, and these feathers and the down are used in assembling the mask.) Food was also given to the Giant Society. The eagle's body was thrown into the river, and the head was placed, with bread and cornmeal, under a rock in a rugged canyon about a mile north of the pueblo. [42]

This burial of the head in a shrine is normally at the direction of, or actually done by, the medicine men. [44] The body of a lion is normally buried by the killer at the spot of the killing, while the skull is removed at the time of the skinning. [3] One informant [3] stated that he did not know about the hunters' heads being washed along with the eagle's head and skin, but since another [92] claimed to have seen recently this part of the ritual, it can be accepted as the present-day, and probably the former, Cochití pattern.

Despite several claims that hunting is on the decline at Cochití and that those who do hunt are very little interested in the rituals involved, it is interesting and undoubtedly significant that the following pairs of "brothers" could be recalled without much hesitation by only a few informants. Note also the dates:

Miguel Ortiz and Sebastian Urina (Miguel trapped a mountain lion)
Juan José Trujillo and Lorenzo Suina, a bear
Juan José Trujillo and José Domingo Quintana, a bear (cared for by the Giant Society)
Celso Montoya and Dolores Pecos, a bear
Celso Montoya and Juan B. Arquero, a bear, 1950 (cared for by the Flint Society)
Pancracio Chalan and Nestor Arquero (father of Juan B.), a bear
Eleuterio Cordero and Juanito Trujillo (?), a bear
Cresencio Toribio and Pancracio Chalan, a bear
Santiago Arquero and Stanley Trujillo, a bear
Santiago Arquero and another man, a bear (on the cacique's hunt)
Paul Trujillo and his son, Gregory, an eagle
Paul Trujillo and Nestor Herrera, an eagle, 1927 (at White Rock Canyon)
Diego Romero and several brothers (resulting from various eagles he has killed)

Juan José Suina and Lorenzo Herrera, an eagle, 1948 (Juan José killed it
   after Cipriano Chávez, a Progressive, had trapped it but did not want it)
Juan José Suina and his daughter, Santana Suina, an eagle (Juan José
   killed it after it had been first caught by Santiago Romero; Santiago had
   tied its feet and was in the process of resetting the trap when the eagle
   flew off and Juan José shot it)

Individual Hunting. With the advent of rifles and the gradual disappearance of big game, communal hunting has lapsed. At present,
three or four relatives or friends go hunting together, with no attention paid to control, direction, or guidance by any of the ceremonial
personnel or societies. These informal groups frequently adopt various rules such as those agreed to by the members of a larger and
more formal group. [92] This decline in the ceremonial aspects of
hunting is not an entirely recent development, as indicated by similar
observations by Goldfrank (1927: 85).

With the great increase in non-Indian hunters in the Jemez country,
and the concomitant decreases in quantity of game, many Cochití
have ceased hunting. A few continue, and several are described as
"getting a buck every year." However, most claim they are "too old,"
"too busy," or have other reasons for their current inactivity, though
the basic reason appears to be the relative scarcity of game.

When the men hunt, they generally go into the Jemez Mountains,
where Cochití have hunted for generations. Despite the availability
of trucks and other transportation to areas of more plentiful game,
there is little interest in hunting elsewhere. "We know the Jemez
country" seems to express their attitude. [2, 3, 15, 42, 49]

As nearly as can be determined from informants, the maximum
combined bag for any year seldom amounts to more than a half-
dozen bucks. There is no hunting season on the reservation, but deer
are rarely seen at that altitude in the warmer months. [1, 2, 44]
Farmers shoot rabbits near their fields, though this appears to be
done more to protect the crops than to obtain meat.

Skunks and "blue" (gray?) foxes were formerly hunted both communally and by individuals. Sporadic hunting of skunks still occurs,
as they are valued for their fur which is made into anklets, or guards,
for dance costumes. Bandelier, in his journal of November 17, 1880,
described the boys, on a communal hunt, digging up skunks. "They
dig up the hole on the north side, stopping the entrance as they proceed, and when the animal sticks out his head, they knock him in the

head." The modern Cochití obtain skunks almost entirely by means of metal spring-traps. [92]

Foxskins were noted in Bandelier's journal of November 17, 1880, as worth $1.00 to $1.25; at present, better-grade foxskins are priced at $5.00, though occasionally a good one can be obtained for as little as $3.00. [92] Foxskins are worn as pendant skins at the back of the man's dance kilt. In addition to those obtained locally, many are obtained from the Navaho. [20, 45, 58]

Bears and mountain lions are increasingly rare. Some individuals said that even if they saw one while hunting deer, they did not think they should bother to kill it. "There is too much ceremony with something like that." [47, 48] This is a strange statement in view of the previously mentioned lack of ritual knowledge. Perhaps it signifies a reluctance to start something they do not know how to finish, or it may be an easy rationalization of why they no longer hunt these relatively scarce animals.

An interesting note was found in Bandelier's journal of March 31, 1882. Jac. Gold, a Santa Fe trader, had told Bandelier that the Cochití never sold puma skins, or mountain-lion skins; on an earlier occasion, he had purchased one, but the *principales* of the tribe sent back the Indian who sold it with firm orders to buy the skin back again. Gold was also said to have stated that he never was able to purchase skunk-skins from the Cochití.

Hawks, ducks, and other birds whose feathers are part of the specific ceremonial paraphernalia are hunted as opportunities present themselves. Feathers are stored carefully in special wooden boxes and are reused repeatedly. [3, 45, 49, 50]

The present hunting situation at Cochití can be characterized as follows. Although only a small number of men still engage in big-game hunting, many participate in rabbit hunts, held either for the cacique or for the people themselves. Other small game, such as pack rats, are seldom hunted, though they are often included in the kill during rabbit drives. A good hunter enjoys a certain prestige, but this is expressed by the mere statement that "he always gets a buck" rather than by a desire to emulate him. Hunting stories are among the favorites (see Appendix 10 for selected hunting and other tales), and animal or hunting dances of the winter ceremonial season are favorites with both young and old people. Aside from these attitudes and some slight nostalgia over good times on the hunting trails, the Cochití appear to have resigned themselves to the passing of their hunting activities.

Fishing

Generalized references to fish and fishing occur in the early Spanish sources, but Bandelier's journal of April 4, 1882, provides the earliest detailed account of fishing among the Cochití (the same data appeared in his Final Report [1892: 149]):

> He [the informant] began by describing their mode of fishing in former times, with long nets made of the threads of the Palmillo ancho (Yucca baccata) which were stretched across the river, weighed down by stones, and kept floating by "Guajes" and skins. One party, with ropes, dragged them up the river on one bank, another on the opposite bank, while one man with a rod, walked behind in the middle of the stream, to keep the net from bursting. After they dredged in this manner awhile it was hauled across by one party crossing the river and then pulled out of the water with the fish in it.

In his published account of this, Bandelier added that the more shallow stretches of the river were fished in this manner so that the man was able to walk behind the net. He further commented (1892: 149): "In this manner portions of the river were almost despoiled of fish. The same improvidence prevailed as in hunting, and the useful animals were gradually killed off. After each fishing expedition, the product was divided among the clans *pro rata,* and a part set aside for the highest religious officers and for the communal stores." Another reference to fishing, found in Dumarest's notes on "Occupations" (1919: 146), says that "fish are blocked up in little bights and caught in a *sarape* or blanket or by a fork or even by hand."

These statements are interesting in relation to present fishing activities. The term for fish, "ka'sh," is not further qualified aside from designations as to size. Informants under fifty years old have no recollection of communal fishing. Older persons have vague recollections of it but question the implications of Bandelier's description. They can recall seeing the fiber fishing nets hanging on the walls of the war captain's home. They agree with the inference from this fact that the war captains were in charge of the use of these nets. One older informant could recall seeing the Cochití nets and added that "the people at Santo Domingo still use nets like them under the war captains." [25] Cochití informants are of the opinion that fishing was done voluntarily under the war captains, "or maybe anyone else that they let borrow the nets." [25, 52, 70] They believe that the catch was divided among the men who had done the work and that each one did as he pleased with his share. Informants are skeptical of the fish's having been divided on a clan basis. No one has any idea about the kinds, sizes, or numbers of fish caught. Instead of the fishing's being done at White Rock, as Bandelier described, one man thought that nets were used in the river just east of the pueblo, "or anywhere they thought there would be fish." [50]

When these data are analyzed, it becomes obvious that Bandelier's description was of a phase of communal effort essentially extinct as of 1882. If his notation that "the product was divided among the clans *pro rata,* and a part set aside for the highest religious officers and for the communal stores" is true, it is in contrast to more recent procedure as recalled by, or known to, present-day Cochití. It would seem that toward the end of the last century the war captains maintained control of the nets, but the general interest in this aspect of fishing has declined. Dumarest, at Cochití in the final years of the last century, made no mention of the nets and described fishing by means of *serapes,* blankets, forks, and even hands. All these items imply individual or small-group activity.

This individual and small-group nature of fishing characterizes present-day practices. A very few men, some boys, and occasionally women and girls, participate. That the catch is seldom impressive undoubtedly tends to reduce the enthusiasm of others for fishing. Hayforks, small nets, ordinary hook-and-lines with worms and insects, and hands are all used. No evidence of poisoning fish has been found. There is also no evidence that fish have ever been of any ceremonial importance. When asked, the Cochití usually claim that they like fish, though not as well as other meats. "Sometimes we sell fish to the Spanish people at Peña Blanca." [25]

Gathering of Minerals

General gathering activities, including those related to minerals, also have declined in relative importance. This decline, however, is not as complete as in the case of hunting because of the continued use of certain items which remain accessible and culturally satisfactory. Gathering differs from hunting in being on an individual, or small-group, basis, not on a communal basis. It is done, for the most part, with no ritual and without control by officers or societies. Because of these distinctions from hunting, data on gathering are presented as a roster of items utilized by the Cochití.

Salt. Salt was formerly procured from Estancia Valley salt lakes, almost one hundred miles southeast of Cochití. The last trips were made about sixty years ago. Older persons remember parties leaving and returning, but no one was found who had actually made a trip. It is the unanimous opinion that official permission to go did not have to be obtained from anyone, such as the war captain. Any older man who had been on previous trips and "knew how" would announce that he was going for salt. Any man· was welcome to join these parties, generally some ten or twenty men, that went out almost monthly. [50] Women did not go "because the men went into the lakes naked." [25] (A modern rationalization of former forgotten ritualism?) Burros carried provisions and brought the salt home.

On arrival at the salt lakes, the men removed all clothing and jewelry before entering the water. "If someone forgot something, he must throw it in the lake." They took off even the woven ties that bound their hair. "They went in just like they were born." Informants disagreed on whether the hair was allowed to flow free, or whether it was tied with amole, or yucca. The men used amole baskets, woven loosely so that the water could drain out, leaving the salt. These were like the baskets used for washing wheat. [25, 49, 50] The salt was carried to the shore and emptied into sacks. While working in the lakes, no one spoke, laughed, smiled, or made any noise, and no one could look back as he left the lake. [25, 49, 50]

Trips for salt took one or two weeks, sometimes longer. During this time no food, sex, or other taboos were observed either by the men or by members of their families who remained at home. [25, 49, 50, 70] The trips were always to Estancia, never to Zuñi or elsewhere. "Since the lakes became private property and were fenced in, the Indians don't go any more. If they went now, they would have to pay for the salt. It's easier to get salt from the stores." [2] The same informant readily admitted many Indians preferred native salt if it were given them, but neither the desire nor need to obtain it has been felt in recent years.

Salt is used primarily for seasoning food. Ceremonial uses were unknown to most informants. One cited the following use, offering the opinion that "now the young women, all the young people, don't know nothing. In the old days when going on a trip, to town or to another pueblo, the mother would put salt in her mouth and then spit it lightly all over the body of her young baby. Then no harm would come to the baby while they were away from Cochití. Today, the babies are often sick when they come home, and their mothers can't understand why this is. They just don't know these things." [25]

These data agree very closely with information gathered by Goldfrank (1927: 9) a generation ago:

> The gathering of salt, a partly economic, partly religious ceremony, is not in charge of a clan, such as the Parrot clan at Laguna, but while retaining some of its ritualistic character and religious setting may be undertaken at Cochiti by an individual as leader regardless of his clan affiliations. Salt is gathered at Salt Place, *mina teka*, a lake to the southeast of the pueblo on the other side of the San Pedro Mountains. Anyone knowing where the lake is might lead an expedition. Here, as at Laguna, there is a Salt Woman, who must be propitiated, so no one laughs or talks while getting the salt, and all move slowly from the lake when they have obtained it. The men go in naked and do not wear jewelry. If they did, it would have to be sacrificed to the Salt Woman. It is not a place of divination here as it is at Laguna. Today expeditions are practically never made, the salt being bought at the store.

Turquoise. Turquoise has been valued at Cochití for many generations. Bandelier, in his entry of September 27, 1880, stated that a stone worth a dollar was doubled in value when cut. While no comparable figures could be obtained for the present, the general opinion is that the value has increased even more, undoubtedly reflecting a greater premium on the time and skill involved.

Traditions still exist concerning the quarrying of turquoise in the Cerrillos Hills, east of the reservation. One of the last attempts to mine turquoise was made by four Cochití early in this century. This was after the mines had passed into private hands; hence their entrance was illegal. While in the tunnel, the four men were captured by the owners, and subsequently they received prison sentences. [25]

At present, turquoise is obtained almost completely through trade or other commercial transactions. [15, 40, 70]

Gypsum. Bandelier noted, October 21, 1880, that *yeso*, or gypsum, was found near San Felipe. It was burned, ground on a metate, and mixed with water to make whitewash for the house walls. As mentioned (p. 49), the preparatory process was attributed to the Spaniards. As noted also (p. 53), it is prepared for the interior and often the exterior kiva walls at the time of the annual feast. Most of the gypsum today comes from the mesa slopes near old La Bajada. [21, 45]

Adobe. Although a large portion of the alluvial plain on which the pueblo is located is adobe, there are certain areas where "good" adobe is obtained. "This kind sticks better." [45] Adobe from particular arroyo cuts is hauled by wagon to the pueblo for making bricks and plastering, and for other purposes. [15, 17] (Plate 15a)

Ceramic Clays. There are also beds of highly valued pottery clay. Some families attempt to keep these sources secret. Deposits are near the mouth of Cañada de Cochití, near the tunnel of the east-side irrigation canal north of Cochití, and on the slopes of the big mesa east of Peña Blanca. Formerly, clay was also obtained from a cave near Santo Domingo, but the Santo Domingo boarded up this cave and locked the entrance. Their plan was to sell the clay to the Cochití, but the latter merely located new beds. [16, 33]

Miscellaneous. The Cochití also gather a reddish sandstone near the mouth of Cañada de Cochití. This forms the base of the reddish paint used on the lower portion of interior house walls. Basalt and tuff for building are obtained in the mountains. Basalt is used in lower courses of house walls and also for grinding-implements, especially the metates on which chili is ground. Various ceremonial effigies, animal and human, are likewise made from basalt. The tuff, lighter in weight, is used to construct the domed outdoor ovens. Such building materials are salvaged and reused when old structures are demolished. To prevent moth damage,[1] small chunks and powdered fragments of tuff are placed in special boxes in which ceremonial feathers are stored. [17, 27, 28, 45] Outcrops of yellow and red ochre, green malachite, and other minerals are exploited for pigments used in painting ceremonial items.

In his journal of November 17, 1880, Bandelier mentioned rattles (kat'zañī) made of fibrous stone, such as petrified wood, but gave no details of their construction. In another entry, April 12, 1882, he reported, in a discussion of gourd rattles, that he was told "that the stone rattles were the original and that the principals would not, at

---

[1] A specimen of this tuff was analyzed by Stephen E. Clabaugh (February 23, 1954), of the Geology Department, University of Texas. An excerpt from his report reads: "There does not seem to be anything unusual about the tuff that might make it valuable as a preservative. There isn't even enough clay to make it a good humidifier, although the broken glass may be able to absorb some moisture from the air."

first, permit the metallic ones. The stone is gathered from the Cerro del Oso, about 28 to 30 miles west of Cochití."

Bandelier stated, October 27, 1880, that the Cochití had no specific name for gold, silver, or copper. For *money*, they used a term borrowed from the Spanish, "pa'so," or their own term for *round*, 'shque-e-ri-tzie."

Gathering of Plants

Piñon (*Pinus edulis* Engelm.). The Cochití are very fond of piñon nuts. Piñons grow in the higher area in the northwestern corner of the reservation and above in the Santa Fe National Forest. Drought in recent years has resulted in poor harvests. When there is a good one, most people go into the hills with their wagons to gather what has fallen, and spread canvas or blankets to catch nuts when the trees are shaken. Nuts are roasted and eaten through the winter. A few people acquire a surplus to sell, but no one has done this recently. Piñon wood is used for fuel, though not as extensively as is juniper. The resin is used as a glue or cement.

Juniper (*Juniperus monosperma* Engelm.). Though seldom mentioned in the literature, the economic importance of juniper (erroneously but popularly known as red cedar) should be emphasized. Juniper is utilized in great quantities in a variety of ways at Cochití.

Its greatest use is for firewood. While a few families use kerosene stoves, and, more recently, electric hot plates, the great majority use wood ranges and corner fireplaces. Paper, corncobs, pine, and cottonwood are all used as fuel but not to the extent that juniper is. Each house has its pile of firewood, chopping block, and ax. One of the most common sounds in the pueblo, summer and winter, is that of the wood choppers at work. Days off from field work and other tasks are spent in the mountains gathering firewood. Deadwood of any kind on the reservation belongs to the finder, but no living trees are supposed to be cut on the reservation. For many years, the Cochití have had to go into the national forest for fuel. Juniper is also utilized in corral fences and is the most common material used for fence posts. As of 1946, a charge of $1.50 per hundred posts was made for cutting in the national forest. [1]

Bandelier, in his journal of November 4, 1880, noted that the juniper berries (*bellotas*) were then being gathered. He added that they require a year to ripen, and that they were used to make a tea for colds. Juniper berries continue to be of some importance in the diet. They may be eaten raw, or may be boiled until soft before being eaten. They are gathered after they have ripened, dried, and fallen to the ground. [2, 3, 15, 44, 92] A medicinal tea is made from the juniper leaves also. For four months after childbirth, a mother must drink nothing but juniper tea if she is to remain in good health. [42, 44, 62]

Pine (*Pinus ponderosa* Dougl.). Western yellow, or ponderosa, pine trees have not grown on the reservation for many years. Roof vigas are cut in the national forest with permission of the ranger, who marks the trees, and can be bought for a nominal fee. Formerly, the Cochití cut many vigas on the Cañada de Cochití Grant; the present owner was said to permit this no longer. Vigas are often cut in the autumn, piled in a somewhat secluded spot, and allowed to dry for a year. They are also lighter then, requiring fewer trips with the wagon. In addition to its use for building, pine is used for firewood. [3, 15] Pitch pine—dried stumps and roots (*ocote*)—is a favorite, being excellent for heat, easy to light and, in the older days, the source of illumination.

Douglas Fir (*Pseudotsuga taxifolia* Britton; *P. mucronata* [Raf.]). This is commonly referred to as "red spruce" by the Cochití ("false spruce" in our culture). It is perhaps the most important plant in the ceremonial life of Cochití and many of the neighboring tribes. Fir twigs are carried by both men and women dancers; they are used as collars for many ka'tsína masks. The references to "spruce" for such circumstances, which fill the literature, are invariably to this fir. (Numerous specimens of evergreen from *Tablita* dances were gathered during the summer of 1951 from several Keresan and other pueblos; specimens were identified by the Cochití as identical with the type used for their own dance costumes, masked or unmasked. All specimens were later identified by Dr. Howard J. Dittmer, University of New Mexico, as Douglas fir.) The pole that is prominent in the *Tablita* Dance is also of Douglas fir. Pine and other woods could not stand the strain to which this pole is subjected, according to informants. Another explanation was that this wood had to be used because it was this type of tree which the ancestors had climbed in their ascent from the lower worlds. [3, 44, 62] In former times, these boughs were gathered by wagons; today a truck is used. [44, 53]

Cottonwood (*Populus* spp.). In the Cochití area there are two types of cottonwoods, the valley cottonwood (*P. wizlizeni*) along the river banks and the mountain cottonwood (*P. angustifolia*) in the canyons above Cochití. Both are used for firewood, mostly in the form of driftwood, easily collected along the banks of the Rio Grande. Boughs, often saplings, are cut to form sunshades and arbors during the summer months. Of the two, the mountain type is more highly valued. This is the wood used for drums. When a mountain cotton-wood dies, its center rots away, making the hollowing process easier for the drum-makers. Since a large proportion of the men make drums, considerable man-hours are spent in the mountain canyons in search of dead cottonwoods. Occasionally, a tree is girdled to kill it, but usually a search is made for a dead one. Logs are cut in about ten-foot lengths and loaded on wagons to be taken to the village. These logs can be seen in many corral sheds and storerooms, where they remain dry until the owner has time to work them. Log sections vary in diameter from three to four inches for small souvenir drums to two feet or more for the large dance drums. [3, 15, 16, 17, 25, 62]

Mountain Mahogany (*Cercocarpus breviflorus*). This shrub is found in the mountains above Cochití and is used in several ways. Its bark is utilized to produce a reddish-brown dye for coloring moc-casins and leggings. Shreds of bark are placed in a half-gallon of hot water, to which a tablespoon of lime is added. The color is tested with a white corncob; the more lime used, the darker the color. The suds are spread over the buckskin until it reaches the desired shade. Mashed roots, used in this dyeing process, are used also in the tan-ning process before dyeing. As noted earlier, this wood was formerly used for implements such as digging sticks. [21, 44, 45]

Rocky Mountain Bee Weed (*Cleome serrulata* Pursh; *Peritoma serrulatum* D. C.). Informants pointed this plant out as the source of *guaco*, the black paint used in decorating the characteristic black-on-cream Cochití pottery. This black paint is also used in decorating ceremonial objects and the participants. When young, the plant is used for table greens, being boiled or fried. Seeds are eaten in the form of cakes or gruel. [3, 16, 17, 28, 45, 49, 53, 88]

Yucca (*Yucca baccata* Torr. and *Y. glauca* Nutt.). Soapweed; datil. These yuccas are, and have been, important plants to the Cochití. Bandelier, in his journal of April 4, 1882, gave the following account of the preparation of the yucca used in making the nets mentioned in the discussion of fishing (p. 140). (A portion of this appeared in Robbins, Harrington, and Freire-Marreco [1916: 51].)

The thread of the *Palmillo ancho* was prepared as follows: In May or June, the Governor sent out men to cut the leaves of the plants and gather them in "hands." Then they dug a hole in the ground (pozo) and kindled a large fire in it. After the ground had become thoroughly heated, the embers and ashes were cleaned out and the leaves placed in carefully, covered with brush, then stones, and finally a layer of earth. On top of this another large fire was built and left burning overnight; the leaves were, thus, well baked. Then the hands were carried to the pueblo, and, as the leaves became very sweet, the boys chewed them up, extracting the fibre "Ha-tyañi-q'o-gomen," which they carefully laid aside, each bundle for itself [,] returning it to the house where it belonged. That fibre was twisted into thread, and strips of netting made of it, which were handed to the officers, and then the whole net made.

Other uses of yucca as food, included in the same discussion by Bandelier, have already been noted (pp. 122–123). While this usage is perhaps not as extensive as formerly, considerable use is still made of the yucca fruit. The fruit of the broad-leafed yucca (*Y. baccata*) is preferred; the fleshy portion is baked like a sweet potato. This is "wild banana" (hosh'kañī) and the Cochití refer to the broad-leafed yucca as "hai'kʸuñī" in contrast to "harsh'tʸᵃ," the narrow-leafed form. Modern Cochití insist that this latter form is better for string and the roots of it are better for shampoos. [16, 28, 44]

Bandelier, in his journal of November 18, 1880, said that amole roots were pounded and the pulp was stirred in water for shampoo suds; the large species was mixed with hot water; the small, with cold. He noted also that soap was sometimes used with the amole. Three days later, his journal records the use of amole foam as an ingredient of paint, the claim being made that such paint was more cohesive than that made with water. In his entry of April 23, 1882, he noted the use of the froth, or foam, of amole for lung disease. The "hearts" of yucca are also used for food. Pounded and cooked in plain water, they produce a pudding something like junket. [44]

Today, both yuccas are also referred to as "amole." The narrow-leafed form is the one used in making baskets that are used for washing wheat, and formerly those used in gathering salt. Pieces of soap-weed root are often thrown to the crowd on feast days as part of the *gallo*, or present-throwing; they are received as enthusiastically today as in former times, for this form of shampoo is still common, if not the most common. [13, 17, 44] Bandelier mentioned the use of paint brushes made from shredded *palmillo*, November 21, 1880.

The heart of the amole is also pounded and boiled in water to make a tea for urinary disorders. After about a week's treatment with this tea, the disorder is usually gone. [34, 37]

Miscellaneous. A wide range of native plants has been, and still is, used by the Cochití as food, medicine, raw materials for basketry, dyes, and other purposes. Some have been mentioned in earlier discussions of foods and diet. In the list that follows, original specimens were identified by Dr. Howard J. Dittmer, University of New Mexico (marked HJD), in the fall of 1951; other specimens I was able to identify with the aid of data provided in Castetter (1935), Robbins, Harrington, and Freire-Marreco (1916), and other sources.

Achillea lanulosa Nutt (HJD) Western yarrow; known to the Cochití by its Spanish name, *Plumahilla.* Used to treat chills; the leaves are put in cold water for a day to make a tea that is drunk until the chills disappear.

Allium sp. (HJD) Wild onion; known as tzī'na ha'truñí, or turkey onion. The bulb may be eaten raw or used in cooking as is the garden variety of onion.

Amaranthus sp. Pigweed, *alegria, quelite*; used as table greens.

Arctostaphylus pungens H. B. K. (HJD) Pointleaf manzanita; Jemez punche; dry leaves are used for smoking, either alone or mixed with other wild "punches," or with some form of tobacco.

Atriplex sp. Saltbush; used for both seasoning and as greens.

Bouteloua curtipendula (Michx.) Torr. Side-oats grama; mesquite grass. Gathered in late summer or autumn in the mountains; dried stems bound and used for hairbrushes and brooms. Bandelier, October 25, 1880, noted the gathering of zacate in the mountains for brooms and for mattresses. He stated that it was cut with iron sickles and bound into bunches to be sold farther south where it did not grow (Santo Domingo, etc.); the men he observed were on the Potrero de las Vacas and were gathering piñon nuts at the same time. Three bundles of zacate were equal in value to a string of green chili two meters long, or two strings of red chili of equal length.

Chenopodium sp. Lambsquarter; used as table greens.

Croton texensis (Klotzsch). (HJD) Doveweed; used for earache; the leaves are made into a moist wad and placed in the ear opening.

Eupatorium sp. (HJD) Thoroughwart; Rat punche; dry leaves used for smoking, either alone or mixed with other wild "punches," or with some form of tobacco.

Euphorbia sp. (also *Chamaesyce* sp.) (HJD) Spurge; called *la golondrina* by the Spanish. "Swallow medicine"; sē'sē ka-wa-wa. The entire plant is ground up, and the powder placed on the sore, burn, or cut.

Grindelia (*sclerosa?*). (HJD) Gum weed; Spanish "Bull eye." The sticky blossom is placed on an aching tooth.

Helianthus annuus and *H. petiolanus.* (HJD) Sunflower. The seeds are ground into flour, which is baked in cakes; juice from the stalks is placed on open wounds to stop bleeding; also appears to act as a disinfectant, or perhaps more accurately, as a seal against germs and dirt, as the Cochití unanimously insist there is "never an infection" if this is used.

Hymenoxys floribunda (A. Gray). (HJD) Colorado rubber plant; gum plant; nūk'tsh; Spanish name, *pinguay.* Bark and roots can be chewed "just like bubble gum."

Lathyrus decaphyllus Pursh. Wild pea; "duck peas"; entire seed pod is eaten.

Martynia sp. Devil's claw. Dried fruit pods are wrapped with yarn or used in other ways in making ceremonial paraphernalia. In recent years, these pods have been painted with bright poster paints to resemble birds and are sold as tourist items.

Monarda menthaefolia Graham. (HJD) Horsemint. Dry leaves used in cooking; they are mixed with the fresh blood of an animal, bran, fat, and onions and placed in a big intestine "like baloney."

Muhlenbergia sp. The long-stemmed species of this genus is used in the same way as *Bouteloua curtipendula.*

Opuntia sp. Prickly-pear cactus. Flat stems and fruit are eaten. Flat stems are burned and powdered after spines have been removed. The powder is placed over the spot where a pimple or boil is forming to cause it to head more quickly.

Phellopterus bulbosus (A. Nels.). Wild celery; eaten either raw or cooked.

Portulaca oleracea L. (HJD) Common purslane; *verdolaga.* Eaten as greens, boiled or fried in lard.

Prunus melanocarpa Rybd. (also *Padus melanocarpa*). Chokecherry. Called a'po, or, by the Spanish, *capulin.* Known also as "bear berry," referring to the red fruit which is eaten like cherries. Made into jam or jelly or meal cakes.

Quercus utahensis D. C. Scrub oak: Ha'pañī, the designation of one clan. Acorns are made into flour; wood was formerly a popular source of implement handles.

Rhus cismontana. (HJD) Sumac; Comanche punche. Dry leaves used for smoking, either alone or mixed with other wild "punches," or with some form of tobacco.

Ribes inebriens Lindl. (HJD) Wild currant; Spanish *manzanita.* Berries are eaten; formerly wood was used for bows and other articles.

Rumex spp. (HJD) Dock; *canaigre.* Leaves used as table greens when the plant is young; young stems eaten as rhubarb; roots used in tanning.

Bandelier, April 1, 1882, stated that the "caña agria" was sprouting and was told by the padre that the Cochití used it for pottery paint. On the twenty-sixth of the same month, he noted that "caña agria" was used by the Mexicans for tanning; he also noted in an earlier entry (April 5) that this plant was found only east of the river. Possibly a reference to *Rumex hymenosepalus* Torr., known also as *canaigre*, or wild rhubarb, in contrast to *R. mexicanus* Meisn., or Mexican dock, which may have a wider distribution since the present specimen gathered in 1951 was found in the mountains above Cochití. Again, Bandelier may not have been precisely correct in his distribution of *R. hymenosepalus*.

Salvia reflexa. (HJD) Called both "bell flower" and O'shatsh, or "sun." Leaves are chewed, the juice being used to treat diarrhea.

Solanum eleagnifolium. (HJD) "Ku-sha'lï beads," or "clown beads." Bull nettle; silver nightshade; *trompillo.* When ripe, the yellow berries are strung and worn as beads by the Ku-sha'lï members; also, when dry, berries are powdered in the fingers and used like snuff; "they are bitter, like tobacco."

Sphaeralcea coccinea. (HJD) Globemallow; "pink flowers." Used to treat rheumatism; leaves are ground into powder, moistened, and patted on the afflicted joint, which is then wrapped in cloth overnight.

Thelesperma gracile (Torr.) A. Gray. (HJD) Wild tea, or Indian tea. The stems, leaves, and blossoms are picked fresh and used immediately or dried for future use.

At present, the Cochití are using these wild plants to an ever decreasing degree, though most older people are familiar with the plants and their uses. From comments made by several informants, it would seem that a considerable amount of the Cochití knowledge of ethnobotanical matters stems from their Spanish contacts. [16, 28, 34, 44, 45]

It would be extremely valuable to learn to what extent the Spaniards actually expanded the number of species utilized as well as the number of uses to which these plants were put. There can be no doubt that many present-day Indian usages in foods, flavorings, medicines, and magical potions had their origins in the culture of the Spanish immigrants. Bandelier, April 17, 1882, gave a remedy acquired from Juan José for treatment of a sore lip, "Yerba de San Pedro." The plant was ground and applied to the sore. "It is true that it dries up with the greatest rapidity. It is a Mexican, not an Indian remedy, but he says that the Indians have, in one of their plants, a specific against cancer, but keep it very quiet."

The widest use of wild plants at present is among those families living on their ranchitos during the summer months. There the people are closer to the plants, and store commodities are less accessible.

Trading

Trading has been and continues to be an important aspect of Cochití economics. Bandelier (1890: 36) remarked, "It may be said that no two tribes were ever so hostile as never to trade, or so intimately connected in friendship as never to fight each other." In his journal of October 21, 1880, he mentioned that there had been Navaho in the village, trading *tilmas,* or cloaks. In a later entry (November 26, 1882), he noted that the Cochití were very eager to get "Plumas de Guacamayo," macaw feathers. Starr, in his diary of September 25, 1897, noted "the Brother Syrian peddlers, whom I saw here three months ago, appeared for supper."

Curtis (1926: 73–74) described the rather extensive travels of the Cochití, generally for purposes of trading. He stated that they went on trading journeys as far west as the Hopi towns and, in company with the Hopi, went to the Havasupai to trade for deerskins. Northward, the Cochití went as far as Taos, and eastward into Oklahoma, or Indian Territory. Both in the north and the east, bread and corn-meal were traded for horses and buffalohides with the Comanches and other Plains tribes. Southward they ranged as far as the plains of central New Mexico, principally to hunt antelope but also to trade. Curtis also told of one informant's father who traveled to Sonora to buy horses. According to another story, three men once went as far as Mexico City to inquire about a land grant. In 1875, Santiago Quintana and two others went on foot to California by way of Prescott, Arizona, and the Gila River. They visited and worked in San Luís Obispo, Bakersfield, and Los Angeles, returning three years later with horses. Curtis observed that these longer trips were exceptional.

Data about trading from the Eickemeyers' visit (1895: 96–97, 101) in 1894 are likewise of value in adding time perspective to this phase of economics:

The Pueblos get most of their horses from the Navajoes, who make a special business of horse-raising and travel from village to village with droves of Indian ponies or cayuses, which they trade for beads that the Pueblo Indians make in great quantities. Four of these strings of beads will buy a horse. Five dollars will also buy a horse; but, strange to say, five dollars will not buy the beads. This method of financiering was quite contrary to any we had ever heard of, but it seemed to suit the Indians, who place a much higher value on beads than they do on money. This is probably owing to the fact that to manufacture them necessitates a great deal of tedious and hard labor.

. . . .

The Indian is very reluctant to sell these drums. In fact, we could not buy one at any price, although we tried at several places. When an Indian will not sell his blankets, pottery, beadwork, or dance costume, it shows he has plenty to eat and is thoroughly prosperous.

In light of data obtained from informants as well as from personal observations, these references and citations of one and two generations ago reveal several interesting features. As noted by Bandelier, despite long-standing hostilities with the Apache, Navaho, Comanche, and various Pueblo tribes, the Cochití have maintained trading relations with these tribes into present times, except for the more distant Comanche. [3, 15]

As one would expect, trading journeys have expanded as means of transportation have improved. Trains, buses, trucks, and cars facilitate these changes, perhaps not so much in actual radius of travel but certainly in the frequency of the trips.

Another factor contributing to expanding travel has been the increasing number of fairs, expositions, and other celebrations which encourage Indians from many tribes to participate. Sante Fe, Albuquerque, Gallup, Window Rock, Flagstaff, Prescott, Los Angeles, San Francisco, and Chicago have all been visited by Cochití who attended such events to present tribal ceremonies, "see the country," and, even more vital to them, meet old and new friends from other tribes and areas with the chance to trade.

In addition to these opportunities, created principally by non-Indians, there is a continual sequence of ceremonies at neighboring pueblos. The El Pueblo Bus Line (during its brief span of business), the community truck, privately owned automobiles and trucks, and for the shorter trips, especially in former times, wagons, all have carried people to these celebrations. The people look forward to such days to see the dances and renew old friendships, both as a change from the normal routine of daily life and as an economic enterprise. If a person cannot go on a trip, he often sends his wares with a relative, who makes as good trades or sales as possible. Personal arrangements are made, with sometimes a "commission" being paid; at other times perhaps a gift, or merely an expression of thanks, suffices. If the trading is poor, it is accepted as unfortunate. [13, 45] While sales to the many tourists are anticipated, there is also a good deal of interest in trading bread, corn, fruit, drums, jewelry, cloth, skins, and almost any other form of property with other Indians. From them, the Cochití favor blankets, jewelry, basketry, pottery wares (especially watertight vessels from Zia, Acoma, and Zuñi), olivella, abalone, and other shells from the Pacific Coast and other areas beyond the bounds of their normal travel. (See Brand 1935 and 1938 for further details.)

Prior to ceremonies, people are busily occupied for days in preparing jewelry, drums, curios, agricultural produce, and breadstuff for trading. Families seek space for at least one member on vehicles leaving first. These individuals are carefully instructed to secure the best location to display wares—"under a certain *ramada*, or porch," "under a particular tree," or "in the shadow of the church," and other time-proven locations with an optimum combination of comfort and potential sales. (Plate 24*b*)

Some ceremonies are recognized as offering better trading opportunities than others. Usually this is determined by the nature of the celebration itself, and, even more, by the variety of tribes and number of people attending. Trading at the Navaho Fair at Window Rock is considered good, but Window Rock is too far for many to go. The Jemez Feast Day (November 12) provides an opportunity to trade nearer home with the Navaho and Apache. The Laguna Feast Day (September 19) is an even better opportunity to contact Navaho and exchange chili, watermelons, and especially bread for turquoise, silver, blankets, and saddles. [15, 20, 44, 53]

When visiting other pueblos, someone in the party usually has a friend or relative at whose home all are welcome and where trading can be done. "We always go to their house." [15, 16, 17, 20, 44, 49, 70] Friendships may result from boarding-school acquaintances, or they may develop from interfamily relations that have existed for several generations. Other instances include families who have, or had, intermarried with a Cochití family. Though written from the viewpoint of Navaho trading practices, Hill's comments (1948: 390) are of interest here:

The institution of "friend" existed among the Pueblos, though this relationship appears to have been defined less rigidly and was more ephemeral than among the Ute. Pueblo "friends" traded with the Navaho. They also acted as agents; sometimes they furnished a room in which the goods were displayed. They were consulted from time to time during trading negotiations with other Pueblos. If a Navaho considered he had obtained a fair bargain he returned to the same family at a later date; if not, a new relationship would be entered into and another friend secured.

Trading is actively engaged in during the intervals between the ceremonies or other special occasions. During even our few months' residence in Cochití, we have had traders from Hopi and Santo Domingo stop at our house. Two Zuñi men were encountered in another Cochití home. Later, informants commented that these two men and others came regularly every year to trade, hitch-hiking their way to and from the Rio Grande pueblos. The Zuñi were trading jewelry, as was the man from Santo Domingo. The Hopi had women's belts for fifteen dollars and *mantas* for eighty-five, as well as dance kilts at an undetermined price. Cochití friends stated that these were about standard postwar prices. [20, 24, 28, 45, 53]

One form of trading, though not consciously considered as such, is an exchange of gifts of approximately equal value, sometimes involving considerable delay before the exchange is considered complete. Typical of this was a Cochití's gift of a drum to his friend from Taos who had admired it. The following year when the two met again, the Cochití was given a pair of beaded moccasins. [62]

The preceding discussion creates the impression that trading and widespread travel are essentially universal among the Cochití. Actually, this is true of the majority. There are, however, some individuals who have never been to various neighboring pueblos, or to certain ceremonies, or other celebrations.

Earlier descriptions of Cochití trading make frequent reference to horse trading. Emphasis is placed by the Cochití now on offering bread, corn, and similar agricultural produce, and the objects they desire in return are jewelry, meat, and blankets, not horses. Horses are costly to keep, and there is less use for them at present. Actually, with grazing limitations becoming recognized, the tendency to accumulate wealth in the form of any livestock is decreasing. True, meat is always a welcome relief from the normal pueblo vegetarian diet, but turquoise, jewelry, blankets, hides, and similar items are easy to store and handle, and with the development of the tourist trade throughout New Mexico and the entire Southwest, these goods can easily be converted to cash, which is of increasing importance to the Indians.

The Eickemeyers' observations on the preference of beads to money is interesting in light of present practices. Much inter-Indian trading is still barter, though considerable cash transactions are made. Non-Indians sometimes barter, too—usually to the advantage of the Indians; the more common form of exchange involves cash. Getting to town is easy enough now to make money more satisfactory than formerly. Occasionally, items are bartered to better advantage than if it were a cash transaction. For instance, when an individual has specific immediate need for an item, such as a carpenter's tool or a certain caliber of ammunition, he will overpay to save a trip to town. Generally, values are well known; if a satisfactory exchange cannot be arranged, the individual borrows what he needs from a relative until such time as he can go to town and buy it at standard prices. In most cases, the Indian has the advantage of being able to wait for a suitable exchange or trade. Non-Indians are often handicapped by the pressure of time or are influenced by their immediate desires—factors well appreciated by the Indians.

Intrapueblo trade among the Cochití is by either barter or purchase. While this is usually on a person-to-person basis, as is other trading, there are occasions when one member of a family acts in behalf of the actual owner or the person desiring the goods. If a child is involved in trading, he may be allowed complete freedom to exercise his judgment, learning from his experiences. If a parent sees that too much advantage is being taken of a child, he may intervene with advice. [62]

Another aspect of trading is the attempt to monopolize a trading opportunity until it has been exhausted. After that, an effort is made to control the news of a possible trade by informing relatives of it first, or by urging the trader to visit the relative's home next.

The Eickemeyers' unsuccessful efforts to obtain a drum from the Cochití despite several attempts is again interesting in light of subsequent developments. At present, the sale of drums, an item for which Cochití is especially famous, is one of their important sources of income. This is derived from both a great assortment of drums made for the tourist trade and from large ceremonial dance drums sought by other pueblos.

Informants are generally unwilling to give any comparative values for trade commodities. "You just have to take your things around and see what someone will offer you for them. Sometimes you can do real well, and other times nobody wants anything." [15, 16] Several informants volunteered to buy blankets or jewelry for me from other Indians at various ceremonials. "Navahos always stick the white people for lots of money." [15, 16, 20, 24, 44]

Hill (1948: 379), encountering much the same situation among the Navaho, made the following comments: "Informants were generally unwilling to quote prices or were quick to point out that they applied only to a single case. Published reports give little concrete material on this subject."

In addition to the stores currently operated by the Spanish-Americans (see Chapter 2), there have been a few stores run by the Cochití. One was that of Santiago Quintana (Cyrus Dixon), located in the house block known as "Butterfly Group." A second was that of Marcial Quintana, which ceased operation about 1924 after too much credit had been extended and a disagreement arose over a check. The case was handled by Juan de Jesús Pancho (John Dixon), a more or less self-appointed "judge," who was a leader of the Progressive faction and was backed to some extent by Indian Service officials. The case went against Marcial, who was one of the Conservative leaders, and subsequently the store was abandoned. [45, 53, 65]

Shortly before the United States entered the Second World War, a loan was made by the Cochití Council of *Principales* to Lawrence Chávez, who wanted to start a store in the pueblo. Informants disagreed as to whether this money had remained on deposit at the agency to the credit of this Indian. They did feel, however, that if such a store could be started by a Cochití and if the selection of goods was comparable in variety and price to that in the present stores, such an enterprise would be very popular among other Cochití. Not only would additional competition be welcomed, but the possibility that a strong Indian-owned store might drive out the Spanish storekeepers and their families was pointed out by several. Others felt that having a new store would not necessarily alter the situation appreciably and might only create ill feelings among the Indians themselves. At present, the Cochití appear relatively united against the Spanish-American traders, though they have little alternative other than to trade with them. [15, 16, 42, 44, 52, 70]

Material Culture

As brought out at the end of Chapter 2, much of the material production of modern Cochití reflects the increasing importance of the tourist trade among the Southwestern Indians. However, details of this variety of crafts are included here also because in the majority of instances the curios are based upon traditional forms and methods. While there have been changes in the materials and especially in the tools utilized, there has been a strong tendency to retain the use of the customary media. Included in this section are pottery, basketry, weaving, hides and pelts, beadwork, jewelry, wooden and stone objects, drums and rattles, and painting.

Pottery. In the introductory remarks to *The Pottery of Pecos,* Kidder (1931: 3) wrote:

Like all Pueblo Indians, the Pecos were diligent potters. Their way of life required the use of many vessels for cooking and serving food and for carrying and storing water, and their supply of these fragile utensils naturally needed constant replenishment. So throughout the centuries the making of pottery never ceased; the potter's art was never at a standstill; styles grew and changed, new wares developed or were introduced and old ones dropped out of use.

In a brief note in his journal of November 19, 1880, Bandelier reported being told by a woman that the thumbnail was allowed to grow to make the indentation of the rim of their pottery. In a more detailed account, April 3, 1882, he recorded the complete process of pottery-making:

They are making pottery now. The clay is yellow. They wet it, and when they take it out it is grey before wetting. They build up the vessel making first a bottom, and then wind Strings of clay on top of it, keeping the clay moist, so as, if it is a tinaja, to give it the form of a wide-mouthed Jug. It is properly a pile of clay sausages. The whole mass is kept wet, so that it can be shaped by pressure as they like. The opening on top is kept open, large enough for the hand to get in. The vessel is placed in a flat basket. When the upper rim is done, all by the thumb, they scrape and smoothen the outside and inside with the hand and a little scraper of calabash or wooden. At the same time, by gently pushing from the inside, they make the sides bulge out so as to give the vessel the true form when it is complete, and then left to dry. When dry, it is smoothed, or scraped outside with a stone-scraper, patched if there were any cracks, and then painted with "Guáco." This is a decoction of a plant which I do not know as yet. [Rocky Mountain Bee Weed—see p. 147]. Its liquid is yellow, so is the color, but after burning, it turns black. The red color they make of red ochre, and burn it in. They burn only once, unless it should fail the first time, when they burn it over again. Before painting it with Guáco, they put diluted white Earth on it. That clay, which burns yellow, they get from the other side of the River. . . . I saw them burn their pottery. They make a ring of stones, in the middle of which they put wood, and set their vessels on it. Then cover it with a perfect vault of cow-dung. Thus the clay is gradually baked all over.

Another brief description of early Cochití pottery-making was given by the Eickemeyers (1895: 101–102):

At another house three squaws were making pottery in their skillful although crude way, by working the clay into shape by hand, guided only by the eye. The jars, after being rubbed and worked into shape, are allowed to dry slowly before baking, which is done in the bake oven in front of each house. These ovens are made of stone and adobe mortar and resemble in shape the old beehive. Many of the jars are artistically decorated with odd conventional designs, and one which we purchased had on the inside two broods of game chickens and two game-cocks. The rooster figured quite prominently on much of the pottery, probably owing to the fondness the people have for the game of "gallo."

Although the great majority of household utensils are of modern manufacture and are obtained from outside sources, pottery made at Cochití and other pueblos is still extensively used. This is particularly true of large storage jars, which are handed down from mother to daughter and highly prized. Smaller bowls are used for chili. "Chili tastes better out of one of these dishes." [28, 45] In many, grease has penetrated the bowl walls, making them more waterproof. Local pottery, though fairly well-made and often watertight, is considered by the Cochití to be inferior to many Zia water jars. A few families still use pottery water "buckets" in preference to metal pails. "The pottery keeps water lots cooler, and it tastes better." [23, 38]

Clay is brought home from special beds by wagon and is sifted and stored until needed. The men help in gathering clay, but the women do the actual pottery-making. The temper is either ground tuff or fine sand. Pottery is made during the warm period of the year; during the cold months it does not dry well, and firing is not as successful. Patching cracks, as noted by Bandelier in his comments on the prefiring stage, is almost never done by modern pottery-makers. [16, 17, 23, 27, 33, 34]

"Potteries," as the Cochití call them, are made both at home in the pueblo and in the ranch houses. Usually they are made indoors so that the freshly formed vessels will dry slowly and evenly, away from drafts. The base is molded in the hand and coils of clay are

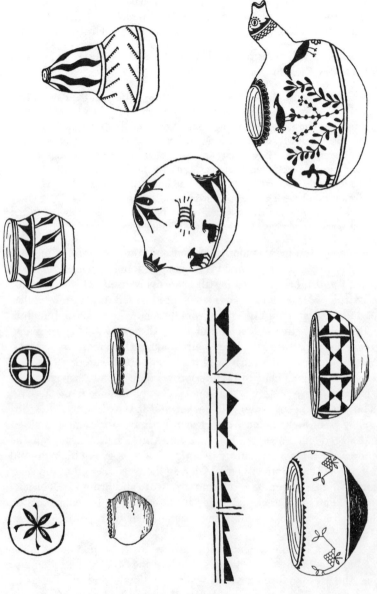

Fig. 13.—Pottery Designs. (Based largely, but not exclusively, on data in Stevenson [1883: 405–409].)

added in concentric circles. Gourd fragments are used to scrape and thin the walls; smooth pebbles are used to polish the surface. Next, the slips of cream and brick-red are added, and the black designs are painted over them. (Plate 17a)

Before final firing, pottery is sometimes heated in the oven of a wood range to reduce the danger of its cracking. [16] Firing is usually done early in the morning so that the workers can escape the heat of the day, not for any technical reason. Vessels are placed in a makeshift oven, made with a frame, or shell, of sheets of iron roofing, or flattened washtubs, wire mesh, and other items. Fuel, usually manure from a corral, but sometimes corncobs, is heaped over the frame. If the frame and fuel touch the pottery, it becomes smudged. Contrary to the observations of the Eickemeyers, outdoor baking ovens are never used now for firing pottery. Some women are more experienced in firing than others, and some are considered to have greater luck. Both are sought by other pottery-makers to help in firing. [16, 17, 18, 23, 27, 28]

Cochití pottery has traditionally been black-on-cream, often combined with brick-red surfaces on the exterior bottoms and the complete interiors of bowls and *ollas*. In some pieces the cream becomes almost a silver. Leaf and geometric designs predominate, and many finished products are very similar to Santo Domingo pieces. (For additional details, see Douglas 1933: 11.) The women generally decorate the pottery, though a few men are recognized as capable ˜nd are willing to assist. Some men make designs on paper first, a few patterns being copied from sherds of prehistoric wares found in the vicinity. These designs are borrowed and copied by others, invariably by relatives. Favorite designs are kept in notebooks so that they may be used again. [16, 20, 24, 27] A few designs are illustrated in Figure 13.

Most present-day Cochití pottery is intended for the tourist trade. This results in smaller pieces, since they can be more easily transported or shipped and are much easier to make. Eccentric items are becoming more common, for example, such pieces as ash trays in the shape of adobe houses and outdoor ovens. Animal effigies, often to be used as small coin-banks, are also being made in answer to the demands of various trading posts. Normally, these eccentric forms are in the traditional black, cream, and brick-red colors. One of the first women known to have made pottery eccentrics in the form of large dolls, or human figures, was Maria Seferina Arquero, wife of

Juan José Suina. She was said to have begun this work in the 1890's.
[65] Several examples are in the Laboratory of Anthropology collections in Santa Fe. (See Stevenson [1883: 405–409] for illustrations
of early Cochití pottery forms and designs.)

Very few women feel capable of making large jars and *ollas*. Some
of this feeling results from an unwillingness to do the work necessary
for a large vessel. It is easier to earn money in other ways and buy a
large vessel from another person, either at Cochití or another pueblo.
[33, 34] At present, informants know only four women who are able
or willing to attempt to produce large pottery pieces: Estefanita Herrera, Teresita Chávez Romero, Ascención Chávez Benada (she did
some pottery firing in October, 1933, for the technical observations of
Anna O. Shepard [1936: 457] in conjunction with her analysis of
Pecos Pueblo pottery), and Agrapina Ortiz Quintana. The last two
women have not made any large pieces for a number of years. [16,
17, 18, 23, 28, 33, 34]

An informant told an interesting account of a large *olla* made by
Agrapina. The family was living at its ranchito at the time, several
years ago. Agrapina made this especially large and fine *olla* inside the
ranch house so that it would dry better and be protected from any
possible damage by rain. When it was at last ready for firing, they
found it was too large to go through the door. After considerable
talking, her husband, Marcial, was persuaded to remove some of the
adobes and the timbers comprising the door jamb. The firing was
accomplished successfully, the door was repaired, and the *olla*, still in
use by the family, frequently reminds them of this comic episode. [18]

The children learn pottery-making "if they want to." Small boys
as well as girls play at modeling the clay. However, as this is women's
work, it is not many years before the boys shift their interests and
efforts elsewhere.

Several informants stated that pottery-making has declined at Cochití because it is too much work for the return received. After the
labor of gathering and preparing the clays, the forming of the vessel
itself, and the finishing and decoration, the piece can still be spoiled
during firing. If the firing goes well, there remains the problem of
transporting the fragile wares for trade or sale. "Other things, like
beadwork and drums, are a lot easier, and you get more money for
them." [16, 20, 24, 44, 70]

Basketry. Basket-making is virtually a lost art at Cochití; at present, only a few people know it and they are seldom active in this

craft. Both men and women do such work and apparently this represents no change from the past. In the collection of Starr photographs of about 1897 is a picture of a man in the beginning stages of making a large flat washing basket (Plate 18a). In the unpublished field notes of Boas for 1922 (Book IX: 947) is the following comment: "Intending basketmakers must fast for four days and take emetics. After that a woman will appear to them who will help them in making baskets." Present-day basket-makers do not follow this preparatory procedure. [92] Basket-makers living today include Juan José Suina; Santiago Cordero (before his blindness); his wife, Damesia; Cipriano Quintana (also before his blindness); and his wife, Clemencia (Plate 26a).

All baskets are wide, shallow, and loosely woven. Materials used include the long leaves of the amole, or soapweed (*Yucca glauca*); a rod of willow, bound into a hoop, serves as the rim foundation. After the leaves have been soaked in water to make them pliable, they are laid on a flat surface, usually the floor. They are interwoven at right angles to one another in a simple twill. The weaver normally places his feet (as in Plate 18a) on the finished portion to hold the leaves in place while he completes the remainder. Finally, the hoop is incorporated, with the yucca leaves being bent upward to form a basin. The leaves are tied around the rim and trimmed off evenly to form a simple decorative fringe on the outside. The baskets are neither painted nor dyed. They vary in diameter from 10 to 30 inches, normally being about 20, and are 4 to 6 inches deep.

This is the only form of basketry made by the Cochití; informants stated that there had never been any other. At present, many also have the more tightly woven Apache, or Ute, "wedding basket," which they use a great deal. Although Cochití baskets are used primarily for washing grain, they are also used as general containers. Formerly, as stated earlier, they were used in the gathering of salt. [3, 13, 16, 45]

While at present sandals woven of yucca and similar fibers are known only from museum displays and the like, Bandelier noted (October 9, 1885) that the Cochití called yucca sandals "shoes for the snow." In view of the present lack of acquaintance with such footgear, it would seem that Bandelier was recording information virtually extinct, if not completely so, as of 1885.

Weaving. The art of weaving has also all but vanished from Cochití. Estefanita Herrera formerly wove but has not done so recently.

Juan Velasquez, a native of San Felipe who married a Cochití in 1924, is the only man referred to as a weaver, and he has not done any weaving in recent years because of the high cost of yarn and because of other interests.

The great decline in weaving among Pueblo people, in general, is interesting in view of the large quantities of *mantas*, and other articles—first of cotton, buffalo, and dog hair, and in post-Spanish times of wool—that are mentioned in documentary sources. Fray Cayetano Fore, in 1794, commented as follows regarding Cochití (Biblioteca Nacional, *Legajo X:* Document 70):

The industry of the Indians of this nation is limited to weaving, and they make mantas of wool and cotton with which they clothe their women. They sell them to those of other nations, which although they are able to weave them, they do not, either through laziness, or because they have no wool, or they are unable to raise sheep as these do. Also, they sell them to the *genízaros* for their wives who use them the same way. They weave and also make wide capes, which they call "Cotones," with which they dress themselves.

In describing Navaho weaving, Matthews (1884: 375) made the following comments regarding the decline of Pueblo weaving, as of the 1880's:

The superiority of the Navajo to the Pueblo work results not only from a constant advance of the weaver's art among the former, but from a constant deterioration of it among the latter. The chief cause of this deterioration is that the Pueblos find it more remunerative to buy, at least the finer *serapes*, from the Navajos, and give their time to other pursuits, than to manufacture for themselves; they are nearer the white settlements and can get better prices for their produce; they give more attention to agriculture; they have within their country, mines of turquoise which the Navajo prize, and they have no trouble in procuring whisky, which some of the Navajo prize even more than gems. Consequently, while the wilder Indian has incentives to improve his art, the more advanced has many temptations to abandon it all together. In some pueblos the skill of the loom has been almost forgotten. A growing fondness for European clothing has also had its influence, no doubt.

In Bandelier's journal there are several references to weaving at Cochití. On November 22, 1880, he mentioned that he "found old man Chávez and his wife, both weaving. They were making serapes, and when he sat down to talk, she took his place." In an entry of December 1, 1882, he noted, "The large loom, for broad girdles and scarfs, is tied to a stake stuck in the floor, and the man sits down to it, stretching his legs in the direction of the stake." He also mentioned the loom for small girdles and garters, "opash-tya-nasht." This was "tied to a post and thus stretched with one hand while with the other they twist and weave." Of interest in relation to the larger loom mentioned by Bandelier is a Starr photograph, of about 1897 (Plate 17*b*), showing a man, Cleito, using such a loom; an extended footbrace had been added, apparently to accommodate the longer sash being woven.

In the last years before its complete cessation, Cochití weaving consisted entirely of women's belts, narrow garters, and ties for the hair; *mantas* and other large pieces were no longer made. [44, 70] Simple looms with either continuous or discontinuous warps were used. (See Spier 1924: 64–85 for details.) Matthews (1884: 391) said he had been told by Bandelier that the Indians at Cochití "make the narrow garters and hair-bands after the manner of the Zuñis, and the broad belts after the manner of the Navajos." According to the descriptions in Matthews' and Spier's records, the smaller and, especially, the shorter articles were made on warps that could not be moved, each end being secured to the beam, or bar. Longer belts were made on warps that formed complete circles around two beams. In this way, the weaver of a long belt could keep his working point within convenient reach by rotating the warp as the work progressed. In his discussion of Zuñi weaving, Spier noted that long belts were made by a "tubular weaving" process, referring to the continuous warps. He cautioned that this technique should not be confused with belt-loom weaving, which simply refers to the method of securing one end of the loom to the weaver's waist, or his knees, with the tautness of the warp adjusted by his forward or backward movements. Spier felt that Zuñi and Hopi weavers were tending to prefer upright looms to belt looms. At Cochití, Spier (1924: 74–77) found that the belt loom was known but, as in the case of these other pueblos, the upright loom was preferred, a preference confirmed by my informants. [21, 44, 70]

The great number of dance kilts, *mantas*, sashes, belts, hair-ties, and knitted leggings, which, except for the belts and hair-ties, are restricted to ceremonial uses, are carefully kept by the owners. It is well recognized by the Cochití that there are few weavers continuing this art. With these items increasingly difficult to find, prices are steadily rising. The primary sources of woven articles at present are the Hopi and Zuñi, who capitalize on their virtual monopoly. [20, 24, 44, 45, 53]

Of interest also was a remark in Bandelier's journal of April 6, 1882, in which he noted that "Juan José has been all day sewing a white shirt for himself. He does it well." With no further elaboration, one wonders if this might have been the type of embroidered dress shirt now associated primarily with the men of Isleta Pueblo. No comparable statement has been found for Cochití, and the point could not be checked with informants.

Hides and Pelts. Again, in Bandelier's journals, there are several references to the working of leather items. On November 9, 1880, he noted a man pounding a hide with a stone to prepare it for moccasins. This is still done but only for the stiffer hide which is used for moccasin soles. [92] A few days later, on the fifteenth, Bandelier was shown two shields. The larger one was of double buffalohide, decorated with a painting of a bull's head on a half-moon. The smaller one, of a very thick single hide, had a cover of deerskin on which stars had been painted. On the eighteenth, Bandelier was shown a shield by Juan José that his father had made more than fifty years earlier. "His father pounded the hide with a smooth stone in a hole in the ground twice until it was perfectly smooth on both sides. It could be turned and used either way." (Plate 24c) In an entry of April 16, 1882, he gave the term "a'tshañi" for well-cured buffalo leather and called it the best for moccasin soles. A buffalohide with full hair was called "tsha-rana"; one with short hair, used, was called "mitze."

Hides and pelts are still valued by the Cochití, but their use is limited to ceremonial garments, moccasins, leggings, and drum heads. Historical accounts frequently mentioned buffalo- and deer-hides used for robes and other articles of clothing. When the Eicke-meyers (1895: 97) were in one home in 1894, they noted on the floor "several old buffalo skins with very little fur left on the surface, showing they had been trampled upon for many years."

Hides of various animals are prepared in a similar manner. The hide is split up the belly and removed in one piece, though the hide of the head, tail, and lower limbs is not removed ordinarily (Plate 16b). Then it is placed in a large bucket and soaked in a mixture of brains, or sometimes of oak bark and roots, or mountain mahogany. After being placed over a log and allowed to dry partially, a blunt draw-shave, or similar beaming tool, is used to scrape off the hair. If it does not come off readily, the hide is soaked again. Hide intended for leggings or moccasin uppers is rubbed with brains to soften it; for moccasin soles and drum heads, the last step is unnecessary. [21, 44]

Adult moccasins—ha'sh^yūme, *zapatos*, "shoes"—currently sell for about $6.00 a pair, $9.00 or $10.00 if leggings are attached. Many women prefer moccasins with detachable leggings because of the convenience. For reasons of comfort, leggings are seldom worn in the homes. For ceremonial dances and other occasions they are put on and, when carefully wrapped, look the same as the long, old-fashioned, attached type.

Since deerskins are scarce, most moccasins and leggings are made of cowhide. Drum heads are of cowhide, horsehide, or sometimes burrohide. Deerskins were formerly used for drum heads but are seldom used in this way at present. Hides are often blackened with liquid shoe polish after the heads are on the drum. Moccasins and leggings are either left white or stained a reddish-brown with dye made from mountain mahogany roots and bark mixed with lime. Both colors are used by both sexes, according to personal preference. For dances and special occasions, soles of the white moccasins are often blackened with shoe polish; those of red moccasins are generally left as they are, white or light tan. Tendon from the legs and spinal area of deer or cattle is used to sew the moccasins and they are fastened with either thongs or silver buttons. They are seldom beaded.

At dances, anklets, or ankle guards, of skunkskin are used, both for the masked and unmasked ceremonies. These are separate, are made from half a skin, and are tied over the moccasin around the ankle. Bourke (1884: 38) observed the Santo Domingo dancers in 1881 wearing moccasins trimmed with goat hair. It would be interesting to know whether this observation was accurate (most of Bourke's are considered valid), and, if so, how long ago skunkskin began to be used for this purpose, and why. Although the observations made by Bourke were for Santo Domingo, that pueblo and Cochití have been so similar in their culture that it is possible they shared a common experience in this particular feature.

At present most men, women, and especially children wear shoes bought from stores. High-heeled cowboy boots, saddle shoes, and street shoes and boots are commonly worn. Unlike the Santo Domingo (White 1935: 23), the Cochití approved of heeled footgear quite some time ago.

The Cochití still have a few of the old buffalohide ka'tsína masks; for new masks, the usual material is cowhide, since deerhide is not rigid enough. In some instances, commercial harness or boot leather is used for the masks as well as for other objects, such as wrist or arm bands.

Beadwork. In his journal of April 4, 1882, Bandelier mentioned having been shown by the war captain, Pomocena, how they drilled the bits of sea shell of which they made necklaces. The drilling went very rapidly: "They need but one hand for the drill, the other holds the shell in a little concavity, scraped out in a piece of wood." Among the photographs taken by Starr at the end of the last century is one of a man engaged in this work. (See Plate 18*b*.)

In his diary of September 19, 1897, Starr said that according to Santiago Quintana the Cochití used iron points for drilling shell beads and flint points for turquoise. He was also told:

> The pump drill has come in only within a little time—perhaps seventeen or eighteen years; . . . before then the turquoise bit was held in a block on one knee and the simple drill shaft was rolled between the open palm and the right leg; . . . it was very slow work; . . . even now it takes time and he spent two days in drilling one thin plate of turquoise he showed me. As for the shell, it is now brought on the train by the barrels full to the trader. Formerly, parties went from here to the Coast and then brought back burro loads of it. Then a little string—three inches long—cost $5; now 50 cents. Navajo are crazy for turquoise beads, giving a blanket for a single fair-sized plate; . . . Mokis, Zuñis, and others all desire it and pay a fine price—though less than the Navajos.

The discrepancy between Starr and Bandelier about the ease of drilling may be due to the fact that Starr had reference to drilling turquoise whereas Bandelier watched the drilling of shell. Starr's note concerning the appearance of the pump drill there is also of interest, though its recency may have been somewhat overstated.

The Eickemeyers (1895: 97) described the manufacture of shell beads at Cochití as follows: "They are made of shells obtained from the traders, and are strung after holes have been bored in them with hand drills, then all together are ground in a circular form with a stone used for the purpose." Beads of shell and stone are still made in the same way. A hand, or pump, drill is used to bore individual beads, after which they are strung on wire and ground down evenly on a fine-grained slab of sandstone. [15, 40, 44, 53] In 1939, Lucinda Cordero Suina of Cochití was awarded a first prize at the New Mexico State Fair for her shell beadwork. (United Pueblos Agency, *Quarterly Bulletin*, I: 1: 39) By trade, purchase, or gift from white friends, the Cochití acquire such shells as abalone and olivella to enhance their ceremonial paraphernalia.

While some beads continue to be made and used in the traditional way, the women currently do most of the beadwork with glass and other beads obtained through trade channels. Leather bags, decorated with both beads and tinklers cut from pieces of tin cans, are made for ceremonial use and the tourist trade. ("Condensed-milk cans are better; they have a prettier sound." [16]) Belts and a few vests and gloves are similarly beaded. Favorite designs include flags, flowers, Indian profiles with war bonnets, bows and arrows, and geometric patterns.

The most prevalent form of beadwork is the lapel ornament, made from scraps of dyed leather obtained from trading posts. These are decorated with beadwork and are sewed in numerous patterns, including drums, horseshoes, butterflies, rabbit's feet, miniature moccasins, sombreros, and Plainslike cradle boards and papooses. Each is attached to a small safety pin, and cards of various assortments are seen in practically all trading posts. Women spend hours of their free time sitting together under a *ramada*, talking and doing beadwork. Beads of assorted colors are purchased by the tube and usually placed in a shallow dish for the women to choose as they need them. Some cut out leather pieces with small scissors for others to assemble and bead. This is a year-round industry, receiving special emphasis before the Santa Fe Fiesta early in September and before each weekend trip to Santa Fe or Albuquerque. Some trinkets are sold singly, usually for about twenty-five cents. Many are sold at half this price in lots of one hundred, or several hundred, on orders from trading posts. [13, 16, 18, 23, 24, 27, 28]

Another form of handicraft comparable to beadwork is the assortment of necklaces and bracelets made from dyed muskmelon seeds and corn kernels, dyed or unstained, which are strung on leather strips. These, again, are made by almost every family. The seeds are generally dyed with stain obtained by soaking colored crepe paper in water. [28, 45]

Jewelry. Silver pieces are the most outstanding form of jewelry manufactured at Cochití. An attempt to fix a date of origin for this work was not very successful.

According to Adair (1944: 194), silverwork was first done at Isleta in 1879, at Santo Domingo about 1893, at Santa Ana about 1890, at Santa Clara about 1880, and at San Ildefonso about 1930, with no data offered for Cochití. One informant was of the opinion that a Navaho had been brought to Cochití to teach silversmithing, though he could not remember the date. [50] Another stated that there were no silversmiths in Cochití in 1910, but he could not remember how soon after that the trade was started, nor by whom. [45] They concurred in the belief that silver was not worked at Cochití prior to this century. [38, 40, 44, 45, 47, 50, 70, 71]

According to others, Reyes D. Suina was the first man at Cochití to do silversmithing, beginning in 1918. The following year he was joined by Rosendo Trujillo, and in 1929, by Salvador Arquero. [55, 64] After several years, a number of others took up the art. Others working silver in recent years have been Alfred Herrera (began in 1932?) and Selviano Quintana. These two earn their livelihood entirely from this occupation. Part-time workers include: Aloysius Pecos, Juan Estévan Chávez, Gerónimo Quintana, Cresencio Suina (began in 1938?), José María Suina, and Solomon Suina. Celestino Quintana has done silverwork for a trading post in Santa Fe. Two women—Reyecita Ortiz Bowannie, formerly married to a Zuñi, and María Crucita Quintana—are the only women at Cochití who have worked silver. The older smiths learned their trade from Mr. Julius Gans, a Santa Fe trader, for whom a number of Cochití are presently working. Younger boys are learning the craft at the Indian schools, but several older smiths do not feel they are being taught properly. [3, 15, 20, 38, 40, 50, 55, 70]

Adair (1944: 208) wrote about the Cochití silversmiths as follows: "At Cochití there are five smiths who do work for a company in Santa Fe and bring their work into town periodically. Joe Quintana is one of the most successful of these smiths. He reported that he had made $1,000 from working silver during the last year, working at his bench from nine to ten hours a day. In design the silver made at this pueblo is Navajo in type." In 1947 the silversmith named by Adair had given up the trade in favor of a welding business in the pueblo, which in turn was abandoned in 1948 when he went to Bakersfield, California, to work on a sheep ranch where his father-in-law, Juan

Estévan Chalan, had worked for many winters. By 1951, Joe had returned to New Mexico and was again employed as a silversmith for a trading post near Cochití. Incomes of other silversmiths were not obtained.

Most Cochití silversmiths who work at home do contract jobs for trading posts. The trader furnishes a bench and some tools, though most smiths own the greater portion of their equipment. The trader gives the smiths an order for so many rings, bracelets, or, occasionally, other items, of specific styles and patterns. Settings of turquoise or petrified wood are sometimes mounted there, or the silver work may be returned to the trader to pass on to other workmen to cut, polish, and mount the stones. Traders know exactly how much silver has been allotted, and the same amount in finished products, with scraps, must be returned. In recent years, a much greater variety of articles —spoons, pins, cigarette cases, flasks, and complete place settings— is being made. Copper articles are also produced. [38, 40, 47, 71]

The concluding remarks of Adair's study (1944: 188–189) are summarized here because they are pertinent in emphasizing the conformity of certain aspects of Cochití silversmithing with those of other Eastern Pueblos and in pointing out still other features of Cochití silverworking which deviate from patterns found in neighboring pueblos.

Silversmithing in the Eastern Pueblos was a thriving trade from 1880 to 1900, with a decrease in the number of smiths during the next twenty years. "About 1920 many young men took up the craft, but they did not learn it from the older smiths in the Pueblos. For the next ten years the population of smiths increased." In this time span, Cochití apparently escaped the nineteenth-century surge, but it did join in the development about 1920, with a Santa Fe trader instigating the movement, according to Adair:

As more tourists flocked to the Southwest, the demand for "tourist silver" increased. This steadily growing market created a demand for more and more smiths. The returned students in the pueblos were quick to realize that here was a trade which did not require long years of professional training, and the craft could be carried on in the pueblo, or one could get a job at one of the bench-shops in Santa Fe or Albuquerque. The owners of these bench-shops found that it was difficult to keep Navajo smiths on the job. They would continually run off to the reservation to attend a squaw-dance or a Yeibichai. Therefore, the shop owners began to hire Pueblo boys.

We find a complete break in the tradition of pueblo silversmithing. The smith of fifty years ago worked in the pueblo and made jewelry of fine design for the residents of his village. His craft was but a part-time occupation.

The modern pueblo smith, for the most part, makes silver in the bench-shop of the near-by cities. The silver which he makes is sold to the white man and is apt to be light in weight and stereotyped in design. For him the craft has become a full-time factory worker's job.

Thus we see that silversmithing, although a comparatively recently acquired craft among the Navajo and Pueblo Indians, is nevertheless of importance in their culture and their economy.

While the increase in the number of smiths in recent years is evident at Cochití, the pueblo has not experienced the general break in the tradition of Pueblo silversmithing which Adair described for the Eastern Pueblos in general. Most Cochití have continued the trade as a part-time homecraft. Two smiths work full time in the pueblo. Perfecto Herrera and several others from Cochití are working in Santa Fe bench-shops. (Such shops as Gans's in Santa Fe and Maisel's and Bell's in Albuquerque have employed many Indian workers with specialized skills. Work is generally organized on "assembly line" principles to expedite mass production.)

Wooden Objects. Bandelier, in his journal of October 27, 1880, mentioned that Juan José made saddle braces of cottonwood for burro saddles. The Eickemeyers (1895: 95) saw "saddles made in the pueblo, similar to our roping saddles, having pommels and rolls." No Cochití recalls any saddle-makers, except those who made the crude packsaddles for burros.

In Bandelier's entry of December 9, 1880, there were comments that bows were impregnated with tallow to make them bend more easily; also that arrowshafts were smoothed with stones which had a groove running lengthwise. The arrow was rubbed until it was smooth, polished, and straight. Bows and arrows, formerly of utilitarian value, are made at present almost entirely for ceremonial equipment or the tourist trade. They are often carried by chorus members in the Comanche Dance and various animal, or hunting, dances. In contrast are the observations of the Eickemeyers (1895: 98): "On the walls of the room were bows and arrows, some in course of construction, while others looked as if they had been used in killing birds and rabbits, a sport of which the Indian boy is fond. They all handle the bow and arrow with great skill."

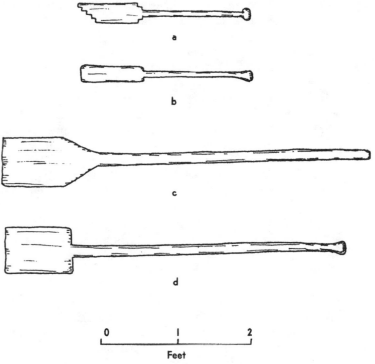

Fig. 14.—Stirring Sticks (a, b) and Oven Paddles (c, d).

Dumarest (1919: 152–153) noted in connection with cures by medicine men that "the invalid will have placed behind his head a bow and arrow, the proper means with which to frighten witches. They are the weapons of *masewa* [the war captain] and *masewa* fights against witches."

Until 1951 woodworking consisted primarily of implement repair, such as the shaping of new handles, generally of oak. Rabbit sticks are made, though they require little work other than stripping bark from the handle area. Stirring sticks for large cooking vessels and bread paddles are also made, usually of pine. Normally these are undecorated, though occasionally a stepped design is carved on the edges of the stirring-stick blades. (Fig. 14a)

Boys at boarding school are taught furniture-making, simple tables, chairs, stools, and chests being visible results of this training. Many families have well-constructed small wooden boxes, locally made, with sliding, grooved covers, in which ceremonial feathers are stored. [19, 44, 45]

In 1951 a training program for veterans was established at Peña Blanca in which several Cochití veterans, with others from Santo Domingo and Peña Blanca, were taught furniture-making. Their training included preparing and interpreting blue prints, compiling statements on materials and costs, and the actual cutting, assembling, and finishing of the pieces. Most articles were of a simple Spanish Colonial style with carving of Indian-design motifs incorporated. Veterans agreed not to dispose of any object for two years; after that time they could do as they pleased. It was hoped that at least some of them would pursue this potentially lucrative craft, and an inspection of finished articles and others in the process of completion late in the summer of 1951 indicated that many of these men had real talent. Whether it will be a development in the future economy of the pueblo, which now has electricity to run the power machines, remains to be seen. (It would seem from a brief visit in 1957 that this activity had already lapsed.)

Ceremonial objects are not commonly seen at Cochití, and data regarding them are difficult to obtain. Shrine offerings are prepared by the medicine men and deposited by them, the nonsociety members knowing virtually nothing of such matters. Ka'tsīna images seen on the walls of Cochití homes are from Hopi and elsewhere, the local ka'tsīnas not being reproduced in this manner.

Bourke (Bloom 1938: 234) observed carved images of saints, or *santos*, on the walls of various Cochití homes. Few of them were actually made by the Cochití; today even these have disappeared for the most part, their places having been taken by printed pictures of the saints and general religious subjects.

Stone Objects. Utilitarian objects of stone consist primarily of grinding tools—metates and manos. The Eickemeyers (1895: 95) saw "many stone implements such as spear, arrow, axe heads, and old mortars and pestles cut out of lava." Informants were unanimous that they had never seen stone axes used, though one roof, or ceiling, was pointed out as made of pine slabs hewn with a stone ax. [16, 44] Manos and metates are still in common use, and hammerstones are used to sharpen these implements, especially the manos. The mortars and pestles seen by the Eickemeyers were most likely metates and manos, as the other forms were unknown except for small mortars and pestles obtained from the Spaniards. Most items of stone at present are of a ceremonial nature; these are seldom seen by non-Cochití except where they have become a part of various museum collections.

Drums and Rattles. Among traders, many tourists, and other Southwestern tribes, Cochití is perhaps best known for its drums. This fame developed both from drums made for the tourist trade and from those used at Cochití. Drums of the latter type are obtained by other tribes for their own ceremonies. In comparison, comments of the Eickemeyers (1895: 100–101) again provide interesting data in time perspective:

> From the ceiling were suspended ten or eleven drums, which the Indians consider sacred.
> The beating of the drum is not an uncommon sound at any hour of the night in the pueblo, whether at a sacred meeting in the estufa or a gathering in the plaza. The Indian is very reluctant to sell these drums. In fact, we could not buy one at any price, although we tried at several places.

Thus, it would seem that the Eickemeyers, visiting in 1894, preceded the development of drums for the tourist trade; to a non-Cochití, or at least a non-Indian, the ceremonial drums were not for sale.

The attempt to date the transition from the attitude encountered by the Eickemeyers brought from one informant the explanation that in 1926 a small drum, perhaps a toy, was taken to Rael's store and sold for fifteen cents. This preceded a secret dance, and the seller needed money for some purchase. The drum was shown by Rael to a wholesaler as an example of Cochití craft, and, as a result, an order was given to Rael for a hundred, or more, like it. Thus began the tourist trade in drums at Cochití. [65]

Drums for the tourist trade are essentially the same as those for domestic use. The principal difference is that those for the Indians are usually larger (12 to 30 inches in diameter and the same range in height); a few are medium-sized. All drums are referred to by the same term, "o-ya-pom'potz." Drum sticks are "o'patz." The old commercial snare drum used on the Feast Day and to accompany the little horse that appears on Santiago's Day is called "o-ya-pī'nitz." [3, 15, 48, 49, 53] One informant stated that these are the only terms used to refer to drums, no other designations or specific names being applied. [25] But another informant stated that the large drums used for the dances are also referred to as "Pai'yat-yama," a term meaning "youth," "young gentleman," "master," or some similar concept of honor. [55] Confirmation and elaboration of this point was not obtained.

An informant, about sixty years old, remembered seeing a single-headed flat drum used in the pueblo. "These were used by the Cochití for their Comanche Dances." The stick used was the hoop-stick. This informant claimed the Cochití also used the basket drum, made of buckskin stretched tightly over an Apache basket; it was beaten with the same hoop-stick. "This made a quieter, dull sound, not like our drums now." [49] All informants, several of whom had seen Navaho and Apache pottery, or water, drums, said they were never used at Cochití.

Among the drum-makers at Cochití, Lorenzo Herrera, Marcelo Quintana (Plate 26b), Pablo Trujillo, and Santiago Herrera are recognized by the Cochití as outstanding. Others include Epitacio Arquero, Eufrasio Suina, Juan José Suina, José Rey Suina, Fernando Cordero, Ramón Herrera (Plate 16a), Lorenzo Cordero, Eleuterio Cordero, and Juan Velasquez. At one time or another, most Cochití men have manufactured drums, though not all continue actively engaged in the work. The women often paint the sides and heads and occasionally mount the drum heads.

Mountain cottonwood, or aspen (hī'ash-kŭ-lī), is used for drum sides (Plate 16a). Heads are of cow- or horsehide, rarely deerhide. The Eickemeyers (1895: 67) stated that heads were made of sheepskin, but informants doubted this. Formerly, burrohides were occasionally used. Well-made drums have one head of flank hide and the other of the thicker hide from the back of the animal. This difference in thickness causes the drum to have two "voices." The same effect is achieved by making the surface of one head greater than the other. Dance drums normally have two voices, but commercial drums are rarely prepared in this way intentionally. [62] Both in the dance drums and the larger ones made for tourists, one-eighth-inch holes are drilled in the sides (two close together [25]; one on each side [23]) under the tie thongs enables the air to escape more easily as the drum is beaten. [24, 62, 88]

Some drums are undecorated, but most, whether for the tourist trade or for ceremonial purposes, are painted on the sides. If ceremonial drums are repainted, they are redecorated in exactly the original manner. Thus, a drum can always be recognized by its colors and pattern, for no two are alike. [55] Heads are most commonly blackened with shoe polish. Tourist drums are generally painted with poster paint, whereas the more permanent native pigments are used for the dance drums. [16, 27, 44, 45, 49]

As of 1951, cowhides costing about three dollars were used for heads. For drums 8 to 10 inches in diameter, about twenty heads could be cut; the thick hide from the neck and chest is not used. [62]

At the Golden Gate International Exposition, twenty-one Cochití Indians were reported to have made total sales of $254.25, mostly from drums. (This was second high to sales of $282.55 for twenty-eight Indians of Santa Clara Pueblo.) "A drum maker from Cochití who has won several prizes for his products received the largest amount, $135.70, of all Pueblo contributors." (United Pueblos Agency, *Quarterly Bulletin*, I: 2: p. 15). At the 1939 New Mexico State Fair, "Fernando Cordero illustrated for spectators the process of drum-making from seasoned aspen block to finished product" (*ibid.*, I: 1: p. 7). Elsewhere in the same bulletin it was noted that a drum of Eleuterio Cordero of Cochití was awarded first prize (*ibid.*: 39). At the 1940 Fair, Lorenzo Herrera, lieutenant governor of Cochití, demonstrated drum-making (*ibid.*, II: 1: p. 3), and José Rey Suina received first prize for his drum (*ibid.*: 6). Several Cochití have demonstrated drum-making at these and other expositions of Indian arts and crafts, and the Cochití consistently monopolize awards in this particular craft.

Drum-making is done the year around, with more men working during the winter when they are free from farm work. Tourist drums are generally made in groups, i.e., several log sections are hollowed, smoothed, and shaped; the heads are placed on the whole group; finally all are painted at the same time, though colors vary. [62] Drum-stick heads are best made of layers of hide, but cloth is often substituted on those destined for the tourist trade. [23, 32]

Large dance drums sell from $30.00 to $60.00 or more, depending upon the size, workmanship, and "voice." Drums about 10 inches in diameter and 18 inches high sell between $8.00 and $20.00. One drum-maker has all but ceased making drums because of the excessive time spent in relation to income received. He has changed to small rattles which look like drums. For seventy-five cents he buys a goatskin from which he cuts heads for several dozen rattles. He uses river cottonwood (more easily available than the mountain cottonwood) and drills out the centers with brace and bit. For these drum-rattles—the size of a small tin of canned milk—he receives

0   6   12

Inches

Fig. 15.—Gourd Rattles.

fifty cents apiece wholesale or from seventy-five cents to a dollar retail. With electricity now available, he plans to replace his hand drill with an electric drill. With all materials on hand, he can make a five-hundred-unit order in a few days of steady work. Painting with poster paints takes most of the time. However, the profit is much greater in relation to the time spent than if he were making drums.

In Bandelier's journal of April 12, 1882, he recorded an account by Juan José of how to make gourd rattles and various utensils:

[He] told me how they prepared their calabashes or gourds to make vessels out of them. After cutting off the stem end, they cooked it with pounded seeds of water-melons. Then poured water inside so as to rot the flesh, grain, fibre, etc. When the inside is all rotten they pour water again mixed with broken flint or obsidian and shake it well, thus grinding and polishing the inside, until no trace of a stench is left.

Essentially the same procedure is followed today, except that with rattles, a hole is cut on each side rather than on the stem end. After being cleaned out, a handle is fitted on, the shaft going through the gourd, with a small wooden pin inserted to keep the handle on. Before the final assembling, a handful of small pebbles is placed inside. [42] (Fig. 15)

Painting. Watercolors and oil paintings are among the more recent forms of art among Pueblo and other Southwestern tribes. Dutton (1948: 52–56) and Tanner and Forbes (1948: 365–367) placed the origin at the end of the last century, when two Hopi, at Fewkes's suggestion, began drawing ka'tsīnas. Chapman and Hewett were also instrumental in developing hidden talents they found among various New Mexico Indians. Much of the original impetus occurred at San Ildefonso about 1910 (Tanner and Forbes 1948: 373–375).

At Cochití, one of the most famous painters was Tonita Peña, who was born at San Ildefonso in 1894 and died at Cochití in 1950. Upon the death of her parents, very early in life, Tonita went to Cochití to live with her mother's sister. At fourteen, she married Juan Rosario Chávez. Thus, at the time of the San Ildefonso art development, Tonita was already residing at Cochití. For many years, she was one of the few women artists, and her artistic development was largely an independent one. Tanner and Forbes (1948: 365–377) characterized her work as follows:

Charm of hand work and accuracy of reproduction are combined in the several paintings of Cochiti pottery by Tonita Peña. The same clean line-work is carried over to her paintings of dance figures. No grounds appear in any of the examples of this Collection, as is also characteristic of the artist in question. Her work reveals a delicacy of figure, fine detail, a softness of line. Flat colors predominate, with an occasional bit of shading or modeling suggested in simple line-work. As is true of several of these artists, Tonita Peña reveals certain little traits in facial treatment which generally may be noted in her paintings. For example, both men and women are thick-lipped, the men particularly have long straight noses, and there is a vertical line between the mouth and cheek.

Tonita stated that there had been little objection at Cochití to her painting dance figures. There had been trouble during a year in which her third husband, Epitacio Arquero, was governor. He defended her by pointing out that since she was drawing only those dancers who could be seen by any outsider it was no more harmful for her to do this than it was for others to make their pottery and sell it. This reasoning apparently satisfied the objectors. After that, she had continued to paint only figures of an exoteric nature. Examples of her work include murals at the La Fonda Hotel in Santa Fe and several items in the New Mexico Art Museum in Santa Fe.

Possibly because of the influence of Tonita and because of encouragement from museum personnel and Indian School officials, others at Cochití have become well known in art circles. Among the younger painters are José Hilario Herrera (son of Tonita Peña), Teodore Suina, Cipriana Romero, Manuel "Bob" Chávez, Andrew Trujillo, and Victor Herrera. In 1940, Ben Quintana of Cochití won the Youth Administration Prize of $1,000 in competition with more than fifty thousand contestants. (Dutton 1948: 54–55) In this same contest, Cipriana Romero won third prize.

Some art work is done in school, but the greatest part is done at home, generally as part-time work, though two or three individuals devote most of their time to painting. Work is done almost exclusively with casein water colors on high-grade art paper obtained from traders, the museum, or schools. Subjects include dancers, group ceremonials, scenes from daily life, and many animals, especially horses, rabbits, deer, and bears. Traditional styles, without horizon or perspective, are followed by most artists.

Perhaps the most deviant art forms have come in recent years from José Hilario Herrera. In a discussion of his work, Dunn (1952: 367) commented:

Joe Herrera, in two summer exhibitions at the Art Gallery of the Museum of New Mexico, has convincingly demonstrated the fact that current American Indian painting which incorporates prehistoric design and techniques can be entirely modern. His paintings are thoroughly contemporary in style, but that is due to the coincidence of their appearing at a time when the general trend in painting is toward the symbolic, the abstract, and the non-objective. His motifs are abstract, although to the casual observer certain of them might appear non-objective. They are symbolic of forms, events, and powers in aboriginal America, many of them as valid today as they were in pre-Columbian times. Herrera paints clouds and rain, stars and planets, the corn, man and his fellow animals, the sacred serpent and supernatural beings not unlike their interpretations on rock and adobe walls in ancient days.

Actually, there is very little in this new phase of Herrera's art that is not natively Indian. Paper, adopted by Indian painters of late years, is really its only non-native component. The paint, casein tempera combined by the artist in natural-toned palette, has its counterpart in native earthcolors which were frequently mixed with milk. The techniques of spray and brush have been employed for untold years in Pueblo painting, with mouth as atomizer and yucca fibre as tuft. The newness of this painting lies in Herrera's own imaginative use of techniques, materials, and motifs that have belonged to American Indian art for centuries.

Several informants stated that formerly, in school and elsewhere, they had enjoyed painting and drawing. Several had considerable talent and expressed hopes of painting again, attracted perhaps by the relative success of other artists. [45, 52, 53, 62] Individuals, sitting idly talking with a group, often amuse themselves and any nearby children by drawing horses, eagles, and similar figures in the smoothed-off adobe ground.

Nonagricultural Community Work

Nonagricultural communal tasks have greatly decreased in recent years. These include church repairs; cleaning up; the raking, sweeping, and hauling of debris before the annual Feast Day; repair of roads, bridges, and other communal works; the repair or construction of houses for the several societies that function for the common good; and the renovation of kivas and community houses before Feast Day. Such work is nonincome-producing, but it is of economic significance in its demands upon the time and labor of the people.

The war captains, assisted by the Ku-sha'lĭ or Kwe'rana members, depending upon who has the responsibility for a particular year, supervise the annual village cleanup and renovation of the kivas and community houses. Each family cleans up its own yard and piles the debris along the roadways, or, if there is a great amount, hauls it to a distant arroyo. Pueblo members rake the streets and roadways, and wagons haul off the debris. The plaza is not only raked, but swept. Before the winter dances, shovels and push boards are used to remove the snow. Again, this is communal labor directed by the war captains. As in other matters, there appears to be a growing laxity on the part of many people to join in this labor, while the usual public-spirited group of "old faithfuls" help repeatedly. Officialdom seems to be yielding to this trend, except for extreme cases of malingering, when public opinion can be depended upon to support whatever disciplinary action is taken. [20, 21, 42, 44, 45, 49, 70]

If a society needs more adequate quarters for its functions, it can request a new house of the governor and council. "Then the people would have to build it for them." Such work is under the supervision of the governor and war captain, in consultation with society members. [3, 44, 45] For moiety work, as on a kiva or community house, workers are recruited by the kiva head, with the close co-operation of the war captain or the assistant war captain, whoever belongs to the kiva in question.

Road work and similar tasks are directed by the governor and his lieutenant. The two *fiscales* also help in these activities, and, in turn, they are assisted by the governor and his lieutenant in supervising the upkeep of the church. Present care of the church consists of re-plastering in preparation for the annual Feast Day and constructing the temporary booth, or shrine, in the plaza for the statue of the patron saint. The *fiscales* also keep the church grounds clean and supply firewood during Masses in the cold months. [3, 20, 45, 52, 53]

In the Domínguez report of 1776 (Biblioteca Nacional, *Legajo X: Document 43*), the *convento* staff at Cochití included a weekly shift of herders for the priests' sheep, cattle, chickens, pigs, and horses. In addition there were, as permanent positions, one *fiscal mayor*, three assistants, eight sacristáns, a head sacristán, eight cooks, and four bakers. Service was so rotated that each week there were on duty one *fiscal*, two sacristáns, two cooks with two boys to carry water, and a baker. The report also noted that the pueblo furnished all necessities for the maintenance of the mission. In former times, when a resident priest was in the pueblo, such community effort necessary for his support created additional work and provoked many protests from the Indians of abuses by the friars. (See Chap. 2, n. 5.)

Another form of community labor, not performed in the last twenty or thirty years, was the operation of the ferryboat which facilitated travel between Cochití and Peña Blanca. This work was discontinued after the construction of the highway bridge, but the older men clearly recall serving as crew members in their youth. The ferryboat was operated under the supervision of the governor by crews of three men who changed daily. One man poled, or paddled, on each side while the third guided the ferry from the stern. Another informant stated that there were sometimes four crew members, the additional one standing at the prow to secure the ferry to the shore (apparently at those times when the current was running more swiftly). [3] Others stated that this fourth man was simply the one whose wagon was being ferried across. Fees were charged non-Cochití. [40, 50, 53,

59] (See Bandelier's description of this boat, p. 60.) Footbridges were also maintained by community labor, as described on pages 57–60.

Community Licenses and Fees

The tribal treasury benefits from licenses and fees, sold by the governor and other officers, or by the council as a whole, to outsiders who wish to conduct various business ventures on the reservation. The funds they provide are spent for the good of the community on such things as machinery and other necessary equipment..

Soon after the Second World War, a lease was sold to a company to mine pumice in the northwestern corner of the reservation. Several such mines were already operating on the adjacent Santa Fe National Forest lands. Before operations began, the lease was canceled by the council for some unstated reason. No lease for mining pumice has been granted since that time. [3, 45, 53]

Another form of license, or permit, is issued by the governor to proprietors of numerous concessions operated in the pueblo on feast days, especially that of July 14. Such stands are seldom operated by the Cochití. There have been a number of concessionaires who make a continual round of Pueblo feast days and fiestas of Spanish-American communities of New Mexico. Fees vary from year to year, depending upon the general economic situation, the moods of the officers and councilmen, and to a great extent upon whether the particular feast falls on a week end—which means a larger crowd, and, hence, the likelihood of charging a higher fee. In years when Feast Day falls on a week end, there are entire carnival units, complete with Ferris wheels and other attractions, as well as the smaller stands. In 1947, local Spanish traders arranged a *baile*, or Spanish dance, the night before, and of, Feast Day, erecting a board platform, or dance floor, covered with a large, open-sided tent. They paid a fee of $25 for this. In 1948, a similar request met the council's demand for a fee of $50, and the *baile* plans were abandoned. Very likely, the council had such a result in mind in asking this fee, since Feast Day was not on a week end. [3, 15, 20, 21, 45]

At the 1948 Feast Day, cars were charged twenty-five cents for parking in the pueblo, unless the owners were friends of some specific family and parked in their yard. This was the first time a charge had been made for parking at Cochití. [20, 42, 54] In 1947, during the dancing, a visiting Kwe'rana from Tesuque who participated in the dancing took up a collection from the spectators. Informants said afterwards numerous Cochití had not liked this innovation (though the proceeds went to the tribe); such a collection had never been taken before at their pueblo. [3, 23, 27, 44, 45] It may be that the 1948 charge for parking was a compromise measure; it brought in revenue for the pueblo and yet was not connected with the ceremony as such. In other pueblos—San Felipe, Santo Domingo, and some Tewa villages—the practice of taking a collection from spectators, generally from non-Indians only, has been in force for several years. Parking charges are also common.

At the 1951 Cochití Feast Day, a parking charge was made within the near vicinity of the plaza. When officers approached several cars, the occupants informed them that they had already paid a parking fee as they crossed the steel bridge north of the pueblo. Several officers went in a pickup truck to investigate and found three young men from Santo Domingo at the bridge illegally collecting from the unsuspecting visitors. Charges against the three were presented to the Santo Domingo governor, who brought the men to a subsequent meeting of the Cochití council. After some discussion, they were fined $15.00 each by the Cochití council, and the Santo Domingo governor guaranteed that the fines would be paid as soon as possible. By the end of the summer, one had paid $5.00; the other fines were still outstanding. [20, 42, 44, 45]

In many pueblos a fee is assessed for photographing. Cochití has charged commercial photographers for some years, the amount being an arbitrary assessment by the governor who gives, or withholds, permission. In 1951, a fee of $2.50 was initiated for uncommercial photography as well; under the officers of 1952, it was set at $1.50. In the absence of the governor, another officer can give permission. This permission allows the photographing of anything in the pueblo or on the reservation except the kivas (a restriction imposed to pacify the "old people" [71]). Pictures of persons are matters of individual arrangement. Most ceremonies cannot be photographed, sketched, or noted. A few exceptions occur during the Christmas dancing season, when there are dances "that aren't our own, like the Laguna, or Hopi, or Zuñi dances." As these are ceremonies, nevertheless, permission to photograph them must be obtained not from the governor but from the war captain. Fees from such permits also go into the tribal treasury. [20, 42, 44, 45, 53]

Wage-earning within the Pueblo

There are occasional opportunities to work for wages within the pueblo, or on the reservation. However, over a period of years, income from these sources has been relatively negligible.

Among the Cochití who reside in the pueblo, agriculture is the basic economic interest. The labor is done by the owner of the field, or livestock; when additional help is required, members of the immediate or extended family are called to help. Payment for such services invariably takes the form of reciprocal aid—a principle practiced in the nonagricultural economy as well. Repairing or building a house is a project shared in by members of a family. [23, 32, 38 45]

In his journal of November 28, 1882, Bandelier noted some details of house construction. Whether this was a private dwelling or a tribal society house is not stated:

> They are building a roof on the house. The adobes (very irregular) are up, and a number of boys throw the dirt up with shovels, while men and boys equalize it and stamp it on the Roof. Women and girls carry water in large Tinajas, Caxetes, etc. A fire is burning near, and it is a source of enjoyment rather than toil. It is communal work, and the workers change in and out as they please. Some of the Principals appear to superintend it.

If Bandelier's identification was correct, the presence of *principales* in a supervisory capacity would suggest a public project; on the other hand, it may have been simply a coincidence that certain *principales* were related to the private builders. Still another possibility is that under the older and more rigid control of daily life, the tribal leaders actually had a voice in the construction of private dwellings. Even today, they retain the right to assign tracts of land for building purposes.

While the traditional mode of operation is still generally in force, paying cash wages to workers who are not related is not unknown. An example of this occurred when three men were employed in building a home (Plate 15*b*) for José Hilario Herrera, the artist, in 1948. Joe's stepfather, Epitacio Arquero, served as the foreman. He was assisted by Lorenzo Cordero, whose only "relationship" was that his wife, Priciliana Roybal, was born in San Ildefonso, as was Joe's mother, Tonita Peña. However, the two women were unrelated, aside from the fact that all San Ildefonso people had affiliated with the Oak Clan upon their arrival in Cochití, regardless of their earlier affiliations at San Ildefonso. [3, 16, 17, 45, 55, 70] The third workman was Nicanor Cordero, for whom no relationship with the owner of the new home was found. Although the wages paid were not learned, it was understood that payment was on a cash basis. [17, 45, 55] Before these workers were hired, an attempt had been made to employ José Rey Suina, another unrelated man, to construct the house. He had had considerable experience and was recognized as an excellent builder. José Rey had said that he was too busy with his farming, drum-making, and other work to undertake this job, despite the cash wages offered. [3, 32, 38, 45, 55]

The Spanish-American traders occasionally hire part-time labor. Some cash wages are paid, but a large part is paid in extended credits —again a form of barter, services for supplies. [20, 44, 45]

Part-time work is obtainable on projects such as the bridge repairs that were carried on by the State Highway Department north of the pueblo in the summer of 1947. The foremen and some specialists were regular employees of the Highway Department, but the men and older boys of Cochití made up the rest of the crew. Such jobs are popular, as they allow the workers to remain at home, and the pay is relatively high. [47]

In 1931/32 many Cochití were employed on the construction projects of the Middle Rio Grande Conservancy District. [40, 53] This included the construction of Cochití Dam, a few miles north of the pueblo, and the irrigation canals on each side of the river.

Since the original construction, part-time jobs have been available with the District. This agency employs regular repair crews, maintenance personnel, and ditch riders, but it has periodic need for men to repair minor washouts and cut weeds along the canals. Clofe Arquero, a Cochití, has consistently been employed as a ditch rider on the west side; on the east side, various men, mostly Spanish-Americans, have worked. Their part-time helpers are invariably men from Santo Domingo or Spanish-Americans from Peña Blanca or Sile. The reason for this has been that other Cochití are usually busy with farming, craftwork, and other activities, and they are seldom interested in such steady employment. District ditch riders were hired, as of 1951, at the rate of eighty-one cents per hour for a forty-four-hour week during the irrigation season, normally about seven months long. [15, 44, 45]

The acquisition of the community combine harvester has provided wage-earning opportunities for a crew of two for approximately a month each summer. Harvesting begins about mid-July and lasts several weeks, with time off for Sundays, feast days of neighboring pueblos, and wet weather. Crew members are paid half in wheat and half in cash, ordinarily; some years the men have been paid entirely in cash. [20, 38, 44, 45]

The community formerly hired a fence rider, whom they paid $45 per month ($40 in 1946/47). The duties of this position, and details concerning it, are discussed on pages 218–219. Other remunerative positions include those of driver, or chauffeur, of the community-owned truck. They are also discussed in detail on page 219.

Wage-earning away from the Pueblo

Through the years there has been a tendency for a few Cochití to seek employment away from the pueblo. The case of Santiago Quintana, "Old Man Guerro," and his two companions' spending several years on the West Coast has been mentioned. Likewise, the cases of Juan Estévan Chalan and his son-in-law, Joe H. Quintana, who worked on sheep ranches near Bakersfield, California, and Isidro Cordero, who spent much of his life away from the pueblo while herding sheep in the Estancia area, have been cited. Bandelier mentioned a young man's leaving to herd sheep in the Navaho country (p. 111), and Starr noted in his diary of September 17, 1897, that Anastacio was "shepherding some sixty miles away."

For about three months, ending with the Armistice in November, 1918, about 13 Cochití men (among them were Clofe Arquero, Epitacio Arquero, Antonio Montoya, Juan B. Pancho, Justo Pérez, and Benigno Quintana), along with 10 from San Felipe and about 30 from Taos, worked at a large munitions plant near Nashville, Tennessee. There they worked with whites and Negroes, all under white supervision. Their bosses were surprised to learn that they were Indians—whom they had considered too lazy to work; they had concluded the men were Filipinos. Although segregation was enforced regarding the Negroes, the Indians went where they pleased, as there seemed to be no rules set up for them. [161]

In the First World War, no Cochití was in service. [44] In contrast, 33 served in the Second World War. Several individuals worked throughout the war years, or until the time they entered service, in various war industries, particularly on the West Coast. Social and other effects of these experiences are discussed more fully in subsequent chapters. Economically, the war years resulted in an appreciable increase in cash income for the pueblo as a whole, derived from industrial wages, service pay, and allotment checks sent to dependents of servicemen. Isabel Chávez Montoya, a lieutenant in the Army Nursing Corps, was the only woman in service.

The following Cochití were in service: Alvin Arquero, Nestor Arquero, Santiago Benada, Pancracio Chalan, Francisco Chávez, José Vivian Chávez, Juan Manuel Chávez, Lorenzo Chávez, Eleuterio Cordero, José Domingo Herrera, José Hilario Herrera, Justino Herrera, Lorenzo Herrera, Perfecto Herrera, Stephen Herrera, Juan R. Melchior, Isabel Chávez Montoya, Antonio Naranjo, Aloysius Pecos, José Dolores Pecos, Alfonso Pérez, Juan Pérez, Benigno Quintana, Delphine Quintana, José Adolfo Quintana, José Salvador Romero, Santiago Romero, José María Suina, José Solomon Suina, Octavio Suina, Teodoro Suina, and Onofre Trujillo.

Of 32 Cochití men, 22 saw overseas duty, 12 in Europe and 10 in the Pacific. Nineteen were in the Army; 7 were in the Navy; 4 were in the Air Corps; and 2 were in the Marine Corps. The highest rank attained was that of sergeant (Stephen Herrera, Aloysius Pecos, and Juan Pérez) and its Navy equivalent, seaman third-class (Pancracio Chalan and Francisco Chávez). Three died in the war: José Salvador Romero, in Europe; Alfonso Pérez, in a Japanese prison camp following Bataan; and Ben Quintana, in the Battle of Leyte. Ben was awarded the Silver Star posthumously. [15, 44, 49, 58, 70]

Of 30 veterans returning, 14 were in the pueblo and 16 resided elsewhere, as of the summer of 1948. Five had re-enlisted; of the 11 others who were living away, the majority were individuals who had already left the pueblo before their military service. Thus, no great change was indicated by their wage-earning away from the pueblo. [86] It was believed that no Cochití veteran, as of 1951, had maintained his government insurance following his discharge from the service. [20, 44, 55, 92]

By the summer of 1951, with the fighting in Korea and the general rebuilding of the armed forces, 24 Cochití were in service. These men were as follows (Second World War veterans marked with asterisk): Nestor Arquero,° Sam Arquero, Candelario Benada, Santiago Benada,° Phillip Herrera, Stephen Herrera,° Victor Herrera, Ralph Martin, Willy Martin, Santiago Naranjo, Natividad Pecos, Albert Pérez, Larry Pérez, José Adolfo Quintana,° Guadalupe Ortiz, Florentino Romero, Santiago Romero,° Pedro Suina, Tony Suina, Victor

Suina, Andrew Trujillo, Gabriel Trujillo, Juan Trujillo, and Lawrence Velasquez. Eighteen were in the Army; 4, in the Marines; and 1, each, in the Air Corps and Navy. Eight were in Korea or Japan; 2 were in Germany; the others were still in the United States. [20, 34, 44, 45, 62]

The present-day importance of wage-earning away from Cochití is probably best emphasized in the single statement (Payne 1942: 11) that in 1942 labor (most of which can be assumed to have been off-reservation employment) was the primary source of Cochití income, amounting to $20,214.49. The second highest source of income was from agriculture ($8,060.00), and the third highest was from stock-raising ($6,069.00). Allowing for the considerable home consumption known to have taken place with agricultural and stock produce, the importance of outside wage-earning remains unquestionably strong.

In the summer of 1948 and again in the summer of 1951, a complete census of Cochití was taken by the author, and an effort made, in each case, to ascertain the whereabouts of every individual on the tribal roll. While it is obvious that such a listing can be accurate only at the moment of compilation, it is clear evidence of the considerable part that wage-earning away from the pueblo plays in the total Cochití economy. Comparative analysis of these rosters reveals the following data: In 1948, of a total population of 423, there were 110 individuals (26 per cent) who did not normally enter into the life of the pueblo. Of the 110, two were confined in hospitals; 33 men and 30 women were gainfully employed; and 45 were members of families whose head was gainfully employed. Of the 110 away from the pueblo, 62 resided in Santa Fe and 19 in Albuquerque, both within sixty miles of Cochití. Twenty-nine lived in other places, ranging as far away as Washington, D.C., New York City, Wisconsin Dells, Denver, California, and Japan.

In contrast, in 1951 there was a total population of 438, of whom 154 individuals (35 per cent) did not normally enter into pueblo life. Of the 154 absentees, 24 (15.5 per cent) were in military service. Of the 154, at least 85 were gainfully employed. In addition, members of their families worked part-time and engaged in handicrafts of various types, which also produced additional income. Of the 154 absentees, 108 lived within sixty miles of Cochití, primarily in Santa Fe or Albuquerque.

Each week end a considerable number of these people return for a few hours' visit with their relatives. July 14 Feast Day, Christmas, and Easter are times when most absentees return for the day, at least, and some for several days. Not as many return for other celebrations, the lesser feast days, or native ceremonials.

Returning absentees rarely participate in actual ceremonies. Most are interested spectators, and some are hardly that, simply coming home to see relatives and friends and apparently holding themselves aloof from native aspects of celebration. Some tend to show more interest in the Spanish *baile* and similar activities. It is interesting that many absentees have married not only non-Cochití but, in several cases, non-Indians.

Economically, the exodus of these individuals from the pueblo has had several effects. There is less demand for agricultural lands. Working conditions and employer-employee relationships are outside the control of pueblo officials, thereby eliminating many forms of economic sanction formerly levied against those who deviated from the main cultural stream. Community-labor projects and tribal offices must be borne by fewer individuals, thereby increasing the economic disadvantages involved. If families seriously need financial aid, the absentee wage-earners are most likely to help. Pueblo community responsibility is thereby displaced by competitive considerations. Pueblo residents visiting the city homes of these absentees become envious of various conveniences and want the same, or comparable, improvements in their pueblo homes. The power of money is emphasized repeatedly in many situations, causing increased exodus from the village to wage-paying opportunities. Those who remain in the pueblo have reacted by a tendency to shift from subsistence, all-purpose agriculture to fewer and selected crops which can provide cash income. In some cases, agricultural pursuits have been completely forsaken in favor of commercial arts and crafts and for wage-earning.

7 POLITICAL ORGANIZATION

General Statements

AT COCHITÍ, political organization is an important factor, or influence, in the lives of the pueblo residents and also those who dwell away from the village more or less permanently. Conversely, the feelings of both groups are of direct concern to the officers who constitute the tribal governing personnel. In governing, Cochití officers are guided by no written laws, or a constitution, as are the officials of Laguna, Santa Clara, and Isleta. Instead, problems are met by the officers and council by means of innumerable "regulations," comprising a body of common law. This body of unwritten, yet efficacious, law is both rigid and flexible, as the situation demands, a generality that has been commented upon by Hoebel (1949: 370–371):

> Law exists in order to channel behavior so that conflicts of interest do not come to overt clash. It comes into existence to clear up the muddle when interests do clash. New decisions are ideally so shaped as to determine which interests best accord with the accepted standards of what is good for the society.

As Aberle (1948: 24) indicated, nothing is known of Pueblo civil organization, or government, in the pre-Spanish era: "Compared to the present-day civil organization, the pre-Spanish administration must have been considerably smaller and simpler, corresponding to the aboriginal economy." Parsons (1939: 1125–1126) was of the opinion that pre-Spanish political organization involved a town chief (cacique) and a war chief (outside chief), and that the duties of both were primarily religious and only secondarily civil. As Aberle and others have noted, present-day Pueblo offices known to have been set up by the Spanish may well have been native offices redesignated. On the other hand, they may have been complete innovations, in part if not in entirety. Regardless of whether or not the secular officers are wholly or partially native in origin, the influence of the religious leaders in secular matters has been, and, in most pueblos, continues to be, strong. Appendix 17 shows in diagram form the interrelationships existing between various parts of the political and ceremonial organizations.

However, at Cochití the religious hierarchy and the Conservatives, whom they regularly appoint to the secular offices, have slowly lost their control, a condition they are becoming increasingly aware of. They are eager to find some means of regaining this lost authority, though they desire as little change in the traditional system as possible. Whereas the people were formerly very sensitive to economic sanctions such as land confiscation and to punishments such as whipping, this is no longer true. Though retaining some control, the traditional government has become steadily weaker and is currently close to the point of being completely ineffectual. (See Lange 1952a.)

The six major secular officers—war captain and lieutenant war captain, governor and lieutenant governor, and *fiscale* and lieutenant *fiscale*—are chosen each year by the heads of the three medicine societies. The six *alguacilitos*, assistants to the war captains, are selected from among the younger men of the pueblo by members of the Council of *Principales*, each of whom is a former, or current, major officer, thereby demonstrating views consonant with those of the shamans.

Ordinarily, replacements are selected each year, though the same men are sometimes retained. If one officer is retained, it is customary to return the entire group of major officers to office. They can be retained only two consecutive years, after which they must be given at least one year's freedom from public office in order to regain their feet economically. Officers serve without monetary compensation, and the numerous meetings and other duties take much time ordinarily devoted to supporting their families. In recognition of this, major officers and their assistants are selected from the various households in such a way that no household in any year suffers the economic loss of more than one of its adult males. A few individuals have suggested that the officers be paid on a monetary basis, or at least be provided the community assistance in the same way that the cacique (and formerly the resident priest) is aided. While quite a number have expressed approval of such compensation, no one has been found who has any idea, or at least one who will commit himself, concerning what or how much this compensation should be. Thus far, no action has been taken. [3, 62]

According to pueblo "regulations," the three head officers are chosen from one kiva, and the three lieutenants, or "tenyets" (*tenientes*), from the other. The following year, unless the same men are returned to office, the head officers and lieutenants are alternated between the kivas. Formerly, according to Goldfrank (1927: 26) and my informants, the division of officers between kivas was on a somewhat different basis. The governor and war captain were picked from opposite kivas, with their lieutenants also alternated. The *fiscales*, under this former system, came from the same kiva as did the governors. [2, 25, 52]

One informant stated that this system is still followed at Santo Domingo, where, in 1952, there was a Turquoise governor and a Pumpkin war captain. He volunteered the additional comment that the present Cochití system, wherein all major officers are of one kiva, is not as good, i.e., it lacks the traditional balance which pervades the Pueblo world. [42] As noted by Bandelier, October 7, 1880, the clans "have nothing to do with the government proper."

Rosters of Cochití officers (Appendices 11–13) reveal that the current deviation of choosing all major officers from one kiva has been practiced for many years. According to representatives from both kivas, the monopoly of the head offices by the Turquoise membership began many years ago when all three head medicine men were of the Turquoise Kiva. (Some stated it began about 1930 [49]; others said it was before that time. [70])

The majority placed this shift as occurring at the time of, and involved with, the Conservative-Progressive controversy, in which the greater proportion of the Progressives came from the Pumpkin Kiva. One Turquoise member stated that the reason the Pumpkin men were not given head offices was that they were drinking too heavily. [45] Others stated that the lack of balance was caused purely by the personal bias of the head shamans. In the matter of interkiva feelings, an entry of Bandelier's for April 12, 1882, is of interest:

He then said that those of the Estufa of "Shyu-amo" [Turquoise] were always against the Pueblo, and that in consequence of it, there had been constant squabbles between them and the "Tanyi" [Pumpkin, the kiva of Bandelier's informant]. . . . The former went to Mexico to secure the citizenship of the Pueblo, still he says it was in the times of Spain. The latter sent a delegation also, who reached the City of Mexico after the former had already ret'd home. The citizenship was revoked, but in the meantime the Mexicans had already occupied the lands near Peña Blanca, and the Pueblo was split up. Subsequently came the epidemic, then the surrender of the Idols, which he also attributes to the "Shyu-amo," and the Pueblo was so reduced that only 25 men at arms were left at one time. This fixes the foundation of Peña Blanca to between 1816 and 1819. It also shows that the Estufa really indicated a phratry, or a cluster of gentes associating for purposes of dancing, and, through custom, of government.

Further political dissension has already been cited (p. 14). Again, on April 4, 1882, Bandelier made the following comments: "He says that there are at present two parties in all the pueblos, a conservative party, which clings to the old democratic customs, and a new one, which makes of the administration of justice rather a one-sided affair."

The present emphasis upon the Turquoise Kiva's recent monopoly of the senior offices is interesting in light of an observation by Dumarest (1919: 200) that at the end of the last century the governor was José Hilario Montoya, and that he had served in that capacity for almost ten years. The inference seems justified that this man—a member of the Pumpkin Kiva—held this office for the "almost ten years" consecutively. This point was noted too late to ask informants about it, but it is odd that no Turquoise Kiva member had mentioned it as a balancing factor for their resented monopoly of recent times.

As one council member of many years' experience commented, "Anyone who thinks that everything in an Indian pueblo is all calm and co-operation just simply doesn't know anything about pueblo politics." [3]

Installation of the Annually Selected Officers

The six major secular officers are selected each year by the three medicine-society headmen. The war captain and his lieutenant are

selected by the Flint head (the cacique); the governor and his lieutenant are selected by the Giant head; and the *fiscale* and his lieutenant, by the Shī'kame head. [3, 15, 92] Dumarest's statement
(1919: 197) that the cacique nominated all these officers was rejected by every informant as having ever been the case; no support
for the statement was found in Cochití or any other tribal data.

The ceremonies installing these officers extend over almost a week.
The incumbent officers go to the cacique on the evening of December 26 and inform him that they have worked hard throughout the
year and that their personal affairs have suffered from neglect; they
then request him to replace them. [44, 92] White (1942: 110) reported this same procedure for Santa Ana. Despite the fact that this
is regular procedure, it was interesting that a man of about sixty at
Cochití, one who had never served as an officer, was completely
unaware of this step. [53]

About this time of year the cacique (the head Flint shaman) calls
the Giant head—his "left hand"—and the Shī'kame head—his "right
hand"—to a meeting. [2] The terminology used here provides an interesting instance of culture change. The designations above came
from one of the oldest informants, a man of recognized knowledge.
When this point was checked, all other informants gave the Giant
head as the "right hand" of the cacique and agreed that the Giant
head is the first assistant; the Shī'kame is second. While the statement of the first informant was taken initially to be an error, it is
quite likely that he was correct and all the others were in error. At
Cochití, the greatest animal helper of the medicine men is the bear.
For some reason thus far unexplained, the bear is considered to be
left-handed. Thus, in structuring the relationship of the three head
medicine men, it would follow in Cochití logic that the Number One
assistant should be designated the "left hand." Most Cochití have become so familiar with the Anglo vernacular "right-hand man" that
the original Cochití connotation has likely been lost.

At this meeting, the three head medicine men select the six major
officers for the coming year. Although precise details of the actual
procedure could not be learned, it appears that each man proposes
his selections independently of the others; if there is a conflict—i.e.,
if the same man is selected for two offices—priority goes to the cacique, then to the Giant head, and finally to the Shī'kame. [44, 45,
49, 92]

On the night of December 29, the Christmas season dancing over, the adult males of the tribe assemble in the Turquoise community house. (In 1948, this meeting was shifted to the Pumpkin community house because of the personal bias of that year's governor. [92]) Goldfrank (1927: 25) stated that the meeting was attended by council members and the head medicine men. My informants insisted that attendance is not restricted to them, and the data provided by Curtis (1926: 85) support their opinion.

When all have assembled (the Progressives do not ordinarily attend), there are preliminary talks ("preaching") by the war captain, the lieutenant war captain, the governor, and the lieutenant governor, in that order. These talks review events of the past year and range from suggestions to virtual demands that pueblo affairs be improved in the way of upright living. It should be noted here that the *fiscale* and his lieutenant do not speak at this meeting; this brings to mind a statement in Bandelier's journal of October 7, 1880, in which he pointed out "but the fiscal himself is not a *principal.*"

When the four officers finish speaking, they go to the Flint–Kusha'lī house (ho'chanī-ītsa) to bring the three head shamans who have been waiting there. When re-entering the community house, the war captain goes first, followed by his lieutenant, then the Giant head, the cacique, and the Shī'kame head; the governor and his lieutenant bring up the rear. These men all sit, and the same four who talked earlier now make a few additional comments on the subject of upright living, co-operation, and proper citizenship.

The meeting is then turned over to the cacique, who, making a short speech concerning the significance of the session, concludes with the matter of choosing a war captain and an assistant. He then makes the announcement with the statement, "Now I'll say his name, ——." He asks whether this selection is agreeable to all, and the answer is inevitably "Yes." He then asks the nominee whether he is willing to serve, and again the inevitable reply, "Yes." The same procedure is followed in the selection of the other officers; the Giant head announces his choices when the cacique has finished, and finally the Shī'kame head makes his selections known, concluding the December 29 meeting.

Frequently there is a brief discussion of the selections, and occasionally a nominee makes a feeble attempt to decline the office. However, this is largely routine, and in the vast majority of instances the medicine men—the tribal religious leaders—appear to retain relatively firm control of the nominally secular affair. [3, 15, 62] Bandelier, in an entry of October 7, 1880, stated that the cacique called upon the people for their choices but that they always abstained, passing the duty back to him. Present-day Cochití do not believe this was accurate, and they express doubt about Bandelier's next statement: "If the parties chosen refuse to accept the charge, then they are imprisoned so long until they take it."

Sporadic dissension does occur, as exemplified by a meeting about 1930 at which a Pumpkin member was proposed as governor. He refused to accept it, however, on the grounds that the three medicine men had not been able to make their selections without interference. This was a part of the controversy over failure to rotate the offices between the kiva groups equitably. Although the nominee was a Pumpkin, he and his side rejected the conciliatory gesture because it had not been arrived at through traditional channels and they refused to be a party to such deviation. [62, 92]

In a more recent meeting, about 1943, Juan José Trujillo is said to have left the meeting when he became dissatisfied with some turn of events. By withdrawing, he "left the pueblo," i.e., became affiliated with the Progressive faction. After about two years he returned to the Conservative group, and in 1947 served a term as governor, [42, 92]

On January 1, each retiring officer brings his cane (*vara*), the symbol of his respective office, to the church, where the cacique takes it at the door. He passes it to the new officer amid a general exchange of congratulations and well-wishing. This transfer follows the widespread Pueblo custom of breathing in, and out, the power which is believed to be seated in these canes. Informants were careful to point out, however, that even though giving up his cane the past officer retains his power, which enables him to speak wisely at council meetings and similar affairs. [42, 92]

Some men, when returning a cane, tie fresh ribbons to it; if one fails to do this, the officer receiving it may do so. This is done simply as decoration, and there are no set colors or combinations of colors for any cane. [20] If the same officers have been continued in office, the canes are still brought to the church at the time of the January 1 Mass, given to the cacique, and received back again with the accompanying congratulations and blessings. The new officers bring the canes back once again on January 6 for the Catholic priest to place on the altar and bless in the course of the Mass that day. [92] From the time the new officers accept the canes on January 1, they hold all the authority vested in their respective offices. These canes are supposed to be in the pueblo at all times.

Following the January 1 Mass, the people gather around to hear speeches, either in the churchyard or in the church, depending upon the weather. The cacique speaks first, followed by the retiring governor and the new governor. As they make various points, emphasizing obedience to the new officers, co-operation with the governing authorities, and general good citizenship, approval is voiced repeatedly by the other new officers standing nearby and anyone else who is so moved. Informants commented that in the speeches the officers often use such "big words," though not particularly archaic ones, that frequently the younger people miss the full significance of their remarks. [25, 44, 49] Goldfrank (1927: 26) stated that all new officers speak at this time; my informants stated that this is no longer true.

After the speeches, the people return home but go shortly thereafter to the homes of the new officers for feasts. Upon entering the home of a new officer, they first offer their congratulations, shaking his hand and speaking to him. In cases of relationship or close friendship, there is commonly an embrace. In speaking, both spontaneous words of congratulation and what appears to be a more stereotyped form of address, or prayer, are used. After this, the people turn to their host's official cane leaning against the wall. Ordinarily, it stands on the floor upon a small Navaho blanket, surrounded by baskets of native bread and bowls of chili. There is also a bowl of blue-corn prayer meal, a pinch of which each person sprinkles on the cane, with or without an audible comment. They are then seated at the feast table, where they may linger to talk if others are not waiting. From this home, the people go to the homes of other officers and the general procedure is repeated.

There is no set order in which new officers' homes are visited. The sequence is determined by the degree of relationship involved, the proximity as neighbors, and the location. While there are more individuals who visit the new officers' homes than there are who visit the homes of celebrants of the various saints' days, by no means do they comprise a complete tribal roster. [3, 16, 23, 45, 53]

After their installation on January 1, the officers are called by the governor to their first meeting that same evening. After a brief session, usually at the governor's home or that of another officer if the governor's is unsuitable, the new officers meet with the entire Council of *Principales* in the Flint–Ku-sha'lī house. At this meeting, the new officers ask for advice from those who have served previously, and general plans for the coming year are considered. Subsequently meetings of the officers, with or without the council, are called as required. Sunday-evening meetings occur quite regularly throughout the year. If the meeting is of the six officers, it is generally held in one of their homes; meetings of the entire council generally take place in the Turquoise community house.

At their first meeting, the officers and the council select six *alguacilitos* from among the young men who have never held a major office and do not belong to a medicine society. The *alguacilitos* are the assistants to the war captains and enjoy greater prestige, but also greater responsibility, than do the *fiscalitos*, who serve as helpers for the governors and *fiscales*. The *alguacilitos* are chosen evenly, three from each kiva, with the council members of each kiva having a voice in the selection of its three only. One other qualification is that the *alguacilitos* must already belong to the Ka'tsīnas, the esoteric masked dancers. The six *fiscalitos*, in contrast, are selected individually by the retiring *fiscalitos*. Since this is done on an individual basis with less influence of public pressure, there is more frequent rejection of their proposals. There is no rule of equal division between the two kivas, and consequently, in any given year one kiva may boast all or none, or any intervening number, of these six offices. With increasing regularity, the *fiscalitos* are being forced to remain in office another year, being unsuccessful in finding another boy to accept the cane. [3, 42, 44, 45, 62]

Assuming that these assistants prove themselves conscientious and capable workers, they are eventually chosen for some major office. Traditionally, *alguacilitos* move up to the position of war captain or lieutenant; *fiscalitos* advance to the position of governor or *fiscale*. Ordinarily, when a young man begins in one of these, he is not chosen for the other. In recent years, however, this "regulation" has not been strictly followed, and considerable interchange has occurred.

Duties of the Annually Selected Officers

War Captain and Lieutenant War Captain. The war captain (sī'at yoyo; also ma'sēwa) and the lieutenant, or assistant, war captain (sī'at yoyo tenyet; also o'yoyēwa) are selected annually by the cacique. Curtis (1926: 84) mentioned that the titles "Masēwa" and

"Ōyōyēwa" were taken from legendary war leaders and were used ceremonially. One informant expressed surprise when told that "Masewa" and "Oyoyewa" are terms commonly found in the literature. "Those names are very secret." Curtis (1926: 85) stated that the assistant war captain was less an assistant than a colleague, the two officers working together with virtually equal status. This observation was confirmed both by my informants and by my observations during ceremonies and other events.

It is the duty of the war captains to call the cacique to task if he is failing in his ceremonial duties. Also they maintain surveillance over the head of each secret society among the Cochití; this is but one facet of their over-all responsibility for the proper functioning of the ceremonial life of the pueblo. They have control of personnel shifts from kiva to kiva and similar changes, even those of a temporary nature. This control also includes direct leadership and supervision of certain rituals and communal hunts for the cacique and the people. It likewise involves the protection of those engaged in ceremonial rites for the common good. Thus, the war captains keep guard over the retreats of the medicine men so that no harm can befall them during these activities. Goldfrank (1927: 24–25) classified the war captains as secular officers because of their annual replacement and regular membership in the council, as well as because of their mode of nomination.

There is some uncertainty as to how the war captains and the war chief (nahī'ya) divided their functions in former times. Whether the war captains have assumed the former duties of the now-extinct office of nahī'ya upon the disappearance of the Warriors Society is difficult to ascertain. The war captains were active in leading Cochití warriors against enemies such as the Navaho during the Spanish era. In this, their functions appear to have overlapped those of the nahī'ya. With the disappearance of both the armed enemies of the tribe and the Warriors Society (and nahī'ya), the war captains continue to lead the fight against enemies of the pueblo.[1] [3, 15, 44, 70]

---

[1] Considerable speculation has been made on the origins of the offices of war captain and lieutenant war captain. Clear evidence as to whether they were of native, or Spanish, origin is lacking. Parsons (1939: 1125–1126) felt that the origin could be traced to the Spanish Decree of 1621. Among other provisions, this decree, a result of the conflict between Church and State, gave ultimate authority to the State. It included instructions that each pueblo should choose, without interference from the Spanish authorities, various civil officials every January 1. (Scholes 1937: 78–79) Parsons stated that just as the governor and

Public enemies are at present in two major categories. First, there are numerous witches that the Indians believe cause harm. Witches appear to be of several types, including some who are harmful only to Indians, some who harm non-Indians (and are of no concern to the Indians), and others who are dangerous to anyone. Since the medicine men are the leaders in thwarting these witches, the war captains and the *alguacilitos* are the logical ones to safeguard them while they perform such community benefits. Secondly, war captains contend with those enemies who would destroy the way of life of the people of Cochití. These include both outsiders and native Cochití. The Conservatives feel that everything good is to be gained by following the old ways. Native religious ceremonies, societies, and traditional attitudes are the best guarantee of a successful and happy life. By failing to adhere to the old ways (a departure characteristic of essentially every Cochití in at least some respect—hence an obvious source of intracultural conflict when tolerable limits are considered), by completely substituting the Catholic faith for native theology, and by adopting other "alien" (variously interpreted) elements of culture, the Cochití, specifically the Progressives, are injuring both themselves and the entire pueblo. [53, 62, 88] However, as a leading member of the Conservatives once pointed out, the officers (and people) of Cochití are "more reasonable" than those of Santo Domingo. For example, the Cochití feel that equally good and efficacious ceremonies can be held in spite of the fact that their water system is protected by covered wells and frequent testing and that electricity is in their homes; they see no inconsistency in this merging of the old and the new. [3, 45, 53, 62, 88]

Since the war captains, who are temporary, and to a considerable degree secular, officers, supervise the activities of the secret societies,

---

his staff became the "mouthpiece and executive" for the cacique, the war captains and their staff "functioned similarly" for the war chief, or nahĩ'ya. Aberle (1948: 38) commented on the war chief as follows: "War Chief, a term not found in the colonial Spanish villages, is used consistently in this paper to designate a man chosen each year who may have civil as well as religious duties. Within the pueblo, though this chief is ordinarily called War Chief, he may be called War Captain, Hunt Chief, Outside Chief, etc. The differences in title are significant of the differences in the actual position of the War Chiefs in different villages. In no other position does there exist the degree of inconsistency between the idea of the officer's duties and the duties he actually performs."

White (1942: 104) wrote that "the chiefs [captains], formerly military officers and leaders, are today the most important (in fact, but not in theory) officers in Santa Ana."

Parsons and others believe these positions were of importance in aboriginal times. They referred to the war captains as "outside chiefs."

Among the Conservatives there is no doubt that the word of the war captain outweighs that of the governor; among the Progressives, however, the reverse is true. In fact, it is the failure to acknowledge the authority of the war captains in their supervision of native ceremonialism that denotes one as a member of the Progressives as much as any other single factor.

Divulgence of tribal secrets or similar acts deemed detrimental to the common good come under the jurisdiction of the war captains, who may call for support from the Council of *Principales*. For infringements of this nature, the war captains either administer the punishment or delegate this duty to the *alguacilitos*.

Informants were most reluctant to discuss details of punishment, though whipping was acknowledged (cf. p. 54). Starr (Scrapbook) mentioned the case of Antonio Melchior: "Melchior is a man with a history. His age is given as 60. His features are fine and his hair is gray, a phenomenon almost unknown among the Indians. Many years ago Melchoir had a misunderstanding with his tribe and was publicly whipped. In a speech, fierce with resentment, he forswore allegiance to his tribe and moved outside the village."

"Standing in a circle," a form of punishment seen publicly invoked as recently as the Feast Day of 1951 at Zia Pueblo (Lange 1952), was admitted by the Cochití as having been administered in "the old days" though never in public, that is to say, never in view of the whites. A few implied that this form has not actually been abandoned. That stocks and hanging by the wrists, practices mentioned in the literature, could not be associated with present practices may perhaps be an admission that these, or similar techniques, have not yet been entirely discarded. (For a discussion of such practices, see Curtis [1926: 77–82]; Dumarest [1919: 200–202]; and Goldfrank [1927: 96, 98].)

Informants stated that formerly the war captains were active in recruiting new members for the secret societies, thereby ensuring that there would be adequate personnel to perpetuate the functions of each group. However, several new members who had been pressured in this way soon became discontented with the duties and responsibilities of membership, the long hours of fasting and other observances required during society retreats, the relative confinement to the pueblo during society activities, and other hardships. At present, rather than have members who are unhappy in their religious roles and thereby ineffectual (if not actually detrimental), there appears to be a widespread attitude in the pueblo that, important as the societies are, it is better for them to become extinct than to be composed of members unwilling to perform their functions with the proper "feelings." Consequently, there is little, if any, recruiting of society members by the war captains or anyone else. [42, 44, 48, 52, 53, 55, 62, 88]

The war captains guard, preserve, and pass down to succeeding generations much of the tribal lore, esoteric and exoteric, or encourage others to do so. One older man, widely recognized as one who "knows the most about the old days," stated that he acquired much of his knowledge many years ago when he was assistant war captain and Teodosio Cordero was war captain. Teodosio had taught him many things about the customs and beliefs and "how things should be done." [25] (As revealed in Bandelier's journal of October 6, 1880, it was this same Teodosio who was the first Cochití Bandelier met, "*principal* of the tribe, and who had been governor two years ago.")

In describing Cochití officers, Dumarest (1919: 200) stated "the foremost is the captain of war (*tsiatoio*), the *masewa*." He mentioned that the captain of war was the guardian of customs, and when the customs were not observed, the war captains inflicted punishment. The war captain worked closely with his assistant in these duties. Curtis (1926: 85) described the office of the war captain as formerly one held for life; later it was changed to an annual appointment. He listed four chief duties of the war captains: to maintain order, to inaugurate and direct communal hunts, to announce ceremonies, and to guard participants in esoteric rites. He said that formerly the war captains decided when it was necessary to choose a new location for the village, and led in repelling enemies. That this power to move the village to another site has not been lost or forgotten, despite Cochití's remaining in one location for about seven centuries, was obvious from the chance remark by a young Conservative that it was very pretty in the mountains around "Old Cochití" (on the mesa above Cañada) and that some day he was going to be war captain and "make the people move back up there." [35]

A brief discussion of former duties of the war captains is contained in Bandelier's journal of October 9, 1880:

Thus, he said that before any expedition was sent out, a general meeting is held. The captain first presents his gun, etc. to his teniente or the oldest *principal*, who examines the weapons, and after finding them correct, he examines the arms of the teniente. Then each goes around his own way in the circle of men, visiting the arms of each man, and if any are found to be out of order, he is ordered to prepare for such and such a time. If then he fails to be in trim, the captain imprisons him without further delay. This he has the right to do without consulting any of the *principals*, for in military affairs the captain is supreme, and can act as he pleases.

Like the governors, the war captains have canes of office. The canes are carried on January 6, for any of the hunting or animal dances other than the Parrot Dance, at the Spring Dance, for the ha'ñĩko (solstice ceremonies), and for all the ka'tsĩna ceremonies. For ha'ñĩko and the ka'tsĩna ceremonies, the *alguacilitos* must also carry their canes.

Appendix 11 provides a roster of the war captains and the lieutenants from 1920 through 1953. Again, the Turquoise Kiva monopoly of the senior office is apparent.

Governor and Lieutenant Governor. A governor (da'pop) and a lieutenant governor (da'pop ten'yet) are selected each year by the Giant Society head.[2] The governor invariably will have served previously as lieutenant governor, or as a *fiscale*, having earlier demonstrated as a *fiscalito* that he would be a satisfactory official. The lieutenant governor is generally a younger man, frequently with no prior public service other than one or more terms as a *fiscalito*. He moves up to the position of governor after several terms as lieutenant or as one of the *fiscales* and as the group of men from whom the governors are chosen becomes reduced by senility and death.

Governors are chosen without regard for their clan affiliations. They may be members of Ku-sha'lĩ, Kwe'rana, or any other society with the exception of the three medicine societies. There was some disagreement on this point regarding all major offices. However, in 1948, of the five living members of the three medicine societies, the only one who had belonged to the council (thereby indicating one-time service as a major officer) was Marcelo Quintana, the cacique. Many years before, Marcelo had served as lieutenant *fiscale* and ap-

---

[2] The traditional system, under which the governor and lieutenant governor were named by the Giant Medicine Society head, has become extinct with the death of the last Giant head (and sole remaining member). This happened about 1955—after my field work and completion of the manuscript. (Lange, 1958: 399–404.)

parently joined the Flint Society subsequently. When he became cacique in 1946, he withdrew from the council. [3, 20, 45, 70]

Some older men have been concerned over the past failure of the head medicine men to observe the regulation that *alguacilitos* should become war captains and *fiscalitos* should become either governors or *fiscales*. Even more bitterly resented, however, has been the past failure to observe the annual alternation of the head offices between the kivas. From 1920 to 1946, the only years in which there was a governor from the Pumpkin Kiva were 1927 and 1937, when Alcario Montoya, a Ku-sha'lī member and sacristán at those times, was selected. Goldfrank (1927: 30–31) noted that as of her stay (during the early 1920's) Alcario had already served several times as governor and had represented the pueblo in Washington, D.C., in a vain effort to have John Dixon, Progressive and self-styled "judge," removed. Dumarest (1919: 200) noted that José Hilario Montoya, father of Alcario, was governor for almost ten years during the late-nineteenth century.

Opposition to the Turquoise Kiva monopoly became so strong, mounting through the years under the leadership of Lorenzo Herrera, Clofe Arquero, and others, that finally, in 1946, Clofe Arquero was selected as governor from the Pumpkin Kiva. In 1947, Juan José Trujillo, Turquoise Kiva, succeeded him; in 1948, Juan José Suina, another Pumpkin man, was governor and was followed in 1949 by José Domingo Quintana of the Turquoise Kiva. In 1950, the governorship was again in the hands of a Pumpkin Kiva man, Salvador Arquero, who served his first term as governor after several terms as lieutenant governor; in 1951, the Turquoise Kiva furnished the governor, Epitacio Arquero. In 1952, Ramón Herrera, Pumpkin Kiva, served his first term as governor, and in 1953, José Domingo Quintana, Turquoise Kiva, was returned to office. Thus, the rotation of the governorship appears to be well established again, to the satisfaction of all.

Duties of the governor and his lieutenant are primarily civil. As mentioned, these offices, and many of the associated duties, are believed by some Pueblo specialists to have been introduced by the Spanish. Outsiders are referred to the governor or, in his absence, to the lieutenant, if they wish to sell various commodities, erect concession stands for any of the ceremonial days, or fiestas, or take photographs in and around the pueblo. The photographing of individuals is a private matter individually arranged, the governor having no authority to speak for them. Requests to photograph ceremonial subjects are referred to the war captains, whose jurisdiction covers all ritual matters. [3, 45, 49, 88]

The people have developed the habit, primarily to avoid any chance for criticism from their neighbors, of answering many requests for aid or co-operation of different forms with the question "Does the Governor [and inferentially, the Council] know about this?" If not, the proceedings are halted until permission has been obtained. The governor (or his lieutenant) makes decisions largely on the basis of precedent. In the absence of both, either the *fiscales* or the war captains are consulted, with decisions given on the same basis. If no one of these officers is present, which rarely occurs, the decision is simply postponed; nothing is considered so urgent that it must be settled before one of them returns. [20, 42, 44, 45, 62]

If a problem has never arisen before, the governor may refuse to decide or to allow his fellow officers to share in a decision. Instead, a meeting (O'wī-tya) of the Council of *Principales* is called and the matter is discussed until a decision is reached. If the council cannot reach a virtually unanimous decision, the problem reverts to the six major officers. In this way a decision is ultimately reached, thereby setting a precedent to be followed in the future. [15] In recent years, there has developed a tendency to abandon the tradition of unanimity and to abide by the rule of the majority. However, there is some reluctance to act by majority rule, especially when the margin of dominance is small. [20, 42, 88]

It is also the governor's duty to work with Indian Service officials, particularly those of the United Pueblos Agency. While any of the Cochití may talk with the agency field representative, it is customary to channel questions and requests through the governor. [20, 44, 45] The governor acts as spokesman for the pueblo in dealing with federal education and health officials. Although he works in close cooperation with his lieutenant, it is the governor to whom mail is addressed and whom these officials call upon for assistance and consultation. [15] If the children of pueblo families become involved in trouble at boarding school, the governor investigates. [44]

The increasingly frequent offers to participate in such events as the Gallup Inter-tribal Ceremonials are directed to the governor, who ordinarily presents them to the entire council for consideration. Also he is called in to arbitrate disputes which arise between individuals and families within, and often outside, the pueblo. [16, 44, 45, 48, 53]

Dumarest (1919: 200) said that the governor "has the church

built and repaired and he keeps in good repair the estufa or ceremonial room." Informants claimed this was completely erroneous, since the *fiscales* are responsible for the church, though they do receive some assistance from the governors; the war captains, together with the kiva heads, are responsible for the upkeep of the kiva structures. [3, 15, 25, 48, 53] Dumarest also said that the governor assigned work at the time of communal planting for the cacique, but informants stated that if the planting is for the cacique, the war captains and either the Ku-sha'lï or Kwe'rana members supervise. In former times, when work was done for the resident priest, *fiscales* directed it. [3, 45, 70] The Eickemeyers (1895: 76) gave the following observations on labor assignments made by the governor (June 25, 1894): "At sunrise the following morning the governor called loudly from his position in the center of the pueblo, assigning to the men assembled in the doorways the work they were to perform that day. As the different names were called the owners disappeared within the houses to prepare for the work allotted to them, and hurried to the scene of action to do their share of the labor."

At present, public announcements are made by the governor, or any other officer, from three locations in the pueblo in regular sequence. First, the call is made from a point between the community corral and the Turquoise Kiva; then it is repeated from the center of the plaza; the final call is made from the arroyo edge just southwest of the church. From a study of the village map (Map 2), it is readily apparent that as the people spread out around the peripheries these three points are becoming less and less adequate. This is partly remedied by the fact that the *fiscalitos* go from house to house and repeat certain announcements; however, with less efficient work being done by these minor officers, important word is either spread personally by the major officers, adding to their official burdens, or the tribal communication system is deficient and co-ordination suffers accordingly.

Notes of Bandelier (April 4, 1882) on the use of yucca in making the community fishing net also mention the governor's authority: "In May or June, the governor sent out men to cut the leaves of the plants and gather them in 'hands.'" This duty is no longer a part of the governor's office. Formerly he also had charge of the community work on the ferry across the Rio Grande. [44]

The governor determines punishments, sometimes after consulting with other officers or the entire council. In turn, he, or any other officer, may be punished or removed from office for misconduct. [3, 15, 44] As with the religious officers, the kiva balance between the secular officers is maintained. If a governor, or any other officer, dies in office or is removed, the medicine men choose his successor from the same kiva. Normally they choose someone who has served previously in the particular office. All other officers remain *status quo* in order to preserve the balance of kiva representation and to provide the full complement of fellow officials with whom consultation can be held. [3, 49, 53]

Appendix 12 lists the governors and lieutenants for those years for which data could be obtained, with their ages at the time of assuming office and their clan and kiva affiliations.

Fiscale and Lieutenant Fiscale. The *fiscale* (pirsh'kalī; also pirsh'kalī mayorī) and lieutenant *fiscale* (pirsh'kalī tenyet, or *teniente*) are selected each year by the Shī'kame head. In correct Spanish this title would be *fiscal* rather than *fiscale*. However, in actual usage, the final *e* is added at Cochití and apparently elsewhere in the Rio Grande Pueblos, as evidenced by the discussion on Santa Ana (White 1942: 108, 173–178). At Santo Domingo, White (1935: 44–45) found the term "bickari," which is somewhat closer to the Cochití "pirsh'kalī" than to "*fiscale*."

The primary duties of these men are in connection with the physical structure of the church. They are responsible for its upkeep, its heating, maintaining an adequate supply of firewood, supervision of the *fiscalitos* in their church duties, and assisting the governors in supervising civil community work, such as ditch cleaning and road repairs.

In his entry of October 8, 1880, Bandelier commented that the *fiscale* had nothing to do except care for the church. "He is not even a *principal* necessarily." Whether Bandelier underestimated the authority of these officers, or whether the additional authority of the present time accompanied their inclusion as council members could not be learned. [3, 42, 44, 92]

Dumarest (1919: 202) stated that the "office of *fiscal* appears to be a recent institution. The *fiscals* were originally the servants of the priest when there was a priest in every pueblo." He further commented that the head *fiscale*, as of the end of the last century, still had charge of church repairs, cultivating and irrigating the priest's lands, harvesting them, looking after the priest's horse, and preparing his meals when he was in the pueblo.

The *fiscale* and his lieutenant are responsible for seeing that the *fiscalitos* make proper announcement of the arrival of the priest in the village and the preparations for Mass. This is done by ringing the church bell, and the following signals are used: one short bell announces the priest's arrival; this is followed by three long bells, at brief intervals, the third and final one signifying that the time for the beginning of the Mass is at hand. Formerly the bell was rung by means of a special long, thin stone. This striker was either broken or disposed of in some other way; it has not been seen for many years. [44]

As the *fiscalitos* become increasingly lax in executing their duties, this task falls more and more to the lot of the *fiscales*. In addition to the bell-ringing, which is more a rather frantic clanging than anything else, the *fiscale* or his assistant serves as *pregonero*, or public crier, announcing church call at the same three spots and in the same sequence as that noted for the governor's and war captain's public announcements. These calls are given at the time of the second long bell. [42, 92] The bell is also rung on the evenings before Mass, for other rites such as the Rosary, and to signal special occasions, such as V-E Day. [20, 42, 44]

In former times the *fiscales*, or their helpers, visited every home in the pueblo before a church service. Anyone caught away from the service after a certain time was flogged with a long whip. My middle-aged informant had never seen this but had merely been told of its happening "in the old days." [42]

After every Mass and sermon the people remain inside the church to listen to the *fiscale* deliver a brief sermon, concerned primarily with general behavior and upright living. If the *fiscale* is absent from the pueblo, this is done by the lieutenant; if both are absent, the governor or some other officer delivers this sermon. Informants were unanimous that this practice occurs after every Mass. [3, 20, 42, 44, 62] While the claim that "everyone in Cochití is a good Catholic" can be supported by such tangibles as widespread attendance at services, it is by just such ways as these final sermons that the native theocracy, through its secular appointees, retains "the last say." Thus, any comments made by the priest in the course of the church service can be edited, restated, or countermanded; even if his remarks need no such alteration, the Cochití officers still implant the final message and thought in the mind of the people as they go to their homes and daily routines.

That the *fiscales* are secondary in relation to the governors and war captains is again revealed in the fact that on numerous occasions throughout the year the official canes of office must be carried by these higher officers but not by the *fiscales*. Such events include January 6, any of the Buffalo, Eagle, Deer, or Animal dances, the Spring Dance, ha'ñīko, and any of the masked, or ka'tsīna, dances. For some of these, not only do the *fiscales* not carry their canes but they actually have no official duty to perform. [20, 42, 92]

It also comes within the province of the *fiscales* to grant permission to bury in the old *Campo Santo,* the churchyard, rather than in the new cemetery west of the village. This privilege is associated with their responsibility for the physical plant of the church. The actual site of the grave is drawn out by the sacristán, and the grave is dug by the *fiscalitos.* [42]

The roster of *fiscales* and the lieutenants shown in Appendix 13 again demonstrates the long-standing monopoly of the senior offices by the Turquoise Kiva membership.

Alguacilitos. Six *alguacilitos* (go'at-chīnī) are selected by the Council of *Principales* at its first meeting of the year on the night of January 1 in the Flint–Ku-sha'lī house. It must choose three from each kiva, and these junior officers serve as assistants to the war captain and his lieutenant. This position is one of considerable responsibility, and those who prove themselves in it are certain to be selected later for a major office. In former times *alguacilitos* always advanced to the position of war captain, or lieutenant, never to that of governor or *fiscale.* At present, with fewer boys and young men interested, the traditional separation has vanished. Anyone selected for this position must already have been initiated into the ka'tsīna cult. This requirement reflects the need for a truly "Conservative" outlook inasmuch as the *alguacilitos* are associated with the ka'tsīna and other esoteric events in their role of guards. While the *alguacilitos* have more prestige than is accorded the *fiscalitos,* their responsibilities are also greater. At present, the position is not particularly sought after.

The roster of *alguacilitos* (Appendix 14) shows a trend toward choosing older men. Although persons selected for these positions are referred to as "young boys" by various informants, including several council members, the roster reveals several middle-aged adults. Of this aspect, remarks in Bandelier's journal of April 13, 1882, are of interest: "It is queer how the Indians defer to age, also how a man of

50 years is still called a 'muchacho.' Age makes the man with them. Only an old man is 'hombre.' I am yet a 'muchacho.'" Bandelier apparently failed to grasp the full significance of his observation. Then, as now, age was deferred to; however, age alone is not enough. If one has not served in a responsible position or otherwise proved himself, he remains a boy—"muchacho"—regardless of his actual age.

The trend toward selecting older individuals as minor officers appears to be a shift that the Cochití are not yet conscious of. It has resulted primarily from the continuous search for new, or potential, officer material. Fewer and fewer young men are interested in serving as officers, partly because they are unsympathetic to the old way of life and partly because they do not care to bind themselves to a career in which their opportunities for economic advancement will suffer. Some "boys" intentionally fail to do well or to work enthusiastically, thereby obviating the possibility of being selected again. Many of the present councilmen are aware of this growing weakness in the traditional pattern of government and are increasingly eager to find some solution to the problem. [3, 20, 21, 42, 44, 45, 62, 88]

As helpers of the war captains, *alguacilitos* are frequently called upon to protect the medicine men and the pueblo at large from the evils of witchcraft and from the ill effects of other intruders. Whenever a society meets, the *alguacilitos*, singly or in pairs, take turns guarding the society house. They may be inside the house when there is nothing of an esoteric nature going on; the rest of the time, they generally take up posts on the roof in order to see anyone who approaches and, if necessary, to prevent any interference. In recent years, it has appeared somewhat incongruous to see these ceremonial guards lying on the roof, casually reading newspapers, magazines, and comic books.

Alguacilitos also act as messengers for the war captains and aid in many lesser tasks. They prepare smokes and light the cigarettes of councilmen or medicine men who are holding a meeting on some ceremonial problem. Before Feast Day they help grind gypsum from which plaster for the kivas is made, gather roosters and prizes for the *gallo* games and foot races on the various saints' days, and direct the foot races. They patrol the ka'tsína dances or any other ceremonies closed to certain people and assist the war captains in detecting breaches of tribal secrets or any other activities considered deleterious to the community welfare. Traditionally, they are expected to report daily to the war captains to see whether there are any tasks or errands for them, but very few are faithful in this respect today and some even avoid being seen by a captain.

Dumarest (1919: 202) mentioned a "head *alguacil,*" who "obeys both the governor and the war captain." He also mentioned his "teniente." These positions were unfamiliar to my informants, who claimed that the six *alguacilitos* are not, and never have been, ranked. Nor could they recall the use of these terms for any other officers. [3, 15, 44, 48, 53, 88]

Fiscalitos. Six *fiscalitos* (pirsh'kalī go'at-chīnī) are also selected each year, but their mode of selection deviates from those mentioned for other officers. At the close of the year, each *fiscalito* is obligated to pass his official cane of office to some young man who has not yet served as a major officer and who does not come from a household that already will lose one adult male as an officer. As pointed out, this system has frequently resulted in an uneven division of these offices between the two kivas. However, since the status of the *fiscalito* is somewhat lower than that of the *alguacilito,* there does not appear to be great concern over this point. [3, 15, 20, 42, 45, 53] *Fiscalitos,* like the *alguacilitos,* are quite often older than the common term of reference to them—"young boys"—implies, and for the same reasons. Appendix 15 provides a roster of the recent *fiscalitos.*

Duties of these minor officers include running errands for the governor, to whom they should (but very seldom do at present) report for instructions at least daily, or to his lieutenant or the *fiscales.* Also, they make announcements for these officers, help with the maintenance of the church, assume responsibility for ringing the church bell, dig graves as designated by the sacristán, and act as pallbearers. The *fiscalitos* also serve as minor peace officers, helping maintain order in the pueblo. At council meetings, they provide tobacco and cornhusks for cigarettes for the councilmen. They also provide punks of corncobs, cattail, or sunflower stem, which they carry to any member wishing to light his cigarette. [42, 45, 88] In former times no *fiscalito* smoked in the presence of these elders, if at all [92], and only native tobacco in cornhusks could be smoked at council meetings. Today commercial tobaccos are used. [2, 70]

Canes of the *fiscalitos* are of two types. Three of them have a short crossbar near the top which forms a cross; the bearers of these canes tend to work with the *fiscales* more than with the governors. This is not a rigid division, however, any more than is the tendency of the three who carry the simple straight canes—the so-called "whippers" —to work with the governors. [42, 44, 45, 92]

The Council of *Principales*

The Council of *Principales* is currently, and has been for as far back as any Cochití can recall, composed of all men who have served, or are serving, as one of the six major officers of the pueblo. As already pointed out in Bandelier's and Dumarest's comments and as indicated by the analysis of the functions of these offices, it may be that the inclusion of the *fiscales* as members of the council is a relatively recent innovation.

As already explained, the present basis for council membership tends to place authority in the hands of the older men. One member stated that many of the younger men are critical of the council's actions, but he added that if they were members, they would find its work is not so simple. [49] It appears that ultimately certain of these younger men will be called upon to serve in governing capacities. The informant's conclusion, coupled with the probability that some of the younger men's ideas will be accepted, will undoubtedly reduce many of these criticisms. Another council member reported considerable criticism from the Progressive faction on the council's decisions, or failure to make decisions, and the fact that the officers and councilmen were "riding around the country in the community-owned truck at the expense of the tribe" and similar complaints. From time to time, this man and others like him had actively sought to have Progressives join in the council meetings (O'wī-tya) and take part in the discussions, regardless of whether they were qualified in the traditional sense or not. To some extent this has accomplished the intended result of quieting much of this type of criticism and at the same time has increased general understanding of current tribal problems and, consequently, co-operation in attempting to solve these problems. [3, 88]

Membership in the council is for life. A man can be ousted for malconduct, but this has seldom occurred. Some individuals who have ceased attending for reasons of poor health, old age, or similar causes are theoretically still members. There are also members of the Progressives who belonged to the council in years past but who no longer attend its meetings. Informants differed in their explanation of this. Some stated that these men were no longer invited to the meetings by the governors acting through the *fiscalitos*. Others stated that the Progressives were formerly invited but declined to participate; hence, their present failure to attend is voluntary. In the summer of 1951, one of the Progressives, Francisco Chávez, who also served as assistant sacristán, began to attend council meetings once more (having served as *Fiscale Mayor* about 1900). [3, 42, 52, 53] Councilmen who later become medicine men or cacique—as in the case of the present cacique, Marcelo Quintana—cease attending the meetings unless they are specifically called to provide special data of some sort. [44]

The antiquity of the council is unknown. Since its members are either past or present officers, it might be supposed that the origins are identical with those of the various offices, though a council selected by other criteria may well have existed earlier. Nevertheless, the importance of the council should not be underestimated. The authority carried by a council decision is all-powerful so far as tribal members are concerned, whether living in the pueblo or away from it, and also so far as nontribal members who wish to deal with the tribe or individual members of it are concerned. Its importance appears to have been slighted in data published on the Cochití. Dumarest (1919: 198–199) simply referred to their endorsing nominations of new officers and mentioned them only briefly elsewhere. Curtis (1926:85) likewise devoted little attention to them. Goldfrank (1927: 25) provided more complete data, including material regarding the nomination (selection) of new officers: "The power of the principales is purely nominal as they always accept the names offered them by the nominating groups." The error in this statement—restricting the voice of acceptance to the *principales* only—has already been noted (p. 196). Elsewhere Goldfrank (1927: 27) added the following comments:

It is difficult to state just how much power rests with the principales. Although their action with regard to nominations is merely one of ratification, still they, no doubt, influence the nominating committees and keep them from presenting candidates who would be rejected. Their influence in other directions seems similar to this. They are essentially a body of consultants, the governor bringing various civil matters before them such as land renting and at times punishments and fines. They are informed by the war captains when a person seeks adoption by one of the clans or when a witch is to be tried. However, their sanction is of great importance, since they are honored members of the community, and it is doubtful whether the governor or war captain would act in direct opposition to their expressed will.

There is no connection between society membership and membership in the principales, a member of any society being eligible for any office, although, for the most part, only members of non-curing societies are represented. Nevertheless, a person belonging to no society may also be elected to office.

Meetings are normally called by the governor, though anyone can request him to call one to discuss a problem. Nonmembers occasionally speak at meetings to present information unknown to members, and the family of a member whose house is being used for the meeting, usually that of one of the current officers, can sit in an adjoining room and listen if they so desire. After the governor announces the purpose of the meeting, members are free to express themselves. This they do until everyone has had a chance to speak. If the council's opinion proves to be unanimous, the matter is settled. If there is disagreement, the discussion continues, sometimes for several evenings if a final decision is not urgent. In former times, when a unanimous decision was mandatory, this occasionally meant that meetings extended over several days, or even weeks, with very little interruption. At present, there is a growing tendency to abide by the will of the majority, particularly when the decision is rather heavily weighted toward one view. [3, 20, 42, 44, 45]

If an immediate decision must be reached and the council is about evenly divided, the matter is referred to the governor and the major officers, who act as a sort of higher council, or *ad hoc* committee. Thus, the council acts as both a legislative and a judiciary body. Occasionally it even assumes executive functions, though these are commonly left to the officers.

Curtis (1926: 85) mentioned the "principales grandes," composed of the heads of the three medicine societies and the heads of the Ku-sha'lī, Kwe'rana, and Shrū'tzī societies. Such a group no longer functions at Cochití, and several informants questioned whether these society heads had ever constituted any sort of formal body. [3, 15, 42]

Council meetings are usually held in the home of the governor, but if this is not large enough or is otherwise inconvenient, the home of another officer is used. Sometimes the Turquoise community house is used. As noted (p. 54), kivas are never used for this purpose. Most council members attend meetings faithfully. Appendix 16 provides a roster as of 1948–1952. Within this interval, there were few new members and an increasing number of men who no longer attend due to illness, senility, or general discontent with the turn of events. As of 1948, 6 of the 34 members were considered by informants to have an inadequate command of English. (Interesting for its comparative value is Starr's notation in his diary of September 15, 1897, that there were 20 council members at that time.) New members since 1948 have all had reasonable facility in English. Of the 6 listed as inadequate in this respect, all but 1 had served as war captain or lieutenant war captain. The one exception is a man who had served numerous terms as governor. The appointment of a governor who lacked a command of English—an ability of prime importance in this role of contact man with the outside world—is somewhat baffling to the writer and also to several informants. Aside from this one deficiency, the man seems to have done a very satisfactory job as governor.

As indicated, the Council of *Principales* has duties of a legislative, judiciary, and executive nature, though this last category is carried out primarily by the officers of any given year. These officers also share judicial responsibilities with the council and, to a very limited extent, the legislative functions. To a considerable degree, the council and the current officers share such responsibilities not only within the Cochití tribe but in conjunction with neighboring pueblos or in co-operation with one specific tribe that may call in the Cochití officials to serve as consultants on various problems. Several such examples are included in the section "Law and Order."

Duties of the Special Officers

Special officers comprise a heterogeneous group appointed by the Council of *Principales*. The position of sacristán is approximately as old as the Catholic faith in Cochití, but most of these positions are of relatively recent date. Almost without exception, they reflect the economic changes which have occurred in the culture.

Sacristán and Assistant Sacristán. Dumarest (1919: 202) noted that "the sacristan is appointed for life, but he has no stick of office and is not considered an officer. However, he is over the *fiscals*." This evaluation of relative authority is valid at present in matters where church services are directly concerned; in other matters, the *fiscales*, as major pueblo officers, wield the greater authority. [45, 62, 70, 92]

The duties of the sacristán are more closely associated with the services of the church than with its physical plant. He assists the priest in his preparations for Mass and in serving it. He occasionally substitutes for the priest in baptisms and burials, usually in cases of emergency. In former times the sacristán also performed marriages, but modern transportation and improved roads now enable the priest to keep a more dependable schedule of visits to the pueblo, making it unnecessary for the sacristán to perform other than emergency rites. [3, 42, 50, 62, 70] Bandelier, in his journal of November 5, 1880, noted that the "padre ate at the home of the sacristán." Today it is more common for the *fiscale* and the lieutenant *fiscale* to alternate in this responsibility. As noted earlier, it is the sacristán who decides upon the location for a new grave after the *fiscales* have passed upon which *Campo Santo* is to be used. [92]

A partial roster of sacristáns was compiled. The first named was Tomas Arquero, of the Oak Clan and the Pumpkin Kiva. He was born in 1884 and served at the close of the last century, obviously as a very young man. Tomas was not a society member so far as could be learned. [88, 92] The next sacristán was Mariano Chávez, of the Cottonwood Clan and Pumpkin Kiva; born about 1857, he served from early in this century until his death in 1917. He was followed by Alcario Montoya, Corn Clan and Pumpkin Kiva, who was born about 1879. He served until 1947, when he resigned. It is interesting to note that both Mariano and Alcario were councilmen and members of Ku-sha′lī at the time they served as sacristán. Following Alcario, Alfred Herrera, Cottonwood Clan and Pumpkin Kiva, born 1915, served until January, 1952, when he was named *fiscale*. Since that time, Francisco Chávez, son of Mariano, and of the Water Clan and Pumpkin Kiva, born in 1883, has served. This last-named sacristán is the first one to come from the Progressive faction.

In return for his work with the church, the sacristán is relieved of all other community duties, such as care of the cacique's fields, road repairs, and ditch maintenance. [53, 62] Beginning with Alcario's tenure, at which time he was also serving as interpreter for the All-Pueblo Council and as a Ku-sha′lī member, an assistant sacristán, Francisco Chávez, was appointed by the council. When Francisco became sacristán in 1952, no assistant was appointed for him. He had been offered the position when it was vacant in 1947, but had declined it, supposedly because of age. [71]

It is interesting that prior to this present sacristán, not only have the holders of this office been Conservative but for many years they also have held membership in the Ku-sha'lī. This may appear strange in view of the close relationship between the sacristán and Catholicism. It is not strange, however, when one takes into account the attitude held regarding the Church and the fact that it is the Council of *Principales*—a completely Conservative body—that makes the appointment. A last point of interest is the fact that all sacristáns, currently recalled, have been members of the Pumpkin Kiva.

Secretary-Treasurer. This official is named by the Council of *Principales*. This office is held on an annual basis, and it has existed among the Cochití since the beginning of the present century. Since that time, there has been an increasing awareness of the need to have a literate person to keep records and accounts and to carry on the correspondence involved in conducting tribal business. This need for keeping written records was emphasized in 1951 as the deadline for filing claims for compensation approached. The Cochití, in filing for compensation for the loss of the La Bajada Grant, east of the Cochití Reservation, came to regret their past negligence in caring for various documents which they felt would aid their case in the courts. Emphasizing this aroused interest in preserving records was the attempt by the officers to trade a rather small safe for a considerably larger one. The safe is normally kept in the house of the secretary-treasurer and is a repository for documents of value to the tribe. [3, 20, 42, 44, 45, 88]

Santiago Quintana (Cyrus Dixon) was the first man to hold this office, or perhaps more accurately, the first to perform this role. Since the turn of the century, others who have served in this capacity include Salvador Arquero, Eleuterio Suina, Alcario Montoya, Celestino Quintana, and Juan José Trujillo. In 1951, Alfred Herrera, the sacristán, also served as secretary-treasurer; in 1952, when Alfred was named *fiscale*, Salvador Arquero again assumed these responsibilities. [44, 45, 62, 92]

Brand Inspector. This position has been filled for many years by José Melchior. Until Francisco Chávez became assistant sacristán and later sacristán, this has been the only office filled by the council with an appointee from the Progressive faction. However, in this case there was little alternative, for Melchior has been the largest cattle owner in the pueblo for many years, being at times almost the only cattleman.

Fence Rider. The fence rider is chosen by the council. This position was created in 1930, the year the reservation was first completely fenced. Before that time, it was the responsibility of those people who had stock to safeguard them on the range. In the earlier years, this officer rode every day except Sundays. He inspected the south half of the fence every other day through the summer. In winter, he rode every other day, alternating a southern trip with a northern.

The rider's duties included the maintenance of the fence enclosing the reservation. He repaired what breaks he could and reported others to the governor, who sent out a repair crew. The rider also watched the condition of the stock and looked for signs of predatory animals, fires, rustlers, and any unusual happenings. [3, 15, 20, 21, 42, 70] A partial roster of fence riders was gathered: 1951, Juan Velasquez; 1948, Fernando Cordero; 1947, Pablo Trujillo; 1946, Fernando Cordero. The first rider, 1930, was Juan Velasquez. It is interesting that in 1952 the pueblo, as an economy measure, did not appoint a range rider, leaving the duties to be carried out voluntarily by those men who had cattle or other stock on the range. [3, 21, 42]

Chauffeurs. Two men, generally one from each kiva, share this remunerative job. They alternate in transporting the people to town, to neighboring fiestas, or to the mountains for timber or other materials. For this, they are paid three dollars a trip, regardless of the distance or time involved. In driving pueblo officials on official business, the drivers are not paid. Other duties include keeping the truck in good repair and maintaining records of income they receive from the passengers. This income is turned over to the tribal treasurer. [20, 42, 44, 45, 92]

Combine Harvester Operators. As noted earlier, this position is also of recent date. The first season in which the community owned a machine, 1947, Philip Cooka (a Hopi married to a Cochití) and Pancracio Chalan (a G.I.) formed the crew. In 1948, these duties were performed by Eleuterio Cordero (a G.I.) and Fernando Cordero (1947 lieutenant governor). When Eleuterio returned to his regular job in a sawmill near Grants, New Mexico, Philip Cooka replaced him. In 1951, the crew was made up of Antonio Suina (a G.I.) and Cresencio Suina (not related); in 1952, Cresencio was again on the combine, this time with Ivan Lewis, a veteran from Acoma who had married a Cochití. The 1952 crew members were both in the Turquoise Kiva, the first time the crew had not included a member of each kiva. In 1948, each crew member was paid $2.00

a day and one sack of wheat, valued at $2.00; the pay was the same in 1951. [20, 70, 92]

Law and Order

Cochití law, as it has developed through the years, is a composite of secular and ecclesiastical rulings and regulations. Legislative, judicial, and executive aspects reveal a dichotomy of responsibility divided between the governors—secular—and the war captains—ecclesiastical, or ceremonial. The council actively participates in the secular phases, less openly in the ceremonial, their places being taken by the medicine men, headed by the cacique, who, it will be remembered, appoints the war captains and who, in turn, is responsible to the war captains.

Further involvement and overlapping result from the fact that all officers and all council members come into such position by virtue of appointment from one of the head shamans. Thus, regardless of whether a specific topic is technically secular or ceremonial, it is apparent that its interpretation and the ultimate resulting action will be strongly colored by the attitudes and values of the ruling theocracy. From the standpoint of cultural dynamics, it is equally apparent that in former times ecclesiastical, or ceremonial, aspects were heavily preponderant; as the theocratic powers have gradually waned, as described in some detail in the next chapter, the secular aspects have increased in importance, though, for the above-stated reasons, it is still often difficult to distinguish between the two approaches to law.

Historical documents for the centuries following the initial European contact contained references in varying detail to diverse complaints and proceedings. However, in essentially all instances these pertain to affairs in which the Spanish civil or ecclesiastical authorities were involved. While these proceedings undoubtedly contributed to Cochití jurisprudence, they are omitted here in deference to instances in which the controversy and questions of law and order were more or less exclusively Cochití. Principles of water rights and the fundamental concepts of ownership and inheritance have already been discussed in Chapter 3.

In an entry of October 9, 1880, Bandelier commented: ". . . for in military affairs the captain is supreme, and can act as he pleases (very important). In cases of crimes, of disputes, etc., the governor is the party to apply to, but then the council first investigates and decides upon the offense. They are the judges, and the governor is but the executive." Later, on the twenty-second of the same month, he noted that "the *principales* have been sitting all night at the house of the *capitan de la guerra* about the case of a man and woman who have been living separate, and whom they want to live together again. Divorce unknown." Such proceedings are carried on even at present. [92] While it is readily apparent that Bandelier's final statement was an exaggeration, the incident points up the fact that the community, through the council, did take, and continues to take, an active interest in affairs that could easily be interpreted as private matters. In these specific cases, the council has been reinforced by the stand of the Catholic Church.

In his journal of November 5, 1880, Bandelier gave the following account of a land dispute:

This morning an old man came to complain to the Padre, while we were at the house of the sacristán, that a certain Teodosio Cordero had taken a field on the left bank of the Rio for himself, which he had first broken. The Padre sent for the governor, who explained the case as follows: The old man, while indeed being the first one to break the ground, abandoned his crops after sowing them. The other worked the field afterwards, and so, when the old man complained about it, they sent two arbiters who divided the field equally between them. Against this the old man complained, but the governor was firm notwithstanding the Padre's intercession, and I did not witness the end of the dispute, but spoke to Juan José afterwards, who said the governor was right, that although the old man had broken the ground first and sowed or planted in it for two years, he had every year abandoned the crops, so that they decided to divide the ground by a line from east to west, leaving the old man to cultivate the southern half and as much beyond it as he pleases, and Cordero the northern half with as much beyond as he wishes. He adds that anyone who fails to cultivate his land for five years loses the claim to it.

The interpretation given here contradicts earlier statements in this book (pp. 40–41) where "homesteading," i.e., original clearing of a tract, is discussed. The discrepancy may well be the result of the difference between theory and practice, along with the pressure of "practical politics." Thus, even though the old man had homesteaded the disputed tract, he was not farming it as efficiently as others might have, or at least that was the claim advanced. It may also be recalled that Teodosio Cordero was a leading figure in the pueblo at that time and apparently was able to obtain what he wanted by going through the official channels, leaving the old man with no higher authority to appeal to. It might be further noted that Cordero received the northern half of the tract, a location which would probably be preferable in light of the ditch system and water supply.

The same entry contains further commentaries upon Cochití law by Bandelier:

There is, at present, considerable disturbance about the new railroad. [While not specified, it seems likely that this was a spur to the Rio Grande running across the Cochití Reservation from Wallace, built by the Santa Barbara Pole and Tie Company to haul timber from the mountains.] Padre Ribera offers to secure compensation for the damage done, the damage to communal lands to be distributed among all, but that to cultivated plots to be paid to the individual tillers, which is perfectly correct.

. . . .

Inquired after punishments. They never punish with death, but if anyone should kill another, or should commit rape, he may be flogged or shut up for as much as a month, also banished from the tribe. The murderers, etc., with crim. con. are turned over to the courts; the council decides their case, and then the *alguaciles* seize him. One is selected to flog him, and if he refuses to inflict the punishment required, he receives the same himself. The *capitan de la guerra* is criminal executor, the governor has civil cases, and the cacique attends only when he is called upon; otherwise, he takes no part in such things.

In his journal of November 6, 1880, Bandelier continued his account of a rabbit hunt, given already in part on pages 125–126, with a description of the controversy between Juan José and Agustín's son-in-law:

At the instance of Agustín, I went to see him [the son-in-law]; he was sitting on a stool, bleeding profusely. Women and children were standing and shouting about, crying and yelling. Agustín called in two Mexicans as witnesses, as he was going to accuse Juan José. I was frightened, and after talking awhile with Victoriano, the war lieutenant, I went home. Found Juan José much dejected, although, from all appearances, he but acted in self defense. I offered to mediate in order to prevent recourse to the laws and courts. My mediation was thankfully accepted, and so I went again to the house of the patient, found his head bound up and he, himself, talking and smiling fairly. All is well. Looked for the cacique but in vain. Juan José requested me to offer Agustín $2.00 for damages, and I did so in presence of Zashua and Juan de Jesús Pancho [John Dixon], but

Agustín refused, stating that he wanted no money, but revenge of some other kind. At night, after Juan José had returned from Peña Blanca, where he had gone in quest of boys who had this afternoon broken the *tinaja* of Ignacia [his daughter], he was summoned before the council and went at night. . . .

November 7. . . . The council at the house of the governor lasted all night, and things look bad. Agustín demands the expulsion of Juan José from the pueblo, and the latter said that if the *principales* would not agree upon a compensation, he would simply accept the conditions of Agustín. Thus the case rests, but meanwhile there are two parties forming in the pueblo. Juan José is quiet, but suffers from headache in consequence of the strokes he received. I went to see the governor and the cacique; the latter was invisible. [This is another of Bandelier's intriguing choices of literal usage.] The governor said that the *principales* were not disposed to banish Juan José (that at all events they could not force him to leave his house, etc.), nor to deprive him of his rights as a member of the tribe, but that if Juan José made any offer of compensation suitable to their understanding of the case, he, the governor, had the power to compel Agustín to accept it. [This procedure is still adhered to at the present time. (88, 92)] Then, in order to protect Juan José, I felt it my duty to call him in, and showed him the ornaments which I had purchased from Agustín for Stevenson. He was thunderstruck. I easily ascertained, then, that these are indeed sacred objects, never to be sold; that it is a great crime to sell them; and that they are distributed among the "braves" without their knowing even who manufactures them. [At present, they are made by the cacique, and possibly other medicine men. (42, 92)] It surprised them greatly when I told them that the cacique made them. Even Ventura (who is one of the *entremeseros*—what that is, I do not know, but they are the dancers [this term generally refers to members of the Ku-sha'lĭ, the "clowns"] and whom Juan José thinks is well informed, was perfectly thunderstruck, and inquired all about it. I shall now wait, but if Agustín does not stop, I shall finally accuse him of the transaction. . . . Afternoon, Agustín goes to Peña Blanca with a letter, probably to bring suit. I finally spoke to the governor in my room. He was perfectly surprised. These ornaments belong to the tribe, and not to the individual who wears them, and they cannot be sold without permission of the tribe. Therefore, I concluded to return them to Agustín, who evidently is very mad at it— but in doing so I avoided his punishment, which otherwise would have been severe. The governor immediately went to the war captain, who fortunately was not at home; otherwise Agustín would have been seized and severely punished. This gives me a deep insight into their customs. At my intercession, the governor was quiet, but if Agustín should do any harm, he will be immediately seized and badly punished. It appears that the war captain has this duty. Notwithstanding this Agustín has brought suit. . . . Juan José is suffering from his whipping. . . .

November 8.   . . . Agustín paid me the $10.00 . . .

November 9.   . . . Juan José has been summoned to Peña Blanca before the J.P. by Agustín. . . . Juan José has settled his affair by paying the costs, $18.50. This was foolish on his part.

It would seem that this might have closed the issue, but in the journal of December 13, 1880, Bandelier noted: "It appears that the junta of last night was again about Agustín and Juan José. The former now wants the latter to be punished by the pueblo. Juan José very sensibly replied that the case was now settled, and that he had paid the cost."

Apparently, this officially closed the incident, though there is little doubt that the factions formed in the course of this controversy did not immediately dissolve. Unpredictable incidents such as this, together with their ramifications to other individuals and other events, are important factors in the daily routine of living. Remaining latent and all but forgotten, they may burst unexpectedly and influentially upon any situation for many years after they first occur.

In the course of this extended dispute, other points of law and order were briefly noted in Bandelier's journal. On November 9, he mentioned that "there is another trouble in the pueblo tonight—a squabble between one of the boys and a Mexican, and so all the boys are cited before the governor. They came to see me, each carrying a stick of firewood. They go begging for it from house to house." While Bandelier did not comment further upon this, it would appear that this was a form of social control, or punishment, whereby these boys, being assigned the menial task of gathering wood from each of the pueblo homes, were exposed to general ridicule.

On December 8, Bandelier noted that Juan José and the governor of Zia Pueblo had had a long talk about robberies which were being committed on the Santa Ana and Zia people; cattle were being stolen, and when the thieves were pursued, they fired upon the tribesmen. A Pueblo *junta* was proposed which could place the collective grievances before Congress. It was suggested that Bandelier might serve as a representative in this.

An entry of April 9, 1882, typified the rather common practice of respected elders, or councilmen, of one pueblo becoming involved in the affairs of another village: "Juan José is very busy with a trial that those of Sta. Ana have with a Mexican, and in which he is going to figure as attorney. In general, he is a kind of country lawyer for the

Indians." And another incident in which some Cochití participated was recorded in Bandelier's entry of July 25, 1885, when he was at San Felipe:

> Afterwards there was a Junta in the house of Santiago, the sacristán, all the *principals* appeared, among them the two "*Shay-qatze*," but the "Hotshan-yi" was not present. The case was curious. A young man of the tribe, who had been to Carlisle-school, & wore American dress, had not only grossly insulted his uncle (one of the *Principals*), but also the other *principals*, given out false reports about the priest and other matters. José Hilario [of Cochití] spoke with great vehemence & the discussion was earnest and violent. At the suggestion of the Priest [Father Navet], two alternatives were left to the boy: either to beg the pardon of each, or to be expelled from the Pueblo. He finally, though with bad grace, took choice of the former, pulled off his shirt, knelt down with only his pants on & begged off. Then he was pardoned and the three *principals* most offended: the Governor, Lieutenant Governor, and his own uncle, stood up, and embraced him one after another. Then he went around and shook hands with the rest, finally the Padre forgave him also.

During the summer of 1951, the Cochití displayed considerable interest in the news that the governor of San Lorenzo (Picurís) Pueblo had been removed by action of the tribe for habitual and excessive drunkenness. They indicated that the same situation could arise, with the same solution, at Cochití. However, no case of a Cochití governor's having been removed for this or any other reason could be recalled by any informant. [3, 44, 45, 62, 70]

Accusations are still presented to the governor, who investigates as best he can and makes a decision on the basis of precedent. If this is not feasible, he convenes a court including his lieutenant and some or all of the other council members. There should be a full complement, but often only a part of the council is present. [92] This appears to be more a matter of chance as to which members are available rather than that any particular men are actually selected. Witnesses, as well as the accuser and the accused, are questioned. After exhausting the evidence, the merits of the two sides are discussed, and a decision is reached. The governor announces this decision, which fixes the blame or absolves it. Punishment may be in the form of monetary fines, such as five dollars for the first offense of drunkenness, ten for the second, or it may take the form of a certain amount of community labor, or, more commonly, so many lashes with the whip kept by the governor. These lashes are administered by one of the three "whipper" *fiscalitos*. This official is closely watched and if it can be detected that he is making the strokes lighter than they should be, another *fiscalito* is designated to complete the sentence on the back of the whipper. One of the last cases of a whipping was that administered to an old woman in 1948, who was convicted of spreading malicious gossip concerning another woman of the tribe. Four lashes on the bared back were ordered in this instance. At any such trial and pronouncement of sentence, the governor and his lieutenant must have their official canes of office in hand. [20, 42]

At present, this traditional system of authority and law enforcement continues, though at an increasingly unsatisfactory level. Monetary fines are difficult to collect; local imprisonment is not possible because there are no facilities, and using jails elsewhere not only costs the tribe money but it does not serve as an effective deterrent to the individual concerned; whippings and economic sanctions such as land confiscation are reluctantly imposed, for they have the cumulative effect of driving the person and often his family with him from the village. Realizing the ineffectiveness of the current system, more and more individuals are tempted to break existing "regulations." Tribal officials are increasingly aware of these failings, but they cannot seem to concur on any practicable solution. With the traditional tribal value system disintegrating, new social controls must be developed. The situation will undoubtedly grow worse before it grows better. (See Lange 1952a.)

8 CEREMONIAL ORGANIZATION

General Statements

PUEBLO CEREMONIALISM has been of great interest in anthropology for many years, partly because of the spectacular and often esoteric nature of many of the rites and partly because of its pervasion throughout the total culture. Comments by Parsons (1939: xi–xiii) about Pueblo ceremonialism in general are equally applicable to Cochití:

However differentiated, all the Pueblos have a well-developed ceremonial life. The Pueblo genius tends strongly toward group rather than individual experience, and this tendency makes for ritual rather than mysticism. Pueblos outchurch the most rigid churchmen. Consequently, of all aspects of their life, their ceremonialism has attracted most attention and inspired most interest in most observers. . . .

Thus in all aspects Pueblo religion is far from a system external to the rest of life. What the outsider from another age or culture calls religion is felt by the insider as an integral part of his life. Descriptions of religious complexes or particulars as borrowed or disintegrated or marginal is also the outsider's classification. To those concerned, a religious fragment, indeed any social fragment, may be as vital and significant, be it loan or survival, as any self-developed or intact unit. In the pueblos, a dance horse is as sacred as a dance deer, and dancing in honor of their saint seems to the townspeople quite as much their own *costumbre* as dancing kachina.

Parson's last sentence is of particular interest in the present discussion, for it appears to have been based on material pertaining to Cochití as recorded by Goldfrank (1927: 46).

Cosmology and Basic Beliefs

Tales of origin and other explanatory accounts of how things have come to be as they are (see Benedict 1931) used to occupy an important position in Cochití life. The past tense is used here because these stories are, at present, known to virtually none of the younger generations. The young people, increasingly exposed to formal education and its teachings, show little interest in such stories; it is the older individual who knows of such matters. This knowledge is possessed by a declining number with the passing years, and among those who do have it, there is less inclination to adhere strictly to details. These details, which in the past have served as the justification for, or the explanation of, the reason certain procedures are followed, steadily lose their significance as they decline in importance or completely disappear from the culture.

Since Benedict and others have already recorded origin and other stories in some detail, they will not be included here. Briefly summarized, the Cochití, as many neighboring tribes do, place the beginning of their ancient existence on earth at "White House," far to the north where they lived with "all the people of the world" following the emergence from Shī'pap after a great flood. Bandelier (October 10, 1880) mentioned the Cochití "Montezuma tale," in which the tribal beginnings are placed at "Tehuayu," to the northwest and north, where "the pueblos were all together in one." Divisions of these peoples both produced and accompanied subsequent migrations, generally in a southerly direction. In the course of these travels, hindrances and aids were contributed by various deities, culture heroes, and animal helpers. Abilities were taught and material possessions were given by them to the Cochití.

In many tales, present-day medicine societies and various tribal officials are mentioned, indicating either their considerable antiquity or a subsequent inclusion through rationalization of these important features into the tribal origin story. Details of the account become clearer and more consistent as the Cochití established residence in Frijoles Cañon, and the final divisions, such as that with San Felipe, occurred. (Such traditions still lack archaeological verification; if they are true, verification should be demonstrable by archaeological excavation, a project the author hopes to pursue.)

Details regarding the nature of the universe are rather few in the literature on Cochití, and little was obtained from my informants on this subject. It is likely that the Cochití beliefs closely parallel those described for Santa Ana by White (1942: 80–88). The world is viewed as a stationary flat, with four underground realms. There is confusion about whether the last of these is "Shī'pap" or whether this term refers to the place at which the ancestors emerged upon the surface of the earth. These worlds are referred to as "rooms," sometimes represented as being located in sequence and sometimes as being arranged concentrically, the last being the innermost one.

The Sun (O'shatsh, or Pai'yat-yama), "the source of life itself," is most closely associated with the east. A former custom, noted by Bandelier in his journal of November 7–8, 1880, was that of the people's greeting the rising sun each morning by going to the river. Here they offered a pinch of corn meal or pollen to the east, the Sun, while looking eastward, and then they proceeded to bathe. Present-day informants had done this themselves as children, but the practice is no longer followed. [42, 92] In his journal of November 10, 1880, Bandelier noted a variation of this—that of adoring the sun from the house tops at sunrise each morning; this practice has also been allowed to lapse. [42, 92] The Sun is personified in many tales and thought of as beginning his travels in the east, passing to the west, where, in setting, he is said "to go home." Masewa and Oyoyewa, the twin war gods, are considered among the most important supernaturals, and the war captains, who bear these names in their official capacities, reflect this prestige and authority in the present-day culture. The home of the Kwe'rana is in the east; that of the Ku-sha'lĭ, though they are more closely associated with the sun, is considered more in the vicinity of Cochití itself, which is the center of the universe. The various ka'tsīnas are linked with Wē'nimats, to the west, where the dead go. Individual ka'tsīnas, many of them still impersonated, figure prominently in various tales. Animal and bird life is personified in the tales, as are the various forces of nature. In contrast to the sun and moon, very few planets and stars are singled out for specific names and distinguishing characteristics. Shī'kwit-koi-matz is the Morning Star; clouds, or more specifically, rainclouds, are Shī'wana. This term is another designation for the ka'tsīnas and is also the name of a secret society, commonly referred to as the "Thundercloud," or "Thunder," Society. It is of interest that membership in this society is limited to women.

In songs (o'wai-yots—"asking for help"), prayers, and general world orientation, the cardinal directions are associated with colors, animals, and trees or plants. While virtually unknown to many present-day Cochití these associations have figured prominently in the ceremonialism and in ritual references. When the hunters sing the hunting songs, the animals are "called" to help them. These songs, as well as those of the medicine men and ka'tsīnas, are commonly sung in traditional but obsolete words, which many of the younger people do not fully comprehend. [44]

It would appear that the numbers *four* and *six* play important parts in Cochití symbolism. Of the two, *four* has a more thorough conceptual development and is usually the pattern of most ceremonials. [3] In relating such details, it is customary to proceed in a counterclockwise circuit, the same pattern followed in dances and other ritual procedures. Individuals vary somewhat among themselves in choosing the starting point; some begin with the east, or, if they consider that they are already figuratively located in the east, they begin with the north. These associations, in sequence of color, animal, and tree or plant, are as follows: North (ka'wish-tēma): yellow, bear, and yellow pine (ha'ñī); West (tsī'pīna): blue-gray, lion, and Douglas fir (ha'kak); South (ta'otyūma): red, badger, and oak (ha'pañī); East (kū¹'chana): white, wolf, and sage (hūash'pa); Up, or zenith (ko'-wa-tyūma): all colors (one informant [45] gave brown for the color here), eagle, and no tree or plant; Down, or nadir (shtī'ya-chana): black, mai't^{yup} (a small molelike animal, seemingly mythical [one informant (15) listed the weasel as the animal for nadir]), and no tree or plant.

Mai't^{yup} appears quite frequently in references to the nadir and also in hunting stories. Although the Cochití say it is a small molelike animal, they insist it is clearly distinguishable from this well-known rodent. It is about mouse size, and it reputedly enters the anus of the deer and chews on the intestines, eventually killing the animal. "Old Man Guerro claimed to have found a buck killed in that way." [3]

These directional names were pointed out as "old," the connotation of the term being that they were used in a ceremonial frame of reference and were unknown to many of the younger people today, who know the directions by the names noted earlier (p. 48). It will be noticed that no tree associations were known for the zenith and nadir. Similarly, these two directions have no "animal hunters" affiliated with them. The animal hunters for the other directions are: North, mo'katch, lion; West, ko'tsana, a little gray hawk with a "pretty whistle," or dya'ñī, the eagle; South, dya't[io], bobcat; and East, ho'pa, or all the Shai'yak (hunters) together. These references, in part contradictory to the usual animal associations, again are limited to hunting rituals and are unknown to many present-day Cochití. [42, 44, 88]

Further directional associations used in composing songs were given as follows: North—associated with the old paths, the ways the old people trod, and olden times, mountains, and clouds; West— lake, home, and origin of all the ka'tsīnas; East and zenith—sun and moon, the sun as the source of life itself, growth, and similar ideas; all four directions—the fields of crops, corn, light breezes blowing, rain, flowing water, corn growing, corn waving, and happy people. [48]

This ceremonial emphasis upon corn reflects the importance of this crop in the food economy, especially before the introduction of wheat and other grains in the post-European era. Corn meal (shka'līna, *Kunque*), particularly blue corn meal, is offered as an accompaniment for any ceremonial request, and in former times, for many requests for labor assistance and other nonceremonial activities. If the person accepts this token offering of meal, it is "offered to the sun" through the act of tossing a pinch of it to the east or toward whatever direction the position of the sun happens to be, and the request is thereby granted.

Corn pollen (ha'tawē) is used in a similar fashion. While the corn is still green, the women gather the pollen and sift it onto a clean cloth in a basket; after cleaning, it is stored in a jar or can. Its use is restricted primarily to adults, especially the medicine men or male and female members of the various secret societies. Ku-sha'lī women gather it for the Ku-sha'lī and also for the Flint medicine men; Kwe'rana women perform this service for their own society and for the Shī'kame Medicine Society; Shī'wana women gather it for the Giant Society members.

The offering or sprinkling of meal and pollen, a relatively simple and often seemingly unconscious gesture, has been an act of great significance in Cochití culture. It invokes supernatural assistance in the matter at hand; it bestows religious sanction upon the proposed activity. Such an act creates a clear-cut distinction between certain items of ceremonial paraphernalia. For the *tablitas* which are worn by the women in certain dances given at the Inter-tribal Ceremonials at Gallup, for example, no meal or pollen is involved in the request for making them or in the actual making of them; hence they may be so used away from the pueblo. However, for the *tablitas* worn at the home ceremonies, meal or pollen does accompany the request to make, or redecorate, the *tablita*. This sanctifies the object. Although the two objects may outwardly appear virtually identical, the one is a sacred object which must be handled in certain ways, kept within the confines of the village or reservation, and never be sold or given to another; the other is mundane and may be seen by aliens and may be sold or given away without incurring the penalties invoked for sacrilegious behavior. [88, 92]

A fundamental belief in the religious orientation of the Cochití is that supernatural power is believed to be held by certain individuals at specific times because these powers have been transmitted to cultural predecessors from supernatural beings during various eras of the past. These specific powers vary in accordance with the person's official capacity, or status, and also to the extent to which he is worthy of that status. Worthiness is evaluated as a person's measuring up to certain cultural ideals; these include industry, kindness, helpfulness, an interest in, but not intense curiosity concerning, others' affairs, an awareness of communal responsibility, providence, honesty, and sincere respect for traditional items and beliefs that are Cochití.

While this is an important concept in the understanding of the Cochití religious attitudes, it is equally important to realize the limitations with which these supernatural powers are viewed. Generally speaking, these powers are functional only with the official duties and responsibilities of the individual. When he is not participating in an event as a society member, for example, he is hardly different from a nonsociety member. Although members of various societies are accorded certain prestige, they do not have unusually fine homes, fields, or other material possessions. No particular privileges are granted them because of their affiliations; none are expected. Membership is assumed to fulfill a promise or vow, through deference to the wishes of some relative (this is increasingly rare, for the Cochití believe that desire for membership must come from the individual), or because of interest in the society's functions and a wish to "help" for the good of all.

These attitudes carry over to the men appointed to secular offices by the theocratic leadership. Authority is vested in these men while they are in office; it passes to their successors subsequently. Respect is paid to the ex-officer, who remains a council member, out of regard for his wisdom and experience, perhaps his age, but not because he is ex-governor, or any other ex-official.

In the same way, it is interesting that despite the extremely close ties between the agricultural economy and the religion, the fields of the medicine men are not especially choice nor is there any feeling that their crops are supposed to be better or freer from insects and other damaging agents.

A possible exception to these generalities is the cacique, especially as of former times. While this rather consistent and omnipresent attitude of reverent awe and respect toward him has weakened, as will be noted in the section dealing with this specific office, it is still apparent among the Conservatives. One cannot but wonder if this feeling toward the cacique may be the surviving remnant of a former prevailing attitude generally accorded all medicine men.

Another facet of Cochití religion is that of the guardian-spirit concept. In Benedict's (1923: 40) paper dealing with this topic for the North American area, she commented as follows:

There are present then in the Southwest most of the elements that we have seen to be associated with the vision-guardian-spirit complex over the rest of the continent. It is the guardian spirit itself that is lacking as an institutionalized element of religion. Under the influence of the concept of group-ceremonial as the proper way of approaching the gods, who here took more and more definite form, individual experience as a means to this end became less and less important, though we are not without evidence that it is present still.

Carrying out this theme, Benedict had earlier (1923: 39) noted, "It is from Cochiti that we have abundance of evidence of the sought vision in the Southwest as an element of contemporary religious practice." For specific examples, she offered excerpts from the Boas manuscripts. In order to provide greater detail here, the original manuscripts were consulted and are presented here in more complete form (Boas 1922):

Men would go out and fast for four days and four nights. They ate only a little mouthful of food and took a mouthful of water once each day. They sang and prayed. If they fasted properly they would see a bear or a mountain lion, coyote, wolf, or eagle, who would come to them and say, "I will help you hunt and catch deer." If the faster asks for rain, the animals may appear and give him rain.

When a person wishes to be a gambler, a person may appear to him and give him power in gambling.

John Dixon remembers a man to whom a bear appeared. He was a good deer hunter. He believed that the bear had spoken to him and promised to help him. This happened while the hunter was in the mountains in a deep canyon. Suddenly, he heard something calling from the distance, "Hu, hu!" It sounded like the growl of a bear. He stopped to listen, then he heard the roaring coming nearer. He did not know what it was and went into hiding. He remained hidden in the bushes and held his gun in readiness. Finally, the noise came very near, and he saw a bear which came close to him. The animal was supernatural (mai'mai) and stopped right in front of him. The bear spoke, "Friend, do not shoot me. I know that if I don't talk to you, you will shoot, for you are holding your gun in readiness. I want to be your friend. Do not shoot me. I am going to help you when you go out hunting deer. You will get as many as you want." Then the man put down his gun. From that time on the hunter could get as many deer as he wanted. In telling about this adventure, he said that the bear was really a person and that he was only wearing a bearskin.

After he had killed many deer, the bear spoke to him and said, "Now, friend, go home. Carry as much of the medicine as you can take along. But you must come back for the rest of the medicine. When you reach home, tell your wife to make wafer bread and when you come back, bring some of it." The man obeyed, and when he came back he carried some wafer bread. He met the bear and gave it to him. The bear returned to his home in the mountains. The man carried the deer home. For four days, his wife made wafer bread and pachute (?) for the man and the bear. For four days he went back into the mountains, but he did not see the bear. He left it on the ground so that the bear could get it.

All kinds of people believe that the bear is their friend. They carry bears' claws and act like bears. The bear is supernatural and a shaman. When a person is cured, wafer bread is made for two days. This is given to the shaman who gives it to the bears. The mountain lion and eagle are also friends of the shamans. When a shaman wants to go to a distant country, the eagle carries him there. The mountain lion is their protector on account of his scent.

Elsewhere (1922: 947) Boas noted that "intending basketmakers must fast four days and take emetics. After that a woman will appear to them who will help them in making baskets." Boas (1922: 994) also noted the procedure followed by warriors who wished to obtain assistance from the supernaturals:

If a person wants to become a brave warrior he must bring many sacrifices at midnight to a place on the Rio Grande called Muskrat House. He must take off all his clothing and throw down sacred cornmeal. He must go into the water and sit in it so that the water reaches up to his neck. Then he will feel that somebody is pulling him. After sitting in the water for some time, he dresses again and goes home. He is not allowed to look backward, and may not run, but he walks home very slowly. Then he will feel that somebody is pulling him and trying to induce him to look back. If he should be frightened and look back on the way, he loses his life, or at least he will not be successful in his endeavor. If he is not afraid, he will become a great warrior.

This account by Boas is interesting in comparison with a similar statement by Dumarest (1919: 145). Young men were led to the river to bathe; upon leaving, they did not dare look back or they would receive wounds in battle. Further parallels may be noted in the procedure followed in gathering salt (cf. pp. 142–143). Still another account was noted by Boas (1922: 994):

People also go to a short, deep canyon in the Peralta. It is a short, deep canyon which runs northward and is called Ga'ectaya, that is, Windy. Four days before starting, the man must purify himself by taking cedar emetics. He must go to the place at midnight. When they arrive there, they must sacrifice cornmeal to the Supernatural Beings. Finally, they arrive at a waterfall. There he must take off his clothing and stand there looking northward. He sacrifices again and prays to the Supernatural Being (Mai'-mai) who lives in the canyon. He also sacrifices turkey feathers (yectde). He asks to be made brave and to be able to withstand the Apache and Navaho. After praying, he draws in his breath four times, holding his hand in front of his mouth, and goes back. As soon as he turns, terrific noises are heard as though rocks are falling down. He feels as if people are pulling him, and a tornado is rushing through the canyon. He must go out slowly without looking back. If he goes out slowly, the noise finally ceases as soon as he leaves the canyon. As soon as he leaves the canyon, he has to turn back and draw in the breath four times through his hands and then he prays.

This general practice of breathing in from the hands or some object, or the reverse of breathing upon either hands or various objects, either to derive or impart power is not only Cochití but is typical of the Southwestern Pueblos in general. (See Parsons 1939: 419–423.) The Cochití term for "power," in any of these supernatural aspects, is īañī.

Still another account recorded by Boas (1922: 947) pertains to the experiences of warriors and the supernatural:

> There is a small black mesa near Peña Blanca which is also used in order to obtain power for the warrior. The applicant must go up slowly and has to look southward. There he sacrifices the same way as in the canyon. Then he turns back and goes home slowly. Formerly, there was a small trail that was followed, but it has now disappeared. As soon as he turns back thunder is heard and there is a whirlwind. He sees fire come from the mountain, and there are unearthly cries. He feels people pulling him backward. To the south of the hill is a small arroyo. As soon as he has crossed this, walking slowly without turning back, the noises cease. Then he must turn back and sacrifice and pray.

> The information in regard to these sacred places was given to the informant by a shaman who claimed to have visited them all. He also heard it from the former Naihya [nahī'ya], Francisco Nambé, his father. He had visited these places, was never wounded, and Francisco was only once slightly wounded, while they themselves were able to kill a great many enemies. When the informant, his older brother and cousins were young, his father told them about these places, but advised them not to go there because it would be too hard for them.

The Office of Cacique

Within the ranks of the Conservatives, the office of cacique is currently considered the most important position in the tribe. This evaluation has remained constant for many years, especially since the complete disappearance of the position of nahī'ya, or head of the Warriors Society, about the end of the last century. In earlier times, the nahī'ya and the cacique shared responsibilities, the nahī'ya assuming charge during intertribal hostilities and in matters concerned with war, and the cacique dominating in peaceful times and activities. With the passing of the nahī'ya from the culture, certain authority and prestige formerly accorded this official passed in part to the cacique and in part to the war captains.

At present, it is recognized that the cacique, despite his prominent status and role, can be called to account by the war captains for any dereliction of official duties. If found guilty, the cacique may be punished or even deposed; in extreme cases, he may be executed by the war captains. No case of deposition or punishment could be recalled by informants (one might well wonder whether this was actually true or merely an ethnocentric view for the benefit of an outsider). It is the cacique, it will be recalled, who appoints the war captain and his assistant each year. Thus, while the war captains are undoubtedly powerful figures, as discussed in the preceding chapter, the cacique too is influential, belonging also to the Flint Medicine Society. Furthermore, he is reinforced by a considerable body of tradition, a circumstance which justifies and enhances his position in the omnipresent religious life of the tribe. Appendix 17 consists of a diagram explaining Cochití political and ceremonial organization.

Despite the extremely esoteric nature of the Cochití religious structure and the position occupied by the cacique within that structure, there is a surprisingly large body of data regarding this office. However, because of the general lack of detailed knowledge on the part of most informants and a common reluctance to reveal more than fragments of this knowledge, the data are confusing, contradictory, and incomplete. The following discourse appears in Bandelier's journal of June 20, 1886:

> The Cacique, at the same time, is "Hishtanyi-Chayan" [Flint medicine man], "Shui-Chayan" [Snake medicine man], "Mash-tshi-Chayan," "Potsho-Asht-Chayan," "Hakanyi-Chayan" [Fire medicine man], and "Capina-Chayan" [K'apina medicine man (according to White [1930: 604] this group had not been reported for Cochití)]. He is also the medicine man of war, and in the night before the campaign, blesses and paints the weapons. He goes along or sends along some of his household [Qoye] to represent him. [Here, one wonders whether Bandelier meant "family household" or one of his official "household," i.e., members of the Flint Society or perhaps any of the medicine societies. Present-day Cochití frequently fail to distinguish between ceremonial societies and kinship groupings in their use of the term "clan."] His death in battle is always considered as a very great misfortune, a sign of utter defeat! He told me of an incident in the campaign against the Yutes, when the *Hishtanyi Chayan* was felled to the ground by a shot which merely perforated his shield, & his people were terribly frightened, thinking all was lost. But he recovered, and they finally whipped the Yutes.
>
> This is interesting as in regard the battle of Otumpan, & the real office held by the chieftain whose death decided the fate of that engagement. "*Maseua*" and "*Oyoyaua*" were brothers—twins, but "*Cenquitye*" made everything. He also made two twin-sisters, "*Nau-tzi-te*" and "*Osh-tzi-te*." These quarrelled at the Casa Blanca near the Spanish Peaks in Colorado,

and fought. The older one, *"Nautzite,"* won, and took the middle line [down the Rio Grande]—there were the Pueblos; the other took the western line, and she was mother to the Navahos! *"Oeshtzite"* left a peculiar medicine and a song in the Navaho language, and while the other Pueblos have the medicine and song of *"Nautzite"* alone, those of Cochiti and Jemez possess also the former.

Therefore, the people of Cochiti have a song in the Navaho language, and when the cacique there dies without a successor having been designated, and there is none able to step in his shoes, then they go to Jemez for a new cacique and also those of Jemez come to Cochiti for a cacique in similar instances. There is consequently a connection between those two Pueblos and the Navahos, which the latter acknowledge & they fear them in war since they have the same medicine. That medicine is called by him also "comer lumbre," fire eating. Therefore the cacique is called *"Hakanyi Chayan."* The stick called "Potsho-äsht", lightning [Pot'ro-esht (92)], is used by him in the Estufa, and it is a part of that medicine too. When the Pueblos met at Jemez, those of Zia, Sᵃ Ana, etc., to go to war against the Navahos, the warriors of Cochiti secretly meet those of Jemez in the Estufa and have their weapons blessed by the Cacique of Jemez also.

And he records in his journal entry of July 26, 1888:

It is the rule, that Ho'chañī [cacique] is always Flint headman, Hish-Ta-Nyi Cha-Yan mayor, Na-Ua. He it is who holds in his power all the higher medicines. The Shkuy-Chayan [Giant head] and the Shī'kame Chayan [head] are his assistants in so far that these three together are the Yaya, since they are those who intercede with the Yaya-Tesh or higher good spirits, who fast and pray for the good of the tribe in general. But only the Ho'chañī has the medicines, the others have to go to him for what they need. The Flint head has also the great war medicine and he it is who prepares and fits out the warrior, previous to starting out for a campaign. This, the putting on of the war paint and annointing of the weapons with sacred paints, is done in the night before departure. Only the Flint head or one of his assistants has the right and the power to do this. For it seems that the three great Chayani are but the heads of so many departments so to say:—The Flint has under him a certain number of what might be called Assistant Flints, the Giant, a certain number of Assistant Giants, and the Shī'kame, also a band of Shī'kame assistants. All are medicine men, doctors, in addition to their higher arts and duties. I gather that the Uisht-Ya-ka is also the Giant head, and the Shay-ka-tse is the Shī'kame head. So there would be only three Yaya. These are not permitted to listen to anything conducive to disorder or strife within the tribe. If in any meeting an angry discussion arises, or there are any signs of trouble, the Yayas must leave forthwith; and should they refuse, it is the duty of the Maseua and of his brother, or lieutenant, to *compel* them to leave.

When a war party returns with trophies, the Flint head is the only one who dares to go out to receive them, conduct them with triumph to the Pueblo, and prepare them afterwards for the solemn dance of the scalps. Neither of the other two or any of their assistants can touch these matters. If they do it, they would be exposed to grave punishment.

A cacique, according to Bandelier (1890: 280–282), was considered ad interim until capable of assuming office. His "education" was conducted by various assistants, other medicine men, and the war captain: "At Cochiti, until two years ago, there was but a cacique *ad interim*. Now the 'legitimate' chief penitent has succeeded, but there is no trace of the two assistants."

The reference to "two assistants" is clarified by a journal entry of July 14, 1885, in which Bandelier stated that there were formerly three caciques: ho'tshan-yi, the leading figure; Shay-qa-tze, the second; and Uisht-yagga, the third one. The entry on the following day added that when there had been three caciques, the ho'tshan-yi appointed the war captains; Shayqatze appointed the governor. The captain was considered the chief officer, and devoted more time to the warriors. Uishtyagga attended to the personal wants of the leading cacique, and he cooked for the three whenever they were together. This indicated to Bandelier that the three were at times isolated together. The parallels suggested here are interesting in relation to the functions of the cacique and the heads of the Giant and Shī'kame societies discussed later in this section. Whether Bandelier recorded a confused account of the personnel involved, or whether the present situation is simply the eventual product of culture change is difficult to determine.

Regarding the point of membership in the Flint Society, one informant [88] stated that according to his father, who had served as a war captain and had been an important figure in the tribe, the cacique was not supposed to belong to any society. In other words, he should be classified as a si^{rr}'shtī, or *Crudo*, or "one of the general public." The connotation of the term "si^{rr}'shtī" appears to be that the person is "raw" in the sense of being unripe, immature, or unfinished. In contrast, there are those described as kē'nat, or "cooked"; this designation appears to be reserved for only the members of Ku-sha'lī and Kwe'rana. It is interesting that members with other society affiliations, e.g., those of the medicine or ka'tsīna groups, are differenti-

ated, along with nonmembers, as "raw." The implication may perhaps be one of relative antiquity of these societies, or it may be
simply one of rationalizing certain tribal traditions. "Cooked" carries
the connotation of being "done" rather than "raw" or "half-baked";
perhaps even better, "cooked" refers to the condition of "having arrived," i.e., of being "in" on the sacred knowledge of the tribe or of
being ceremonially and culturally mature. All this is in contrast to
those who belong to no society, or at least not the Ku-sha'lī or
Kwe'rana societies.

As noted in Appendix 18, the roster of caciques during the last
sixty years or more reveals that all five caciques have been Ku-sha'lī
members as well as Flint. Just how this change from an unaffiliated
status occurred, if it occurred at all, could not be learned. While these
two societies are very closely bound, dual membership is not necessary [88], a fact confirmed by the roster of Flint members in Appendix 19 and the roster of Ku-sha'lī members, Appendix 27. The
same informant [88] had the impression that the current cacique of
both Tesuque and Jemez pueblos were *Crudos*—"That's the way it
should be." White (1932a: 41) noted that the Acoma cacique "is not
a medicine man."

A conflicting viewpoint on the matter of society affiliations was
expressed by another informant [52], who stated that the present
Cochití cacique is not actually qualified for office since he holds
membership only in Flint (and Ku-sha'lī) and not in the Snake and
Fire medicine societies into which he should also have been initiated.
He further complained that the preceding cacique had, so far as he
knew, never belonged to the Fire Society. Bandelier, in his journal of
August 21, 1888, stated that the cacique at that time was the only
member of the Fire Medicine Society. "Formerly, there used to be
three or four of them."

As noted by White (1942: 96) and others, the term *cacique* is
Spanish; the Cochití normally use a shortened form, referring to this
official as "ka'sīk." Recent caciques have also been called Flint
headman (hiʳ'shtī-añī na'waiya) and, together with the Giant and
Shī'kame heads, the cacique has been known as "tshrai'katse." No
meaning was learned for this term, but as Goldfrank (1927: 46)
noted, it is encountered in connection with hunting activities. The
cacique is also called "ho'chañī," or chief. Still another term is
"shtē'ya-moñī," the meaning of which was not learned. White (1942:
96) credited Boas with the translation of this term as "leader."

"Shtē'ya-moñī," in addition, is used in reference to a sacred-stone fetish kept by the cacique. This fetish, and the cacique, are both also referred to as "yaya," or mother.

There is likewise some feeling that the cacique is the "father" of his people. Bandelier, in his journal of October 7, 1880, stated: "The cacique himself is the father of the tribe or pueblo; he appoints his own successor, and he has to receive at his house and entertain all strangers coming into the pueblo." The "father" aspect may be a relatively recent addition which followed the disappearance of the nahī'ya (head of the Warriors), or it may have developed through cumulative influence from Christianity. White (1942: 96; 1942a: 305–306) has cited parallels for most of these terms among the other Keresan tribes.

Bandelier reported (October 5, 1880) being told by Teodosio Cordero, a council member, that the cacique "commands everything" (*manda todo el pueblo*). It can be safely said that the power and influence of the position of cacique, as the religious head of a traditional theocracy such as Cochití, undoubtedly varied with the individuals holding the office. In cases of strong-willed and able persons, this power approached the absolute. While the present cacique is by no means an absolute ruler, he still wields considerable influence among the Conservatives of the tribe.

Goldfrank (1927: 43) stated that only a Ku-sha'lī member was eligible to become Flint head, who, according to her data, was a different person from the cacique. My informants. on the other hand, said the offices of cacique and Flint Society head are, and have always been, simultaneously filled by the same man. [3, 15, 70, 92] Goldfrank stated that there was a feeling, as of the time of her studies, that all Flint shamans must also be Ku-sha'lī and this undoubtedly stemmed from the fact that the Flint head had to be Ku-sha'lī.

If this was an ideal at that time, the actual instances (see Appendix 19) of a Flint member's not being Ku-sha'lī are interesting. White (1930: 612) merely commented that there was a close relationship between the Flint and Ku-sha'lī societies. Curtis (1926: 84) stated that the Flint headman was also cacique. Dumarest (1919: 196) said the cacique was the Flint shaman who had been a member the longest period of time. At the point of death, he named his successor, but he was obligated to name the man who had been a member the next longest time after himself. Bandelier, in his journal of April 4, 1882, stated, "But the cacique never selects his successor from his own family." Whether this was ever a formal rule could not be learned. The list of caciques contains one instance of a son and father both serving. However, two other caciques served between the terms of these men. (See Appendix 18.)

The procedure related by Dumarest was confirmed by my inform-ants, and in light of this, the succession of caciques in December, 1946, is noteworthy. The rule of succession was, in this case, broken when Victoriano Cordero, the incumbent, died on December 12, and Marcelo Quintana became cacique on December 18. When Victori-ano became ill shortly before his death, he named Marcelo as cacique pro tem. This violated the Cochití rule, for another Flint shaman, Juanito Trujillo, had been a member for a longer time than Marcelo. One explanation was that Juanito himself had refused the office on the ground that he was an old man (sixty-four at the time) and a widower with no one to care for him. [52] Other informants had not heard of this and simply stated they did not understand why nor how the deviation had occurred. Still another [92] claimed that Victoriano died without actually having named a successor, though Marcelo was acting as cacique pro tem. Under the circumstances, the war cap-tain (Epifanio Pecos) and the assistant war captain (Diego Romero) had simply told the council that Marcelo should be cacique, having already been designated cacique pro tem because of his greater ex-perience and knowledge. This opinion was supported by the council. From comments by several councilmen, it would seem that Victoriano had not been a popular cacique and also that Juanito was not a par-ticularly popular person, either. Thus the council, aware of Marcelo's general popularity, willingly bypassed the traditional procedure in the hope that a more popular cacique would be successful in leading the tribe into better times.

Though contrary to most of the data, still another account held that the new cacique was selected by a group composed of the two war captains and the headmen of the medicine societies. [52] It may well be that such a procedure, still not ideally recognized, is being followed in a present-day attempt to depart from the former rigid control of the cacique by transferring the control to such a group as indicated. Thus, while the theocracy is outwardly unchanged, the line of succession is gradually becoming somewhat democratized, though still controlled by the Conservative leaders.

A precedent for the war captain's taking the lead in naming a new cacique in cases where the incumbent dies without designating his successor was noted in Bandelier's journal of April 4, 1882:

> He told me that the Cacique often, and even commonly, selected his successor while yet a boy, and then began to train him. If the Cacique saw his end nearing, and that successor was yet too young, he called for another man who enjoyed his confidence, entrusted him with the secrets of his office, and with the care of the young man. When the latter became fit for office, then the *"interim"* turns over the office to him. . . . If the cacique dies without naming his successor, the Captain (which is also named "Masaua") called together the pueblo, and they appoint a new cacique.

Regarding the "secrets of his office," an earlier journal entry of Bandelier's (November 18, 1880) is of interest: "What the secret of the cacique is, he alone knows. It must be a weighty one, since Juan José says the caciques hardly last longer than twenty years in office." A more plausible explanation might be that by the time an individual has mastered sufficient knowledge to assume this office, he has reached an age at which, under the general life expectancy of the Cochití, he could rarely anticipate more than another twenty years of life.

While the full details of installing a new cacique were not obtained, the following account provides the broad outlines of the procedure as enacted at the time of Marcelo Quintana's installation, December 18, 1946. Following the decision to convert Marcelo's pro tempore designation to that of full-fledged cacique, the war captain called a meeting of all the people at the Turquoise Kiva. They began to assemble in the late afternoon, about five o'clock, and seated themselves in the kiva in about the order in which they arrived, no areas being reserved for any particular group. On such an occasion as this, once a person is in the kiva, he is not allowed to leave. If it is necessary for someone to relieve himself, there are ollas available.

After some waiting, the war captain, the Giant headman, Marcelo, the Shī'kame headman, and, finally, the lieutenant war captain entered, in that order. Descending the ladder, they moved along the wall of the kiva in a counterclockwise manner to the north wall. (Fig. 16) While standing, the war captain, Epifanio Pecos, spoke to the people, and his lieutenant, Diego Romero, added some comments. Both spoke of the respect that everyone owed the cacique and pointed out that the cacique must respect the people and his position

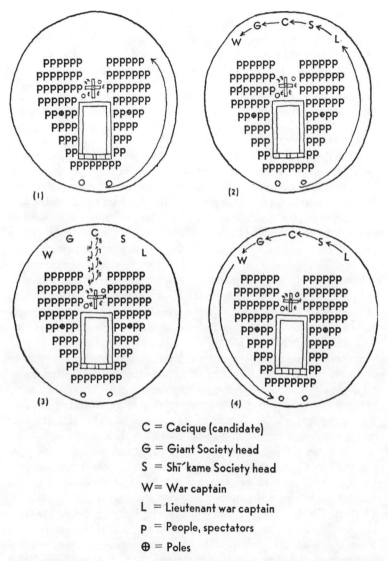

C = Cacique (candidate)

G = Giant Society head

S = Shī´kame Society head

W = War captain

L = Lieutenant war captain

p = People, spectators

⊕ = Poles

Fig. 16.—Arrangement and Movement of Various Individuals During the Installation of a Cacique.

so that the people could, in turn, respect him. Then the five men seated themselves in their places along the north wall. Marcelo next got to his feet and spoke, telling the people that he was to take Victoriano's place and that, in contrast, he was a very young man (relatively inexperienced) but would do his best. (Plate 26b)

After this speech, the people all rose and turned, facing south. The Giant and Shī'kame heads joined in a medicine song, after which Marcelo took four steps south, toward mo'katch, the fire box (in which there was no fire). He was then standing close to a sort of "sand painting" made of a mixture of white and blue corn meal which had been spread in the form of a cross, the arms of which were about 18 inches long. At the center stood the large fetish, shtē'ya-moñī (also known as the cacique's "yaya"). This figure, about 6 inches in diameter and 15 inches in height, is made of black lava, but it appears to be of a red substance owing to the long-standing practice of sprinkling it with red ochre, or *almagre*. It is in approximately a kneeling position, with the arms crossed on the chest. The figure is adorned with necklaces of turquoise and coral beads and with abalone (wa'-ponu) earrings.

As the Giant and Shī'kame heads sang several songs, they arranged around the figure and cross of meal various stone animals and bowls, some containing corn meal and some containing water. Various pantomimes accompanied the songs, and water from the bowls was sprinkled by dipping eagle feathers (actually two complete eagle wings) in the water.

The cacique remained standing before these ceremonial objects until each person had touched the fetish, in the process of which each one breathed from it, absorbing ī'añī, or power. At the conclusion of this phase of the ritual, the cacique took four steps back to his first position or, as one informant described it, "four jumps," in the course of which he was said to be "returning from the outer world" with power. The touching of the fetish by all enabled the cacique to then "pick up all the people" (i.e., all the Pueblos, like Taos, Isleta, Hopi, and the others, but not the Navaho or Apache). This was "just a motion" which symbolized that he embraced them with his care and protection.

Upon returning to his position along the north wall, the cacique talked further to the assembled people. Then the war captain added certain comments, as did the lieutenant. With that the five men left the kiva in the same order in which they had entered, continuing

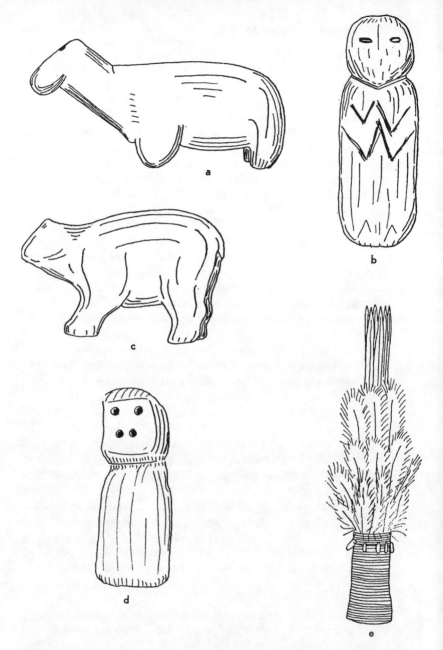

Fig. 17.—Stone Idols and I'ar-iko. The idols (*a, b, c,* and *d*) average about three inches in length; the ī'ar-īko (*e*) stands about fifteen inches in height.

the counterclockwise circuit back to the ladder. The people remained in their places until the war captain returned after a few minutes and dismissed them.

No feasting followed, as is customary following the installation of the new secular officers each year. The medicine men other than the heads—Juanito Trujillo of the Flint and Vicente Suina of the Giants —did not appear during the above proceedings. Informants were of the opinion that they were "busy" with other matters in their respective society houses. The three head medicine men returned to the ho'chanī-ītsa, from which they emerged after a short time.

For this occasion, the war captain and his lieutenant were dressed in their nicest clothing, such as they would wear as a member of a chorus for a *Tablita* Dance. The three medicine men were naked except for a black breechcloth. Their hair was fastened in *chongo* fashion, and they wore no moccasins, no feathers, nor any body paint. The cacique wore a necklace of bear claws and had a streak of red paint across his cheeks and the nasal bridge. The other two medicine men were similarly dressed; informants did not agree as to whether they wore a bear-claw necklace or not. One informant [55] stated that the cacique had a streak of black paint on his chin; another [42] did not recall such a streak and was of the opinion that it was not there. Each of the three medicine men had a bowl of medicine water placed on the floor in front of him. [42, 55, 92, 93]

The cacique keeps for the Flint Society the shtē'ya-moñī mentioned in the above account, and each of the other medicine societies has a similar "yaya," though they are not as large. In addition, the cacique, as does every other medicine man, has his own sacred fetish, basically a perfect ear of corn with various feathers arranged on it, the ī'arīko. (Fig. 17e) Any of these fetishes, as well as ka'tsīnas and other deities, may be referred to under the heading of "ko'pirsh-tai-a." This term has several connotations—that of a deity or supernatural, a ghost, a soul—somewhat comparable to the conception of the Holy Ghost, according to one informant [55]. Its use in reference to the ka'tsīnas, specifically, appears to be rather unusual, being limited to the less tangible aspects of the ka'tsīnas and almost never to the actual dances. [42, 92]

Another instance of confusion in the succession of caciques occurred early in this century, according to one informant. [88] Guadalupe Romero, the cacique, died about 1905. He wanted a man by the name of Ko'hai-o (Bear) to succeed him, the same man mentioned later as one of the last Warriors at Cochití. However, Ko'hai-o was bypassed (the informant thought because he was not a medicine man), and Antonio Suina became cacique. This explanation by the informant is noteworthy in view of the already-mentioned opinion of another informant that the cacique should be a *Crudo* only (pp. 239–240). In any event, it is interesting that the incumbent cacique should even have considered for his successor a man who was not properly qualified. It was said that it was at this time that many of the "old" tribal secrets were lost forever; additional losses occurred in the intrapueblo dispute between Conservatives and Progressives in the early 1920's. [65]

The loss of secrets and ceremonial paraphernalia, including those from sales of equipment, is interesting not so much for the fact that it has existed and continues even at present as for the personnel involved. Frequent mention is made throughout the Bandelier journals of the collecting activities by various representatives of scientific institutions. While all transactions regarding ceremonial paraphernalia were conducted in more or less strict secrecy, there was seldom any suggestion that contacts were difficult to arrange. Sellers or traders of the small stone idols—the ī'arīko, hunting fetishes, and the like (Fig. 17), for the most part reputed to have been made by the cacique as a part of his responsibilities—included a fairly diverse group of individuals. In his journal of November 7, 1880, Bandelier noted, "These ornaments belong to the tribe, and not to the individual who wears them, and they cannot be sold without permission of the tribe." Later, June 20, 1888, Bandelier mentioned the cacique's making the "I'yiare Qo," and using them in curing. He added, "The cacique is also making them for sale!"

The attempt to compile a roster of caciques (Appendix 18) with their terms of office was only partially successful. [3, 15, 25, 42, 44, 70, 88] A rather striking revelation is contained in this roster. Because of the strong affiliations among the Flint, Ku-sha'lī, and Turquoise Kiva memberships, it has often been assumed that a cacique should be a member of the Turquoise Kiva. From the roster, it is apparent that not only is a Pumpkin Kiva man permitted to become cacique, but at Cochití, four of the six caciques that are remembered there have been Pumpkin Kiva members. The shift to the Turquoise Kiva appears to have been a recent development, not only in the choice of caciques but in the entire membership of the Flint Society, as the roster (Appendix 19) indicates. The ramifications of the shift in headship of the Flint Society is discussed in greater detail in the chapter on political organization, where it is noted that the balance between the two moiety groups, the Turquoise and Pumpkin, has been badly upset in the last thirty years or more.

Bandelier, in his journal of October 16, 1880, stated, "Ceremonial councils are held at the home of the cacique, not in the estufas." Such meetings are still held at ho'chañī-ītsa [92]. My informants stated that in the past the Cochití built a new house for each cacique when he first took office. This house contained living quarters for him and his family as well as a room set aside for his official functions as tribal religious leader. Antonio Suina was the last cacique for whom a house was specifically constructed about 1905; this house, just west of the Turquoise Kiva, is still used as a residence by his descendants. When Victoriano Cordero became cacique, the pueblo built the present "office" for him, close to his own home. This office has never been used as a residence; it comprises the eastern half of the Ku-sha'lī Society house, and its entrance is through the western room which is used by the Ku-sha'lī. At present, the cacique continues to use these quarters for official purposes while maintaining his residence at some distance. That one of the cacique's duties is to observe the sun and its marches north and south on the eastern horizon is indicated by the framed aperture high on the eastern wall of his office. Informants thus far, cannot, or will not, give any details of these solstice observations other than to comment that they are still made by the cacique at certain times of the year. [44, 45, 53]

Traditionally, the cacique has been the person to care for the jar of scalps taken by Cochití warriors. He "feeds" the scalps periodically (this commonly involves the sprinkling of corn meal and pollen on them—in much the same way the drums are "fed" [44, 52, 92]) and sees that they cause no harm to his people. This function brought the cacique into close relationship with the Warriors Society, or Ompī, during its existence. However, this group, as noted later in this chapter, has been extinct since about the close of the last century.

In his journal of October 22, 1880, Bandelier stated:

When a war party returns, they appear in front of Juan José's house. The man who does the first killing, not the man who kills the most, leads the file; the war captain goes by his side. Then they deposit the scalps at the cemetery entrance and enter the church to pay their devotion to San Buenaventura. Afterwards, they go around the pueblo singing and finally they go into the kiva [always the Turquoise Kiva for this (92)] where they report to the people about the campaign. Finally, the war dance and war song are performed, and the crowd disperses. The scalps are preserved by the cacique at his own house, hung to a round shield.

On the preceding day, Bandelier had written: "In the estufas they also hang up the scalps, for they cut off the scalps with the ears and suspend them on the rim of a shield on a pole painted red." One of my informants [92] claimed to have seen this assemblage but stated that "it is gone now."

The following is an entry in the diary of Starr for September 19, 1897, the source being named as John Dixon:

Formerly there were many scalps here. The whole hairy covering including at times the ears themselves or parts of them was taken. It was stretched and dried upon a little ring. These scalps—of this kind—were taken by all the Pueblos. Formerly there was a great bunch of them, which were brought out in the Scalp Dance. This was conducted by a society—"the Warriors," membership in which was secured by the simple taking of a Navaho scalp, by any man. If any are left now they would be in charge of the Cacique or of the chief of the warriors who happens to be the father of Andres—Antonio's late son-in-law.

Six days later Starr recorded a futile attempt to view the scalps "in the hands of the Cacique." He was told that "many still are left—all in Cacique's possession—but the hair has all disappeared."

Information pertaining to the present feeding of the scalps varied greatly. According to three informants, the cacique still washes and feeds the scalps [44, 52, 92]; according to another, the previous cacique was the last one to do this [49]; another stated that a still earlier cacique had been the last one to care for them [70]; and still another disclaimed any knowledge of the subject [25]. This last statement came from an individual who, had he so chosen, was probably the best qualified to answer of any informant with whom the matter was discussed. Hence, his reply was taken as indicating a complete unwillingness to discuss the matter, at least with an outsider, and in all probability an unconscious revelation that at least certain phases of caring for the scalps are still practiced at Cochití, as the first three informants indicated.

Bandelier (1890: 281–282) wrote that the cacique was the great medicine man of war. He had "Yerba del Mansa" (*Anemopsis californica*), pulverized leaves and stems from herbs of the lizard's-tail family, which strengthened his warriors and struck terror in the hearts of the enemy. He painted warriors to make them terrible and also invulnerable. He was a powerful doctor, and in war the cacique tended the wounded as a surgeon and nurse. In his journal of April 4, 1880, Bandelier stated, "He is also the medicine-man of the pueblo; even for the Mexicans."

The cacique is supposed to devote his time to the spiritual and physical welfare of his people. In addition to making sun observations, he spends much time in rituals and periods of fasting and meditation. For example, on the day his field is planted and again when the community harvests the corn crop, he spends the day in seclusion at ho'chañi-itsa with the Giant and Shi'kame heads. On such retreats a single go'atchīnī guards them from any outside intrusion. [92] He also joins in activities of the Flint Society and is an ex officio member of the other medicine societies. It seems that the cacique's working in his personal fields and his continuing as a drum-maker for commercial purposes constitute a break from the old pattern in which the pueblo completely supported their religious leader and his family. The present cacique's playing baseball in 1947, the year following his installation in office, was likewise a departure from a cacique's former aloofness from mundane affairs. According to informants, pressure from the older people has corrected this last-named breach with the traditions of the office.

Formerly, the cacique exercised control over the people in such matters as their leaving the pueblo. Bandelier noted such an instance in his journal of October 18, 1880, stating that Juan José had spoken to the cacique about leaving the pueblo with Bandelier, "and that the cacique had told him there was nothing in the way, but that if anything should transpire calling for his stay, one of his sons might go with me. This shows that they (at least the *principales*) are careful to inform the cacique of their actions and it may even prove that they need his consent.(?)"

This custom has all but lapsed at present-day Cochití. Few officers or society members feel obligated to mention their plans to leave to the cacique. Instead, society members normally clear such plans with the society head, and officers do likewise with the governor. The cacique himself is much freer to leave and remain away from the pueblo than was formerly the case. [92]

One informant recalled that in his childhood, a half-century ago, it was customary for one to go to the cacique and ask his blessing before he left the village on a trip. If the cacique had recently completed some ceremonial and had a bowl of water or prayer meal on hand, he would sprinkle this on the person's head, "like holy water." The same procedure was likely to be followed upon the traveler's return [88], perhaps as a purification rite commonly followed in the pueblos after contact with the outside world.

If a man is a council member at the time he becomes cacique, he gives up his council duties upon assuming office. Bandelier (1890: 282) said that the cacique opened the council meeting with a speech or, more properly, a prayer. Normally, he then retired and did not listen to, or engage in, the discussions. Occasionally, he remained and presented his views. My informants stated that, as of the present, he does not attend council meetings, not even to open them. If he happens to have personal knowledge of a problem under discussion, he may be called upon to present this information. When he has finished, he immediately leaves, for it "isn't right for the cacique to hear arguments or sarcasm." [3, 15, 92]

The cacique, as head of the Flint Society, has another important function. This is the annual selection of the two war captains, whose principal duties are to preserve tribal traditions and secrets and to lead the fight against tribal enemies. In recent years, these enemies are conceived of as being more internal than alien. An important phase of the war captains' duties involves the combating of the harmful effects of witches. Thus, the war captains are placed in a position of close co-operation with the cacique and all other medicine men who have the primary duty of combating ills caused by witchcraft.

Witchcraft and Superstition

Witchcraft among the Cochití is by no means an extinct phenomenon. As indicated for the Navaho by Kluckhohn (1944: 9–12), the fact that this topic is not mentioned in general conversation is not an indication of its absence in the culture; rather, it is a clear-cut manifestation that witchcraft is not a topic to be considered lightly. Even those who do not personally believe in witchcraft respect the danger of becoming implicated in charges of witchcraft by those who do hold such beliefs. This is explained as a simple recognition of the power and influence of those who maintain dominant control in this culture, i.e., the cacique and other medicine men and, through them, the secular officers and council members.

Witches, or "bad people" (ka'nat-yai-ya) appear frequently in the literature. They are believed to appear in many forms—human, animal, and bird—and in different well-known forms, such as deer, coyotes, owls, and others, or as such objects as "fireballs," 6 to 12 inches in diameter, which consist of a black center with a surrounding surface of fiery, red flames. The "bad people" may appear in any of these forms before any person—Cochití, other Indians, Spaniards, or Anglos. They speak in the language of the person addressed, calling to him, threatening him, seeking to involve him in evil doings. The medicine men, with the help and protection of the war captains, are the most successful opponents of these evil ones.

Council measures may be employed in certain circumstances, usually with the assistance of the medicine men; even then it is recognized that it is not always possible to overcome these forces. It is in such periods that the welfare of individuals and possibly of the entire community suffers. There appears to be a tacit faith that eventually the good forces will emerge victorious, but this victory is not seen as either quickly or easily gained.

In his journal of October 19, 1880, Bandelier quoted Agustín Herrera as saying that he believed "in witches and sorcerers, both of Pueblos and of Mexicans; they change themselves into snakes, toads, frogs, etc. They have the evil-eye. They have the superstition of a cat crossing the path, and also of Friday. . . . Some of them live in the pueblo." In an entry the next day, Bandelier quoted the padre as saying that there was a superstition among the Indians (Cochití) that if anyone wished to injure another, he made a "mono," an image made of earth, or clay, of the one he wished to hurt. If possible, the earth where this person had urinated was chosen. He then pierced the image with cactus spines at the places where he wished to inflict pain. Present-day Cochití seem familiar with such practices, but they steadfastly insist that they are no longer followed. [42, 92]

In an entry of November 29, 1880, Bandelier noted two stories in which a Cochití was pursued by an animal believed to be a *brujo*, or witch. One story concerned pursuit by a coyote in the vicinity of the old Bajada Hill; the other account told of the man's being chased by a large deer in the Cuesta Colorado. Finally, the Cochití succeeded in shooting and killing the animal. In an entry of December 6, 1880, Bandelier observed that the Cochití were familiar with the pueblo of Isleta del Sur, south of El Paso, Texas, but were not enthusiastic about visiting there or having any contact with it because of the great number of *brujos* believed to be there.

In his entry of June 21, 1886, Bandelier recorded that the death penalty for practicing witchcraft was certain. He noted that the sentence was carried out secretly and that afterwards the information of it was communicated secretly to "all the other tribes." He was told that some five or six years before, two witches were killed at Zia "in a quiet way." "They did not use poison, but clubbed them to death."

One informant [62] was of the opinion that the recent increase in the Cochití population was due to their having a cacique "with better thoughts and more awake to the doings of the bad people. In earlier times, most children died very young; the bad people, lots of them Spanish, were to blame. Now there are fewer Spanish, a better cacique [the incumbent had been in only two years at this time], and things are lots better here." From other informants, the impression was gained that the past cacique may well have engaged in some witchery himself; no one actually made this statement, but the implication was that he had not fought the witches to the limit of his ability and may even have sympathized with their activities.

In an entry of November 14, 1880, Bandelier noted that when the coyotes howled, it was regarded as a "bad sign"—a presage of bad weather, cold, or ill luck. While some present-day Cochití have retained such beliefs, others have adopted the interpretation that when the coyotes howl it means rain—good luck. There appears to be an increasing tendency to attach no significance whatsoever to such signs. Another superstition is the belief that when the left eye winks, bad luck is inevitable—nothing can be done to avoid it. If someone drops something and it sticks in the ground in an upright position, this is a sign of good luck. [62, 92]

Innumerable accounts indicate that the subjects of witchcraft and superstition are not yet dead at Cochití; a number of illustrative incidents are related in Appendix 20.

Medicine Societies

Of the various secret societies among the Cochití, those of the chai'añí, or medicine men, have traditionally held the greatest preeminence. (See Appendix 17 for a chart explaining the various Cochití secret societies and general ceremonial organization.) In times past, this dominance rested upon the leading roles played by the medicine societies in the theocratically seated controls of this culture. The medicine societies, either working alone, or at times in unison or sequence, protect the community as well as individuals from harm of various categories. Within their ranks, the medicine men include the cacique, specifically, as head of the Flint Medicine Society, whose importance has already been discussed.

White (1930: 618) made the following evaluation of the functions of Keresan medicine societies:

> The three major functions, then, of the medicine societies are the curing of disease, retreats for rain, and the selection of pueblo officers, of which the first is most fundamental. In former times, no doubt, war functions were as important as retreats, or perhaps more important, at least as far as the Flint society was concerned. The medicine-men are really secondary at solstices; although they carry much of the burden, it is really the cacique who is in charge. The assistance of the medicine-men at masked dances is, too, a rather minor function, as well as their custody of masks.

While the pre-eminence of these societies continues as of the present moment, there is little doubt that the over-all prestige of the societies and of the medicine men themselves is declining. In recent years, the decline has been in what might be termed the overt aspects of their functions. In matters of curing, weather control, combating the evil doings of witches, and similar activities, there is a growing tendency to withhold respect for, and to lose faith in, the abilities and powers of these shamans. This development is the result of various factors, such as economic changes, improved education, and contacts with the outside world. (Lange 1952a, 1953) Thus far, the medicine societies have retained to a surprising degree certain covert functions, including such related matters as social controls and community well-being. All this they have accomplished, despite the declining respect for the medicine men and their activities, because the medicine men have been able to retain the power to select the secular officers who ostensibly govern the tribe. By selecting men whose sympathies are compatible with their own values and viewpoints, the medicine men continue to exercise theocratic controls.

While it is commonly recognized that there are situations in the pueblo which are not ideal and that the present governmental machinery is deficient in some respects and hence partly to blame, there has not been any concerted effort to overthrow the control of the medicine men since the restoration of outward peace following the Conservative-Progressive controversy in the middle 1920's (see pp. 30–32). However, at present, the Flint Society has but two members, and the Giant and Shī'kame societies have but one member each. Thus, the current balance that rests upon having each of these society heads name two of the six secular officers is likely to be upset at any time. Whether the surviving societies would absorb this function of the extinct society remains to be seen. Ultimately, one society head would be naming all officers if this plan of adjustment should be followed.

If the current system should be abandoned and some form of constitutional government adopted, as has happened in certain other villages, such as Laguna, Santa Clara, and Isleta, then the nominating—and hence the controlling—function of the medicine societies would be lost—assuming that the societies, one or all, have not themselves become extinct during this period. With the constantly improving level of general education and comprehension of world knowledge within the pueblo, as well as with the continued opposition from the Catholic Church, the medicine societies would be virtually powerless without the nominating power. Another solution might shift the nominating power to the nonmedicine societies. It is virtually impossible to obtain from the Cochití predictions of such eventualities. When the need arises in actual and not hypothetical circumstances, a decision will be reached. Until then, no suggestion of the solution is offered by anyone. This situation is a further manifestation of the temporal orientation of this culture to the present, rather than to the past or future.

Cochití medicine men, as do others among the Pueblo tribes, assign great curing powers to the bear. As noted in the discussion of hunting (pp. 134–138), the bear is given many human qualities, and the killing of a bear is surrounded by ceremonialism in which the medicine men play prominent roles. Bear paws are worn by the medicine men as a part of performing their cures and in counteracting the powers of witches. They are also worn as necklaces or bracelets. In such paraphernalia, the left front paw and claws are most prized, since the bear, for reasons unknown, is considered to be left-handed. Small stone bears are used as elements in the laying out of an altar (ait'shīn), symbolizing the presence and assistance of these animals in the associated rituals. The over-all importance of the bear in various aspects of the medicine society is perhaps best indicated by the fact that in routine thought and conversation, the societies are referred to as "Bear societies" and the medicine men as "Bears."

It appears that recent conceptions of past conditions existing in these medicine societies have tended to envisage rather large and comprehensive memberships—in contrast to the limited memberships found today. So far as Cochití is concerned, such notions are erroneous. Dumarest (1919: 187) recorded the Flint Society membership as "five or six" at the end of the last century. In 1924, Curtis (1926: 87) found only one member of the Flint Society, the cacique himself. Goldfrank (1927: 117), for about the same time, listed Victoriano Cordero (the cacique) and José Domingo Chalan, "about to be initiated." During the period 1947–1953, Marcelo Quintana (the cacique) and Juanito Trujillo were the only members of the Flint Society. The rosters of the Giant and Shí'kame societies reveal similarly small memberships, both at present and as far back as data can be obtained.

In view of the present minimal membership of the society rosters and also in recognition of the changes which will have to come if one or more of the societies should become extinct, it would seem that some effort would be made to recruit members and thereby strengthen the societies. Several informants were of the opinion that the medicine men are currently handicapped in presenting complete rituals because of lack of personnel. However, no recruiting is being done. This was explained by the fact that membership must be voluntarily sought, whether in the medicine society or any other type of society. Enforced recruiting, practiced many years ago, led to members who were discontent with their official roles. One of the basic criteria is a "good heart and mind," meaning that the member is happy in his society work, interested in performing it to the utmost of his ability, and believes wholeheartedly in the efficacy of it. Drafting members results in obtaining opposite qualities; hence, despite a recognized need for the continuance of these societies, on the part of at least the Conservatives, there is equal recognition that the tribe will be better off without them than to have them composed of unwilling members.

This general attitude and other data regarding medicine-society membership are contained in this entry from the July 26, 1888, journal of Bandelier:

Ha-yo-ue told me that the Cha-ya-ni are invested by the Capitan a guerra and by his lieutenant, the O-yo-ya-ua. The party who wishes to become Chayani has to make the application himself directly. On the day set, the Maseua (*capitan de la guerra*) and his brother, the Oyoyaua, go to the place where the candidate is and sit on both sides of him, the Maseua to the right and the Oyoyaua to the left. Therefore, the Maseua and his brother are obliged to protect the Chayani all; they also have the duty to punish them, in case they do wrong.

Further details of becoming a member of a medicine society at Cochití were obtained. For the most part, these substantiate the details already published by Goldfrank (1927: 56–57) and are included here as briefly as possible. The long and arduous process of becoming a member and the declining prestige of the medicine men quite adequately explain the failure of an individual to join one of the three societies during recent years.

Having arrived at the decision to become a medicine man, the candidate makes known his intentions to the war captain and the head of the society. The next four years are spent in fasting and in continence. After successfully completing this preliminary stage, the candidate observes a four-day period of fasting and vomiting. At the conclusion of this more intense period, the society goes into a four-day retreat during which the candidate remains at his home until the last night of the society's retreat.

On the last evening, society members come to the candidate's home to prepare him for the actual initiation. He is naked except for a black breechcloth secured with a yucca belt, and his face is covered with black paint that has flecks of mica shining through. His hair is free from any band or ties. He is then escorted to the society house, where he is placed before an altar. This is an arrangement, or assemblage, of bowls of medicine, corn meal, prayer sticks, and various animal and human fetishes. The war captains are present, as well as the society membership, each of whom has his corn fetish (ĭ'arĭko) standing upright on the floor in front of where he is seated.

Knowledge of ritual details leaves much to be desired at this point. There appear to be some songs, prayers, and ceremonial whipping, administered both to the initiate and to his ceremonial father. Then the new member receives a new name, and after some dancing in which he joins, he takes his seat behind his newly acquired corn fetish which is given him by the society head. His position is at the end of the line of shamans. As the older members die and new members join, this individual's position moves toward the middle position, which he will occupy eventually as the oldest member and, simultaneously, as the society head. [3, 42, 88, 92]

The corn fetish is a fundamental part of the paraphernalia of each medicine man. Basically, it is a perfect ear of blue corn with its tassel intact. On this foundation, various feathers are arranged (Fig. 17e). This sacred object is also called a "mother," or "yaya." Upon the death of the medicine man, other society members take the fetish apart, shell the ear of corn, and distribute the kernels to relatives of the deceased to mix with the supply of regular seed corn. The power (ī'añī) of the fetish kernels is absorbed by the seed, thus assuring a good crop. [88]

While present-day Cochití seem vaguely aware that in times past the various societies had special skills in curing specific illnesses, they are quite agreed that today the societies are about equally competent. A person who is sick is likely to call upon any of the societies simply because of family relationship, friendship, or similar grounds. If any preference is shown, it is normally in favor of the Flint, owing to the fact that the cacique is a member of this society.

When a person becomes sick or has suffered periodic illness over a span of time, a relative is sent with a present of corn meal to the medicine-society headman. If the illness is not severe, an individual medicine man may be contacted, though this is seldom done. (It should be remembered that at present three of the four practicing shamans are society heads.) The shaman soon comes, alone, to the patient's home, where he enters into a discussion with the patient and his relatives as to the time, place, and other arrangements for the cure. This may be planned for the following week, or the following year; the sicker the person is, the more immediately will the cure be scheduled.

Taking the basket of corn meal—and thereby accepting the request to cure the patient—the Bear takes the meal to the other Bears. It was pointed out here that in the case of either the Giant or the Shī'kame societies, the Cochití organization functions alone. However, if the Flint Society is consulted, the meal is then taken by the cacique to the Bear—in this case, Flint—Society at Tesuque Pueblo to enlist its aid because the Cochití society is the "parent" of the Tesuque group and, as such, enjoys reciprocal aid relationships with it. [88, 92] To digress slightly, it is of interest that informants added that formerly the Cochití Flint Society was over the Santa Clara society but that the present Santa Clara society is now under the Jemez Bear Society. The Cochití Flint Society was also at one time over the Santo Domingo Flint, but this is no longer true. Similarly, the Cochití Shī'kame Society was once under that of Santo Domingo but is no longer. When a society is about to initiate a candidate, the affiliates from other pueblos gather at the initiate's village to assist in his induction. [88] These interpueblo ties, a subject about which relatively little is known, are worthy of future investigation.

To return to the subject, on the day set for the cure, the family takes the sick person to the society house and the Bears receive him when they have completed their preparations. Any other persons may go along "if they want to help." While the cure is being carried on inside, the proceedings are protected by the six *alguacilitos,* who watch all the first night, starting about nightfall and continuing until early dawn. Thereafter, they take turns in standing guard.

Following a cure by a society, the family of the patient is expected to give a basket of blue corn meal to the society. Some families have given commercial flour in recent years; it is generally considered, however, that this is not proper. Although it is readily admitted that this gift is virtually obligatory, it is spoken of as a "present" and not as a "payment."

If the cure is not successful, the medicine men are not considered to be at fault. They are still paid in flour, meal, or some native food-stuff, though perhaps not in the same quantity, as if it had been suc-cessful. In time, another society may be approached to try its powers in effecting a cure. In 1952, informants could recall two cures effected by the Flint Society. One was that of Juan Benada and the other, of Reyes Melchior, thirty-six and twenty-nine years old, respectively. While details are lacking, both cases, judging from statements of various informants, appear to have been of a psychosomatic nature. Both were generally considered to have been successful cures. [3, 42, 44, 92] Later in 1952, Reyes fatally shot his nephew with a hunting rifle early one morning while the rest of the family was still sleeping. Efforts had been made before and after the slaying to have him com-mitted to the state institution at Las Vegas, but family objections had prevented this from being done. Further developments have not been ascertained. The case is cited simply to illustrate the nature of one type of illness with which the medicine men are asked to deal.

In contrasting present practices with those of several decades ago, it is interesting to read an account in Bandelier's journal for Decem-ber 6, 1885:

He says that when one falls sick, the Chayani, three of them, & an old woman, sit up with the patient, four days & four nights, praying & watching, fasting rigidly. They are not allowed to eat anything except some cornmeal in water, once every twenty-four hours, and there is a guard placed on the house to prevent any Mexican, every female or male relative, from entering the building or even to approach it. About 2 A.M. of the 5th day, they go to the river to wash & bathe themselves. Then food is brought to them from the house of the patient. The medicine is mostly herbs, incantations, and prayers to their Idols. The "Qoshare" sing, pray, and dance only the first day, the other three days they simply fast and remain quiet in their Estufa.

Although this account has several points of value for time perspective, it also contains some rather confusing data. First, the inclusion of the Ku-sha'lī ("Qoshare") is unexpected unless Bandelier's informant had reference to a Flint Society cure in which the affiliated Ku-sha'lī played a minor role. Second, the reference to the Ku-sha'lī's fasting in their kiva would appear to be an outright error, the place in all probability having been the society house. [42, 92]

Many of the functions of the medicine societies are performed as single-society activities (and hence are discussed in relation to the specific society later in this chapter), but the three societies do co-operate on numerous occasions. For example, in the spring before the annual cleaning of the irrigation ditches, the societies plant prayer sticks in each of the two Cochití ditches. The Flint Society plants its sticks at the head of the ditch; the Giant, in the middle; and the Shī'kame Society at the foot of the ditch. [42, 44] The late December meeting, at which the three society heads confer on the secular officers for the coming year, has already been noted. They also co-operate in the installation of a new cacique.

The three society headmen pick the side dancers and guards for the ka'tsīna dances. In these affairs, the war captain decides on the time of the dance, and the Shrū'tzī head decides how the dance is to be done and the costumes to be worn. If there should be any dispute over details, the Shrū'tzī head's opinion normally carries the more weight.

Further collaboration is shown at times when general conditions in the village are considered to be in obvious need of improvement. At the instigation of someone—usually the war captain—a general overall cure for the village is performed. While these cures are not called for with any frequency, they do occur from time to time. The rites take place only in the Turquoise Kiva and are attended by nonmembers as well as members of the societies. In the course of the rites, the nonmembers are said to experience what the medicine men do, especially the young men who take part in the dancing. [92]

Two of the ceremonial highlights of any year are háñī-gīt°, held sometime in February to "bring the sun back" (from the south), and ha'ñīko, held toward the end of November as a farewell to the sun at the close of the agricultural season. These two ceremonies are given each year, there being no option as is true for certain other ceremonies. All the tribe participates. All-night rituals are performed in the three medicine houses; the Flint is joined by the Ku-sha'lī, the Giant by the Shrū'tzī, and the Shī'kame by the Kwe'rana. Altars (ai'tshīn—"tzī'pañī ai'tshīn," when used in the summer, and "kash'-stī-etsa ai'tshīn," when used in the winter) are set up in the society houses and there is dancing by both men and women. The public is not permitted in the Flint or Shī'kame houses on either of these occasions; visitors are welcome, however, in the Giant house, for this society, together with Shrū'tzī, is considered to be more closely affiliated with the common man. During these rites, protection is furnished each house by the war captains, their helpers, and the *fiscalitos*. At night they usually stand guard just inside the door, and during the daylight and in good weather, they usually keep watch while sitting on the roof. The war captain and the governor are present at the Flint house; the lieutenant of each of these officers is at the Giant house; and the two *fiscales* stay at the Shī'kame house. In addition, there are two *alguacilitos* and two *fiscalitos* at each of the medicine houses.

From time to time, usually beginning in early summer but also at any time when it is decided that improvement is needed in the over-all situation, the medicine societies lead the pueblo in a series of fasts (go'wa-tyash), or retreats. Such retreats involve certain taboos, or restrictions, such as continence. Food taboos are strictest during the first retreat of each group, when only one meal per day is eaten, a light noon meal consisting of bread and stew. For the following three retreats, some variety of food is brought to the house and may be eaten often.

If there should be four members in retreat, two remain in the house throughout the four days and nights, resting there and using pottery jars when there is need to relieve themselves. The other two are allowed to "come out" early each morning, carry on a normal day's routine, and return to the society house early in the evening. For the next three retreats, the pairs alternate these roles. The society head makes the assignments as he sees fit, and the over-all proper functioning of the society is supervised by the war captains, as mentioned. [42]

In each series, the Flint, joined by Ku-sha'lī, leads off, followed by Giant, and, in turn, Shī'kame, assisted by the Kwe'rana. Each group fasts one week; this actually means that the society "goes in" on Monday evening and "comes out" late Friday afternoon. As in other retreats or cures, the societies are protected by the war captains and their helpers. One informant stated that two go'atchīnī should watch over each fast, but another, a society member, stated that there was a definite composition of the personnel involved.

The war captain and one go'atchīnī watch over the first Flint retreat; the *teniente* and one go'atchīnī watch the first Giant fast; and two go'atchīnī protect the first Shī'kame retreat. For the second round, the two go'atchīnī who did not help the first time watch the Flint; another pair of go'atchīnī serve the Giant, and still another, the Shī'kame. The third and fourth times are the same. The war captain and his lieutenant might help in any of these, but there is no obligation for either to do so. If the fasts do not achieve the desired results —rain, or improved community health, or whatever was declared to be the object of the fasts—a new series of four retreats by each society is begun. This sequence is partially confirmed by a journal entry of September 6, 1886, by Bandelier, who noted that the cacique and the Ku-sha'lī had fasted the previous week and that the Giant medicine men were fasting at the time he wrote.

Dumarest (1919: 205) stated that if conditions became grave, as in case of severe drought, the fasting sequence was "irshteani, shikarne, schkoio, quirana, shreutse." My informants insisted that this sequence was confused, and furthermore, that the Shrū'tzī do not join in these, though the Ku-sha'lī do help the Flint. [3, 42, 88, 92]

In his journal of December 4, 1882, Bandelier commented that "it appears that Romero Chávez and Rafael are the head medicine men. They wear a species of 'Cotones' with wide sleeves, the cacique wears it with black and red stripes." Present-day evidence fails to reveal any distinctive garb of either the society headmen or any of the society members. Informants confirmed this impression, though it may be that there is some culture loss involved.

In discussing the recent introduction of electric power in the pueblo, it was interesting to note that in addition to its use in private homes, it was used in the two community houses and the two kivas by means of extension cords from adjacent homes. However, it was stated with certainty that electric lights are not used in medicine-society houses and there appeared to be little likelihood that they would be in the near future. Here again is an interesting insight into the relative values inherent in the medicine-society activities and those which occur in the kivas.

Flint Society. An all-time roster of Flint members (hir'shtīañī chai'añī) was compiled with the aid of several informants and appears as Appendix 19. It is regretted that more complete data on these men could not be obtained in order to uncover possible clues to the type, or types, of individuals from whom the caciques have been selected.

Members of the Flint Society need not belong to any particular clan or kiva. Goldfrank (1927: 43) was told that "at present only Koshari may become members of the Flint Society." But she called attention to two exceptions that she found. One, Antonio Trujillo, was a Flint member for years before he sought membership in the Ku-sha'lī Society immediately before his death. My informants were of the opinion that he never did actually join the Ku-sha'lī. [3, 45] Luís Romero joined Ku-sha'lī after he became a Flint shaman. Goldfrank commented that this procedure was tolerated but it was not considered orthodox.

My informants, in compiling an all-time roster of this society (meaning the inclusion of all members, living or deceased, of whom any informants had any recollection), indicated several men who had been Flint but never Ku-sha'lī. It is also interesting to note their exclusive affiliation with the Pumpkin Kiva rather than Turquoise except for the last three Flint members.

The Flint, together with other medicine men, are considered primarily as doctors, curing illnesses, setting fractures, and helping the people combat witchcraft. In their retreats, they help bring rain and make prayer sticks for the Ku-sha'lī. Flint shamans are called upon, as are other medicine men, in case of birth, naming, or death. There appears to be little bias in favor of any particular society's ability, though, perhaps because the Flint headman is the cacique, the Flint seems to be favored. Dumarest (1919: 188) said that Flint shamans were especially able in case of wounds, a statement which correlates with Bandelier's remarks (pp. 250–251).

Dumarest further stated: "But to all curing societies women may be admitted. Because of timidity, however, they rarely apply." He

(1919: 189) mentioned one woman doctor but neglected to specify the society to which she belonged. Present-day Cochití insist that women are ineligible for the Flint, or any other medicine society. They say that in the society's retreats, the members are waited upon by the women of the affiliated Ku-sha'lī Society but that these women could not in any way be considered as members of the Flint Society.

The Flint Society house, which is shared with the Ku-sha'lī, is the cacique's "office." In the inner room, the cacique is said to make solstice observations, though precise details of this are lacking. Also in this inner room the animal impersonators for various hunting dances are prepared. This should be done at the Shī'kame house, for the Shī'kame Society has fallen heir to the functions of the Shai'yak, or Hunting, Society. However, since there is not adequate room there, the Flint house is now used for this purpose. The choruses of the two kiva groups "pick up" and "drop" the "animals" at this house as they go from the community houses to the plaza on days when these ceremonies are given. [3, 92]

Snake Society. The Snake medicine men (Shrū'wē chai'añī) are extinct at Cochití. Goldfrank (1927: 42) stated that the membership of the Snake Society had to be drawn from men who were Flint, and she further pointed out that initiation into one ordinarily involved initiation into the other, as well as into the Fire Society.

In view of these statements, it is somewhat surprising to find that the Snake Society became extinct upon the death of the former cacique, Victoriano Cordero. Why the remaining Flint shamans—Marcelo Quintana and Juanito Trujillo—have never joined the Snake (and Fire) Society is not known, if membership in the Flint is generally mutually inclusive of the Snake and Fire.

Perhaps this is not as unusual as first appears, however. The all-time Snake membership roster (Appendix 21), as compiled by informants, is appreciably shorter than that of the Flint, causing one to wonder about the accuracy of Goldfrank's informant on this point. It is also interesting to note that the last-named of the three Snake shamans—José Montoya—was omitted by my informants in their listing of the Flint medicine men. [3, 15, 44]

Dumarest (1919: 188) stated that the Snake Society was considered most proficient in treating the bite of the rattlesnake and other poisonous animals.

In ethnographic accounts, the Snake Society appears to have been evaluated as a "degree" within the Flint Society. Curtis (1926: 88) felt that formerly it was perhaps completely independent of the Flint and that a reduction in numbers brought about the survivors' absorption by the Flint Society. The numerical strength of the Snake Society, or "degree," was not provided in any of the accounts.

Fire Medicine Society. The Fire medicine men (Ha'kañī chai'añī) constituted another "degree" within the Flint Society. Like the Snake Society, the Fire Society is now extinct at Cochití. That informants did not agree on when this had occurred is an interesting commentary on the pueblo "layman's" awareness of the functions of these societies upon his life. Several stated that Victoriano Cordero was the last member. [15, 44] Others claimed that Victoriano, though both Flint and Snake, had never gone through the initiation rites of the Fire Society. [52, 70] Little was learned from the published data on the Fire Society, and the membership roster is very brief, with only Antonio Suina as an unquestioned member and Victoriano as a doubtful one. Since data on these men are given in the short Snake roster, they are not repeated separately for Fire.

Specialties of the Fire Society were the treatment of burns and fevers. In other respects, it was similar to the other medicine societies in its functions. [3, 70] Curtis (1926: 87–88) reported that the Fire shamans did such tricks as extinguishing fire in their mouths.

In Bandelier's entry of August 21, 1888, a few notes were made regarding the Fire Society:

There exists a kind of Chayani called: Fire-Chayani, "Ha-Ka-nyi Chayani." They are a subdivision of the Hish-tanyi, and the Ho-tsha-nyi [cacique] is now, at Cochití, the only Fire-Chayani still existing. Formerly, there used to be three or four of them. Hayoue recollects distinctly having seen that they *Ate Fire!* This was done in a case of sickness and used as a cure. He describes the process as follows:

The Chayani met in the room of the sick individual. Each one held in his hand a little broom-like tuft of grass (Popote). They began to sing and at a certain part of the song the Ha-ka-nyi Na-ua, who is the Cacique always, bit off a part of the end of that broom which had previously been set on fire. The broom was waved to the North, West, South, East, Above, and Below, in succession, and each time the Cacique took a bite of the flaming grass and chewed it. After the Na-ua had done this, the others performed the same operation in turn. Then the chewed ashes were spat into the face and on the body of the sick party and he was thoroughly besmeared with them. This was the *Cure.*—He assures that the Chayani did all this with perfect impunity and he attributes it to the 4 or 5 days rigorous and absolute fasting which precedes such a ceremony

Always.—If the fasting is done with perfect free will and carried out fully, then the Chayani will eat the fire with total (absolute) impunity, if *not,* they will suffer from it themselves. The same is the case with the *Fire-Dance.* In it, the Chayani one after another jump into a flaming pyre and dance, in the very center of the flames. But should any of them fast irregularly, he will be scorched; if not, he can brave the fire.

Bandelier did not specify the society involved in the following account, but the performance described was included in the journal entry with the preceding account and is kept in the same order here:

He also mentioned, among others, one very remarkable trick which he himself saw performed, at his father's house. Some of the Chayani placed a white screen in the background of a darkened room. Behind it and on the floor they placed a round disk painted yellow, representing the *Sun.* Then they began to sing and at the song the disk began to rise on the East corner of the screen, like the sun would in the heavens. When it reached the highest point of the curve (which corresponded with the middle of the screen) the song was interrupted,—and the sun also stopped. When the singing began again the sun resumed its motion gradually declining toward the West until it touched the floor at that corner of the screen. He attributes this clever performance to the efficacy of the Song exclusively.—Another very pretty trick is also done with an empty gourd, the top of which is perforated and has four Eagle's plumes fastened to it. The bottom of that gourd is of course convex and cannot stand. Nevertheless, as soon as the song of the Chayani begins, one of them gives it a very slight blow with the hand and this causes it to stand up and remain thus as long as the singing lasts, while the plumes quiver in a dancing motion.—Finally, he asserts that the growing and ripening of a Maize-plant in one day—between *Sunrise* and *Sunset* is performed by the Navajos today yet. The Pueblos did it also, but the *Song that produces it is lost now!*

Everything is attributed by him to the magic powers of the *Song* alone.

Po'shai-añī Society. Although White (1930) discussed the Flint, Snake, and Fire societies, he made no mention at all of the Po'shai-añī shamans (Po'shai-añī chai'añī). In the ethnographic data published on Cochití, this group has been mentioned only by Curtis (1926: 87–88). He stated that this group was the highest of the three degrees—Snake, Fire, and Po'shai-añī—within the Flint Society. Members of this were assistants and understudies to the Flint head, the cacique. Curtis also referred to them as "Whipper shamans."

In his journal of August 4, 1891, Bandelier stated that the "true

name for Montezuma is 'Pu'shaya,'" and he added that the term
Montezuma was modern. One wonders whether this recording of this
name is not another form of the name of this society. If so, it may also
provide a clue about the origin or nature of the society.

No data on this society as such were obtained from any of my informants, but a reference to the term "Po'shai-añī" was made by one
informant concerning another matter. In discussing the celebration
of Santiago's Day, July 25, 1948, and the appearance of "The Little
Horse" (Santiago), he stated that the horse is also called "yaya"
("mother") and "Ka'waio san'tīak" by the Cochití. Then he mentioned another name for this impersonation which is, he said, known
to very few of the Cochití themselves—"Po'shai-añī." [52]

This term is known among the Santo Domingo as "Poshaiyanyi," a
deity who fought a series of contests with the Christian God long
ago, defeating Him in each phase of the contest (White 1935: 178–
179). The term "Bocaiyanyi" is used at Santa Ana to designate one of
the two "horses" that appear on Santiago's Day and Santa Ana's Day,
July 25 and July 26, respectively (White 1942: 256–263). No reference to a Po'shai-añī Society in any other Keresan pueblo has been
found. Stevenson (1894: 59–67) related a rather lengthy tale from
Zia in which the leading character is the deity "Po'shaiÿänne."

Giant Society. Next to the Flint Society, the Giant Society is the
most important Cochití medicine society at present. There is but one
member (Shko'yo chai'añī)—Cipriano Quintana. As the na'wai-ya,
or head, he attempts to carry on the traditional functions of the society. Cipriano, the second oldest man and third oldest person in the
village, is considerably hampered in this task, however; he has been
completely blind for several years and in recent years has become
increasingly senile. Even with all one's faculties, there appears to be
considerable doubt that any one person would be able to carry on a
society's work in an ideal fashion.

Until recently, Cipriano had the assistance of a second Giant shaman. This much younger man was generally believed to lack much
of the knowledge that he should have, especially as the successor to
Cipriano as society head. About the winter of 1950/51, he is reputed
to have left Cochití with his Spanish-American wife and her children
and gone to the West Coast. While this was a serious ceremonial loss
to the pueblo, the Cochití were even more bitter over the fact that
he is said to have taken with him two suitcases filled with Giant

paraphernalia for the alleged purpose of selling them. [3, 15, 20, 44, 45, 62, 88] Several mentioned that upon a return visit at Christmas time, 1951, this man had just stayed at home all the time and had not gone to see anyone "like a person should." This added to the suspicions. When asked why the war captains had failed to press any charges, the general response was that they were waiting for "more proof." [3, 42, 44, 92, 94] One cannot help but wonder, in retrospect, whether the evidence was not actually sufficient but that the situation was rationalized in this way in order that the war captains not be confronted with a trial and certain conviction. This could result in no alternative other than death, and acculturation has seemingly advanced so far even with the war captains, guardians of tribal traditions, that they can no longer force the issue to such an extreme conclusion.

Dumarest (1919: 187) noted six or seven members of the Giant Society at the end of the last century. Curtis (1926: 87) stated that there were four in 1924, and Goldfrank (1927: 117) likewise noted four. An all-time roster of Giant members appears in Appendix 22. In this roster are two women: Priciliana Roybal Cordero, still living, and Trinidad Melchior Montoya, who died in 1946. These were the only women named by informants as actually belonging to a medicine society. Their inclusion appears to be due to their membership in the Thundercloud Society, which is limited to women and is especially close to the Giant Society, meeting in the same house, though several informants stated that it also has connections with the Flint and Shi'kame medicine societies. Thundercloud is not connected with the Shrū'tzī Society. [15, 42, 45, 70] This exclusion may stem from the close association of the Shrū'tzī Society with the Ka'tsīna Society, which is restricted to male membership. However, as listed in the roster of the Shrū'tzī Society (Appendix 25), Lucia Romero was reported to have been a member of that society.

In 1951, Reyes Suina Chalan, an older woman who has been active in pueblo rituals, was said to be participating, as a member of the Thundercloud group, in the retreats of the Giant Society following the death of her husband, Juan Estévan Chalan. [42] Other informants said that she had not joined any society but did join in certain phases of the Giant retreats, as is the privilege and custom of any person classified as a *Crudo*, i.e., one who belongs to no society. The Flint and Shī'kame medicine societies specifically care for the members of the Ku-sha'li and Kwe'rana, respectively, and the Giant Society cares for the *Crudos*. [3, 44, 88]

When in retreat, the Giant Society, unlike the Flint or Shī'kame societies for whom the rule is optional, must keep a fire burning in the society house. The fuel is ordinary firewood, gathered by the go'atchīnī at the direction of the war captains. Women of the Thundercloud Society normally tend the fire and make certain that it does not burn out before the end of the retreat. It is interesting that despite this fire's being ritually important, there is no compulsion, at least at present nor supposedly at any time in the past, to ignite it by friction or some other native device; the use of commercially produced matches appears to be perfectly proper. [92]

Dumarest (1919: 188) stated that Giant shamans specialized in the treatment of fevers. Curtis (1926: 87) simply designated them as healers. Goldfrank (1927: 49, 76) in several instances said that Giant shamans were preferred in cases of childbirth and death, though my informants said they knew of no such preference. [44, 45, 52, 55, 70] Bandelier's data (1890: 280) were divergent here, stating that the Giant Society (rather than the Shī'kame Society?) was concerned with the hunt. In view of the unanimity among other sources, it appears that Bandelier was in error on this point.

The head Giant, also known by the terms "tshrai'katse" and "Shko'yo na'waiya," is spoken of as "assistant to the cacique," or as "the cacique's right hand" (cf. p. 239). The data of Goldfrank (1927: 41) and Curtis (1926: 84) confirm this, but according to Dumarest (1919: 197) the Giant head was the second assistant to the cacique rather than the first. My informants thought Dumarest's statement was an error, as the present arrangement has always been true so far as they knew. Again, it is quite possible that Dumarest's work was at an early enough date that he actually was told the Giant was the "left hand." In light of the explanation already given on page 195, it may be that Dumarest interpreted this to mean "second" assistant rather than "first."

It is interesting that in spite of the concept of the Giant head's being assistant cacique, or "right hand," it is the next man in line within the Flint Society, not the Giant or Shī'kame head, who becomes the acting cacique if the cacique is ill or momentarily incapacitated. [3] This is explained as consistent with the need for the cacique to have the special knowledge of the Flint members and also with the fact that the other society heads must remain in their respective offices in order to maintain the balance necessary in pueblo ceremonial life. Furthermore, it leaves the Giant and Shī'kame heads available for consultations with the acting cacique if he so desires. [3, 44]

The Giant head, as is discussed in Chapter 7, chooses the governor and lieutenant governor each year.

Shī'kame Society. There is only one Shī'kame medicine man (Shī'kame chai'an) at present—Eufrasio Suina. Dumarest (1919; 187) stated there were five or six at the end of the century. Curtis (1926: 87) noted that there were four in 1924, and Goldfrank (1927: 117) named three. Informants compiled an all-time roster of nine Shī'kame medicine men (see Appendix 23).

Most informants stated that this society is an exclusively male organization; one man, however, a member of the affiliated Kwe'rana Society [94], insisted that he knew of women's belonging in the past, though he could not name any of them. In its retreats, the Shī'kame Society is aided by the Kwe'rana women, but the women are excluded from the esoteric aspects of the Shī'kame. As revealed in the roster, all Shī'kame members have also been Kwe'rana members, though informants insisted that this was not actually necessary. The two societies are very closely affiliated and they share the same house. A member of one society cannot enter this house while the other group is in retreat unless he is a member of both groups. [44, 70]

Although Dumarest (1919: 197) stated that the Shī'kame head is the first assistant to the cacique, all other published data and my informants claim that he is the second assistant. Dumarest did not give the special abilities of this group of shamans, but he did comment on certain food restrictions observed only by these men (1919: 189):

Shikarne chaiani are much afraid of a medical plant called *shietretse wawa* (medicine), in Spanish *osha.* They believe they will fall ill from its very smell. To eat it would be death. For a like reason *shikarne chaiani* keep from eating *wako,* a plant which is eaten when young after it is cut up like spinach and boiled. For *shikarne chaiani,* rabbit meat is also a poison. Nothing edible is abstained from by *irshteani* or by *schkoio* chaiani.

As Parsons indicated in an editorial note to the above quoted statement, "*wako*" (guaco) is the Rocky Mountain bee plant, taboos of which, along with jack-rabbit meat, "are also observed by the *shikani-kurena cheani* of Laguna and by the *shi'wanakwe* of Zuñi."

Use of the Rocky Mountain bee plant and of rabbit meat, in connection with the Shī′kame's assuming the duties of the extinct Hunters Society, has been noted on page 130.

Bandelier (1890:280) stated that the Shī′kame head was the leader of the medicine shamans and that the Giant head was the head shaman of the hunt. This is the reverse of the present situation and, unless it was merely an error in recording, which appears most probable, is an unexplained case of shift in role and emphasis by these two medicine societies.

As head of the third most-important medicine society in the pueblo, the Shī′kame head (Shī′kame na′wai-ya)—the third tshrai′katse— also shares in the selection of the secular officers, choosing each year the *fiscale* and assistant *fiscale*.

In addition to the normal duties of a medicine society—curing, weather control, and some of the direction of the masked dances— the Shī′kame have taken over duties formerly executed by the Hunters Society. In spite of this added responsibility, the Shī′kame is represented by only one man at present. One informant was quite insistent that the Shī′kame head should also be referred to as "Shai′-yak," or Hunter. [42] Others were equally insistent that this absorption of the Hunters Society by the Shī′kame was one of title primarily, and that essentially none of the Hunters' ritual and ceremonial knowledge was included. [3, 15, 44, 45] In contrast to their own situation, several Cochití stated that there is still a functioning Shai′-yak Society at Santo Domingo. "This is the real thing." [42, 44, 88]

In the section on the Flint Society, it is pointed out that Snake, Fire, and possibly Po′shai-añi constitute "degrees" within the Flint Society, or did so until they became extinct. Similarly, according to Curtis (1926: 88), the Shī′kame Society was said to include a "degree" called "Mūkat[sa]," or "Cougar." Curtis felt that this was true simply because the duties of the Hunters Society had been absorbed by the Shī′kame, including the role of Cougar Man in the communal hunts. None of my informants knew of any such degree within the Shī′kame Society.

Two journal entries by Bandelier are of interest in providing possible clues to the former situation here. On November 18, 1880, he noted, "When I mentioned to Juan Chávez the pumas [mo′katch] and the name *shyayaq*, asking him whether this was his name, he replied, 'Es su oficio.' " Later, on September 6, 1886, he noted, "Hayoua says that Shikame chayan is one of the Shyayaq, and whenever they went to a big hunt (buffalo, etc.), he had to fit them out."

Other Secret Societies

The functions of the nonmedicine societies duplicate to some extent those of the medicine societies. Part of this duplication, such as the curing by the Ku-sha'lī and Kwe'rana societies, appears to be of considerable antiquity; other duplications have resulted from the readjustments made necessary when certain societies became extinct and their functions, or a portion of them, were absorbed by surviving societies. Under this classification are the following societies: Warriors, Tū-ba'jī, Hunters, Thundercloud (or Thunder), Women's, Shrū'tzī, Ka'tsīna, Ku-sha'lī, Kwe'rana, Turquoise Kiva, Pumpkin Kiva, and the Drummers, who are associated with one or the other of the two kivas. (See Appendix 17.)

Of these societies only two, the Turquoise and Pumpkin kiva groups, acquire their members partly as a result of kinship. A person is born into the kiva group of his father. However, even in these two cases, this affiliation is not a hard-and-fast one; a woman normally changes her kiva to that of her husband if the marriage is an exogamous one. At any time in life, a person or a family may request permission from the war captains and the two kiva heads to change kiva affiliation; such a request is never refused. All Conservatives belong to one or the other kiva; the Progressives, while no longer active in kiva matters, are more or less subconsciously associated with one of the two kivas.

The other societies, as will be brought out in the detailed discussions of each, are either extinct or, with only a few exceptions, are handicapped by small memberships. The Ka'tsīna group, formerly composed of all adult males and older boys, is now more restricted in its membership. All of these forgo the recruiting of new members, for, as noted earlier, constructive membership depends upon voluntary affiliation.

Warriors Society. The society of the Warriors (Ompī) has been extinct for several decades. One of my informants, born in the late 1880's, remembered seeing a Scalp Dance of the Ompī as a small child and stated that the dancers came out of the Turquoise Kiva and moved into the plaza. Further details were lacking, however. [15]

While no details of an actual Scalp Dance are to be found in any published data, the entry of October 24, 1880, of Bandelier's journal reveals the following account of the "war dance" as performed by the *Matalotes* (Ompī):

> The war dance is very costly. There are but few men in the pueblo who dance it. (He calls them *"matalotes,"* but it should be *matadores*.) It costs at least $20.00 to each one of them. The *capitan de la guerra* decides when the dance shall take place, but if, for some cause whatever, any one of the heroes cannot accumulate enough for the costs of the dance during the spring and summer, it is deferred until another year. Eight days previous, both the *matalote* (there are fourteen in the pueblo) and the *malinche* (the woman who is to dance with him, and who is selected by the *capitan*) become abstemious. For the first four days, the man keeps only apart from his wife, but on the fifth day he only eats a little in the morning and nothing until noon of the next day, then nothing until evening of the seventh day, then nothing until the close of the dance. (It lasts two days.) The close of the dance is made by a virgin *malinche*, and when she stops, the bell is tolled from the church, and while the *matalote* and his *malinche* go home to eat, the remainder go to prayer on their knees.

Several years later, Bandelier provided added details in his journal of December 26, 1885. Earlier, on December 21, he had referred to this ceremony as *"baile de la cabellera"* and mentioned that there would be six *matalotes* and six *malinches* from each kiva:

> They were dancing the "Ah-ta Tanyi." It is not the Scalp-dance proper, but an imitation of it. The "Matadores" (or Matalotes) or *Umpa* are painted black, the front hair combed down on the forehead and painted with almagre. There is a crown of white down [eagle's] over the head and down the side locks, and there is a feather of the painted eagle hanging from the topknot. They are dressed in buckskin and white shirt, the buckskin hanging down almost to the ankles. Bead-strings around the neck and an iridescent shell suspended to them. In the left hand a bow painted red, with eagle feathers at each end, and some red-painted arrows. In the right hand, a wooden or iron hatchet, also red. The Estufas alternated, "Tanyi" and "Shyuamo" [Pumpkin and Turquoise], and each had its malinche, or "Tzimat at Anyi" [Tzi'amatá (92)] or "Cu-cu" [ko'ko (92)]. One had two "Umpa," the other three. They came in, the Tanyi with the Cacique, who was not painted, but wore three little plumes, white, one on each side-lock and one behind, and carried a black folded cape with red trimmings or embroidery without sleeves. It is strapped round the waist, and the arms are bare from above the elbows. Some of the men are painted

yellow, but most of them red. The Qoshare are dressed, they wear twigs of the "Pino real" on the head, and wreaths of the same around the body and neck. Cheeks painted bluish-white in a streak across the cheekbones. The Malinche dressed like always, with the exception of a tuft of parrot-plumes instead of the *tablita*. To the right wrist a coyote skin was hanging. [The Santo Domingo Ku-sha'lī still use a coyote skin for this dance (92).] The song was the same as always. They danced first in a cluster, then in four rows, the Malinche between them. Finally, they knelt down in two rows, only the Cacique and the Umpa standing. Then the Malinche, with arms gracefully uplifted, and with an arrow in the right hand, hopped from one end of the line to the other, between, thus blessing alternately each row. The Cacique was directing the motions of her arms and hands, by indicating the motions with his arms. She acted very gracefully. Then another woman joined her, and another, so that three of them performed the blessing inside of the rows together. The Malinche was a woman, the 2 others were "widows." This blessing was the last performance, and during it, muskets and pistols were fired off from behind the lines by men standing. Previous to the blessing, however, those of one Estufa (the one who had previously danced) sent a delegation of men with fruits, corn, onions, chile, etc. etc. which they threw to the dancers. They caught them, and then women came in from the houses and threw also, very much like the "Tunles-Jian," and the dancers threw them to the children and people on the housetops. . . . At the next to the last dance, a little boy came, dressed as a Matalote, and then there was another dance by the "Tanyi" wherein the Malinche was a young girl. Otherwise, the Malinches are young married women. At the real scalp-dance, the Matalotes are naked, painted black with "Marmaja," and have bands of white down around the knees, white feathers on the head, and leatherstraps around the neck and shoulders. Four days total abstinence except for once every twenty-four hours are observed by both Matalotes and Malinches. The "Umpa," in this case, are only men who have killed beast of prey: eagles, bears, mountain-lions, wolves [one of my informants (92) insisted that the wolf should not be in this list], and *those animals who are nearest to man!* A real scalp-dance can only be celebrated when a fresh scalp is taken, in which case all those who have taken scalps previously celebrate the new one and "wash it in blood." Along with the "Shyuamo" there was an old man with two eagle plumes on the head. The dance stopped at sun-down.

The Warriors Society included men who had taken the scalp (na'kats) of an enemy. It also included those who had "counted coup," either first or second, on a mountain lion, bear, or eagle, as described previously (see pp. 134–135). The two men who had touched one of these animals of prey—considered almost human—

entered into a "brother" relationship and were also eligible for membership in the Warriors Society. At present, a few "brothers" are known in the pueblo, but the society has been extinct for some time. [25, 44, 45, 53] Bandelier's remarks (1890: 300) suggested that this animal type of Ompī may have been a compensatory measure as the actual man-killers began to disappear. He also noted that this transference indicated the high regard of the Cochití for these animals. According to one informant, the animal Ompī came in when someone wanted a *Matalote* Dance. Since only one man knew the songs, he needed others to help him, and the animal Ompī were designated after obtaining the *Principales*' permission. [44] While this incident was dated about 1900 by the informant, it is quite evident from Bandelier's journal that the animal Ompī originated sometime earlier. His account would also tend to show this form of Ompī more as an alternative form to the man-killers rather than as merely a substitute.

The head of the Warriors Society, called nahī'ya and also Ompī na'wai-ya, was looked upon as the "father" of his people. He was the warrior who had taken the most scalps. Apparently this accounting was done at the time a new headman became necessary through the death of the incumbent. There seems to be no evidence that he was ever displaced by another warrior who might have happened to take a greater number of scalps later on. One informant stated that a man should have taken at least four scalps before he became the society head. [44]

Dumarest (1919: 198–199) stated that the nahī'ya, or "war priest," was second in the hierarchy, subordinate only to the cacique. He also stated that the office was shared by two of the *principales*. It was a lifetime office and the nahī'ya, like the cacique, named his successor. He was chosen from men who were not shamans. Dumarest described this office as follows:

The *nahia* is chosen for his intelligence and his memory, for he is both advisor to the Cacique and guardian of traditions unknown in part even to the *principales* and sometimes even to the Cacique. He is also counsellor to *masewa*. He supervises the *principales*, the *chaiani*, the *shiwanna*. He is chief and organizer of secret dances. He maintains the customs. Like the Cacique he is called yaya, for by his fasting and prayers he too brings rain. This office of paramount authority was created when the people left *shipapu* for the south. *Masewa* called a meeting and asked for an adjutant to serve him when he went to war. The *nahia* is the same as *masewa* and *oyoyawa*.

In editorial notes, Parsons commented that elsewhere Dumarest referred to the *"nahia"* as *"hotshani,"* a general Keresan term for "chief." Likewise, she pointed out that the nahia was the "older brother" and the assistant was the "younger brother," emulating the twin war gods, Masewa and Oyoyewa. In the same passage cited, Dumarest added the following:

The *nahia (shreutse nawaia)* is head of the *crudos.*

. . . .

To the office of *nahia* is sometimes added the office of the head of the *matalotes (taiwa),* men who have killed one or more Navajo and brought back the scalps or who have killed at least some mountain lions or bears. The head of the organization is he who has the greatest number of kills to his credit. The head of the *matalotes* is the leader in the war dances. The Cacique is not necessarily *matalote,* but he has the right in the war dances to assign each dancer his *malinche* or female partner. Recently, at Cochiti, this right was usurped by the *nahia* who is also head of the *matalotes.* He was on his way to fetch to the dance one of the women he had chosen when the Cacique met him and had him make the poor woman change from her dance dress and give it over to the woman the Cacique himself had chosen. The episode made considerable noise.

According to my informants, several errors appeared in Dumarest's account. They questioned that the nahī'ya was actually a member of the *principales,* on the grounds that the cacique is not a member of this group. They claimed that this was a single officer, comparable to the cacique, and never a dual office such as that of the war captains. It was felt that when this office became extinct, certain of the functions were absorbed by the cacique, some by the war captains, and certain others by the Shrū'tzī head, particularly those which pertained to the Ka'tsīnas. It was agreed that the nahī'ya was not a medicine man, as Dumarest also suggests by pointing out that the nahī'ya was chosen from men who were not shamans; however, the statement that he supervised the chai'añī was held to be an error. [3, 44, 88]

Curtis (1926) made no mention of the position of nahī'ya, but Goldfrank (1927:39) gave considerable information, though it did not agree with much of that reported by Dumarest:

Today there no longer exists the office of *nahia*, a life position and formerly the highest official in the tribe. Dumarest has made some notes on this office, which was still flourishing in his time. However, there is one discrepancy between his data and mine. According to him the cacique is the head religious officer of the village, the nahia under him. According to my informant the nahia, a member of the ompi[c] (warriors or those who have scalped a Navajo) was designated by his predecessor and installed by the cacique, but thereafter was the superior officer of the village although the one was primarily war chief, the other religious head of the village. The same procedure is followed in the case of the war captain and cacique today.

White's data (1935: 39–40) on the office of nahī'ya at Santo Domingo provided little help for resolving the discrepancies in the accounts of Dumarest and Goldfrank. One of my informants asserted positively, however, that there are still Ompī at Santo Domingo and San Felipe. [55]

Present-day informants' opinions tend to support Goldfrank's position concerning the two offices of nahī'ya and cacique. In the segmented, yet overlapping, responsibilities of the several pueblo officials, it is probable that the Cochití themselves never had a rigid concept that one of these offices was superior to the other. In rather typical pueblo fashion, it would appear that the two officers were essentially equal in over-all prestige and authority, with the cacique having the final word in matters of peace, or internal welfare, while the nahī'ya assumed charge in times of war. [44, 88]

In the discussion of the cacique, his close connection with war was mentioned; this, however, concerned his association with "medicine," i.e., with making his own warriors invulnerable, striking terror in the enemy by magical powers, and treating wounds (curing). But the cacique was not concerned with war as an armed combatant. He and other medicine men were the highest authorities in matters of general welfare to the people, such as weather control and curing. A comment by Parsons (1939: 144) is applicable here to these two officers, the cacique and the nahī'ya: ". . . the general Pueblo attitude is that the chief of a ceremony being performed is paramount or general chief for the time being."

An older informant could recall five members of the Ompī by their native names, but he could not give their Spanish names. These men were Ko'hai-o, Yē'ma, Stait'yama, Kī'ma-tīwa, and Ka'wa-tīwa. [25] The first man, whose name means "bear," was the person mentioned as the proposed successor to Guadalupe Romero as cacique but rejected in favor of Antonio Suina (pp. 247–248). Yē'ma was listed by Starr (1899: 34) as Juan de Jesús Patagordo, of the Sun clan;

Kī'ma-tīwa was listed (1899: 40) as José Cordero, of the Corn clan. José was said to have been the last Ompī at Cochití, and his death was placed at about the turn of the century. He was said to have become eligible for membership after killing a bear. [52] He was a member of the Turquoise Kiva and was the father of José Nicanor Cordero, present Shrū'tzī head, and Santiago Cordero, very active in the Turquoise Kiva ceremonial life until he became blind in recent years. Data on the other two men could not be obtained.

From other informants came the names of a few additional Ompī. One was José Ortiz, who died late in the last century and was the father of Miguel Ortiz. José also belonged to the Shrū'tzī Society. [44] José María Quintana was an earlier nahī'ya. He was born about 1850 and was a member of the Turquoise Clan. [52] According to Starr (1899: 34) his Indian name was Hakaya-tiwa.

In regard to the paraphernalia involved with the Ompī, it is interesting that in Bandelier's journal of November 23, 1880, he noted that when he had asked the cacique for permission to paint the ornaments of the *malinche*, the cacique "most graciously consented. . . . As soon as I said that the cacique had given the permission, everything was all right." The fact that permission was asked of, and granted by, the cacique rather than the Ompī na'wai-ya, as of 1880, is also of interest. In view of data obtained from my informants it is strange that Bandelier makes no mention of meeting or becoming acquainted with the nahī'ya. So far as I can recall, Bandelier makes no reference to this official by the title *nahī'ya* in any of his publications or journals. On November 25 and 26, 1880, Bandelier noted:

This dress of the *malinche* is regarded as a very valuable piece. Juan José says that his mother made it about thirty years ago, and that while there used to be two in the pueblo, this is the only one now extant, but that in every pueblo there are similar patterns, though not identical. The pattern of each pueblo is, however, consecrated, and if one manta is used up, it is faithfully copied. The *manta* is property of Juan José's sister, or rather, she has it in trust, but her father bought the cloth, or rather, had it woven.

.   .   .   .

At night, Juan José finally told me the secret of the paintings on the *manta*. The upper zigzag lines signify lightning (*el rayo*, not *el relámpago*); the lower, the cloud which brings rain and thus fructifies the earth, symbol of good times. It is also the clouds dripping rain, and the outer figures are rain clouds—raindrops, too. The crown signifies the rainbow. The

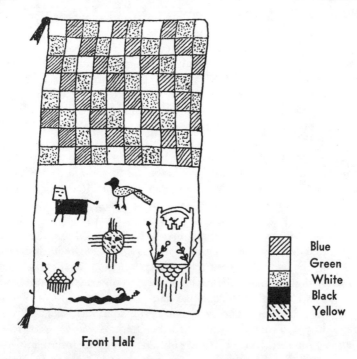

Blue
Green
White
Black
Yellow

Front Half

Fig. 18.—MALINCHE MANTA.

whole also belongs to the *Cachinas*. . . . He also says that in such paintings there is no red tolerated, as red is the color of hail, epidemics, war, and starvation, and if, at a *"baile de la cabellera"* there is no such manta in the pueblo, they go to another one to borrow one. There is, consequently, great superstition attached to it.

When checking this account with present-day Cochití, several discrepancies came to light. The *manta* of the *malinche*, since the disappearance of the Ompī, is now used in the dances of the Ku-sha′lī and the Kwe′rana—but not in Ka′tsīna dances. There are two *mantas* now at Cochití, essentially identical. They are also used in the Deer Dance, which is given on Reyes Day, January 6. It was stated in still another discussion that the *mantas* are currently kept for the tribe by Alcario Montoya (some doubt was expressed that the one kept by Alcario was still extant), Vicente Romero (head Kwe′rana), and Juan Velasquez. This suggests that there were at least three rather than two at some time not very long ago. This particular type of *manta* is given the name "tsīa'matu"; the designs were also said to be embroidered on the black wool *manta* with various-colored wool yarns—in contrast to Bandelier's reference to "paintings" on the *manta* he was copying. Figure 18 shows the front portion of a tsīa'matu. [42, 92]

As to the actual procedures followed in warfare, very little information can be learned today. In Bandelier's journal of November 20, 1880, is the notation that in making up a war party the war captain named the leaders and divided the group into squads of ten men each. No details were found regarding either fighting tactics or the rituals involved in warfare.

Informants unanimously agreed that no native rites were performed when the young men left for service during the Second World War, nor was there any ceremonial reception for them upon their return. Masses were said in the church in behalf of certain servicemen, but nothing else of a ceremonial nature was associated with this war service. "All that went with the Ompī, and now nobody knows about such things." [48, 49, 55, 58, 62, 70, 88]

Tū-ba'ĭ Society. No data on this society or its membership could be learned from my informants. Dumarest (1919: 194–195) claimed that the society existed only for purposes of divination. It was more active in winter than in summer, and the members' appearance in the village in a group signified a snowfall. They also performed magical rites in the kiva, though Dumarest did not specify which kiva. He described performances in the kiva in which scarecrows of the fields were made to speak, sometimes revealing good or bad behavior on the part of various individuals. Concerning this point, White (personal communication, spring, 1952) noted, "I cannot help being skeptical about Dumarest here."

Goldfrank (1927: 40) was told that the cacique, Victoriano Cordero, was a member of "Tubahi, a curing society that functioned formerly," but she was unable to get any elaboration of this.

Hunters (Hunting) Society. The Hunters (Hunting) (Shai'yak), Society has been extinct at Cochití for many years, though one informant was quite insistent that it was proper to refer to the Shī'kame head as "Shai'yak." Bandelier (1890: 276), in a general statement on this society in the Keresan pueblos, commented, "They are fast dying out, however, and have almost disappeared in several villages." Dumarest (1919) failed to mention this society, and Goldfrank (1927) did not obtain a membership roster for it. That informants likewise were unable to recall any members indicates that it had become extinct sometime before the end of the last century. Curtis (1926: 87) simply noted it was extinct. Goldfrank (1927: 46–47) collected some data on this society which she presented in the present tense, though, as noted, the society was probably already extinct:

Lastly, there is the Hunting society whose membership in Cochiti is identical with that of the Cikame society. The officers of the Cikame society are called by the same name as the supernaturals in charge of the hunt (caiak, djaikatse, dreikatse).

.   .   .   .

Just how the Hunting society became identical with the Cikame I did not learn. I believe that, as in the other villages, the Hunting society was originally independent. Today practically no one hunts, although my informant was able to give me many details of former days, and with the lessening of interest and the falling off of membership, perhaps the functions and ritual were assumed by the Cikame.

As already noted, Bandelier stated that the Giant Society, rather than the Shī'kame, was concerned with hunting and controlling the animals. If this was not an error, as it most likely is, it is interesting that when the Hunters, or Shai'yak, became extinct, their functions were absorbed by the Shī'kame instead of the Giant. Overlapping memberships could have played a role in this transition, though without a membership roster for the Shai'yak there is no way of reconstructing the actual circumstances. Goldfrank's idea of identical memberships in the Shī'kame and the Hunters societies does not appear valid except as mere circumstances. There seems to have been a transfer of functions from one society to the other, perhaps simply by default, but there is no evidence of mandatory duplicate memberships.

Thundercloud (Thunder) Society. The Thundercloud, or Thunder (Shī'wana), Society has already been mentioned in its association with the Giant Society. It is composed of women only and has its closest association with the Giant Society, though it also has some relationships with the Flint and Shī'kame societies. [3] At present, there is only one member, Priciliana Roybal Cordero. Personal data are given for her in connection with her membership in the Giant Society (Appendix 22). Trinidad Melchior Montoya was also a member of this society until her death in 1946; her personal data are also included in the roster for the Giant Society. The only other member that informants could recall was Ignacia Archibeque Herrera. She was of the Water Clan and Pumpkin Kiva. She was born February 5, 1860, and her death is unrecorded. As noted in discussing the Giant Society, one informant [42] said Reyes Suina Chalan was a member of the Thundercloud Society; other informants were not of this opinion, however.

Women's Society. At present, there are four members of the Women's Society (Ko'yawē) at Cochití; Juanita Chávez Romero, head; Reyes Suina Chalan, Damesia Suina Cordero, and Lucinda Cordero Suina. In compiling an all-time roster of members, only two other names were added: Inez Moquino Arquero and Juana Herrera Herrera. (See Appendix 24.)

Informants insisted that this society has had no connection with scalps or war. The principal function of the group is the ceremonial grinding of corn to make prayer meal for the cacique. [44, 70, 88] According to Curtis (1926: 88), these women invite other women, recognized as skillful grinders, to bring corn and assist in grinding it for the cacique. Curtis called this group a "pseudo-society," apparently because of his failure to find evidence of formal organization. However, according to my informants, the society has a head, and membership in it is recognized among the people.

An interesting point arose when Inez Moquino Arquero was mentioned by one informant as formerly assisting in the care (washing and feeding) of the scalps in association with certain scalp rituals, sometimes having to do with the *Matalotes,* or Warriors. The informant stated that this woman was the one who carried the scalps on a flat, wooden cradle-board and sang lullabies to them; whether she did this because of her membership in the Women's Society, the Ku-sha'lī, the Sage Clan, or for some other reason, such as personally volunteering for this duty and being accepted as a "dependable" person, the informant was unable to say. [95] The possibility that she performed this service as a member of the Women's Society was not mentioned by the informant, but it also must be considered as a possibility. However, the fact that the society exists after this duty is no longer performed by any member would tend to discount the association, though this may simply constitute an instance of culture loss. But as noted (pp. 249–250), at least some informants claim that the scalps are still being washed and fed by the cacique.

Shrū'tzī Society. This society is represented at present by two members—José Nicanor Cordero, head, and Guadalupe Ortiz, grandson of the Giant Society head and nephew of the cacique. An all-time roster of the society's membership shows eleven names, including that of one woman (Appendix 25). Goldfrank (1927: 44) pointed out that women were not eligible for membership in this society owing to its close connections with the all-male Ka'tsīna organization. In view of this, it is interesting that informants gave Lucia Romero Montoya as a past Shrū'tzī member. [3, 15, 42, 53] While it was unanimously stated by my informants that the Ka'tsīna Cult is a male group at Cochití, Boas (1922: 730) was told first that women do not become Ka'tsīna and later was told that "a few might." It is noteworthy, by comparison, to find that at Zia Pueblo, Stevenson (1894: 116) stated in regard to the Ka'tsīnas there that "females sometimes, though seldom, join this order." Also of interest is White's report (1942: 137–138) of women's joining the Santa Ana Ka'tsīna societies and actually portraying certain masked characters (the female Ka'-tsīnas).

Informants stated that "Shrū'tzī" is a difficult word to translate. It refers to those who do not belong to either Ku-sha'lī or Kwe'rana; Shrū'tzī members do not belong to any other society. There are instances, as in the case of Vicente Suina, of Shrū'tzī members withdrawing from this society to join another, most commonly the Giant Medicine Society, with which the Shrū'tzī has the closest affiliations except for the Ka'tsīna Cult. These points are corroborated by Goldfrank's findings a generation ago. Shrū'tzī members may be sometimes referred to as "raw," or *Crudos*, in contrast to the "cooked" or "roasted" status assigned to Ku-sha'lī or Kwe'rana members (see p. 239). [3, 15, 44] Another informant gave Shrū'tzī members a midposition, stating that they were neither "raw" nor "cooked." [55]

The Shrū'tzī Society cares for the ka'tsīna masks and other paraphernalia, equipment consisting of a considerable array—leather-helmet masks, face masks, ball eyes, assorted forms of beaks, and ears. These are assembled and decorated with fresh paint, feathers, hair, yarn, fur, and evergreen for each specific ceremony in which an impersonation appears. Dancers of either kiva may impersonate any of the characterizations that are appropriate for the scheduled ceremony. There appears to be no ka'tsīna ceremony specifically reserved for either kiva. [88, 92]

Estephanita Herrera, a Ku-sha'lī and an active participant in native ceremonials, has lent the society the use of a house located on the south side of the house block just south of the church. [44, 45] The Shrū'tzī head is responsible for preparing the necessary equipment for the ka'tsīna performers which occur periodically throughout the year. [3, 42, 45, 70] This procedure will be discussed at greater length in the following section, which deals specifically with the Ka'tsīna Cult.

It appears that both the Shrū'tzī and the Ka'tsīna organizations are slowly losing their former prominence at Cochití. As noted previously in connection with the making of dolls and other ritual paraphernalia, Goldfrank (1927: 76) was told by informants that the Shrū'tzī members were lazy and were not performing their jobs well.

Dumarest (1919: 199) stated that "the *nahia* (*shreutse-nawaia*) is the head of the *crudos*" (the uninitiated). Curtis (1926: 87–88) recorded this society as the "Siusti" and pointed out that the term "society" was applicable to neither the Siusti nor the Shī'wana, or Ka'tsīnas. He called the society head "nawaya," as he did other headmen, and stated that the head kept and maintained the ka'tsīna masks. Goldfrank (1927: 44–45) added still another spelling: "Curdzi." However, in her phonetic recording *c* has an *sh* value, which makes the pronunciation quite similar to the pronunciation recorded here.

Goldfrank (1927: 44) gained the impression that the Shrū'tzī Society was related to the Giant Society as a "managing society" in much the same way that the Ku-sha'lī was related to the Flint and the Kwe'rana, to the Shī'kame:

The relation between the Curdzi and the Giant society is less apparent but no less real. Some Curdzi do join the Giant society, but upon so doing, they must relinquish their membership in the Curdzi society, as a Curdzi may not join any other organization. The Curdzi and Giant societies have their respective houses. However, it is the Giant society that fashions prayer sticks for the Curdzi, as these may only be made by members of the curing societies. The Curdzi go into retreat on the first night of the retreats of the Giant society and both groups visit the chief Curdzi shrine, the house of Ganadyani.

These data agree generally with those obtained from my informants. A few exceptions occur. In Goldfrank's time, the house of the Shrū'tzī head was too small to accommodate the ka'tsīna paraphernalia, and the Giant head consented to keep it for him. At present, with the loan of a house, the Shrū'tzī again have direct charge

of the paraphernalia. For the most part, my informants seemed unaware of the close connection between the Shrū'tzī and Giants suggested by Goldfrank. However, this is interpreted as change occurring
over the span of a generation rather than as any error in the respective data.

Dumarest's notes (1919: 198–199) are both interesting and confusing in reference to the Shrū'tzī. He appeared to distinguish between the *"nahia"* (head of the Warriors) and the *"shreutse-nawaia"*
(Shrū'tzī head). He then stated that the *"nahia (shreutse-nawaia)*
is the head of the *crudos."* This seems to say that the Warrior head
was also the Shrū'tzī head, which means, in turn, that he was also in
charge of the Ka'tsīnas. If so, this adds still another function to the
former office of nahī'ya and indicates further change and adjustment
when this office became extinct. Again, it may have been simply a
case of careless use of the term *"nahia"* by Dumarest.

At present, with José Nicanor Cordero, the head, becoming increasingly handicapped by age, and the other member, Guadalupe
Ortiz, away from the pueblo in the armed forces, this society is weak.
Although individual informants would undoubtedly deny the trend,
it is apparent from numerous statements and implications that
ka'tsīna matters have already begun to be controlled to an increasing
degree by the war captains and by the other ceremonial leaders,
especially kiva officials.

Ka'tsīna Cult. At Cochití, the term "Ka'tsīna" is used interchange-
ably with "Shī'wana" in designating the cult of tribal deities, together with the masked impersonations of these supernaturals. Boas
(1922: 731) noted another term, "Kopictayo," which applied to this
complex; according to my informants this term has more of the connotation of "spirits." Curtis (1926: 87–88) felt that the term "society"
was not properly applicable to the ka'tsīnas. The fact that the membership, at least formerly, embraced essentially all adult males of the
tribe and that they functioned with a minimum of organization other
than the supervision of the Shrū'tzī Society would tend to support his
view.

At present, the participation in this group is much less universal.
It remains, without any distinctive organization, under the theoreti-
cal control of the Shrū'tzī members. However, in practice, the
Shrū'tzī control is less effective for the reasons indicated in the section discussing that society. Sharing the control with the Shrū'tzī is
an informal group which amounts to a ceremonial council. This is

composed of the cacique (Flint head), Giant head, Shī'kame head, Ku-sha'lī head, Kwe'rana head, war captain, assistant war captain, Turquoise Kiva head, Pumpkin Kiva head, and the governor. (See Appendix 17.) Often the members of what might be termed a ceremonial nucleus of each kiva are included. This duplicates the Council of *Principales* only partially, leaving out the younger *Principales* and adding the medicine men. [3, 44, 88, 92]

While the Ka'tsīnas are commonly viewed as tribal, it would appear that in recent years, with increasing emphasis upon kiva membership and activities, a virtual dichotomy within the Ka'tsīna structure has developed, as suggested at the end of the preceding section. This appears to be rather recent, but it may actually be much older, even traditional, and it may be simply a matter of having been undiscovered in earlier research. The close association between the ka'tsīna groups (five of them) and the medicine societies at Santa Ana, as reported by White (1942: 133–142), is in distinct contrast to the situation at Cochití. The importance, in practice if not in theory, of the kiva groups in ka'tsīna activities aligns Cochití more closely to such pueblos as Santo Domingo and San Felipe.

Formerly, when all adult males joined the Ka'tsīna Cult, tribal initiations were held about every four years. Today, the cult is more a secret society than it is the manifestation of a general adult male status. The present procedure in obtaining members is for the so-called "ceremonial council" to decide among themselves that a certain older boy or young man is discreet enough to protect the secrets of the group if he should join them. This appraisal is communicated to the boy's father, or some other older and reliable male relative who knows the boy well. If this person is of the opinion that the appraisal is accurate and, equally important, that the boy would be interested in affiliating with the cult, he passes this information on to the boy. He tells the boy when he is to be ready, and at that time an *alguacilito* comes to escort him from his home to the Shrū'tzī house. The boy is taken to the inner room there; he comes face to face with the members of the "ceremonial council" and receives instructions concerning his obligations as a member of the Ka'tsīnas.

Informants insisted that there are no rites of initiation beyond this rather matter-of-fact indoctrination session. If true, it would seem probable that this simple procedure is recent and represents a sloughing off of a more elaborate routine in past times. One would expect at least a minimum use of meal or pollen to accompany the various stages of the negotiations with the nominee, the presence of a "Ka'-tsīna father," and a purifying, or ceremonial, whipping. (See White [1942: 133–135] for comparative data from Santa Ana Pueblo.)

In the summer of 1952, the following data regarding participation in the Ka'tsīna Cult were gathered for the Cochití adult males (arbitrarily set at those over fifteen years of age): sixty-three were not members of the cult; thirteen had been active but had dropped out because of old age, blindness, or some other physical handicap; fifty-eight were active in Ka'tsīna performances. Of the first group, there were some who had never joined and others who had once belonged but had dropped out as a part of their shift to the ranks of the Progressives. The youngest active member was a young man of twenty-one, who had joined in 1950 at the age of nineteen; few of his age group or of those only several years older had chosen to join the Ka'tsīnas. It is quite clear that recruits are becoming increasingly rare. [3, 15, 45, 48, 49, 53, 55, 62, 88, 92]

Ka'tsīna ceremonies are held in various locations, including isolated level sites on the river bank both above and below the pueblo; a spot in the saddle between two hills, ga'ash-kona ("White Hills"), a mile northwest of the village; in the plaza; and in the Pumpkin (but not the Turquoise) Kiva. In former times, informants recalled dances by the Ka'tsīnas in some of the larger private homes, a favorite being that of Juan Chávez, located just northwest of the plaza where, in 1952, Nestor Herrera and his family lived. It is interesting that Bandelier noted the same use of this house in his journal of December 12, 1880.

In recent years there have been no ka'tsīna rites along the river and in the plaza because these spots cannot be adequately guarded against intruders. Bandelier, in the entry noted above, recorded that "he [the informant] frankly confessed it was not permitted to see them although he formally denied they danced naked. . . . He says that the Cachinas may perhaps be free to me when I return [from a short trip to Mexico], and that they are perfectly decent." Earlier, on November 28, 1880, he had commented in a similar fashion: "*Cachinas.* He represents them as good, not bad, and as intercession "por el bien del pueblo," but that the Mexicans are strictly forbidden to see them. They are held in the timber. A few years ago, Telísforo Lucero was nearly killed by the Indians of Cochití on that account."

Present-day Cochití say that they cannot recall a ka'tsīna ceremony in the Turquoise Kiva; this they attribute to the fact that for many years this kiva has been more or less surrounded by homes of several Spanish families, whereas there have been only Indian homes in the vicinity of the Pumpkin Kiva. The fact that the Spanish families have been removed from the area of the Turquoise Kiva in recent times has failed to alter the established pattern, however.

Thus, at present, the Ka'tsīnas perform in the Pumpkin Kiva during the winter months and during the hours of darkness; there are daylight and occasional evening performances during the warm months at ga'ash-kona, the site a mile northwest of the village. During these ceremonies, the *alguacilitos* constantly patrol the horizon and near vicinity to ward off any disturbing influence. [3, 44, 53, 55, 70, 88]

Ka'tsīna ceremonies may be asked for, specifically, by any member. The request is first taken up with the Shrū'tzī head who, in turn, conveys it to the war captain and his assistant. Next, the matter is discussed with the mayorlī of the kiva which is to perform the ceremony, a position filled in recent years by Eleuterio Suina for the Turquoise and Lorenzo Herrera for the Pumpkin. In addition, this meeting is attended by the cacique and other members of the "ceremonial council" already mentioned. No one could recall an instance of a request's not being honored.

The majority of the ka'tsīna impersonations are done by older men who regularly sing in the choruses for the public dances. Occasionally, their ranks are supplemented by some of the younger men. When the formality of agreeing that the ceremony should be held has been observed, the same group selects the impersonators who are to take part. Sometimes a member volunteers to take part or to perform a certain impersonation; generally, the participants are simply designated by the headmen. A member is notified of his selection in secret —the usual procedure being to find him alone at a corral or stock tank or en route to his fields. He is told that he has been chosen and that he should come to the Shrū'tzī house at a particular time to get ready for the performance. Commenting on this "sly" manner of making plans known only to the members, one man observed, "And the women are the first to know." [55]

In making these choices, care is taken to choose a person known to be willing and capable, and he should have no distinctive scars, deformities, or any other identifying physical feature. Individuals having such identification can be given only those roles in which the appropriate costume obscures it.

It is theoretically the decision of the Shrū'tzī head to determine whether a specific ka'tsīna is being properly cast and portrayed. This responsibility is causing some uneasiness at present, owing to the fact that the head, José Nicanor Cordero, is somewhat handicapped by old age. The only other member is young and, according to general opinion, has many details yet to learn; moreover, as of 1952, he had been away from the pueblo for several years because of military service.

It is customary for the three medicine-society heads to name the side dancers and the ka'tsīna guards who are to be included; the other impersonators, as noted, are picked by the assembled headmen. Numerous practices are held in preparation for any ceremony; each time the costumes are used, they are assembled and freshly decorated by specific individuals—men designated as "kwirsh'ke-shē" ("blue") —whose duty it is to gather the pigments and other materials for preparing the ceremonial equipment needed by either kiva group. For the Turquoise Kiva, the work is shared by Lorenzo Suina and Juan Velasquez (he recently replaced Santiago Cordero, who was forced to give up this position when he became blind); for the Pumpkin Kiva, the work is done by Lorenzo Herrera and Nestor Herrera. These four men help the Shrū'tzī Society in preparing paraphernalia (in recent years, owing to circumstances already noted, they have taken over an increasing amount of this work) for the ka'tsīnas and also that for the public dances given by their respective kivas.

Despite certain manifestations of a decline in general interest in the ka'tsīnas, it appears that the preparation of ka'tsīna equipment and also for the ka'tsīna performances is much more meticulous than that for the public dances. Among those who continue to follow the ka'tsīna beliefs and practices, the general attitudes toward them and their standards of perfection remain surprisingly unimpaired. However, in the less obvious aspects, so far as other individuals are concerned, at least, there are signs that the significance attached to certain practices is diminishing.

Those who have been chosen to participate should fast and vomit for four days prior to the ceremony. The fasting includes a sex taboo and a limit of one meal, eaten about noon, each day. This meal is minimal and should consist of only native foods. Food from a store is taboo for such occasions. Vomiting is done in private outside the individual's home first thing in the morning. The procedure to induce vomiting is to drink a warm tea made of juniper leaves; tickling the throat with a finger or a feather is not practiced. "It isn't necessary." [88] Another informant, somewhat younger, stated that fasting and vomiting are not so strictly observed as formerly. "Now it's up to the person; some of the older ones do, but there are lots who don't." [55]

Masks, either the helmet ("bucket") or the face type, are cleaned and painted with care. The proper pigment is mixed with water and applied with a brush of yucca. Then the juice obtained by straining the contents of pumpkin seeds is sprayed by mouth over the mask as evenly as possible. (For modern, exoteric application of this technique, see p. 181.) This darkens the paint and "fixes" it. While this is still moist and sticky, the worker chews mica and sprays it evenly over the mask to give it a glistening appearance. Deerskin is unsatisfactory as the basic element of the mask, for it is too pliable to keep the desired form. Formerly buffalohide was the usual material used, but at present masks are most commonly of cowhide; a few are made of commercial boot leather or horsehide.

Set times for ka'tsīna performances are few. In early January, on a date decided by the war captains, there is a ka'tsīna dance in honor of the new officers. There is always a ka'tsīna dance on Easter Evening. For time perspective, it is interesting that Bandelier (April 9, 1882) noted a "Cachina Dance" on Easter Evening. Apparently all other dances are held at the suggestion of the war captains, others of the "ceremonial council," or any member of the Ka'tsīna Cult. Such suggestions may have been made initially by a woman or child who is not actually a member but expresses a desire to see the ka'tsīnas, perhaps a specific group of them.

On the third day of formal preparations, the Ku-sha'lī members, in typical costume, go from house to house throughout the village and announce that the ceremony is to take place the following day, giving the location and time. Some contradiction was encountered as to precisely who receives this invitation from the Ku-sha'lī. It was stated that "everybody is invited," and this included the Progressives as well as the Conservatives. It was added, however, that the Progressives do not attend. In attempting to find the reason for this, wondering if perhaps certain ka'tsīna characters might single out the Progressives for special ridicule and hence cause them to remain away, I was told by other informants that the Progressives were not invited. It was their view that the Progressives, in abandoning the beliefs and practices of the Ka'tsīna Cult, had, in effect, placed themselves in an identical position with other taboo nonbelievers such as

the Spanish, Anglos, and any other outsider. [42, 44, 92] On the point
of exclusion of outsiders (see p. 18), it is interesting to find an entry
of Bandelier's (April 5, 1882) confirming that the Cochití "Cachina"
was secret and was performed "in the sierra"; one exception—Jemez
—was pointed out to Bandelier. There "Americans are allowed to
assist. But the other pueblos do not like it at all." This may have been
true in 1882; if so, the discrepancy had been eradicated by the time
of Parsons' work there. Her comments (1925: 7–8) are of interest
not only for Jemez but for Cochití and other pueblos of the area:
"As far as I can learn, in recent years no White has seen, except accidentally in passing, a k'ats'ana or masked dance at Jemez. . . . There
is an unswayable determination, I believe, that no White is to see the
k'ats'ana and this determination is based, not on the character or
behavior of the contemporaneous White, but on tradition."

In light of these comments, it is surprising to note that Bandelier,
in his journal of April 8, 1882, recorded that an Indian came late that
evening and invited him to a "Cachina Dance" at one of the kivas.
Bandelier's reaction to this invitation is—in terms of field method-
ology—as surprising as the invitation itself: "I declined, telling him
that I did not feel authorized to go, since it was my duty to publish
everything I saw and as the dance was secret, it would be of no benefit to me and might injure him. So he went, telling me that tomorrow
he would tell me all about it."

Despite the exclusion of the Progressives, one of the Conservative
leaders pointed out that although this group have eliminated themselves from such activities, they continue to criticize the quality and
other aspects of the ka'tsīna performances. Summing up, he added,
partly with resentment and partly with damaged pride, "They're
characters." [96]

Before the ceremony is to begin, the members of the audience—
women, children, and nonparticipating men—take their places. It is
considered highly improper, if not virtually impossible, to arrive late
or to leave early when there is a ka'tsīna performance. The idea that
one must remain throughout a ka'tsīna performance corresponds to
the practice reported for Santo Domingo by White (1943a: 331); apparently this feature is less rigidly enforced by the Santa Ana and
Acoma (1943a: 331).

If the dance is outdoors—at ga'ash-kona, for example—the women
and children sit on the ground in a cluster on the east side, facing
northward. To their left, or to the west, the men who are "in" on the

ka'tsīna secrets gather. If the dance is in the kiva, the women and children huddle about the firebox, on the south side. The men form a band across the front of this area, between it and the area where the ka'tsīnas dance, and also arrange themselves along the sides and behind the women and children, thus completing a cordon between these and the dancers as they enter and leave the kiva. In this way those who "do not know about these things" are effectively kept from coming into close contact with the dancers, thereby minimizing the chances of their detecting any unwarranted knowledge.

There are prescribed dress and behavior customs for the spectators to follow. All men must wear a bowguard, but informants did not agree on whether this requirement applied also to boys. An inspection for this is made by the ka'tsīna side dancers, or guards, and whippings are administered to anyone who has forgotten to wear this item. Similarly, moccasins (not shoes) must be worn by all— men and women, boys and girls. Other items of dress should be of the type still worn by chorus members on Feast Day; while some latitude is developing for the men, this dress is still preferred. For the women, traditional *mantas* are worn without the underdress which has recently come in. This leaves the arms bare, and if the weather is cold another *manta* or blanket is worn. While they await the appearance of the dancers, the women rearrange their hair from the customary *chongo* style to two braids which hang in front. One informant added that this particular custom is limited to the married women. It was also stated that no jewelry or anything shiny could be worn by anyone [44, 88]; another opinion was that this was applicable only to the men and that women could wear jewelry if they cared to. [55, 92, 96]

For all ka'tsīna ceremonies, the first characters to appear are two or three Ku-sha'lī, in typical costume. They slip in slyly and speak rather quietly. After a short time, they register great surprise upon finding the audience present—"You might say they find reality." [96] Then the Ku-sha'lī begin to make jokes, gesture in ridiculous ways, and otherwise entertain the people. They tease certain women about their husbands or a widow about some man. They make many exaggerated statements and tell numerous jokes. It would appear that this comic introduction is partially institutionalized in the sense that one woman who is ceremonially prominent, Damesia Suina Cordero, was mentioned by several informants as being the particular object of many of these jokes. "She talks right back to them, too."

Generally, the first impersonation to appear is He'rūta, the head

Ka'tsīna of the Cochití. He, like all other Ka'tsīnas, speaks no recognizable language; instead, communication is by means of gestures and strange birdlike calls and whistles. These are understood by the Ku-sha'lī, of course, and one or more of them serve as interpreter. The conversation (see Dumarest [1919: 177–178] for a fairly detailed recording of a typical conversation) includes several exchanges concerning the purpose of He'rūta's coming. He states that he has brought some dancers with him from Wē'nimats, and he asks whether the people would care to see them and their dancing. When a Ku-sha'lī turns to the people and relays this question to them, they respond affirmatively. It appears that He'rūta has suddenly become quite deaf, necessitating several repetitions. When the question is asked and answered a magical fourth time—in the process of which interest and tension mount—He'rūta acknowledges their enthusiasm and departs to bring the dancers. If the performance is in the kiva, he enters from the right and leaves by the left, thus conforming to the counterclockwise ceremonial pattern. If it is outdoors, he enters the "stage" (ka'katch, or plaza) from the west, symbolically the home of the Ka'tsīnas, or Wē'nimats, and also departs in that direction to get them.

Upon returning, He'rūta is at the head of a line of performers. First come the guards, the so-called "whipper" Ka'tsīnas, whose duty it is to keep the audience from getting too close to the dancers, to assist in keeping the dancers' costumes in proper repair, and to police the proceedings generally. Next follow the war captain and his lieutenant, who carry their canes of office: upon entering, they leave the dancers and take their seats among the men in the audience. In the policing of the crowd, the governor, who must carry his official cane for any ka'tsīna dance, may assist the Ka'tsīna guards. It was stated by some that the lieutenant governor and the *fiscale* and his lieutenant do not carry their canes [3, 44], but others insisted that official canes are carried by all six of the major officers for any ka'tsīna performance. [42, 92]

The line of dancers appears next, led by a Ku-sha'lī dressed not in typical ceremonial garb but in his "nicest clothing." He carries a small basket of corn meal and wears a bit of cornhusk in his hair. At the rear of the line is a Kwe'rana member, similarly dressed but wearing a fluffy eagle feather on top of his head and hawk feathers in his side hair. He carries a willow wand. Informants stated that Dumarest (1919: 205) was in error in saying the Ku-sha'lī carried goose feathers in the right hand and a basket in his left and the Kwe'rana carried goose and hawk feathers in the right and evergreen in the left. This discrepancy may well represent the product of culture change which informants, thus far, have quite vigorously denied for most aspects of such a sacred topic.

The lead and rear positions of the Ku-sha'lī and Kwe'rana, respectively, are never shifted, despite the fact that a ceremony may take place in a year during which the Kwe'rana Society has ceremonial control of the tribe. This is the order followed except for the few instances indicated in the detailed account of individual ka'tsīnas in Appendix 26.

The general pattern for a ka'tsīna dance is for the line of dancers to enter and, maintaining their individual places in the line, dance facing toward the east for one song. They then reverse themselves, turning as a line, not as individuals, and dance facing westward. This routine constitutes "one time," or "one round." The Shrū'tzī head, the war captain, and the kiva mayorlī agree beforehand on how many songs ("times") there will be. In the kiva, there are four, the dancers departing at the end of each round. In the old days there were often five, but the "regulation" is four and this number has been reverted to in recent years. When the performance is held outdoors, there are normally four rounds before noon and four after. About noon, the women bring food for the Ka'tsīnas, depositing it near the western exit for the men who "know about such things" to take to "Wē'-nimats," where the Ka'tsīnas eat.

This practice appears to be an added security feature regarding the Ka'tsīnas; White (1943a: 331) mentions that at Acoma "the old ladies carrying food" actually go behind the church where the Ka'-tsīnas are resting. This practice was noted as not so strict as that of Santo Domingo, where the side dancers try to prevent anyone from seeing even "the old ladies carrying food to the dancers." Here it is not clear whether the women themselves take the food to the dancers, as at Acoma, or merely take it "toward" the Ka'tsīnas for the men to receive and present to the dancers, as at Cochití.

The war captain and his assistant enter at the time of the first round and do not leave until the conclusion of the final one, when they take the same places in the line of departing performers that they had upon entering.

In the course of the dancing, certain Ka'tsīnas—most often the side dancers—go to various members of the audience and present them

with gifts concealed in their costumes—certain traditional foods, a
rattle, a small bow and arrow for a man, or a small wooden doll
(o'aka) and cradle for a woman. As the dancers leave for the last
time, He'rūta tells the Ku-sha'lī members to inform the people that
it is the end of the ceremony and they should return to their homes.
[55, 88, 92]

Several informants were of the opinion that all ka'tsīnas known
at the end of the last century could be correctly impersonated today,
both in costume and in portrayal. They admitted that numerous ka'-
tsīnas have not been seen for almost that long, but they hastened to
point out that one is not justified in declaring certain ka'tsīnas "extinct" simply because they have never been regularly portrayed. It
was interesting that in some instances where an informant stated he
had never seen a particular impersonation himself, he could nevertheless provide a description of the ka'tsīna sufficiently accurate to
be corroborated by another, speaking independently of him, who had
seen it. [3, 15, 88, 92, 96]

Data regarding various ka'tsīnas are presented in Appendix 26.
To summarize briefly here, the names and descriptions for eleven
distinct ka'tsīna individuals, twenty-one guards or attendants, and
twenty-one dances in which a line of similarly costumed performers
participate were obtained from various informants. The few masks
and related data provided in Dumarest's account (1919: Plates V–
VI; Figs. 22, 24, 25; pp. 176–185) were generally confirmed by my
informants, a few shifts in colors and design being noted. These
deviations are discussed in Appendix 26 with the specific impersonation involved.

Considerable concern was voiced by several Cochití over the increasing intervals between ka'tsīna ceremonies. With the great majority of them on no regular schedule, it is becoming quite easy to
allow performances to slip by. Although it is perhaps unfair to de-
clare any of the dances or impersonations actually extinct, for reasons
already noted, there are increasing apprehension and expressions of
doubt regarding the ability of the tribe to perpetuate these. It was in
a sincere effort to safeguard against such an eventuality that certain
informants voluntarily opened this esoteric topic for discussion with
the writer and expressed their desire to have these data faithfully
recorded. While much remains to be gathered on this subject, this
section and the material in Appendix 26 constitute an appreciable as
well as a fundamentally sound base from which to do further re-

Plate 1.—Cochiti and Vicinity, 1947. Aerial photograph. *Photograph by C. E. Fullerton.*

Plate 2.—Cochití Pueblo, 1947. This aerial photograph, looking toward the south-west, shows the ground plan of the major portion of the pueblo. In the foreground are the fields and the Middle Rio Grande Conservancy District canal; in the center are the rectangular juniper-pole community corral, the plaza, and the two round kivas (the near kiva is the Turquoise and the far one, the Pumpkin); to the left is the Mission of San Buenaventura de Cochití. *Photograph by C. E. Fullerton.*

Plate 3.—STONE LIONS ON THE POTRERO DE LAS VACAS. *a(above)*. This well-known pair of stone lions is now within the area of Bandelier National Monument; Cochití hunters still make some use of this shrine (see p. 132). *Photograph by C. F. Lummis, 1890; Neg. No. 266, Southwest Museum.*

b(below). Close-up of the stone lions, Potrero de las Vacas. *Photograph by W. Henry Brown, no date; Neg. No. MNM 03436, Museum of New Mexico.*

THE STONE PUMA, POTRERO DE LOS IDOLOS.

Plate 4.—STONE LIONS ON THE POTRERO DE LOS IDOLOS. *a(above).* Arrow points to the remaining lion of a pair located on the Potrero de los Idolos; this one-time shrine had been completely forgotten and "lost" until relocated by a Cochití and the author in 1952 (see p. 8, n. 3). *Photograph by C. F. Lummis, about 1890; Neg. No. 3756, Southwest Museum.*

b(below). Close-up of the stone lion, Potrero de los Idolos. *Photograph by C. F. Lummis, about 1890; Neg. No. MNM 04565, Museum of New Mexico, and also Neg. No. 699, Southwest Museum.*

Plate 5.—Mission of San Buenaventura de Cochiti. *a(above)*. This photograph, of unknown date and source, shows the church in poor repair. From the remarks of Bourke (p. 46) and Kubler (p. 61), this picture was probably taken in the early 1880s. The *Campo Santo* was fenced but not walled, as it was in later years. *Neg. No. SAR 1504.7, School of American Research, Museum of New Mexico.*

b(below). This photograph, by Vroman, 1900, shows the church in much better repair, freshly whitewashed, with murals about the entrance, and the *Campo Santo* walled. *Neg. No. 2171b, Bureau of American Ethnology, Smithsonian Institution.*

Plate 6.—The Altar: Mission of San Buenaventura de Cochiti. This interior view was made by Vroman in 1900. Barely distinguishable on the ceiling above the altar is a series of painted native designs. *Neg. No. 2172, Bureau of American Ethnology, Smithsonian Institution.*

Plate 7.—*a(above)*. A COCHITI FUNERAL, ABOUT 1897. The body, wrapped in a blanket, is being carried on a house-ladder. *Photograph by F. Starr; Neg. No. 15669, Museum of the American Indian, Heye Foundation.*

b(below). THE COCHITI MISSION AFTER REMODELING. The gabled roof and tall cupola were added in 1912; the wall around the *Campo Santo* was also replaced with a wire fence. *Neg. No. SAR 1504.9, School of American Research, Museum of New Mexico.*

Plate 8.—*a(above)*. MISSION OF SAN BUENAVENTURA DE COCHITI, 1951. The short steeple replaced the tall one (Plate 7) shortly after 1912 because the wind created too much strain on the walls of the main structure. *Photograph by C. H. Lange.*

b(below). THE FLINT—KU-SHA'LI HOUSE, 1951. Only a few yards north of the mission, this structure figures prominently in native ceremonialism. On the shady east wall, facing the camera, the aperture high in the center of the wall allows the rays of the rising sun to be used in certain ritual calculations of the cacique, whose "office" is the room on that side of the building. *Photograph by C. H. Lange.*

Plate 9.—TURQUOISE KIVA, COCHITI, 1900. Northeastern sector of the pueblo in the background, with La Tetilla on the horizon at extreme right. Note at right the woman walking with an *olla* balanced on her head (this is no longer seen at Cochiti). *Photograph by Vroman; Neg. No. 2169, Bureau of American Ethnology, Smithsonian Institution.*

Plate 10.—Cochiti Bridge-building, 1897. *a(above)*. Preparations are being made to set a "caisson" in the Rio Grande (pp. 57, 59 f.). Various ceremonial officials are standing in the background. *Photograph by F. Starr; Neg. No. 15666, Museum of the American Indian, Heye Foundation.*

b(below). The completed bridge. *Photograph by F. Starr; Neg. No. 15668, Museum of the American Indian, Heye Foundation.*

Plate 11.—AGRICULTURAL FIELDS, COCHITÍ. *a(above)*. Irrigation "beds" located in an arroyo bottom to take advantage of flood waters. Note the diversion structure on the upstream side for spreading the water. *Photograph by F. Starr, 1897; Neg. No. 15629, Museum of the American Indian, Heye Foundation.*

b(below). View across the valley immediately north of Cochití; on the far horizon is La Tetilla; irrigated fields west of the river can be seen at center; a "ranchito" stands on the high ground above the fields; in the foreground, the fenced pasture encloses fields that formerly were dry-farmed and that also utilized flood waters from the "Long Arroyo," which empties just to the left of this scene. Rocks in right foreground are the remains of a small house archaeological site. *Photograph, 1951, by C. H. Lange.*

Plate 12.—Cochiti Stores. *a(above).* This photograph, of unknown date and source, was probably taken about 1900. It shows the store of Juan José Romero, which was located in the house block south of the church from about 1895 to 1916. Note the strands of chilis hanging from the walls and the baby being carried upon the woman's back. The wagon standing before the last unit on the right is similar to the type still in use at the pueblo today. *Neg. No. SAR 1504.4, School of American Research, Museum of New Mexico.*

b(below). The store and home of Leopoldo Rael was built in 1923 on the site of a store operated by José A. Rivera from 1900 to 1923. The building was enlarged in 1947/48; in the late winter of 1954 it was destroyed by fire. *Photograph (1951) by C. H. Lange.*

Plate 13.—Panoramic View, Cochiti, 1900. Jemez Mountains in the distant background; between the mountains and the pueblo are the juniper-covered foothills; at center and at middle right-hand margin are threshing floors, enclosed by wire and post fences. On the near side of the *Campo Santo* wall an improvised fenced addition is visible. *Photograph by Vroman; Neg. No. 2165, Bureau of American Ethnology, Smithsonian Institution.*

Plate 14.—*a(above).* COMMUNITY-OWNED COMBINE HARVESTER AND TRACTOR, 1951.
The advantages of this modern agricultural equipment, purchased in 1947 despite
some protest, resulted in plans, as of 1952, to purchase a second combine. *Photograph
by C. H. Lange.*

b(below). WINNOWING WHEAT, 1951. Despite the modern methods of harvesting,
winnowing continues in the centuries-honored ways. *Photograph by C. H. Lange.*

Plate 15.—*a(above)*. REPLASTERING HOUSE WALLS, 1948. This work, done by the women, is carried on today in the same way that it has been done for centuries. *Photograph by C. H. Lange.*

b(below). NEW HOME CONSTRUCTION, 1951. Time-honored materials continue to be used, though with occasional adopted techniques aimed at increasing precision in building. This home was designed to include the first inside bathroom in the village. *Photograph by C. H. Lange.*

Plate 16.—Drum-making, 1951. *a(above).* Hollowing out the log section. The consistently high quality of Cochití drums is widely recognized. *Photograph by C. H. Lange.*

b(below). Skinning a horse for drumheads. *Photograph by C. H. Lange.*

Plate 17.—Cochiti Crafts. *a(above).* Pottery-making. The form is being built up and shaped prior to scraping, polishing, and firing. Note the selenite window in the background; formerly common, these have completely disappeared from Cochití. *Photograph by F. Starr, about 1897; Neg. No. 15621, Museum of the American Indian, Heye Foundation.*

b(below). Belt-making. Although such looms are often secured to house posts, the arrangement here permits greater mobility and serves the purpose equally well. *Photograph by F. Starr, about 1897; Neg. No. 15623, Museum of the American Indian, Heye Foundation.*

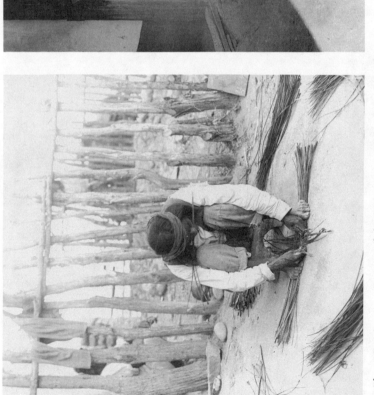

Plate 18.—Cochiti Crafts. *a(left)*. Basket-weaving. Note the materials conveniently arranged about the weaver and also that he uses his hands, feet, and mouth. This is a washing, or winnowing, basket. *Photograph by F. Starr, about 1897; Neg. No. 15744, Museum of the American Indian, Heye Foundation.*

b(right). Bead-drilling. This pump drill is still used for such purposes today. *Photograph by F. Starr, about 1897; Neg. No. 15749, Museum of the American Indian, Heye Foundation.*

Plate 19.—Two Views of a Kwe'rana Dance, 1897. Kwe'rana men and women in a ceremony in the plaza. *Photographs by F. Starr; Neg. Nos. 15641 and 15640, Museum of the American Indian, Heye Foundation.*

Plate 20.—TWO VIEWS OF THE MATACHINA DANCE. Note the Spanish violinists seated in front of the kneeling dancers in the plaza; also note the *malinche* (in white) and the *avuelo*. The costume of the *avuelo*, masked, approximates that of the River Men in the festivities of May 3 (pp. 337 f.). *Photographs of the Christmas dances, 1925, in the Elsie Clews Parsons Collections, American Philosophical Society.*

Plate 21.—Saints' Day Festivities. *a(above)*. San Juan's Day *Gallo*, or Rooster-pull, 1948. The war captain and several *alguacilitos* (foreground) are supervising the contesting horsemen. *Photograph by C. H. Lange.*

b(below). San Lorenzo's Day *Gallo*, or Present-throwing, 1947. In addition to the variety of presents thrown to the crowd, an important part is the throwing of water on the people—usually by the cupful, but here an entire pailful. This is largely done for amusement at the present time, but it is safe to assume an origin in the symbolic magic of rain-making. *Photograph by C. H. Lange.*

Plate 22.—TABLITA DANCE. *a(above).* Turquoise Kiva dancers in front of the church; the pole-carrier is swinging ka-arsh′ti-trūma (pp. 347 f.) over the heads of the dancers; a Ku-sha′lī side dancer is standing between the camera and the chorus at the right. (The community corral is visible in the background.) *Photograph by C. F. Lummis, about 1888; Neg. No. MNM 4831, Museum of New Mexico.*

b(below). Turquoise Kiva dancers in the plaza; Kwe′rana members are the side dancers in this picture. *Photograph by F. Starr, about 1897; Neg. No. 15645, Museum of the American Indian, Heye Foundation.*

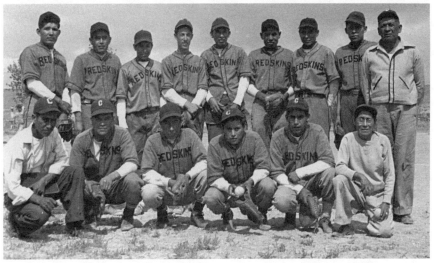

Plate 23.—*a(above)*. TABLITA DANCE. Close-up of Turquoise Kiva dancers in the plaza; Kwe'rana side dancer with his willow wands is standing at the left of the dance lines. *Photograph by F. Starr, about 1897; Neg. No. 15644, Museum of the American Indian, Heye Foundation.*

b(below). COCHITI BASEBALL TEAM, 1948. The Redskins were considered the "first team," the Braves the "second." Squad members included Conservatives and Progressives, veterans and nonveterans. Fourth player from the left, standing, is a son of one of the Spanish families in the village. *Photograph by C. H. Lange.*

Plate 24.—a(above). WOMAN ON HOUSE-LADDER. These two-storied structures were formerly common at Cochití, but there are none left at present. Note the vent for the ground-floor inner room at the right-hand margin. Photograph by F. Starr, about 1897; Neg. No. 15743, Museum of the American Indian, Heye Foundation.

b(below). "THE PORCH," SANTA FE. The front of the State Museum is a favorite spot for trading with tourists. Photograph (1948) by C. H. Lange.

c(above). JUAN JOSE MONTOYA AND HIS DAUGHTER. As revealed in Bandelier's journal, Juan José was one of his principal informants. This obviously posed picture, of unknown date and photographer, is included for the items of material culture illustrated. Neg. No. MNM 4845, Museum of New Mexico.

d(below). EL PUEBLO BUS LINE, 1948. Passengers boarding a bus for trip to Santa Fe. Photograph by C. H. Lange.

Plate 25.—*a(above)*. Cochiti Family Group, 1897. This picture helps dispel the impression that present-day contrasts between the clothing of the two sexes is a recent trend. *Photograph by F. Starr, 1897; Neg. No. 15590, Museum of the American Indian, Heye Foundation.*

b(below). Double Wedding Party, December 26, 1947. The couple stands in the middle of each row between their respective *padrinos*. Note that both pictures show a contrast in clothing styles for men and women. *Photograph by C. H. Lange.*

Plate 26.—a(left). Cipriano Quintana and His Wife, Clemencia, 1951. At the time of this picture, Cipriano was head of the Giant Society and continued to fulfill his role at least partially despite almost complete blindness and his seventy-nine years. This man had served as *padrino* more often than any other person at Cochití, indicating the esteem with which he is regarded. Clemencia is a member of the Ku-sha'li Society. *Photograph by C. H. Lange.*

b(right). Marcelo Quintana, Cacique, 1951. Marcelo, son of Cipriano, is a member of the Flint Society and also of Ku-sha'li. He became cacique in December, 1947. *Photograph by C. H. Lange.*

Plate 27.—*a and b(above).* SANTIAGO QUINTANA. These photographs were taken by Jack Hillers, about 1879. *Neg. Nos. 2159b and 2159a, Bureau of American Ethnology, Smithsonian Institution.*

c and d(below). SANTIAGO QUINTANA. These photographs were taken by De L. Gill in 1913. The four pictures clearly show the physical changes over a period of about thirty-four years. *Neg. Nos. 2163b and 2163a, Bureau of American Ethnology, Smithsonian Institution.*

Plate 28.—a(above, left). Jose Hilario Montoya. Many times governor of Cochití in the closing years of the last century, this man was a close friend of numerous early anthropologists who visited the pueblo at that time. *Photograph by C. F. Lummis, 1891; Neg. No. 701, Southwest Museum.*

b(above, right). Jose Alcario Montoya. The son of José Hilario, Alcario has continued to hold a prominent position in the life of his tribe until very recent years. This picture, by F. Starr, was taken in 1897 when Alcario was about eighteen years old. *Neg. No. 15500, Museum of the American Indian, Heye Foundation.*

c and d(below). Jose Alcario Montoya. Taken about sixteen years after *b*. *Photograph by De L. Gill, 1913; Neg. Nos. 2162a and 2162b, Bureau of American Ethnology, Smithsonian Institution.*

search. It is in this spirit of presenting all data available that the following miscellaneous remarks regarding the ka'tsīnas are made. The face mask can be worn only by men who have long hair, for the hair is necessary to conceal the edges of the mask. Thus far wigs have not been permitted. The helmet mask is, in most cases, so snug that a dancer who has long hair cannot wear it in the ordinary *chongo* style. Long hair is never permitted to flow nor to be seen below the mask, as pictured in an illustration (Plate V) in Dumarest's report (1919). Instead, the hair is braided and wrapped around the dancer's neck, where it is out of the way and also out of view. [3, 44]

Sleigh bells and zigzag lines drawn in the white paint on the hands and body are characteristic of public dancers but not Ka'tsīnas. The only exceptions are a very few guards, recently acquired impersonations (?), who do wear sleigh bells. The ka'tsīna dance lines all have rattles of turtle shell and deer hooves. [44, 88]

When asked what they think about in the course of dances in which they themselves are impersonators, informants consistently gave "orthodox" replies—rain, good harvests ("the same as in other dances"), the good of the people, and concern that they were doing everything just right ("that the war captains won't notice any mistakes").

In response to a query as to which was a favorite dance in which to be a participant, one replied, "Tsē'adyū-wītsa"; as noted in Appendix 26, this is one of the dances performed most commonly by the Cochití, apparently an indication that it is a favorite of other participants as well. Another favorite, from the viewpoint of personally doing the impersonation, was Shka'shrūtz. This impersonation was said to have been brought in in rather recent years from Acoma by a member of that tribe who married into Cochití. As steps and movements of this dance are lively and fast, the impersonators chosen for it are generally the unusually agile younger men. This dance has been given as a public dance at the Christmas season, with several unmasked young men performing the steps. [42]

In reference to this recent importation from Acoma, an entry in Starr's diary for September 25, 1897, is of interest:

Antonio announced the presence of two masked figures, different from any we had seen and beautiful, who were making a tour of the place [Cochití]. They were dressed as Acomas, and spoke the language of Acoma; they, however, are truly Cochiteños. They were apparently going around for general good influences. He felt sure a few cents would secure their retratos. We failed to find them, however, and the commandante [war captain?] refused to grant permission.

In public dances the number of dancers is variable and not especially important, but the line of Ka'tsīnas is always made up of an odd number, with the leading dancer in the middle. The others take their cues from him.

Ku-sha'lī Society. The Ku-sha'lī Society is one of the more widely known Pueblo Indian societies. At Cochití, it is especially famous due to Bandelier's book *The Delight Makers.* This appellation, in use partly before and partly after the appearance of Bandelier's title, has become synonymous with the members of this society and their public antics. Another designation for them which is frequently encountered is the Spanish *Entremesero,* or "clown." Of major concern to the Ku-sha'lī Society are weather control, fertility of the animal and plant worlds, and, related to these, the supervision of many ceremonies. [55, 92, 96] It is primarily this last function that caused Goldfrank (1927: 37 ff.) to designate the Ku-sha'lī, as well as the Kwe'rana and Shrū'tzī, as "Managing Societies."

Dumarest (1919: 191) stated: "The *koshare* are *chaiani* at a certain age. In their cures they do not suck. Their only method is 'the brushing way.' The invalid is the only witness of the ceremony; nobody is admitted. The invalid becomes an *entremesero* (clown)."

It is interesting that my informants often failed to mention the curing function of the Ku-sha'lī Society. It may be that the obligation to join the society following a cure—a feature not associated with the medicine societies—has caused some reluctance to call upon the Ku-sha'lī for this purpose and that through the years this function has almost completely lapsed. Some went so far as to say that the obligation to join after a cure had been effected was unknown and that such an impression was probably incorrect. Others, however, confirmed the practice, though stating that it had seldom occurred in recent years.

Curing by the Ku-sha'lī was said to be more like that practiced by the clans rather than that conducted by the medicine societies. After the Ku-sha'lī have cured an individual, the society members can, and often do, call upon this person, as their "child," to help them in various ceremonial capacities, perhaps dancing with them or helping to provide a feast for some special occasion such as an initiation. [42, 44, 92] White (1935: 54) noted that neither the Ku-sha'lī nor the

Kwe'rana perform cures at Santo Domingo, San Felipe, or Zia. Within recent years, the Cochití Ku-sha'lī conducted a curing rite for
Clemencia Quintana, a Ku-sha'lī member, who was afflicted with a
chronic throat ailment. [88]

Much of the ceremonial control exercised by the Ku-sha'lī is alternated annually with the Kwe'rana Society. In certain instances, the
rotation means that one society has direct supervision, with the other
group playing a minor role of assistance; in other cases, it means the
society has exclusive charge of certain functions. [55, 92]

As mentioned (p. 239), members of both Ku-sha'lī and Kwe'rana
are referred to as "cooked," or "roasted," in contrast to nonsociety
members, who are "raw" (si^r'shtī). It is common knowledge that a
Ku-sha'lī was the "first man"; this is the justification for the Turquoise Kiva dancers' taking precedence over those of the Pumpkin,
for the Ku-sha'lī Society is closely affiliated with the Turquoise Kiva.
[88]

In an entry of July 26, 1888, Bandelier noted that there were still
songs which stated that the Ku-sha'lī came down the east bank of
the Rio Grande and the Kwe'rana came down the west bank. He
further noted that these tales were the subject of many songs known
only to the initiated and that many were being lost with the death of
the old men. Whether these bits of evidence constitute clues to the
relative age of various societies is dubious; on the other hand, it
would perhaps be short-sighted to ignore them completely.

The society head, or na'wai-ya, assigns duties to other members on
such occasions as the annual Feast Day *Tablita* Dance. Certain members are selected as side dancers and others are placed in one or the
other chorus or given other duties. At such times, the Cochití members may be assisted by members from other pueblos. This exchange
of personnel was said to have occurred often in past times but not for
some years now. [42, 55, 92]

Every few years, theoretically every four, the Ku-sha'lī hold a
public dance, often in conjunction with the initiation of new members. The initiation ceremony, which should be held in February, is
sponsored by some one of the women who belong to the Ku-sha'lī.
For it, the hair may be arranged in either one or two "topknots," [55,
92] and the members' faces and bodies are painted according to
their groups within the society. Some have black and white stripes;
some, black circles; others have yellow and blue patterns. Appendix
27, containing a roster of Ku-sha'lī members, provides a list of the

designations; but no ranking by the various color-groupings was implied. The significance of such groups within the Ku-sha'lī has not been determined, and the knowledge of their very existence constitutes new data. The implications of these categories remain in need of elaboration. According to one informant, each initiate has from the society membership a ceremonial father and mother, who need not be husband and wife, and the initiate receives the same designation as his ceremonial mother. [55]

For other ceremonial occasions, the more usual Ku-sha'lī costume is worn. For the men, this means painting the body completely with alternate bands of black and white, with black rings around the eyes and mouth. Bandoliers, wristlets, and anklets of rabbit fur are worn, and a black breechcloth is used. Dual "horns" of cornhusks are worn in the hair, and owl feathers are attached to the head. The women wear the traditional *manta* and have their faces painted white.

Membership, as noted, is open to both sexes. Male members, however, are the principal participants, with the women acting more as food preparators during the retreats and other functions of the male membership. The Ku-sha'lī women have similar responsibilities toward the affiliated Flint medicine men. Ku-sha'lī women are supposed to help in plastering the society-house walls. If unable to help, a woman may be excused, but she is expected to do more than her normal share on some subsequent society project. If her excuse is not considered very good, a portion of the wall may simply be left for her to do as soon as she is able. [88] At present there are eight male and five female members, though two or three of the older men have become almost completely inactive in society affairs. (See Appendix 27.)

In the journal of Bandelier, there are two descriptions of Ku-sha'lī dances. Since these have not been published, they are included here in their entirety (ellipses indicate material irrelevant to the subject). The first was dated November 9–10, 1880, and the time is evening:

Soon after, a drum was heard, and José Hilario not being here, I went to his house. There was a whole crowd of boys and women, all in serapes, tramping about in the plaza, singing to the sound of a drum. Suddenly they would all together cower down to the ground, and thus remain for a while, during which time the leader kept on singing at a slow measure and occasionally touching his drum. Suddenly they all arose with a yell and peals of laughter, and went farther, singing at the top of their voices, and with regular tripping or trampling. . . . Thus they went in the moonlight around the pueblo, and this is the introduction for tomorrow's "*Baile de los Entremeseros.*" Juan José tells me that these *entremeseros,* when they dance in the summer, and also when they go out as messengers to gather the people for a public work like at the acequia, etc., are dressed in black mantles, with their hair very long, their faces blackened, and white circles painted around their eyes and mouth. . . .

November 10.   . . . I went several times during the day to witness the performance, which is nothing else than a theatrical performance, accompanied by and intermingled with dancing. The men are all naked except the *maxtlatl* [kilt], bracelets on their ankles, wrists, and collars. These ornaments are nearly all dark. [These are black rags; as at Santo Domingo, the Cochití Ku-sha'lī also use rabbitskins for this purpose—if they have them. (92)] The hair is tied back, and a tuft of corn leaves, sliced, is tied on top of the head. They are painted variously—white, black, and brown or copper colored—and look really like devils, or like the Mingo Indians in the German translation (by Hoffmann) of Fenimore Cooper's *Deerslayer,* etc. Some have figures painted on their body, among which I noted, on one particularly ugly devil, a large open hand on one side of the body, painted dark on an ashy gray surface. The faces are particularly ugly. If the body is black, the face is white, or the reverse, but in all cases white is the prevailing tinge of the face, so that it looks like that of a clown. *Malinche, tzima-ta-tañi.* It is the one with the painted hand which beats the drum. The drum is painted light brown all over, and, as far as I could see, about 0.75' long and 0.30' in diameter. It is not suspended from the shoulder, but held in the left hand near the top, against the knee, slightly bent, and thus beaten with one stick with a round, big knob. The women are also painted, but dressed, and all the women wear their serapes like shawls to their knees on their backs. Some of them carried children of eight to ten years on their back. One of the women was painted yellow in the face, others, blue, white, or black. The aspect of all is simply hideous. They came in a body, singing and rattling. The rattles, of deer hoofs and tortoise shells, are suspended from the wrists, others on the ankles, others to the belts. Hands are free, and they hold sometimes *guayaves, tortillas,* etc. etc. The gait is a very light trot and therefore slow. They went around the pueblo, entering the plaza from the northeast corner, and returning by the southwest corner, around the eastern row of houses, passing that of the cacique. For a while they remained in the plaza, and while a part of them stood in a body looking quietly, others, principally men, performed all sorts of tricks—not always graceful—chasing each other, dragging each other through the dust, climbing house tops, men and women, some with children who were freely bundled about very roughly. The roof of the houses in the rear (west) of the cacique's was particularly the scene of exploits. One woman went into an oven on top of it, and was afterwards dragged from it by the man, and her child (eight or ten years old) handed down very unceremoniously from the roof. About an hour later, I heard the drum and went to the plaza again. The *malinche* was with him. She is an exceptional figure. A jacket of deer-skin, a large conch shell painted brilliant rose, with green tinge iridescent, as breastpin. Around the waist, and as high up to support the breasts, a woolen garment, wound around, with two scarf-like pendants to below the knees, hanging down behind as far as the dress or petticoat. This garment is peculiar. Color is dark green, with patterns of green and yellow. It has been worn evidently, but is otherwise in good condition. Her headdress is peculiar. The bows were green, and the upper one had, in the middle, a dark band; still, I could not distinguish as to whether it was brown or black. They soon formed in two rows, the women on the south side, and the men on the north, single file, some of the men continuing to chase and swarm around them like clowns. They teased the bystanders, now very numerous (many Mexicans), entered the houses, took out lines, vases, skins, tortillas, pelted each other. (This headdress is called *o-ta-tiushit* [*tablita* (92)], and Juan José says that it signifies crown. The feathers on each side are eagle feathers, the tuft behind of parrots, *guacamayos*, *shia-uat*. Behind is a tress of resplendent green feathers of *shia-uat* also.) The feathers of owls and crows are regarded as *fieros*, and are used by *brujos* and the *baile de los Comanches*. This *baile* is called *peshari-pashca*. The manta is called *tzi-ma-ti*. The pattern is a standing one, and if the one is used up, the new one has to be made after the same pattern. There are always two in each pueblo, one for each estufa, as for the *baile de la cabellera*, two are used. It is of black wool, and the designs are needle work, in this case made by the mother of Juan José, whose property also was the conch shell. Both are now in possession of the sister of Juan José, the wife of Luis Montoya. Formerly, the sack was of white cotton, but there is no cotton cloth in the pueblo any more. The legs and feet were in the ordinary deerskin, but nice. At the sound of the drum, which was beaten by the black fellow standing outside of the northern row, while the children were mixed according to sexes, the two lines began to hop (with both feet, turning about in sections, the eastern section being last). Could not dare to count them, but there may have been forty, perhaps thirty-five in all. Then the *malinche*, while the others were hopping on the spot, hopped slowly and not ungracefully sideways up and down through the lines, blessing or fanning them alternately with a tuft of eagle's feath-ers which she held in each hand. Finally, both rows went down on their knees, all the while clapping their hands so as to keep the rattles going, and the *malinche* kept on hopping back and forth and blessing them be-tween the lines. During this time the skirmishers kept acting around them. One of them who was particularly fond of rolling in the dust, was at last dragged about and through the lines by his companions until he was completely naked, and there took place an exhibition of obscenities hard to describe. Sodomy, coitus, masturbation, etc., was performed to greatest perfection, men accoupling with each other on the ground or standing, and to the greatest delight of the spectators (certainly over one hundred), men, women, girls and boys, Mexicans and Indians looking on with the greatest ingenuity and innocence, not the slightest indecent look on the part of the women, and applauding the vilest motions. I was terribly ashamed, but nobody seemed to take any concern about it. The *malinche* slowly withdrew, followed by the drummer and the crowd, but without anything like an exhibition of shame or haste. The dance was ended, and so she went. The clowns followed them with their abominable gestures, and actually carried back one girl, threw her down, and while one was performing the coitus from behind, another was doing it against her head. Of course, all was simulated, and not the real act, as the women were dressed. The naked fellow performed masturbation in the center of the plaza or very near it, alternately with a black rug and with his hand. Everybody laughed. I went home. About 3 p.m., hearing the drums again, I found them in a cluster around the *malinche*, forming a round group (not a ring), and hopping around her. Afterwards, they again formed in a row of two, as before, and also knelt down, with the *malinche* hopping between. The clowns, outside, imitated drunkenness perfectly; one had a shield, bow, and arrow, and they went about as usual, cracking jokes, teasing each other and the people, pelting tortillas and *guayaves*, etc. etc. The exit was always to the southeast, but not to the estufas. [The Ku-sha'lī house was, and is today, southeast of the plaza.] I heard the drum last at 4 o'clock, about. The clowns remained in the plaza all the while for the diversion of the people. . . .

Reading the above account, present-day informants found it generally true for current practices as well as for the 1880's. Obscenities are still the ceremonial privilege of the Ku-sha'lī clowns, though these aspects are becoming less frequent and less pronounced with the passing years and accompanying acculturation. [42, 55, 92] Further elaboration of the headdress and *manta* of the *malinche* was made by my informants. The *tablita* is painted "all colors—like a rainbow"; the earrings are cornhusk cones. Around the neck are worn several necklaces of yellow "Ku-sha'lī beads" (p. 151); the face is painted white with black circles around the eyes and mouth. (See Fig. 19.) In each hand, she carries a piece consisting of two eagle tail-feathers inserted in a cornstalk.

Bandelier witnessed another Ku-sha'lī ceremony two years later,

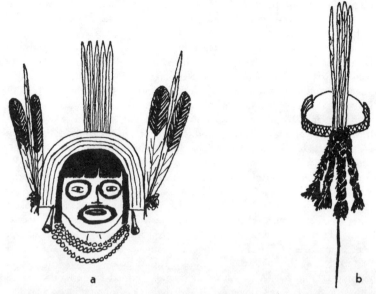

a   b

Fig. 19.—Ku-sha'li Malinche Headdress (*a*). Stick (*b*) woven into *manta;* beaded band across back of head with thong passing in front under the bangs.

a description of it being included in his entry for November 30, 1882:

At 9 a.m. the chorus of singers opened the ball by passing before the house of the Cacique to the Estufa of Shyuama [Turquoise], singing. . . . At intervals, some of the Qoshare—commonly 9 men and 4 women—came singing into the plaza and formed into a row, alternately on the South and North side. They held twigs of Sabinos and bowing down all together seemed apparently to plant corn; although it was hardly intended for it at all. It was 3 p.m. until the dance proper began, and it was an exact repetition of the figures and also in part of the obscenities practiced in 1880. The whole is a filthy, obscene affair. Drinking Urine out of bowls and Jars used as Privies on the house-tops, eating excrements and dirt, ashes and clay, washing each others' faces with Urine and with every imaginable dirt, imitating cohabitation and Sodomy, were the principal "jokes" of the abominable leaders of the "Qoshare." The dancers were all painted in a sinfully ugly manner, white and black prevailing. The *Malinche* had the face painted blue. Santiago, the Governor, had the body painted light Indigo-blue. Red was not visible. I succeeded in getting a very poor photograph, as no persuasion could induce them to stop any length of time. The 3 leaders seemed particularly anxious to prevent my taking any view.

In her discussion of clans, Goldfrank (1927: 10) noted, "There is no direct relation between clan and society membership, but there is a tendency for members of a family to affiliate with the same society." This opinion is substantiated by the roster gathered from my informants for the Ku-sha'lī and other societies. In several cases where society affiliations differ within a family, as between man and wife, this has frequently been the result of later, i.e., second or third, marriages.

As noted earlier, the Ku-sha'lī share a house, located near the southeastern corner of the plaza, with the Flint Society. When the Ku-sha'lī are "busy" in the house, it can be entered only by those Flint members who are also Ku-sha'lī. [3, 55, 70, 92]

Goldfrank (1927: 37, 42–43) designated the Ku-sha'lī as a "managing society" for the Turquoise Kiva. At present Lorenzo Cordero, a Ku-sha'lī, is head of the Turquoise Kiva and, as such, is called "Toad" (Pa'lak). He also has served as head Ku-sha'lī since December, 1946. As kiva head, he designates who is to sing in a chorus for a dance, who is to dance, and who may be excused from participation in any ceremonial event. As Ku-sha'lī head, he directs the activities of the society and the ceremonial efforts of the members. In such supervisory roles, he, in turn, is observed and checked by the war captains, in whom rests the ultimate ceremonial control.

While there are Ku-sha'lī members with longer terms of membership than Lorenzo's, they are all members of the Pumpkin Kiva with three exceptions: Isidro Cordero, the oldest man in the pueblo and too feeble to assume the responsibilities of head, and Juanito Trujillo and Marcelo Quintana, both Flint medicine men and, hence, ineligible. [3, 16, 53]

Thus the relationship of the Ku-sha'lī to the Turquoise Kiva is maintained as it should be. In this matter, it is interesting to note that several Ku-sha'lī are members of the Pumpkin Kiva, a somewhat unexpected situation but one which appears to have been true for many years. The kiva head, together with the war captains, is also responsible for the upkeep of the kiva structure and for the proper execution of the kiva, or moiety, ceremonials in general. [42, 44, 45] It will be interesting to note what policy is followed in the future when it becomes necessary to name a new kiva head. Assuming that there have been no new members in the meantime, it will mean that a Pumpkin member will become head of the Turquoise Kiva. While it would seem quite simple for this person to change his kiva affiliation, it is interesting that in a similar situation with the Kwe'rana and the Pumpkin Kiva, the succeeding head chose to remain with the Turquoise Kiva and, despite some protests, has shown no disposition to change. (For discussion, see p. 390.)

Of the present Ku-sha'lī members, only one, Cleto Arquero, is relatively young; he was "put in" by his grandparents as a very small boy. Under such circumstances, the initiate is taken to the door of the society house, where he is taken charge of by his Ku-sha'lī father and mother. Four days of preparations precede this act, and there is a day of public dancing in the plaza following the initiate's reception into the society. Initiations, as noted, occur in February. Another Ku-sha'lī dance may be given in the fall after the harvest, though this does not necessarily occur each year; it appears to be given if the Ku-sha'lī head so decides or if the war captain requests it. [55, 92] At such dances, the membership may be assisted by "Little Ku-sha'līs"—those individuals who have been cured by the society and in the process of which have acquired a Ku-sha'lī "father" and "mother." No particular attention is paid to age in this instance. The ceremonial couple, much in the fashion of an adopting clan father and mother, can call upon their "child" to help the society at such times.

At the Ku-sha'lī dances, relatives throw presents to the members, who commonly throw them back to the spectators. The tribal leaders, the "sages," sitting on the west side of the plaza, also receive presents; in some cases specific individuals are called upon to come forward for a particular gift. This practice is an obvious parallel to the "*gallo*," which is a part of many of the Catholic feast day celebrations; which is antecedent remains to be learned. Limited notes on this occurrence in other neighboring pueblos, but not in Spanish-American communities, suggest that the throwing of presents as a part of the Catholic feast days actually has its origin in these native rites of the Ku-sha'lī and the companion Kwe'rana societies.

At Santo Domingo, White (1935: 53–54) found the use of "Crusti Koshairi" and "Crusti Quiraina." These were nonmembers selected to impersonate real Ku-sha'lī and Kwe'rana during such ceremonies as the August 4 Feast Day Dance. My informants said that this was not the custom at Cochití. Only actual members of either society, or their "children," function as such; on feast days and similar occasions only the members carry on these duties. While unwilling to predict, they admitted the possibility that such a development might come at Cochití if there should be a serious drop in memberships. At the same time, they professed considerable amazement that the substitution was already allowed at Santo Domingo, where the society rosters have been larger and, seemingly, adequate for that pueblo's ceremonial needs. [3, 15, 42, 45, 62]

Except for the clowning in conjunction with their own ceremonies and the annual Feast Day dance on alternate years (in which the Ku-sha'lī serve as side dancers), Ku-sha'lī buffoonery has disappeared. It was formerly a part of the Kings' Day celebration, but it has not been included for a number of years. [44] As described in the following chapter, the Ku-sha'lī are responsible for the celebration of Santiago's Day, July 25. Clowning is a part of these proceedings, especially at those times when Santiago, or "the Little Horse," comes, though the characters do not appear with the traditional black and white paint on body and face. [44, 92]

The ceremonial control of the pueblo is assumed by the Ku-sha'lī following rabbit hunts held in October, or in November, prior to the harvesting of the cacique's fields. Although the war captain calls the hunt, it is supervised by either the Ku-sha'lī or Kwe'rana Society. At the close of the hunt, participated in by both men and women, the supervising society head goes to the war captain and states that his society has worked hard and faithfully during the past year for the good of the people and that it is now time they should be relieved of this burden. The war captain agrees, and going to the head of the other society, informs him that his group is now responsible for the welfare of the tribe during the coming year. [88]

Kwe'rana Society. The Kwe'rana Society, in its relationship to the Pumpkin Kiva, is the counterpart of the Ku-sha'lī in its relationship to the Turquoise. The Pumpkin head, with the same duties in relation to that kiva, is called "Pumpkin Father" (Dañi na'wai-ya).

At present, the Kwe'rana head is Vicente Romero, who belongs to the Turquoise Kiva, as does the entire male Kwe'rana membership. Vicente was also head Kwe'rana at the time of Goldfrank's stay at Cochití in the early twenties. [3, 44]

The Kwe'rana Society is "equal" to the Ku-sha'lī and commonly shares duties of ceremonial management with that group, but there are certain basic differences. The Ku-sha'lī, often referred to as

Entremeseros, are normally considered a clown society. Although the Kwe'rana Society is also referred to in the literature as a "clown society," all informants consistently held that clowning is not an aspect of its official behavior. The Kwe'rana do not paint their bodies in any way, nor do they wear unusual costumes as the Ku-sha'lī do (and as do the Kwe'rana of such pueblos as Santo Domingo). While some informants stated that "Kwe'rana always wear their nicest clothes when they dance or do other work," others implied that in former times the Cochití Kwe'rana also painted their bodies and faces. [42, 55] One of the distinctive bits identifying members of this society is a tuft of sparrow-hawk and blue-jay tail feathers tied in the hair. These two birds were said to be very closely associated with this society, though precise details of this relationship could not be learned. White (1942: 130) has noted the association of the sparrow hawk with other Keresan Kwe'rana.

As mentioned, the Kwe'rana are associated with the Shī'kame Society just as the Ku-sha'lī are linked with the Flint Society. The Kwe'rana and Shī'kame societies share a house on the eastern side of the plaza. Again, when one society is "working," only those members of the other society who belong to both can enter the house. Like the Ku-sha'lī, the Kwe'rana Society is concerned very little with curing or witchcraft, but concentrates upon weather control, fertility, and supervising, "managing" those ceremonies directed primarily at the first two goals. [42, 48, 55, 70]

The Kwe'rana, again like the Ku-sha'lī, accepts both men and women; at present, there are seven male and seven female members. One of these married a San Felipe woman and moved there many years ago, though he frequently joins with the Cochití Kwe'rana in various ceremonial functions. The all-time roster includes twenty-one males and fifteen females. (See Appendix 28.)

In his entry for April 19, 1882, Bandelier noted that the Kwe'rana Society possessed no distinctive headdress such as that worn by the Ku-sha'lī *ma¹ᵢnche* (Fig. 19). This statement was confirmed by present-day informants, who stated that Kwe'rana women, in the dancing of the society, wear such traditional costumes as they do in the *tablita* dances except that there is no *tablita* of any sort.

The Kwe'rana, like the Ku-sha'lī, have a distinctive dance that is held about harvest time, either before or after; it is completely independent of the Ku-sha'lī Dance, which may also occur at harvest time. The public portion of this dance, beginning before sunrise and continuing until late afternoon, is preceded by four days of preparations. Although some stated that the Kwe'rana men wear "their best clothes" for this ceremony, another informant said that the body is painted, the painting varying with a person's status within the society. As in the case of the Ku-sha'lī, no additional data could be learned about "degrees." These dances are sponsored by some woman who belongs to the society. Present-throwing—"gallo"—is again a part of the occasion. It may or may not coincide with an initiation rite; Kwe'rana initiations should occur only in November and there has not been one for several years now. [42, 55, 92] (Plate 19a, b)

The Cochití Kwe'rana sometimes go to Tesuque Pueblo to dance either on their own initiative or at the request of the Tesuque Kwe'-rana. (92) In recent years there has been some reciprocity; a Tesuque Kwe'rana, Candido, comes to Cochití to help at the July 14 Feast Day Dance, particularly in those years when the Kwe'rana are in charge. [55]

In an entry of December 6, 1885, Bandelier briefly noted that he had returned to Cochití in time for the close of the dances of the "*Quirana*": "They only wear a little plume of the eagle's (rather down) on one side, & a down of 'Cernicalo' [sparrow hawk] on the other side of the head, above each ear, fastened to the hair; paint: red. Good blankets, etc., but no other costumes."

Turquoise Kiva Society. As noted in the discussion of the Ku-sha'lī Society, the Turquoise Kiva group takes ceremonial precedence over the Pumpkin group owing to the fact that a Ku-sha'lī is said to have been the "first man" and the Ku-sha'lī Society has a close affiliation with the Turquoise Kiva.

Curtis (1926: 86) referred to the kiva groups as "religio-social parties." Earlier statements by Bandelier were cited by White (1942: 142) to the effect that "all the inhabitants of the pueblo, grouped by kins [clans], belong to one or the other estufa, one set of kins meeting at the calabash [kiva], the other at the turquoise." Elsewhere, Bandelier (1890:301) stated that the people "assort themselves respectively in these two meeting places, the estufas, that are named after two of the most prominent clans: the Turquoise, Shyuamo, and the Calabash, Tanyi."

The social aspects are discussed at greater length in Chapter 10, but it may be noted at this point that present-day clans are represented in both kivas, and if kiva membership was ever strictly endogamous, it must have been quite some time ago. A person does receive his kiva designation from his father, and a wife normally joins the kiva of her husband if she is not already a member, but present-day kiva membership can hardly be compared with clan membership. Unlike a clan affiliation, a kiva membership can be shifted at virtually any time. Permission to change must be obtained from the two kiva heads and the war captains, but since there is no record of such a request's being refused, it can be seen that kiva affiliation is flexible. Hence more and more emphasis is being put upon the ceremonial aspects, at the expense of kinship or social considerations.

The Turquoise Kiva (Ha'nanī chīt'ya, "East-inside kiva") is northeast of the plaza; the kiva group also has a community house southwest of the plaza. At present, the affairs of the kiva are in charge of a headman, referred to as "Toad" (Pa'lak). The reason for this could not be ascertained: "That's just the way it is, that's all." The incumbent is Lorenzo Cordero, the Ku-sha'lī head, as noted. The mayorlī is Eleuterio Suina, who came into this position after Luís Ortiz was unable to continue, about 1947/48. These two men more or less share the leadership of the kiva, though the mayorlī has more direct responsibility for leadership in songs and other aspects of the ceremonies. The mayorlī's principal helpers are Diego Arquero, Epitacio Arquero, and Juan Velasquez.

Other important kiva leaders are those designated as "blue" (kwirsh'ke-shē). This may refer to one or two men whose duty it is to decorate the *tablitas* and the long pole carried in the *Tablita* Dance. At present this work is done by Eleuterio Suina and Juan Velasquez; formerly, Santiago Cordero and Lorenzo Suina did it. As noted, these men perform similar duties in relation to ka'tsīna ceremonies. According to one informant, they should be Ku-sha'lī members, but it is interesting to note that not one of the four men named is a Ku-sha'lī, nor do they hold membership in any other society except the Ka'tsīna.

Curtis (1926: 86) stated that "the kivas play no part in the masked dances, but in other dances either one kiva party has charge or both divisions participate as such." As already indicated in the discussion of the Ka'tsīna Cult, the kiva groups are important factors. Whether this is a relatively recent development or whether Curtis was in error could not be determined.

In recent times, the kiva structure has been used only a few times each year; the greatest amount of activity takes place in the community house. This is true for the specific functions of the Turquoise Kiva group and also, because of its greater size, for certain tribal meetings as well. Before the construction of the separate house (1938), such affairs were held in the larger private homes; it would seem that the common use of the kiva—as suggested in earlier accounts in the literature—had not occurred at Cochití for many years, if at all.

The chorus for the kiva dancers is selected from the older men, usually those who are members of the Council of *Principales*. There are occasional exceptions made in the case of a young man who shows unusual talent in singing, in composing words or melodies, or who excels in learning songs from local sources or elsewhere.

In addition to their own songs, the Cochití also use Hopi, Navaho, Zuñi, Santo Domingo, and other tribal songs for their dances. The song is customarily used for a complete "round," or phase, of the dance and not just as an inserted line or word. In many, the singing is mere humming, or the intoning of meaningless or "nonsense words." For example, the Buffalo Dance songs are said to consist almost entirely of melody, with no true words. In special dance songs, the melodies are said to have remained unchanged through the years, though the words are revised each year. In other dances, neither the melody nor the words can be changed. New melodies or words may be contributed by any kiva member, though most come from the mayorlī or his chief helpers. [3, 20, 42, 45, 70]

To obtain new songs, a person may go to another village or tribe and memorize songs that he hears there. This is not considered plagiarism, and the song is equal in value to one consciously taught by another tribe or composed by one of the Cochití. No payment, as such, is involved for teaching songs to another person or tribe. "Anyone is happy to teach another and is pleased to hear his song sung at another village." [44] However, when a specific song is taught to a person upon request, it is customary to give a present to the teacher. This is voluntary, and it is considered more a matter of courtesy than a formal business transaction. [3, 70]

When a person desires a certain part, or role, in a dance that has only a few performers, he can make this request of the kiva head. He is then tested for the part unless there is no question of his ability or lack of it. The principal men of the kiva decide who is to perform. Almost all ceremonies are preceded by four nights of practice in the community house of that kiva group. Dancers are taught and rehearsed in their roles while the chorus and drummers practice the songs. [20, 42, 45, 88]

Sometimes a kiva leader asks a person, possibly a relative, whether he would like to perform a certain role, at the same time urging his participation. Sometimes the person complies; at other times he rejects the proposal on the grounds that the steps are too difficult or that he is not an accomplished enough dancer or for some similar reason. [20, 38, 45]

In addition to the practicing and the actual ceremony, the dancers —including the girl, or *malinche,* if there is one—for such dances as the deer, eagle, buffalo, and animal observe continence and fast four days. The fasting involves a diet restricted to native foods and vomiting each morning for the four days, the fourth being the morning of the ceremony. If the dance is put on at the request of the war captain and, thus, is basically religious, the fasting and vomiting are necessary for the dancers but not for the chorus members, though an individual may simply decide to do so on his own. If the dances are part of the more recreational ceremonies at Christmas, the fasting and vomiting are not required but are often done voluntarily.

For the Feast Day *Tablita* Dance (but not those at New Year's, Easter, and Santa Cruz Day), the chorus and the dancers must fast and vomit for four days. On Feast Day, the participants vomit, have a light breakfast of native foods, and then must not eat again until after four dances. After this intermission period, there are more dances, formerly four but more recently three and sometimes only two.

After a dance has finished, the performers, both in ka'tsīna rites and in public dances, go to the river to wash off their paint and change to ordinary clothing before returning home. Then, in many cases, the people bring them presents of food, jewelry, and other items, thank them for their performance and the good that has come to the village because of the ceremony, and generally congratulate them. [34, 42, 44, 88]

As stated in the discussion of social organization, the Turquoise Kiva is considerably larger than the Pumpkin so far as active personnel is concerned. While the Pumpkin people are actually more numerous, many have become Progressives and do not participate in the ceremonial aspects of the kiva organization. An interesting development has taken place partly as a result of this numerical inequality.

This is the desire of certain individuals to "help the other side," usually in a *Tablita* Dance, especially that of July 14. This can be done by either group, though it is generally the Turquoise people who "go over" to the Pumpkin side to dance or to sing in the chorus. Permission of the war captain and kiva heads must be obtained, but this is seldom, if ever, refused. Following the specific ceremony, the people revert to their own kivas. [13, 18, 45, 70] Such "helping" also occurs between various pueblos, as for example, people of Cochití dancing at Santo Domingo or elsewhere. It is customary, on such occasions, that a person will help the kiva of the other tribe that corresponds to his own kiva, though this is not mandatory. [42, 45, 88, 92]

Pumpkin Kiva Society. Much of the material in the discussion of the Turquoise Kiva applies to the Pumpkin as well. The kiva head bears no such title as "Toad," being known simply as "Pumpkin headman" (Dañī na'wai-ya). The incumbent is Pablo Trujillo, who is a Kwe'rana member as he should be but who, strangely enough, has not relinquished his membership in the Turquoise Kiva, as noted earlier (p. 306). While considerable protest has been voiced over this breach of custom, the situation remains unchanged. The position of Pumpkin mayorlī is filled today, as it has been for many years, by Lorenzo Herrera. In native terms, this position is called gya'ya-jū-nī ("in the middle"), which refers to this leader's position in the center of his chorus. He, like his Turquoise counterpart, is the song leader— supervising words, melodies, dancers' movements, and similar details. He works closely with the kiva head, and also with his chief assistants, who at present are Juan José Suina, Clofe Arquero, Salvador Arquero, and Fernando Cordero.

In the Pumpkin Kiva, the duty of decorating *tablitas* and other ceremonial items is performed by Lorenzo Herrera and Nestor Herrera. Nestor assumed this role following the death of Juan Estévan Chalan, a Kwe'rana member, who also was kiva head. While the decorators should be Kwe'rana members, neither of the present men is; in fact, one of them, Lorenzo Herrera, is a Ku-sha'lī; Nestor has no affiliation other than that with the ka'tsīnas. Thus it would seem that in order to have the ceremonial positions filled at all it is necessary at present to have men in office who do not have the proper ceremonial qualifications or affiliations. Either this is a new development or the inability to force the freshly installed incumbent to align himself properly is a recent development. In either case, the integration and balance of the ceremonial structure are being lost.

Further disintegration of the traditional ceremonial patterns is revealed in a statement by one informant. While acknowledging that the Turquoise dancers theoretically have taken precedence over those from the Pumpkin Kiva, he stated that "now it depends on who is ready first." He claimed to have seen violations of the traditional order in many of the ceremonies, though that of the July 14 Feast Day has actually adhered to the traditional ideal. The greatest deviation occurs during the series of Christmas dances, which appear to be more in the realm of entertainment than religion. This is also indicated by the fact that in past years certain war captains have been known to grant permission to photograph some of the Christmas dances but no others.

In the matter of kiva precedence in ceremonial procedures, it is interesting to find that Cochití informants maintain that at both San Felipe and Jemez, the Pumpkin dancers appear before those of the Turquoise Kiva. Further research in the various pueblos on this point and the associated traditional explanations would be well worth while.

Drummers Society. This society has never been reported for the Cochití nor for various neighboring tribes. Further evidence may indicate that a plural designation, reflecting the dual kiva organization, is more accurate. Present information remains disappointingly meager, and some readers might well question the actual designation on the basis of the present data.

However, each kiva does have a group of men who are the official ceremonial drummers (kī'ya pom-potz, "drummer"), ideally four or more; these form a type of society within each kiva organization. The drummers are said to be chosen by the "councilmen of the kiva." For the Turquoise Kiva, Eleuterio Suina is the head; others are Epitacio Arquero (one informant [42] named this man as the head Turquoise drummer), Gerónimo Quintana, Diego Romero, Pablo Trujillo, and José Rey Suina. Lorenzo Herrera is the head Pumpkin drummer, and he is assisted by Epifanio Pecos, Fernando Cordero, and Justo Pérez. [88]

It is interesting that each head drummer also serves as the mayorlí of his kiva; this would appear to be nothing more than coincidence, however, for the preceding Turquoise mayorlí, Luís Ortiz, who died in 1949, was not a drummer. One further comment regarding the drummer personnel is noteworthy. Additional flaunting of tradition is apparent in the fact that Pablo Trujillo, Pumpkin Kiva head, is a drummer for the Turquoise. Pablo's predecessor as Pumpkin Kiva head, Juan Estévan Chalan, was a Pumpkin drummer.

Informants believed that new drummers were picked to fill vacancies because they possessed the necessary aptitudes. There was some feeling that a man might volunteer to serve in this capacity after a vow, but others did not believe that this was possible. One informant stated that drummers, at least formerly, prayed for power and success at a spot near White Rock Canyon, north of Cochití, "where the current and rapids thunder like drums." [83] Others claimed to know nothing of this; if it had once been done, they insisted it must have been some time ago. [42, 44, 88]

Drummers customarily keep their drums at home; there is some confusion about whether they merely serve as trustees of these drums or whether they actually own them. Drums used in the actual ceremonies are not used for practice. [49, 70]

On dance days, the drums are brought to the kiva community houses, where the drummers, while alone, warm them by the fire to obtain the proper "voice." Corn meal is "fed" to the drums as a form of blessing and request for power. After the dance, singers toss a pinch of meal on the drum and inhale from the drum, rubbing meal on their throats, thereby assuring the continuance of their own voice and general well-being. The drums are returned to the community houses where they are again "fed"; the cacique comes to each house and thanks the drums for their help in the day's activities. He "draws out their breath." After this, the drums are taken to the drummers' homes until they are needed again. [42, 52, 55]

Old drums, no longer used, are stored in the front room of the Shī'kame–Kwe'rana house; it was said that these should be fed and treated as though they were to be used on each dance day. Others were of the opinion that this was not necessary, perhaps a rationalization of the current negligence in adhering to traditional behavior patterns.

Cochití drums typically have two tones, one head giving a lower tone than the other. This is achieved by using different thicknesses of hide or by making the areal surface of the heads different. High or low tones are called for by specific portions of many dance songs, as in the case of the *Tablita* Dance, which begins on a low tone, alternates several times, and concludes on a high tone. [55] The Cochití have no knowledge of a device for changing the tone of a drum which was described by Curtis (1926: 169) for Santo Domingo drums. A small block of wood was suspended from the interior sides of the drum in such a way that it rested on one head but not on the other if the drum should be reversed. In this way, a tonal distinction was created.

9 CEREMONIES: CALENDAR AND PARAPHERNALIA

Ceremonialism

MUCH HAS BEEN WRITTEN concerning the richness of Pueblo Indian ceremonialism, and attention has been called repeatedly to its pervasiveness throughout Pueblo culture. The data from Cochití simply add corroborative evidence to the over-all picture.

As noted earlier, Cochití ceremonialism may conveniently be divided into two categories, esoteric and exoteric. Not only is this dichotomy of value for purposes of analysis; it also reveals a duality which is commonly recognized by the Cochití themselves. A great number of ceremonies, undoubtedly even more numerous in times past, can be viewed by only specific segments of the Cochití population—society members but not nonmembers, the initiated but not the uninitiated, or Conservatives but not Progressives. Others can be witnessed by Cochití and other Pueblo Indians but not by Spanish-Americans, Anglos, or other outsiders. Still other ceremonies are open to anyone interested in watching. It appears that from time to time specific ceremonies have been shifted from one category to the other, but the categories themselves remain valid components of Cochití ceremonialism. In an entry of April 9, 1882, Bandelier recorded various "classes," or types, of "Cachina" dances and added the interesting comment, "The other dances, he says, are imitations of the Cachina, and have even the same words." This similarity, but distinction nevertheless, between masked and maskless ceremonies has been noted for other pueblos (Santa Ana, Santo Domingo [White 1942: 218]). Its existence in modern Cochití ceremonialism has been confirmed by my informants [42, 88, 92]. (Also see p. 297.)

Another dualism which is apparent only in part to the Cochití as well as to others, including ethnologists, is the distinction between ceremonies of native origin and those derived from contact with the Catholic Church. This distinction, or duality, is often more apparent to the outsider interested in cultural antecedents than it is to the Cochití tribesman. There are elements in either category that are deeply valued and still others that are of only minor significance. Again, while some elements are readily recognizable as to their origins, many others have become so thoroughly integrated in the overall ceremonialism as to defy efforts to discover the circumstances of their inception.

Regardless of the origins of specific features, Cochití ceremonialism has retained its supposed aboriginal emphases upon curing (personal and community welfare being involved here), fertility (relating to the plant and animal kingdoms, including man, with an ethnocentric emphasis on matters relating to the Cochití), and weather control (primarily directed at securing seasonable and adequate precipitation and at the same time avoiding such catastrophic events as hail, strong wind, unseasonal freezing, and drouth). What shifts in emphasis from one to another of these basic concerns have occurred during past times is impossible to say, though it would appear safe to assume that such shifts have occurred. To offer an evaluation of the relative merits of each in present-day Cochití life would be to assign values or the absence of values to these activities and interests which do not exist among the Cochití as a tribe. One can only state that where such weighting of relative importance does occur, it is primarily a matter of individual interest, knowledge, and opinion.

The task of recognizing and evaluating actual changes in the Cochití ceremonial calendar and in the associated paraphernalia is not an easy one. Perhaps the greatest difficulty stems from the fact that much of this phase of the culture is esoteric, especially in regard to non-Cochití. A related handicap arising from this secrecy is that it has permitted very little accurate detail to be recorded in times past.

In lieu of recorded data, it is necessary to rely upon memory, which, despite its increased acuity in nonliterate societies, is nevertheless fallible.

The fact that virtually any inquiry regarding religious matters, aside from observations of overt behavior and certain paraphernalia, is met with evasive replies, claims of ignorance, and similar responses indicates that esoteric aspects of ceremonialism still exist in an appreciable amount. Close observation reveals that existing societies meet and conduct retreats regularly. Informants vary in their estimates of how efficiently or how completely these societies currently discharge their respective duties. It must be remembered that ignorance of such matters on the part of many informants may be actual and not merely alleged; in such cases, lack of information does not warrant the conclusion that these activities are defunct. To further complicate matters, the irregular appearances and occurrences of specific dancers, rituals, and items of paraphernalia are perfectly legitimate. Such sporadic occurrences make it difficult to pronounce many aspects irretrievably lost from the culture, despite the fact that they may not have been seen for a successive number of years.

Much of the foregoing discussion suggests the stability and continuing nature of Cochití ceremonialism, but there is no doubt that this ceremonialism has experienced many changes, calendrical, ritual, and material. While never large in memberships, the present societies are seriously weakened by the death of each older member. Younger members are increasingly fewer and appear less capable of properly continuing the activities of their group. Also, the proportion of the pueblo interested in whether or not the societies are functioning properly is constantly diminishing. Much of this disinterest can be attributed to such factors as the development of nonagricultural economic activities, e.g., silver-working; wage-earning; the health programs of the Indian Service; doctrines of the Catholic Church; and the Middle Rio Grande Conservancy District's improvements. All have contributed to the freeing of individual Cochití from reliance on the societies' efforts relating to curing, fertility, and weather control.

Informants several times expressed the opinion that present-day secret-society members do not possess the ceremonial know-how of their predecessors. This attitude is undoubtedly founded to some extent on fact. Also to be remembered is the point that these adult informants were evaluating this alleged decadence with mature judgments rather than with their youthful impressions.

In spite of the acknowledged difficulty of evaluating ceremonial changes and the lack of success in recording esoteric ceremonial details, it is still apparent that certain changes have occurred, are occurring, and in the future will occur with compounded intensity. Each death among the individual society members means that a continually diminishing portion of the core of this native religion remains. Much that does exist does so only as a hollow shell, appealing to a constantly shrinking proportion of the pueblo populace. Barring some unforeseen event, the decline appears certain to continue. The final disappearance of this ceremonialism is, on the other hand, nowhere in sight. The merging of native ceremonialism with Catholicism has served, as it undoubtedly will serve in the future, to perpetuate at least some features of native religion. If for no reason other than tribal pride in folklore and tradition (rather than religious interest), the continuation of these rites, or portions of them, may be anticipated for many years.

Ceremonial Calendar

Chronologically another dual division can be established. This, too, is one which facilitates analysis and is a dichotomy realized by the Cochití. One division consists of those ceremonies which must occur according to a rigid calendar; the other, of those which occur sporadically and largely at the instigation of specific individuals, such as the war captain. Ceremonies in this latter category may not be seen for several successive years; on the other hand, they may appear a number of times in any one calendar year.

In either series, variations in details are apparent. Some are optional, and their occurrence is neither surprising nor particularly significant. Others, at least in theory, are impossible; these are, of course, the more difficult to discover. In the absence of personal observation over an extended period and without the aid of recorded descriptions of earlier performances, one is forced to depend upon the word of an informant. Most individuals, relying on memory, cannot help but be influenced by the tradition that ceremonial variation or change should not—hence, cannot—occur. However, since there is an increasing awareness among the more discerning Cochití that changes have occurred and are continuing to occur in increasing number and degree, this very fact has prompted a certain amount of collaboration in having these events recorded in their "proper form" as this is currently interpreted, at least by a particular individual.

Still another classification of ceremonies from a chronological viewpoint emphasizes the dichotomy of winter and summer. In the field notes of Boas (1921: 535) this distinction is brought out, "chalchihuitl" (turquoise) being associated with winter and "Dahni (or any crop)" (pumpkin) being associated with summer. Other related concepts noted were those of "hard" and "dry" (ts'e·'p'an^{y}i) for the winter dancing and "soft" and "damp" (ga·'cp^i^{c}t) for the summer dancing. These terms are applied without discrimination to the performances of both the Turquoise and the Pumpkin kiva groups.

A comparable though somewhat contradictory classification was given by one informant [55] in discussing the Buffalo Dance. Since these data appear contradictory, they are being withheld until they can be clarified. They do confirm the continued existence of the seasonal dichotomy as indicated by Boas a generation or so ago. In this regard, it would be worth knowing the seasonal association, or absence of it, for each specific ceremony currently performed or remembered. Little data on this subject has been gathered as yet.

As mentioned (p. 262), ha'ñi-gīt°, in February, and ha'ñiko, in late November, are perhaps the two high points, ceremonially speaking, in any year. These ceremonial peaks are theoretically associated with the two solstices, "bringing the sun back" (from the south) and bidding it farewell following the agricultural season. It is noteworthy that the two dates do not coincide with the actual occurrences of the solstices. A similar situation was reported for Santa Ana by White (1942: 205-207), where the solstice rites are held "sometime in May" and "about November 13 or 15—'shortly after the Jemez fiesta [November 12].'" White added, "One informant said that it is sometimes held as early as the latter part of April: 'sometimes the Masewi hurries it up to make the summer longer.'" This deviation is also characteristic of Cochití.

White found no satisfactory explanation for this calendrical deviation, though his informant's comment may hold the solution. With the traditional agricultural emphasis in the culture, it may be that the time set for "calling the sun back" intentionally preceded the true solstice in order that it could be claimed that the recall was actually achieved. Similarly, late in the fall, after the main harvests, the reversal of the sun's course along the eastern horizon might have been intentionally anticipated in an effort to impress the laymen with the powers of the medicine societies.

In contrast to a popular conception of American Indian "moon counts" for the months of the year, it is interesting that no such reckoning is found among the Cochití. Modern references to the months of the year are in Spanish or English, and there is no Keresan counterpart; this appears to have been true in the past also. The word for *moon* is ta'watsh; *month* is tzash'tye-ta'watsh, and there appears to be no elaboration of these terms. The year is divided into specifically named seasons, however; *winter, spring, summer,* and *autumn* are, respectively: kok', tī'tsha, ka^r'sha-tī, and shto'na. [48] Another informant added that the *middle of winter* ("Christmas") is termed sun'kok; *mid-summer* is, similarly, sun'ka^r-shat^i. An additional calendrical point is the last half of July, "wheat-cutting time"— lersh'shī-nī ("little") shto'na ("fall"). [49] One cannot help wondering whether perhaps the "sun'kok" and "sun'ka^r-shat^i" designations may not more nearly approximate the actual date of the solstices than do the dates observed but that because of unknown reasons they have been allowed to fade into relative obscurity.

The remaining material in this chapter is discussed on the basis of the twelve calendar months as recognized in our own culture. This procedure may appear open to criticism on the grounds of imposing an alien frame of reference, but it has the merit of conforming in numerous respects to the Cochití way of thinking of various ceremonial occurrences. These ceremonies are here arranged in the sequence of their occurrence or, in the case of legitimate variation, the ceremony is discussed at the time of the year when one might anticipate its performance. While the roster of ceremonies described is by no means complete, either in respect to roster or to detail, the series well illustrates the fact that the amount of time, thought, and energy devoted to ceremonial activities remains undeniably impressive even at the present time.

January

January 1. New Year's Day is also referred to as "Fiesta de la Primarera" (Bandelier, November 8, 1880) and Feast of the Circumcision. It is celebrated with Mass and the associated transfer of the official canes to the incoming secular officers (pp. 197–198); there is general visiting and congratulating of these men later in the morning. During the afternoon, there is a *Tablita,* or Corn, Dance, which is considered to be mainly in honor of, and as a blessing for, the new officers. *Tablita* dances, in general, are held to entreat for rain and good harvests.

For the January 1 dance, old songs are used, in contrast to the *Tablita* Dance of the July 14 Feast Day, for which new songs are generally prepared. For the New Year's Day dance, the community house of each kiva group is used, not the kiva structure. The long, decorated pole, described in greater detail in connection with the July 14 dance (see Fig. 23), is also used on January 1, but in place of the July Feast Day side dancers who urge the dancers along and help keep their costumes in order, the members of the Turquoise and Pumpkin choruses perform this function. The various phases of this dance are similar to those of the July 14 performance with the important exception that the January 1 dance is only half as long, being confined solely to the afternoon.

Following the dance, the *alguacilitos* for the coming year are selected; that evening at the first meeting of the council with the six new major officers, the *alguacilitos* and the *fiscalitos* are given their canes of office. As noted (p. 198), it is customary for the governor to call the new officers to his home for a brief meeting before they join in the session of the entire council at the Ku-sha'lī house.

Bandelier, in his journal of November 8, 1880, recorded that on this day a stew was prepared "composed of all herbs which they feed on during the year. Sometimes they put meat into it. With thin tortillas." In the same entry, Bandelier states that the January 1 dance was called "Qqa-shati-mae pashca." Here again slight confusion is indicated. As noted, "ka^r'sha-tī" is the term given by one of my informants [48] as referring to summer; "pash-ko" refers to any public dance [88]. Hence it would seem that Bandelier was given the native reference for the *Tablita* Dance in terms of its most important performance on July 14, the Feast of San Buenaventura, the patron saint of Cochití. An even more common designation for this dance is "ai'ya-shtīo-kutz"; this term also applies specifically to the second of the two phases into which this dance is divided. (Plate 22*a, b* and Plate 23*a*)

January 6. Kings' Day, Reyes Day, Day of Epiphany, Twelfth Night. This day is celebrated, again, with a ritual blend of Catholicism and native ceremonialism. In the morning there is a Mass at which the official canes of office are blessed by the priest (p. 197).

In the afternoon, there is some form of animal dance. "On January 6, all dances should be Shai'yak dances," commented one informant [42]. There appears to be considerably more importance placed upon the participating personnel for this occasion than is true of other animal dances. Parsons (1929: Plate 25*b*) illustrates a "Dance of horned animals, Cochiti, January 6, 1925." The animal dances for January 6 are arranged in a three-year cycle. For the first year (as in 1950), the Turquoise Kiva has an Eagle Dance, in which the two eagles must be impersonated by medicine men. In recent years this has been done by Marcelo Quintana, cacique, and Eufrasio Suina, Shī'kame head. The two girls who dance with the "eagles" are chosen for their excellence in dancing. Four or five drums and a chorus accompany them. For Eagle dances on other days, there are no requirements other than recognized ability in dancing. [55] In recent years the Eagle Dance has been performed only by the Turquoise people; when the Pumpkin group does give this dance, it is performed by only the two men impersonating the eagles—no women accompany them. [62]

Paired with the Turquoise Eagle Dance, the Pumpkin group has an Elk Dance. This is performed by two elk dancers and fifteen or twenty "Comanche" (tīs'nē) dancers. The term "Comanche" is generally applied to a popular stereotype of a Plains warrior dancer, most commonly with a feathered war bonnet and often with a feather bustle. These men dance and gesture in mimicry of the hunt. Four drummers ordinarily are a part of this chorus. [42]

For the second year (as in 1951), both the Turquoise group and the Pumpkin group present a Deer-Antelope Dance. This dance, as performed by each side, shows several deviations from the usual hunting dance. No drums are used; dancers are accompanied solely by a chorus that keeps time with gourd rattles. Each group of dancers consists of two "deer," two "antelope," and two hunters. One informant [42] added two small boys to each group, though their roles were never made clear. The "animals" are driven in from the mountains about dawn by a party of hunters; the dancers are taken to the Flint–Ku-sha'lī house, where they rest until about ten o'clock in the morning. When they are brought out by the ceremonial leaders of their respective kivas (the Turquoise appearing first), they dance in front of the church—just outside the *Campo Santo* in the same location that other ceremonies, such as the *Tablita* Dance, are begun. Following this, they move to the plaza, where they dance again. There is next a diversionary bit of play and joking on the part of the *Viejos*. It was not learned who these clowns are nor how they are chosen, but it is quite likely that they are Ku-sha'lī, *fiscalitos*, or simply members of the ceremonial nucleus of each kiva.

After the clowning, the hunters "kill" the deer and the antelope and the carcasses are carried to a predetermined house—usually that of a close relative who has agreed as a public duty to serve as a sort of sponsor for the dancer. A present is given to the hunter, and the dancer is carried into the house just as a real animal would be upon the return of a successful hunter.

The "animal's" costume is removed and he is ceremonially bathed and shampooed. It is then that the family presents the dancer with a new outfit of clothing, including a blanket. Relatives often give other presents to the dancer, and it is they who secretly return his costume to the Flint–Ku-sha'lī house. The clothing and other presents are viewed as a fair exchange for the blessings this dancer has bestowed upon the household by his presence there. [42, 92]

On January 6 of the third and last year of the cycle (as in 1952), both kivas present a Buffalo Dance. Each group is accompanied by a chorus and four or five drums. For each, there are two buffaloes (mo'shatsh), a hunter (Shai'yak), and a girl (*malinche*). Statements from various informants indicate clearly that differences in costume occur, not only between the two kivas' impersonations but also within either kiva, depending upon the occasion and the season of the year. Details here are admittedly confused, but they are offered simply as a hypothetical framework which can be pursued, corrected, and supplemented sometime in the future.

For the Turquoise, the buffaloes wear white kilts on which a plumed serpent extends the entire width of the piece. (See Fig. 20 for items used in Buffalo dances.) Along the bottom edge is a fringe with metal tinklers. The visible parts of the body are completely covered with black paint. Variations include knitted leggings, a kilt consisting of an ordinary *manta*, and a white shirt. A long woven belt may be tied either at the right side or in back, where it is allowed to hang, "like a tail." The headpieces of actual buffaloskin (with the hair intact) are said to be "old," and lack the more spectacular bulk of newer but less sacred buffalo headpieces. The horns are blackened and tipped with fluffy eagle feathers; one informant [55] mentioned that in some Buffalo dances one horn is painted yellow and the other, blue—a combination commonly found in the decoration of ceremo-

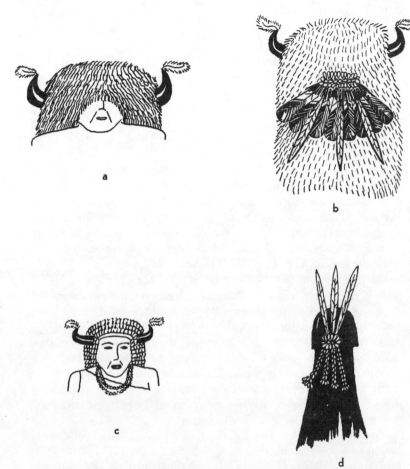

Fig. 20.—BUFFALO DANCE PARAPHERNALIA. *a.*, *b.* Buffalo headdress, front and back; *c. Malinche* headdress, front; *d. Malinche* feathered assemblage.

nial paraphernalia. Moccasins are worn, but statements conflicted as to whether these are plain, beaded, or dyed. Perhaps the point was formerly significant but may have become currently inconsequential. In the right hand is a medicine man's polished black rattle of untanned hide with a buffalo-tail handle; in the left, a bow and several (usually four) arrows. Another account described the "buffalo" as carrying a stick similar to that used by other animal dancers and on which he leans as he assumes various postures in imitation of this animal. Still another version was that the rattles on this day were the ordinary yellow-gourd type, and the black hide rattles were used at all other Buffalo dances. This point needs clarification. At the back of the head is a colorful, fanlike arrangement of eagle and parrot tail-feathers, the bases of which are obscured by a cluster of smaller parrot feathers.

The hunter is usually dressed in buckskins, somewhat in the fashion of a Plains Indian, though there is no headdress like that popularly associated with the Plains tribes. The *malinche* wears a white *manta* as a skirt, or dress, with a long woven belt tied about the waist; occasionally the *manta* is supplemented with a woven kilt worn over the upper trunk. She wears the fanlike arrangement of eagle and parrot tail-feathers between her shoulders; a variation of this description had four ropes of braided parrot feathers worn in this position. For a headdress, one account mentioned an elaborate piece, which looks like the buffalo headdress from a distance but is actually made of turkey breast-feathers. One blue horn and one yellow complete this item. Her face is well covered with white paint. The girl carries a pair of eagle tail-feathers and several twigs of fir in her right hand, and a small basket-like piece full of small parrot feathers in her left. Another informant [55] gave a second piece identical with that mentioned for the right hand as the correct item for the left hand as well. Long wrapped white leggings and moccasins, with skunk-skin anklets, complete her costume.

Pumpkin buffaloes were said to wear kilts of white *mantas* and long-sleeved white shirts. In other details, they appear very similar to the Turquoise dancers. The Pumpkin hunter is essentially the same, but the *malinche* differs considerably in appearance from her Turquoise counterpart. She wears a black *manta*, and her face is blackened. The headdress is similar to that of the Turquoise *malinche* except that the horns are black. She carries a fan of eagle and parrot feathers in each hand.

Additional variables pointed out by other informants include the following: according to one, the Turquoise side has lost its headdress of turkey feathers worn by the *malinche* and, in its place, the girl now wears two eagle tail-feathers with a long parrot feather standing erect between them at the back of her head. When the Buffalo Dance is presented later in the spring, regular moccasins rather than beaded ones are worn, and the forearms and lower legs of the buffaloes are painted red. When this dance is requested and presented later in the year, two women instead of one accompany the buffaloes. In the winter Buffalo Dance the chorus members daub eagle down in their hair and paint their faces and the buffaloes wear black paint, but at performances later in the spring these features are omitted, for they are believed to bring snow, "and no one wants snow in the springtime." [3, 44, 55, 88]

The buffalo is considered to have unusual curative powers, "like the bear, only not quite so much." If a person has been sick and there is a Buffalo Dance being planned, he may ask the war captain to relay a request to the dancers to perform at his home. The request is invariably complied with, and the dancers appear for one "round" in the yard or in front of the door. This is spoken of as "bringing good medicine," amounting to a blessing. One specific instance of this was cited as having occurred during the Christmas season of 1947 following the somewhat prolonged illness of Alfred Herrera. His subsequent series of official capacities and general activity in community affairs are considered tacit proof of the efficacy of the Buffalo Dance in such matters. [42, 55, 92]

On the evening of January 6, there are numerous groups of dancers who go to homes of the new officers and also, since this is Kings' Day, to those of any person having the name "Rey" or "Reyes." Occasionally the dancers visit homes of retiring officers as well. In 1947, this series was witnessed by the writer; included were a Laguna Dance, two Comanche Dance groups, a group of black-faced clowns who spoke primarily in Spanish (the most popular of all groups), and an Eagle Dance group. This last-named actually consisted of three girls, two of them the daughters of a local trader (see p. 19); despite this unorthodox personnel, it was well received by the Cochití.

In an entry for July 16, 1885, Bandelier mentioned that Father Navet saw the "Venado," or Deer Dance, performed "for his reception." Since the brief description noted "two solo-dancers with antlers," his following comment is puzzling: "No headdresses, neither male nor female." Father Navet also saw a "Cibolo," or Buffalo Dance, which he described as "with only one woman in the center & the ear of corn, which she holds out to the men who wear buffalo-heads, & who surround her as if attracted by the corn."

A more recent account of a January dance was found in "Cochiti Ancient Hunting Dance," by Applegate (1929: 117–118). Excerpts from this description follow:

In January 1929 they performed one of these dramas which they call, "Ancient Hunting Dance." This is an interpretative dance that is seldom given, and it is performed by several of the different clans of the pueblo, taking place in the old plaza.

.   .   .   .

My father used to tell me that a long time ago the Indians brought trees from the mountains when they gave this dance and set them up in the plaza like a woods and that one of the trees always had squirrels and birds in it, and the Indians, who were dressed as eagles, deer, hunters, and grandfather spirits, danced among the trees, but there are not so many of us now and we do not bring trees from the mountains any more.

While open to suspicion in certain details, it may well be that this description, contained in a popular account, provides a clue to the common practice of placing several fir trees, usually four or five feet high, in the plaza when various dances are held. This is especially true of animal, or hunting, dances; often there are but two of these trees, one at either end of the actual dancing area. Occasionally, on special days such as the July 14 Feast Day *Tablita* Dance, many more trees are used, including branches of cottonwood. In addition to those in the plaza, one or more of the main approaches to the plaza by which the dancers file in and out are lined on either side by these trees, placed several feet apart. Further mention of these trees will be made in the discussion of Santiago's Day, July 25.

Early in January, each year, a Ka'tsína Dance, of unspecified type, is held in honor of the newly selected officers.

February

February is one of the few months in which there appear to be no set ceremonies. However, it is not a month of ceremonial inactivity. This is a popular month for additional animal, or hunting, dances as well as for Ka'tsína performances. It is also the time (cf. pp. 262, 321), for hañí'gĭt°, and there is the additional possibility of cures and retreats by the several medicine or other secret societies.

March

Ditch-Cleaning Ceremonies. In March, the adult males traditionally turn out for the cleaning of the irrigation ditches. As more and more individuals forsake agriculture, this burden is being carried by a diminishing percentage of the tribal labor force, though, as noted, the increasing population has enabled the numerical strength of this force to remain little changed. While there is a growing tendency to abandon various ritual aspects in favor of more scientific procedures, the opening of the community ditches is still done with traditional rites of the medicine societies, as mentioned on page 261. Further details, still incomplete, are included here. A few days before the spring ditch-cleaning begins, members of the three medicine socie-ties—Flint, Giant, and Shī'kame—unite in a purification, or blessing, ceremony at the heads of the two Cochití ditches. Since in this ritual they are supposedly alone, carefully guarded from a distance by the war captains and the *alguacilitos*, nonsociety members are ignorant of further details. Informants were unable to state whether the gov-ernor and officers pick the day for ditch-cleaning according to a ritual schedule of the societies or whether the societies operate flex-ibly after the day has been set by the secular officers. [44, 45, 53, 70] At least in the past, it seems probable that this date was set by the societies.

Goldfrank was told that sometime before the filling of the ditches, in February or March, the Flint shamans place a bunch of feathers on each side of the head of the ditch, sprinkling corn meal four times and praying for successful crops. The Giant shamans place theirs in the middle section of the ditches; the Shī'kame place theirs at the lower ends. The feathers are washed away when the water enters. Minor discrepancies between certain statements of my informants and Goldfrank's notes (1927: 91–92) may have resulted from the more complete knowledge of her informants. On the other hand, the discrepancies may reflect the simplification of these rituals in the intervening quarter-century.

Spring Dance (O'wē). Usually before (occasionally after) the cleaning of the irrigation ditches, the Spring Dance is performed to assure good crops in the coming growing season. It is held at night in the two kivas, and both men and women dance. Members of each kiva dance first in their own kiva and later in the other one. Costumes are very simple: "Everyone wears his nicest clothing." For men, this is European clothing with the inevitable headband. For women, it is the traditional Pueblo woman's *manta* (pot'chana), buckskin leg-gings, and woven sashes. Goldfrank (1927: 107) described eagle feathers in the men's headbands, but my informants stated that this is rarely seen at present. [70]

For this dance, the entire tribe assemble in their respective kivas. For many years, Spanish-Americans, Anglos, and non-Cochití Indians were permitted in the kivas. In the spring of 1947, this practice was stopped by several older Pumpkin Kiva members, acting on the grounds that the pueblo was increasing in population and the outsiders overcrowded the kivas. In the case of the Pumpkin Kiva, the ban was extended to include the Cochití Progressives, the great majority of whom formerly belonged to that kiva. Ironically, these Pumpkin Progressives were admitted that year, in fact were invited, to the Turquoise Kiva ceremonies. [20, 44, 45, 52, 53, 55, 70]

Goldfrank (1927: 107) stated that the Spring Dance was followed by a feast, and after four days the dance was repeated. Informants said they knew nothing of this repetition, now or at any time in the past. Goldfrank also credited Parsons with the statement that the Spring Dance at Cochití had been borrowed from Jemez, where it was known as "su'we'e" dance. White (1942: 243) described an essentially identical ceremony, "ao-wε," or "o-wε," at Santa Ana. He did not mention the ceremony in his Santo Domingo report. Of interest in time perspective, Bandelier (November 18, 1880) noted that the Turquoise dancers first went to dance in the Pumpkin Kiva; then all went together to dance in the Turquoise Kiva. He added that there was no separation according to clans for this ceremony.

Present-day informants both confirmed and clarified Bandelier's account. Each group of dancers performs in its own kiva first; then the Turquoise go to the Pumpkin Kiva to dance "for the Pumpkins." Returning to their own kiva, they are joined by the Pumpkin group who "dance for the Turquoise people." Later, both groups join in dancing in the Turquoise Kiva. [3, 42, 92]

Agricultural Rites. Following the ditch-openings and the O'wē, the war captains decide on the time for the planting of the cacique's fields (pp. 83–84). This may be either before or after others plant their fields; in the fall, however, the cacique's fields should be harvested first. [42, 44, 45]

Because this opening of the agricultural season is done amid considerable ceremonialism, it is appropriate to pause and discuss this aspect of Cochití life in greater detail. Numerous references in the literature have stressed the close relationships between Pueblo agriculture and religion. This association was commented upon by Forde (1937: 243) in specific reference to the Hopi:

In the more elaborate ceremonies several motives are inextricably inter-woven, but the needs of agriculture and the hazards of the environment feature prominently in many of them. There are rites for every stage in cultivation; ceremonial activities throughout the year have nearly always some reference to agricultural prosperity, while corn is used symbolically at every turn.

Forde's remarks are generally applicable to Cochití in past times particularly; in recent years, however, the influence of extension agents in the Indian Service and other innovations have slowly shifted the emphasis in agriculture away from ceremonialism.

The continued planting of prayer sticks before opening the irriga-tion ditches has been cited. But today there is no use of prayer sticks or meal in dedicating the fields at the time of planting or at any other point in the agricultural season, nor was there any such use at the time of Goldfrank's investigations. However, she did state (1927: 92–94) that the women carried seed corn to the cacique so that he might sprinkle medicine water upon it, and later the women sprinkled corn meal upon it. As mentioned, planting was begun on the edge of the field, and the planter worked in a diminishing spiral, finishing at the center. In storing corn, four ears, called "the mothers," were not husked. One was placed in each corner of the stack, and the husked corn was stacked on top of these four. When entering the room in which the corn was stored, it was necessary for one to remove his shoes. Also, yucca roots were never stored near corn or wheat, as it was believed that the grain would disappear as rapidly as the foam of the yucca.

At present, certain changes, all indicating the loss of agricultural ceremonialism, are apparent. Corn is planted in rows without pre-pared mounds, and throughout the pueblo less blue corn, the type most closely associated with the ritual, is being grown. Corn is fre-quently stored in bins in sheds without using "mothers," and the proximity of yucca roots is ignored. A few older people still remove their shoes upon entering a storeroom, but almost no one observes this when entering a shed. [15, 27, 52, 53, 70]

A few aspects of agricultural ceremonialism have continued in relatively unchanged form. One of the more obvious of these is the series of activities associated with the community's care of the cacique's corn field. The work required to farm these two acres of blue corn, given to the cacique primarily for ceremonial purposes, comes under the supervision of either the Ku-sha'lī or the Kwe'rana society, depending upon whose year it is to be in charge of this and other ritual activities. [3, 42, 45]

The planting of the cacique's fields, being a ceremonial affair, is initiated by the war captain. He calls a meeting of the Council at the cacique's "office," the Flint–Ku-sha'lī house. He tells them that it is time to plant for the cacique; everyone there agrees that it is time. The following day the war captain leads the men on a rabbit hunt, going out in the direction designated by the Council. The Shī'kame, functioning in place of the extinct Shai'yak, perform the religious aspects of the hunt. The hunters return in the evening with their bag, usually twenty-five or thirty cottontail or jack rabbits and other small rodents, which they take to the cacique's home and present to him. This game is prepared for a large *fiesta*, or feast, which is served the men the following day after they have completed the planting of the cacique's fields. The feast is prepared by various women who volunteer for this work, baking loaves of bread, making paper bread, and cooking meat stews.

Depending upon whose year it is, either the Ku-sha'lī or the Kwe'rana members get the blue seed corn early in the morning from the cacique and the heads of the other two medicine societies. It is blessed by these three men and then is carried by the society members through all the streets of the pueblo. As they pass by each house, the women pour water on both the seeds and the members. (The possibility that this practice is an antecedent of the pouring of water over the assembled crowd at various present-throwing *gallos* cannot be ignored nor can it be proven. See details under the several summer feast day celebrations.) After this, the women members of the society bring dry clothing to the Turquoise Kiva for the men. (A recent innovation?) Next, they proceed to the cacique's fields, followed by all the men (but no women) for the planting.

April

Easter. Aside from those ceremonies retained to inaugurate a new agricultural season and the various optional ceremonies, either masked or unmasked, which may be held, the next fixed observance is a series of events associated with Easter Sunday. As in any Catho-

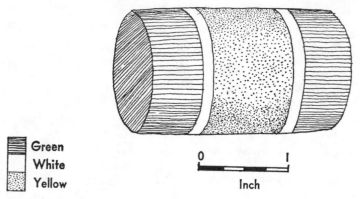

Green
White
Yellow

0   I

Inch

Fig. 21.–Kick Stick.

lic community, the observances of the Lenten season and Holy Week
are important to the Cochití. Again, however, there is a blending of
native religious practices and Catholicism. Prior to Easter, there are
various observances according to the Catholic calendar, but Easter
Evening (p. 291) is reserved for a masked ka'tsina performance.

The morning of Easter Sunday begins with Mass. Later in the
morning, the first of a series of four kick-stick races is held. There
are two "sticks," one for each kiva, which are made by the medicine
men. (Fig. 21) The races continue during the following three days.
The race is run each day toward a different cardinal direction, the
sequence being north, west, south, and east, i.e., counterclockwise.
For each race the runners go out from the village and return; after
circling the village by the streets outside the plaza, they stop at the
Turquoise Kiva and then the Pumpkin. The runners try to kick the
two small blocks of wood with their toes or moccasins and keep them
far enough ahead that it is not necessary to break their strides. On
reaching the kivas, they "pick up" the sticks with their feet, lifting
them to the kiva roof; another runner kicks them down through the
hatchway. Other runners within the kiva "are supposed to kick the
sticks out again—but maybe they throw them, sometimes." From the
Pumpkin Kiva, the runners kick the sticks to the Flint–Ku-sha'lī
house where the race ends. [55]

Though termed a "race," with each side "trying to win each day,"
these events have more of a ceremonial than a competitive athletic

character. Theoretically, each kiva membership has its designated stick, but a runner is as likely to kick one stick as the other, depending upon which comes within reach of his foot. Despite the fact that the runners expend considerable energy, there is little interkiva or even interpersonal feeling manifested. Certain runners are acknowledged as "good," while the remainder join in simply as an obligation to the community or to be a part of the group. One informant was of the opinion that in recent years more of a competitive spirit has been developing in these races. [55] Symbolically, the races were explained as "sending out a call for rain in each of the directions." [42, 55, 62, 88] [During archeological field work on the Cochití Reservation in the summer of 1958, it was stated that the Easter kick-stick races had not been run for several years—with the implication that they would probably never be resumed. It was also stated that the Easter *Tablita* dances are no longer given except for the performance on Easter Day itself. (35)]

One might suggest as a reconstruction of these events that formerly they were participated in by most adult males rather than by the older boys of today's races. The duties have fallen upon the older boys who, with the decline in the belief of the efficacy of such events, are neither convinced of the value of the magical symbolism nor especially enthusiastic about athletic performances. This absence of a deep-seated competitive spirit in athletics is often apparent in the attitudes of the baseball teams (see p. 19 and the final pages of Chapter 10), especially in instances in which the opposing team succeeds in obtaining an early lead.

In the afternoon of Easter Sunday, there is also the first of a series of four *Tablita* Dances. In the dance of the first day, members of each kiva perform as units. On the second day, the Ku-sha'lí members dance together with the Turquoise Kiva members, and on the third, the Kwe'rana take over with the Pumpkin members. "These are for the 'cooked' ones." On the fourth and last day, when the individuals classed as "raw" dance, the Shrū'tzī are in charge. Only on this day of the Easter series is the "pole" used by each kiva. [55] Also in contrast to other Easter season dances and those of New Year's Day and Santa Cruz Day, the dancers wear body paint. A more complete account of this *Tablita* Dance will be found in the discussion of the July 14 Feast Day Dance.

Bandelier reported (April 5, 1882) being told that the Easter

Dance was an intercession for the productivity of crops to be planted. It was said to be "emblematical of the acts of planting and growing various crops."

Time perspective for various details related by present-day informants is again furnished by Bandelier's journal entries of April 9–12, 1882, in which he recorded his observations of the Easter Sunday dance and those of the following three days as well. Since these have not previously appeared in print, his notes on the *Tablita* Dance are presented here in full (the ellipses indicate his digressions):

9th April 1882. (Easter.) "Bayle de la Tabla." About 3 P.M. went to the Plaza. A drum with 6 or 8 men was stationed in the S.E. corner. The drum was yellow ochre, and the men were in clean, gaudy clothes. The dancers came in from the S.E. corner. In pairs, 2 men preceding 2 women. . . . Meantime another cluster had formed and was gradually advancing. . . . The men stamped and the women hopped. Every dance lasted about 20 minutes, so they alternated, changing drums at each time. They invariably went out to the East, in the alley N. of the house of the Cacique, and came in by the S.E. corner. The sight is very picturesque.

Dancers, when in double file: "Q'aatsh," when in lines facing each other "Q'a-ya-shtui-go-tza." [Ai'ya-shtiu-kutz (92)] Dance stopped at sunset. The Scarf: "Fajare-tovaji." "Q'ash-pa." The Kilt: "Otze." [Ot'zin (92)] The dress of the dancers was exactly as painted in Gl. Simpson's Report. The men were naked to the Girdle, the breast and arms painted white. The hair long and flowing, a tuft of green feathers on the top of the head. Below the waist a scarf, originally white and a Kilt embroidered on the fringe like that of the *Malinche*. No leggings but moccasins with a skunk-skin about the heel. A fox-skin hanging down from the waist behind. All carried a calabash rattle [wē'a-shī-katz (92)] in one, and a green bough of Sabino ["Wrong, it should be *Pinabete,*" (spruce) (92); see page 146 also.] in the other hand. The women had nothing particular except the headdress, "O-pash-tia-uasht" [O'ta-shtīa-wisht (92)]. . . .

10th of April 1882. . . . The dance began at 3 P.M. and there was but one party represented, the "Q'u-share." There were in all about 10–12 pairs. The women had a headdress like that of those of yesterday, with the difference that it is slightly higher, and has a bow or arch on top of it and 2 points. The men had the same dress. But all the faces were painted *white.* [White is a prominent color of the Ku-sha'lĭ.] There appear to be two sets of dancers in the Pueblo: the "Qu-share" and the "Q'i-ranna." This, coupled with the division into 2 Estufas, the "Tanyi," or calabash, and the "Shu-amo," indicate two phratries. . . .

11th of April 1882. . . . The dance began early, the dancers entering from the N.W. corner and going out the same way. The flag "Qash-tetshume" [Ka-arsh'tītrū-ma (88, 92)] was carried in front. [This is in obvious disagreement with the ceremony of today; entrance now is from the southeast corner and there is no pole on this occasion.] All had, on the left side of the head, a bunch of feathers of the Cernícola [sparrow-hawk, symbol of the Kwe'rana]. They are all painted red, and they have the same headdress as yesterday. [According to present-day informants (see Fig. 23), Bandelier's observations here were not keen enough; instead of the middle "rainbow" at the top of the *tablita*, this group should have a third "cloud." (3, 42)] The banner is said to be "la mera bandera de Montezuma." . . .

12th of April 1882. . . . The dance began again at 1 P.M. . . . The dancers were all in one body, the flag at their head. They came in from the S.W. corner, and their number was twice that of the last two days. At certain points, . . . the flag was inclined over the heads of the dancers. Every move or change of direction in the promenade was indicated by rattling, and the beginning of every dance, after a pause, by a shrill tremulous shout of the singers. The dancers themselves never shouted. Each dance lasted also about 20 minutes, and the same figures were always repeated. . . . Many small, very small, children danced along. There were old men who regulated the dance, putting the dancers in line whenever the younger and less trained ones got out of order. . . . The fact that one party went out by one corner and the other by another, is that the places where the drums are kept were in that direction. Thus, Romero Chavez' was the place where they painted themselves today. Their motions are clumsy, the men paw the ground, and women vibrate on the palms, not on the toes. The singers generally do like the women, but today some of them stamped and pawed too. . . .

Additional comments on the *Tablita* Dance and upon Bandelier's observations are to be found in conjunction with the description of the July 14 ceremonies.

May

May 3. Aside from the unpredictable incidence of masked and curing rites, the major ceremonial for May is that of May 3—Holy Cross, or *Santa Cruz*, Day. Mass is again combined with native rites consisting primarily of another *Tablita* Dance very similar to those of the other days but with a few exceptions.

As noted earlier, the decorated pole is not used for the May 3 dance, nor are the kivas used, the choruses and dancers being centered about the two community houses instead. A distinctive feature

of this dance is the fact that the side dancers are "the River Men."
(See Fig. 22.) These impersonations are done by the *fiscalitos*, the
exact number—six or fewer—being the decision of the war captains.
The River Men are also called "*Avuelos*," or "*Grandfathers*." Masked
and dressed as tramps, they carry quirts or whips, which they crack
loudly. They supposedly speak nothing but Spanish. Again, there is
the common blending of amusement at their antics and fear of their
taunts and ridicule.

In the *Cochiti Newsletter* for May, 1945 (a mimeographed sheet
sent to Cochití servicemen), was the following item: "The 'River
Men' paid us their annual visit on May 3rd. They didn't come to
school after us as they did last year. We all danced in the afternoon.
We had school the following Saturday morning to make up our
time." A young mother, discussing the "bogeyman" aspects of the
River Men, told of how the younger children ran from their sight and
of how her own nine-year-old son hid under the bed when he heard
of their coming. [38]

During the dancing, the River Men, as side dancers, urge the
dancers along and see that their costumes remain in good repair. This
is the only appearance of these characters during the year. Their
origin, native or Spanish, remains obscure; in either case, there has
been an obvious blending.

June

June 13. San Antonio's Day. This is typically celebrated with Mass in
the morning and subsequent feasting in the homes of the Antonios,
Antonitas, and Tonitas. In the afternoon, there may be a rooster pull
(*Juego de gallo,* or, more commonly, *gallo*) if the war captains and
alguacilitos have succeeded in obtaining a few roosters. While this
feature is optional, there is generally a series of foot races. These are
participated in by the children, usually those from about eight to
twelve years of age. Runners are grouped in several heats, determined
on the basis of sex and size. Within any heat, the runners may be
given a handicap of a few feet according to the decision of the *alguacilito* in charge.

The runners line up, and the *alguacilito* gives the signal by beating
on the ground with an improvised staff three or four feet in length.
At the fourth measured beat, the runners start. The course is about
fifty or seventy-five yards, and the finish line is marked by a series of

Fig. 22.—River Man.

prizes—dishes, a box of Cracker Jack, or some similar object. Runners are not restricted by lanes; they simply aim for the prize they most desire and believe they have the best chance of reaching first. For a group of six runners, there are frequently as many as four prizes. The prizes are donated by various families, often those that have a member celebrating his Feast Day.

After the conclusion of the foot races, the crowd begins its tour of the village, an occasion also referred to locally as "*gallo.*" The crowd visits each home of a feast celebrant. On the roof of the house or on a more favorably located neighbor's roof, the celebrant's family awaits the throng. As the people crowd about the house, presents of a wide variety are thrown to them by the family. When the supplies have been exhausted, the crowd moves on to the next house and the next, until each one has been visited. Those who throw presents from one roof are privileged to join the crowd at any of the other homes. (Detailed accounts of such *gallos* may be found in Lange: 1950b and 1952b; the first of these relates to Santo Domingo and the second, to Cochití.)

As in the case of the kick-stick races and multiple days of *Tablita* dances at Easter time, informants in the summer of 1958 considered rooster pulls a thing of the past in Cochití. Although horses and roosters were both seen less frequently, it appeared that the greatest lack was human interest. [20, 35, 98, 99]

Because there is no Cochití term for this present-throwing other than "*gallo,*" it has been hypothesized that the custom is of Spanish origin. However, no precise parallel can be found elsewhere in Span-

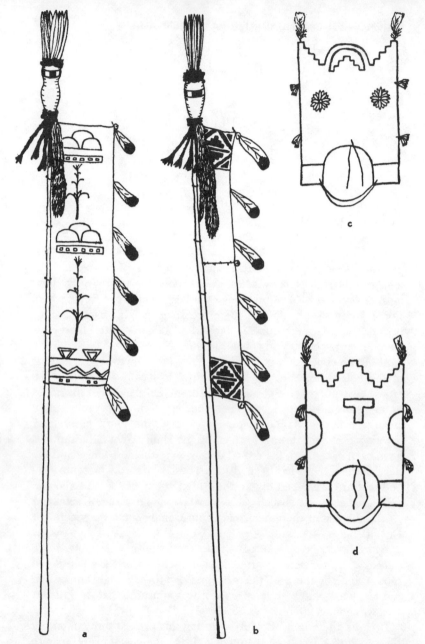

Fig. 23.—TABLITA DANCE PARAPHERNALIA. Ka-arsh'tī-trūma (decorated pole):
a. Turquoise, *b.* Pumpkin; *Tablitas*: *c.* Turquoise, *d.* Pumpkin.

ish America or in the Spanish heritage itself. The nearest parallels are seen in the present-throwing described in association with initiation and other rites of the Ku-sha'lī and Kwe'rana societies (p. 306). The process whereby the custom received its Spanish designation remains obscure for the present.

June 24. San Juan's Day. Since this celebration, both as the Eickemeyers witnessed it in 1894 (1895: 63–75) and as the writer saw it in 1947, has already been described in print (Lange: 1952b), only the main events as they now occur will be summarized here. The day begins with a Mass, and feasting follows at the homes of the Juans and Juanitas. In the afternoon, there is likely to be a rooster pull and foot races, but, regardless of the presence or absence of these events, there is the present-throwing by the families of the principal celebrants. (Plate 21*a*)

June 29. San Pedro's and San Pablo's Day. The events of this day duplicate those of San Juan's Day except that the Pedros, Pablos, and their feminine counterparts are the honored celebrants. In recent years, an occasional baseball game has been scheduled with some visiting team for this day. However, as in the case of other feast days, there still appears to be considerable feeling that this is not an appropriate form of celebration, despite the general enthusiasm within the pueblo for baseball. As of the summer of 1958, a number of baseball games were played on various feast days, though not on the principal feast day—July 14.

July

July 14. The Feast of San Buenaventura, the patron saint of Cochití. July 14 is the calendrical date of this celebration, but the preparations for this, as is true for many important celebrations, precede the specific date by many days. Owing to the importance of this event in the lives of the Cochití, a full discussion is included here simply to keep the relevant data within a unified description.

While the term "Corn Dance" is popularly applied to this ceremony, the Cochití insist that this is a misnomer. A more accurate designation is "*Tablita* Dance," the term being derived from the thin headboards of wood (o'ta-sht[io]-wisht, or *tablita* [48]) worn by the women. (Fig. 23 *c* and *d*) That the *tablitas* have special significance was demonstrated in an incident occurring in 1948. When an informant was asked whether a picture of his wife and himself in dance costume could be taken, he replied that he would be happy to oblige. The officers, however, did not want pictures taken of the women while wearing *tablitas*. [3] In 1947, pictures of men and women in costume had been taken with no difficulty at the time; apparently, however, there had been repercussions. Later, some enlightenment was obtained in a conversation with another informant. When a request of a ceremonial nature is made, it is customary to accompany it with a gift of tobacco or corn meal. A request so made is much more demanding, and the actions involved assume unusual seriousness. When the kiva head requests two men of his kiva to prepare and decorate these *tablitas* for a dance, he does this with tobacco or corn meal. Since the *tablitas* are thus the product of this ceremonial request, they are sacred and are due a respect not accorded ordinary objects. [44] This principle applies to other aspects of ceremonial paraphernalia and procedure. [88]

An interesting perspective on *tablitas* of earlier times was found in a description contained in Bandelier's ethnographic novel *The Delight Makers*. In this account (1946: 130), *tablitas* are described as made of painted buffalohides which have been flattened and stiffened. No archaeological or ethnological verification of this is known; present-day Cochití have no knowledge of such a *tablita*. Until such evidence appears, one can only conclude that the description was simply an invention of Bandelier.

Bandelier's description of the *Tablita* Dance in his novel was undoubtedly based upon several which he had actually witnessed at Cochití, on the main Feast Day or on other occasions. His notes for the July 14 dance and associated activities in 1882, previously unpublished, follow (the ellipses indicate his digressions):

14th of July 1882. . . . The Pueblo is gradually filling with strangers. As far as I can see, the following Pueblos are represented: Cia, S. Domingo, San Felipe, Sa. Ana, Jemez, Sandia, Tesuque, S. Juan, Sa. Clara, S. Ildefonso. Men and women on horseback, and such a display of turquoise and of Navajo-blankets, silver-trinkets, Navajo-bridles, skirts, etc. One woman of Tesuque had a peculiarly handsome and very large turquoise on her breast. Every house was open and each one entering was at once fed. Mass was said at 10 A.M. A great number of Mexicans were here too. . . . It grew very hot about noon. At that time, the 3 "Qu-share," among them Juan Luís, almost naked and painted like at the "Baile de los Entremeseros," opened the dance as usual, singing: "Ho-a." Previously, the procession had gone forth and placed S. Buenaventura in a little niche made with green boughs and Navajo blankets at the edge of the portal of José Hilario's house. As the dancers delayed, I went with Juan José to the Estufa of "Tanyi" where they were dressing up and painting. The sight was a very picturesque one. The singers were squatting on the floor, singing and beating the drum. Each Estufa had its banner tied to the ladder above the Roof. At last, about 2 P.M., the Estufa of "Shyu-amo" made their appearance, about 25 pairs, dressed and painted as in the Spring, but they did not go to the Plaza, directly to the Churchyard, and danced in front of it, surrounded by an Ellipse of about 200 Indians on horseback, all gaudily dressed, presenting a very striking appearance with their gay hankerchiefs [sic] and blankets. Soon after the "Tan-yi" arrived also, then the former left for the Plaza, the latter danced in front of the churchyard and then followed to the Plaza again, where the remainder of the dance was conducted during the day. All the while, the three "Qu-share" were cutting up their capers, sometimes very filthy, though not properly obscene. . . . while Bennett and I remained to photograph. This was a hard job. We got the 3 "Qu-share" however, and one plate of the dancers. But the weather was very unfavorable and the people in a great hurry to dance, so that the "Qu-share" who had the management of the "floor" in every respect, took the groups away from us whenever they formed. Much work and very small profits. Occasional sprinkles and blasts of Sand alternated with terribly hot sunshine. Thunder around us. For the rest, the dance was identical with that of Easter-time. The horsemen filled the entrance to the plaza and made it look very gay. Jac. Gold bought Pottery, old things, Victoriano's shield, and rubbish in general. About 5 P.M. Rooster-pulling began, but it was a tame affair, and only led to squabbles between the Indians and Mexicans, and among the Mexicans themselves. I saw some Whiskey-flasks circulating on the sly, but otherwise there were no disorders. We left at sunset. . . .

Another description, as of about 1890, is in an account by Lummis (1928: 257–270). The participation of the Spanish, or Mexican, people in the Catholic aspects of the Feast Day celebration was noted. The gathering of Indians from nearby pueblos and some from more distant ones was again mentioned. Lummis stated that the first dance of the day was held in front of the church in honor of the priest, who was a spectator. A chorus of a dozen men and a single drummer accompanied the dancers. At the head of two columns of dancers, alternating male and female in each column, was a man carrying a long pole to which was attached a banner, "the Holy Flag of the Sun." "The banner is a priceless bit of work in beaded buckskin, bearing, with its pole, the general shape of a giant feather, and fringed and tufted at sides and top with eagle feathers."

Lummis described the costumes in considerable detail, and he
noted the arrangement of the dancers in "a long row by pairs—first
two women and then two men—. . ." He also noted that the women
danced barefoot and the men wore moccasins. Along the rows of
dancers he noted three Ku-sha'lī men who "were the most important
characters of the day." In the second group of dancers (the other
moiety), he noted that the *tablita* tops were arched rather than ser-
rated, commenting that this was the only distinguishing feature marking the two groups. Also mentioned in his account was a pool of
water from recent rains in the plaza where Ku-sha'lī members engaged at length in antics to amuse the crowd. He stated that a cedar
booth in the plaza sheltered "the gracious lady of the day, San Buena
Ventura, in paint and plaster." Two Mexicans "with a tub of alleged
lemonade, and a Santo Domingo Indian with a big box of apricots
the size and flavor of a musty dried prune" were also noted. He
further observed that little business was done by these vendors except with the visiting Spaniards:

> For two hours a furious sand-storm has been sweeping down the valley,
> nearly blinding everybody but the performers. The dance would be kept
> up till sunset, but at three o'clock it begins to rain emphatically, and
> though eyes are no object, all that feast-day finery is, and the dance ends
> in short order.

As activities supplementary to the principal event, the *Tablita*
Dance, Lummis observed a rooster pull being engaged in by the
Spanish visitors while some Indians engaged in a struggle along the
river banks to catch a greased pig, which one man finally succeeded
in carrying home. In conclusion, Lummis commented on the Spanish
people's moving across the Rio Grande to Peña Blanca, where a *baile*
was to be held that night under the stars.

Lummis' notes contain numerous deviations from the celebration
of recent Feast Days of San Buenaventura. First, his error in referring
to the Patron Saint as a "gracious lady" should be corrected. San
Buenaventura, a man, was considered a famous doctor in addition to
his religious activities. The church at Cochití has honored San Buenaventura as its patron since at least 1667 and probably earlier (Scholes
1929:54–55). In 1794, there was a reference to the Cochití church as
"Nuestro Señor Doctor San Buenaventura de Cochití." (Biblioteca
Nacional, *Legajo X:* Document 82)

In describing the arrangement of personnel in the dance lines,

Lummis differed from current practices of placing a man at the head of each line. This lead man is the head dancer in his line in such instances as the *Tablita* Dance, where the lines are composed of both sexes; in cases where there are only males, the head dancer is placed in the middle of a line. [44, 49, 70] Lummis' account appears to be in error, since informants said dance lines have been headed by men throughout their memory, the span of which in some cases would antedate the time of Lummis' observations. (This was further confirmed in conversations following the Feast Day Dance at Santa Ana Pueblo, 1951. There, the Pumpkin dancers were led by two women said to be Ku-sha'lī members. They wore the regular *manta* costume with white boots; their faces were painted white; in contrast to the other women, they wore no *tablitas* but had a tuft of parrot feathers on top of their heads; their hair was confined in *chongo* fashion, more in the fashion worn by men. Investigation revealed that this practice had also occurred in 1950 [23]; on the other hand, several Cochití said they had never seen it before anywhere. [20, 38, 42, 62] Again, one wonders whether Lummis was in error, or whether present-day Cochití memories are short about this detail.)

In the summer of 1958, I again observed the Santa Ana Feast Day ceremonies. The Ku-sha'lī women were much in evidence, functioning almost in identical manner as the male society members. Their hair was arranged with tufts of corn husks and plastered with white clay; the exposed parts of their arms and legs were painted with black and white bands. That women should dance barefooted is still recognized by the Cochití, but the practice has not been followed because sandburs have recently begun to grow in the area in front of the churchyard, where the first part of the dance is held. In 1947, the first two women in the Turquoise dance lines, Agrapina Quintana and Juanita Trujillo, began dancing barefooted, but after a few moments they were forced to drop out until someone brought moccasins from their homes. In later rounds of the dance in the plaza, a few women took off their moccasins, but the great majority wore them throughout the day. In 1948, no attempt was made to dance barefooted.

Lummis' statement that the Ku-sha'lī were the most important persons of the day is questionable. Since every other year at Cochití, the Ku-sha'lī, as an organization, takes no part in the Feast Day celebration, alternating these functions with the Kwe'rana Society, it would seem unjustified, generally speaking, on the basis of informants' statements to designate any persons, or group, as the "most important" participants. In typical Pueblo Indian philosophy, "everyone has something to do," the implication being that the contribution of each is equally essential. [15, 44, 49]

The cessation of the ceremonies because of rain, as recorded by Lummis (1928: 269) is certainly questionable in view of current practices. At present, it is considered a most successful dance if there is rain during or soon after the dancing. If it falls during the dancing, there is no idea of stopping; rather, it most often means the dancers continue with renewed enthusiasm. [15, 44, 49, 53] When during the summer of 1951, I reported that rain, falling in torrents had momentarily halted a *Tablita* Dance at another village, the Cochití expressed both interest and obvious amusement, almost scorn, that the dancing had been interrupted for such a reason.

Lummis' statement that the first dance of each moiety was held in front of the churchyard is still true today. However, his statement that it is in honor of the priest and is witnessed by him appears to have resulted from a lack of understanding. Informants stated that the first round is danced in front of the church in honor of the patron saint whose church it is; there is little, if any, feeling that this dancing honors the priest. [48, 49, 55, 62, 70]

Following the Mass, there is a procession in which the priest marches. The procession escorts the image of the Patron Saint from the church to the plaza, where a temporary shelter of evergreen or cottonwood boughs has been erected. (Which of the three images, noted on p. 62—assuming that all three are still present and there have been no subsequent additions—is carried, or whether there is any alternation practiced from one year to another are points which remain unknown at present.) After the procession disbands, the priest generally leaves the pueblo. Other priests and nuns are often observed later among the throngs of spectators, but the priest serving Cochití seldom remains for the proceedings after the procession. [48, 49, 53]

A final difference in the Feast Day as described by Lummis is the complete absence of a *gallo,* a pig chase, or any other such diversion. These were formerly staged by the Spanish people, and as their numbers have diminished within the pueblo, Cochití officials have succeeded in eliminating them. The commercial concessions, on the other hand, have greatly expanded, with an occasional "Spanish

Dance," or *baile*, included. This is especially true when July 14 happens to fall on a week end. However, the *baile* is never held at the same time as the *Tablita* Dance; it is limited to the evening before and the evening of Feast Day, and is patronized primarily by Spanish-Americans. Some younger Cochití, particularly the boys, attend, but more often than not, they are merely spectators. [44, 45, 53, 58]

Intrigued by the remarks of White in his study of Santa Ana Pueblo, I attempted to learn more about the pole and banner used in the *Tablita* Dance. As White (1942: 343–345) pointed out, in spite of the prominence of this bit of paraphernalia in the Eastern Pueblos, extremely little is known about it. Efforts to obtain data on this at Cochití emphasized the reasons for White's statement. From the general hesitancy to discuss the subject, it was obvious that this is a very sacred object. It appears to be on a par with the Patron Saint, even, at least in the minds of the Conservative Indians, to surpass him in importance.

At Santa Ana, White (1942: 343–345) was given the name "kastotcoma" for this decorated pole. At Cochití several names were obtained for it, the most common being "ka-arsh'tī-trūma." [44, 45, 48, 52, 53, 88] Another term is "Pai'yat-yama." [21, 42, 44, 62, 70] One informant replied, when asked, "Oh, that's a hard name," referring to pronunciation, probably of one of the foregoing terms. After a brief pause, however (while seeking a way out of his slip?), he said, "pa'ño" (perhaps a derivation of Spanish *bandero*, "banner." An even closer connection may be the word *baño*, meaning "bath," for with frequent references in Spanish journals to the kivas as *estufas*, and the associated sweat baths, it is possible that some derivation of this meaning was applied to the pole of each kiva.)

Even though informants were inclined to insist that the make-up of this important item of paraphernalia has been stable, certain innovations in it have been dated. First, surprisingly enough at Santo Domingo in 1948, the Pumpkin Kiva banner had a corn stalk embroidered down most of its length. The Turquoise Kiva banner remained unchanged. Observing this introduction, the Cochití Turquoise Kiva later adopted the idea and its banner appeared similarly decorated for the first time for the Feast Day in 1951. The embroidery was done by girls who had learned this skill at the Santa Fe Indian School. Commenting after the 1951 Feast Day, a Cochití Pumpkin man stated: "They're going to make one like that for the Pumpkins next year. It looks real pretty—nice that way." [49] However, this was not done in 1952; whether it has been done since then I cannot say. (See Fig. 23.)

Though Cochití informants claimed that the poles used by each kiva, and those in other pueblos, have always been decorated as they are now, Bourke (1884: Plate IV) illustrated a pole from Santo Domingo with the sash wrapped around the pole as a kilt rather than extended at full length along the pole, as is commonly seen at present. (The only known exception was observed at the 1958 Feast Day at Santa Ana Pueblo where the pole of the Turquoise Kiva was decorated in a kilt-like manner. The pole of the Pumpkin Kiva had been accidentally broken, just before the dance, and that group danced without a pole.) If this kilt arrangement was formerly true at Cochití also, the assembled pole would be much closer to representation of a person, or more likely, a ka′tsīna. This comparison was confirmed by some informants [44, 88], but it differs from the interpretation offered by another informant: that it symbolizes a corn plant [62]. The description by Lummis of this banner as a "priceless bit of work in beaded buckskin" is likewise intriguing, especially as informants and the published data were unanimous in mentioning only embroidered cotton dance sashes.

Informants stated that the pole must be reassembled each time it is used; after a ceremony, it is dismantled, and the parts are returned to the individuals who lent them. Parts include the parrot and eagle feathers, the ovoid blue sphere fashioned of solid wood (one informant [52] stated that this ball was a hollow gourd with no seeds or anything else in it; this does not appear to be true any longer, though it may well be the "way it is supposed to be"), the foxskin, sash, and ropes of braided parrot feathers. Another informant [42] made the comment that it is this ovoid sphere that is specifically "Pai′yat-yama." When assembled, the complete unit becomes "ka-arsh′tí-trūma."

The pole itself is of Douglas fir ("spruce"), the tree which the people ascended in their emergence myth. Informants insisted this was the only wood resilient enough to withstand the strain of being shaken over the heads of the dancers. No one could recall a pole's breaking during a ceremony.

According to one informant [3], both the pole and the blue ball are stored in the ceiling of each kiva; another stated these are kept in the community houses. The men who decorate these (kwirsh'ke-shē) are also the ones who decorate the *tablitas* for their respective kivas. Since the *tablitas* at Cochití are prepared for each kiva by these specific functionaries, there is much greater consistency in the shapes and decorations. At Santo Domingo and Zia, where this work is delegated to families or individuals [44, 45], much more variation occurs, though even here general stereotyped limits are observed.

When the men at Cochití who do the decorating are asked by the kiva heads to perform their duties, the request is accompanied by corn meal, corn pollen, or tobacco, thereby making it sacred. [44] The reassembling of the pole is done very early in the morning on the day of the dance; it is dismantled that same evening. [3, 44, 62] Several days are devoted to repairing the *tablitas* before they are used. [92]

The use of the term "Pai'yat-yama" with reference to the pole is interesting in light of other usages of this term. "Pai'yat-yama" is also used in reference to the dance drums of the pueblo, though never for the smaller, tourist type of drum. [55, 62] This usage was denied by several other informants, but in such a manner as to be interpreted as an attempt to withhold this information. Curtis (1926: 168) listed several specific names for Santo Domingo drums, the first being "Paiyatyama." Several of my informants said that Cochití drums do not have specific names. They stated that some boys are given "Pai'-yat-yama" as a personal name; it means "youth," or "master," i.e., "young gentleman." [44, 45, 48, 53, 55] At other pueblos, such as Zuñi, 'Paiyatyama" is a legendary culture hero, always a youthful representation when appearing as a Ka'tsína (Bunzel 1932: 1016, Plate 37b). The term was used by Benedict (1931: 71, 86) as the name of a youthful Cochití culture hero "Payatamu," with many similarities to the Zuñi. Among the Cochití, it is also a Ka'tsína impersonation. (See Appendix 26.)

As mentioned, the Ku-sha'lī and Kwe'rana alternate each year in supervising the July 14 celebration. This supervision involves the gathering of dancers for rehearsals, directing the pueblo-wide clean-up prior to the Feast Day, and performing important ceremonial roles before and during the dance. The two groups, each with its affiliated kiva group, never appear the same year, as is the Santo Domingo custom. On the day of the dance, the members of the managing society "call the dancers." They go from their own society house to their kiva, to the other kiva, and then circle the streets outside the plaza. Then they enter the plaza singing and calling. They go to the rear of the church, where they divide into pairs and then go to each home. [44] Individuals who appear on these occasions at Cochití are full-fledged members and not nonmembers dressed to portray society members. Frequently, members of the society from another pueblo help with the Cochití dance, particularly when such a society has been set up by the Cochití society. Reciprocally, Cochití members participate in such ceremonies of other pueblos.

"Helping" other pueblos is also characteristic of nonsociety members. The assistance may take the form of dancing, singing in the chorus, or some other function. For many years, one of the Cochití Turquoise Kiva lines has been led annually by a man from Isleta Pueblo (whose wife is a Cochití) who vowed during an illness that if he recovered, he would "dance for Cochití every Feast Day." In 1951, following further illness, this man joined the chorus and sang rather than participating in the more strenuous dancing. Such vows are quite common, though they usually cover shorter periods of time. Participation is with the permission of the war captains and kiva heads, and a request is almost always allowed. [44, 45, 48, 49, 52, 53, 55] Connections are particularly strong between Cochití Kwe'rana and those of the Tewa Pueblos, especially of Tesuque, Nambé, and San Ildefonso. At least one Tesuque Kwe'rana member is a regular performer in the Cochití July 14 dance. [44, 55]

In 1948, I noticed that the dancing was at a faster tempo than that customarily practiced in Rio Grande *Tablita* Dances. Several informants confirmed this observation, saying that the boys, i.e., the young men, "wanted to step it up." They also used more intricate dance movements. This appeared to be especially characteristic of the dancing of the Pumpkin Kiva group. (This increase in tempo and in intricacy of line movement was also noted by Fred Eggan, who considered the Cochití dancing of 1948 as more like that of the Hopi villages than that of the other Eastern Pueblos.)

For any other *Tablita* Dance, old songs are used, but new ones are required for July 14. At a meeting of the two kiva heads and the war captains, the number of songs to be prepared by each side is agreed upon. Traditionally, the number is supposed to be eight, but this is no longer true. Formerly, each side sang four song sets, and after an intermission during which they ate, they sang four more. The two kivas must sing the same number of songs on any given day; in 1947, for example, each kiva sang seven songs for Feast Day. (Each dance round is accompanied by one song set.) At present, each side dances twice or perhaps four times for *Tablita* dances other than that on Feast Day. [3, 15, 44, 48, 49, 70]

In preparation for the July 14 Feast Day, the kiva mayorĩ reminds the chorus members as early as May to begin thinking of songs. He makes the final selections, and the choruses begin practice about June 15. For about two weeks, they meet in their respective community houses every evening to work out words and melodies. The following entry from Starr's diary of September 15, 1897, data primarily from Santiago Quintana, is of interest: "He told me that the Cochiti are great singers and the young men know Ute, Comanche, Navaho, and Apache songs—in fact, every nation's songs they have ever heard. Then there are many songs of their own; they have many kinds, among them, war songs." One interesting note on the interchange of songs among the Pueblos was revealed in the comment of one man [62] that he had heard Cochití war songs sung as a part of the regular Shalako ceremony at Zuñi many years ago. It is noteworthy also that this ceremony had elements with a definite war association among the Zuñi (Bunzel 1932: 970).

After July 1, practices are held every other evening until the last four evenings before the Feast Day. For the last four practices, the choruses meet in their kivas with the dancers. At these sessions, the correct order of the dancers is irrelevant, and various movements of the dance lines are not rehearsed. Smaller children, especially boys who have not danced before, are given extra drill at home by their families. On the day of the dance, various dance formations and movements are shown and explained to the men before each round. "The girls don't need to know this; all they do is follow the boys." [20, 24]

The kiva structures are used only for the July 14 *Tablita* Dance. The women dress in them, and the men dress at home except for a few finishing touches. All the dancers gather in their respective kivas with the chorus members and side dancers. [53] Body paint is usually red for the Turquoise men and light-blue or gray for the Pumpkin men. Contrary to early sources, present-day Cochití insist that body paint is used only for the July 14 dance. [3, 44, 88]

In any *Tablita* Dance (ai'ya-shtĩo-kutz) there are two major phases within each round.[1] The first phase includes the entrance and the circling of the plaza; during this time the two dance lines are parallel, with the leader of one dancing beside the leader of the other line. The two leaders are directly behind the pole-carrier, or, on occasions when the pole is not used, actually in front. This phase is termed "ha'wē-na-ai-ya." (The Hopi, in their Butterfly Dance, were said by one informant [55] to call this "ho'wē-na-ai-ya.") For the second phase the two lines face each other, with the leader of one line opposite the tail of the other line. From these basic positions, the two lines break into several segments that join with corresponding segments of the opposite line in forming a series of circles and other formations as they weave back and forth between their original positions. This is "ai'ya-shtīo-kutz," the phase which is also the designation for the entire ceremony. This is usually at a faster tempo. At times, usually later in the dancing of any day—commonly the last round—a "yo'rañī" is danced. This is done at a slower tempo than ai'ya-shtīo-kutz, and the drum beat has a heavier and slower pattern. In each of the phases, the drumming begins at a low pitch and ends on a higher pitch as the drummer shifts to the other head of the drum. [55]

Following any dance, such as the *Tablita* Dance, the evergreen worn or carried by the dancers is gathered in the kiva or community house and several young men are designated to throw it all into the river as "an offering." Also, dancers are supposed to wash off their paint in the river, "but now they go to the schoolhouse and use the showers there." [55]

Much remains to be known about the *Tablita* Dance in the entire Rio Grande Pueblo area. As at Cochití, it is held almost entirely in association with Catholic feast days, both major and minor, so far as specific pueblos are concerned. While it is a public ceremony, in contrast to the Rio Grande ka'tsīna rites, there are elements of the *Tablita* Dance—the pole and the *tablitas* themselves—which are held very sacred. The accuracy of Poore's statement (1895: 437) that the ceremony is an ancient native rite which the Church has taken over for its own designs is difficult to evaluate but appears essentially

[1] The analysis presented in this paragraph is a revision of that made in an earlier account (Lange 1957: 68) in which three major phases, or divisions, were designated. The analysis presented here also correlates with that made by Kurath in Appendix 43 of this volume.

valid. That the celebration represents a merger of native and Catholic rites cannot be disputed. (PLATES 22, *a* and *b*, and 23*a*)

July 25. Santiago's Day. At Cochití, this celebration is combined with that of Santa Ana's Day. Santa Ana Day was formerly celebrated on the proper date (July 26), but with fewer Anas in the pueblo and with the major feast day of neighboring Santa Ana Pueblo occurring on July 26, the two celebrations have been merged at Cochití.

In many respects the celebration of Santiago's Day duplicates those of other saints' days. On the evening preceding Santiago's Day, there are bonfires in front of the celebrants' homes. Fireworks, rockets, and guns are fired. Following Mass and feasts at homes of the Santiagos, Diegos, Anas, and Anitas, *gallo* is played, foot races are held, and presents are thrown from the roofs of the homes of the principal celebrants.

Most important of all these elements of the Cochití celebration is the characterization of Santiago, or the "Little Horse." This masked impersonation was not portrayed in 1946 and 1947; it was done in 1948. His failure to appear in certain years was explained as due to the people's not asking for him soon enough in a particular year for adequate preparations to be made "for his coming." However, it was said that Santiago appeared again in 1952 despite the fact that there had been no formal request from the lay public for his appearance. [42]

The Little Horse consists of a horse "body" worn by a man, Santiago, who appears as the rider. (Fig. 24*b*) The horse's head is very small, about the size of a fox terrier's, and at Cochití it is always white. Behind Santiago is the rump of the horse, complete with white tail. From the body of the horse a white sheet and a gaily-colored shawl hang down to conceal the lower portion of the man's body, though the lower part of his legs and feet are visible. (Informants stated that Santiago always rides a white horse at Cochití whereas at Santo Domingo there are two horses, one black and one brown. [20, 21, 34]) Santiago himself is dressed in a black stovepipe hat and black swallow-tailed coat. He carries a long thin sword in his right hand, and his face, except for the eyes and forehead, is covered by a black scarf. A long braid of hair, decorated with bright ribbons, hangs down his back. In 1948, false hair had to be used because the impersonator, Lorenzo Cordero, had short hair. This impersonation

Fig. 24.—Santiago's Day Impersonations.

had previously been done by Alcario Montoya and, before him, by Victoriano Cordero. [55] He wears regular dance moccasins with skunkskin anklets, and his steps mimic the prancing of a spirited steed. He is accompanied by a snare drum (o'ya-pī-nutz); in 1948 the drummer was Octavio Suina, an *alguacilito*, but not a Ku-sha'lī member. This celebration is traditionally an all-Ku-sha'lī affair, and, until senility prevented it, the drumming had been done by Isidro Cordero. Why another Ku-sha'lī had not replaced Isidro was not explained.

In addition to "Little Horse" and "Santiago" this impersonation is referred to by the Cochití as "Our Mother." [65] Other names are "Ka'wai-yo san'tī-ak" [48] and reputedly a very esoteric name— "Po'shai-añi." [52]. This last term was discussed earlier (pp. 267–268) as a reported degree within the Flint Society, which is closely affiliated with the Ku-sha'lī.

Some informants stated that this impersonation takes a long time to prepare. If the people want it, they must so inform the war captains about Easter, and they, in turn, inform the Ku-sha'lī Society, whose function it is to supervise Santiago's Day. This prerogative is never alternated with the Kwe'rana Society. [20, 24, 34] Other informants stated that in the old days, the request was made in early spring before planting; now it is commonly done about a month before Santiago's Day. [25, 49]

On the evening of July 24, 1948, I heard considerable laughter and general commotion in the plaza. Investigation showed that most of the pueblo was present, ranged around the edges of the plaza. In the middle of the plaza, a *ramada* of cottonwood boughs had been erected, and a table and benches had been placed under it. Seated at the table were the war captains, the *fiscales*, and the lieutenant governor (the governor was absent from the pueblo at the time). There were also the Giant Society head and Octavio Suina, an *alguacilito* who had been chosen to serve as drummer.

In addition, two Ku-sha'lī men were present, dressed as old men (*viejos* or *viejitos*, son'daro) (but never called *abuelos* on this occasion [48]), with sheepskin wigs and beards, blackened faces, and large straw hats. (Fig. 24a) They are also called *entremeseros*, or clowns; some simply refer to them as Ku-sha'lī. [65] One, "Jerry," recently impersonated by Juanito Trujillo, was seated under the *ramada* while the other, "Tūtī," played by Lorenzo Herrera, stood in the middle of the plaza, reading from a blank sheet of paper:

DEAR MR. GOVERNOR JUAN JOSÉ SUINA AND GOVERNOR TENYET JERRY QUINTANA:

I am Tony Tūtī and this is my *compadre*, Albert Einstein. We have traveled five thousand miles and have eighteen miles left to go. Our feet are nothing but blisters. We have had a lot of work and a lot of trouble for you, and tomorrow the "Horse" is going to come. Everybody must obey us and be nice to us. We have had a lot of work to do to get ready. The war captain said to me, "Tomorrow, you are in charge of the pueblo." I said, "O.K." Everyone must be nice to us. We need lots of food and a place to sleep. We are not married. If you don't like my partner, here I am. The Little Horse needs a place to sleep. He is just fifteen years old. I am fifteen and a half years old. Any girl who will sleep with the Little Horse raise your hand. [He raised his right hand, but no one else did.] If you will sleep with me, raise both hands. Be nice to us tomorrow, and everyone obey. No drunkenness allowed. Everybody have a good time tomorrow. That's all.

Then the second *viejo*, "Jerry," walked to the center of the plaza and also read from a blank sheet of paper:

DEAR MR. GOVERNOR JUAN JOSÉ SUINA AND TENIENTE JERRY QUINTANA:

Tomorrow is a big day. The Little Horse is coming. Everyone be good to us. We have had lots of work to bring the Little Horse. Everyone get dressed up. All you girls put on your lipstick. Come alone—we don't want to see your boy friends. Everyone have a good time. No one—Mexicans, Indians, or no one else—should take pictures of the Little Horse. He will come about 7:30 in the morning. Get up at five o'clock, everyone, and be ready. That's all.

While the above versions are accurate in general phrasing, detail, and theme, the actual speeches were somewhat longer. They were accompanied by constant laughter from the steadily increasing audience. That evening, there were fireworks, bonfires, and on several houses *luminarios* burned. Drumming continued for the third consecutive night.

The next morning all the boys and young men were busily saddling and decorating their horses. Soon after seven o'clock, the two war captains walked northwestward from the village past the Pumpkin Kiva. A large group followed them, and the horsemen trailed a short distance behind. The officers walked to the northern edge of the pueblo and sat down to wait for the Little Horse. Soon drumming was heard in an arroyo half a mile north, and at a signal all the horse-men rode out and circled Santiago, who had appeared in the com-pany of the drummer and two *viejos*. At the edge of the village, the people gathered around this party, pushing coins into the hand of Santiago and pinning bright ribbons at the neck of the Little Horse. Meanwhile, the horsemen circled and whooped. The war captains were now joined by the cacique, who remained thereafter close to the Little Horse, the Kwe'rana head, and the Shī'kame head. Several women next approached and sprinkled corn meal on the horse and placed coins in his neck, presumably in some container concealed there. From the arroyo, the party moved past the Pumpkin Kiva and on to Rael's store, where they turned eastward toward the church. Then by a swift move, apparently through the side entrance of the church, Santiago and the *viejos*, together with the drummer, eluded the crowd. The church bell clanged wildly at this moment, and the people gathered outside the churchyard but made no effort to enter it or the church. Suddenly there was a second clanging of the bell, and the party of principals emerged from the front of the church and joined the crowd once more. Then all moved to the community cor-ral, where the leading characters entered. Led by the war captains, they circled the corral four times, moving clockwise (one of the few ceremonial procedures noted in which the movement was not counterclockwise). The captains and others sprinkled corn meal or pollen as they walked. Two horses had been brought into the corral (animals are almost never kept there anymore), and several men kept them from escaping as the party made its rounds. After this, Santiago and an attendant entered the Ku-sha'lī house and the other principals returned to the *ramada* in the plaza. The remainder of the morning was spent in feasting at various homes, and no further activi-ties occurred in the plaza.

During the afternoon, Santiago came out of the Ku-sha'lī house periodically, each time making four rounds, counterclockwise, of the plaza. He was accompanied by the cacique and three *viejos*, whose chief function was to prevent him from dashing out of the plaza as he continually threatened to do. His steps varied from tiny prances to a long-gaited waltzing step, interspersed with quick, darting runs at which the *viejos* raised their walking sticks to bar the way and shouted "Whoa!" or "Whoa, Baby!"

As the dancers made their rounds of the plaza, the people, both

Indians and Spanish-Americans, came forward and again placed ribbons around the neck of the Little Horse, put coins in the container at his neck, and sometimes placed food and other items in the hand of Santiago. These last were quickly transferred to the cacique.

Several families, all Indians, brought their young sons, ranging in age from several months to about five years, to the Horse and put them on its back behind Santiago. The younger ones were held on by their fathers; the older ones were left alone, hanging to Santiago's shoulders. Santiago darted back and forth, attempting to buck off the extra load. These attempts were met with cries of "Whoa!" and "Steady, Baby!" from the attending *viejos*. No one was thrown, and all but one or two of the youngest ones appeared to enjoy their experience. (In 1952, there was none of this "riding"; Tūtī had instructed the people not to do this any more. [42])

On his last appearance (fourth?) in the plaza, Santiago was met by the usual group of helpers. Suddenly the cacique took Santiago's sword, replacing it with a rooster with which Santiago chased the three *viejos* and anyone else he could reach. The oldest *viejo* (and oldest man in the pueblo), Isidro Cordero, was caught and was knocked flat when Santiago struck him with the rooster. He picked himself up promptly, and the fun went on. One *alguacilito* rode his pinto horse into the plaza, where he sparred with Santiago for a time. After a few moments, he succeeded in taking the rooster from Santiago and galloped out of the plaza with all the other riders in hot pursuit. In the meantime, Santiago, sword in hand again, entered the Ku-sha'lī house and did not appear again.

Just before the rooster pull began, the *viejos*, who the evening before had claimed that the war captains had transferred their authority to them (as Ku-sha'lī) for the day, were interrupted by the war captains during their banter with some women. These officers told them to get on with their business, thereby asserting their ultimate control of this ceremonial, as in the case of all others.

The *gallo* and foot races were held south of the church, and at the conclusion of these events, the crowd assembled to go from house to house to scramble for presents from the Santiagos, Diegos, and Anas. The first house visited was the Flint–Ku-sha'lī house, where Ku-sha'lī women had gathered on the roof to throw presents in honor of Santiago himself. From there, the crowd made its way to a dozen or more houses before the day's festivities were concluded.

The previous year, 1947, Santiago's Day festivities were also observed by the writer. It was explained that "the people were too busy this year to bring in the horse." Nevertheless, considerable activity was observed, and the prominent place of the Ku-sha'lī Society was manifest. Isidro Cordero was seen drumming numerous times in the streets of the village: "He is the only one who knows how to drum for the horse." [23, 32] (This was an interesting comment in view of the drumming by Octavio Suina noted in 1948; as mentioned, Octavio was not a Ku-sha'lī member.)

The war captain issued a call about an hour after noon, and a number of horsemen gathered in the street north of the plaza. From here, they followed a single-file procession of three Ku-sha'lī members who came from their society house and went to a shrine just beyond the northernmost house (that of Diego Romero). The society members—Alcario Montoya, Lorenzo Cordero, and Juanito Trujillo—carried meal in bowls of old Cochití manufacture with terraced edges. Alcario also carried an American flag, about two feet by three, with yellow and pink ribbons tied to the top of the stick.

At the shrine, the group was joined by the war captain; Isidro continued his drumming in the plaza. Suddenly the horsemen, about twenty of them, left the shrine, galloping around the western periphery of the village and entering the plaza at the northeast corner. This circuit was counterclockwise, conforming to the usual Cochití pattern. In the plaza, they were met by the war captain and Alcario, who took back the flag which had been carried by the leading horseman and carried it into the Ku-sha'lī house. From this time on, the war captains and the *alguacilitos* supervised a rooster pull with birds brought out from the Ku-sha'lī house. There were also foot races for the children, after which the crowd went from house to house for the present-throwing.

In concluding this discussion of ceremonials and changes found therein, it is only fair to say that there is considerable difficulty in obtaining definite data. Early and reliable recorded accounts are virtually nonexistent, and either from pride or lack of awareness, many informants insist that there have been no ceremonial changes. However, several informants provided data which proved to be an almost hopeless maze of conflicting detail but which, at the same time, disproves the contention that no changes have occurred. These data on Santiago's Day are included here to illustrate the need for rechecking information with numerous informants before reliable reconstructions can be made.

Goldfrank (1927: 46) gave a brief account of the festivities of Santiago's Day:

> The Flint society to restore the equilibrium has adopted a horse, surely a recent innovation. The stuffed horse's head is carefully fed by the cacique, as a member of the Flint Society, and is ridden by him or a Koshare on St. James's Day, July 25. Three Koshare helpers of the cacique attend the "Horse Saint" (*gawaya santiak*). One of the attendants plays a drum and the populace is encouraged to throw coins. This dance is followed by a rooster pull. The rider of the horse is the first to carry the rooster. The whole get-up of the horse and rider who wears a high hat and long black coat give the ceremony a strong Mexican tang. In olden times a tree and squirrel were brought down from the mountains and placed in the plaza, but this is no longer done and my informant added, "They don't know how to do their sacred things any more."

Several attempts were made to obtain from informants an account of this former celebration. Goldfrank's version corresponds closely with the 1948 procedure except that my informants claimed it was, and had always been, a Ku-sha'li affair rather than Flint. [20, 44, 45, 70] Her remarks on the "olden times" indicated considerable change for which more data were sought. It seems safe to state that "olden times" signified a time predating the first-hand experience of any Cochití living in 1948.

Recollections of various informants achieved little unanimity. One version was that Santiago formerly came from an arroyo north of the pueblo as he did in 1948. This informant doubted another account in which Santiago came across the river from the sharp peak referred to as *La Tetilla*. When Santiago reached the arroyo by the Pumpkin Kiva, the riders swung to the west and came up behind him. Having reached the arroyo, Santiago "flew" across the arroyo and reached the church before any horseman could catch him. (The informant's use of the word "flew" to describe the movement of Santiago across the arroyo and then later in entering the kiva was challenged for clarification. He insisted that Santiago flew a few feet above the ground, never touching it nor using the steps or ladder of the kiva. [65])

From the church he went to the Turquoise Kiva, but he did not use the steps. He again flew to the roof and then entered the kiva. He started down once but came up again. He tried again but came back up. The third time (Christian symbolism rather than native, which would be the fourth) he was successful and disappeared into the kiva without using the ladder.

There was no recollection of large pines or squirrels on Santiago's Day, but rather an association of these items with Reyes Day, January 6, which agreed with Applegate's description (p. 329). Four large evergreens, possibly firs, were brought from the mountains in wagons. They were concealed in the arroyo north of the pueblo. At dusk, the war captains told everyone to remain indoors and keep his windows covered. In the morning, four large fir trees were in the plaza with live squirrels in their tops. The squirrels remained in the treetops "without any sort of leash." (?) After this there were certain animal dances just as they still have. Trees and squirrels appeared only on Reyes Day. [65] For many Cochití dances, particularly hunting dances, an evergreen tree from two to four feet high is often placed at each end of the plaza. This has also been observed at Santo Domingo, Jemez, and elsewhere, and may represent a survival of the former use of more numerous and larger trees. At present, no animals or birds or any form of decoration or offering has ever been noted in these small trees.

Another informant insisted that the Little Horse came not on Santiago's Day but in connection with bringing in the horses for the grain threshing. If the Horse came on Santiago's Day, he did not return that same year. It was only with his appearance at threshing time that the pine trees and squirrels had appeared in the plaza. [25]

Another informant, about sixty-five years old, had been told by his grandmother that the impersonator of Santiago had to fast for one year prior to the dance. Fasting involved continence only; there were no food restrictions. If the fast was observed faithfully, then the man and Horse had power to help the pueblo; otherwise, they had no power. This informant recalled that in his childhood the Horse came in September but not necessarily every year. [52]

Another informant, about sixty years old, had heard of trees and squirrels in connection with Santiago's Day. However, he had not seen them himself and believed this custom had been lost by the time of his early childhood. [70]

Another informant, about sixty-five years old, claimed that the impersonator of Santiago went to a shrine near the top of *La Tetilla*, where he fasted four days before the celebration and burned a candle. On the night before the dance, he was joined by other Ku-sha'lī who were to play important roles in the ceremony. That morning the people rode almost to *La Tetilla* to meet Santiago and escort him to the pueblo. They returned to the village, crossing the river on the ferry. [50]

August

August 10. San Lorenzo's Day. This day is celebrated by Mass, feasting at the homes of the Lorenzos and Lorenzas (Lorencitas), rooster pulls, foot races, and present-throwing. Until it was revived in 1948, this celebration had been considerably curtailed in recent years in an intentional move to discourage outsiders, particularly men from Santo Domingo, from attending. The attendance of these outsiders, for some reason on this particular date, led to an unusually large number of fights. "They don't play [in the rooster pulls]; they take it all so seriously." [23] (Plate 21*b*)

Whether this explanation has any foundation in fact is unknown; it may be that the "īañī," or power, believed to be absorbed by anyone on whom some of the rooster's blood spills, was looked upon as an aid to be sought with greater fervor by some of these outsiders than by many Cochití.

Although this is the only August celebration at their own village, the people of Cochití are busy throughout the month with ceremonies elsewhere. August 2 at Jemez, August 4 at Santo Domingo, August 10 at Picurís (San Lorenzo), August 12 at Santa Clara, August 15 at Zia, and the Inter-tribal Indian Ceremonial at Gallup are events attended by many Cochití and participated in by at least some in almost any year. In addition, there are September feasts at Laguna and Taos as well as the Santa Fe Fiesta, all of which have religious and social significance as well as providing economic opportunities.

September

Aside from the outside celebrations noted in the August discussion and in ka'tsīna and curing ceremonies which may possibly occur, September's activities are largely devoted to the harvest.

October

Harvest Rites. Activities of October largely continue those of the preceding month. It is during the autumn that the war captain again calls the council members to the cacique's "office" and announces the completion of the growing season begun earlier that year. He says that it is time to harvest the cacique's fields, and a rabbit hunt for all the men is announced for the following day. The Shī'kame (Shai'yak) assists ceremonially in this, and all the game is taken to the cacique's home. On the second day, there is another hunt, this time both men and women participating. The women get the animals, and the first to reach either an animal or a man who has picked one up, gets it. Four days later this present is repaid by the woman's making a present, usually of corn meal, to the man, or men, from whom she received rabbits. On the third day, harvesting of the cacique's fields is begun. Men and women both go to the fields at this time. The men pick the ears from the stalks, and the women do the husking. After the corn is all picked, the men help the women finish the husking. It is taken to the Flint–Ku-sha'li house and laid out on the roof to dry. Members of the Women's Society examine the corn and take out all the perfect ears, the "ko'tona." Then the war captain tells the people they are free to harvest their own fields. The Conservatives wait for this permission; the Progressives no longer do, harvesting according to the condition of their crops. [42]

Although the war captain calls these rabbit hunts, such related points as giving permission to be absent from them come under the jurisdiction of either the Ku-sha'li or the Kwe'rana. The head of the supervising society which has held control during the year goes to the war captain soon after the last hunt. He says that his society has performed its duties for the good of the pueblo and that now it is time for some other group to do this. The war captain accepts this "resignation," and then goes to the head of the other society, informing him to tell his society members that they are to have charge of these matters for the good of the pueblo during the coming year. [88]

November

November 1. All Saints' Day. This day is celebrated with a Mass. In the afternoon, little cookies and other food are taken into the hills, "anywhere," and left there.

November 2. All Souls' Day. After the Mass, presents of food are made to the children, there is feasting in the homes, and gifts of food are brought to the church also. This is in the form of the *primicia,* or "offering of the first fruits." According to one source, the Spanish families generally contribute a dollar and a half, and some Indian families do the same, though there is no particular compulsion to pay anything.

In addition, gifts of corn or wheat are presented in honor of the dead to the Church, "the padres"; candy is given to the children. In former times, this grain was milled for use of the local priests, sold for necessary cash, or distributed to needy families. At present, the two latter uses are more common that the first. Formerly, food and other presents were placed on graves in the *Campo Santo* as "an offering to the spirits." [65]

The quantity of the gift varies according to the individual family's means; formerly, the standard of measurement was the *almor* (local variant of *almud*), seemingly about a twelfth of a *fanega* or bushel. The measure was described as a box ten inches square and four inches high. For wheat, the contents should be level; for corn or beans, the measure was heaping. This measure was formerly also the standard unit in sales or trades at the local trading posts. [65]

Goldfrank (1927: 74–75) provided additional material on the customs of November 2. The retreats of the medicine societies in a general purification of the whole tribe which she mentioned continue at the present time; other aspects mentioned have, for the most part, been lost.

December

December 13. Guadalupe's Day. Although the celebration of Guadalupe's Day is actually December 12, there is a postponement of one day at Cochití. Since Guadalupe is the Patroness of the Peña Blanca church and the priests are busy there on that day, the Cochití have their Mass and feasting in the homes of the Guadalupes on the following day. There are no rooster pulls, foot races, or present-throwing at this time.

December 25. Christmas. There are Christmas Eve and Christmas morning Masses; the remainder of the morning is occupied with feasting, visiting, and a celebration of the day much as it is observed by Spanish or Anglo families.

In the afternoon, there is dancing by both kiva memberships. Considerable variation is allowed. In his journal of December 21, 1885, Bandelier noted that there was to be a *Matachina* Dance on Christmas Day. It is interesting that in 1946 a *Matachina* Dance was presented by the Turquoise Kiva; it was noted that "this is the first time in over fifteen years we have had the *Matachinas*." [44, 45] In Parsons' Tewa study, she included two photographs of a Cochití *Matachina* as of "Christmas-tide, 1925" (1929: Plate 38*a, b*). (Other *Matachina* photographs of Parsons' are shown here as Plate 20.) For the Pumpkin side in 1946, there was a Buffalo Dance. In both 1947 and 1948, both kivas presented Buffalo Dances.

The writer was informed by Mr. Peter Kunstadter that in 1953 there had been animal dances by both kivas. They were described as composed essentially of the same number and types of "animals." In each case, there were two antelope, two deer, and two buffalo dancers accompanied by one *malinche*. An interesting innovation occurred when a red pickup truck was driven into the plaza midway through the dancing, and Santa Claus emerged. Kunstadter was told that this was the first time this had ever been seen at Cochití. As the pickup came to a halt, Santa jumped to the ground, greeted the officers, and began to distribute candy to the children, the dancers, and members of the chorus. Somewhat larger packages were distributed to various people gathered in the plaza to watch the dancing.

Christmas Season Dancing. During the afternoons of the four days following Christmas, the festive atmosphere is continued, with each kiva presenting a dance, normally no two alike, each day. These are looked upon more as recreational than religious, though the war captains continue to be in charge. Proof that these dances are looked upon with somewhat less reverence is seen in the fact that occasionally permission is granted by the war captains to photograph this dance. Except for this one series, photographing the dances is not allowed in the pueblo.

Bandelier, in an entry of December 26, 1885, described a dance, the "Ah-ta Tanyi." His detailed account of this has already been included (pp. 274–275). Comments by Ickes (1933: 207–208) confirm certain of the foregoing remarks for a period assumed to have been slightly prior to her date of publication. She referred to the Christmas ceremonies as "pleasure dances, not ritual." At the time of her visit at Cochití, three days after Christmas, the "dancers were out," both the Turquoise and the Squash (Pumpkin) people dancing. On this day, the Turquoise people presented a Comanche Dance. A long line of Plainslike warriors, including small children, danced. The other kiva had two lines of dancers, seemingly composed primarily of women, but "led by two large men dressed as women." On the side of their heads they wore the symbolic squash blossom made of yarn woven upon radiating sticks.

In 1946, the following dances were presented on the indicated dates (the dance of the Turquoise is listed first and that of the Pumpkin second, in each case): December 26—no dances were held out of respect for the death on December 23 of Trinidad Montoya, who had been very prominent in the tribal ceremonial life; December 27 —Buffalo and Mixed Animal dances; December 28—Parrot Dance and a six-man unmasked Acoma dance (see also p. 297) by the Turquoise and an Eagle Dance by the Pumpkins; December 29— Zuñi and Comanche dances.

In 1947, the following were presented: December 26—Comanche and Navaho Yeibeichai dances; December 27—Laguna and Taos dances; December 28—Bow and Hopi dances; and December 29— Jicarilla and Navaho dances.

Often, on the evenings of December 26 and 27, various dance groups go from house to house. [55]

December 29. This is the last of the four days of dancing after Christmas. Following the conclusion of the afternoon's dancing, the people go home. In the evening, there is the meeting of the adult males in the Turquoise community house, where they hear the medicine-society headmen announce their selections of the secular officers for the coming year.

While the foregoing listing and individual descriptions can be considered fairly complete, there are obviously omissions of what might occur in the course of any year. Considered as a whole, there is little doubt that the ceremonial calendar at Cochití is less full today than formerly. Equally certain is the fact that both in quantity and precise specifications, associated paraphernalia have been allowed to deteriorate. However, the calendar still occupies a major proportion of many individuals' time, thought, and energy, especially of the Conservatives; to a much lesser degree, the same is true for Progressives as well.

10 SOCIAL ORGANIZATION

Kinship Groupings

Family. Among the Cochití, the conjugal, or nuclear, family is the basic social unit. In spite of certain polygynous families in mythology (Benedict 1931: 60–62; and others), which defy explanation by present-day Cochití, they claim to have always been a monogamous people. No statement in the literature, aside from mythology, contradicts this claim.

While the family may be correctly considered as the base of social organization, it is rivaled in many instances by the household. Reflecting the matrilineal clan system, Cochití households have been traditionally matrilocal. However, with patrilineal moieties (kiva organizations) and Spanish and Anglo influences, this traditional dominance has been much less pronounced in recent decades. As of 1880, Bandelier (September 23, 1880) was told there were 60 to 70 *escaleras* at Cochití. This term, translated literally as "ladders," referred to families in the sense of households, often including grandparents and grandchildren. This term is no longer used. [92] In a later entry of November 5, 1880, shortly after the observances of All Souls' Day (pp. 363–364), Bandelier noted that *primicias* had been paid by 63 *escaleras.*

In his journal of November 26, 1880, Bandelier reported on a census taken by Andrés Cabeza de Vaca, assisted by José Hilario Montoya. The results listed 268 Indians, 54 houses, and 68 families, with one family refusing to co-operate. (Bandelier added that a similar census at Santo Domingo had shown 1,135 Indians, with 7 families not co-operating "despite the governor's accompanying him.") This suspicion and unwillingness to divulge personal information persists to the present time. The person, a Cochití, designated by the Indian Agency to report vital statistics complained that "there are a couple of families here at Cochití that won't tell you anything like that."

As of August, 1951, there were 92 households (one less than in 1948). For the most part, these consisted of the head of the house, his wife, and their children. Variations included one or two grandparents, paternal or maternal; stepchildren; grandchildren; siblings of either parent; and children of deceased siblings of either parent.

It is interesting that in his *Final Report* (1890: 142), Bandelier, speaking of the time of initial Spanish contact, stated, "The Pueblo Indians had in fact no home life." Explanation for this comment appears to lie in his discussion on pages 143–145 of the *Final Report,* where he repeated the commonly-held belief that, at least at the time of the Conquest, the men lived somewhat apart and concentrated their activities in their respective kivas, from which the women were more or less banned. (See Winship 1896: 520–521.)

If one may assume that this description was relatively accurate for the middle sixteenth century, it is interesting that today (and for some appreciable time into the past) the kivas are used at Cochití only for a very few days during any year, and there is little suggestion of sex segregation in their use.

Additional insight is obtained in observations from Starr's scrapbook of December 12, 1897, which resulted from his visits to Cochití late in the last century: "Among the Cochitis, the woman is boss. The high offices are held by men, but in the household and in the councils of the clans, woman is supreme. The 'new woman' is old among the Cochitis. She has been the arbiter of destinies of the tribe for centuries." In the same article, Starr related how he had been able to secure a plaster bust of one man "at the dictation" of his wife. Farther on, he refers to "Inez Moquino, wife of the war captain . . . but she is nevertheless ruler of the Cochitis."

In the writer's own experiences during field work, it was repeatedly observed that the women, while not actually holding formal office, were influential. In reference to one specific inquiry as to whether it would be permissible to do something, several men—council members, at that—stated without hesitation that they saw no reason for not doing it. "But don't let that old lady see you," they warned, pointing with their lips at a particular home. The implication was quite clear that if this woman had raised an objection, these officials would have been forced to rescind their permission.

The status and role of individual family members among the Cochití at present show many parallels with patterns among modern Anglo-American families. Both in comparative importance and in nature, changes in specific status attributes and role functions have undoubtedly occurred during recent decades. These changes can, in some instances, be correlated with shifts which have occurred in the clan and moiety (kiva) organizations, to be discussed later in this chapter. Lack of specific evidence makes it difficult to state with certainty whether the changes in family and those in clan-moiety aspects should be designated as cause or result. Since they are affiliated by their bearing on kinship, it appears wiser to consider them together and to attempt an analysis or hypothetical reconstruction of the over-all changes that have brought about the present situation.

Discounting the inevitable variations in unusual instances, the typical present-day Cochití family is characterized by a blend of four attributes, each of which becomes momentarily dominant in specific situations: father domination; equality of the father and mother; domination by the mother; and a rather consistent respect for any individual—old, middle-aged, or young. Throughout these interrelationships, there is a deference shown by younger individuals to those who are older, whether or not they are relatives. It would be misleading to single out any one attribute as "typical of the Cochití family."

So far as ownership is concerned, personal property is a well-recognized concept; fields and buildings may be owned by either sex. Produce from the fields formerly passed into the possession of the woman when it entered the home, but there has been an increasing shift in recent years for the men to retain possession of it. While in the past home ownership was largely by the women, men are becoming owners more and more commonly.

Disposal of possessions is predominantly a matter for the owner to decide. Considerable latitude is allowed children and young people, though older members of a family may intervene if they see that unfair advantage is being taken of a child. Occasionally, a child is permitted to go through with a disadvantageous exchange—"Then he'll be wiser the next time." [62, 88] (See Chap. 3.)

While co-operation among family members is still expected in many tasks of housekeeping or work in the fields and care of the live-stock, modern machinery and appliances are making it possible for smaller groups or even individuals to do the same amount of work in less time. Small children remain near the house, though they occasionally accompany their parents or others to the fields. Their activities include general play, with a common tendency to mimic the work of older persons. During the early years, little attention is paid to dividing up labor on the basis of sex; as the child grows older, usually at some time between six and ten years, it becomes important to adhere to activities assigned to the appropriate sex. Adult co-operation is shifting from former patterns based on clan affiliation to consanguineous ties and even ties of friendship, regardless of kinship. Assistance is given to those of genetic kinship as well as to those related by marriage. Whether these developments can be attributed to an increased adoption of Anglo-American ways or to the fact that the patrilineal moiety system has gradually equalled, or perhaps surpassed, the matrilineal clan system, is difficult to judge. Undoubtedly, the presence of both Spanish and Anglo influences and the presence of patrilineal moieties have served to facilitate the acceptance of additional stress upon the prominence of the male.

Activities relating to the community, whether political or ceremonial, are pursued by the individual with rather complete freedom from his family. He is encouraged but certainly not pressured to become a member of a society or to serve in some official capacity. Once he is involved, his goings and comings from such "business" are accepted with a minimum of inquisitiveness, at least overtly. An example of such personal independence was seen in the case of a tribal officer and society member who was unexpectedly wanted by one of the officials. When inquiry was made at the man's home, his family was completely unable to say where he was. It was later learned that he had left the village on a trip of several days' duration; he had considered himself under no obligation to inform anyone of his family, society, or tribal government that he was leaving. While this may represent a somewhat extreme instance, it illustrates the degree to which a person feels free to act. It was equally revealing that no member of this man's family, society, or the government expressed any real disapproval. When this point was queried, several replied that this had happened before—both in the case of this individual and also in the case of others—and there was really nothing unusual about it. [42, 45, 62, 88, 92]

Along similar lines, inquiry was made as to what answers were given by participants in Ka'tsīna or similar events when their children, or others, asked concerning their whereabouts after these persons had failed to sit with other family members or had failed even to appear among the spectators. The reply was, "They never ask about such things." While by comparison with attitudes in our own culture and at first thought such an attitude is somewhat surprising, it becomes more understandable when one remembers that household members are constantly leaving for, and arriving from, work in the fields, errands or visits to the homes of relatives, meetings of the council, officers, societies, and similar events. Despite the ideal of expressing no curiosity in the affairs of others, there would appear to be at least occasional deviations, especially by younger ones who are not yet enculturated. In such cases, the transgression may be countered by silence or by any number of evasive, yet momentarily satisfactory, replies which cumulatively may be calculated to discourage any tendency toward undue prying. That much of this is "ideal" rather than actual is seen in the statement (p. 289) that despite the fact Ka'tsīna affairs are only for cult members (excluding women), "the women are the first to know." [55]

In daily living, the family typically rises about six or seven o'clock; rising times vary with the seasons and according to plans for the specific day. Often one of the family will be up and about an hour or more before the others. Meals are eaten together unless a member needs to be elsewhere. Ideal behavior for children, young people, and adults is described in terms of "good manners." When asked to elaborate upon this concept, it was stated that one should show respect for his elders; he should work hard at the tasks given him and not be lazy; he should be helpful and co-operative without becoming meddlesome; he should avoid idle gossip; and he should respect property and privacy of others.

The Cochití would be among the first to deny that "Indian children are always well-behaved and do not need to be punished." Several factors should be mentioned in respect to disciplinary matters. To the outsider and particularly the casual visitor, the children invariably appear well-behaved. Children, especially the younger ones, are often somewhat overawed, though simultaneously curious, with strangers present; at times they may be bashful enough to leave, going to a nearby relative's home until the strangers depart. They may simply keep on with their routine play, in the process of which they are relatively unrestricted by the myriad "don'ts" often found in our culture. Reasons for fewer "don'ts" may be found in fewer items of the "untouchable" category; damaged surfaces of walls or floors are easily repaired; numerous and readily available siblings, cousins, or neighbors provide playmates and tend to reduce the individual child's desire or need for attention-demanding tantrums and other exhibitions. Older children assume many of the responsibilities of "baby-sitting," thereby freeing the adults for other activities.

These children do occasionally misbehave, however, and when they do, measures are taken to correct the transgression or prevent its recurrence. Ridicule may be directed at the child, at times severely and at some length, but generally effectively. If he acts with an outburst of temper, the mocking or taunting is merely increased or renewed. Such correctional means may be applied in the presence of comparative strangers. Cultural bogeys, such as the "River Men" (p. 338), are used as threats by parents and others. Corporal punishment, such as whipping with a strap or switch, is used for more extreme cases but rarely in the presence of nonfamily members—as is true in most families of our own culture.

Playmates are most often children of neighboring families, cousins, or siblings. Generally speaking, in a village of this size, most children are acquainted. If the occasion arises, they quickly join in play. On the other hand, there are certain children who are rather widely looked upon as "wild," or "rough," or "trouble-makers." Playing with these individuals is avoided whenever possible; if unavoidable, it is more closely supervised than usual by older people.

One final observation regarding the play, work, and other activities of children and their enculturation is that these processes are far more of a community matter than is typical in most segments of our culture. Instead of discipline or correction or effective supervision being limited to the immediate family, members not only of the extended family but of the entire community may participate. By presenting a virtually united front to the younger generations, the general standards of the adult generations are more effectively transferred and maintained. While this united front has been subjected to stress resulting from conflicts accompanying the accentuated changes of recent years and has been weakened accordingly, it is still of sufficient homogeneity to act as a community-wide reinforcement of family and household values. As illustrated in the discussion of the increasing ineffectiveness of the political system (pp. 220–226), the more pronounced changes of recent decades are having their effect upon the organization of the Cochití family and household in its task of enculturation.

As of August, 1951, a census showed a tribal total of 438 persons —226 males and 212 females. (In 1948, there were 423 persons—217 males and 206 females; see Appendix 2 for other census data.) The average household size was 4.76 persons (compared with 4.55 in 1948), with a range of from one to ten members and in no case including more than three generations.

Further analysis of the population and family data revealed that 155 individuals did not regularly reside in the pueblo. Of the 283 who lived in the village (as compared with 313 in 1948), the average household size was 4.17 persons with 68 units being counted.

In comparing these data for the two years 1951 and 1948, several important points became clear. While the Cochití as a tribe had a steady increase, the actual pueblo community had numerically decreased. Analysis of those remaining in the pueblo indicated a high percentage of small children and a gradually shrinking core of the older generations. The exodus had occurred primarily among the young and middle-aged adults; repercussions of their leaving have become apparent in not only social organization but in political, ceremonial, and other phases of the culture as well.

From gathering data on kinship terminology and from remarks made by numerous informants, it was clear that the Cochití family, both in its use of native terminology and adopted Spanish and English terminology and in the conceptual shifts accompanying these usages, had become increasingly closer to the neighboring non-Indian family. This change is illustrated in the contrast between the present discussion—an entire subsection devoted to a consideration of the family—and the published literature on Cochití which all but ignores the family while emphasizing discussions of clan and moiety. At the same time, accounts of the clan are essentially unanimous in pointing out the declining significance of the clan structure at Cochití. It is evident that as this decline has continued, the family has become increasingly important. With a steadily-growing proportion of the Cochití being educated away from the pueblo, finding employment away from the village, and marrying individuals who have no kinship affiliations which fit into the traditional structure of the tribe, it is not surprising that this change in emphasis has occurred.

Clan. The Cochití clan (ha'no) is essentially a kinship group, being matrilineal and exogamous; residence, as noted, tends to be matrilocal—especially in the early months after marriage. The clans are named after plants, animals, and natural phenomena such as the sun, water, and turquoise. No ideas of "totemic" relationships are involved, and no taboos of food or other usages are observed. There appear to be, or to have been, few clan rituals or officers in special capacities dependent upon clan affiliation. An occasional clan adoption or a clan curing rite is still held, and it is customary to refer to the oldest woman of a clan as its "head." This "headship" is virtually nonfunctional aside from a slight prestige (slight in the sense that few Cochití know what clans are still extant and whatever deference is paid comes from the recognition given to age) and some responsibility in the occasional clan rituals.

In his entry of October 7, 1880, Bandelier noted that the clan name was a person's *"apelativo,"* observing that children obtained it from their mother and not the father. In an entry on October 16, he noted that "then came Agustín 'Yaqqua' [Corn Clan]."

At present, except for that of a diminishing number of older people, especially women, relatively little interest is shown in clan personnel, structure, or functions. In the literature describing this aspect some decades back, clan matters have considerably more prominence. Even though this may have resulted from an artificially imposed emphasis reflecting anthropological interests, this former importance is attested to by present-day Cochití as well.

One of the earliest listings of Cochití clans is that contained in Bandelier's journal of October 7, 1880:

In Cochiti, a gens, Coyote, "Shu-tsuna"; a gens, maize, "Yaga." Water, "Tzitz"; calabash, "Tañe"; sun, "Oshatch"; encina [oak], "Ha-pañee"; "Shipewe" [a kind of sage]; turquoise, "Shu-amo"; light [fire (92)], "Ha-kañeh." These *"generaciones"* have their *principales,* which are tacitly acknowledged on account of their age and experience. They have nothing to do with the government proper. . . . The *principales* of the *"gentes"* call together their male members for the dances. Thus the *gentes* come in still. Those of the same name cannot marry, even if they do not live in the same pueblo.

Other clans recorded elsewhere in Bandelier's journal include Yssi or yedra (Ivy); Huashpa, or chamiza (Mexican Sage); Hiithsha-añy

(cottonwood); and Ho-goqqa, or *Tortolita* (Dove). It is interesting
that Bandelier used the term "gens," though he was clearly aware of
the matrilineal descent; he may well have been following the terminology of Morgan in his *Ancient Society* (1877). Of even greater
significance is Bandelier's reference to the older males of the various
clans as *principales*, with the added note on their association with
ceremonial leadership. If this was true in Bandelier's time and not
merely his transference of this pattern from some culture such as the
Iroquois or Hopi, it is noteworthy that this aspect of clan function
has been entirely lost to modern Cochití, not only in practice but
even in the realm of traditional knowledge.

Another roster of clans was compiled by Bandelier about 1882,
though it was not published until 1890 (*Final Report*: 273). Included
were the following: Sun, Water, Cottonwood, Turquoise, Panther,
Bear, Calabash, Mexican Sage, Coyote, Corn, Scrub-oak, Fire, and
Ivy. However, he recognized this as probably incomplete since the
census on which it was based was only a partial one.

Another early listing of clans was done by Bourke in 1881 (Bloom
1938: 235). In gathering these data, Bourke noted that the governor
was very reluctant to discuss "Janos," but he succeeded in obtaining
the following list from the lieutenant governor: Huacamayo or Si-
Shi-wati (Macaw); Melon (Ish-hanni); Eagle; Sol (Sun); Agua
(Water); Encina (Oak); Verenda (Antelope); Tejon (Badger);
Maiz (Corn); Oso (Bear); Turkey; and Coyote—with an added
comment that neither Snake nor Frog was present.

When Starr (1899: 42–43) took his complete census of Cochití on
September 28, 1897, the following data on clans were obtained:

Eleven clans exist today at Cochiti according to this census. Their English names in the order given above are calabash, scrub-oak, water, cottonwood, coyote, Mexican sage, sun, ivy, turquoise, sage (Shipewe), maize.
Comparing this list with the one given by Bandelier we fail to find three
that he names—panther, bear, fire. On the other hand he fails to name one
that occurs here—probably "Shipewe"—"a kind of sage." Santiago Quintana says he does not think there has been a clan of the panther, or of the
bear; at all events there have been no such within his memory. He has
known several that have died within that period—viz.: Kūtz (wood),
Hā-kū-ni (fire), and Kīr-shrā (elk).

Dumarest (1919), writing as of the end of the last century, did not
compile a clan roster, but his notes included mention of the Sun,
Water, Fire, Eagle, Antelope, and Rattlesnake clans.

Hodge (1907: I: 318) listed the following clans for Cochití: Sun, Water, Cottonwood, Turquoise, Mountain Lion, Bear, Calabash, Coyote, Oak, Corn, and Fire. He listed as extinct: Eagle, Turkey, Antelope, Dance-kilt, and Reindeer (?). (Elk) In addition, Hodge noted that Bandelier named Ivy and Mexican Sage as present.

As of the early 1920's, Goldfrank (1927: 15) made the following statements regarding Cochití clans: "The clans existing at Cochití today are Oak, Cottonwood, Corn, Coyote, Turquoise, Ivy, Squash, Cipewe, Sage, Water. The Sun clan, mentioned by Starr in his census, has since become extinct, the last surviving male having died in August, 1921."

Cochití data gathered for Curtis (1926: 85–86) revealed that, as of 1924, the following clans existed: Sun, Turquoise, Water, Shipewe, Ear-corn, Eagle, Scrub-oak, Sage, Coyote, Cottonwood, Squash, and Mustard. His information indicated that the Ear-corn (Corn) Clan was very near extinction, having only two members, therein agreeing with Goldfrank's findings. Curtis felt that the clan Bandelier recorded as Ivy should have been the Mustard Clan. However, Bandelier's Ivy was later confirmed by both Starr in 1897 and Goldfrank in 1923, as well as by my own data for 1947–1952. On an ethnobotanical trip, one informant identified a poison-ivy plant as the one bearing the same name as the clan. [3] [No other source listed Mustard as a Cochití clan, though White (1935: 71) listed it for Santo Domingo and Hodge (1907: II: 433), for San Felipe.] Curtis listed the Fire, Elk, Turkey, Antelope, and Cougar clans as extinct. The fact that he did not include Sun as extinct probably indicates that these lists were compiled for Curtis early in the 1920's—in view of Goldfrank's notation on that clan. His informants said the Bear and Rattlesnake clans had never been at Cochití. Curtis corrected Hodge's Dance-kilt Clan as being the Sage Clan; "Kàspa" (the wide white cotton belt) had been confused with "Waspa" (sage), according to Curtis.

In 1947–1952, my informants listed the following clans: Antelope (Kutz), Bear (Ko'hai-o), Corn (Ya'ak), Cottonwood (Hī'tra-añī), Coyote (Shrū'tzūna), Dove (Hū'ka), Ivy (I'sī), Oak (Ha'pañī), Pumpkin (Da'ñī), Red Shell (Yarch), Sage (Huash'pa), Shī'pewe (a kind of sage), Sun (O'shatsh), Turkey (Tzī'na), Turquoise (Sho'ame), and Water (Tzitz). Of these, the Dove, Sun, and Turkey clans were extinct. The Dove had been represented only by Juan Bautisto Valencia and Lorenzo Valencia, brothers and natives of San Felipe who had married into Cochití. (Juan had belonged to the

Turquoise Kiva and Lorenzo, to the Pumpkin. [3]) Of the existing clans, the Antelope is represented by Ivan Lewis, an Acoma married to a Cochití; the Bear is represented by Philip Cooka, a Hopi who married in; and the Red Shell, by Juan Velasquez, another San Felipe married to a Cochití. [16, 44, 45]

Efforts to determine true names of clans were only partially successful. "Corn" is correct rather than "Ear-corn"; "Cottonwood" refers to the species which grows along the river (Hī'tra-añī) rather than the mountain cottonwood, or aspen (Hī'ash-kūlī). "Coyote" is the correct clan name; "shrū'tzūna" means "coyote" rather than "fox," the skin of which is used in many dance costumes. The fox is designated as "Blue (grey?) Fox," or "kwirsh'ke-shē shrū'tzūna." Bourke (Bloom 1938: 223) raised this same question regarding the Coyote Clan at Jemez, concluding, however, that it must have actually been "Fox."

"Pumpkin" is used consistently by informants in preference to "Squash," which has been a common designation for both the clan and moiety in many Pueblo ethnographies and actual local vernacular. However, from an ethnobotanical viewpoint, "Pumpkin" appears to be the more accurate designation. (This opinion is shared by Donald D. Brand, according to a conversation of November, 1947.)

All other clans mentioned in the various ethnographic reports have been checked with my informants. With the exceptions of the Dove, Sun, and Turkey clans, already mentioned as extinct, they disclaimed knowledge of any clans at Cochití other than those they named as present today. Until prompted, they excluded those brought in from other pueblos by the three men (Antelope, Bear, and Red Shell), an omission perhaps reflecting an attitude which may account for certain discrepancies in earlier lists. In compiling this list of clans, it was revealing that a majority of the informants needed prompting before a complete roster could be made. (Comparative clan rosters are found in Appendix 29.)

Here again was clear evidence of the decline of clans in the consciousness of the Cochití as a tribe. Several others stated they knew little or nothing of clans and preferred to talk about other topics. This, it should be pointed out, was not the reluctance to discuss clans which was noted by Bourke; rather, it was a lack of interest and knowledge in clan matters and clan affiliations. The Cochití admitted that knowledge of clan membership is possessed by a relatively few people, most of whom were then more than fifty years old. Others whose age is that of this older group and almost all of the younger generations do not know even their own clan affiliations. [16, 18, 44, 45, 49, 52, 70, 92]

The decline of clan significance is not a particularly new development, but it has become accelerated in recent years. Dumarest (1919: 147), at the end of the last century, recognized that clan exogamy was occasionally breached. Starr (1899: 43–44) noted four intraclan marriages. These, he said, occurred in the Cottonwood and Ivy clans, two in each. The Ivy cases, however, were due to an error in recording; in each instance, the wives—Lupita Archibeque and Maria Ignacia Archibeque, sisters—were actually members of the Water Clan. [44, 53] Starr's comments remain pertinent, nevertheless:

> Several times in the tables . . . we observe a striking fact, the marriage of members of the same clan. Such a thing was not tolerated under the old system. . . . The sanction of the new creed has here broken down the ancient barrier. Membership in one clan is not necessarily relationship so close as to fall under the ban of the Church of Rome. The Indian yields to the church decision and to inclination and the wedding takes place.

In the partial census made by Goldfrank, additional deviations from strict clan exogamy were noted. Goldfrank (1927: 12) summarized her findings as follows:

> Clan exogamy is still an all important feature of the social organization. I have noted a number of cases of intermarriage within the clan, as has also Professor Starr. From these few cases it is hard to determine whether they are the result of the lessening of clan feeling or merely the accidents that are bound to occur in any community. . . . On the whole, I believe, the villagers are very conscious of the exogamic law and very anxious to adhere to it.

Curtis (1926: 86) merely commented that Cochití clans were exogamous and matrilineal, but "the rule of exogamy is in abeyance." Data gathered during the period 1947–1952 indicated a continuation of the findings of earlier investigators. (See Appendix 30 for a comparison of 1897 and 1948 interclan marriages.) Occasional exceptions to clan exogamy appear to be what Goldfrank termed "merely the accidents that are bound to occur in any community." In an effort to obtain material from as far back as possible, I examined the records kept by the Franciscan Fathers at Peña Blanca. Marriages recorded there were later checked with informants to ascertain clan affiliations. Baptism (and birth) records provided the ages of individuals who participated in intraclan marriages. (For the compiled list, see Appendix 31.)

This list includes 16 marriages involving clan endogamy. Of the 16 cases, all but one were recorded by the priests at Peña Blanca. This one marriage occurred earlier than any other marriage listed here, but it is also true that as of that time the Church records were quite incomplete. As of 1948, there were records of 428 marriages, including an estimated 50 between a Cochití and a non-Cochití. (Appendix 32 presents an analysis of these marriages.)

Of the 379 marriages involving two Cochití, clan affiliations for both man and woman could be learned for only 195 marriages. It is obvious that 16 known breaches of clan exogamy constitute a small proportion (8.2 per cent) of the total marriages for which both persons' clan is known. These intraclan marriages have occurred at intervals varying from three to sixteen years, with no obvious clustering at any one period of time.

A consideration of the persons involved in the 16 intraclan marriages reveals several interesting facts. Seven occurred in the Oak Clan; 5, in the Cottonwood; 3, in the Sage; and 1, in the Water Clan. The 3 Sage marriages occurred between 1904 and 1915 in unbroken sequence. Intraclan marriages between 1918 and 1947 have been exclusively Oak affairs with the exception of 1 Cottonwood marriage in 1929. Four other Cottonwood marriages comprised all endogamous marriages from about 1857 to 1892, except for the 1 Water endogamous marriage in 1874.

Of the 7 Oak marriages, 2 involved women from San Ildefonso who had joined the Oak Clan upon their arrival in Cochití. Two involved sons of two other women from San Ildefonso who also had joined the Oak people. Thus, relationships in these cases were obviously quite distant. Two other Oak marriages involved daughters of families recognized as Progressives. The husbands in these cases were brothers and veterans of the Second World War. Both men participated in ceremonials with the Conservatives, and the two marriages occurred in the postwar years 1945 and 1947.

Of the 5 Cottonwood marriages, that of 1857 involved the parents of Ignacia Montoya, who in 1892 also married within her clan. Her husband, Juan Pedro Melchior, became a leader in the Progressive movement, and in turn, his son, Joe Melchior, has been a Progressive for many years. Joe's daughter, Caroline, a member of the Oak Clan through her mother who came to Cochití from San Ildefonso, married another Oak member, José Dolores Pecos, in 1947, the last marriage referred to at the close of the preceding paragraph.

Although it would seem from the foregoing data that it has been members of the Progressives who have been involved in intraclan marriages, this impression is not supported by the evidence. Cleto Urina was a Kwe'rana Society member, as was Lucia Romero; José Nicanor Cordero has been Head Shrū'tzī for many years. Diego Arquero was a member of the *Principales* and was active in the Turquoise Kiva; Miguel Ortiz and his wife, Zeferina, were both Kwe'-rana; Manuel Ortiz was Head Shī'kame and a member of Kwe'rana; his wife, Victoria Martinez, was Ku-sha'lī; Pasqual Suina was active in Pumpkin Kiva ceremonies, serving as a drummer at the time of his death; Salvador Arquero is a member of the *Principales* and an active participant in Pumpkin Kiva ceremonies; Ricardo Chávez joined the Ku-sha'lī shortly before his death; Damasio Quintana and his wife, Cresencia Arquero, are both active members of the Turquoise Kiva; and Aloysius Pecos and José Dolores Pecos are both active in the Pumpkin Kiva.

In view of these data, Bandelier's comment (1890: 140) that the Christian rites of marriage and baptism tend to destroy the clans, which "are now merely a survival" is of particular interest when one considers the time it was written. Starr's observation, "The Indian yields to the church decision and to inclination and the wedding takes place" and Goldfrank's "On the whole, I believe, the villagers are very conscious of the exogamic law and very anxious to adhere to it" quite accurately summarize contemporary attitudes regarding clans and marriage. If any modifications of these statements are warranted, they are first in Starr's feeling about the complete impossibility of such marriages "under the old system" and second in the emphasis with which Goldfrank said the Cochití regard clan exogamy. There are increasingly fewer individuals who know the clan affiliations of others in the pueblo; nevertheless, there are enough whose attitudes are respected for clan exogamy to continue as the common practice. The available marriage records indicate that deviations are not appreciably more prevalent at present than they have been at any time in the past. (See Appendix 32.)

Another basic factor to be considered is the effects of this numerical strength of the various clans upon the potential choice of mate open to the individual. A comparison of clan strengths as noted by Starr and as determined for 1948 is contained in Appendix 33.

If we keep in mind the dates of the intraclan marriages, Starr's view that these had occurred within the larger clans where it was possible to have endogamous marriages and still not violate Catholic marriage laws is confirmed by figures computed by Starr and those of the present writer. The influx of San Ildefonso people and their joining the Oak Clan (and in most instances, the Pumpkin Kiva) at Cochití resulted in such a notable increase that it has been the largest of Cochití clans for several decades. (The arrival of the Martinez, Peña, and Roybal families from San Ildefonso about 1910 is but one instance of interpueblo migrations. In this case, as in others, the people moved to a tribe of distinctly divergent linguistic affiliation. Although they are undated, there appear to have been still earlier movements of relatives of these people to Cochití; in general, their reception among the Cochití has been very cordial. [44, 45, 55])

In 1948, the Cottonwood Clan, with the second highest number of intraclan marriages, was the third largest clan; at the time most of these marriages occurred, however, the Cottonwood was the largest clan of the pueblo. The second largest clan in 1948, the Sage, has had the third highest number of endogamous marriages, and the Water Clan, fourth largest in 1948 though not as large formerly, had had one intraclan marriage.

Goldfrank (1927: 9) was told that at Santo Domingo, in addition to the rule of clan exogamy, there were rules against marriage between members of the Turquoise and Pumpkin clans. Her informant said that no such rule existed at Cochití (as did mine [55]), though Goldfrank found no such marriage at the time of her stay at Cochití. She did find one instance of such a marriage in Starr's census, but a check with one of my own informants indicated that Starr's identification was erroneous, the man actually being Oak (Ha'pañi) instead of Pumpkin (Da'ñi). [3] Thus, so far as is known, there has been no intermarriage between the Turquoise and Pumpkin clans at Cochití. Goldfrank (1927: 13) commented further on clan marriage:

I noted upwards of one hundred and fifty names with clans, and from these it would seem that there is no objection to marriage into any of the clans, except one's own. However, often preferences arose in families and we find several members of one family marrying related members of another clan, or a man picking his second wife from the clan to which his first wife belonged. This is, however, unconnected with any idea of levirate or sororate, but rather, as occurs in our own culture, is the result of a previous intimate relation with a certain family.

In examining family records accumulated through a study of the Church records for Cochití, ample supporting evidence for Gold-frank's views was found. It was clear that there was some tendency for two clans to become intertwined in succeeding-generation marriages. (See Appendix 34.) However, as Goldfrank stated, there was no evidence of a sororate or a levirate in any form. Likewise, there was no tendency for preferred marriages between certain clans. Further, there was no restriction against marrying into the clan of one's father, despite the matrilineal system, such as White (1942: 153) found at Santa Ana. White noted, "Marriage into the father's clan was said to be 'all right if she (he) is not too close to you,' by most of the informants. One informant said, 'they ought not to do it but some of them do.'"

In her other remarks concerning clans, Goldfrank pointed out that at Cochití, the clans, in contrast to those among the Western Pueblos, had little or nothing to do with ceremonial life. (In this respect, the comments of Bandelier [p. 374] are of interest.) Goldfrank believed that the degeneration of the clans had perhaps been hastened by the "newer Mexican and white influence." She learned that clans were still functioning in ceremonial cures. In cases of persistent, but not virulent, illnesses, a woman of a strong clan was chosen as a ceremonial mother. Usually her husband, normally of another clan, became the ceremonial father. In this way, the patient acquired a special relationship with these two clans, though retaining his relationship to the clan of his birth. Goldfrank (1927: 8, 118) was told that clan cures were to obtain greater security for the individual and with less expense than if medicine men were called. She listed eight individuals who had experienced clan cures. The ceremony involved was described as essentially the same as that when an actual clan adoption is made.

If one attempts to delineate the two ceremonies more precisely, the following distinctions may be drawn. A clan cure may be requested by anyone; the person experiencing this rite retains his original clan affiliation and acquires those of his sponsors in addition. Following a curing rite, a woman's children inherit only her original clan membership and not those derived from the curing ceremony. [42, 44, 45] An adoption is possible only for those who have no previous clan affiliation or none of significance among the Cochití. In such cases—normally limited to women—her offspring inherit this clan designation from her.

My informants knew of the eight cures listed by Goldfrank, but they could add very few from recent years. Clan cures, with the approximate date of their occurrence, included the following: Cresencia Arquero Quintana (Oak), by Victoria Quintana Pecos (Oak) and her husband, Epifanio Pecos (Ivy), 1952; Genevieve Pecos (Oak), by Margaret Ortiz Quintana (Water) and her husband, Geronimo Quintana (Oak), 1951; Martina Herrera (Cottonwood), by Reyes Quintana Romero (Oak) and her husband, Vicente Romero (Sage), about 1948; and Pasqual Suina (Oak), by Felipita Herrera Trujillo (Coyote) and her husband, Pablo Trujillo (Turquoise), also about 1948. It is interesting that in two of the four cases, the clan of the patient was the same as that of one of the sponsors. It would appear that perhaps half of the potential benefit to be derived from these cures was knowingly waived!

These rites are held at the home of the sponsors; if the sponsors are not wife and husband, they generally take place at the woman's home, unless such practical matters as better facilities favor the man's home. [3, 42, 44] The procedure followed in these recent cures was, briefly, described as follows. After some period of generally poor health, the patient informed her father that she would like to have a curing rite held for her. The father, agreeing that this was a good idea, called a meeting of various relatives (specifically stated to have included siblings and *padrinos* but not members of the clan at large) for the relatives to concur. In a few weeks there was a second meeting, at which corn meal was presented to the agreed-upon sponsors, who in this case happened to be a married couple. "They had to say 'Yes.'" The husband, upon agreeing to serve, stated that the curing ceremony would be held the following autumn, approximately a year after the initial request had been made.

The man and his wife then called a meeting of their respective clan members. The request was relayed to them, properly sanctified with corn meal. If members had failed to appear at this meeting, they would have been approached individually the day after and informed of the matter. The following autumn, an announcement was made one evening, four days ahead of the scheduled cure.

On the set day, members of both sponsoring clans gathered at the sponsors' home; members of the patient's clan gathered at her home.

"Big *fiestas* were made." When the sponsors were ready, they took the patient to their home. The sponsors and all their clan members joined in washing the patient's head. All these people also brought presents for her—corn, rabbits, melons, "anything to eat."

Then the two clans returned the patient to her own home and relatives; from there, additional food was taken back to the sponsors' home and the sponsoring clans had a final feast. In general, this is the routine followed, though if the patient is considered to be in somewhat more critical condition (and yet not requiring attention from the medicine societies), the interval between the request and the curing may be appreciably shortened. [42, 92] The patient's status, following such a ceremony, was defined in the words of one informant: "If an Ivy is cured by Sage and Oak, he is still Ivy—but also he is a 'little' Sage and a 'little' Oak. Later if a Pumpkin asks the Sage or the Oak to be cured, then the Ivy who is 'little' Sage or Oak goes along to help out." [92]

An interesting comparison, involving a generation's difference in time, is revealed in a description of a clan adoption found in Boas' 1921/22 field notes (Book IX: 992). Since this has not been published, the notes are presented here in essentially complete form:

When a person wants to give his child to another clan, he first invites his own relatives and then the man and his wife who are to adopt the child. When they are all in, the father of the child delivers a speech and says: "Father and Mother, we have invited you and you have come; we will tell you our wishes. We want to give our child to you, to your clan (naming the man), and to that of your wife. You will wash his head and body. Then our child will be known as your child and your clan's child."

The couple reply: "It is well. We are glad to accept him as our child, and we will wash his head and his body. We are going to invite both our clans."

Then the day for the invitation is agreed upon. The ceremony must be performed in the fall of the year. They are given corn meal (ckilena) in a husk, and the couple take it home. When the formal adoption has been celebrated, the woman who is to adopt the child goes in the evening to all the houses of her clan and to those of her husband's. She tells them that they are going to adopt a child and that they are going to wash his head and that it will be a child of the clan. While delivering this speech, she gives to each person some sacred meal and she announces the child's name and clan and tells them that this is done according to the wish of the child's parents in order to secure health and long life for the child. Then everyone takes some of the sacred meal and goes out of doors and throws it as a sacrifice to the Kopictaya.

The actual day for the adoption is always set in fall after the harvest. A man belonging either to the father's or mother's clan is sent out to gather soapweed. A woman is selected to give a pottery tub in which the child will be washed. One woman must give a belt, another a water jar, still another one a cooking vessel, still another one a pottery pan. The man to whom the child is given must give a pair of shoes to it. If it is a girl, she is given a manta. After the child has been washed, it is dressed by the couple who adopt it. After sunset, the child is taken into the house. The child is placed in the middle of the house and is given presents of corn and other small objects. In the evening before sunset the child is taken to the kopictaya who are asked to give it health. Then the parents of the child give a feast.

The child continues to live with its own parents. He does not really belong to the clan into which he has been adopted; he remains a child of his own clan, but he is called child (s'ahwicye) by the members of the new clan into which he has been adopted. This is done principally to secure good health for the child.

Other clan ceremonialism, as noted by Goldfrank, has practically disappeared. Kick-stick races have moved from clan participation to an event in which the two kiva groups, or moieties, take part. Also, "There is no direct relation between clan and society membership, but there is a tendency for members of a family to affiliate with the same society." (Goldfrank 1927: 10) These observations still hold true at Cochití, as is shown in society rosters in the various appendices.

The following statement of Goldfrank (1927: 9) has already been commented upon in the chapters on economics: "The clans are again important when they are called upon as a whole by an individual to assist in his planting, harvesting, plastering, house building, grinding." Briefly, as the waning importance of the clan has been replaced by the family, we see again in the pueblo an increasing similarity to Spanish and Anglo family structure. When projects mentioned by Goldfrank are to take place, it is no longer the members of a clan, but rather the members of the extended family that co-operate and from whom reciprocal co-operation is expected. In addition to one's own parents, siblings, or grandparents, the extended family often includes the *padrinos* acquired in the Catholic rites of baptism and marriage. The *padrinos* may or may not be the same in both ceremonies; while they are often selected from members of the family, and even from the same clan, this is by no means a prerequisite. In this regard, it is interesting to speculate on whether the Spanish and Catholic role of *padrino* has not slowly but surely displaced the clan role of responsibility, mutual aid, and general significance. (Similar developments have been noted elsewhere, perhaps most clearly by Spicer [1940] in his Yaqui study of Pascua.)

To summarize the data on clans, it is evident that clan exogamy is still largely adhered to by the Cochití. However, a steadily increasing proportion of the Cochití have no knowledge of, and generally little interest in, their clan structure. Those older individuals who do know have sufficient influence to maintain clan exogamy except for a few cases, a situation which has existed for many decades, possibly centuries—even when clan matters were of greater general importance. More profound changes, at present not much more than indicated, are to be expected. These will occur after the deaths of the older people who have insisted on traditional clan exogamy and to an even greater extent will result from the growing tendency of Cochití men to marry women whose clans have not existed at Cochití, or, as in the case of several others, to marry women who have had no clan and, hence, their children have no clans. Thus, in future marriages, the incest rules of Catholicism will increasingly be the determinants of marriage rather than tribal customs. As outside employment is sought in preference to economic effort within the pueblo, and as outside formal education is sought in preparation for such employment, more contacts will be made with non-Cochití people. Clan rules of marriage, and clans themselves, will continue to hold less and less significance for the Cochití.

Kinship Terminology

In his *Havasupai Ethnography*, Spier (1928: 213) opened his discussion of kinship with the following observations:

> The individual is oriented among his tribesmen by his relationships. His family is for him a group of kinsmen; beyond them are more distant relatives and in the outer circle the unrelated members of the tribe.

> To the question who are kinsmen the answer comes patly enough, blood relatives, but blood relatives are always a group defined by arbitrary limits.

The contrasts between Havasupai and Cochití structures—patrilineal versus matrilineal, polygamous versus monogamous, and family alone versus family, clan, and moiety—do not negate the pertinence of Spier's comments to Cochití social organization and kinship terminology.

Eggan (1950: 10) has provided the following appraisal of kinship systems:

> The kinship system consists of socially recognized relations between individuals who are genealogically and affinally connected, plus the set of social usages which normally prevails among them. . . . Between each pair of relatives there are rights and duties which define their relation; these relations are usually organized in such a way that they are consistent with one another and result in a minimum of conflict under ordinary circumstances. . . . From this standpoint the emphasis on terms of relationship as strictly linguistic phenomena is not warranted.

Since, as the comments of both Spier and Eggan indicate, a kinship system is an arbitrarily (i.e., culturally rather than naturally) established and socially recognized facet of culture, it can, and does, change in ways similar to and reflecting those ways in which the culture itself is changing. With the changes described in the economic, political, and ceremonial phases of Cochití culture and with the changes that have occurred in the family and clan concepts of the Cochití people, it is not surprising to find changes in kinship terminology, changes in the usage of these terms, and changes in the associated attitudes.

Kinship terms were collected, somewhat haphazardly, but never published by Bandelier. Organized presentations were made by Curtis (1926), Goldfrank (1927), and Parsons (1932), though most of Parsons' data were based upon Goldfrank's material. Additional terms were found in Boas' unpublished field notes for 1921/22. I gathered additional data during field work from 1947 to 1952. In the earlier part of the work, I intentionally avoided close consultation with published terminology; at the end of it, alternative terms and other discrepancies were specifically checked with several informants. Appendix 35, based on data gathered in 1947/48, provides comparisons of terms published by Curtis, Goldfrank, and Parsons and those gathered by myself.

An important feature which is not readily apparent from data in Appendix 35 should be noted. In attempts to obtain terminology, it proved most difficult to get terms for relatives beyond the range of the nuclear family and grandparents from informants less than fifty years old. Terms for more distant relatives are little known: "I get all mixed up on those things because we just use Spanish or English now." Thus, the greatest portion of the 1947–1952 data was obtained from a few informants and they were more than fifty years old; some individuals in even this age group seemed to have inadequate knowledge in this realm. In order to substantiate or disprove this impression, it would be extremely worth while to conduct a survey among those who were largely ignored in the present study because of their reputedly incomplete knowledge. Such a survey would ascertain the precise degree and nature of these inadequacies, and it is highly probable that the study, in itself, would be revealing as to the type and amount of change occurring in the kinship system.

After analyzing my 1947/48 data, Eggan (March 15, 1949) commented as follows: "In general, my guess is that Cochiti once had a kinship structure based on the matrilineal lineage and household, but that it has been the most acculturated [of the Keresans] toward Tewa and/or Spanish patterns."

Evidences of the transition referred to by Eggan are seen in the use of Spanish terms, such as *"bisavuelo"* (greatgrandfather), and hybrid terms, such as "momo *avuelo.*" Goldfrank and Parsons listed "mumu" for both grandfather and greatgrandfather, male speaking. In his journal of October 22, 1880, Bandelier gave "sa-na-uma-qqo" for this term and "sa-na-papa-sse" for greatgrandmother. Present-day informants claimed to be completely unfamiliar with both terms.

The tendency to reduce the number, or variety, of terms is also apparent in reference to other relatives, such as uncles, aunts, and cousins. "Sa'oshē," used traditionally by either parent in reference to either a son or a daughter, is now applied to both parallel and cross-cousins, reckoning bilaterally. (See Appendix 36 for details.) The terms "wa'tī" and "pī'hīᵃ,"—brother- and sister-in-law, respectively —are being increasingly applied to any in-law, again bilaterally reckoning. In this reduction of terms, or shift from denotative to classificatory emphasis, the process has included both a redefinition of native terminology and a replacement of alien (Spanish or English) terms. The terms "aunt," "uncle," and similar ones are becoming increasingly common, not only in conversations with non-Cochiti but among themselves.

The process of simplification, or redefinition, may be merely an elaboration of a long-standing custom—that of using the specific terms for "mother" or "father" as an expression of respect when referring to any person older than the speaker. If the ages of the speaker and the person addressed are considerably different, or if the speaker wishes to emphasize his respect, the terms for "grandfather" or "grandmother" are similarly employed. In more recent times, these terms have been used in situations calling for general respect for one's elders and also in referring to the siblings of one's parents who were formerly addressed by denotative terms. [25, 88, 92]

Still another result of acculturative influences accompanying the decline in the clan structure has been the retraction of kinship terms referring to more distant relatives. Another shift, again reflecting the diminishing emphasis upon matrilineal clans and the corresponding elevation in the importance of patrilineal aspects, is the extension of terminology applicable to the mother's clan members to include those of the father's clan as well—but only within the more restricted range already noted for the mother's clan members.

Finally, a characteristic most apparent at present and presumably absent or at least much less prominent in times past is the widespread confusion and disagreement regarding the proper application and range of inclusion of specific terms. (See Appendix 36.) This situation, as it continues and expands, can only result in the further disintegration of the traditional system and the concomitant acquisition of features from the Anglo-American system.

Non-Kin Groupings

Moieties. One would normally expect moieties to be included in the discussion of groupings based upon kinship. (According to Lowie [1940: 547] a moiety is "one of two intermarrying exogamous tribal halves, either undivided or comprising lesser clans. Sometimes the term is applied to the clearly defined half of a tribe irrespective of marriage regulations.") At Cochití, the two moieties—the kiva groups, Turquoise (Sho'ame) and Pumpkin (Da'ñī)—have social, political, and religious significance. Their political and ceremonial aspects have been discussed in previous chapters. As social groupings, the two moieties, as was formerly true of the series of clans, included all members of the tribe as well as those people who had married into Cochití and were participating in the life of the pueblo. Most informants could give the kiva group ("side") to which any person in the pueblo belonged, a situation which differed markedly from that in regard to clan affiliations.

However, in analyzing the moiety affiliations of the entire population, it is evident that kinship is not the automatically determining factor that it is in the clans. Several considerations are involved in moiety membership. First, a person belongs to the kiva of his father. This applies to both male and female with the exception of a woman who transfers to her husband's kiva at the time of marriage. It would be impossible to transfer from one clan to another. Still another feature, again differing from clan organization, allows a man to change his "side" if personal difficulties with members of his present kiva make his membership unpleasant. As the difficulties pass, he can return to his original kiva. In these shifts, he ordinarily takes his wife and children with him. However, as the children, especially the sons, become older, they may or may not follow the father in his shift to the other "side." [3, 16, 17, 42, 45, 48]

Shifting from one kiva to another, and possibly back again, has to be done with the permission of the kiva heads and the war captains each time. This is largely a matter of formality, and permission is rarely, if ever, denied. Here is additional justification for considering the moieties as groups based on free association rather than groups based upon kinship.

Various examples of specific kiva shifts illustrate that this is a common, if not widespread, practice. After initially changing from the Pumpkin Kiva, personal difficulties with several others in the Turquoise caused Antonio Trujillo to shift back to the Pumpkin; his sons, Juan José and Pablo, accompanied him. Upon the death of the father, the two sons again affiliated with the Turquoise.

As of the summer of 1958, Pablo Trujillo, who as a Kwe'rana member, had become head of the Pumpkin Kiva upon the death of Juan Estevan Chalan, had once again changed his affiliation to the Pumpkin Kiva. His wife and younger children accompanied him in this shift.

Rosendo and Juanito Trujillo, brothers of Antonio, were Pumpkin members until Rosendo withdrew from kiva activities as a Progressive; subsequently, Juanito changed to the Turquoise. Fernando Cordero shifted from the Turquoise to the Pumpkin; Santiago Herrera and his entire family left the Pumpkin Kiva in favor of the Turquoise upon the death of the father, Juan Herrera. Epitacio Arquero shifted to the Pumpkin Kiva for a time and then returned to the Turquoise. Juan B. Arquero and Patricio Arquero were originally Pumpkin members; upon the death of their parents, both went to the household of Vicente Romero to live and shifted to Vicente's Turquoise Kiva. Following the death of Vicente, Juan and Patricio again became members of the Pumpkin Kiva. Lorenzo and Juan Valencia, San Felipe brothers who married Cochití wives, were members of the Pumpkin and Turquoise kivas, respectively. Numerous other examples have undoubtedly occurred.

Another point demonstrates this basic distinction between clans and moieties in the minds of the Cochití. Every Cochití is a member of a clan; in contrast, a considerable number of the Cochití are said to belong to neither kiva. In spite of this nonmembership, or lack of participation, almost anyone can still name the kiva to which these persons formerly belonged. There are two vaguely differentiated groups of these inactives. One is composed of those who have left the pueblo and are inactive because of their current absence. "They don't dance anymore." Many are young adults who "don't have costumes anymore" and who, for similar reasons, no longer participate in pueblo ceremonials. Informants were not unanimous in declaring such individuals as nonmembers; some preferred to call them "inactive." It is their involuntary inactivity that distinguishes them from the second group, members of the so-called Progressive faction, who not only "don't dance" but no longer acknowledge the authority of the war captains as it pertains to native ceremonials. Many of these reside in the pueblo but have withdrawn from all activities associated with the kivas and other aspects of native religion.

As shown in Appendix 37, the numerical strengths of the moieties roughly divided the pueblo population of 1948 in half—204 in the Turquoise and 219 in the Pumpkin. This division need not have been so nearly balanced; it simply happened to be true in 1948. However, further analysis of these two groups shows that the larger proportion of Progressives currently withdrawn from the Pumpkin moiety greatly reduces the actual strength of this group. This is particularly significant in political and ceremonial matters, as has been indicated in previous chapters.

The dichotomy between Conservatives and Progressives has frequently been discussed and referred to elsewhere. A statement from Bandelier's *Final Report* (1890: 301) is of interest in relation to these terms: "Recently, that is, since the beginning of this century, each of these estufas seems to represent also a certain tendency, or what might be called a party. Usually the people of Tanyi [Pumpkin] represent the progressive, the Shyu-amo [Turquoise] the conservative element. Whether this division is accidental, or whether some religious conception underlies it, I am unable to say."

If one accepts Bandelier's characterization of the two groups as accurate for that time, the subsequent developments are noteworthy. As already indicated, the larger proportion of the Progressives has come from the Pumpkin membership. However, in the present active membership, it appears that those who have remained Pumpkins tend to be more rigid and more conservative in their adherence to ceremonial traditions than do the Turquoise. Whether this conservatism is a reaction resulting from the withdrawal of the various Progressives—a form of revival—is uncertain. It may have actually preceded the withdrawal of these Progressives; in fact, the defection of these Progressives may well have been effected by the relatively extreme views of the dominant Pumpkin leaders. The Turquoise members, adhering to a more "middle-of-the-road" attitude, may have retained their numerical strength by preserving interest without alienating certain members by overzealousness.

Appendix 38 shows the 1948 intermarriages between the moieties and subdivisions of each. This includes "aliens" (non-Cochití) who married into the pueblo and adopted varying attitudes toward the moieties. Some joined the moiety which paralleled the one with which they were affiliated in their home pueblo; others, coming from tribes with no moieties, joined the moiety of their mates; and others, with or without previous affiliations, never joined either Cochití group. Informants disagreed on the exogamous or endogamous nature of the kiva groups. Several concluded that there was no rule of either procedure of which they had ever heard. [44, 45, 62] One informant was of the opinion that marriage in former times was on the basis of moiety endogamy but that this had not been followed for some time. [52] The absence of a recognized rule, at least in recent decades, is brought out in Appendix 38, which presents an analysis of all marriages for which the moiety of both the husband and wife could be learned. Considered in twenty-five-year periods, there is no appreciable shift between endogamous and exogamous marriages in the moieties.

Starr (1899), reporting his census of Cochití in 1897, showed considerable concern with clan organization, yet he made no mention of the two kiva groups. Dumarest (1919: 171, 184, 206) provided little more in the way of data on these organizations, merely noting that there were two, the Turquoise and the Squash, and designating them as *estufas* with ceremonial functions. In his discussion of marriage, only the clans received brief mention.

Curtis (1926: 86) provided better comparative data from a quarter of a century ago. He stated that there were two "religio-social parties": "Táhñitits^a," Squashes, who met in the Póna'ni-chítya (West-inside kiva) and the "Syohoeminatits^a," Turquoises, who met in Hánani-chítya (East-inside kiva). Curtis noted that these were said to have been endogamous but that this principle was abandoned when the population declined appreciably. In support of this, some Cochití had told Curtis that certain clans were once entirely within one or the other moiety. Bandelier (1890: 301) concluded that the endogamous arrangement of certain clans within each moiety suggested the one-time presence of phratries. Earlier in his field studies (October 16, 1880), Bandelier had gone so far as to state, "This clearly establishes the phratry."

A generation ago, Curtis found that in the Turquoise Kiva there were most of the Sun, Turquoise, Water, and Shī'pewe people; in the Pumpkin Kiva there were most of the Corn, Eagle, Ivy, Sage, Cottonwood, and Pumpkin, with the Coyote about evenly divided. His data indicated that a woman transferred to the moiety of her husband upon marriage and, upon his death, she returned to her own group.

Present-day informants believed the statement that a widow returns to her original kiva is unwarranted by actual cases. While a few women do, others do not. Transfers because of, or to avoid, discord are still made, occasionally with subsequent returns. It would be interesting to know whether there have been more transfers in families where exogamous marriages provided greater familiarity with the other group. Indications in 1948 were that it made little difference, but more complete data might alter this impression.

Informants believed that there is little significance regarding endogamous or exogamous marriages when the moieties are concerned. The data presented in Appendix 38 show approximately as many marriages (as of 1948) between the moieties as within them. Appendix 39 presents the clan strengths within each moiety as of 1948. Whatever tendency certain clans had to concentrate within one moiety or the other a generation ago has been dissipated, as one would anticipate when moiety endogamy, if it ever existed, was abandoned.

Goldfrank's material (1927: 115) on moieties, gathered at about the same time as Curtis', partially confirmed his, though it gave less suggestion of one-time moiety endogamy:

> Sons belong to the estufa of their fathers; wives to that of their husbands. However, membership may be changed due to a quarrel. The clans represented in my list for Turquoise estufa are Fox, Squash, Sage, Turquoise, Oak, Cipewe, Water, and Cottonwood. In the Squash estufa are found Sage, Turquoise, Oak, Water, Cottonwood, Ivy, and Corn. These lists made no attempt at completeness and are merely an indication of the type of membership found and the lack of correlation between clan and estufa membership.

In attempting to gain some perspective of the time of changes at Cochití and to place Cochití with its contemporary Keresan neighbors with respect to moiety organization, the following remarks of White (1942: 142) are helpful:

> Santa Ana again appears as unique: at no other Keresan pueblo does kiva membership depend upon clan affiliation so far as we know. At Santo Domingo, San Felipe, Cochiti, and Acoma a child joins the kiva of his father. The situation at Laguna and Sia is not clear, but we are reasonably sure that kiva membership is not determined by clan affiliation.

White offered no explanation of this, though in discussing the problem, he cited Bandelier's statement that "all the inhabitants of the pueblo, grouped by kins [clans], belong to one or the other estufa, one set of kins meeting at the calabash [kiva], the other at the turquoise." Bandelier (1890: 301) had also stated that the clans "assort themselves respectively in these two meeting places," the estufas that "are named after two of the most prominent clans: the Turquoise, Shyuamo, and the Calabash, or Gourd, Tanyi."

No other source nor any informant gave any impression that the Turquoise Clan and Turquoise Kiva and the Pumpkin Clan and Pumpkin Kiva have any special relationship.

Age Groups. Except for the general tribal initiation of boys into the Ka'tsīna Cult, normally held every four years, as described in Chapter 8, age groups have never played a prominent part in Cochití culture. Once the boys are initiated, they are undifferentiated from all others who have undergone previous initiation rites. Secret societies for either male or female members provide the only other formal groupings, though membership is not based on age and only partially on sex.

While not a rigidly stable group, the younger men of Cochití have been bound for many years by an interest in pueblo baseball teams. During the summer months, this sport is a focal point for the entire pueblo, either as players or spectators. From informants' accounts and from numerous old photographs of these teams, it is apparent that this interest goes back, at least, to the beginning of the present century. As far as can be determined, the teams have always been an all-pueblo affair, without consideration of clan, kiva, society, or political faction. In recent years, interest has been so intense that two teams were formed, with occasional mention of forming a third. [19, 20, 24, 45] (Plate 23b)

In discussing these baseball teams, an interesting situation came to light in regard to Marcelo Quintana, the cacique. In his younger days and prior to becoming cacique in 1946, Marcelo had been a good pitcher. In 1947, he was among the older men who still played on the second team, being unable to devote the time necessary to play on the first team. In several appearances as pitcher, he was received with enthusiasm by the crowd, composed of a good representation of the Cochití populace, including all ages, both sexes, medicine men, and Progressives. When an informant was asked in 1948 if Marcelo was again pitching, he replied that "some of the old people" had made objections to Marcelo's playing ball on the ground that it was not proper for the cacique to do such things, and so Marcelo no longer played, though he continued to watch the games. [19, 20, 24, 44] In 1951 Marcelo again figured prominently—this time in the role of coach for the second team. [20, 21, 45]

A potential age group that has thus far failed to materialize is that of war veterans at Cochití. In talking with veterans and others in the pueblo, several reasons for this became evident. In pueblos where strong in-group veteran feeling exists, as at Santo Domingo with its local American Legion Post, there is a greater cleavage between ideas and attitudes of the younger men, mainly veterans, and the older men who are in positions of authority in the tribe. At Cochití, as evidenced by the general interest and widespread participation either as players or spectators in the ball games, there are fewer of these conflicting attitudes. Stated positively, at Cochití the two groups have more common interests. Also, at Cochití the division between the Conservatives and the Progressives occurred more than a generation earlier.

While there is still ill-feeling regarding certain phases of the dispute, in general there is little overt bitterness on either side, and a tolerant attitude is held by most members of the two groups.

Veterans who did not return to the pueblo after the war were primarily those who had left the village before the war. Those who did return to the village have adjusted to it with relatively little conflict. Several veterans regularly residing out of the pueblo return on week ends to play for the pueblo teams. Several Cochití volunteered the opinion that Santo Domingo would have much less trouble with its boys if the officers would encourage them to play ball and engage in similar activities rather than forbidding them to do so.

It is evident that social groups based on free association are weakly represented in Cochití culture; what manifestations there are appear to be relatively recent innovations.

11 LIFE CYCLE

General Statements

EACH CULTURE, consciously and unconsciously, molds, or attempts to mold, the behavior of its members, encouraging certain modes of conduct, tolerating others, and banning still others. This enculturation is a learning process which continues throughout the life span of each individual member of the society, or participant in the culture. Involved in this life cycle are certain exceptional and unusually significant times, commonly referred to as "crises." In this chapter, only those crises are considered which are commonly experienced by the majority of the Cochití. Emphasis is again placed on change and the nature of such change in the various stages of individual development.

Material of the type offered here is most commonly discussed much earlier than the final chapter in an ethnographic or community study. In this study it seemed wisest to postpone its consideration until now in order for the reader to have already acquired some appreciation of the cultural matrix in which the individual tribal member finds himself and in which he experiences life. The specific crises take on additional significance when they can be related to the various facets comprising the structural framework of the culture, and accordingly, their importance can be better evaluated.

As will be revealed in the discussion of an individual crisis, the importance and/or the nature of these aspects have shifted with the passage of time; again the interrelationships among the several facets of any culture are clearly demonstrated.

Birth

Attitudes regarding pregnancy and birth have changed somewhat in the last twenty-five or fifty years at Cochití. In the discussions of Dumarest (1919: 141–144) and Goldfrank (1927: 76–78), there was general agreement on details. Briefly summarized, the medicine man and the general magical procedures, of an imitative type, played conspicuous roles in safeguarding the well-being of the mother and the child. Dumarest (1919: 141) noted that pregnant women and also those who desired a child received carved wooden images (o'ak^a) from the Shī'wanna, or Ka'tsīnas. Goldfrank's informants (1927: 76) claimed never to have seen these dolls but knew that members of the Shrū'tzī Society, in their retreats, were supposed to make them. However, "in recent years, the members were very lazy and none had been made during their retreats, so that they were no longer given away at dances."

In the more conservative families, some of the magical practices mentioned by Goldfrank are still followed. [3, 17, 45] These include keeping a perfect ear of corn (ko'tona) in the home during pregnancy; at the first labor pains, the shoes, stockings, belt, and jewelry are removed and the woman loosens her hair so that the child will descend more rapidly. Formerly, more than today, a pregnant woman nearing delivery would grind and engage in other rather strenuous activities to induce labor. This and other vigorous physical exercise throughout the course of pregnancy are slowly being abandoned as more care is exerted to prevent miscarriages and related difficulties. The influence of knowledge acquired through visiting nurses, health education, and similar sources is being felt to an increasing extent.

At the time of a birth, the woman sits, or kneels, with her legs spread, or she may lie on a bed. A midwife, often the woman's mother, washes the baby with warm water and a soapstone. Midwives, of whom Lucinda Suina, Estephanita Herrera, Reyes Romero, and Luisa Pancho are the most in demand, usually assist at births; the medicine men often arrive too late. "It's just like in the hospital where the nurses help if the doctor doesn't show up." [48] Medicine men are still commonly called for births in the pueblo. If the birth is at all difficult, the medicine man is definitely called, and it is generally he who cuts the umbilical cord (any sharp knife being used). [42, 48, 53] Goldfrank (1927: 76) stated that a Giant shaman was the preferred medicine man at birth. This was not confirmed by my informants, who said that the choice of the medicine man was a matter of family preference and was rather evenly spread among the various medicine men. [16, 42, 48, 49]

In recent years an increasing number of confinements have been in hospitals, usually in Santa Fe. "It's easier on the mothers that way, and the babies get a better start." [48, 70] A further change has been the increasing use of visiting government nurses and doctors who periodically examine pregnant women, babies, and older children. Few instances remain at present of the type described by Bandelier in his entry of November 10, 1880, in which he recorded his visit to the home of the governor: ". . . his wife lay on the floor with a newly born baby, wrapped in a serape, by her side. She was wrapped up in a serape to her chin, face flushed, but healthy and smiling. Baby one day old."

Following a birth, the mother remains indoors and relatively quiet for four days; on the morning of the fourth day a medicine man, who is also the godfather, comes just before dawn for the naming rites. During this four-day period the baby is kept on a hard-backed cradle board; as long as the baby remains on this board, a stick used in stirring *atole* (a gruel made from corn meal) and a perfect ear of blue corn are kept near the cradle as protection. These objects are the only ones used in this manner, regardless of the sex of the baby. [42]

A baby normally nurses for about a year and a half unless he is displaced by a new-born child. For four months after a birth the mother is not supposed to drink any water; she should drink only a tea made from juniper sprigs. As long as the mother continues drinking this tea, continence is observed. However, present-day mothers are not as bound by such "regulations" as were those of preceding generations. Again, the advice of visiting nurses and the knowledge of general diet and hygiene are displacing the traditional beliefs and practices. [3, 42, 62, 88, 92]

Based on Church baptism records at Peña Blanca and, hence, incomplete, Appendix 40 does give some idea of the frequency of births in different years, with males and females indicated. It is virtually impossible to gather reliable statistics on the number of miscarriages, though it is certain that there is a fairly high percentage. However, the annual totals provide some indication of birth-rate changes which cannot be obtained from informants. The annual total of recorded births varied from 6 to 27, with an average of 15. No year since 1900 has had more than 19 births, but several years prior to this date had more than 20. Low totals of 6 and 7 occurred in 1901, 1919, and 1943. The 1901 low was a result of a severe epidemic of "*Los Frios*" which swept the pueblo in 1900, and the 1919 low reflected the nationwide influenza epidemic of 1917/18. The 1943 low was undoubtedly due to the war period, which took many of the younger adults away from the pueblo, either in service or industry. In some cases, families accompanied these people, and babies born during that time were often baptized elsewhere, though some births had been reported back to Peña Blanca.

Also shown in Appendix 40 is the incidence of twinning. Informants recalled that triplets were born to the wife of Isidro Perez early in this century; however, no notation of this was found in the baptism records, and informants believed that the babies lived only a short time. [42, 44, 92] Informants generally felt that twins are "lucky." i.e., that parents are fortunate in having them. The occurrence of twins was given no unusual meaning or significance. (It is interesting that Esther Schiff [Goldfrank] found twins were considered "a misfortune" at Laguna—a Western Keresan pueblo [1921: 387].) In contrast to Spier's discovery (1933:314) among the Maricopa that the older twin is considered to be the second-born, the Cochití stated that the older twin was the first-born. The same matter-of-fact replies were made to other questions of this type. The sex of the first-born child is unimportant. "Maybe the father wants a boy, and the mother, a girl—but it doesn't matter to most people." As the size of the family grows, it is better to have both sons and daughters, but "the most important thing is if the babies are healthy." [62] Left-handedness has no significance; it occurs "because he is born that way. Sometimes a baby hurts the other hand when it is little." Regardless of the reason, if a child shows left-handed tendencies, "it's better not to change it." [62, 88, 92]

In the seventy-three years for which the record extended, with a total birth record of 1,098, there have been 12 pairs of twins. This was an incidence of 1 in 91.5 as compared with the normal incidence of 1 in 85 (Romer 1941: 382). Of the 12 occurrences, an analysis of the people involved showed the following genealogical facts. Twins were born in 1897 to Natividad Arquero and Juanita Chávez; in 1899, twins were born to Santiago Quintana and Cresencia Arquero, a sister of Natividad. Twins were born in 1932 to Pablo Trujillo and Felipita Herrera, and in 1945 twins were born to Josephine Trujillo. Pablo and Josephine are children of Antonio Chávez Trujillo and Estanislado Trujillo, who had different mothers but the same father, José Antonio Trujillo. The twins of Pablo Trujillo and Felipita Herrera, born in 1932, were also related to twins born in 1946 to Santiago Herrera, a brother of Felipita, and Rosaria Suina. Additional relationships between the known pairs of twins could probably be established with more complete family data. The foregoing instances demonstrate the known tendency for twins to appear more frequently in certain lineages.

The incidence of illegitimate children has increased somewhat in the last decade, though the rate of incidence in this century is below that of the last. Several factors may have been involved in these trends. One is the increasing awareness of Anglo cultural attitudes combined with a growing interest in following these attitudes. This feeling was exposed by one informant who said, "Now there is more of an idea that illegitimate births hurt the mother's chances of getting married later on—or at least it hurts the chance of a good marriage." [62]

An examination of the 97 cases of illegitimate children indicated the following. Seventeen mothers bore 36 of these children, with the highest number being 3 in two instances. There was a tendency for the pattern of illegitimacy to recur within several families, ranging from mother to daughter to granddaughter to cases of a mother and two daughters or two and three sisters being noted. The average age in 65 cases where the mother's age was known was 20.8 years, the range extending from 14 to 36 and the mode being 16 years. Within this range, there were no instances for the ages of 28 through 30, the majority of cases occurring in the years below this gap. An explanation for the gap may be that there was an increase in the number of illegitimates among women in the early thirties who had lost their husbands and had not as yet remarried.

While there is considerable attempt to conform to Catholic law and general Anglo attitudes on extra- and premarital relations, the traditional Cochití attitude of nondiscrimination toward children born of such relations has been maintained. On the bases of their personalities and abilities these children are accepted by playmates; later, they are considered peers by other adolescents. As adults, if their experience and conduct warrant it, they are placed in prominent positions in the ceremonial and political life of the pueblo. So far as can be determined, there has been a similar lack of discrimination against the parents of these children.

The incidence of illegitimate births between 1875 and 1947 is shown in Appendix 40. The continued frequency is evidence of little change in attitude among the Cochití. Their unchanged attitude is also demonstrated in Appendix 41, which shows marriage dates and the dates of birth of first-born children.

Naming

Indian Names. On the fourth day after birth, the godfather (ka'-na^rshtīo, "his father," [55]) comes to the house just before dawn. The family members and others remain indoors while the godfather, and in most cases the godmother (ka'nai-ya) also, takes the child outside as the sun appears on the horizon. The child is presented to the sun and is given an Indian name. Invariably this godfather is a medicine man, often the same one who assisted at the birth. [42, 48, 53]

One informant stated that the woman who accompanies the medicine man in this naming is the one who served as midwife. [42] Others stated that she was more often the wife of the medicine man. The child receives several names from various sources, however, and while that given him by the medicine man is most likely to be his "official" name, this is not necessarily so. One informant designated the medicine man's suggested name as the "real one," adding that the others were "more like nicknames." [42]

Bandelier, in his journal of October 10, 1880, noted that "when a father is informed of the birth of a child, he names that child after the first object (inanimate or not) which he meets after receiving the information." A week later, October 18, Bandelier recorded, "He says that Indian names are given by the fathers and mothers, after birth." One of my informants stated that the father may offer corn meal to the Ka'tsīnas in order to have them name the baby for him; in such cases, they are free to choose any name of their liking. The corn meal passes from the father to a go-between, who offers the meal to the Ka'tsīnas for an idea. [55] No special names acquired as members of societies or as a Ka'tsīna are found at Cochití, in contrast to the situation reported for Jemez by Parsons (1925: 31). Curtis (1926: 77) noted that Cochití names seldom had ancestral connotations.

People who come to the house following a birth can also suggest names for the baby, according to my informants. The name used is the one that is easiest to remember or which appeals most to the family and other relatives; this may or may not be the one given by the medicine man. The name of a deceased relative, most commonly that of a grandparent, is sometimes used; or it may be the name of a bird, an animal, or a Ka'tsīna. "Maybe it is just sounds that go together and don't mean anything at all." [48] This explanation appears to refer to those names used because they are easily remembered.

Published data indicate several variations in the naming procedure. According to Dumarest (1919: 143–144), both a godfather and a godmother took the baby, with the woman carrying it and presenting it to the sun as the man announced the name. Curtis (1926: 77) was told that only the godparents went out with the child while all others remained in the house. The godmother held the child, "up in full view of the sun," and the godfather bestowed the name. Goldfrank (1927: 49) stated that everyone except the mother accompanied the godparents. The shaman often gave the child several names, "although only the first one is commonly used."

Boas (1922: 2), in a brief and somewhat incomplete discussion of the act of naming, said that after the medicine man arrives, he inquires as to the clan of the mother and the father; he then prays, naming several deities and calling upon them to safeguard the child. He gives the mother "food" (pollen) to use in the child's behalf:

Then he says again, "Enough, here it is, my daughter. Hold on to this feather. Here it is. Now stand up." Then she rises and next her mother (that is, the child's mother's mother) takes up the cradle in which the child lies. She picks it up and puts beads on the baby. Then, "Now it is enough so far," he says, "next I shall take you out." Then they go out and then they stand there. Then again the shaman prays. He says, "Enough, Mother Sun, Chief, you who are coming up in the east this morning; everything, cultivated plants are growing, and get old. Now give this your new born baby health too, also growth and your happiness, that is what we wish. Here is life (food). Take it, this pollen and meal. On account of this, you will give health. Thus is her name, Ciaidyu-its'a. She wants health and growth and old age and that her mother and father after she has grown may love her, that is what we wish." That is all.

From an examination of the names listed by Starr (1899) and according to present-day Cochití, "-tīwa" is a common masculine suffix and "-utz" a common feminine suffix. [3, 45, 52] Curtis (1926: 77) also noted the "-tiwa" masculine suffix, with the remark that the same is true at Zuñi and Hopi. Informants' statements regarding meaningless names were substantiated by Starr's findings (1899: 42): "Surprisingly few of the Indian names are significant; it is certain that some which are significant have not been translated, but it is equally sure that a large number of them are today 'simply names.'" Starr's expression "simply names" is especially noteworthy, for statements of the same nature were made by my informants. An unsolved question is whether these names are, and have always been, meaningless combinations of sounds or whether the names represent archaic linguistic survivals, the meanings of which have been lost to modern Cochití. In the opinion of most informants, the answer is that these names never had meanings and are selected simply as euphonious sounds. [3, 45, 53]

As Goldfrank (1927: 22) stated, personal names are not used in direct address. Some informants thought that there has been a growing tendency to adopt this practice in recent years, perhaps because of additional contacts with outside peoples. [3, 45, 53] If one requests them, however, Indian names are given without hesitation, the same situation that Goldfrank reported. The increasing use of personal names, as indicated in the section on kinship terms, involves many of Spanish provenience. In former times, clan members greeted one another with "A-hai'tē, Ha'pañí!" ("Hello, Oak!"). Only a few of the older members of the Oak clan, the largest in the pueblo, continue this custom at present. [25, 45, 52] Teknonymy exists, as Goldfrank noted, though it too is being replaced to a considerable extent by the use of Spanish names.

Still another form of reference is the practice of saying something belongs "to that man who lives over there," or "to that family," when the house or land of these individuals happens to be in view of the speaker. At such times, as is customary among Navaho and other Indians of the Southwest, it is common for the Cochití, man or woman, to protrude the lips, thereby pointing to the person or object of reference. (See p. 369 for an instance of this.) Whether this form of circumlocution is common among themselves, or whether it occurs more as an evasive technique when speaking with an outsider has not been determined. Very likely, it is used among the Cochití themselves.

Spanish Names. In addition to an Indian name, all Cochití have Spanish names which are being used increasingly among themselves, and almost exclusively when dealing with outsiders. These names are received at the time of baptism. There is no set time for this rite, though it is usually within a week or two after birth. When a child is to be baptized, the *padrinos* chosen by the parents come to the house for the baby. The woman carries it to the church and the *padrinos* present it to the priest. Most *padrinos* ask the parents if they have selected a name for the child. Often they have done so, frequently one in honor of one of the *padrinos;* if they have not, they ask the *padrinos* to choose a name. "It is really the say of the *padrinos;* but if they are polite, they ask the parents first." [70] In cases of emergency, the child receives Christian baptism before the native naming rite is performed; ordinarily, however, baptism occurs after the four-day period which marks the naming by the medicine man. [42, 44]

Padrinos may be the same individuals who served, or would serve, as godparents in bestowing the Indian name on the child. *Padrinos* are ordinarily a married couple who are considered outstanding persons and who can be depended upon to supervise and augment the parents' rearing of the child. In 1948, the person who had served most often as a *padrino* was Cipriano Quintana, second oldest man in the pueblo and head of the Giant Medicine Society. Informants insisted that Cipriano had been selected (together with his first and second wives) because of the general respect with which he (they) was regarded in the village. The fact that he was head Giant, or even a member of that society (in view of Goldfrank's notes), was considered coincidental. Informants conceded that his being a medicine man may have influenced the selection in some cases, but the fact that he was a Giant had no particular bearing. [25, 44, 45, 53] In cases of illegitimate children, there is a tendency to pick *padrinos* closely related to the mother. Her parents, her mother and brother, sister and brother, grandparents, or *padrinos* are normally selected.

Clan and moiety affiliations have little bearing upon the choice of *padrinos.* Selections appear to be based on family relationships, or friendships, rather than clan or moiety considerations.

It was noted in examining the baptism records of the Church that given names of the *padrinos* are often chosen, revealing a possible factor in the selection of *padrinos*. Whether these cases are cause or effect is unknown. There is also a tendency to use the names of deceased relatives, as was noted with the Indian names. Another interesting practice is that of bestowing upon a subsequent child the name of one who has died, especially if death occurred in very early life.

Surnames at Cochití are also of interest. At present, they are almost entirely Spanish, as they have been for many years. Starr's census (1899) indicates that this was true at the end of the last century, and this was also revealed in the various records kept by the Franciscan Fathers. Strangely enough, however, prior to 1875 it was much less apparent. Names were recorded as "Juana Maria Natural," or even more commonly as "José Antonio N——," or merely "José Domingo." "Natural" most commonly referred to illegitimates, though in some cases it appears to have had more the connotation of "native" as contrasted to Spanish or Mexican, especially in those instance where surnames were unknown or actually lacking. For these entries, it seems that while Christian, or baptismal, names were in general use prior to 1875, the use of surnames was not firmly established, owing in part, perhaps, to the unfamiliarity of the priests with the individuals of the several towns and pueblos of which they had charge. Another contributing factor was undoubtedly the periodic change which many Indians made in their names, especially the surnames. This practice was revealed several times in working out genealogical data from the Church records with the aid of various informants.

Two observations from Bandelier's journal are of interest here. In the entry of October 4, 1880, he noted that within the record-keeping span of individual *padres*, the details were most complete in the initial years (contrary to the opinion expressed in the above paragraph); as time passed, details were ignored as they became better acquainted with the people. He noted that in these later years the first name was often used alone. On the same date, Bandelier stated that the last baptism at Cochití where an Indian family name was mentioned was recorded by Fray Sebastian Alvarez, November 29, 1823, when Maria Taiye was noted as the godmother. (In view of other data, Bandelier's precise meaning is ambiguous.) Bandelier noted that subsequently Indians were mentioned by their baptismal names and appear only with Spanish family names. The last marriage recording an Indian name was celebrated December 5, 1823, according to Bandelier. While the precise accuracy of these notations may be questioned, they are noteworthy in attempting to determine chronological changes in naming practices.

Starr (1899: 42) noted that male members of a family used the surname "Arcero" and female members "Arcera." At present, these people use "Arquero" (Spanish for "archer"). Informants also stated that in their early years, boys of a family used the name "Chiquiui-tero," from "Chiquichuitero" ("basket-maker"). Girls of the same family used the surname "Panocha," the name of a sweet pudding made of fermented grain. [3, 15, 44, 70]

Surnames were also changed in case of duplication. For instance, Santiago Quintana became Santiago Melchior to avoid confusion, and Natividad Arquero became Natividad Quintana. A somewhat different practice occurred, however, when Juan de Jesus Pancho and Santiago Quintana, while attending Carlisle and after their return to Cochití, were known, respectively, as John Dixon and Cyrus Dixon. Isidro Cordero, who went to Carlisle with these two men, retained his original name.

Several Cochití surnames reveal implications of interpueblo migrations, or transfers. The Pecos family is said to have come originally from Pecos Pueblo, though no concept of the chronology involved can be ascertained. Such a movement is plausible enough, despite linguistic difficulties, though the final survivors of Pecos appear to have gone as a unit to their linguistic kinsmen at Jemez Pueblo. (Parsons 1925: 3–4) While there are no Moquinos living at Cochití at present, there were several during the latter half of the last century and their descendants are still at Cochití. The Moquinos, as the name suggests, are reputed to have come from the Hopi villages. Again, chronology is lacking, but one suggestion is found in documents translated and edited by Thomas (1932: 242–245). According to this source, the Moquinos may well have arrived in Cochití (and other pueblos of the Rio Grande) about 1780.

The Anglicizing of Spanish personal names and surnames is becoming more prevalent as the people have increased contact with Anglo-American culture. Many of these are used as nicknames, but others are used almost exclusively in signatures and in daily references about the village. Francisco becomes Frank; Juan, John; José, Joe; Florencia, Florence; Helena, Helen; Martinez, Martin. A few non-Spanish names are found in the Church records, especially among the recent baptisms, but the great majority have remained

Spanish. The fact that Indian names are still important was revealed
in numerous conversations when informants could give the Indian
name but not the Spanish name, at least not immediately. In speaking
of others, especially when an older person is being spoken of by a
younger one, it is very common to precede the Spanish name with
"Mr." or "Mrs."

Puberty

Unlike many American Indian tribes, the Cochití take little notice of
puberty in the case of either a girl or boy. So far as can be learned,
this has been true in the past as well.

Girls' Puberty. Goldfrank (1927: 83) obtained the following data
on girls' puberty: "There is no ceremony when the girl arrives at
adolescence. She is told about menstruation before it occurs and
boys are also informed of this function in women. After the arrival of
menstruation, the girl does not play as freely with the boys as formerly." My informants stated that they knew of no formal recognition
of the beginning of a girl's menstruation. They also said that the Cochití have never made formal recognition of a woman's reaching the
menopause. [45, 49, 52, 53]

Boys' Puberty. No ceremony, tribal or other, marks a boy's reaching puberty. At approximately four-year intervals, an initiation of
boys into the tribal Ka'tsīna Cult is held, but the age at initiation
depends upon the wish of the boy, his family (usually just the father,
but sometimes other older males), and the tribal authorities. The boy
must be judged by all concerned to be reliable, responsible, and
capable of maintaining the esoteric nature of this society. [3, 44, 88]

In former times, boys were inducted into the Ka'tsīnas and taught
the secrets at an earlier age and at more regular intervals, usually in
four-year cycles. There followed a time when, for reasons of security
against loss of tribal secrets, initiations were postponed for those boys
who were going to attend the various boarding schools; when they
returned, they were initiated. At present, an increasing number of
boys are not interested in joining the Ka'tsīnas when they do return
to the pueblo. Hence the Ka'tsīna Cult, closely allied with the
Shrū'tzī Society, has become less of a universal tribal male group.
During recent years, it has become increasingly comparable to other
secret societies and the medicine societies in that only a portion of
the male population participates. As of 1951, there were 58 active

members of the Ka'tsīnas with an additional 13 who had become inactive due to old age or poor health. In contrast, there were 63 males over sixteen years old who were not members; with the exception of a few of the older Progressives, these 63 had never been initiated and it was likely that few of them would be. [44, 88] Thus, while the Ka'tsīna initiation has never been an actual puberty rite, it has lost its universality among the adult males of the tribe. [3, 44, 45, 48, 49]

Goldfrank (1927: 57) was told that all members of the pueblo joined the Ka'tsīna Society but that the initiates varied in age at the time of their induction. Curtis (1926: 86) stated that all boys, when about thirteen or fourteen years old, joined this society. In 1951, the youngest member of the society was eighteen; how long he had been a member was not ascertained. Dumarest (1919: 146) was told that the initiation was held whenever the boy was considered capable of keeping the secrets from the women and uninitiated children. This statement is of interest, both in providing time perspective to my informants' statements and in the implication, by omission, that all adult males were initiated. An initiation described by Dumarest was believed by Goldfrank (1927: 58) to pertain to the Warrior group, a society which became extinct about the time Dumarest was at Cochití.

Membership in the Ka'tsīna Society at present is gained in much the same way as that in other secret societies. It can be pledged during an illness, or other time of crisis, or it can be sought by a mature man or a young man. The attitude of the Cochití, as a whole, seems to be that membership in the Ka'tsīnas, or in any other secret society, must come as a voluntary move on the part of the individual. Formerly, some limited recruiting was done by the war captains, but this has ceased because several who had been urged to join became unhappy and embittered with their subsequent duties, obligations, and restrictions. [44, 45, 48, 49, 55] Thus, at present, the culture gives no formal recognition to male puberty.

Adolescence and Enculturation. Although these aspects have been already noted in the previous discussion of the family, certain phases of this topic merit elaboration at this point. Curtis (1926: 77) noted the lack of formal instruction of the children; instead, they learn by observation and in the family are taught "by precept and example how to perform the customary acts of religion and what constitutes good conduct." While this statement corroborates material mentioned earlier (pp. 369–373), he included additional data which is certainly open to question. Even though Curtis (1926: 77–78) used the present tense in the material below, the implication was that the custom described was no longer practiced at Cochití at that time—a generation ago. There is no denying that the existence, and even the appreciable frequency, of premarital relations is amply demonstrated by such tangible evidence as the data in Appendix 41, but even the one-time existence of such organized procedures as described by Curtis appears to be gross exaggeration if not near-fabrication:

> In order to induce children to cohabit and reproduce at an early age, boys and girls, as soon as they reach puberty, are (or formerly were) placed in a room together, many at a time, and an old man and an old woman remain with them to lead them through an inevitable period of embarrassment. The children remain there all night, and many girls become pregnant in this manner. This is still the custom at Santo Domingo. In many localities there is a progressive element that opposes the practice, but usually they are powerless against the force of custom.

Bandelier, in journal entries of November 26 and 28, 1882, made the following comments which would appear more reliable: "Pedro tells me that when a boy and girl are engaged, it is customary for the boy to sleep with the girl every night. Adelaido, indeed, goes out every night. . . . Ventura also told me that the boys and girls go to sleep together in the presence of the parents if the girl likes the boy. . . . He asked for money 'to go sleep with the neighbors' girl.' Thus, it seems that presents are given, expected, and received." In his *Final Report,* Bandelier (1890: 141) commented that chastity was an act of penitence and that promiscuity within the village was an established fact. Data from Church records and the opinions of my informants suggest that Bandelier's appraisal was, and continues to be, more valid than Curtis'. On the other hand, it is apparent that there are numerous individuals who adhere rigidly, on personal grounds attributable to Christian doctrines, or otherwise, to taboos on pre- and extramarital relations.

Present-day informants stated that family members customarily sleep in the same room and the siblings of opposite sex need not be separated until "they are eight or nine years old." [42, 62, 92]

In reply to inquiries about the age at which a boy is considered to be a man and a girl, a woman, the attitude noted by Bandelier (p. 210) was reiterated by present-day Cochití. For males, the shift generally appears to occur at about thirty years of age—"when they get to be officers." For women, the change was described as occurring at about thirty-five years of age. [42, 62, 92]

These estimates may appear surprisingly at variance with attitudes prevailing in our culture, but they emphasize that to the Cochití, "man" or "woman" is a social concept to a much greater extent than it is a physiological one. While a married status and the achievement of parenthood are certainly contributing factors in the attainment of adulthood, there are other considerations which must be satisfied before a person is commonly recognized as a "man" or a "woman" among the Cochití.

Marriage

It has already been pointed out in the discussion of clans that marriage among the Cochití is monogamous. This characteristic has been constant for the Cochití and other Pueblo peoples as far back as we have records. Marriage at Cochití has been based on the principle of clan exogamy for as long as we have knowledge, though there have been a few endogamous marriages steadily through the years. As indicated in the discussion of moieties, there appears to be some evidence of former moiety endogamy. This, however, if true at any time in the past, seems to have dissipated some time ago, possibly at some critical period when a sharp decline in population forced some relaxation of these rules. Goldfrank (1927: 84) found that residence was formerly entirely matrilocal for a brief period following marriage. A tendency toward this has continued into present times, though residence with the husband's parents or in an independent dwelling, often belonging to the husband, is becoming more common.

In regard to intertribal marriages, Bandelier (September 26, 1880) noted that "on the 24th, Padre Ribera told me that while intermarriages with other tribes occur, they are very violently resisted. An Indian of Cochití married a Cia girl sometime ago, but under violent protests from both tribes. According to the Roman (church) law, no marriage is valid unless celebrated at the parish of the woman." This closing statement was said to be true even at the present time [92]; however, Bandelier himself in another entry of November 29, 1880, commented that "José Hilario married from Cia, and there appears to be little opposition to intermarriage between other pueblos," plainly contradicting Padre Ribera's statement. In his entry of October 8, 1880, Bandelier noted the presence of "two Piro Indians from Senecu at Cochití who still speak their idiom. One of them is the son of a Cochití man who married a Piro woman." Elsewhere in Bandelier's statements, in the data gained from informants, and from examining the records of the Franciscan Fathers, intertribal marriages are repeatedly mentioned, though the frequencies are in the minority of total marriages. The tribes most often encountered are other Keresans, though there are a surprising number from the Tewa villages to the north of Cochití.

In discussions of these intertribal marriages there were several statements which indicated that this form of marriage was not "ideal." "Marriage should be inside the pueblo; outsiders often leave their wives here. Wives are taken care of better if the man is willing and wants to farm here at Cochití." "If a person marries outside, the other Keres are next best; maybe an Anglo is the next best choice." "It's better if all the people in town are Cochití—better spirit and more co-operation then." Despite such attitudes, most Cochití seemed reconciled to the fact that marriages with outsiders will continue and undoubtedly increase as contacts with outsiders through Indian boarding schools and other media become more numerous.

In generalizations regarding marriage, it was widely felt that a person should marry. Individuals who never married have been quite rare in the memory of present-day Cochití: "Those people were just unlucky, I guess," was a typical comment. While the physical attributes of potential spouses can hardly be termed irrelevant, it is certain that these aspects are relatively unimportant in the preliminary considerations of marriage. Desired criteria were stated in such vague terms as "not too tall," "not too short," "nice-looking face," "medium build," and similar expressions. When more definite expressions or standards were sought, informants were unable (rather than unwilling) to develop such concepts. On the other hand, they were quickly and freely able to term "ideal" spouses as those who "work hard," "minded their own affairs," "are kind," and display other behaviorally-oriented rather than physically-oriented characteristics. Contacts with contemporary American culture may in time alter these views, but it is interesting that the traditional criteria have continued to be so firmly implanted.

Bandelier (October 29, 1880) stated that the proposal of marriage was made by the boy's father or some male relative substituting for him. Curtis (1926: 88) said that soon after puberty a father told his son to look for a wife. If the son could not find one, his father helped. The matter was discussed with the girl's parents, and a price (or "present"), such as an unusual shell ornament or a pair of moccasins, was agreed upon. If necessary, the girl's family persuaded her to accept the boy. If the arrangement was satisfactory, other presents followed through a period of "trial" for the suitor. Sometimes several boys competed, with the girl finally taking the favorite as her husband.

Goldfrank's data (1927: 84) were generally confirmed by my informants as true for the present time as well: A wedding feast was prepared by the family of each principal. First, the girl's family went to the boy's home, and later, all went to the girl's. "Today this is considered as a preliminary ceremony to the Church wedding, but formerly these exchanges sanctioned the marriage." Father Dumarest's notes (1919: 150–151) described the marriage procedure much as it is observed at present.

Present-day procedure and views regarding marriage may be summarized as follows. Either the boy or the girl may take the initiative, but it is more commonly the boy. One informant believed a person should be at least sixteen before marrying [42], while another thought thirty the proper age [62]. After the couple has become well acquainted, the boy goes to his father who in turn goes to the girl's father with the proposal. Occasionally, the boy's *padrino* serves as the go-between. [62] The girl's father tells him to wait, perhaps a day or two, while he consults her relatives. If the proposal is accepted, the boy's father is notified. Then the two families prepare a *fiesta;* everyone goes to the girl's home first, then to the boy's. (This is the reverse of the procedure reported by Goldfrank.) At this time, the relatives express their willingness and desire to give their own relative to the intended spouse. Next, the boy and girl select their *padrinos* and notify the Catholic priest of their intentions. On the wedding day, the couple and most of the village attend Mass before the wedding. After this, the wedding party, their relatives and friends (most of the village) return to the girl's home where her family, assisted by the boy's, serves *fiesta* to all. "There used to be two of these *fiestas,* but now it is just at her house." [42] The couple, the *padrinos,* the priest, closest relatives, and special friends are seated at the table first. The girl's mother, often with the aid of some woman, such as Juanita Trujillo, supervises the preparations and the serving, and the girl's father serves as host, greeting all guests at the door. It is interesting that the immediate families of the couple are often so involved in preparing this feast that they do not attend the Mass and wedding ceremony in the church. This has been interpreted as an indication of the relative importance between the Church ritual and the feast—a survival of pre-European practices—in the minds of these Indians. When the people at the first table finish eating, they move to chairs and benches in the main room, where the remaining guests come to congratulate the couple, the *padrinos,* and the parents before eating. Presents are given the couple, and they are greeted with the characteristic embrace and handshake.

After the majority of the guests have eaten, the *padrinos* and various older and respected tribesmen—kinsmen or not—make rather lengthy speeches, concentrating upon advice to the newly-weds on how to live."When trouble comes, the couple can remember this advice and profit from it." [44] Several informants were of the opinion that this feast and speech-making comprised the wedding prior to the arrival of Catholicism in the village. [3, 15, 17, 42] (This confirmed Goldfrank's opinion.) A double wedding in 1947 (Plate 25*b*) was interesting in that both bridegrooms (veterans) wore business suits and the brides wore traditional Pueblo clothing. At another wedding in 1947, the bridegroom, again a veteran, wore a business suit and the bride a flowing white dress and veil.

The *padrinos* at a marriage are often those who served as baptismal *padrinos* for one of the couple. Sometimes the *padrinos* are of the same generation as the couple, though they are more commonly chosen from the parental generation. Similarity in clan or kiva affiliation is common but by no means the rule. Again, where similarity is found, it is more likely to be due to family relationships, or common society memberships, or political sympathies than it is to clan or moiety affiliations. [3, 16, 17, 25, 45, 53]

As of 1948, all Cochití marriages but one had been performed in a Catholic church, either in the pueblo, in another pueblo, or in a city. The one exception was performed by a nearby justice of the peace; in a reference to this couple as "man and wife," a twelve-year-old girl volunteered the observation that this woman was not the man's wife, "he just lives with her." [30] In spite of this deviation from the norm, the couple and their children play prominent roles in the life of the pueblo, and, except by a minority who disapprove of the marriage, they are well regarded in the community. The statement has been made by several that "we are all good Catholics here at Cochití."

Hence, divorce is not recognized, though there are several individuals in the tribe who are separated from their mates, almost all of them non-Cochití men.

An investigation was made of the ages of the men and women of Cochití at the time of their marriage. This was based on records of the church at Peña Blanca. It would be valuable to know whether numerous missing marriage records are due to accidents of recording by the priests, to the failure to forward to Peña Blanca the records of marriages away from the pueblo, or to marriages outside the Church —either civil or according to native rites alone. While the data are incomplete, several points are noteworthy.

Contrary to the impression gained from various sources (e.g., the citation from Curtis), the majority of the marriages of the last century did not involve particularly young persons. Some instances did occur in the earlier Church records. No cases of brides under seventeen years old were noted after 1910. Ages prior to 1910 dropped to thirteen, with a considerable number ranging from seventeen to twenty-one. For the bridegrooms, eighteen was the youngest age recorded since 1910. Before this date, the age dropped to sixteen. This was exceptional, however, with the majority being about twenty. Correlations of ages of marriage mates were variable. Instances ran the full gamut from equal ages to either the husband or wife being as much as twenty-five years older than the mate.

From the marriage records it was also apparent that remarriage was preferable to the status of widow or widower. A few individuals never remarried, but the great majority did, some as many as two or three times. Adults of either sex who never married were unusual. Transvestites are known to the Cochití from contacts with the Zuñi and some other tribes. Informants were unanimous in stating that there had been no transvestites at Cochití; despite this, they have a word, "kō'kwēma," for these individuals. [53, 70, 88]

Death

In his journal of November 10, 1880, Bandelier recorded the following regarding death and the afterlife:

Juan José this evening confesses to me that the Indians believe in a return to this earth of the spirits of the deceased [Ko'pish-taiª (92)], and of a steady communication of these with the living. Also of a punishment of the dead on this earth, and that those spirits who come to weep and make noise in houses, etc., do it to instigate the living to pray for them. Therefore the custom to strew crumbs of tortillas, etc., etc., at night, in the morning before sunrise when the boys get up to the river to wash themselves, and to scatter crumbs for the spirits of the dead. They pray to God for them.

These things are still believed by some. [92] In another entry of April 16, 1882, Bandelier, discussing the words to an Easter season *Tablita* Dance, continued with comments relating to death and associated topics:

It results from these [words of the songs], that Ma-se-ua is the spirit of Rain who dwells in the lagune of "Shipap." This Lagune is said to be to the North, beyond the "Conejos," and is described to be very round and deep. Many streams flow into it, but it has no issue. Out of this Lagune came forth the Indians and in it dwells "Te-tsha-na," our mother, from which sprang the Indian race. Those who die go to heaven above where God judges them and while the bad ones go to perdition forever, the good ones return to their mother in the said Lagune. They admit that God punishes even the good ones after their death, but that after that they still go to their mother. There is a singular admixture of Christian and pagan beliefs in this.

Bandelier's account of the handling of the dead was reported in his journal of July 26, 1888:

When anybody dies, they place in a corner of the room or where he or she has expired, an ear of *Blue Corn* with barbs at the point, called Ko-ton-a. This ear represents the soul of the deceased, which still hovers about the place. Alongside of it, they put a small club. At the close of the fourth day, the three Chayanis go there. One of them sings and prays, while another one takes away the club and ear of corn to some unknown place.—I forgot to state that when they first place the ear and the club, they surround these objects with a circle of crosses scratched in the floor. These crosses are as follows: X X and are intended for the footprints of the bird called Sha-shua or the Paisano [Road Runner]. From the shape of such tracks, it is impossible to determine if the bird goes forward or backward. These tokens constitute a magic circle for the purpose of preventing evil spirits or Brujos to find out where the soul of the deceased goes and thus protect that soul from their persecutions. When the ear of corn and the club are removed, the last ceremony performed, while the singing and praying is going on, is the obliteration of these X-marks, by one of the medicine men—and with the plume of an eagle. When the marks are all destroyed, the ceremony is over.

In regard to the souls of good men he asserts that they are going to our mother. An ear of *Blue* corn is the symbol of such a soul. They are Ko-Pish-Tai, also Shiuana.

For comparative purposes for a generation or more later, the unpublished notes of Boas (1922: 66–67) provided the following account of a Cochití funeral which is presented here in its entirety:

If anybody dies, first he will be nicely placed on his bed. At that time, a new suit will be put on for the last time, and his body will be washed for the last time by his father's sisters. These will wash him. When he is dressed entirely, next the tc'ai-ya·nʸi comes. He will put eagle feathers on the crown of his head, and also he will paint his face, and also put beads around his neck. And also he will put on turquoise ear-rings. When this is done, the chaiani will speak thus: "This is done, poor child. Today your breath from this place on earth and from under the sunshine will go. Next to another world you will go. You are happy in our father's house and in our mother's house. Thus I send you back there to our father and our mother where they live. Thus it will be for long ago it came to be thus. You will come to the place where our mother's and our father's life and breath are. Thus it is. We are poor. I give back to them your life. On our earth everybody will be thus, Mother I'atyikᵘᶜ and Father Itctsitʸi, please admit this (man or woman) to your house which you have in heaven. (The gratifying place which you have above.) This I want, mother, father. Now he is ready to be buried. Go ahead, go out from the room. Your body shall be earth and dust. Thus it will be.

"Oh, poor one, Mother, Mother Iatyikuc, look at him. With his clouds, with his breath, you will see him, alas. Mother Iatyikuc, look at him. With clouds and fog your Mother and your Father will take you."

Then they carry the body from there to the graveyard. As soon as they get there from here they put it into the ground. Then they put water by its side and also food for his traveling provisions. This is our custom.

Next, after two days the dead one will eat for the last time, but only the vapor of the food. He will eat here on earth (where the sun shines) for the last time. Thus it is. The Tcaianyi will give him to eat. Then the relatives of the dead one sacrifice food for the last time. They burn it on the fire because only the vapor is eaten by the dead one.

After this, the Tcaianyi makes them all go out from the inside of the house where he died. He will whitewash it entirely and clean it from sickness. (The smell like dirt.) He will wash away the bad smell, and odors. Then he will make the inside of the house good again. Thus are the customs of here and Laguna, all the people. Also when a person is dead, a man will watch during the night. He never sleeps for one night where the body lies [lay?].

Present-day informants stated that when a person dies, a woman (mother, wife, sister, or daughter) washes the hair, and the family dresses the body in the person's best clothes. A medicine man, who may be of any of the three societies, is called in to prepare the body for burial. [42, 53] He sprinkles herbs on the face [48], and corn pollen is placed in the mouth of the deceased. [42, 48] Another informant stated that the corn meal is placed in the mouth. [70] No face-painting is done. [42, 48] The medicine man massages the body, whispers some words, and then "takes out something" (the soul) from the body. This "something" is placed in a corner of the room where it remains four days before it is sent on to Wē'nimats, the land of the dead. [53] Another informant said that a bowl containing pollen was placed in a corner of the room and left there for four days. [42]

When the body has been prepared, the medicine man sews it in a blanket; in some cases, a rather crude wooden box is nailed together to serve as a casket. The majority of the people, especially the older ones, prefer burial in a blanket. At this time, the sacristán and the six *fiscalitos,* having dug the grave and placed a cross of large pebbles on the bottom of it, return to the home of the deceased and the sacristán offers a prayer. Then the body is placed on a house-ladder (Plate 7a) and carried to the church, where the sacristán again prays. After this, the body, still on the ladder, is placed on a wagon and carried to the *Campo Santo.* Burial takes place soon after death. If death occurs at night, burial is the next morning; if it occurs during the day, burial takes place that same day. If the deceased is a small child, the sacristán may simply carry the body in his arms to the *Campo Santo.* In former times, when burial was in the churchyard, the ladder was all that was used; since the *Campo Santo* is now some distance west of the village, the wagon has been added. [42]

Graves are dug at a spot designated by the sacristán; the digging is done by the *fiscalitos,* who also serve as pallbearers. There are no family plots in the *Campo Santo;* graves are dug in rows in sequence as they are needed. The body is placed in the grave, on top of the cross of stones, with the head oriented to the west and the body extended. On top of the mound, after the grave has been filled in, another cross of small rocks is formed. There is another prayer by the sacristán at the time of interment. After the burial, the people return to their homes; the *fiscalitos* go home by way of the irrigation ditch, or the river in the winter time, to wash the dirt from their shovels. [42]

It is interesting that the present sacristán (Alfred Herrera) is not a society member. From 1947 back into the last century, the sacristáns (Alcario Montoya and Mariano Chávez) were both members of Ku-sha'lĭ. The position of assistant sacristán, held from the beginning by Francisco Chávez, a son of Mariano, is a relatively new one. It was created because the regular sacristán, Alcario Montoya, was absent from the pueblo many times in his role of interpreter for the All-Pueblo Council and as a Ku-sha'lĭ member participating in rituals at other pueblos. [48, 53] As of 1958, Alfred was no longer sacristán, and the office had been taken over by Francisco Chávez—continuing the tenure of non-Ku-sha'lĭ people—in fact, giving the office, for the first time, to a Progressive.

After four days, the medicine man returns to the deceased's home to get the bowl of pollen, brushing the four walls with the pollen to remove whatever evil effects may still be lingering. [42] Most commonly the sacristán, or his assistant, officiates at the actual burial, since the priest is seldom available. Generally, the priest conducts a blessing at the grave upon his first visit to the pueblo after a burial. [42, 53] Unless the priest happens to be in the pueblo at the time of death, he is not called upon to administer the last sacraments or to officiate at the burial. [26, 39, 44, 70]

The *Campo Santo* used at present is located at the edge of the hills a half-mile west of the pueblo. José Ortiz, father of Miguel, is said to have been the first person buried there, at about the turn of the century. This occurred after a severe epidemic of *"Los Fríos,"* mountain fever, and another of malaria had plagued Cochití in the 1890's and early 1900's. At that time, the numerous deaths in the village, sometimes five or six a day, filled the *Campo Santo* immediately in front of the church, and the new burial ground west of the pueblo was consecrated. Like the Indians, the Spanish families at Cochití have used both *Campo Santos.* [65, 70, 88]

The *Campo Santo* is arranged in north-south rows of graves that are dug as the need arises. There are no family plots, as mentioned, and there is no segregation of the sexes. Most graves are marked by simple white wooden crosses, the legends of many no longer legible. When the churchyard was the only *Campo Santo*, the sexes were segregated, with the males south of the mid-line and the females, north, duplicating their normal division within the church during Mass. [3, 15, 70]

While most burials are in the *Campo Santo* west of the pueblo, an occasional one still takes place in the churchyard. One informant stated that this is usual in case of a sacristán's death. [44] In December, 1946, Trinidad Melchior Montoya, wife of Alcario Montoya, sacristán at the time, died. She had been a very prominent woman in the secret societies and ceremonial life of the pueblo, and had requested that she be buried beside her mother in the north side of the old *Campo Santo*. Alcario took her request to the *fiscales*, who approved it. It was explained that this was done because of her understandable wish, that it had nothing to do with her own importance or the position of her husband. [44, 45, 53] "Anyone else could do it, but most of them don't care. Both places are *Campo Santos*." [26, 42]

Stillborn babies or those not baptized have traditionally been buried beneath the floor—usually near the doorway. This is done by the father, not the medicine men. In earlier field work, this practice was described as one no longer followed. [62] However, in the examination of a ruin excavated on the Cochití Reservation in 1958, the practice was referred to as one still carried on. [97, 99]

Published accounts reveal only slight changes from present burial practices. Dumarest (1919: 166–174) commented upon the very short interval between death and burial, and of the body's being visited by relatives and friends who threw corn meal in the mouth of the corpse as preparation for the four-day journey to Shī'pap, in the north, followed by a journey to Wē'nimats, in the west, where the good people (sinless) go directly after death. The body was carried to the grave on a house-ladder. The major differences between Indian and non-Indian burials at Cochití were the Indians' practice of burying without the assistance of a priest and without a coffin, according to Dumarest.

Goldfrank (1927: 65–66) was told that certain medicine men were summoned in specific instances. If the deceased had been a Ku-sha'lī, a Flint shaman was called; a Shī'kame was called for a Kwe'rana; and a Giant was called for anyone else. A deceased shaman was painted with red ochre by the attending medicine man. Others were sprinkled only with corn meal and corn pollen. The shaman removed the soul of the deceased, and it remained in the house four days. These data were confirmed by my informants as still applicable. [3, 44, 88]

According to Curtis (1926: 83), "Although the mortuary customs are described in the present tense, burial at the present time is from the church. Nevertheless, the rites of the 'day when the dead person is sent away' are still usually observed." This duplication of present practices indicated that the abandonment of native burial rites has been in slow progress for several decades, primarily under the influence of the Catholic Church and the Progressive faction. However, at the present time among the Conservatives, the medicine men prepare bodies for burial and four days later send the soul on its journey from the pueblo to Wē'nimats. Regarding bereavement behavior, Curtis commented that "widows and bereaved parents used to neglect their personal appearance, neither washing their faces nor combing their hair, and the names of the dead were not spoken for about a year. Those who handled the corpse bathed afterwards, but not ritualistically." Trinidad Montoya's death in 1946 occurred on December 23. The regularly scheduled Christmas dances were held on the twenty-fifth, but the dances scheduled for December 26 were canceled. Dances on the following three days were held as scheduled. My informants disagreed with Curtis and minimized overt displays of personal mourning. "Maybe in the old days [the more overt patterns], but not for some time now." [3, 42, 44, 62]

Of the records kept by the Franciscan Fathers at Peña Blanca, those of death are the most incomplete. One priest explained this deficiency as due to the increasing number of Cochití who die away from the pueblo, as in government hospitals. As a result, many of these deaths are never reported back to Peña Blanca. [39]

Another explanation may lie in the Cochití view of the obvious and more tangible immediate life, in which the values of baptism are more real. Having the security of baptism and facing the intangible and less awesome postexistence (which still seems quite strongly associated with Shī'pap and Wē'nimats), the Catholic rituals of death and burial do not appear as urgent or as significant to the Cochití.

Appendix 42 provides data on annual death rates and life expectancy from 1878 through 1947. The high rate of infant mortality from 1890 through 1930 is obvious. That the number of infant and total deaths prior to this time is smaller can be explained by the incomplete recording of these events. Since 1930, the effects of improved health services, e.g., the covered and inspected water supply and fly spraying, and the educational policies of the Indian Service, such as the immunization program, are apparent.

Cochití beliefs associated with death and postmundane potentialities reveal several aspects. There is an obvious retention of the traditional orientation of Wē'nimats and the Ka'tsīnas; particularly among the Progressives, there is at least a blending, if not an actual replacement, with Roman Catholic doctrines. Along with these interpretations, there are those who answer queries on the subject with a simple "I don't know." This reply has been evaluated as a polite refusal to discuss the subject with relative strangers, an attitude we encounter in our own culture. It has also been evaluated as an accurate self-appraisal of the person's life orientation. In part it may reflect an as yet unresolved confusion resulting from the blending of two systems of theology; in part it may reflect the cultural tendency to emphasize the present rather than the future, which makes it all the easier to postpone formulating any definite conclusions on the subject.

At any rate, it rather clearly demonstrates a general lack of definitive theological orientation with the present-day Cochití. It may well be that this lack is a far more universal quality than has frequently been implied for such cultures as those of various American Indian tribes as well as for others. Whether one is justified in injecting such a lack of unanimity into the past or whether the explanation lies more in its being a recent product of acculturation is not very clear. There is, however, little doubt that this manifestation of independent interpretation is associated with similar recent developments of shifting emphasis from the group to the individual, as has been indicated in the preceding chapters on economics, political, ceremonial, and social organization. The implication of the development as it pertains to the acculturation of individual Cochití is that it may well facilitate the acquiring of new values and new systems of belief.

APPENDICES

Appendix 1

CLIMATIC SUMMARY: Selected Stations Surrounding Cochití

Station and County	Temperature					Average Dates of Killing Frost			
	Span (in Years)	Jan. av. °F.	July av. °F.	Maximum °F.	Minimum °F.	Span (in Years)	Last in Spring	First in Fall	Growing Season (Days)
Alamos Ranch, Sandoval	18	27.2	66.7	95	−14	23	May 8	Oct. 18	163
Frijoles Cañon, Sandoval	---	---	---	---	---	---	---	---	---
Santa Fe, Santa Fe	40	29.2	68.9	97	−13	40	Apr. 24	Oct. 19	178

Station and County	Span (in Years)	Average Precipitation (in Inches)												Annual Total
		Jan.	Feb.	Mar.	Apr.	May	June	July	Aug.	Sep.	Oct.	Nov.	Dec.	
Alamos Ranch, Sandoval	28	0.96	0.70	0.98	1.10	1.48	1.46	3.30	3.34	2.05	1.51	0.68	0.71	18.27
Frijoles Cañon, Sandoval	14	0.42	0.90	0.81	0.75	1.59	1.17	2.53	2.55	2.00	1.15	0.59	0.80	15.26
Santa Fe, Santa Fe	40	0.66	0.74	0.81	1.07	1.46	1.19	2.28	1.90	1.68	1.11	0.71	0.58	14.19

Source: U.S. Department of Agriculture 1941: 1011, 1014–1015.

Appendix 2

COCHITI CENSUS DATA, 1680–1952

Date	Total	Males	Females	Families
1952	444	229	215	116
1951	438	226	212	92
1948	423	217	206	93
1944	353			
1943	346	181	165	81
1940	324			
1937	307	163	144	
1936	309	167	142	
1935	309	169	140	
1934	307	165	142	
1933	298	159	139	
1930	280			
1928	272	138	134	
1923	267			
1910	237			
1900	198			
1897°	273	146	127	59
1890	268			
1887	302			
1880	271			
1851	254			
1829	372	182	190	
1821	339	182	157	
1799	505			
1794	667			242
1779				116
1776	486			116
1765	450			150
1749	521			
1744	400			80
1707	500			
1706	520			
1680	300			

° The number had been 309 earlier in this year; 26 died in one week's time.

Sources: 1952, 1951, 1948: author's data; 1944, 1943, 1940, 1937, 1936, 1935, 1934, 1933, 1930, 1928: United Pueblos Agency, *Annual Reports;* 1923: Curtis (1926: 259); 1910, 1900: Bureau of Census, 1915; 1897: Starr diary (9/26/97) and Starr (1899); 1890: 11th Census, 1890; 1887, 1880, 1829: Bandelier journal (9/2/87, 7/16/82, 3/28/82); 1851: Abel (1915: 294); 1821: Bloom (1913: 28); 1799, 1794, 1776: Biblioteca Nacional, *Legajo X:* Documents 74, 70, 82, 43; 1779, 1765, 1707: Thomas (1932: 99); 1749: Kelly (1940: 362–363); 1744, 1706: Hackett (1937: 404, 369); 1680: Hodge (1907: 318).

Appendix 3

COCHITI HOME OWNERSHIP AND OCCUPANCY as of July 14, 1952°

House No.	Number of Rooms	Owner(s)	Occupant(s)	Av. No. at Home
1	3	Diego Romero	owner & daughter's fam.	8
2	2	Diego Romero	storerooms	0
3	3	Epitacio Arquero	owner	2
4	1	Epitacio Arquero	storeroom	0
5	3(?)	José Hilario Herrera	being built	0
6	2 (adding 2)	Juan José Trujillo	owner	2
7	3	Fernando Cordero	owner	7
8	2	Pablo Trujillo	owner	6
9	2	Eufrasio Suina	owner & parents	8
10	3	Delphin Quintana	being built	0
11	3	Cresencio Suina	owner	5
12	3	Rosendo Trujillo	owner	8
13	3	Cipriano Chávez	owner	2
14	2	Juan Francisco Chávez	owner	4
15	2	Francisco Chávez	owner	2
16	4	Juan José Suina	owner	6
17	4	Juan Rosario Melchior	owner	4
18	1	Pumpkin Kiva membership	ceremonial only	0
19	2	José Domingo Quintana	owner & daughter's fam.	8
20	2	Selviano Quintana	vacant	0
21	2	Cresencia Quintana	owner	2
22	2	Alvin and Nestor Arquero	vacant	0
23	3	Vicente Romero	owner	3
24	2	Juan Estévan Chávez	vacant	0
25	1	Vicente Romero	storeroom	0
26	2	Lorenzo Herrera	owner	4
27	2	Aurelia Suina	owner	4
28	2	Marcelo Quintana	owner	4
29	2	José Domingo Quintana	storerooms	0
30	1	Vicente Romero	storeroom	0
31	1	Lorenzo Cordero	storeroom	0
32	3	Juan Velasquez	owner	3
33	3	Magdalena Melchior	owner	1
34	2	Celso Montoya	Epifanio Pecos	5
35	2	Santiago Cordero	owner	6
36	1	Isidro Cordero	owner	1
37	1	Lorenzo Herrera	storeroom	0
38	1	Epifanio Pecos	storeroom	0
39	2	Emilia Hurtado Suina	vacant	0
40	2	Philip Cooka	owner	5

° For locations of these buildings, consult Map 2.

House No.	Number of Rooms	Owner(s)	Occupant(s)	Av. No. at Home
41	1	Juanito Trujillo	storeroom	0
42	3	Clofe Arquero	owner	5
43	2	Antonio Naranjo	owner	4
44	1	Emilia Hurtado Suina	Juanito Trujillo	1
45	3	Reyes Chalan	owner	7
46	2	José Francisco Herrera	owner	4
47	2	Nestor Herrera	owner	9
48	1 (adding 1)	Catherine Garcia	owner	5
49	1	Giant Medicine Society	ceremonial only	0
50	2	Magdalena Melchior	storerooms	0
51	1	Vicente Romero	storeroom	0
52	2	Lorenzo Herrera	storerooms	0
53	2	Cresencio Pecos	owner	3
54	3	Aloysius Pecos	owner	6
55	2	Santiago Herrera	owner	6
56	1	Reyes Chalan	storeroom	0
57	1	Estephanita Herrera	owner	2
58	1	Santiago Herrera	storeroom	0
59	2	Eleuterio Suina	storerooms	0
60	2	José Alcario Montoya	owner	2
61	1	Pablita Ortiz Tecumseh	storeroom	0
62	1	Santiago Cordero	storeroom	0
63	1	Rosendo Trujillo	storeroom	0
64	1	Santiago Cordero	storeroom	0
65	1	Pablo Trujillo	storeroom	0
66	1	Ignacita Arquero	owner (kitchen)	1
67	11	Leopoldo Rael (Spanish)	owner	6
68	1	Ignacita Arquero	owner (bedroom)	1
69	2	Cruz Pérez	owner	2
70	4	Reyesita Bowannie	owner	4
71	3	José Rey Suina	owner	4
72	2	Flint—Ku-sha'lï House	ceremonial only	0
73	1	Lorenzo Suina	storeroom	0
74	2	Kwe'rana Society House	ceremonial only	0
75	1	Diego Romero	storeroom	0
76	2	Lorenzo Suina	owner & daughter's fam.	8
77	2	Maria Ortiz Cordero	owner	7
78	3	Lorenzo Cordero	owner	3
79	2	José Solomon Suina	owner	6
80	2	Lucinda Suina	owner	1
81	3	Ramón Herrera	owner	7
82	4	Juan Bautisto Pancho	owner	7
83	2	Juan B. and Patricio Arquero	owners	2

House No.	Number of Rooms	Owner(s)	Occupant(s)	Av. No. at Home
84	4	Caroline T. Pecos	owner	3
85	2	Ivan Lewis	owner & wife's mother	6
86	2	Ascención Benada	storerooms	0
87	2	Frank D. Herrera (Spanish)	owner	3
88	6	Luciano Gallegos (Spanish)	owner	3
89	3	Alfred Herrera	owner	6
90	2	Community "Farmer's" House	storeroom	0
91	2	Agrapina Quintana	owner	2
92	1	Diego Arquero	owner	1
93	2	Luciana & Guadalupe Ortiz	Cipriano Quintana	3
94	1	José Nicanor Cordero	owner	1
95	1	Turquoise Kiva membership	ceremonial only	0
96	1	Cruz Pérez	storeroom	0
97	1	Justino Herrera	vacant	0
98	1	Cipriano Quintana	storeroom	0
99	1	Santiago Romero	owner	2
100	1	Salvador Arquero	owner	3
101	2	Cresencia Quintana	storerooms	0
102	2	Gerónimo Quintana	owner	6
103	1	Magdalena Quintana Chalan	storeroom	0
104	3	Gabriel & Leonard Trujillo	storerooms	0
105	2	José Dolores Pecos	owner	5
106	1	Cresencia Quintana	storeroom	0
107	1	Eleuterio Cordero	owner	6
108	1	Clemencia Quintana	storeroom	0
109	1	José Alcario Montoya	storeroom	0
110	1	Reyes Chalan	storeroom	0
111	2	José Domingo Melchior	owner	2
112	1	Reyes Chalan	storeroom	0
113	1	José Alcario Montoya	storeroom	0
114	1	Clemencia Quintana	storeroom	0
115	1	Reyes Chalan	in ruins	0
116	2	Salvador Arquero	storerooms	0
117	1	Estephanita Herrera	storeroom	0
118	1	Shrū'tzi Society	ceremonial only	0
119	1	José Domingo Melchior	storeroom	0
120	1	Estephanita Herrera	storeroom	0
121	1	Estephanita Herrera	storeroom	0
122	3	Cristino Tafoya (Spanish)	owner	3
123	4	Ramón Lucero (Spanish)	owner	5
124	1	Reyes Chalan	storeroom	0
125	1	Reyes Chalan	storeroom	0
126	1	Manuelita Chávez	storeroom	0
127	2	Santiago Cordero	storerooms	0

House No.	Number of Rooms	Owner(s)	Occupant(s)	Av. No. at Home
128	1	Reyes Chalan	storeroom	0
129	2	Antonio Ortiz (Spanish)	owner	1
130	1	Penitente *Morada*	ceremonial only	0
131	3	Pancracio Chalan	vacant	0
132	1	Epifanio Pecos	storeroom	0
133	3	Martha & Margaret Pecos	being built	0

Appendix 4

COCHITI USE OF ELECTRICITY: Monthly Consumption of KW-H from October, 1950, through July, 1951. CHART A

Meter No.	Hookup Date	Oct.	Nov.	Dec.	Jan.	Feb.	Mar.	Apr.	May	June	July	Total	Range
101	1/6/50	22	28	28	52	34	36	32	30	32	28	322	22–52
102	1/10/50	22	26	30	26	20	24	16	20	10	12	206	10–30
103	1/10/50	2	34	44	40	34	38	10	8	8	14	232	2–44
104	5/26/50	28	16	14	50	22	18	28	44	62	34	316	14–62
105	1/7/50	32	40	34	44	62	76	40	52	54	64	498	32–76
106	1/6/50	26	156	198	62	40	66	138	60	30	24	800	24–198
107	1/6/50	54	70	56	76	54	68	62	70	66	90	666	54–90
108	1/10/50	12	20	20	42	16	18	20	30	28	28	234	12–42
109	1/6/50	8	10	8	12	8	8	10	8	12	8	92	8–12
110	1/6/50	0	2	6	6	4	6	4	4	0	4	36	0–6
111	1/6/50	18	30	44	56	30	28	16	20	12	16	270	12–56
112	1/6/50	34	50	58	50	34	40	30	34	22	18	370	18–58
113	1/5/50	12	20	22	42	22	26	14	22	20	18	218	12–42
114	1/5/50	8	10	12	12	8	8	6	6	12	20	102	6–20
115	7/13/50	14	22	26	32	22	20	16	16	18	16	202	14–32
116	1/10/50	12	18	18	26	10	26	30	18	16	8	182	8–30
117	7/13/50	22	44	46	46	34	40	32	46	36	70	416	22–70
118	1/6/50	6	4	10	16	8	14	6	16	2	6	88	2–16
119	1/6/50	22	30	30	44	26	34	28	30	28	28	300	22–44
120	1/5/50	60	60	60	68	54	72	62	74	88	102	700	54–102
121	1/5/50	46	30	16	36	16	16	40	48	40	66	354	16–66
122	1/5/50	22	30	30	38	26	32	22	52	64	82	398	22–82
123	1/5/50	34	46	44	56	40	48	42	44	42	110	506	34–110
124	1/5/50	12	10	16	56	24	24	16	16	18	24	216	10–56

Meter No.	Hookup Date	Oct.	Nov.	Dec.	Jan.	Feb.	Mar.	Apr.	May	June	July	Total	Range
125	1/5/50	22	36	40	68	42	78	40	32	14	16	388	14–78
126	1/6/50	12	22	26	40	22	26	14	18	14	20	214	12–40
127	1/6/50	8	2	6	6	8	10	22	34	38	10	144	2–38
128	1/10/50	0	0	2	0	0	0	0	0	2	2	6	0–2
129	1/6/50	6	14	14	26	22	26	12	6	4	6	136	4–26
130	1/6/50	38	28	28	38	24	32	14	16	16	16	250	14–38
131	1/10/50	34	40	44	52	56	28	34	40	58	86	472	28–86
132	1/6/50	18	28	30	42	20	28	26	24	16	18	250	16–42
133	1/6/50	18	26	26	52	24	24	18	16	20	24	248	16–52
134	1/13/50	24	38	34	58	28	36	26	22	18	30	314	18–58
135	3/9/50	16	16	24	268	44	44	42	14	16	14	498	14–268
136	1/10/50	8	2	12	30	26	22	14	16	12	12	154	2–30
137	1/6/50	28	38	34	64	44	50	38	40	22	6	364	6–64
138	1/10/50	26	26	34	44	40	52	44	30	20	32	348	20–52
139	1/6/50	60	66	62	82	52	70	46	78	80	116	712	46–116
140	1/6/50	16	16	20	26	16	20	18	18	14	10	174	10–26
141	1/6/50	42	42	56	58	50	48	38	40	28	32	434	28–58
142	1/6/50	18	26	24	40	24	26	26	30	24	22	260	18–40
143	1/6/50	42	42	32	50	28	34	16	6	2	4	256	2–50
144	1/7/50	12	14	20	36	18	16	16	20	16	22	190	12–36
145	1/10/50	26	36	34	42	26	36	34	28	18	30	310	18–42
146	1/10/50	24	30	36	54	30	30	28	34	24	22	312	22–54
147	1/6/50	24	34	34	70	48	50	42	42	22	26	392	22–70

Total for Cochití Indian homes 14,550 0–268

Day School

	1/26/50	78	94	134	150	120	116	104	98	64	66	1,024	64–150

Church

	1/5/50	4	12	14	42	6	12	6	4	10	14	124	4–42

Spanish-American residences

1	1/10/50	8	14	14	20	18	16	16	8	0	0	114	0–20
2	1/10/50	26	34	28	38	28	30	26	34	30	52	326	26–52

Spanish-American stores

1	1/7/50	290	222	208	200	54	122	116	168	184	436	2,000	54–436
2 (Com)	1/5/50	108	106	106	132	100	118	110	124	124	158	1,186	100–158

Total Cochití Indian residence kw-h consumption	14,550	0–268
Monthly average (total)	1,455	
Monthly average for individual meters	31	
Santa Fe residential reading average for same period	1,022	
Santa Fe monthly average for individual meters	102	

Source: Basic data obtained through the aid of Mr. Ralph Loken, manager, Santa Fe Division, New Mexico Public Service Company, and Mr. William Rose, office manager at Santa Fe.

Monthly Consumption of KW-H from August, 1951, through May, 1952. CHART B.

Meter No.	Hookup Date	Aug.	Sep.	Oct.	Nov.	Dec.	Jan.	Feb.	Mar.	Apr.	May	Total	Range
101	1/6/50	22	24	32	50	50	60	50	36	46	30	400	22–60
102	1/10/50	16	22	24	34	26	34	36	40	36	28	296	16–40
103	1/10/50	14	8	16	34	44	38	32	22	6	4	218	4–44
104	5/26/50	32	40	38	50	48	60	36	46	44	38	432	32–60
105	1/7/50	40	46	50	56	40	62	40	38	44	66	482	38–66
106	1/6/50	36	28	24	72	92	114	74	76	88	62	666	24–114
107	1/6/50	80	56	56	66	66	78	72	72	84	66	696	56–84
108	1/10/50	32	20	20	28	28	36	28	22	28	28	270	20–36
109	1/6/50	6	0	8	10	12	24	14	18	18	12	122	0–24
110	1/6/50	2	0	2	2	6	6	0	2	2	2	24	0–6
111	1/6/50	26	16	16	32	34	58	42	30	22	24	300	16–58
112	1/6/50	22	26	30	48	48	56	36	30	30	22	348	22–56
113	1/5/50	16	8	16	24	22	28	20	24	20	18	196	8–28
114	1/5/50	10	8	6	10	14	30	22	28	42	14	184	6–42
115	7/13/50	24	10	14	24	20	32	20	22	22	20	208	10–32
116	1/10/50	6	58	36	28	20	14	14	16	18	10	220	6–58
117	7/13/50	90	60	38	42	28	38	26	22	50	52	446	22–90
118	1/6/50	2	4	4	4	10	8	2	6	6	2	48	2–10
119	1/6/50	28	26	32	44	38	54	28	24	28	22	324	22–54
120	1/5/50	68	70	52	76	74	138	84	78	92	78	810	52–138
121	1/5/50	62	42	38	34	30	44	18	16	32	36	352	16–62
122	1/5/50	84	60	54	60	52	66	44	30	56	54	560	30–84
123	1/5/50	82	62	50	70	48	54	58	40	68	70	602	40–82
124	1/5/50	22	14	26	34	34	66	26	30	22	16	290	14–66
125	1/5/50	4	4	2	26	34	62	26	36	50	36	280	2–62
126	1/6/50	26	16	18	32	30	42	24	30	32	28	278	16–42
127	1/6/50	52	16	18	20	28	36	26	24	26	18	264	16–52
128	1/10/50	2	0	0	2	0	0	0	8	0	0	12	0–8

Meter No.	Hookup Date	Aug.	Sep.	Oct.	Nov.	Dec.	Jan.	Feb.	Mar.	Apr.	May	Total	Range
129	1/6/50	2	2	8	10	14	28	8	6	6	4	88	2–28
130	1/6/50	24	16	20	32	28	46	28	34	32	24	284	16–46
131	1/10/50	86	50	42	38	30	44	18	16	28	26	378	16–86
132	1/6/50	20	18	24	38	32	46	26	26	34	22	286	18–46
133	1/6/50	28	20	20	30	30	50	26	26	20	28	278	20–50
134	1/13/50	28	34	28	38	28	40	24	22	20	26	288	20–40
135	3/9/50	44	42	48	66	80	86	90	86	84	82	708	42–90
136	1/10/50	6	4	4	16	34	56	26	30	32	18	226	4–56
137	1/6/50	2	0	4	4	2	18	2	2	0	0	34	0–18
138	1/10/50	58	80	48	56	52	64	42	42	46	52	540	42–80
139	1/6/50	38	32	34	52	42	74	56	56	50	34	468	32–74
140	1/6/50	8	10	14	26	18	30	18	34	50	52	260	8–52
141	1/6/50	22	28	34	46	48	58	40	34	46	30	386	22–58
142	1/6/50	22	18	28	48	36	52	30	30	26	24	314	18–52
143	1/6/50	8	6	6	8	6	20	6	4	20	30	114	4–30
144	1/7/50	30	2	10	22	30	38	22	22	20	14	210	2–38
145	1/10/50	38	22	22	34	38	52	38	46	42	38	370	22–52
146	1/10/50	24	28	28	38	36	54	34	36	36	30	344	24–54
147	1/6/50	30	22	20	48	48	98	50	54	48	28	446	20–98
154	10/5/51				18	16	20	10	20	22	12	118	10–22
155	12/20/51						50	34	28	30	24	166	24–50
156	9/13/51			12	10	10	14	10	18	18	14	106	10–18
157	12/18/51						12	10	6	6	0	34	0–12
158	12/18/51						36	18	16	16	8	94	8–36
159	1/18/52							14	20	16	10	60	10–20
160	11/1/51				12	22	32	24	24	22	16	152	12–32

| Total for Cochití Indian homes or other buildings | | | | | | | | | | | | 16,080 | 0–138 |

Day School

	1/26/50	14	72	84	172	218	208	232	156	166	104	1,426	14–232

Church

	1/5/50	10	2	0	10	6	32	4	6	8	6	84	0–32

Spanish-American residences

1	1/10/50	22	44	36	54	44	38	14	32	46	24	354	14–54
2	1/10/50	74	60	56	74	58	68	50	58	60	50	608	50–74

Spanish-American stores

1	1/7/50	710	570	434	352	166	210	226	364	494	512	4,038	166–710
2 (Com)	1/5/50	162	126	114	124	104	136	102	106	136	120	1,230	102–162

Total kw-h consumption for Cochití Indian homes and other buildings
       CHART A (47 meters)   14,550
       CHART B (same 47 meters) 15,350
       CHART B (7 more meters)   730
       CHART B (54 meters)   16,080

Total kw-h consumption for Cochití Day School
       CHART A   1,024
       CHART B   1,426

Total kw-h consumption for Cochití Church
       CHART A   124
       CHART B   84

Total kw-h consumption for Cochití Spanish-American residences
       CHART A   440
       CHART B   962

Total kw-h consumption for Cochití Spanish-American stores
       CHART A   3,186
       CHART B   5,268

Total kw-h consumption for Cochití Spanish Americans
       CHART A   3,626
       CHART B   6,230

Source: Basic data obtained through the aid of Mr. Ralph Loken, manager, Santa Fe Division, New Mexico Public Service Company, and Mr. William Rose, office manager at Santa Fe.

Appendix 5

COCHITI ELECTRICAL APPLIANCES, as of July 14, 1952

Meter No.	Iron	Hot Plate	Radio	Refrigerator	Toaster	Washing Machine	Others
101	x		x			x	phonograph
102	x		x		x		
103	x		x				
104			x				
105	x		x	x		x	
106	x		x		x	x	
107	x	x	x	x	x	x	corn popper; vacuum cleaner
108	x		x			x	
109							
110							
111	x		x			x	
112			x		x	x	
113	x		x			x	
114							
115			x			x	
116	x		x			x	motor (½ hp?)
117	x	x	x	x	x	x	
118							
119	x		x			x	
120	x	x	x	x	x	x	
121	x		x	x		x	
122	x		x	x			
123	x	x	x	x	x	x	
124	x		x			x	
125	x		x			x	
126	x		x	x		x	
127	x		x				
128	x	x	x	x	x	x	
129	x		x				
130	x		x				
131							
132	x		x			x	phonograph
133	x		x			x	
134	x		x			x	
135	x		x			x	
136	x		x				
137	x		x				
138	x		x	x		x	
139	x	x	x	x		x	

Meter No.	Iron	Hot Plate	Radio	Refrigerator	Toaster	Washing Machine	Others
140	x		x	x			
141	x		x			x	phonograph
142	x		x			x	
143	x		x				
144	x	x	x	x	x		
145	x		x			x	water heater
146	x		x			x	
147	x		x			x	
154	x		x				
155	x		x			x	
156	x		x			x	
157							
158	x		x				
159	x		x				
160	x		x			x	

Day School

| | x | x | x | x | x | x | |

Church

| | | | | | | organ |

Spanish-American residences

| 1 | x | | x | x | x | x | water heater |
| 2 | x | | x | x | x | x | water heater |

Spanish-American stores

| 2(Com) | x | | x | x | | | |
| 1 | x | | x | x | | x | |

Appendix 6

INDIVIDUAL PAYMENTS TO COMMUNITY
FOR USE OF THE COMBINE: 1948 and 1951

Farmer	1948	1951
Arquero, Epitacio	5.5	---- [a]
Chalan, Juan Estévan (paid by widow, 1951)	9.5	2.0[b]
Cooka, Philip	2.5	3.0
Cordero, Lorenzo	4.0	---- [a]
Cordero, Santiago	1.5	---- [a]
Herrera, Francisco	1.5	---- [a]
Herrera, Lorenzo	---- [a]	7.0
Herrera, Loretto	4.0	3.25
Herrera, Nestor	4.0	5.0
Lewis, Ivan	---- [a]	5.0[b]
Melchior, Reyes	2.0	---- [a]
Montoya, Alcario	2.0	---- [a]
Pecos, Aloysius	1.5	---- [a]
Pecos, Cresencio	1.5	2.0
Pecos, Epifanio	5.0	---- [a]
Pecos, Santiago	---- [c]	2.0[d]
Pérez, Cruz	1.0	---- [a]
Quintana, Cipriano	7.0	---- [a]
Quintana, Damasio	8.0	---- [a]
Quintana, Delphine	2.0	---- [a]
Quintana, Gerónimo	2.0	---- [a]
Quintana, José Domingo	3.0	---- [a]
Romero, Diego	2.5	8.0
Romero, Santiago	16.0	9.0
Suina, Cresencio	3.0	---- [a]
Suina, José Rey	4.0	3.0
Suina, Juan José	11.5	6.0
Suina, Octavio	---- [c]	7.0[b]
Trujillo, Juan José	5.5	7.0
Trujillo, Pablo	2.0	---- [a]
Trujillo, Rosendo	4.0	---- [a]
Velasquez, Juan	---- [c]	5.0
Total	116.0	74.25

[a] Paid cash at the rate of $2.00 per 100-lb. sack.
[b] Paid half wheat and half cash at the rate of $2.00 per sack.
[c] Raised wheat but exact payment for use of the combine is unknown.
[d] Did not plant wheat.

In 1948 the community collected one out of each six sacks harvested; in 1951 it collected two out of each eleven sacks harvested. In both years, the farmers had a return of between three and four sacks for each sack planted—considered a normal and fair return.

Appendix 7

CROP ACREAGES AND YIELDS

Crop	Acreage	Yield
Maize	270	5,400 bu.
Alfalfa	136	244 T.
Wheat	120	1,440 bu.
Sudan grass & tame hay	41	43 T.
Beans	14	66 bu.
Chili	8	8 T.
Watermelons	6	12 T.
Oats	5	40 bu.
Total acreage	601	

Fruit	Trees & Vines	Yield
Peaches	550	2,200 bu.
Grapes	300	63 bu.
Apples	297	1,485 bu.
Plums	25	100 bu.
Apricots	20	80 bu.
Cherries	15	45 bu.
Pears	5	15 bu.
Total	1,212	3,988 bu.

Source: Field agent's *Annual Report,* United Pueblos Agency. Field-crop data are for 1945; fruit data are for 1941.

Appendix 8

OCCUPATION OF THE PEOPLE: 1880

The following remarks on the economic activities of the Cochití were made by Bandelier in his journal of November 5, 1880:

January. House work. Light work, carrying work. Make *chiquihuites* [quish-te (baskets)]. Hunt rabbits whenever there is fresh snow (also deer).

February. Hunt also. About middle of February, begin to sow wheat. Sometimes irrigate before sowing, but not always, and only if the ground is very dry.

March. Sow wheat. The boys go out to gain money by hiring out as herders.

April. After the 20th of April, the planting is commenced, of corn. The ground is invariably irrigated before the breaking seven or eight days. The breaking is done with ploughs and oxen. There are about thirty or forty ploughs in the pueblo, of which three or four belong to the Indians. They are borrowed from one another. The corn is covered with the plough again. It is not irrigated more for two months, but the ground is pulverized with the shovel or hoe, of iron now.

May to 10th of June. The maize is planted fully. In June and July they pulverize the ground in the cornfields.

In *July* they make the last weeding and with the plough, and then throw up their embankments and let water in, irrigating thence on every week, almost. From the 25th of April to middle of May the chile is planted. In each of the crosses . . . a grain is planted, then covered with the foot, then frequently irrigated. It blooms about the 20th of July, and is therefore irrigated afterwards every seven or eight days. Melons and watermelons are planted in April (late). The breaking and planting is made with the aid of the plough, but the weeding, etc., is done with hoes. In July, maize begins to bloom and to throw out ears *(espiga).* Wheat begins to show ears in June. It is cut about the 10th to the 25th of July, and the common wheat about August 5–10. It is thrashed (with horses) in July, August, and September. . . . Change about every year, wheat lands being changed to corn, etc., and the same place with other fruit or crops. . . . The *punche* is sown in May, and, if it grows, planted in the same month. Frequently irrigated.

Appendix 9

SELECTED TYPES OF FARMS

The following farms, with the exception of the last one, are briefly described here to give some idea of Cochití agriculture as of 1948, with some revisions as of 1951. While these examples include some of the better farms, they present a fairly accurate impression of what farming means to individual Cochití families. The information listed in the last farm described is taken from Bandelier's journal as of October 9, 1880, and is included for its comparative value.

Farm A. The owner of this farm operated about 15 acres on a crop-rotation basis, maize being replaced by wheat, and the wheat replaced in turn by alfalfa, which was allowed to grow for several years. There were 5 acres of maize, a little blue and a little white but mostly yellow. (This was true of the whole pueblo; blue and white corn were formerly the most popular, but yellow corn, primarily for stock-feeding, has supplanted both types.) There were 4 acres of alfalfa, which yielded three to four cuttings per year, depending upon the weather. The alfalfa was not baled but hauled in wagons and stacked high on the sheds in the corral, or placed on the ground in a separate corral where the stock could not reach it. Two acres were planted in wheat, with a normal yield of about 12 sacks. Since 2 sacks went to the community for use of the combine harvester, the net return was 10 sacks. There were smaller tracts of garden vegetables, chili, and watermelons. In 1948, the chili and watermelons planted west of the river dried up, whereas those on the east matured. This was true of all fields, and it remained an unsolved mystery despite soil tests and other tests made by the Agency. Though formerly practicing dry farming, this man had only irrigated fields. He also had a few acres washed out in a flood several years before, and he had not repaired the damage because he did not need the additional land. Since he had homesteaded them, he had no fear of their reverting to the pueblo. He formerly had cattle, as many as 3 head at once, but had none in 1948. There were 3 horses, all draft animals, but one could be used with a saddle. He had never raised sheep or goats. He owned about 30 chickens, which were kept penned, at least at night. Chicken-stealing still occurred at Cochití, but he felt it had declined with the exodus of Spanish families from the pueblo. He had no pigs in 1948, though he had kept some in the past. [73]

Farm B. The operator of this farm cultivated about 16 acres acquired in part through inheritance from his father, mother, and stepfather and in part by homesteading in the *bosque*. There was also some land that had belonged to his wife which he was holding in trust for their children. His fields were scattered throughout the cultivated lands of the pueblo, as was true of almost all holdings. He had done some dry farming and occasionally had done well, "when the rains hit right." He had 8 acres of wheat; 7 of maize (all yellow), and 3 of alfalfa. He also had about a quarter-acre of chili, onions, cabbage, a few grapes, and some young apple trees. He had 1 team of work horses, 6 head of cattle (2 were milk cows), 10 sheep, 3 pigs, and between 35 and 40 chickens. He had used fertilizers of various kinds for as long as he could remember. [74]

Farm C. The operator of this farm had a small garden of lettuce, carrots, chili, and red beans. A quarter-acre tract was used for muskmelons and watermelons. He grew maize, but he planted about 12 acres of oats, which he cut slightly before it matured in order to keep the heads intact. He used the oats for fodder. He had one of the largest cattle herds in the pueblo, grazing as many as 36 head at a time, and also had 8 horses. [75]

Farm D. This farm comprised about 9 acres; of these, about 3 acres were in maize, all yellow. The owner formerly grew white and blue but had not done so recently, using the yellow corn mostly for stock feed. He had about 5 acres of alfalfa, which he had grown for several years in preference to wheat. Although he had grown oats successfully, in 1948 he had none. In a half-acre garden plot he grew chili, onions, and tomatoes. He had never grown tobacco. He had experimented with hybrid corn, importing seed from Iowa which did not grow well; later he tried seed from Illinois, which grew very well. However, he did not care much for it, for it was expensive and had to be bought each year. He had 10 or 11 head of cattle and depended on community-owned bulls for breeding. He had a team and 1 smaller horse which had not yet been broken. In 1951, he had about 10 acres in crops, in tracts of 3 and 7 acres each; in one, he had about 35 fruit trees (apples, peaches, plums, and apricots) and alfalfa; in the other, there were 2 acres of yellow dent corn and 5 of alfalfa. [76]

Farm E. On this farm the owner farmed about 20 acres, the acreage left after about 20 acres had been given his married children. His 20 acres were farmed as follows: about 8 acres of maize, 5 of alfalfa, 3 of wheat, 2 of beans, and 1 of garden produce, including sweet corn, melons, chili, onions, sweet potatoes, and peas. He had 1 heifer, 2 pigs, about 15 chickens, and 3 horses, one still unbroken. He also had 2 hives of bees, the only person in the pueblo keeping bees. (Many Cochití like to gather wild honey in the mountains.) Instead of stacking his hay as most Cochití farmers did, he baled his alfalfa. He obtained the baler from "Rusty" Campbell, a storekeeper in Peña Blanca, and paid every fifth bale for its use. In 1947, he paid 30 bales, leaving 120 for himself. He felt this was worth while since the bales were piled neatly, and more compactly, in sheds. Protecting the hay from the weather made it better feed, and less hay was wasted. He always rotated his crops and had used manure on his fields for as long as he could remember. [77]

Farm F. The owner of this farm cultivated about 20 scattered acres with help from his stepsons. He plowed as soon as the ground thawed, but never during the fall or winter. He plowed moving counterclockwise from the center section of the field outward. Wheat was broadcast and plowed into the ground, normally about three inches. Some farmers harrow and drag the wheat seed, but this man felt that deeper sowing enabled the wheat to withstand dry spells better. "Indians like to plow wheat under." He used any and all kinds of fertilizers, principally manure, and plowed under the stubble to increase the humus in the soil. He had about 8 acres of maize, 4.5 of wheat, 6.5 of alfalfa, and a quarter-acre of chili peppers. He also raised some pinto beans. His rotation sequence went from wheat to maize to wheat to alfalfa for several years before returning to wheat again. Blue and white corn were for family use; yellow corn was for the stock. In the garden he grew onions, pumpkins, garlic, peas, tomatoes, carrots, cabbage, *havas*, and *garbanzas* (a large salty-flavored pea). [78]

Farm G. The owner of this farm had about 30 acres in one unit. He had about 8 acres of yellow corn and 7 of alfalfa. In a small garden he grew cabbage, carrots, onions, sweet potatoes, chili, tomatoes, muskmelons, watermelons, squashes, *havas*, and *garbanzas*. The garden was cared for mainly by his wife and children, and he spent his time with the field crops. *Garbanzas* sell very well in stores catering to the Spanish trade. "Those people like them even better than *frijoles*." In rotating crops, he often planted maize one year, followed with wheat or beans, after which a forage crop such as alfalfa was grown for several years before maize was grown again. His wife tended the chickens and hogs during the summer months; he relieved her of this work in the winter. He had 7 horses, including both draft and saddle horses, in 1948. He also cared for the community stud and used him in his team; no stud fee was charged. By 1951, this horse had died and had not been replaced by the community. He also had a small flock of sheep, normally about 8 or 10 animals, in 1948; by 1951, this flock had been enlarged. These animals were of good quality and yielded a fair return in wool, lambs, and, to some extent, in meat, though he did little butchering since he was attempting to enlarge his flock. [79]

Farm H. In 1951 the owner of this farm was farming 1 acre of yellow dent corn and 1 of hybrid corn east of the river and the following tracts west of the river: 1.25 acres of white corn, a half-acre of four-year-old alfalfa, and 1.25 acres of three-year-old alfalfa. He left alfalfa from three to five years, depending on how well it did, before putting the field into corn for two years, followed by a year of wheat, and then back to alfalfa. He also had about 15 additional acres which he had purposely allowed to lie fallow in 1951 while he served as a major officer. The increased threat of a water shortage forecast for the 1951 season also influenced his decision; normally, this acreage was planted in corn and wheat. He also had a quarter-acre of garden produce. He had 1 fifteen-year-old work horse (its partner had died a year or more earlier), a saddle horse, and a two-year-old colt. He owned 5 head of beef cattle, including a two-year-old heifer. There were also about a dozen chickens. [89]

Farm I. On this farm the operator had 12 acres of wheat, 6 on each side of the river. Of this, 3 acres belonged to a brother-in-law who was in service in 1951. This land was planted in wheat, with an additional 4 acres of his brother-in-law's planted in alfalfa. He owned 1 team of work horses and 1 saddle horse, 3 head of cattle, 1 pig, and 3 chickens. [90]

Farm J. The owner of this farm had a total of about 14 acres, divided as follows: east of the river were two tracts—4 acres of yellow corn and 3.5 of oats and vegetables; west of the river, there were 2 acres lying fallow, 3 acres of alfalfa, and another field of 1.5 acres of alfalfa. He had 1 work team and a saddle horse; he had no cattle, sheep, or pigs. There were about 15 laying hens. [91]

Farm K. Of this farm, Bandelier (October 9, 1880) was told by Juan José Montoya that he had 37 cows, 3 horses, 1 mule, and 1 burro.

Appendix 10

SELECTED HUNTING AND OTHER TALES

A story told by several informants concerned a trip into the upper Pecos drainage to hunt buffalo and antelope at the water holes and salt beds there. While details varied slightly from one informant to another, this appears to be the same story related in Curtis (1926: 77), where a date of about 1868 was assigned. About a dozen men under the war captains and three or four *alguacilitos* went on a hunt for the cacique. Pack burros were taken along and the hunters took their stations in small pits dug around the edge of a salt lake where high grass helped conceal them. A herd of antelope repeatedly returned, and the men killed many of them, cutting the flesh into strips and drying it on poles. Then some mounted Mescaleros attacked. Some Cochití were killed, but they succeeded in driving off the Apache. They returned home without delay. [25, 49, 50]

A hunting party succeeded in getting its meat and was ready to return to Cochití. Two of the men decided to remain behind to do some more hunting. One of these was a witch, who belonged to a society of "bad people." The others, however, did not know this. The next day these two men ran into some Mescaleros, who surrounded them. The two men thought, "No more home to Cochití." They were smart, though, and good runners. The witch ran but was killed. Before he died, he said, "This is our place here." Although wounded by an arrow, the other man escaped and managed to reach a sheepherders' camp. The herders were frightened, but they bandaged his wounds, took care of him, and gave him fresh clothes. "This took place over around the San Pedros, east of Cochití, not as far as the Pecos. Buffalo moved up and down the Pecos and swung all over the country. Hunters hung around the water holes and salt beds." [49]

Up in Colle Canyon, above Cochití, there was one of the last Navaho fights. There were cattle at Cañada where there was water. Two or three men were herding them. It was early morning, and the men were fixing breakfast and making bread. Suddenly stones began to drop down the chimney of the small house they were in. "What's the matter?" one of them asked. Then they saw a long stick coming down the chimney, and it speared the bread cooking over the fire. "Somebody go out and look," one of them said. One man went, and there on the roof was a Navaho, who immediately jumped down and ran. Though pursued, the Navaho got away. As the Cochití returned to their house, they noticed that none of the cattle remained; the Navaho had driven them off. Word was sent back to the pueblo for reinforcements. Trailing the Navaho and the cattle, they caught them near Mesa Cañada. One Navaho jumped down from the mesa, and the other ran away. The one who jumped was chased as far as Mesa Allerton, near the old sawmill, where he climbed another mesa, shouted at the pursuing Cochití, and then disappeared. [49]

A long time ago, one June, just before the big feast of July 14, some men went out to hunt antelope east of the pueblo. They had their hunt and were on the way back; the party included one man who was the grand-father of Epifanio Pecos (also the uncle of Lorenzo Herrera). They were about ten or fifteen miles on their way—one day's journey—when they made the first camp. At that time one of the men discovered he had left a medicine bag at the last camping site. This was a younger man and a brother-in-law of Epifanio's grandfather. So these two men went back. When they reached the camp and found the bag, it was too late to start back to rejoin their party, so they stayed that night. Next day the younger man suggested that they stay and hunt some more. The older man said, "No, they are waiting for us. Let's go." But they did stay that day and another night. That night the older man had a dream. In that dream a stranger, a man, came and talked with him. This stranger told the older man (who had never cut his hair in bangs) to cut his hair and then no harm would come to him. When he told the younger man that, he said, "Why do you believe that?" But the older one had already cut his hair as the stranger had directed. He cut it off with a knife. Then the two men started back.

They came to a valley canyon and looked down. They saw nothing; it was all clear. There were lots of rocks in this canyon and when the two men reached the middle of the valley, lots of people stood up behind the rocks and shouted at them. These were Mescalero Apaches and some from the other pueblos too. As four or five of these ran toward the two, they stripped off their clothing and got their bows and arrows ready. The older man had a gun, but one of the Apaches snatched it away from him. Then someone shot him—wounding him in the arm and also the ribs. He ran, and they pursued him. They chased him into some pines and brush (encino) and willow bushes. Here he hid, and the chasers gave up looking for him. He got up, having stayed there very still, "just like dead." He stayed all day, and about five o'clock got up. Having no shirt, he tore up his kilt and bandaged his wounds. Then he set out to find his comrades.

He traveled four or five miles and then in the night he came upon two Mexican sheepherders at their camp. He saw the fire and when he came out of the night, all bandaged and torn, they were afraid of him. He told them what had happened and they gave him some clothes and the herders joined him and finally he found his comrades. The younger man was killed by the Apaches; he never came back. [25]

The Cochití used to be very dangerous. Once some Navaho stole a girl. Every house had grinding stones for corn, etc. A girl went to another house one night. The people knew that almost every night Navaho raiders came, all wrapped in blankets, and would get either a man or woman who was out alone. They would hide very quickly. If you speak to a Cochití, he answers. But these figures never answered; they were Navaho. One night two girls had to go to the toilet; they went out to a corral. The Navaho caught them; one got free and ran home. The other one was carried off by Navaho on horseback. They put the girl in the saddle, and a man sat behind her and held her. The Cochití had to wait until morning to track them, and then they couldn't catch them.

The girl married the Navaho who stole her. In two years, they had a child; she stayed a long time and was gone many years. Navaho women, neighbors, became very good friends. "Are you lonesome?" "Yes." "Do you have a family back home?" "Yes." "You are my best friend; I like you very much and will tell you how to get away to see your family." "All right." "You make lunch—bake bread; we will go for piñons. Wherever we find them we will camp. Bring along a good sharp knife and hide it in

your buckskin leggings." "All right." "Where we camp you go off a little
bit. Then when ready take good horses." "All right." "Take two or three;
wherever you stop, change to another—keep going. You will be chased
right away. Next morning I'll come over to your place. We are the only
two who know the plan; our husbands do not know. When ready, wash
your husband's hair. Then he will go to sleep. When he is asleep, take out
the knife and scalp him—cut his throat."

The Cochití woman did that; she took two horses and away she went.
She traveled all night and another day; then the Navaho woman went
over and gave the alarm. The Cochití woman got back as far as Valle
Grande; she turned loose one horse and used the other. The Navaho
woman's husband gave the alarm; the men saddled up, took their bows
and arrows, and chased the Cochití woman. About ten miles from Cochití
they almost caught her. They came down to Cañada, eight miles away;
they were very close. Then she found a cave; the horse stood nearby.
After fifteen or twenty minutes, the Navaho came and found just the
horse. Some wanted to come down to Cochití and find the woman, but
others said it was too dangerous. The dead man's relatives were crying for
revenge on her. They wanted to take her scalp back. The others went
home, taking the horse. A half-hour or an hour later, the woman came out;
she figured she was safe. She came down the long arroyo and saw an old
man at the mouth of it. He had a cane and a rope across his chest, going
for wood. The girl watched him, but he didn't see her. Then she spoke to
him. The old man was afraid: "Who are you?" The girl answered, "Don't
you remember, Grandpa? I am the one taken by the Navaho." He just
opened his mouth; he was speechless. "All right, all right, that's fine." She
told him to go back and tell the people to come meet her. "I have my
husband here—this scalp." The old man trotted off. Later two, three, or
four men came in bunches and met her at the little hill—the high place by
the canal just north of the pueblo. Then the people began their custom;
they took the scalp home and were very happy. [49]

One of the favorite stories of the old people comes from the first trip
made by some Cochití to California. They traveled by foot, horseback,
and pack burros. One who went was Santiago Quintana, "Guerro," who
went as a young man together with his wife's father. Another was a very
short man, called "Ha'ro." These men spoke very good Spanish. They
traveled about a month or more on their way out. About the Red
(Colorado) River (at the present California-Arizona line), they had
finished all their food; only one burro was left and they decided to kill it
and eat it. (This appeared to be quite a joke to the informant.) The meat
kept them until they finally reached Los Angeles. The men remained two
or three years in California. Much of the time was spent on large ranches

where the men worked as sheepherders, camp cooks, and similar ranch helpers. Once when the men all lined up to receive their pay, Ha'ro was told that he got only half-pay as he was not large enough to receive full pay (another joke). The men made good money in California, and they returned riding fine horses, with silver trimmings on their bridles and saddles. These horses were very fast, and they always won the races in the pueblo and were also best in the rooster pulls. Later, with this example, others followed their footsteps to California for similar employment. [49]

Appendix 11

COCHITI WAR CAPTAINS AND
LIEUTENANT WAR CAPTAINS, 1923–1954

Year°	War Captain Age and Clan	Kiva	Lieutenant War Captain Age and Clan	Kiva
1954	Santiago Romero 72, Shipewe	P†	Lorenzo Cordero 56, Coyote	T
1953	Juan Velasquez 51, Red Shell	T	Justo Pérez 58, Pumpkin	P
1952	Santiago Romero 70, Shipewe	P	Damasio Quintana 60, Oak	T
1951	Eleuterio Suina 70, Pumpkin	T	Nestor Herrera 60, Cottonwood	P
1950	Epifanio Pecos 56, Ivy	P	Diego Romero 60, Sage	T
1949	Juan Velasquez 47, Red Shell	T	Nestor Herrera 58, Cottonwood	P
1948	Santiago Romero 66, Shipewe	P	Diego Romero 58, Sage	T
1947	Juan Velasquez 45, Red Shell	T	Santiago Arquero 57, Sage	P
1946	Epifanio Pecos 52, Ivy	P	Diego Romero 56, Sage	T
1945	Eleuterio Suina 64, Pumpkin	T	Santiago Pecos 59, Ivy	P

° Records for years not listed were unobtainable.
† "P" refers to Pumpkin Kiva, "T" to Turquoise Kiva.

Year*	War Captain Age and Clan	Kiva	Lieutenant War Captain Age and Clan	Kiva
1944	Santiago Romero 62, Shipewe	P	Vicente Romero 59, Sage	T
1943	Santiago Romero 61, Shipewe	P	Vicente Romero 58, Sage	T
1942	Eleuterio Suina 61, Pumpkin	T	Santiago Pecos 56, Ivy	P
1941	Eleuterio Suina 60, Pumpkin	T	Santiago Pecos 55, Ivy	P
1937	Epifanio Pecos 43, Ivy	P	Epitacio Arquero 47, Sage	T
1933	Santiago Romero 51, Shipewe	P	José Domingo Quintana 46, Oak	T
1932	Eleuterio Suina 51, Pumpkin	T	Santiago Pecos 46, Ivy	P
1931	Eleuterio Suina 50, Pumpkin	T	Santiago Pecos 45, Ivy	P
1930	Marcial Quintana 51, Water	T	Santiago Arquero 40, Sage	P
1923	José Domingo Chalan 44, Corn	P	Santiago Melchior 44, Cottonwood	T

Appendix 12

COCHITI GOVERNORS AND LIEUTENANT GOVERNORS,
1923–1954

Year°	Governor Age and Clan	Kiva	Lieutenant Governor Age and Clan	Kiva
1954	Clofe Arquero 61, Sage	P†	Octavio Suina 48, Ivy	T
1953	José Domingo Quintana 66, Oak	T	Cresencio Pecos 54, Ivy	P
1952	Ramón Herrera 51, Cottonwood	P	Octavio Suina 46, Ivy	T
1951	Epitacio Arquero 61, Sage	T	Fernando Cordero 46, Oak	P
1950	Salvador Arquero 51, Cottonwood	P	Gerónimo Quintana 35, Oak	T
1949	José Domingo Quintana 62, Oak	T	Ramón Herrera 48, Cottonwood	P
1948	Juan José Suina 66, Ivy	P	Gerónimo Quintana 33, Oak	T
1947	Juan José Trujillo 59, Coyote	T	Fernando Cordero 42, Oak	P
1946	Clofe Arquero 53, Sage	P	Gerónimo Quintana 31, Oak	T
1945	Luis Ortiz 64, Turquoise	T	Salvador Arquero 46, Cottonwood	P
1944	Epitacio Arquero 54, Sage	T	Gerónimo Quintana 29, Oak	T
1943	Epitacio Arquero 53, Sage	T	Gerónimo Quintana 28, Oak	T
1942	Luis Ortiz 61, Turquoise	T	Salvador Arquero 43, Cottonwood	P
1941	Luis Ortiz 60, Turquoise	T	Salvador Arquero 42, Cottonwood	P
1940	Epitacio Arquero 50, Sage	T	Lorenzo Herrera 59, Water	P
1939	Luis Ortiz 58, Turquoise	T	Salvador Arquero 40, Cottonwood	P
1938	Luis Ortiz 57, Turquoise	T	Salvador Arquero 39, Cottonwood	P

° Records for years not listed were unobtainable.
† "P" refers to Pumpkin Kiva, "T" to Turquoise Kiva.

Year*	Governor Age and Clan	Kiva	Lieutenant Governor Age and Clan	Kiva
1937	José Alcario Montoya 58, Corn	P	Celestino Quintana 26, Turquoise	T
1936	Luis Ortiz 55, Turquoise	T	Lorenzo Herrera 55, Water	P
1935	Luis Ortiz 54, Turquoise	T	Lorenzo Herrera 54, Water	P
1934	Santiago Cordero 56, Sage	T	Clofe Arquero 41, Sage	P
1933	Luis Ortiz 52, Turquoise	T	Lorenzo Herrera 52, Water	P
1932	Juan José Trujillo 44, Coyote	T	Clofe Arquero 39, Sage	P
1931	Juan José Trujillo 43, Coyote	T	Clofe Arquero 38, Sage	P
1930	Luis Ortiz 49, Turquoise	T	Lorenzo Herrera 49, Water	P
1928	Luis Ortiz 47, Turquoise	T	Lorenzo Herrera 47, Water	P
1927	José Alcario Montoya 48, Corn	P	----------------------------	----
1923	Marcial Quintana 44, Water	T	Lorenzo Herrera 42, Water	P

Appendix 13

COCHITI *FISCALES* AND LIEUTENANT *FISCALES*, 1923–1954

Year°	*Fiscale* Age and Clan	Kiva	Lieutenant *Fiscale* Age and Clan	Kiva
1954	Alfred Herrera 39, Cottonwood	P†	Solomon Suina 39, Shipewe	T
1953	Pablo Trujillo 49, Turquoise	T	Francisco Herrera 60, Cottonwood	P
1952	Alfred Herrera 37, Cottonwood	P	Solomon Suina 37, Shipewe	T
1951	Pablo Trujillo 47, Turquoise	T	Francisco Herrera 58, Cottonwood	P
1950	Cresencio Pecos 51, Ivy	P	Octavio Suina 44, Ivy	T
1949	Damasio Quintana 57, Oak	T	Pancracio Chalan 41, Ivy	P
1948	Cresencio Pecos 49, Ivy	P	Pablo Trujillo 44, Turquoise	T
1947	Lorenzo Suina 63, Pumpkin	T	Ramón Herrera 46, Cottonwood	P
1946	Nestor Herrera 55, Cottonwood	P	Pablo Trujillo 42, Turquoise	T
1945	Diego Romero 55, Sage	T	Cresencio Pecos 46, Ivy	P
1944	Pasqual Suina 44, Oak	P	Santiago Herrera 31, Coyote	T
1943	Pasqual Suina 43, Oak	P	Santiago Herrera 30, Coyote	T
1942	Diego Romero 52, Sage	T	Lorenzo Cordero 44, Coyote	T
1941	Diego Romero 51, Sage	T	Lorenzo Cordero 43, Coyote	T
1939	Diego Romero 49, Sage	T	Pasqual Suina 39, Oak	P
1938	Diego Romero 48, Sage	T	Nestor Arquero 33, Sage	P
1937	Pasqual Suina 37, Oak	P	Marcelo Quintana 33, Cottonwood	T
1932	Epitacio Arquero 42, Sage	T	-------------------------	----
1931	Epitacio Arquero 41, Sage	T	-------------------------	----

° Records for years not listed were unobtainable.
† "P" refers to Pumpkin Kiva, "T" to Turquoise Kiva.

Year°	Fiscale Age and Clan	Kiva	Lieutenant Fiscale Age and Clan	Kiva
1930	Epifanio Pecos 36, Ivy	P	------------------------------	----
1923	Adelaido Montoya 56, Cottonwood	P	Diego Arquero 34, Sage	T

Appendix 14

COCHITI *ALGUACILITOS*, 1945–1952

Year	Alguacilito	Age	Kiva	Clan
1952	Edward Cordero	21	T†	Oak
	Ivan Lewis	33	T	Antelope
	Delphine Quintana	37	T	Cottonwood
	Juan Rosario Melchior	40	P	Pumpkin
	Celso Montoya	38	P	Oak
	Aloysius Pecos	37	P	Oak
1951	Patricio Arquero	20	T	Water
	Eleuterio Cordero	45	T	Oak
	Loretto Herrera	26	T	Coyote
	Antonio Naranjo	33	P	Oak
	José Dolores Pecos	30	P	Oak
	Justo Pérez	56	P	Pumpkin
1950°	Loretto Herrera	25	T	Coyote
	Guadalupe Ortiz	21	T	Cottonwood
	José Rey Suina	40	T	Ivy
1949	No data available			
1948	Cresencio Suina	35	T	Ivy
	Octavio Suina	42	T	Ivy
	Solomon Suina	33	T	Shipewe
	Juan B. Arquero	24	P	Water
	Francisco Herrera	55	P	Cottonwood
	Antonio Suina	21	P	Oak
1947	Santiago Benada	23	T	Sage

° Names of the three Pumpkin *alguacilitos* were unobtainable.
† "T" refers to Turquoise Kiva, "P" to Pumpkin Kiva.

Year	Alguacilito	Age	Kiva	Clan
	Reyes Melchior	24	T	Pumpkin
	Damasio Quintana	55	T	Oak
	Alvin Arquero	28	P	Oak
	Cruz Pérez	67	P	Cottonwood
	Justo Pérez	52	P	Pumpkin
1946	Cresencio Suina	33	T	Ivy
	Octavio Suina	40	T	Ivy
	Solomon Suina	31	T	Shipewe
	Juan B. Arquero	22	P	Water
	Pancracio Chalan	38	P	Ivy
	Fernando Cordero	40	P	Oak
1945	Romulo Cordero	23	T	Corn
	Loretto Herrera	20	T	Coyote
	Juan Velasquez	43	T	Red Shell
	Alvin Arquero	26	P	Oak
	Ramón Herrera	43	P	Cottonwood
	Justo Pérez	50	P	Pumpkin

Appendix 15

COCHITI *FISCALITOS*, 1945–1952

Year	Fiscalito	Age	Kiva	Clan
	Juan Benada	36	T	Sage
1952	Wilfred Herrera	17	T*	Ivy
	José Higenio Quintana	37	T	Cottonwood
	Ernest Suina	15	T	Oak
	Nestor Arquero (in service)	28	P	Oak
	José Abenicio Herrera	17	P	Oak
1951	Juan Benada	35	T	Sage
	José Higenio Quintana	36	T	Cottonwood
	Cresencio Suina	38	T	Ivy
	José Rey Suina	41	T	Ivy
	Nestor Arquero	27	P	Oak
	Cruz Pérez	71	P	Cottonwood
1950	No data available			
1949	Patricio Arquero	18	T	Water
	Loretto Herrera	24	T	Coyote
	Guadalupe Ortiz	20	T	Cottonwood
	José Higenio Quintana	34	T	Cottonwood
	Teodor Suina	31	T	Ivy
	Lorenzo Herrera	22	P	Oak
1948	Philip Cooka	41	T	Bear
	Ivan Lewis	29	T	Antelope
	Pancracio Chalan	40	P	Ivy
	Juan Rosario Melchior	36	P	Pumpkin
	Celso Montoya	34	P	Oak
	Aloysius Pecos	33	P	Oak
1947	Loretto Herrera	22	T	Coyote
	Guadalupe Ortiz	18	T	Cottonwood
	José Rey Suina	37	T	Ivy
	Antonio Naranjo	29	P	Oak
	José Dolores Pecos	26	P	Oak
	Antonio Suina	20	P	Oak
1946	José Hilario Herrera	26	T	Oak
	Delphine Quintana	31	T	Cottonwood
	José Adolfo Quintana	25	T	Turquoise
	Juan B. Arquero	22	P	Water
	Juan Rosario Melchior	34	P	Pumpkin
	Aloysius Pecos	31	P	Oak
1945	Juan Benada	29	T	Sage
	Philip Cooka	38	T	Bear

* "T" refers to Turquoise Kiva, "P" to Pumpkin Kiva.

Year	Fiscalito	Age	Kiva	Clan
	Roberto Martinez	42	T	Oak
	Damasio Quintana	53	T	Oak
	Celso Montoya	31	P	Oak
	--------------------------------	----	P	-----------

Appendix 16

COCHITI COUNCIL OF *PRINCIPALES*: Changes during Period 1948–1952

Principal	Age in '48	Kiva	Clan	'48	'49	'50	'51	'52
Arquero, Clote	55	P°	Sage	a	a	a	a	a
Arquero, Diego	60	T	Sage	r	r	r	r	r
Arquero, Epitacio	58	T	Sage	a	a	a	a	a
Arquero, Salvador	49	P	Cottonwood	a	a	a	a	a
Arquero, Santiago	58	P	Sage	a	d	d	d	d
Chalan, Juan Estévan	70	P	Corn	a	a	d	d	d
Chalan, Pancracio	40	P	Ivy	u	a	a	a	n
Chávez, Cipriano	55	P	Water	p	u	u	u	p
Chávez, Francisco	65	P	Water	a	i	i	i	a
Cordero, Fernando	43	P	Oak	a	a	a	a	a
Cordero, Lorenzo	50	T	Coyote	a	a	a	a	a
Cordero, Nicanor	72	T	Sage	a	a	i	i	i
Cordero, Santiago	70	T	Sage	a	a	i	i	i
Herrera, Francisco	55	P	Cottonwood	u	u	u	a	a
Herrera, Lorenzo	67	P	Water	a	a	a	a	a
Herrera, Nestor	57	P	Cottonwood	a	a	a	a	a
Herrera, Ramón	47	P	Cottonwood	a	a	a	a	a
Herrera, Santiago	35	T	Coyote	i	i	i	i	i
Melchior, José Domingo	59	P	Cottonwood	p	--	--	--	p

Key: a—active member   n—nonresident (seldom active)
      d—deceased   p—participant; never an officer
      i—inactive   r—rarely active
      u—unqualified because of not having served as a major officer (traditional basis
      of eligibility)

° "P" refers to Pumpkin Kiva, "T" to Turquoise Kiva.

Principal	Age in '48	Kiva	Clan	'48	'49	'50	'51	'52
Montoya, José Alcario	69	P	Corn	i	i	i	r	i
Ortiz, Luis	67	T	Turquoise	a	a	d	d	d
Pancho, Juan	60	P	Oak	i	i	i	i	i
Pecos, Cresencio	49	P	Ivy	a	a	a	a	a
Pecos, Epifanio	54	P	Ivy	a	a	a	a	a
Pecos, Santiago	62	P	Ivy	a	a	i	i	a
Quintana, Celestino	37	T	Turquoise	n	n	n	n	n
Quintana, Damasio	56	T	Oak	..	a	a	a	a
Quintana, Gerónimo	33	T	Oak	a	a	a	a	a
Quintana, José Domingo	61	T	Oak	a	a	a	a	a
Romero, Diego	58	T	Sage	a	a	a	a	a
Romero, Santiago	66	P	Shipewe	a	a	a	a	a
Romero, Vicente	63	T	Sage	a	a	i	i	i
Suina, Eleuterio	67	T	Pumpkin	a	a	a	a	a
Suina, Juan José	66	P	Ivy	a	a	a	a	a
Suina, Lorenzo	64	T	Pumpkin	a	a	i	i	i
Suina, Octavio	42	T	Ivy	..	..	a	a	a
Suina, Pasqual	48	P	Oak	a	d	d	d	d
Suina, Solomon	33	T	Shipewe	..	..	..	..	a
Trujillo, Juan José	60	T	Coyote	a	a	a	a	a
Trujillo, Pablo	44	T	Turquoise	a	a	a	a	a
Trujillo, Rosendo	56	P	Sage	p	..	..	..	p
Velasquez, Juan	46	T	Red Shell	a	a	a	a	a

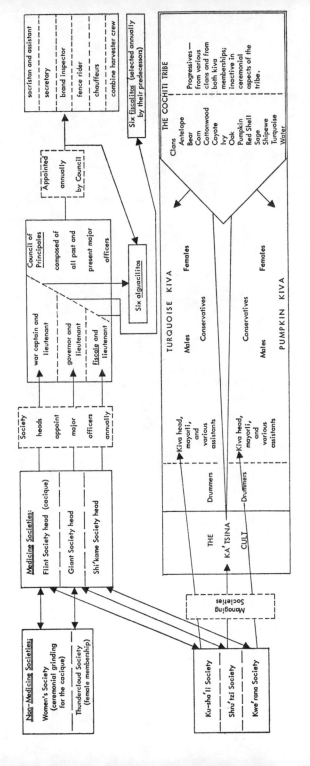

Appendix 17

THE INTERRELATIONSHIPS AMONG COCHITI SOCIAL, POLITICAL, AND CEREMONIAL COMPONENTS

THE COCHITI TRIBE

Clans
Antelope
Bear
Corn
Cottonwood
Coyote
Ivy
Oak
Pumpkin
Red Shell
Sage
Shipewe
Turquoise
Water

Progressives —
from various
clans and from
both kiva
memberships;
inactive in
ceremonial
aspects of the
tribe.

Six fiscalitos (selected annually
by their predecessors)

sacristan and assistant
secretary
brand inspector
fence rider
chauffeurs
combine harvester crew

Appointed
annually
by Council

Council of
Principales
composed of
all past and
present major
officers

Six alguacilitos

war captain and
lieutenant

governor and
lieutenant

fiscals and
lieutenant

Society
heads
appoint
major
officers
annually

Medicine Societies:
Flint Society head (cacique)
Giant Society head
Shi'kame Society head

Non-Medicine Societies:
Women's Society
(ceremonial grinding
for the cacique)
Thundercloud Society
(female membership)

TURQUOISE KIVA
Males   Females
Conservatives

PUMPKIN KIVA
Conservatives
Males   Females

Kiva head,
mayorli,
and
various
assistants

Kiva head,
mayorli,
and
various
assistants

THE
KA'TSINA
CULT

Drummers

Drummers

Managing
Societies

Ku-sha'li Society
Shru'tzi Society
Kwe'rana Society

Extinct Societies: | Snake | Fire | Po'shai-añi | Tuba'ji | Warriors | Hunters

Appendix 18

COCHITI CACIQUE ROSTER

Victoriano Cordero: Shipewe Clan, Turquoise Kiva, born 3/12/76; Flint Society, Snake Society, Fire Society, Ku-sha'lĭ Society; became cacique in December, 1914, and died in office 12/12/46.

Rafaelito Herrera (known also as Semilla and Guayave de Leche): Coyote Clan, Pumpkin Kiva, born 1864; Flint Society, Ku-sha'lĭ Society; became cacique in November, 1911, and died in office 12/22/14.

Marcelo Quintana: Cottonwood Clan, Turquoise Kiva, born 5/15/04; Flint Society, Ku-sha'lĭ Society; became cacique 12/18/46 after serving several days as cacique pro tem.

Guadalupe Romero: Sun Clan, Pumpkin Kiva, birth date unknown; Flint Society, Ku-sha'lĭ Society; became cacique about 1890 and was still holding the office when Starr took his census, 9/28/97.

Antonio Suina: Coyote Clan, Pumpkin Kiva, born 1856; Flint Society, Snake Society, Fire Society, Ku-sha'lĭ Society; became cacique sometime after September, 1897, and died in office 11/8/11.

Appendix 19

COCHITI FLINT SOCIETY ROSTER

Antonio Chalan (father of José Domingo): Cottonwood Clan, Pumpkin Kiva, born about 1842; *not* a Ku-sha'lĭ member; died 3/28/12.

José Domingo Chalan: Water Clan, Pumpkin Kiva, born 5/29/75; Ku-sha'lĭ Society; died 9/15/33.

Victoriano Cordero: Shipewe Clan, Turquoise Kiva, born 3/12/76; Snake Society, Fire Society, Ku-sha'lĭ Society; cacique and Flint head from December, 1914, until his death, 12/12/46.

Rafaelito Herrera (known also as Semilla and Guayave de Leche): Coyote Clan, Pumpkin Kiva, born 1864; Ku-sha'lĭ Society; cacique and Flint head from November, 1911, until his death, 12/22/14.

Marcelo Quintana: Cottonwood Clan, Turquoise Kiva, born 5/15/04; Ku-sha'lĭ Society; cacique and Flint head since 12/18/46.

Guadalupe Romero: Sun Clan, Pumpkin Kiva, birth date unknown; Ku-sha'lĭ Society; cacique and Flint head from about 1890 until his death sometime after 9/28/97.

Luis Romero: Shipewe Clan, Pumpkin Kiva, born 1/31/79; *not* a Ku-sha'lĭ member; died 4/28/20.

Antonio Suina: Coyote Clan, Pumpkin Kiva, born 1856; Snake Society, Fire Society, Ku-sha'lĭ Society; cacique and Flint head from sometime after September, 1897, until his death, 11/8/11.

Antonio "Chávesito" Trujillo: Sun Clan, Pumpkin Kiva (formerly Turquoise), born 2/21/60; *not* a Ku-sha'lĭ member; died 7/31/21.

Juanito Trujillo: Sage Clan, Turquoise Kiva (formerly Pumpkin), born 1/13/81; Ku-sha'lĭ Society.

Appendix 20

SELECTED WITCHCRAFT ACCOUNTS

Witchcraft is something that is practiced by only the old-time Indians. However, this incident actually occurred about 1933. I went to my ranch for about fifteen days. The first day, after supper, two owls called to me from a nearby tree, "Hey! Hey!" I got out my rifle and then closed the door and went to bed. But I couldn't sleep. Every night these two owls came and perched just over the door. I shot at them about twenty times, but it didn't do any good. Then my oldest boy came to the ranch and stayed with me. He heard the same thing. We recognized the voices of R—— C—— and V—— A——. The two of us began to play cards, but the two owls stayed close by. Then my boy took a bullet and cut a cross on its nose with a knife. V—— was close to the gate and R—— was across the arroyo. After the boy shot, the owls disappeared. When we returned to the pueblo, I told my wife about these things, but she would not believe it. I told her to watch and see if V—— didn't go to the store to get medicine the next day; sure enough, V—— came in and asked for medicine. He remained sick about four months. Then V——'s nephew came by and I asked him. He said it was true—V——'s "seat was filled with shot wounds" —and soon after that V—— died. [72]

Soon I went again to my ranch, and again on the way an owl called, "Hey! Hey!" This time I recognized T——'s voice. That night this calling came again, about eleven o'clock. I fired, and there were no more calls. Soon after that T—— went to the hospital with a sick foot; he stayed about nine or ten months before he returned. Soon, T—— and I went to the ranch together for wood; I told T—— that I had shot him. We talked all that night at the ranch, and in the morning T—— said that in two or three days he would die as he had talked too much. Three days later, T—— was dead. [72]

The Cochití word for *witch*, or *bad person*, is "ka'nat-yai-ya." When the Conservancy District canal was dug through the bank where Clofe Arquero now has his barn and corral, the workmen uncovered a sort of cave. It was round, had adobe walls, and was about eight feet in diameter. A bone awl was found in the house by Antonio Calabaza. It is generally believed around the pueblo that this was a witch's house. It was destroyed during the construction, and most people feel that there has been much less witchcraft practiced at Cochití since. [53, 65, 70, 72]

One time the parents of Cruz Pérez were returning to Cochití from Tesuque or San Ildefonso. As they came to the steep hill at Bajada, a coyote jumped from behind a bush, and the horse that Refugia was riding bucked and threw her off. She was sick for four or five months, and then she said she wanted the medicine men to cure her. She spoke to John Dixon, her brother, and to Juan Pedro Melchior, and they agreed to help her. She and her family had to have a big feast to pay the medicine men. Lots of people came; she was in a big room at the southwest corner of the plaza. Her bed was placed by the door, and there was a big fire outside the door. The door was closed, and suddenly there was a terrific noise outside but no one could see what was happening. Then the door opened and a big coyote stuck his head part way inside and then withdrew it. He did this a second time; the third time, the coyote came all the way in. The next day, Refugia was all right again. [72]

One time when I came back from a trip to Santa Fe, I had had a little to drink and was sleepy. So I went to bed and was soon sound asleep. The next day my wife told me that she had seen two balls of fire, about eight inches across, come up out of the chimney of a house next to ours—or close to it—and these balls rolled around the edge of the roof. Then they rolled down to the ground and around the plaza. At this point, my wife ran home. I told her she should have awakened me. However, the following night, the same thing happened, and this time I saw them. I wanted to catch them, but my wife and her cousin held me back. Soon the balls of fire turned to ashes, like burned rags. I kicked them and they fell to pieces. The next day, I reported this to Victoriano [Cordero], the cacique. He said that I should grab just a piece from these balls of ashes, and then the next day I should look around and if I saw a man with a tear or a hole in his pants, or a woman with a tear or hole in her dress, then I would know who these witches were. [72]

About 1924, the husband of A— C— B— was very sick. I was going to get his horses at a corral near where Cruz Pérez now lives. I was called back to get some coal oil for A—. Later that evening, while returning from Sile, I was just passing a large bush south of the arroyo by

Pancracio's house when my horse reared. Looking more closely, I saw a figure huddled in the bush. "So'ka-nī [friend]," he said. I recognized the voice of A——'s ailing husband. I stopped to see if I could help if there was any trouble, but he called to go away. When I talked with Juan Pedro Melchior about this, he said that this was the spirit of A——'s husband—who had died just shortly before this moment. [72]

About 1910, there were lots of burros, two hundred or more, about three hundred horses, and many more cattle than now. Every man, whether or not he owned burros, helped herd them. Every night they were put in the corral that is still by Ramón's [Herrera] house. At this particular time the horses were grazing in the mountains near Bear Head Peak. The war captain sent for the horses to be brought in. Ventura Ortiz, a brother of Luis Ortiz, stayed up in the mountains to hunt. He found some deer tracks; following them, he soon saw the deer, a big one, but he couldn't get a shot. He trailed it for more than a mile. Then he came to a ridge, sloping on one side, but very steep on the other. Somehow the deer surprised Ventura and with his horns pushed him off the ridge and he slid down the side. He was not killed, but he was sick for more than a year. At that time J—— B—— P—— was an *alguacilito;* J—— told me that on the night of the cure by the medicine men, he was dressed in white—shirt, pants, moccasins—and was armed with a bow and arrow as guard. The medicine man "looked like the Devil"—all black, face and body, with a small skirt or kilt. The medicine man ran west to Peralta Peak, followed by the *alguacilito,* whom he soon left behind, and disappeared for a couple of hours. He returned carrying a large buck, whose horns were so large that they could not get them through the door when they returned to the pueblo and the house of the sick man. Then the sick man recovered. [72]

This is the story of the Mat'zī Ko'katz Ka'tsīna. It happened a long time ago, but my father saw the substitute actually appear at Cochití. This is one mask which has been done away with because of what happened while this Ka'tsīna was dancing. This is the only mask I know that has been done away with by the "big men" [ceremonial leaders].

There was a Ka'tsīna Dance in the plaza. Lunch time came, and after a rest, the first dance after noon began. A guard Ka'tsīna came into the plaza. He was a stranger who had never been seen at Cochití before. However, the people showed their respect and allowed him to join with the other masked dancers there in the plaza the rest of the afternoon. Near the end of the day, this Ka'tsīna went up to one of the Ku-sha'lī. They "talked" with signs; the Ku-sha'lī was able to understand this stranger.

The Ka'tsīnas have a place where they dress and where they can return during the time of the dance to rest briefly. This Ka'tsīna now went to this place. When he got to this house, he walked a certain way and after entering, he kept his mask on. Other Ka'tsīnas usually take the masks off in order to have a better rest. The Shrū'tzī Society head was there and asked him to take his mask off, but he refused. After a time, he returned with the other Ka'tsīnas to the plaza.

Later, this Ka'tsīna went again to the Ku-sha'lī for a "talk." He asked to race one of the Cochití audience. The Ku-sha'lī went to the middle of the plaza and made an announcement. He particularly put it up to the old men who were sitting in a group at the side for their decision. They agreed that this could be done, and told the Ka'tsīna to pick out someone.

The Ka'tsīna looked about him at the people and at those up on the roofs. There was a man up there who had washed his hair that same morning and it was hanging loose down his back. This man was called down by the Ka'tsīna; he was known to be a pretty good runner. Then the old men and other people went out of the plaza to the northeast, to the corral, where there was an open lane down to the irrigation canal, a "race course."

In ka'tsīna races, it is the rule to run in such a direction as to end in front of the audience. This Ka'tsīna insisted upon running away from the people, and they gave in to his wishes. (Since then, because of what happened at this race, this rule has never been violated again.) The race started about where Aloysius Pecos now has his house [1951]. A starting line was drawn in the sand; the two runners took their place; an officer counted "One, two, three, four, go," hitting the ground with a stick each time. The man immediately went out in front of the Ka'tsīna (probably the Ka'tsīna let him?); halfway down the course, the Ka'tsīna caught up with him. Near the end, they were even. At the end, the runners went down over the crest of the hill (about in front of Philip Cooka's or Clofe Arquero's now—and at that time, there was a greater dropoff than at present) and out of view. There, out of sight of the others, the Ka'tsīna caught the man from behind by his long hair, easily pulling him off balance and throwing him to the ground. He quickly put a handful of dirt in the man's mouth, thereby choking him. Using his flint knife, he scalped him. He was first seen running on out across the fields to the northeast. Then the people went to the end of the race course to see what had become of the other runner. As soon as they realized what had happened, the men got their weapons and on foot and on horseback, they took up the chase.

At that time, the river was very high—perhaps this was about May. Some of the horsemen nearly caught up with the Ka'tsīna about where the steel bridge is now. He jumped from the bank, but instead of sinking in the water, he appeared to run right across the surface. When he left the river, he entered a cave on the eastern bank. The swift-flowing water discouraged the horsemen from attempting to cross. They waited for him to emerge from the cave. While waiting there, one of them saw a big signal smoke coming from somewhere north of La Tetilla. One of the horsemen was chai'añi (medicine man); he knew what that smoke meant. He told the others that there was no use in waiting any longer. They might as well return to the pueblo. The Ka'tsīna had been a witch—not a real Ka'tsīna—and had been "an enemy." This was his way of "getting even" for something with the man chosen to race with him.

Witchery was behind this incident, and three or four years after this actually occurred, an impersonation of this Ka'tsīna was made. The mask and remainder of the costume was copied and it was called the "Blood Mask Ka'tsīna" (Mat'zī Ko'katz Ka'tsīna). Later, when the big men were talking about ka'tsīnas one time, one man suggested doing away with this ka'tsīna as it was not a good one and would best be forgotten or at least no longer impersonated, and was too dangerous to do so. The others agreed and since then this ka'tsīna has never been seen.

"This simply shows that even the big men who have charge of these things for the good of the pueblo are sometimes actually traitors, or bad people, or witches. They use their official positions in order to influence the others to do things which they should not do. Even some of the recent medicine men have been suspected of 'being more on the other side.' It is good for the pueblo that the other big men decided to forget this ka'tsīna." [94]

[Journal of Bandelier, April 25, 1882] In a row of houses near the Peralta Arroyo, now abandoned, there lived two men, both good hunters. One of them was a sorcerer, the other was not. The sorcerer and the other man's wife entered into a compact against the life of the other, in order that they might marry each other. So one night the hunter was in the Cañada late and, not wishing to return home after dark sat down in a rocky recess on the right-hand side of the arroyo. While there, crows and owls began to alight upon the neighboring trees, and then change themselves into the forms of men and women. One of them approached the rock, without noticing the hunter, and the rock opened, revealing a cave inside. Soon that cave filled with sorcerers and witches which all came in the shape of owls and crows. Among them were the friend of his and finally his own wife also. She came late. When asked by the chief of the sorcerers where her husband was, she replied that he was still absent hunting but that she had placed his food on a certain shelf and that, upon his return, the brown corn would speak to him and inform him where the victuals were. It was then agreed upon to have the hunter killed in the morning by a deer, and for that purpose, two of the sorcerers were sent out to fetch in the deer. They brought in the animal. It was called upon to

APPENDICES   **463**

sit down and a cigar was offered to him. After he had begun to smoke, he
threw off his fur and was ready to talk. His task was then assigned to
him, namely: to be on the other side of the arroyo next morning, that the
two hunters would come after him. Then he should charge upon the
doomed one and kill him with his antlers. The deer wept, but said that,
being once under the spell of the cigar, he could not refuse to obey
although it was very wrong. He was then led out again, and the listener
stealthily went home. There, indeed, the corn spoke to him. He seized it,
dipped it into urine, and dashed it against the wall, then took a firebrand
and examined the inner closet where he found, in a small painted cup, the
natural eyes of his wife. These he also dipped into the urine and replaced
them. Then he lay down. After midnight, his wife returned, went into the
closet and remained there. At daybreak, the traitor called him out; they
went and found the deer as agreed. The deer rushed them but killed the
traitor in place of the hunter who dextrously avoided the thrust. He then
went home and found his wife sitting in the dark with her face covered.
Seizing her by the hair, he found that she had the eyes of an owl, not
having been able to use her own. He threw her down, and she died. Such
stories appear to be current. Nambé and Isleta del Sur are great places for
sorcery.

Appendix 21

COCHITI SNAKE SOCIETY ROSTER

Victoriano Cordero: Shipewe Clan, Turquoise Kiva, born 3/12/76; Flint Society, Fire Society, Ku-sha'lĭ Society; cacique and Flint head from December, 1914, until his death, 12/12/46.

José (?) Montoya (son of José Hilario): Corn Clan, Pumpkin Kiva, born about 1873; died about 1908. (This man was named as a member of the Snake Society by only one informant [3]; while his membership may be valid, it is strange that he was not named by others and also that he was not named by any informant as holding membership in societies normally affiliated with the Snake Society.)

Antonio Suina: Coyote Clan, Pumpkin Kiva, born 1856; Flint Society, Fire Society, Ku-sha'lĭ Society; cacique and Flint head from sometime after September, 1897, until his death, 11/8/11.

Appendix 22

COCHITI GIANT SOCIETY ROSTER

Natividad Arquero (later known as Quintana):° Oak Clan, Turquoise Kiva, birth date unknown; Giant head until his death sometime after 1923.

Vicente Arquero: Oak Clan, Pumpkin Kiva, born about 1871; died 11/22/39.

Priciliano Roybal Cordero:°° Oak Clan, Turquoise Kiva, born 1893 (San Ildefonso); Thundercloud Society; said to have requested membership in the Giant Society.

Trinidad Melchior Montoya:°° Cottonwood Clan, Pumpkin Kiva, born 9/13/73; Thundercloud Society; requested membership in the Giant Society; died 12/23/46.

° Named as having been a member of the Shrŭ'tzĭ Society; upon becoming a medicine man, he withdrew from the Shrŭ'tzĭ.

°° As note on page 269, two women (Priciliana Roybal Cordero and Trinidad Melchior Montoya) were named by informants when they were compiling the roster for the Giant Society. Informants disagreed about whether they held actual membership or whether their membership was limited to the closely affiliated Thundercloud Society. Both women were married to Ku-sha'lĭ members: Priciliana, to Lorenzo Cordero, head Ku-sha'lĭ since 1946; and Trinidad, to José Alcario Montoya.

Cipriano Quintana: Water Clan, Turquoise Kiva, born 3/1/72; Giant head since October, 1945.

Francisco Quintana (brother of Cipriano): Water Clan, Turquoise Kiva, born 8/23/69; Giant head at the time of his death, 12/30/16.

Pedro Suina (father of Vicente): Pumpkin Clan, Turquoise Kiva, born 4/6/75; Giant head at the time of his death, 10/24/45.

Vicente Suina:° Shipewe Clan, Turquoise Kiva, born 8/9/20; absent from the pueblo and inactive since late 1950.

Appendix 23

COCHITI SHI'KAME SOCIETY ROSTER

Luis Archibeque: No information could be obtained about this man other than that he was also a member of the Kwe'rana Society.

Antonio Calabaza: Shipewe Clan, Turquoise Kiva, born about 1866; Kwe'rana Society; died 9/20/41.

Manuel Melchior: Turquoise Clan, Turquoise Kiva, born about 1839; Kwe'rana Society; head Shi'kame until his death, 9/19/09.

José Maria Naranjo: Oak Clan, Turquoise Kiva, birth date unknown; Kwe'rana Society; head Shi'kame; death date unknown.

Manuel Ortiz: Oak Clan, Turquoise Kiva, born 4/21/77; Kwe'rana Society; head Shi'kame; death date unknown.

José Vivian Pérez: Water Clan, Pumpkin Kiva, born about 1855; Kwe'rana Society; died 6/22/08.

Santiago Romero: Clan unknown, Turquoise Kiva, birth date unknown; Kwe'rana Society; death date unknown.

Eufrasio Suina: Coyote Clan, Turquoise Kiva (formerly Pumpkin), born 11/17/12; Kwe'rana Society; head Shi'kame.

Anastacio Urina: Water Clan, Pumpkin Kiva, born 4/2/76; Kwe'rana Society; death date unknown.

Appendix 24

COCHITI WOMEN'S SOCIETY ROSTER

Reyes Suina Chalan: Ivy Clan, Pumpkin Kiva, born 4/15/83; Kwe'-rana Society.

Damesia Suina Cordero: Shipewe Clan, Turquoise Kiva, born 11/26/04.

Juana Herrera Herrera: No information could be obtained about this woman other than that she preceded Juanita Chávez Romero as Society head.

Juanita Chávez Romero: Cottonwood Clan, Pumpkin Kiva, born 7/9/72; Ku-sha'lï Society; Society head.

Lucinda Cordero Suina: Shipewe Clan, Turquoise Kiva, born 12/15/78; also Kwe'rana. (This woman is the mother of Damesia [Women's Society] and Vicente [Giant Society]; the widow of Pedro Suina [head Giant]; and the sister of Victoriano [cacique, Flint, Snake, Fire, and Ku-sha'lï].)

Appendix 25

COCHITI SHRU'TZI SOCIETY ROSTER[*]

José de Jesus Quintana Benada: Turquoise Clan, Turquoise Kiva, born 3/13/81; death date unknown.

José Nicanor Cordero: Sage Clan, Turquoise Kiva, born 8/8/76; Society head since December, 1927.

Manuel Cordero: Sage Clan, Turquoise Kiva; birth and death dates unknown.

Juan Pedro Melchior: Cottonwood Clan, Pumpkin Kiva, born about 1860; dropped out of the society and became a Progressive sometime before 1920; died 5/1/35.

Santiago Quintana Melchior: Coyote Clan, Turquoise Kiva, born 6/23/78; died 3/1/31.

Adelaido Montoya: Cottonwood Clan, Pumpkin Kiva, born 12/25/60; died 5/17/26.

Guadalupe Ortiz: Cottonwood Clan, Turquoise Kiva, born 12/10/29.

José Ortiz: No information could be obtained about this member other than that he was also a member of the Warriors Society (Ompï).

[*] Vicente Suina and Natividad Arquero, as noted in Appendix 22, at one time belonged to the Shrū'tzï Society but withdrew at the time they joined the Giant Medicine Society.

Lucia Romero: Cottonwood Clan, Pumpkin Kiva, born 3/22/70; died 1/29/06. (Lucia was the wife of Adelaido Montoya and the daughter of Guadalupe Romero, cacique during the 1890's. See pages 283–284 for a discussion of the unusualness of a woman belonging to the Shrū'tzī Society.)

José Victor Suina: Sage Clan, Turquoise Kiva, born 2/23/53; head Shrū'tzī at the time of his death, 12/19/27.

Abenicio Trujillo: Ivy Clan, Pumpkin Kiva, born 5/5/95; dropped out of the society and became a Progressive about 1920; died 1/30/49.

Appendix 26

COCHITI KA'TSINA CULT

The data in this appendix are presented in two sections. Section A is scarcely more than a roster of the individual characterizations of the Cochití ka'tsīnas. These have been arranged in the categories in which the Cochití normally think of their masked impersonations. Included is an estimate of the frequency of their appearances: "often" indicates at least an annual appearance; "seldom" indicates intervals of more than a year but at least once in three or four years; "rarely" indicates an interval of more than four years and in some of these instances, informants stated that they could not even estimate the time of the figure's last appearance though they could give the proper costume and procedure.

Section B provides a detailed description of each figure, presented by categories in the order in which the figures are listed in Section A. These data, as noted earlier, are highly esoteric so far as non-Pueblo Indians are concerned. Despite this fact and certain risks involved, these data were given voluntarily by several informants in order that they might be recorded before becoming lost to the tribe. The great majority of the descriptions, together with the figures, are believed adequate for an accurate and detailed reconstruction. The roster appeared to have been essentially complete as of 1952.

Section A

I. *Individual Important Ka'tsīnas*

1. He'rūta (Head Ka'tsīna). Only one of these impersonations appears at a time, with the exception of the He'rūta Dance, when a line

of five, seven, or nine identically costumed dancers appears. Called "Ka'tsīna father."   *Often*

2. I'dja-kū. Head, or father, of the Shrū'tzī Society. He is also the head of the Racing Ka'tsīnas.   *Rarely*

3. Ku-sha'lī Kē'a-nasht[10]. Called "Ku-sha'lī father." In recent times, he has been more popularly called "Turtle-shell Carrier." If the Ku-sha'lī Society head prefers, he may replace He'rūta in the Speckled Dance; theoretically, this might happen in virtually any dance, but in practice it is almost never done.   *Often*

4. Wē'korī. Father of the Kwe'rana Society and the Shī'kame Society. His appearance is most usual at initiations of the Kwe'rana, but he may appear briefly at any of the regular masked dances.   *Rarely*

5. Kai'tsame. Brother of Wē'korī. These two always appear together.   *Rarely*

6. Ma'sha-wa (Turkey Buzzard). This mask belongs to the Giant Medicine Society.   *Seldom*

II. *Motion-makers, or Actor Ka'tsīnas*

7. Shka'shrūtz. He appears with the Tsē'adyū-wītsa dances; there is a black one for the Black Speckled Dance and a red one for the Red Speckled Dance.   *Often*

8. Na'wish. He appears for the Dyū'wenī Dance, sometimes with Pai'yat-yarna.   *Often*

9. Pai'yat-yama. He appears in the Dyū'wenī Dance along with Na'wish; Pai'yat-yama enters directly behind the Ku-sha'lī who guides the dancers in. Pai'yat-yama *must* be impersonated by a Ku-sha'lī member.   *Often*

10. Ko'chī-nako (Yellow Woman). Only one of these is ever seen; she always appears at the Big Zuñi Dance.   *Often*

11. Ko'ko-shūlī. One of these always accompanies the Little Zuñi Dance   *Often*

III. *Guards and Attendants, or Side Dancers, for the Ka'tsīnas*

12. Tzī'na (Turkey). He usually, but not necessarily, appears with a line of Turkey dancers.   *Seldom*

13. Ko'hai-o (Bear). He is referred to as "was'tich"—meaning that the impersonation can be done only by a medicine man since medicine men are the only ones who know how to produce the peculiar high-pitched whistle required for this type of ka'tsīna.   *Seldom*

14. Mo'katch (Mountain Lion). He is also "was'tich"; formerly there was one for the north, west, south, and east.   *Seldom*

15. Dya'ñī (Deer).   *Rarely*

16. Kutz (Antelope). There are two types: (*a*) with red body paint; (*b*) with white shirt (confused with line dancers?).   *Rarely*

17. Kash'ko (Mountain Goat).   *Rarely*

18. Kū'kañī Shpū'la (Red Fawn).   *Rarely*

19. Mo'ña-kai Shpū'la (Black Fawn).   *Rarely*

20. O'shatsh (Sun). He is "was'tich."   *Rarely*

21. Hī'ya. He always appears with his brother, E'ka.   *Rarely*
22. E'ka. He is always with his brother, Hī'ya.   *Rarely*
23. Hīl'līl-yīka (Hair-cutter). He always appears with his mate, I'wa-kai-ya.   *Rarely*
24. I'wa-kai-ya (One-Who-Combs). She always accompanies her mate, Hīl'līl-yīka.   *Rarely*
25. Hīū'sa-pats (Hitter) (hard).   *Seldom*
26. Hīū'shta-kats (Hitter) (soft).   *Rarely*
27. Shko'o-ko (Small owl-like bird).   *Rarely*
28. Ko'a-līsh. He is "was'tich."   *Rarely*
29. Hū'hū-ya.   *Rarely*
30. Nʸen'yēka.   *Often*
31. Shrūī'yana. There are four pairs of these—for North, West, South, and Nadir.   *Often*
32. Tsē'ya-mash-ta-ti^{owi}.   *Rarely*
33. Bloody Hand Ka'tsīna. This is the only masked impersonation which informants classified as extinct ("gone"); this classification was based on the fact that tribal leaders were said to have "destroyed" this mask because of the misfortune associated with it.

IV. *Musicians Accompanying Various Ka'tsīna Dance Lines*
34. Ko'chī-nako (Yellow Woman). In contrast to No. 10 (of the same name), two of these appear together for the following dances: Tsē'adyū-wītsa, Dyū'wenī, Cho'watsa, and A'ha-ī-hī. They play on a notched stick held over a dry hollow gourd.   *Often*

V. *Ka'tsīna Dance Lines (Always Composed of an Uneven Number of Dancers)*
35. A'shū-wa Ma'ka-shañī (Big Zuñi Dance). This is said to have come from Zuñi many years ago; there are Zuñi songs, but also songs from Cochití, Hopi, and elsewhere.   *Often*
36. A'shū-wa Lī'ka-shañī (Little Zuñi Dance). Said to have the same general background as No. 35.   *Often*
37. Tsē'adyū-wītsa Dance.   *Often*
38. Tzī'na (Turkey) Dance.   *Often*
39. Dyū'wenī (Frijoles Cañon) Dance.   *Often*
40. Wai'yosh (Duck) Dance.   *Often*
41. Kutz (Antelope) Dance.   *Often*
42. Dya'ñī (Deer) Dance.   *Often*
43. Kū'kañi Kē'awī-charla (Red Speckled Dance).   *Often*
44. Mo'ña-kai Kē'awī-charla (Black Speckled Dance).   *Often*
45. Racing Ka'tsīna Dance. This includes several pairs of racers—Sun Ka'tsīna (different from the guard Sun Ka'tsīna), Longears Ka'tsīna, and Black Foot Ka'tsīna.   *Rarely*
46. Tsē'ya-nom (Even) Dance. This is very similar to the Wai'yosh Dance (No. 40); the songs and steps are the same. The dancers wear shirts and the masks have no beaks; Tsē'ya-nom should be danced only in cold weather.   *Often*

47. Ha'ñi-sat-ya-me (Ka'tsīnas That Live in the East) Dance. *Often*

48. Hiū'shta-kats Dance. The line of dancers is dressed like the guard with this name.   *Rarely*

49. He'rūta Dance. There is an entire line of dancers dressed just like the leader, who fades into the line, thereby losing his identity. The Ku-sha'lī go through all sorts of antics in their search for him, much to the delight of the spectators.   *Rarely*

50. Kash'ko (Mountain Goat) Dance. The dancers use no rattles or whistles (the only dance in which this is true); the words of the songs used "are very peculiar."   *Rarely*

51. Shrūī'yana Dance. The dancers are dressed just like the guards of this name; in this dance, the guards are dressed as Shrūī'yana also; only the leader is distinguished by the rattle he carries.   *Rarely*

52. A'ha-i-hī Dance. The impersonations for this dance should be done only by those who are sir'shtī (nonsociety members [See p. 239 f.]).   *Often*

53. Cho'wa-tsa (Slow) Dance.   *Often*

54. Chīch'she Dance.   *Often*

55. Tsē'ya-mash-ta-ti^{owi} Dance.   *Rarely*

Section B

I. *Individual Important Ka'tsīnas*

1. *He'ruta, Head Ka'tsīna.* He'ruta, called "Ka'tsīna father" by some, appears as a single individual at all masked ceremonies with two exceptions: in the Speckled dances, he is usually replaced by the Ku-sha'lī father; and in the He'ruta Dance, an entire line of dancers dressed in identical costumes play a part in obscuring the true He'ruta as a trick on the Ku-sha'lī. In recent years, the He'ruta impersonations have been done most often by Diego Romero for the Turquoise Kiva and by Cresencio Pecos for the Pumpkin Kiva.

It is interesting that He'ruta is generally recognized by the Cochití as the ka'tsīna leader and, at the same time, he is described with much more variable costuming and paraphernalia than any other individual ka'tsīna. Informants provided descriptions of six quite distinct He'rutas. The details follow; mask sketches appear in Figure 25. Only one form of He'ruta is ever seen on any one occasion.

He'ruta A

Upper trunk: white fringed buckskin shirt that hangs almost to the knees; shirt has V-yoke in front and in back.

Lower trunk: G-string.

Legs: white fringed buckskin leggings; white buckskin moccasins.

Wrists: black leather bowguard on the left; nothing on right.

Hands: right hand free; left hand carries a whole fawnskin bag or pouch filled with all kinds of seeds which he distributes to the crowd after giving general advice at the close of a dance. (These

FIG. 25.—KAʻTSINA MASKS. *a.* Heʻruta A; *b.* Heʻruta B; *c.* Heʻruta C; *d.* Heʻ-ruta D; *e.* Heʻruta E; *f.* Moqui Heʻruta.

seeds are saved by the people to put with other seeds at planting time.) The advice and all conversation is by means of gestures which the impersonator must learn; interpreting is done by the Ku-sha'li.

Mask: helmet, or "bucket," type, basically black (Fig. 25a). Top is covered with buffalohair ("horsehair now"); white zigzag lines encircle the mask vertically; eyes are black with white rings around them; mouth is a small white rectangle; ears are red leather tabs through which there is an eagle feather "earring"; collar is a fox-skin.

On his back, He'ruta carries a bundle of Douglas fir branches about three feet long; placed horizontally at the small of the back, it somewhat obscures the buttocks. In the branches is a yucca whip which he occasionally uses.

He'ruta B

The over-all costume of this ka'tsīna is the same as that of He'ruta A with the exception of the mask painting. The top of buffalohair (horsehair), collar of foxskin, and the red ear tabs with eagle feather "earrings" are identical with those for He'ruta A. The mask, however, is basically white (Fig. 25b), with alternating zigzag lines of green, yellow, and red—four lines of each color—encircling the mask. A green zigzag passes through the right eye (green), a yellow zigzag through the mouth (green), and a red one through the left eye (green).

He'ruta C

This form differs in having no shirt; instead he wears a cape, like a *manta*, of deerskin with the hair still on it (the hair is worn on the outside); this cape hangs to the knees. Arms and legs are painted blue-gray. He carries the bundle of fir on his back and the fawnskin bag of seeds in his hand. Mask (Fig. 25c) is the same except that it is painted green; eyes are white with a black dot in the middle; mouth is a plain circle of red.

He'ruta D

This type (Fig. 25d) is the same as He'ruta C in all its features but one. This ka'tsīna is sometimes called the Kwe'rana He'ruta, and perhaps indicative of this affiliation, he wears a cluster of hawk and blue-jay feathers on the top of his head.

He'ruta E

This He'ruta (Fig. 25e) is also the same as He'ruta C in his general appearance. His mask, however, resembles that of the Moqui He'ruta in having a red oval, outlined in black, for a mouth. His other mask features are the same as for He'ruta C. This He'ruta is called "Ho'to-pa," or "Fawnskin."

He'ruta F, or Moqui He'ruta

As the name suggests, this He'ruta may have come from the Hopi. It is the most divergent in appearance of the Cochití He'rutas.

Upper trunk: painted blue-gray; white band shows just above the top of the kilt.

Lower trunk: Hopi dance kilt, white sash, belt, and foxskin hanging behind.

Legs: white above the knees, blue-gray below.

Feet: white moccasins and skunkskin anklets.

Knees and wrists: one green and one black twist of yarn for each. (On all Ka'tsīnas who wear these twists of yarn, it makes no difference which color is worn on which side except that if the right wrist should happen to have the green yarn then the left knee should also have green.)

Hands: painted white and in each a long yucca whip. This He'ruta does not carry the fawnskin bag of seeds or the bundle of fir that the other forms do.

Mask: helmet type (Fig. 25*f*); green in front and blue-gray in back (color areas are always divided or outlined by a thin black line); red ears with eagle feather earrings; black triangular eyes; red oval, set on the oblique (up, left; down, right); evergreen (fir) collar; white cotton "clouds" covering the top of the mask. At the top of each side there is a "set" of one parrot and two eagle tail-feathers. A cluster of small parrot feathers conceals the point where they are tied to the mask. At the back of the mask, two yucca leaves form a "V," and again a cluster of small parrot feathers conceals the joining. Two turkey breast-feathers are tied near the tip of each yucca leaf.

2. *I'dja-kū*. This ka'tsīna is looked upon as the father of the Shrū'tzi Society and also as the head of the Racing Ka'tsīnas. The impersonator should be a very swift runner; informants stated that this ka'tsīna had not been seen at Cochití since the death of Marcial Quintana in June, 1945. Even though Marcial was more than sixty years old at the time of his death, he had continued to do this impersonation. I'dja-kū sometimes serves as a guard, or side dancer, though he is most often associated with the racers. Costume is as follows:

Upper trunk: painted red, as are the arms and hands.

Lower trunk: yucca belt and G-string; in the belt is folded a yucca whip and also a slightly curved rabbit stick, about three feet long and painted red.

Legs: painted red.

Feet: white moccasins and skunkskin anklets.

He wears a buckskin *manta*, or robe, which hangs to his knees.

Mask: helmet type painted brownish-red and covered with mica specks to make it sparkle (Fig. 26*a*). At the top is a tuft of three downy eagle feathers and a road-runner tail-feather and a yellow

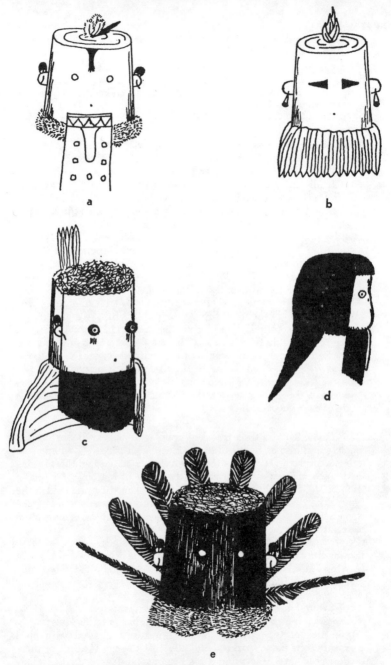

Fig. 26.—KA'TSINA MASKS. a. Ï'dja-kū; b. Ku-sha'lī Kē'a-nash-t[io], or Hē'a-ch[io]; c. Wĕ'korī; d. Kai'tsame; e. Ma'sha-wa, Turkey Buzzard Ka'tsīna.

canary feather. This tuft is attached to a thong at the top of the helmet and falls one way and then another in the wind or as the ka'tsīna moves. In the center of his "forehead" is a tuft of black hair a little less than an inch in diameter and four or five inches long. Ears are red leather tabs with an eagle feather earring in each. Eyes are red dots; mouth extends from a line even with one eye to the other eye and consists of a series of red and white triangular teeth; a red leather tongue four or five inches long hangs from the mouth. Front of the mask has a beard of black horsehair speckled with tufts of eagle down. Back of the mask is concealed by a collar of bobcatskin.

3. *Ku-sha'lī Kē'a-nasht*[io]. In recent years, he has been more popularly referred to as "Hē'a-ch[io]" (Turtle-shell Carrier). He is recognized as the father of the Ku-sha'lī, and the impersonation must be done by a member of that society. He may replace He'ruta in a Speckled Dance if the Ku-sha'lī head should so decide. In practice, this is the only occasion when this substitution occurs, though in theory it could be done any time the Ku-sha'lī head decides. However, since the two kivas took over the Speckled dances from the Ku-sha'lī, Turtle-shell Carrier has not been seen; prior to that time, he was often seen in place of He'ruta. Costume is as follows:

Body: entirely red; wears a buckskin robe which falls to his knees.
Feet: white moccasins with anklets of cornhusks.
Wrists: wristlets of cornhusks.
He wears a broad belt of buckskin, at the back of which is a large turtle shell with several deer-hoof rattles attached. Under the belt and turtle shell, he carries a yucca whip.
Mask: helmet type, painted red (Fig. 26*b*). Eyes are black triangles; red tab ears have earrings of cornhusk cones; at the top of the helmet is a tuft of cornhusks; collar is of purplish-white cornhusks.

4. *Wē'korī*. Wē'korī is the Ka'tsīna father of the Kwe'rana and the Shī'kame societies. He appears—always in the company of his brother, Kai'tsame—most often in conjunction with Kwe'rana initiations, but the two may appear briefly at any of the masked dances. It seems that his appearances are becoming less frequent and are generally at night. The impersonation must be done by a Kwe'rana member. Costume is as follows:

Upper trunk: white shirt with bandolier of black yarn over the left shoulder.
Lower trunk: elaborate kilt of black and yellow designs such as those used in the Kwe'rana Dance. A white sash hangs in back, and there are bells around the waist.
Legs: knitted stockings with the fringes in front.
Knees and wrists: black and green yarn ropes tied to them.
Feet: white moccasins with skunkskin anklets.

Hands: painted white, a deer antler in the right and in the left a small Douglas fir tree which serves as a cane. A small turkey feather is tied at the top of this.

Mask: helmet type; green in front and blue-gray in back (Fig. 26c). Ears are red leather tabs with eagle feather earrings; eyes are protruding black and white balls; no mouth except a tiny circle of black which conceals the air hole; front of the mask has a beard of black horsehair with specks of eagle down in it. Top of the mask is covered over with a cloud of eagle down. At the back of the mask is a collar, or cape, which hangs down far enough to conceal the unbound hair of the impersonator. At the base of the mask a cluster of parrot tail-feathers with a cluster of small parrot feathers conceals the ties. Four braids of parrot feathers, such as those seen on the pole used in the *Tablita* Dance (Fig. 23), hang from this cluster.

5. *Kai'tsame*. He always appears with his brother, Wē'korī. As is true of his brother, Kai'tsame must be impersonated by a Kwe'rana. Costume is as follows:

Upper trunk: white shirt with black yarn bandolier over left shoulder; white cape over both shoulders.

Lower trunk: black and yellow kilt, elaborately decorated, like that used in the Kwe'rana Dance. White sash hangs in back with bells around the waist.

Legs: knitted stockings with the fringes in front.

Knees and wrists: black and green yarn ropes tied to them.

Feet: white moccasins with skunkskin anklets.

Hands: painted white; in the right is a long yucca whip; in the left, a small fir tree, with a turkey feather tied at the top, serves as a cane.

Mask: a face mask (Fig. 26d). Green, with small red circles for eyes; a red leather tongue eight or ten inches long hangs from the mouth; a beard of black horsehair. The impersonator should have hair long enough to conceal the edges of the mask.

6. *Ma'sha-wa (Turkey Buzzard)*. This mask belongs to the Giant Medicine Society; when epidemics occur in the pueblo, the war captain, having first consulted the Giant head who, in turn, confers with the Shrū'tzī head, brings this ka'tsina from house to house to bless and cleanse the community. He may appear briefly at masked dances, especially those immediately after or during a time of numerous illnesses; he is also present at Giant curing rites. In recent years, this impersonation has been seldom seen. Costume is as follows:

Body: all black except for red below elbows and knees; a band of white eagle down separates these two colors.

Waist: buckskin kilt with metal tinklers around the bottom, supported by a woman's belt.

Feet: white moccasins and skunkskin guards.

Knees and wrists: ropes of yucca tied to them and across the chest, serving as a criss-crossed bandolier.

Hands: painted white; nothing carried.

Mask: helmet type painted black and covered with mica to make it shine (Fig. 26e). Eyes are rather small red circles; ears are red leather tabs with eagle feather earrings. No mouth is indicated, though there is a tiny air hole (as is true of most helmet masks). Collar is a bobcatskin, fastened in front. At the back of the mask is a fan of large feathers: six eagle tail-feathers in the middle and one wing-feather at either end. A cluster of hawk ("or any kind") feathers conceals the ties for this fan. Top of the helmet is covered with a cloud of eagle down.

II. *Motion-makers, or Actor Ka'tsīnas*

7. *Shka'shrutz.* This ka'tsīna appears often, accompanying the Speckled dances; there is one for the Red and one for the Black. In the description of this figure, the data pertain to the Red; the Black is exactly the same except for the change in paint colors. He also appears with the Tsē'adyū-wītsa (No. 37) and Dyū-'wenī (No. 39) dancers; Shka'shrūtz is a motion-maker, serving as Na'wish in these ceremonies. Costume is as follows:

Body: all red, with white circles stamped on the red with a gourd stem.

Lower trunk: yarn belt of black and green, each color comprising half the length; embroidered sash is the G-string.

Feet: white moccasins with anklets of fir.

Wrists: bracelets of fir; bandolier of shells worn over left shoulder.

Mask: helmet type, painted red (Fig. 27a) and covered with white circles the size of a quarter-dollar, stamped on with a gourd stem; eyes are black triangles; ears are red leather tabs with cornhusk cone earrings; collar is of fir. On top of the mask, four long turkey tail-feathers, trimmed to the quill except for the tips, form a cross; a cluster of the trimmings conceals the ties.

There is another form of Shka'shrutz; there is some suggestion that he is less associated with the Speckled dances than either the red or the black variation of the first type but this distinction does not seem to be well developed. Costume is as follows:

Body: all red, including arms, hands, and legs (no white circles).

Feet: white moccasins with anklets of fir.

Wrists: bracelets of fir.

Waist: yarn belt, green for half its length, black for the other half; G-string of black or dark blue, "like the chai'anī wear."

Mask: helmet type, painted green (Fig. 27b). Collar of fir; red leather ears and earrings of two turkey rump-feathers on each side; eyes are black triangles, mouth a protruding red ball from which a white serpent zigzags to a point high on the "forehead." On the top is a cluster of four eight-inch turkey rump-feathers; ties are

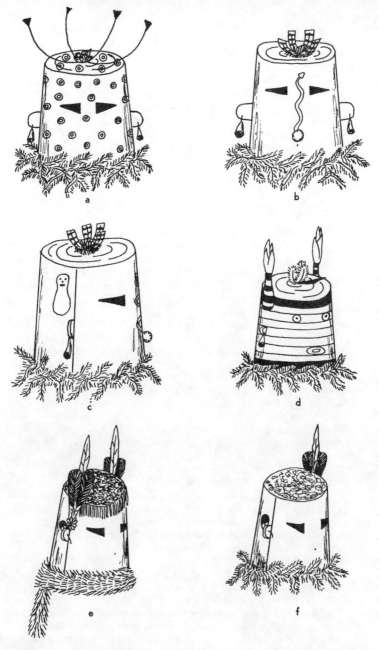

Fig. 27.—KA'TSINA MASKS. a. Shka'shrutz A; b. Shka'shrutz B; c. Na'wish; d. Pai'yat-yama; e. Ko'chī-nako, Yellow Woman (motion-maker); f. Ko'ko-shūlī.

concealed by a cluster of small parrot feathers; entire assemblage rests on a pad of red angora hair.

8. *Na'wish.* This motion-making ka'tsīna is very similar to the second type of Shka'shrūtz; Na'wish appears most commonly with the Tsē'-adyū-wītsa dancers.

Only certain features of the mask distinguish Na'wish from the second form of Shka'shrūtz (Fig. 27c). Instead of the helmet's being painted entirely green, only the front half of the Na'wish mask is green; the back half is red, the top, white. In the red panel, at the front corners above each ear, there is a figure (o'ak[a]) (p. 398) painted white. The green, red, and white areas are separated by a thin black line.

9. *Pai'yat-yama.* This ka'tsīna appears in the Dyū'wenī Dance along with Na'wish; Pai'yat-yama enters directly behind the Ku-sha'lī guide; he must be impersonated by a Ku-sha'lī member. Costume is as follows:

Body: basically white paint, over which colored bands three or four inches wide are painted horizontally on the trunk, arms, and legs. Color sequence on the body duplicates that on the mask, where the stripes are about an inch wide. From the top down, colors are: white, black, white, yellow, white, green, white, red, white, black, white, etc.

Feet: white moccasins.

Ankles and wrists: Douglas fir.

Waist: belt of black and green yarn; woven sash is the G-string.

Hands: painted white; nothing carried.

Mask: helmet type, with painted bands as noted above (Fig. 27d). Douglas fir collar; white oval mouth (with red center) in the red stripe; round white eyes in the yellow stripe; red ears with corn-husk earrings in the green stripe. On top of the helmet is a cluster of downy eagle feathers. On each side a small gourd, painted with black and white bands, is secured so that it protrudes above the helmet like a horn. A tuft of cornhusks extends upward from each gourd.

10. *Ko'chī-nako (Yellow Woman).* This motion-maker mimes the words of the songs of the Big Zuñi Dance. She appears in the place of Na'wish in this particular ceremony. (Women's parts are always enacted by men in ka'tsīnas.) She follows the Ku-sha'lī guide in making her entrance, thereby preceding the line of dancers. Costume is as follows:

Body: black *manta* secured over the right shoulder; woman's belt around the waist.

Legs and feet: white moccasins and wrapped buckskin leggings.

Arms and hands: bare and painted white.

Wrists: one with black yarn, the other with green; in each hand, a prayer stick.

Fig. 28.—KA'TSINA MASKS. *a.* Tzī'na, Turkey; *b.* Ko'hai-o, Bear; *c.* Mo'-katch, Mountain Lion; *d.* Dya'ñī, Deer; *e.* O'shatsh, Sun (side dancer); *f.* head disk worn by O'shatsh.

Mask: helmet type, painted green in front and blue-gray in back (Fig. 27e). Collar is a foxskin (the tail always falls behind the right shoulder); eyes are black triangles; no mouth is indicated; red tab ears with eagle feather earrings; across the forehead are bangs of black horsehair. Top of the mask is covered by a white cloud of eagle down. (It is easiest to build up such "clouds" with cotton; sometimes the cotton is covered with a thin layer of eagle down; other times it is simply left as it is.) Above the ear on each side is a set of one parrot tail-feather and two eagle tail-feathers. A cluster of small parrot feathers conceals the point where these are tied to the helmet.

11. *Ko'ko-shŭli*. This motion-maker appears with the Little Zuñi dancers. She, like Ko'chī-nako, acts out the words in place of Na'wish. Her entrance parallels that of Ko'chī-nako, and her costume is essentially the same except for some differences in the mask.
Mask: this is the same as that of Ko'chī-nako except that the collar is Douglas fir instead of a foxskin; there are no bangs across the forehead; the set of feathers appears only over the left ear instead of both ears (Fig. 27f).

III. *Guards and Attendants, or Side Dancers, for the Ka'tsīnas*

12. *Tzī'na (Turkey)*. This ka'tsīna never appears in a dance line but only as an attendant, or guard; most commonly this is for the Tzī'na Dance. However, he sometimes appears for other dances, though he has seldom been seen in recent years. Costume is as follows:
Upper trunk: long-sleeved, collarless white shirt with special pockets from which piñon nuts drop behind the dancer.
Lower body: Hopi dance kilt.
Hands: painted white; in each, a long whip of narrow-leafed yucca.
Legs and feet: knitted leggings with fringes in front; white moccasins with skunkskin anklets.
Knees: rope of black yarn on one, green on the other; sleigh bells instead of turtle-shell rattle. (Bells are proper for side dancers but are never worn by line dancers except in public dances.)
Wrists: green yarn on one, black on the other.
Mask: helmet type, painted green in front and blue-gray in back (Fig. 28a). Top and back of the mask are covered by a "blanket" of turkey breast-feathers extending to the dancer's shoulder blades; the same type of blanket forms a beard. Ears are red leather tabs, each with an earring of two small turkey feathers; eyes are black triangles; there is a crooked beak made of a gourd segment, also painted green; juncture of the beak and helmet is concealed by a fringe of fluffy red feathers.

13. *Ko'hai-o (Bear)*. This dancer is "was'tich"—meaning that he can be impersonated only by medicine men as they are the ones who

know how to produce the peculiar whistle necessary for this characterization. Costume is as follows:

Body: long-sleeved, collarless white shirt, with a black yarn bandolier over the left shoulder; over both shoulders a cape of white cotton with no embroidery. Cape has four pairs of small turkey feathers, a pair at each shoulder and at each hip, not at the corners. He wears a regular Hopi dance kilt with sash and a foxskin behind.

Legs: knitted stockings with green yarn at one knee, black at the other.

Feet: boots made of bear paws, left and right (it does not matter whether these are front or back paws); boots are knee length.

Hands: painted white, with wristlets of green and black yarn. In the right hand is a broad-leafed yucca leaf used as a whip; in the left is a fir-tree cane with a turkey feather tied at the top.

Mask: helmet type, painted green in front and blue-gray in back (Fig. 28b). Collar is a bobcatskin which fastens in front; ears are red leather tabs, each with an eagle feather earring; eyes and mouth are small red circles; spaced across the forehead are four bear-claw marks painted in brown; top of the mask is covered by a cloud of eagle down. At the back is a cluster of five large eagle feathers: three tail feathers with a wing feather at each end. Ties are concealed by a cluster of hawk feathers on a pad of red angora hair.

14. *Mo'katch (Mountain Lion)*. This ka'tsīna is also "was'tich"; in former times there were four of these, one for each cardinal direction. Though seldom seen in recent times, this ka'tsīna is normally seen in pairs: the North (yellow) and the West (turquoise) appear together, and the South (red) and East (white) come together. Costumes of the four are identical except for the shift in colors; the South (red) is described below. For the other three, the appropriate color should be substituted whenever *red* is mentioned except that the ears of all are almost always red (a few "long-eared" forms have black and white ears). Costume is as follows:

Body: painted black; a buckskin kilt hangs to the knees and is secured with a woman's belt; just above the kilt is a red circle, about four inches in diameter, in front and in back. Circles are outlined with eagle down; below the elbows and knees it is red also, again separated from the black by a line of eagle down. No foxskin hangs from the sash.

Feet: white moccasins with skunkskin anklets.

Hands: painted white; in the left a bow and arrow; in the right a whip of narrow-leafed yucca, three of four feet long.

Mask: helmet type, painted white both behind and on top (Fig. 28c). A bobcatskin collar fastens in front; red leather tab ears have an eagle feather earring. Front of the mask is white, with a large red circle outlined in black. Within this circle are black triangle eyes and a straight bill, "like the duck," black on top and white on the bottom. Its juncture with the helmet is concealed by a fringe of small turkey feathers. If the face (the area inside the black ring) is white for the South, then the rest of the front-half of the mask is turquoise. Across the forehead is a yucca visor; a downy eagle feather at each end and one in the middle. In the back is a fan of three eagle tail-feathers flanked by an eagle tail-feather; ties are concealed by a cluster of hawk feathers and a pad of red angora hair.

15. *Dya′ñi (Deer)*. This ka′tsina is rarely seen at present, though the Deer dancers appear in a line quite often. Costume is as follows:
Upper trunk: painted blue-gray.
Lower trunk: regular dance kilt, white sash, a foxskin behind.
Legs and feet: legs are blue-gray; white moccasins and skunkskin anklets.
Knees and wrists: black and green yarn ropes.
Hands: white, whip of mountain willow in each.
Mask: helmet type, painted blue-gray both front and back (Fig. 28d). Collar is evergreen; ears are red leather tabs with eagle feather earrings; eyes are black triangles; no mouth is indicated. Across the forehead and reaching down almost to the eyes is a large black triangle. Top of the mask is white, with a cluster of parrot feathers tied in the middle. At either side is a deer antler, either white or black. Eagle down conceals the juncture of the antler with the helmet. To the tip of each point is tied a tiny fluffy turkey feather.

16. *Kutz (Antelope)*. This ka′tsina, rarely seen at present, wears the same mask and costume as the line dancers of the same name. The only difference is that in each hand the guard carries a four- or five-foot-long whip made of two or three mountain-willow branches.

17. *Kash′ko (Mountain Goat)*. Rarely seen at present, this ka′tsina is dressed essentially the same as the line dancers of this name. Differences between the two are: in place of the dancer's rattle in the right hand, the guard carries a single large broad-leafed yucca as a whip (o′shai-yan). In place of the regular Hopi kilt, he wears an embroidered black *manta* as a kilt, like that worn by the Ku-sha′lĭ and Hïl′lïl-yïka (No. 23). A plain white sash is tied so that it hangs down in back. Instead of painted legs, the guard wears knitted stockings with black and green yarn at the knees; black and green yarn is also tied at the wrists.

18. *Kŭ′kañĭ Shpū′la (Red Fawn)*. This ka′tsina has been rarely seen in recent times; he is dressed like the line dancers of this name except that the guard carries sleigh bells in his left hand in place of fir twigs. In his right hand, he carries a mountain-willow whip in place of the gourd rattles carried by the dancers.

19. *Mo′ña-kai Shpū′la (Black Fawn)*. Remarks regarding the Red

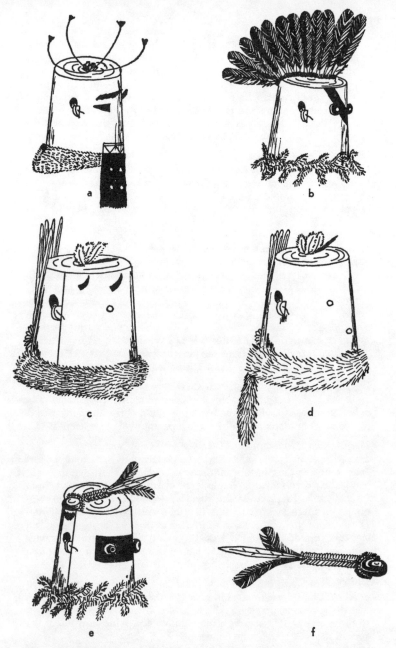

Fig. 29.—Kaʼtsina Masks. *a.* Hī'ya; *b.* Ê'ka; *c.* Hīl'lïl-yīka, Hair-cutter; *d.* I'wa-kai-ya, One-Who-Combs; *e.* Hīū'sa-pats, Hitter (hard); *f.* feathered stick worn on top of the helmet as shown in *e.*

Fawn ka'tsīna apply to this ka'tsīna also; the only difference is the substitution of *black* for *red* in the description of the various features of the costumes.

20. *O'shatsh (Sun)*. Since this ka'tsīna is "was'tich" and must be impersonated by a medicine man only, he has rarely appeared in recent years. Costume is as follows:

Upper trunk: painted blue-gray.

Lower trunk: Hopi dance kilt, white sash, and foxskin.

Legs and feet: painted blue-gray; white moccasins and skunkskin anklets.

Knees and wrists: black and green yarn.

Hands: painted white; in each, a long whip of narrow-leafed yucca.

Mask: face mask, painted green (Fig. 28e). The impersonator's long hair conceals the edges of the mask across the top and sides; the bottom is covered by many strings of beads. Eyes are black triangles. On top of the head is a rawhide disk about four inches in diameter (Fig. 28f). It is painted to represent the face of the sun; eyes are black triangles; mouth is a black dot; around the edge are a fringe of red angora hair and a fluffy eagle feather at each "corner." One informant said this "face" was green, like the mask; another insisted it was yellow.

21. *Hi'ya*. Rarely seen in recent times, Hi'ya should be seen only in the company of his brother, E'ka. Costume is as follows:

Upper body: painted blue-gray; a buckskin cape across the shoulders, reaching to his ankles.

Lower body: yucca belt and G-string; in the belt is folded a single large broad-leafed yucca (a whip).

Hands: painted white but nothing carried.

Wrists and ankles: evergreen.

Feet: white moccasins.

Arms: painted blue-gray; on each upper and lower arm is a daub of eagle down.

Mask: helmet type (Fig. 29a), painted completely green (one informant stated that this was the only mask with a green face that did not have a blue-gray back; an examination of other masks in this list, however, disproves this opinion). A bobcatskin is the collar at the back of the mask, and the front has a black horsehair beard with flecks of eagle down. Ears are red leather tabs with eagle feather earrings; mouth is indicated by a series of red and white teeth, extending about the distance between the outer corners of the black triangular eyes; over each eye is a row of stiff black horsehair lashes, about two inches long. On top, four long turkey feathers, trimmed except for the tips, conceal the ties.

22. *E'ka*. He is always seen with his brother, Hi'ya, though their

appearances have been very infrequent in recent years. Costume is as follows:

Upper trunk: painted blue-gray; a buckskin cape worn over the shoulders hangs almost to his ankles.

Lower trunk: belt and G-string of shredded yucca; a single large broad-leafed yucca whip is folded in the belt.

Upper and lower arms: painted blue-gray, with a daub of eagle down on each.

Legs and feet: painted blue-gray; white moccasins.

Anklets and wristlets: evergreen.

Hands: painted white but nothing carried.

Mask: helmet type, painted green (Fig. 29b). Collar is evergreen; eyes are red leather tabs with eagle feather earrings; no mouth indicated. Black and white ball eyes protrude from the helmet; eyes are made of leather built up on a stick just like a drumstick. From the upper right a black band passes between the eyes to lower left. On a front-to-rear line across the top of the mask is tied a vertical fan composed of an entire eagle tail (twelve feathers). Eagle down obscures the thongs.

23. *Hil'lil-yika (Hair-cutter)*. This ka'tsina always appears with his mate, I'wa-kai-ya; they have rarely appeared in recent times. Costume is as follows:

Upper trunk: long-sleeved, collarless white shirt.

Lower trunk: wears the embroidered black *manta* (tsiᵃ'matī) of the Ku-sha'lī for a kilt; white sash tied behind as a tail.

Legs and feet: knitted leggings; white moccasins and skunkskin anklets.

Knees and wrists: black and green yarn, with a pair of sleigh bells at each knee.

Hands: painted white; in the left, an evergreen-tree walking stick with a small turkey feather at the top. In the right, a large pair of scissors, from which he obtains his name. He looks at the spectators critically and if he finds anyone who has failed to keep his hair looking nice, he promptly trims his bangs.

Mask: helmet type, painted green in front and blue-gray in back (Fig. 29c). Collar is a bobcatskin fastened in front; ears are red leather tabs with eagle feather earrings; eyes and mouth are red circles the size of a dime; across the forehead are four brown bear claws. Top of the mask is white, with a cluster of fluffy white eagle feathers tied in the middle. At the back of the mask, five parrot tail-feathers extend above the mask; ties are concealed by a cluster of small parrot feathers.

24. *I'wa-kai-ya (One-Who-Combs)*. This ka'tsina always appears with her mate, Hil'lil-yika; she combs or brushes the hair of those who have had their hair cut or trimmed by her partner. Rarely seen in recent years. Costume is as follows:

Body: black *manta*, with woman's belt around the waist.

Arms and legs: painted white.

Feet: bare and painted white.

Hands: painted white; left hand is empty; in the right, a brush, or comb, or long grass.

Mask: helmet type, painted white (Fig. 29*d*). Collar is a foxskin, with the tail hanging behind the right shoulder. Ears are red leather tabs with eagle feather earrings; eyes and mouth are red circles about the size of a dime. A cluster of fluffy eagle feathers on top; behind is a plume of five parrot tail-feathers. Ties are covered by a cluster of small parrot feathers.

25. *Hiü'sa-pats (Hitter) (Hard)*. This ka'tsina is seldom seen. His name is derived from the buckskin bag that he carries. Men or women who have on new clothing and appear excessively proud of it are struck with this bag, which leaves a smudge of red ochre on them. Costume is as follows:

Body: a long-sleeved, collarless white shirt; bandolier of black yarn passes over the left shoulder (this should be true for all guards or line dancers who wear such shirts). Hopi dance kilt, white sash, and foxskin.

Legs and feet: painted white above the knee, blue-gray below; white moccasins with skunkskin guards.

Wrists and knees: black and green yarn.

Hands: painted white; in the left is a buckskin bag, covered with red ochre and filled with seeds of all kinds. Ochre is replenished often enough for the bag to leave a mark on anyone struck by it. In the right hand, a single broad-leafed yucca whip.

Mask: helmet type, painted green in front and blue-gray in back (Fig. 29*e*). Collar is Douglas fir; ears are red leather tabs with eagle feather earrings; no mouth is indicated; black and white ball eyes (made by a black ring and dot on a white background) in a black rectangular area. Top of the mask is white; on top of it is a feathered stick (Fig. 29*f*). At one end, on the right side, is a gourd about three inches in diameter, painted green; at its juncture with the stick is a ruff of red angora hair; main shaft of the stick about eight inches long (width of the mask), painted white and covered with parrot feathers; at the opposite end, the left side, a parrot tail-feather and two eagle tail-feathers form a tridentate tip.

26. *Hiü'shta-kats (Hitter) (Soft)*. This ka'tsina rarely appears at present; his name comes from his throwing turkey eggs (filled with corn smut) at individuals who appear to be excessively proud of new clothing. After throwing an egg, he returns to "Wē'nimats" for another one. Costume is as follows:

Body: painted red; black yarn bandolier worn over the left shoulder; Hopi dance kilt, white sash, and a foxskin behind.

Fig. 30.—Ka′tsina Masks. *a.* Hīū′shta-kats, Hitter (soft); *b.* Shko′o-ko, small owl-like bird; *c.* Ko′a-līsh; *d.* Hū′hū-ya; *e.* N^yen′yēka; *f.* Shrūī′yana.

Legs and feet: white above the knee, red below; white moccasins and skunkskin anklets.

Knees and wrists: black and green yarn; sleigh bell at each knee.

Arms: red above the elbows, white below.

Hands: white; in the left hand, a mountain-willow whip of two or three branches; in the right, the turkey shell filled with corn smut.

Mask: helmet type, painted green in front and red behind (Fig. 30a). Collar is Douglas fir; ears are red leather tabs with eagle feather earrings; no mouth indicated; eyes are black triangles. Top of the mask is white; there is a feathered shaft with gourd tip as described for Hiū'sa-pats and drawn in Figure 29f. However, for Hiū'shtakats, the gourd end is at the front and the shaft extends toward the rear.

27. *Shko'o-ko (Small Owl-like Bird)*. Rarely seen at present.

Upper body: long-sleeved, collarless white shirt; black yarn bandolier over left shoulder. Over both shoulders a white embroidered *manta* with four pairs of small turkey feathers attached to it, one at each shoulder and each hip.

Lower body: Hopi kilt, white sash, and a foxskin behind.

Legs and feet: knitted stockings and white moccasins with skunkskin anklets.

Knees and wrists: black and green yarn.

Hands: painted white; in each, a single broad-leafed yucca whip.

Mask: helmet type, painted completely white (Fig. 30b). Collar is a foxskin, with the tail hanging behind the right shoulder. Ears are red leather tabs with eagle feather earrings; eyes and mouth are red circles the size of a dime. On top of the mask a cluster of fluffy eagle feathers; at the back of it, a plume of five parrot tail-feathers extends above the helmet; ties are concealed by a cluster of small parrot feathers; from this point of attachment are four braided ropes of parrot feathers, "like those on the Corn Dance pole."

28. *Ko'a-līsh*. This ka'tsīna is "was'tich"; hence, he can be impersonated only by a medicine man. Rarely seen in recent years. Costume is as follows:

Body: painted black; Hopi kilt, white sash, and a foxskin.

Legs and feet: painted black; white moccasins and skunkskin guards.

Knees and wrists: black and green yarn; sleigh bell at each knee.

Hands: painted white; in each, a mountain-willow whip.

Mask: helmet type, painted black, with a coating of mica to make it glisten (Fig. 30c). Collar in back is a bobcatskin; beard of black horsehair with daubs of eagle down in it. Mouth is indicated by a row of red and white triangular teeth. Ears are red leather tabs with earrings of eagle feathers; eyes are red circles the size of a dime—leather washer-like disks tied to the helmet by a knotted thong. Across the forehead are four bear claws, painted brown. At the back a fan of three eagle tail-feathers with an eagle wing-feather on each side; ties are concealed by a cluster of small parrot feathers and a pad of red angora hair.

29. *Hŭ'hŭ-ya.* This ka'tsĭna rarely appears. Costume is as follows:
Body: white shirt with black yarn bandolier over left shoulder; over both shoulders he wears a white *manta* with embroidered borders. A pair of fluffy turkey feathers at each shoulder and each hip. He wears a Hopi kilt, white sash, and a foxskin behind.
Legs and feet: knitted stockings and white moccasins with skunkskin anklets.
Knees and wrists: green and black yarn.
Hands: painted white; he carries a long pole (one of those used in the *Tablita* Dances) when appearing outdoors. In a kiva or house, he carries a pole only about four feet long. Pole is painted white; at the top is a prickly pear cactus plant covered with eagle down. When used in this way, the pole is not called "Pai'yat-yama."
Mask: helmet type, painted white (Fig. 30*d*). Foxskin collar; eyes and mouth are red circles the size of a dime; ears are long, six or eight inches, and are white from the helmet to a point about mid-way the length; remainder is black. Top of the mask is covered by a cloud of eagle down.

30. *Nᵛen'yēka.* This ka'tsĭna appears often, most commonly with the Shrūī'yana, though he may appear alone. He carries himself proudly; the Ku-sha'lĭ chide him and joke that he has too many children: "Nᵞen'yēka struts all the more." Costume is as follows:
Body: white shirt, with buckskin cape, worn like a *manta,* over the right shoulder and under the left. Hopi kilt, embroidered sash, but no foxskin or white sash.
Legs and feet: knitted stockings with fringe in front (true of all Ka'tsĭnas who wear these stockings and also of the Deer dancers in the public dance); white moccasins and skunkskin anklets.
Knees and wrists: green and black yarn; behind the right knee a turtle-shell rattle.
Hands: painted white; long yucca-leaf whip in each.
Mask: helmet type, with more of a peak in front and sloping to the rear (Fig. 30*e*). Mask is green; ears are red leather tabs with eagle feather earrings; black and white ball eyes in a red rectangu-lar area; mouth is a series of red and white triangular teeth; black horsehair beard with daubs of eagle down in it; collar in back and around under the beard is a foxskin. A skunk tail, attached to the peak of the helmet, and hangs down the back of it.

31. *Shrūī'yana.* These ka'tsĭnas, like the other side dancers, take care of the line dancers and "watch out for things"; they whip any in-truders or late arrivals. There are eight of these, two each of four

kinds. Depending upon the decision of the war captains, they may appear as either two pairs or four pairs; no rule for deciding the actual number seems to exist. They are often seen at present, normally making several appearances during any year. Costume is as follows:

Body: one pair is painted all yellow (North); another pair, blue (West); another, red (South); and the fourth pair, black (Nadir). On the side of each upper and lower arm and leg is a daub of eagle down. Dancer wears a red angora belt with cornhusks covering the G-string; a foxskin hangs behind; in front and back of each leg an eagle wing-feather hangs from the belt.

Feet: white moccasins and skunkskin anklets. No yarn or rattle, but sleigh bells either at the waist or ankles.

Hands: same color as the body (never white); in each, a large broadleafed yucca whip.

Mask: helmet type, painted in three horizontal bands (Fig. 30*f*). The middle band—"the face"—is always green; top and bottom bands are yellow, blue, red, or black, depending upon the direction represented by the wearer. Ears are red leather tabs with eagle feather earrings; eyes are white circles about the size of a dime. Mouth consists of a row of red and white triangular teeth; beard of black horsehair with daubs of eagle down in front, a collar of bobcatskin in back; bobcat's head should be on the right. According to one informant, a small black rectangle, or square, represents a nose; according to another, a mouth (despite the aforementioned series of teeth immediately below). Top of the mask is covered by a cloud of eagle down, in the midst of which is a single large fluffy eagle feather.

32. *Tsē'ya-mash-ta-ti*[owi]. This guard rarely appears at present; his costume is the same as that of the line dancers of this name. The only exception is that the guard carries a whip of mountain willow in each hand in place of the dancers' gourd rattles and branches of Douglas fir.

33. *Bloody Hand Ka'tsīna*. This mask is the only one which informants described as "gone." It was said to have been first worn by a strange intruder many years ago (in mythological times?); it was later reintroduced by "bad people" among the medicine men themselves. Finally, the impersonation was done away with and has not been seen at Cochití for many years. The story of this ka'tsīna is told in Appendix 20 (pp. 460–462). Costume is as follows:

Body: painted red; buckskin kilt with either a yucca belt or a woman's belt; no sash or foxskin. Around the bottom of the kilt are metal jingles; a feathered serpent is painted on the kilt. A shredded yucca bandolier passes over the left shoulder.

Legs and feet: white above the knee (under the kilt); red band around the knees, white below. White moccasins with skunkskin anklets.

Fig. 31.—Ka'tsina Masks. a. Bloody Hand Ka'tsïna; b. notched stick and gourd musical instrument; c. Ko'chī-nako, Yellow Woman (musician); d. A'shu-wa Ma'ka-shañī, Big Zuñi Dancer; e. A'shu-wa Li'ka-shañī, Little Zuñi Dancer.

Wrists: ropes of shredded yucca.

Hands: painted white; in the left, a bow and arrow; in the right, a long flint knife.

Mask: helmet type, painted white (Fig. 31a). Collar is a bobcatskin, fastened in front, head on the right side. Ears are red leather tabs with eagle feather earrings; eyes and mouth are red circles about the size of a dime. On each side, reaching up from the bottom toward the eye, is a red hand with fingers extended. On top of the mask is a tuft of three downy eagle feathers.

IV. *Musicians Accompanying Various Ka'tsina Dance Lines*

34. *Ko'chi-nako (Yellow Woman).* There are two of these, dressed identically, who always appear together; they should not be confused with the motion-maker (No. 10) of the same name. These two musicians appear in the Tsē'adyū-wītsa, Dyū'wenī, Cho'watsa, and A'ha-ī-hī dances. They enter behind the Na'wish and just ahead of the Kwe'rana who brings up the rear as the dance line enters. As in the case of other feminine ka'tsīnas, the impersonators are actually men.

Their instruments are always the same (Fig. 31b). A deer scapula is rubbed over a notched stick across the open top of a hollow gourd, or pumpkin, which has been dried and hardened in an oven. The pumpkin is placed on the ground and serves as a resonance chamber. Pumpkin, stick, and scapula are painted white; a twig or two of fir decorates the scapula. Costume is as follows:

Body: white, embroidered *manta* (ko'po-notz) fastened over the right shoulder; a woman's belt tied around the waist. Over both shoulders a plain white *manta* hangs down to the knees. A pair of fluffy turkey feathers tied at each shoulder and each hip.

Legs and feet: white moccasins and wrapped leggings.

Arms and hands: painted white; in the left hand, the pumpkin shell; in the right, the stick and scapula.

Wrists: green and black yarn.

Mask: face mask, top and side edges of which are concealed by the hair of the impersonator (Fig. 31c). The long hair is arranged in two braids, crossed and tied behind the head. Multiple strands of white beads hide the bottom edge of the mask. The mask is green, with black triangular eyes; no mouth indicated. On top of the head is a single downy eagle feather.

V. *Ka'tsina Dance Lines (Always Composed of an Uneven Number of Dancers)*

35. *A'shū-wa Ma'ka-shañī (Big Zuñi Dance).* This dance is held often at Cochití; the people say that it came originally from Zuñi. The line of dancers consists of an uneven number, with the leader, or mayorlī, in the middle. All are dressed identically except that the leader has a red beard and the others are yellow. The dance is accom-

panied by a number of Zuñi songs, but also there are songs from
Cochití, Hopi, and elsewhere. Personnel appear in the following
sequence:

1. Spectators gather.
2. Two or three Ku-sha'lĭ appear.
3. He'rūta enters and asks, by gestures, whether the people want
   to see the dancers; he leaves to get them.
4. He'rūta returns with the guard Ka'tsīnas, followed by the war
   captain and his lieutenant. These two officials remain until the
   performers make their final departure.
5. Behind the war captains, another Ku-sha'lĭ leads in the dancers.
6. Ko'chī-nako, Yellow Woman, the motion-maker.
7. Line of dancers.
8. A Kwe'rana.

Costume is as follows:

Body: black paint except under the kilt, which is painted white so
that the kilt does not become smudged. Hopi dance kilt, white
sash, and a foxskin behind.

Legs and feet: white above the knees, black below; white moccasins
and skunkskin anklets.

Knees and wrists: black and green yarn; turtle-shell rattle behind the
right knee.

Hands: painted white; left hand, Douglas fir; right, white gourd
rattle.

Mask: face mask, painted green, worn so that the edges are hidden
by the impersonator's hair (Fig. 31d). Eyes are black triangles;
mouth, or teeth, is an arc of black and white squares; row of small
turkey feathers conceals the attachment of the beard to the mask;
beard is yucca, yellow for all except the leader's red beard. A necklace is worn under the beard, and an abalone pendant hangs just
below the tip of the beard. On top of the head is a flat gourd about
three inches in diameter, painted green with a yellow stripe around
it. Extending backward from this is a single parrot tail-feather; a
cluster of small parrot feathers conceals the attachment of the
gourd and tail feather. At the back of the head, in the dancer's
long, flowing hair, a set of four downy eagle feathers spaced along
a black thread is fastened. Top feather stands erect, the other
three hang downward. A small abalone weight keeps feathers in
place.

36. *A'shū-wa Lĭ'ka-shañĭ (Little Zuñi Dance).* General remarks pertaining to the Big Zuñi Dance apply to this ceremony. The dancing
in the Little Zuñi Dance is at a faster tempo, however. The beard
colors are reversed for this dance: the leader's is yellow, and all the
others' are red. In procedure, this dance duplicates the Big Zuñi, the
only change being the substitution of Ko'ko-shūlĭ for Ko'chī-nako.
Costume is as follows:

Body: yellow paint on the back, shoulders, and chest to about the
level of the nipples; this area is divided from the remainder of the
body, which is painted black, by a thin line of white paint. On each
side, over the ribs, and also on the outside of each calf, are two
white rectangles. Hopi kilt, white sash, and a foxskin behind.
Feet: white moccasins and skunkskin anklets.
Knees and wrists: black and green yarn.
Hands: painted white; in the left, Douglas fir; in the right, a gourd
rattle painted white.
Mask: the mask and head feathers (Fig. 31e) are the same as those
described for the Big Zuñi Dance (Fig. 31d). The only difference
is the addition of four triangles which point inward from the edges
of the mask on either side, one above and one below each eye. The
two triangles on the right side are red; those on the left, yellow.

37. *Tsē'adyū-wītsa Dance.* This dance is a favorite of many Cochití
and is often seen. It is one of the three dances which are sometimes
referred to by this name; the others are the Tzī'na (Turkey), and the
Dyū'wenī (Frijoles Cañon) dances. It is particularly close to the
Frijoles Dance since both have a Na'wish (motion-maker), two
Ko'chī-nako musicians, and quite similar masks and costuming.
Order of appearance for this dance is as follows:
1. Spectators take their places.
2. Two or three Ku-sha'lī appear.
3. He'rūta enters and asks, by gestures, whether the people want
   to see the dancers; he leaves to get them.
4. He'rūta re-enters with the guard Ka'tsīnas, followed by the
   war captain and his lieutenant.
5. Behind the war captains, another Ku-sha'lī escorts the dancers.
6. A line of dancers, the leader in the middle.
7. Na'wish (the motion-maker).
8. Two Ko'chī-nakos (musicians).
9. A Kwe'rana.
Costume is as follows:
Body: painted red, with black yarn bandolier over left shoulder; Hopi
kilt, white sash, and a foxskin behind.
Legs and feet: painted red except under the kilt, which is white;
white moccasins and skunkskin anklets.
Knees and wrists: black and green yarn; turtle-shell rattle behind
right knee.
Hands: painted white; in the left, Douglas fir; in the right, white
gourd rattle.
Mask: helmet type, with collar of Douglas fir (Fig. 32a). Mask is
painted red, front and back; ears are red leather tabs with eagle
feather earrings; eyes are black triangles; in the center of the face
a vertical line of black and white squares, four of each, extends
from top to bottom; across the forehead four white scallops, out-

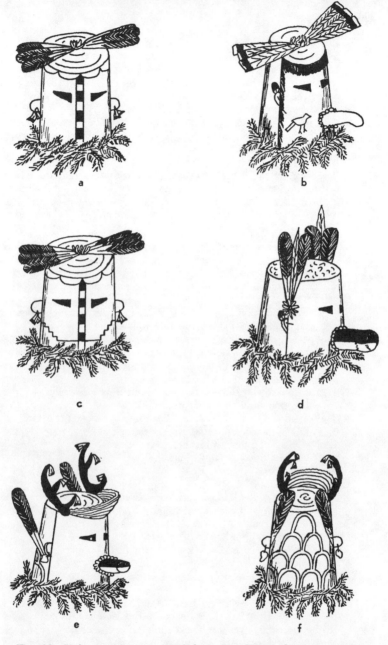

Fig. 32.—KA'TSINA MASKS. *a.* Tsē′adyū-wītsa dancer; *b.* Tzī′na, Turkey, line dancer; *c.* Dyū′wenī, Frijoles Cañon, dancer; *d.* Wai′yosh, Duck, line dancer; *e., f.* Kutz, Antelope, line dancer.

lined in black; top of the mask is white, and at the center three eagle tail-feathers extend outward to each side. Ties are concealed under a cluster of small parrot feathers.

38. *Tzī'na (Turkey) Dance.* This dance is held often at Cochití; it is a favorite for the Easter season. Order of appearance of personnel is identical to that listed for the Tsē'adyū-wītsa Dance. Costume is as follows:

Body: black, with white below the elbows; white under the kilt and below the knee; knees painted black. Bandolier of shell rattles passes over the left shoulder; Hopi kilt, white sash, and a foxskin behind.

Knees and wrists: black and green yarn; turtle-shell rattle behind the right knee.

Hands: painted white; in the left, Douglas fir; in the right, white gourd rattle.

Mask: helmet type, painted blue-gray in the back and green in front (Fig. 32b). Collar is Douglas fir; ears are red leather tabs with eagle feather earrings; eyes are black triangles; tied to the helmet is a curved green beak, made of a gourd stem, with a series of fluffy eagle feathers, dyed red, concealing the juncture. To the right of the beak, facing it, is a yellow profile of a turkey; to the left and facing the beak, is a red one. Sides and forehead enclosed by a fringe of orange angora hair. Top of the mask is white; in the center three turkey tail-feathers point to each side, their attaching thongs concealed by a cluster of small parrot feathers. One informant stated that the orange angora hair completely covered the top and back of the mask, thereby eliminating the white top and blue-gray back described above. This discrepancy has not been clarified.

39. *Dyū'wenī (Frijoles Cañon) Dance.* The mask for this dance is said to have been found in a cliffhouse ruin in Frijoles Cañon, the old home of the Cochití, many years ago. This dance, like the Turkey Dance, is often given at Easter time. The role of motion-maker, usually performed by Na'wish, is often taken over by Pai'yat-yama in this ceremony. Order of appearance of personnel is like that described for the Tsē'adyū-wītsa Dance except for the addition of Pai'yat-yama, who enters directly behind the escorting Ku-sha'lī and ahead of the line of dancers. Costume is as follows:

Body: painted red, with black yarn bandolier over left shoulder; on the back, two narrow white stripes—straight, not zigzag—extend from the collar across the shoulders vertically to the kilt; no lines in front; Hopi kilt, white sash, and a foxskin behind.

Legs and feet: white above and below the knees; white moccasins and skunkskin anklets.

Knees and wrists: green and black yarn; turtle-shell rattle behind right knee.

Hands and forearms: painted white; in the left, Douglas fir; in the right, white gourd rattle.

Mask: helmet type, with Douglas fir collar (Fig. 32c). Back of the mask is blue-gray; front is divided in half by a vertical column of black and white squares, four of each. To the right the face is green, with a bottom sector of yellow. The two sectors are divided by a black line which is horizontal in the center and extends upward at the side in steps; same arrangement on the left, with top sector red and the bottom, green. Ears are red leather tabs with turkey feather earrings, a pair hanging from each ear; eyes are black triangles. Across the forehead are four white scallops outlined in black. Top of mask is white; three eagle tail-feathers extend toward each side, with the ties concealed by a cluster of small parrot feathers.

40. *Wai'yosh (Duck) Dance.* This dance is held often; its songs include frequent imitations of the quacking of ducks. Appearance of personnel is as follows:
   1. Spectators assemble.
   2. Two or three Ku-sha'lī enter.
   3. He'rūta appears and asks, by gestures, whether the people want to see the dancers; he leaves to get them.
   4. He'rūta returns with the guard Ka'tsinas, followed by the war captain and his lieutenant.
   5. Another Ku-sha'lī follows.
   6. Line of dancers.
   7. A Kwe'rana.

No motion-maker or musicians appear for this dance. Costume is as follows:

Body: blue-gray paint; Hopi kilt, white sash, and a foxskin behind.

Legs and feet: blue-gray below the knee and white above; white moccasins and skunkskin anklets.

Knees and wrists: black and green yarn; both colors on each knee and each wrist (this is unique, as indicated earlier).

Hands: painted white; in the left, fir; in the right, gourd rattle.

Mask: helmet type, painted blue-gray in the back and green in front (Fig. 32d). Collar is Douglas fir; ears are red leather tabs with eagle feather earrings; eyes are black triangles. Bill is black on top and white on the bottom, with a slight bulge near the tip. Juncture with the helmet concealed by a fringe of small turkey feathers. Above each ear is a set of two eagle tail-feathers and one parrot tail-feather, which stands erect above the mask; ties are concealed by a cluster of parrot feathers. Top of the mask is covered by a cloud of white cotton.

41. *Kutz (Antelope) Dance.* This dance is held often; the costumes of the guard of this name and those of the line dancers are quite similar. The guard usually appears with the upper trunk painted red

and the line dancers with white shirts, but this distinction does not always exist. Order of appearance of personnel is the same as that described for the Duck Dance except for the addition of a "leader" in the Antelope Dance. He appears directly behind the escorting Ku-sha'lī and ahead of the line of Antelopes. He does not dance but carries a basket of corn meal in his left hand and prayer sticks in his right. Otherwise, he is dressed the same as the other dancers. Costume is as follows:

Body: painted red with white below the elbows, or he may have a white shirt; Hopi kilt, white sash, and a foxskin behind.

Legs and feet: red paint below the knees and white above; white moccasins and skunkskin anklets.

Knees and wrists: black and green yarn; one color on each.

Hands: painted white; in the left, Douglas fir; in the right, white gourd rattle.

Mask: helmet type, painted green in front and either pale red or vermilion in the back (Figs. 32e, f). Collar is Douglas fir; ears are red leather tabs with abalone earrings; eyes are black triangles; bill is black on top and white below, with a ruff of small turkey feathers concealing the juncture with the helmet. Just below each ear an eagle tail-feather extends upward and backward. Across the forehead is a visor formed by a segment of a Jicarilla basket; this is also painted green and the rim is decorated with eagle down. Top of the mask is white; at each side is an antelope horn painted black. Around the base of each horn is eagle down; on each prong a small turkey feather. One informant described the back of the helmet as plain red; another, as red with a series of clouds outlined in white; these arcs were four wide and four high and occupied the greater portion of the back half of the mask. The apparent discrepancy may be explained, perhaps, by the sloughing off of this added decorative feature in more recent times.

42. *Dya'ñi (Deer) Dance.* This dance, often held at Cochití, has the same order of appearance as that described for the Duck Dance. Costume is as follows:

Body: white shirt with black yarn bandolier over left shoulder; Hopi kilt, white sash, and a foxskin behind.

Legs and feet: blue-gray below the knee and white above; white moccasins and skunkskin anklets.

Knees and wrists: black and green yarn; turtle-shell rattle behind the right knee.

Hands: painted white; in the left, a Douglas fir-tree cane with a turkey feather tied at the top of it; in the right, a white gourd rattle.

Mask: helmet type, painted green in front and blue-gray in the back (Fig. 33a). Collar is Douglas fir; ears are red leather tabs with earrings of small turkey feather pairs. Eyes are black triangles.

Fig. 33.—Ka'tsina Masks. *a*. Dya'ñī, Deer, line dancer; *b*. Speckled Dance rattle; *c*. Kū'hañi Kē'awī-charla, Red Speckled dancer; *d*. Racing Ka'tsīna; *e*. Sun Racing Ka'tsīna; *f*. Long Ears.

Bill is black on top and white below, with a ruff of downy turkey feathers around the juncture with the helmet. Across the forehead is a visor of green yucca; fluffy eagle feather at each end and one in middle of visor. Top of helmet is white; on each side is a deer antler, painted black. Around the base of each antler is a ruff of eagle down with a small turkey feather attached to the tips. Dark feathers are preferred for this, though white ones can be used.

43. Kū'kañi Kē'awī-charla (Red Speckled Dance). Often held on Easter Eve, but at other times as well. Identical with the Black Speckled Dance, except for color substitutions. The dance differs from other masked ceremonies in being initiated by the Ku-sha'lī head, rather than the war captain, at least in times past. It is considered as "belonging" to the Ku-sha'lī Society, but since there have been so few Ku-sha'lī members in recent years, it has been taken over by the kivas. Either kiva may give the dance, with the approval of the Ku-sha'lī head. This is the only dance in which red moccasins are worn by the dancers, in which colored gourd rattles are used in place of plain white ones, and in which the green and black yarn on the knees and wrists is replaced by red yarn. It is a very fast dance. Personnel, in order of appearance:

1. Spectators assemble.
2. Two or three Ku-sha'lī enter.
3. He'rūta appears and asks, by gestures, whether the people want to see the dancers; he leaves to get them. (For this dance—theoretically, for any dance—He'rūta may be replaced by Ku-sha'lī Kē'a-nasht[10]; if the Ku-sha'lī father does appear, He'rūta does not come. Since the two kivas took over this dance from the Ku-sha'lī, however, the Ku-sha'lī Kē'a-nasht[10] has not been seen.)
4. He'rūta returns with the guard Ka'tsīnas, followed by the war captain and his lieutenant.
5. Ku-sha'lī escort.
6. Line of dancers.
7. A Kwe'rana.

Costume is as follows:

Body: painted black with white rings stamped on with the cut stem of a gourd. White below elbows and knees. Belt of red angora hair with cornhusks over the front of the G-string and a foxskin hanging behind.

Knees and wrists: red yarn; turtle-shell rattle behind right knee.

Hands: white; in the left, Douglas fir; in the right, gourd rattle. Rattle has a white handle; gourd is white on either side, with a red band around the sides containing a series of white rings (Fig. 33b).

Mask: helmet type, with Douglas fir collar (Fig. 33c). At the top and bottom are red bands with white rings. Top and middle portion of mask is green; ears are red leather tabs with eagle feather earrings;

black and white ball eyes; no mouth indicated. On top of mask, with the gourd in front, is the feathered-stick assemblage described for Hīū'sa-pats and pictured in Figure 29*f*.

44. *Mo'ña-kai Kě'awī-charla (Black Speckled Dance)*. Remarks pertaining to the Red Speckled Dance apply to this dance, the only exception being that the speckled bands on the helmet and on the gourd rattle should be black instead of red.

45. *Racing Ka'tsīna Dance*. This ceremony was formerly held quite often, but since the death of Marcial Quintana in June, 1945, it has not been held. One informant recalled that the last time the dance was given, on an Easter Eve, all the women, remembering the death of a person during the previous performance, cried when the dancers appeared. It could not be ascertained whether the person who died had been a dancer or a spectator.

In addition to the actual racing Ka'tsīnas, there are a Sun Ka'tsīna (not the Sun side dancer previously described), Longears, and Black Foot. Order of appearance of personnel:
1. Spectators gather.
2. Two or three Ku-sha'lī appear.
3. The Head Racer, rather than He'rūta, appears and asks, with gestures, whether the people would like to see the racers; he then leaves to get them.
4. The Head Racer returns with the guard Ka'tsīnas, followed by the war captain and his lieutenant.
5. Ku-sha'lī escort.
6. Line of racers.
7. A Kwe'rana.

The dance may proceed the same as any other masked ceremony, or the racers may challenge spectators to foot races. Members of the crowd are chosen, and a course of about two or three hundred yards, in any direction, is laid out. The Ka'tsīnas have been carefully selected to include the swiftest runners of the tribe. If a Ka'tsīna wins the race, he picks another contestant; if the spectator wins, the Ka'tsīna's partner immediately challenges him. These races are run, one by one, and it is so arranged that the final race is always won by a spectator. (It would mean bad fortune for the tribe if a Ka'tsīna should win this final race.)

Prior to the actual ceremony, the racers observe strict conditioning; this involves "hard" fasting, i.e., four days of vomiting and isolation in the hills, where they practice running, drink very little water, and eat only a mouthful of paper bread each day. This is the only ka'tsīna impersonation that requires this much preparation; the identities of the runners are carefully guarded secrets, known supposedly only to the war captains and head medicine men.

Costume is as follows: The racers are paired and are colored in general agreement with the usual directional colors: yellow, blue, red, black, and lavender. This last color seemingly has no place in the usual scheme of ritual colors. For races, there are usually only two or three pairs (they may appear in any combination); for dances, the entire group appears. Racers are dressed identically except for color; a yellow racer for the North is described below:

Body: yellow; white below knees and elbows; white belt with cornhusks concealing the G-string in front and nothing in the back.

Feet: bare, painted yellow.

Hands: painted white; nothing carried.

Mask: helmet type, painted yellow (Fig. 33d). A foxskin collar, with
the tail hanging behind right shoulder; ears are red leather tabs
with turkey feathers paired as earrings; at the top of helmet on
each side is a cluster of cottontail-rabbit tails. Eyes and mouth are
formed by white rings around a center of white. Eyes are round;
mouth is somewhat elongated horizontally.

With the actual racers, there is a Sun Racer whose name—O'shatsh karch'ta-yanī ("Gets Power from the Sun")—distinguishes him from the guard also referred to as the Sun Ka'tsīna. This Ka'tsīna, or the next one described—Longears—may serve as the leader (mayorlī) of the dance line. Costume of the Sun Racer is as follows:

Body: black; white below elbows and knees; white belt with cornhusks over G-string.

Feet: bare, painted white.

Hands: painted white; nothing carried.

Mask: helmet type, painted black with foxskin collar (Fig. 33e).
Ears are red leather tabs with pairs of small turkey feathers for
earrings; eyes and mouth are white rings with white centers. Eyes
are round; mouth, somewhat elongated horizontally. On top of
mask is a gourd and feathered-stick assemblage already described
for such ka'tsīnas as Hiū'sa-pats and the Red Speckled Dancer.

Also appearing in the group with the racing ka'tsīnas is Longears. This character appears to be lame; he may serve as mayorlī of the dance line if the Sun Racer does not. It is not clear whether the lame-ness is merely a pretense to lure some person into challenging Long-ears to a race (in the course of which the lameness disappears), or whether it is simply a part of the characterization that is maintained throughout the ceremony. Costume is as follows:

Body: black; white below elbows and knees; white belt with cornhusks over G-string; white paint under the area of this belt.

Feet: bare, painted white.

Hands: painted white; nothing carried.

Mask: helmet type, painted black with foxskin collar (Fig. 33f).
Ears are long, pointed, and stiff. Inside half is white and the outer
half, at the tip, is black. On top at each side is a cluster of
cottontail-rabbit tails. Eyes and mouth are white rings with a white
center. Eyes are round; mouth, elongated horizontally.

Still another impersonation included in the racing ceremonies is that

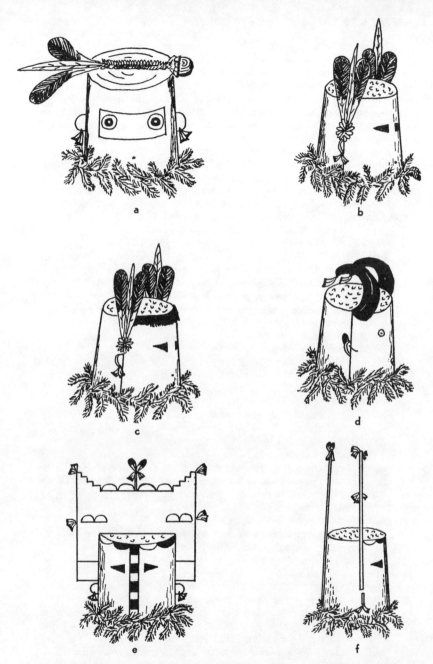

Fig. 34.—KA'TSINA MASKS. *a.* I'yū-be-dik, Black Foot; *b.* Tsē-ya-nom, Even dancer; *c.* Ha'ñī-sat-ya-me dancer; *d.* Kash'ko, Mountain Goat, line dancer; *e.*, *f.* A'ha-ī-hī dancer.

known as I'yū-be-dik (Black Foot). There may be either one or two of these characters. While they are primarily dancers, they occasionally race as well. Costume is as follows:

Body: painted black; white below knees and elbows; Hopi kilt, white sash, and a foxskin behind.

Knees and wrists: green and black yarn.

Feet: bare; painted black with skunkskin anklets.

Hands: painted white; in the left, Douglas fir; in the right, white gourd rattle.

Mask: helmet type, painted black, with an evergreen collar (Fig. 34a). Ears are red leather tabs with earrings of pairs of turkey feathers; no mouth indicated; black and white ball eyes. Around the eyes is a rectangular yellow area. On top of the head, with the gourd at the left side, is the feathered-stick assemblage described earlier for Hiū'sa-pats, Red Speckled Dancer, and the Sun Racer.

46. *Tsé'ya-nom (Even) Dance.* This dance is often held, most commonly during cold weather. Dancers are dressed very much like the Duck dancers except that they do not have beaks on their masks and they do wear shirts. Songs and steps of the Even Dance are the same as those used in the Duck Dance (No. 40). Costume for the Even Dance is like those of the Ha'ñī-sat-ya-me Dance except that the latter has the added feature on its masks of a black horsehair fringe across the forehead. Personnel and order of appearance are the same as that noted for the Duck Dance. Costume is as follows:

Body: white shirt with black yarn bandolier over left shoulder; Hopi kilt, white sash, and a foxskin behind.

Legs and feet: white above the knees; blue-gray below; white moccasins and skunkskin anklets.

Knees and wrists: black and green yarn; turtle-shell rattle behind right knee.

Hands: painted white; in the left, Douglas fir; in the right, white gourd rattle.

Mask: helmet type, painted green in front and blue-gray in the back (Fig. 34b). Collar is Douglas fir; ears are red leather tabs with earrings of pairs of small turkey feathers; no mouth indicated; eyes are black triangles. Top of mask covered by a white cotton cloud. On each side, above the ear, is a set of two eagle tail-feathers and one parrot tail-feather, which protrudes above the helmet; ties concealed by a cluster of parrot feathers.

47. *Ha'ñī-sat-ya-me Dance.* The name refers to the Ka'tsīnas that live in the east; it is another masked dance often held at Cochití. Personnel and the order of appearance are the same as noted for the Duck Dance. The costume, including the mask, is like that described for the Even Dance except that on the Ha'ñī-sat-ya-me mask there is a fringe of black horsehair about an inch long across the forehead (Fig. 34c).

48. *Hiū'shta-kats Dance.* This dance, rarely performed, is given by dancers dressed just like the guard of this name. The only differences are that the dancers carry fir in their left hands and white gourd rattles in their right, in place of the willow whip and turkey egg filled with corn smut. Personnel and the order of appearance are the same as described for the Duck Dance.

49. *He'rūta Dance.* This dance, rarely held, is considered one of the most enjoyable of the masked ceremonies. The costume of the dancers may be any of the six variations described for He'rūta (No. 1). The only requirement is that it be identical with that worn by the actual He'rūta on this particular occasion. Personnel and order of appearance are the same as in the Duck Dance. However, a slight deviation in the routine occurs when He'rūta leaves to bring back the dancers. Instead of leading them in, he becomes a part of the dance line, all dressed identically. This turn of affairs is very baffling to the Ku-sha'lī, who greatly amuse the spectators with their antics as they try to identify the true He'rūta.

50. *Kash'ko (Mountain Goat) Dance.* The unusual absence of the whistle-like calls typical of most other ka'tsīna ceremonies is a distinguishing feature of this dance. The songs were described as including many "peculiar words." Again, personnel and the order of appearance duplicate the account in the Duck Dance.

While details of the costume were given by informants, no one could actually remember having seen the ceremony. Costume is as follows:

Body: white shirt with black yarn bandolier over left shoulder; Hopi kilt, white sash, and a foxskin behind.

Legs and feet: painted white above the knee and blue-gray below; white moccasins and skunkskin guards.

Knees and wrists: black and green yarn.

Hands: painted white; in the left, small Douglas fir-tree cane, with a turkey feather tied at the top; in the right, a white gourd rattle.

Mask: helmet type, painted green in front and blue-gray in the back (Fig. 34d). Collar is Douglas fir; ears are red leather tabs with eagle feather earrings; eyes and mouth are leather washers, painted yellow, about the size of a dime. Top of mask covered with a cloud of eagle down. At each side is a mountain-goat horn, painted black, with a small turkey feather at the tips. Eagle down hides the juncture of each horn with the helmet.

51. *Shrūī'yana Dance.* In this dance, the line is composed of Shrūī'yana dressed just as the individual guards are dressed. Shrūī'yana guards invariably serve as side dancers for this dance. One Shrūī'yana, the mayorlī, is distinguished by the fact that he carries a rattle in his right hand in place of the yucca whip. The dance is rarely held. For costume details, see the description of the Shrūī'yana side dancer (No. 31).

52. *A'ha-ĭ-hĭ Dance.* The ka'tsīna impersonators for this ceremony should be sir'shtĭ, i.e. nonsociety members. The dance is initiated by the Shrū'tzī Society head, or some person who suggests it to him; he then requests of the war captain that it be held. It is a very popular dance, occurring at least once a year and sometimes more often than that. Personnel appear in the following order:

1. Spectators gather.
2. Two or three Ku-sha'lĭ appear.
3. He'rūta enters and asks, by gestures, whether the people want to see the dancers; he leaves to get them.
4. He'rūta returns with the guards, followed by the war captain and his lieutenant.
5. Ku-sha'lĭ escort.
6. Line of dancers.
7. Two Ko'chĭ-nakos (musicians).
8. A Kwe'rana.

As the dancers enter, the leader is in front rather than in the middle; his costume is the same as those of the other dancers except for the addition of a feathered stick at the back of his mask which the others do not have. Costume is as follows:

Body: painted blue-gray; bandolier of shell rattles over left shoulder; Hopi kilt, white sash, and a foxskin behind.

Legs and feet: white above knees and blue-gray below; white moccasins and skunkskin anklets.

Knees and wrists; black and green yarn; turtle-shell rattle behind right knee.

Hands: painted white; in the left, Douglas fir; in the right, white gourd rattle.

Mask: helmet type, with a *tablita* (Figs. 34e, f). Collar is Douglas fir; ears are red leather tabs with pairs of small turkey feathers for earrings; eyes are black triangles; face is divided by a vertical column of black and white squares, four of each; across forehead are four scallops of black and white, alternating. Front of mask is green, back is blue-gray. Top of mask covered by a white cotton cloud. The *tablita* is dominantly green; the designs, the same back and front, are outlined in black, as are the edges of the *tablita*. The bottom, at each side, is yellow; two yellow half-circles—clouds— are midway up each side; the four half-circles across the top are white. At upper corners and midway down each side is a pair of small turkey feathers. On the back of the mask of the leader only is a green stick. At the upper end, just visible from the front over the top of the *tablita*, are two pairs of small feathers: the upper pair, eagle, and the bottom pair, turkey. Ties at base of stick are hidden by a cluster of small parrot feathers.

53. *Cho'wa-tsa (Slow) Dance.* This dance is frequently held at Cochití; any of the Ka'tsīnas may participate. The name is derived

Fig. 35.—KA′TSINA MASKS. *a.*, *b.* Cho′wa-tsa, slow dancer; *c.* Chīch′she dancer; *d.* Tsē′ya-mash-ta-ti^{owi} dancer.

from the movements, which are very slow throughout the ceremony. Order of appearance is like that described for the A′ha-ī-hī Dance (No. 52). Again the line of dancers is immediately preceded by the leader; he is dressed like the others except that he carries a basket of prayer meal in his left hand and a prayer stick in his right in place of the evergreen and gourd rattle carried by each of the other dancers. During the dancing he does not join the line; instead he walks back and forth alongside the dancers. Costume is as follows:

Body: painted blue-gray, with a bandolier of shell rattles over left shoulder; Hopi kilt, white sash, and a foxskin.

Legs and feet: painted white above knees and blue-gray below; white moccasins and skunkskin anklets.

Knees and wrists: black and green yarn; a turtle-shell rattle behind right knee.

Hands: painted white; in the left, Douglas fir; in the right, white gourd rattle.

Mask: helmet type, painted green in front and blue-gray in the back (Figs. 35a, b). Collar is Douglas fir; ears are red leather tabs with pairs of small turkey feathers for earrings; eyes are black triangles. Dividing the face is a vertical column of black and white squares, four of each; across forehead are four scallops, two black and two white, and a visor (o'tan) of yucca. A downy eagle feather at each end and one in the middle. Top of mask covered by a cloud of white cotton. At the back of mask is a stick, whose upper end can be seen from the front. At the upper end are two pairs of feathers: one from under the wing of the eagle and the other, from the turkey. The entire shaft of this stick is covered with small turkey feathers; a cluster of small parrot feathers conceals the ties.

54. *Chich'she Dance.* This dance, held almost every year, is very similar in procedure to the Duck Dance (No. 40). Costume is as follows:

Body: white shirt with black yarn bandolier over left shoulder; Hopi kilt, white sash, and a foxskin behind.

Legs and feet: painted white above the knees and blue-gray below; white moccasins and skunkskin anklets.

Knees and wrists: black and green yarn; turtle-shell rattle behind right knee.

Hands: painted white; in the left, Douglas fir; in the right, white gourd rattle.

Mask: helmet type, painted green in front and blue-gray in the back (Fig. 35c). Collar is evergreen; ears are red leather tabs with earrings of pairs of small turkey feathers; eyes are black triangles; the face is divided by a vertical column of black and white squares, four of each; top of mask is white and in the center is a cluster of downy white eagle feathers. At the back of the helmet is a set of two eagle tail-feathers and one parrot tail-feather; ties are concealed by a cluster of small parrot feathers.

55. *Tsē'ya-mash-ta-ti^{owi} Dance.* This ceremony has been seen rarely at Cochití in recent years. Personnel and the order of appearance are like those in the Duck Dance (No. 40). Costume is as follows:

Body: painted black, with white below elbows; a shell-rattle bandolier passes over left shoulder. Hopi kilt, white sash, and a foxskin behind.

Legs and feet: painted white above and below knees, which are painted black in about a four-inch band.
Knees and wrists: black and green yarn.
Hands: painted white; in the left, Douglas fir; in the right, a white gourd rattle.
Mask: helmet type, painted black and covered with mica to make it glisten (Fig. 35d). (All masks have some mica over the paint; some, such as this one, have more than others, however.) Collar is of cornhusks; ears are red leather tabs with eagle feather earrings; eyes are black and white balls; no mouth indicated. On top of the helmet is a tuft of fluffy white eagle feathers. Arranged in a row up the back of the mask is a fan composed of a complete turkey tail (sixteen feathers). Small hawk or parrot feathers conceal the ties.

Appendix 27

COCHITI KU-SHA'LI SOCIETY ROSTER

Cleto Arquero: Pumpkin Clan, Pumpkin Kiva, born 12/19/34. White.
Inez Moquino Arquero: Sage Clan, Pumpkin Kiva, birth date unknown; Women's Society; died 3/1/19. White.
Juan Arquero: Cottonwood Clan, Pumpkin Kiva, born about 1850; died 2/13/15. Red.
Lucia Naranjo Arquero: Oak Clan, Pumpkin Kiva, born about 1849 (in Santa Clara); died 11/9/14. White.
Merced Montoya Arquero: Sage Clan, Pumpkin Kiva, born 7/28/66; died, 1937. Red.
Reyes Quintana Arquero: Oak Clan, Pumpkin Kiva, born about 1869; died 3/18/29. White.
José Domingo Chalan: Water Clan, Pumpkin Kiva, born 5/29/75; Flint Society; died 9/15/33. White.
Juan Isidro Chávez: Ivy Clan, Turquoise Kiva, born 1858; died 9/12/12. White(?) Red(?).
Juanita Quintana Chávez: Cottonwood Clan, Turquoise Kiva; birth and death dates unknown. Classification in the society unknown.
Mariano Chávez: Cottonwood Clan, Pumpkin Kiva, born about 1857; sacristán at the time of his death, 6/11/17. White.
Ricardo Chávez: Oak Clan, Turquoise Kiva, born 2/4/12; was a member only a few days before his death, 12/31/33. White.
José Maria Che: Cottonwood Clan, kiva unknown, born 2/20/75; death date unknown. Classification within the society unknown.

Manuelita Moquino Che: Sage Clan, Pumpkin Kiva, born 4/22/54; died 8/3/03. Classification in the society unknown.

Isidro Cordero: Shipewe Clan, Turquoise Kiva, born 1867. Red.

Lorenza Arquero Cordero: Oak Clan, Turquoise Kiva, born 3/10/68; death date unknown. White.

Lorenzo Cordero: Coyote Clan, Turquoise Kiva, born 8/2/98; Ku-sha'lī head since December, 1946. White.

Victoriano Cordero: Shipewe Clan, Turquoise Kiva, born 3/12/76; Flint Society, Snake Society, Fire Society; cacique at the time of his death, 12/12/46. White.

Estephanita Arquero Herrera: Coyote Clan, Turquoise Kiva, born 3/18/89. Red.

Lorenzo Herrera: Water Clan, Pumpkin Kiva, born 3/23/81. White.

Rafaelito Herrera (also known as Semilla and Guayave de Leche): Coyote Clan, Pumpkin Kiva, born 1864; Flint Society; was cacique from November, 1911, until his death, 12/22/14. White.

Torivio Herrera: Water Clan, Pumpkin Kiva, born 6/8/78; death date unknown. White.

Alcario Montoya: Corn Clan, Pumpkin Kiva, born 1/26/79; withdrew from active membership in the autumn of 1947, at which time he also resigned as sacristán. Yellow.

Antonio Montoya: Coyote Clan, kiva unknown; birth and death dates unknown; withdrew from the society sometime prior to his death and became affiliated with the Penitentes. White.

Luis Moquino: nothing could be learned about this man except that he was a member of the Ku-sha'lī Society.

Candelaria Trujillo Ortiz: Coyote Clan, Turquoise Kiva, born about 1881; died 11/13/11. White.

Victoria Martinez Ortiz: Oak Clan (Sun? [92]), Turquoise Kiva, birth date (in San Ildefonso) unknown; died 10/21/29. White.

Lorencita Che Pecos: Ivy Clan, Pumpkin Kiva, born about 1864; died 3/7/19. Blue.

Salvador Pecos: Turquoise Clan, Pumpkin Kiva, born 4/9/65; head during the early 1920's; death date unknown. White.

Santiago Pecos: Ivy Clan, Pumpkin Kiva, born 12/20/86. Blue.

Refugia Pancho Pérez: Cottonwood Clan, Pumpkin Kiva, born 10/26/54; died 4/23/38. White.

Clemencia Arquero Quintana: Oak Clan, Turquoise Kiva, born 4/5/95. Red.

Estephanita Montoya Quintana: Cottonwood Clan, Turquoise Kiva, born 9/26/02; died 6/24/35. White.

Marcelo Quintana: Cottonwood Clan, Turquoise Kiva, born 4/15/04;

Flint Society; Ku-sha'lï head until December, 1946, when he became cacique. White.

Petra Herrera Quintana: Water Clan, Turquoise Kiva, born about 1888; died 5/1/10. Classification in the society unknown.

Rosaria Arquero Quintana: Cottonwood Clan, Turquoise Kiva, born 10/9/79; died 6/28/21. White.

Santiago Quintana (known also as Guerro): Pumpkin Clan, Turquoise Kiva; birth and death dates unknown. White.

Zeferina Garcia Quintana: Oak Clan, Turquoise Kiva, born 6/2/58; died 1/5/30. White.

Juanita Chávez Romero: Cottonwood Clan, Pumpkin Kiva, born 7/9/72; Women's Society head. Red.

Salvador Romero: Shipewe Clan, Turquoise Kiva, born 10/7/17; killed in action in the Second World War, death date unknown. White.

Antonio Suina: Coyote Clan, Pumpkin Kiva, born about 1856; Flint Society, Snake Society, Fire Society; cacique at the time of his death, 11/8/11. White.

Dominga Pecos Suina: Coyote Clan, Turquoise Kiva, born 10/1/90. Blue.

Josefa Peña Suina: Oak Clan, Pumpkin Kiva, born about 1880 (in San Ildefonso); died 5/19/15. Red.

Juanito Suina: Oak Clan, Pumpkin Kiva, born 11/27/82; withdrew from active membership many years ago, reputedly because of a Spanish-American wife; death date unknown. White(?).

Victoria Pecos Suina: Ivy Clan, Turquoise Kiva, born 7/6/89; Blue(?) White(?).

Juanito Trujillo: Sage Clan, Turquoise Kiva (formerly Pumpkin), born 1/13/81; Flint Society. Red.

Sebastian Urina: Water Clan, Pumpkin Kiva, born 1/20/90; withdrew from active participation many years ago when he moved to Wisconsin Dells, Wisconsin, where he took an Anglo wife and is known as Chief Evergreen Tree (his Indian name is Ha'kak, "Evergreen"). White(?).

Appendix 28

COCHITI KWE'RANA SOCIETY ROSTER

Luis Archibeque: nothing is known of this man except that he was also a member of the Shī'kame Society.

Antonio Calabaza (known also as Archibeque): Shipewe Clan, Turquoise Kiva, born about 1866; Shī'kame Society; died 9/20/41.

Maria Luisa Trujillo Calabaza: Sage Clan, Turquoise Kiva, born 11/16/76; died 4/14/12.

Juan Estévan Chalan: Corn Clan, Pumpkin Kiva, born 1878; Pumpkin Kiva head until his death, 8/11/49.

Guadalupe Archibeque Chávez: Water Clan, Pumpkin Kiva, born 2/15/70; died 4/12/40.

Pablina Quintana Cooka: Turquoise Clan, Turquoise Kiva, born 6/2/05.

Juana Apodaca Cordero: Shipewe Clan, Turquoise Kiva, birth and death dates unknown. Juana was a Comanche who was captured very young and brought up by a Spanish family in Cochití; she married a Cochití and joined a clan and kiva; several children of this marriage have played important roles in the ceremonial and political life of the tribe.

Lupita Cordero (known also as Panocha) Suina: Pumpkin Clan, Turquoise Kiva, born 2/23/53; died 12/19/27.

José Hilario Herrera: Oak Clan, Turquoise Kiva, born 3/10/20.

José Antonio Melchior: Turquoise Clan, Pumpkin Kiva, born about 1838; died 4/20/18.

Manuel Melchior: Turquoise Clan, Pumpkin Kiva, born about 1839; Shī'kame Society; died 9/19/09.

José Maria Naranjo: Oak Clan, Turquoise Kiva; birth and death dates unknown; Shī'kame Society head at the time of his death.

Luis Ortiz: Turquoise Clan, Turquoise Kiva, born 3/?/81; mayorlī of the Turquoise Kiva during the 1940's; died 9/13/49.

Manuel Ortiz: Oak Clan, Turquoise Kiva, born 4/21/77; Shī'kame Society head at the time of his death, 9/16/45.

Maria Quirina Urina Ortiz: Sage Clan, Turquoise Kiva, born 7/6/68; died 7/19/27.

Miguel Ortiz: Sage Clan, Turquoise Kiva, born about 1873; death date unknown.

Ventura Ortiz: Turquoise Clan, Turquoise Kiva, born 7/1/66; died 9/26/25.

Victoria Ortiz: Turquoise Clan, Turquoise Kiva; birth and death dates unknown.

José Vivian Pérez: Water Clan, Pumpkin Kiva, born about 1855; Shī'-kame Society; died 6/22/08.

Agrapina Ortiz Quintana: Turquoise Clan, Turquoise Kiva, born 5/23/87.

José Adolfo Quintana: Turquoise Clan, Turquoise Kiva, born 2/17/21.

Lucia Romero Quintana: Sage Clan, Pumpkin Kiva, born 7/20/87; death date unknown.

Maria Genevieve Quintana: Cottonwood Clan, Turquoise Kiva, born 1/19/29.

Ramón Quintana: Sage Clan, Turquoise Kiva, born 3/24/98; married a San Felipe woman and has lived there many years, though he returns quite regularly to Cochití to "help" the Kwe'rana.

Diego Romero: Sage Clan, Turquoise Kiva, born 5/18/90.

Santiago Romero: nothing is known of this man except that he was a member of both the Turquoise Kiva and the Shī'kame Society.

Terecita Chávez Romero: Shipewe Clan, Turquoise Kiva, born 5/14/94.

Vicente Romero: Sage Clan, Turquoise Kiva, born about 1885; Kwe'-rana head since the early 1920's.

Anita Trujillo Suina: Oak Clan, Turquoise Kiva, born 2/24/10.

Eufrasio Suina: Coyote Clan, Turquoise Kiva (formerly Pumpkin), born 11/17/12; Shī'kame Society head.

Lucinda Cordero Suina: Shipewe Clan, Turquoise Kiva, born 12/15/78; Women's Society.

Zeferina Arquero Suina: Cottonwood Clan, Pumpkin Kiva, born 7/25/67; died 3/22/37.

Felipita Herrera Trujillo: Coyote Clan, Turquoise Kiva, born 4/27/08.

Pablo Trujillo: Turquoise Clan, Turquoise Kiva (formerly Pumpkin), born 3/31/04. Pumpkin Kiva head since August, 1949.

Anastacio Urina: Water Clan, Pumpkin Kiva, born 4/2/76; Shī'kame Society; death date unknown.

Cleto Urina: Water Clan, Pumpkin Kiva; birth and death dates unknown.

Appendix 29

COCHITI COMPARATIVE CLAN ROSTERS as Recorded in Eight
Sources between 1881–1948

Clan	1881 (1)	1882 (2)	1897 (3)	1899 (4)	1907 (5)	1923 (6)	1924 (7)	1948 (8)
Antelope*	P	U	E	P	E	U	E	P
Badger	P	U	U	U	U	U	U	D
Bear	P	P	D	U	P	U	D	P
Corn	P	P	P	U	P	P	P	P
Cottonwood	U	P	P	U	P	P	P	P
Cougar, Mountain Lion	U	P	D	U	P	U	E	D
Coyote, Fox	P	P	P	U	P	P	P	P
Dove	U	U	U	U	U	U	U	E
Eagle	P	U	U	P	E	U	P	D
Elk†	U	U	E	U	E	U	E	D
Fire	U	P	E	P	P	U	E	D
Frog	D	U	U	U	U	U	U	D
Ivy‡	U	P	P	U	U	P	P	P
Macaw, Parrot	P	U	U	U	U	U	U	D
Oak	P	P	P	U	P	P	P	P
Pumpkin, Squash, Melon	P	P	P	U	P	P	P	P
Rattlesnake	D	U	U	P	E	U	D	D
Red Shell	U	U	U	U	U	U	U	P
Sage**	U	P	P	U	E	P	P	P
Shipewe	U	U	P	U	U	P	P	P
Sun	P	P	P	P	P	P	P	E
Turkey	P	U	U	U	E	U	E	E
Turquoise	U	P	P	U	P	P	P	P
Water	P	P	P	P	P	P	P	P

Key:
(1) Bourke
(2) Bandelier
(3) Starr
(4) Dumarest
(5) Hodge
(6) Goldfrank
(7) Curtis
(8) Lange
P—Present at the time of author's recording of clans
U—Unmentioned
E—Extinct at time of author's recording
D—Denied by informant as ever present

* Recorded by Starr as "Wood."
** Recorded by Hodge as "Dance Kilt."
† Recorded by Hodge as "Reindeer(?)."
‡ Recorded by Curtis as "Mustard."

Appendix 30

COCHITI CLAN INTERMARRIAGES, 1897 and 1948

CHART A: 1897[*]

	Squash	Oak	Water	Cot.	Fox	Sage	Sun	Ivy	Turqu.	Cip.	Corn
Squash	0	1	2	1	0	2	0	0	1	4	0
Oak	1	0	1	5	2	0	0	2	0	0	0
Water	2	1	0	2	0	0	2	0	0	0	1
Cottonwood	1	5	2	2	1	6	1	2	2	0	0
Fox	0	2	0	1	0	2	1	2	1	1	0
Sage	2	0	0	6	2	0	1	2	1	1	2
Sun	0	0	2	1	1	1	0	0	0	0	2
Ivy	0	2	0	2	2	2	0	2	2	1	0
Turquoise	1	0	0	2	1	1	0	2	0	1	0
Cipewe	4	0	0	0	1	1	0	1	1	0	1
Corn	0	0	1	0	2	2	0	0	0	1	0

[*]Goldfrank (1927: 14). Her data were based upon the census of Cochití taken in 1897 by Starr (1899).

CHART B: 1948[†]

	Squash	Oak	Water	Cot.	Fox	Sage	Sun	Ivy	Turqu.	Cip.	Corn
Squash (Pumpkin)	0	0	0	3	1	1	0	1	0	1	0
Oak	0	4	3	5	5	5	0	7	1	0	1
Water	0	3	0	2	0	1	0	0	2	0	0
Cottonwood	3	5	2	0	3	3	0	1	0	1	2
Fox (Coyote)	1	5	0	3	0	0	0	2	1	1	0
Sage	1	5	1	3	0	2	0	0	1	3	0
Sun	0	0	0	0	0	0	0	0	0	0	0
Ivy	1	7	0	1	2	0	0	0	0	1	1
Turquoise	0	1	2	0	1	1	0	0	0	0	0
Cipewe (Shipewe)	1	0	0	1	1	3	0	1	0	0	1
Corn	0	1	0	2	0	0	0	1	0	1	0

[†] Data furnished by Informants 16, 44, 45, 53, 88.

Appendix 31

COCHITI INTRACLAN MARRIAGE ROSTER*

Diego Arquero, 22, and Anita Chávez, 17; Sage Clan; married 4/7/10.

José Arquero, 18, and Cecilia Cordero, about 17; Cottonwood Clan; married 10/16/78.

Salvador Arquero, 30, and Candelaria Montoya, 24; Cottonwood Clan; married 12/6/29.

Ricardo Chávez, 21, and Juana Maria Romero, 15; Oak Clan; married 12/29/33.

José Nicanor Cordero, 28, and Juana Maria Archibeque, age unknown; Sage Clan; married 4/18/04.

Juan Pedro Melchior, about 32, and Ignacia Montoya, 26; Cottonwood Clan; married 3/1/92.

Adelaido Montoya, 27, and Lucia Romero, 17; Cottonwood Clan; married 7/25/87.

Juan José Montoya, born about 1836, and Maria Trinidad Herrera; age unknown, Cottonwood Clan; married about 1857, the year of birth of their first child, according to Church records at Peña Blanca.

Manuel Ortiz, 45, and Victoria Martinez, age unknown; Oak Clan; married 4/9/22.

Miguel Ortiz, 42, and Maria Zeferina Urina, 47; Sage Clan; married 4/11/15.

Onofre Pancho, 21, and Cecilia Roybal, about 20; Oak Clan; married 5/6/18.

Aloysius Pecos, 30, and Sinaida Chávez, 25; Oak Clan; married 11/24/45.

José Dolores Pecos, 26, and Caroline Melchior, 22; Oak Clan; married 12/26/47.

Damasio Quintana, 48, and Cresencia Arquero, 65; Oak Clan; married 3/30/40.

Pasqual Suina, 26, and Aurelia Montoya, 15; Oak Clan; married 8/30/26.

Cleto Urina, age unknown, and Reyes Archibeque, age unknown; Water Clan; married 11/28/74.

* Based on Franciscan church records, Peña Blanca, and Informants 3, 16, 44, 45, 53, 88, and 92.

Appendix 32

COCHITI INTERCLAN MARRIAGES*

	Pum.	Oak	Wa.	Cot.	Coy.	Sage	Sun	Ivy	Turqu.	Sh.	Corn	Bear	Ant.	Dove	R.S.	Un.	A.-S.	Total
Pumpkin	0	1	1	3	2	2	0	1	0	2	0	0	0	0	1	1	0	14
Oak	1	7	8	14	9	12	1	11	1	2	2	0	0	1	0	27	4	100
Water	1	8	1	10	3	2	0	1	4	4	1	0	0	0	0	8	1	44
Cottonwood	3	14	10	5	7	13	0	9	5	2	3	0	0	0	0	23	3	96
Coyote	2	9	3	7	0	4	1	4	3	2	1	0	0	0	0	7	0	43
Sage	2	12	2	13	4	3	1	1	1	5	2	0	1	1	0	26	5	74
Sun	0	1	0	0	1	0	1	1	2	1	0	0	0	0	0	4	0	11
Ivy	1	11	1	9	4	1	1	0	3	1	1	0	1	0	0	4	0	38
Turquoise	0	1	4	5	3	1	2	3	0	0	0	1	0	0	0	12	0	33
Shipewe	2	2	4	2	2	5	1	1	1	0	1	0	0	0	0	13	2	36
Corn	0	2	1	3	1	2	0	1	0	1	0	0	0	0	0	3	1	15
Bear	0	0	0	0	0	0	0	0	1	0	0	0	0	0	0	0	0	1
Antelope	0	0	0	0	0	1	0	0	0	0	0	0	0	0	0	0	0	1
Dove	0	1	0	0	1	0	1	1	0	0	0	0	0	0	0	0	0	3
Red Shell	1	0	0	0	0	0	0	0	0	0	0	0	0	0	0	0	0	1
Unknown	1	27	8	24	26	4	4	4	12	13	3	0	0	0	0	92	3	224
Anglo-Spanish	0	4	1	1	0	0	0	0	0	2	1	0	0	0	0	3	0	14

* Data compiled from records of the Franciscan Fathers, Peña Blanca.

Appendix 33

COCHITI CLAN STRENGTH: 1897 and 1948

Clan	1897 (Starr's Data)			1948 (Lange's Data)		
	Males	Females	Total	Males	Females	Total
Corn	4	1	5	8	9	17
Cottonwood	27	24	51	25	18	43
Coyote (Fox)	10	12	22	13	20	33
Ivy	21	12	33	14	10	24
Pumpkin (Squash)	10	5	15	10	3	13
Oak	12	22	34	60	54	114
Sage	23	20	43	29	30	59
Shipewe (Cipewe)	14	11	25	16	17	33
Sun	4	0	4	0	0	0
Turquoise	13	11	24	9	13	22
Water	6	9	15	12	8	20
Total	144	127	271	196	182	378
Clans unknown (1897)	2	0	2			
Total (1897)	146	127	273			
Other or unknown clans (1948)				21	24	45
Total (1948)				217	206	423

Appendix 34

SEQUENTIAL INTERCLAN MARRIAGES

Clofe Arquero, Sage, married Petra Suina, Oak, 2/9/16; and Cresencia Quintana, Oak, 8/1/19; and Juanita Herrera, Cottonwood, 8/10/29; and Juanita Cordero, Oak, 12/23/36. Clofe's father, Juan Arquero, was of the Cottonwood Clan.

Rafael Arquero, clan unknown, married Maria Concepción Chávez, Cottonwood, date unknown; and Maria Soledad Romero, Cottonwood Clan, date unknown.

Francisco Chávez, Water, married Gregorita Pérez, Cottonwood, 11/11/07; and Miguela Quintana, Cottonwood, 11/28/36. Francisco's father, Mariano Chávez, was of the Cottonwood Clan.

Juan Isidro Chávez, Ivy, married Juana Quintana, Cottonwood, date unknown; and Maria Lorencita Romero, Cottonwood, 2/7/86.

José Francisco Herrera, Cottonwood, married Josefita Roybal, Oak, 4/17/18; his brother, Nestor Herrera, Cottonwood, in his second marriage, married Lorencita Romera, Oak, 1/15/31.

José Montoya, Corn, married Maria Dominga Suina, Sage, 2/8/85. José's father, José Hilario Montoya, was of the Sage Clan.

Epifanio Pecos, Ivy, married Juana Estrella Cordero, Oak, 1/20/17; and Victoria Quintana, Oak, 1/26/28. His brother, Santiago Pecos, Ivy, married Petra Cordero, Oak, 5/4/08.

Tonita Peña, Oak, married Felipe Herrera, Sage, her second husband, 7/14/13; and Epitacio Arquero, Sage, 1/22/22.

Avelina Pérez, Pumpkin, married Salvador Arquero, Cottonwood, 10/9/32; her father, José Maria Pérez, was of the Cottonwood Clan.

Gerónimo Quintana, Oak, married Margaret Ortiz, Water, 4/28/35; his father, Francisco Quintana, was of the Water Clan.

Helen Quintana, Coyote, married Fernando Cordero, Oak, 12/13/32; her father, Pablo Quintana, was of the Oak Clan.

Cresencio Suina, Ivy, married Eusabia Trujillo, Oak, 12/23/40; José Rey Suina, Ivy, married Anita Trujillo, Oak, 1/22/33; and Octavio Suina, Ivy, married Frances Trujillo, Oak, 9/24/33. This is an instance of three brothers marrying three sisters.

Appendix 35

COCHITI KINSHIP TERMINOLOGY[*]

Comparative Data for 1920–1925 and 1947–1948

English Term	1920–1925 Man Speaking	1920–1925 Woman Speaking	1947–1948 Man Speaking	1947–1948 Woman Speaking
I (pronoun)			hīn	hīn
Great-grandfather	mumu (G) (P)	baba (G) sababa (P)	bisavūēlo	bisavūēlo
Great-grandmother	baba (G) sababa (P)	da'o' (G) da'o' (P)	mono avūēlo (*rare*) bisavūēla	tata avūēlo (*rare*) bisavūēla
Father's father	so'momo (C) mumu (G) mumu (P) voc. momo (C)	sa'papa (C) baba (G) sababa (P)	yaya avūēla (*rare*) so'momo voc. momo	yaya avūēla (*rare*) sa'papa ka'papa voc. papa ka'ʳpala (*obs.*)
Mother's father	Same as for *father's father*	Same as for *father's father*	Same as for *father's father*	Same as for *father's father*
Father's mother	sa'papa (C) baba (G) sababa (P)	sa-táo (C) da'o' (G) da'o' (P) voc. táo (C)	sa'papa voc. papa	sa'ta-o
Mother's mother	sa'papa (C) baba (G) sababa (P)	sa-táo (C) da'o' (G)	sa'papa voc. papa	sa'nai-ya voc. yaya kar'la (*obs.*) sa'ta-o voc. ta'o
Father	sá-nas-tyᵘ (C) umu (G) (P) voc. omo (C)	sa'-nas-tyᵘ (C) (sa) nactᵘᶜ (G) wawa, sanashtᵘˢʰ, dada (P) voc. táta (C)	sa'nash-tyᵒ voc. omo	sa'nash-tyᵒ voc. ta'ta

[*] Terms were obtained for 1920–1925 from the published data of Curtis (C), Goldfrank (G), and Parsons (P); for 1947–1948, the data were obtained by the author.

English Term	1920–1925 Man Speaking	1920–1925 Woman Speaking	1947–1948 Man Speaking	1947–1948 Woman Speaking
Mother	sá-naya (C) yaya (G)(P) voc. yáya, náya, náya (C)	Same as man uses	sa'naiya voc. yaya	Same as man uses
Father's brother	sa'-nawashē (C) umu, (s) anawa, (s) anawace, awa wawa (G) umu, wawa (P)	sa-ñeñe (C) nyenye, (sa)nactᵘᶜ (G) nyenye, sanashtᵘˢʰ, dada (P)	sa'na-washē voc. a' wawa omo (obs.)	sa'néñē, sa'na-washē voc. ka'néñē
Mother's brother	sa'-nawashē (C) umu, (s) anawa, (s)anawace, awa wawa (G) umu, wawa, awa, anawa, anawashe (P)	Same as for *father's brother*	Same as for *father's brother*	Same as for *father's brother*
Father's sister	sá-naya (C) yaya (G) (P) voc. yáya, náya (C)	Same as man uses	sa'néñē voc. yaya ka'néñē	sa'néñē voc. ka'néñē
Mother's sister	Same as for *father's sister*	Same as for *father's sister*	sa'nai-ya voc. yaya	Same as for *father's sister*
Wife's father	sá-nastyᵘ (C) voc. omo (C)		sa'nash-tyº, voc. omo	
Husband's father		sa'-nastyᵘ (C) voc. táta (C)	sa'nash-tyº voc. ta'ta	sa'nash-tyº voc. ta'ta
Spouse's mother	sa'-naya (C) voc. yáya, náya (C)	Same as man uses	sa'nai-ya voc. yaya	Same as man uses
Spouse	sô'ko, sá-uko (C) (s)ok'o (G) sok'o (P)	sá-trᵘshē (C) (sa)truce (G) satrushe (P)	sau'ko; also ka'nai-ya (after name of oldest living child)	ka'nash-tyº voc. sa'tre-shē

Spouse's brother	sá-wat'i (C) wat[1c] (G) wat[1], (P) voc. wáṭ'i (C)	sá-mēmē (C) wat[1c] (G) wat[1], (P) voc. meme (C)	sau'ko ka'mēmē voc. sa'tyum-shē	sa'mēmē voc. mēmē
Spouse's sister	sá-mēmē (C) bi²hia (G)(P) voc. mēmē (C)	sa-táo (C) bi²hia (G)(P) Voc. sa-táo, táo (C)	sa'mēmē voc. mēmē	sa'ta-o voc. sa'ta-o, ta'o
Brother	sá-tyûmshe (C)(sa)dyumice teutcume(i)(G) sadʸumishe, chuchumi (P)	sá-mēmē (C) meme (G)(P) voc. mēmē(C)	sa-tyum'shē voc. kar'tyu-mē	sa'mēmē voc. mēmē
Sister	sa'-mēmē (C) meme (G)(P) voc. mēmē (C)	sa-táo (C) ta'o, sooshe, da'ona (G) (P) voc. sa-táo, táo (C)	sa'mēmē voc. mēmē	sa'ta-o voc. sa'ta-o, ta'o
Brother's wife	sá-pihya (C) bi hia (G)(P)	Same as man uses	sa-pi²hi²she voc. pi²hia	Same as man uses
Sister's husband	sa'-wat'i (C) wat[1c] (G) wat[1]' (P)	Same as man uses	sa'wa-ti voc. wa'ti	Same as man uses
Widow	biuda (G)	biuda (G)	biŭda	biŭda
Widower	biudo (G)	biudo (G)	biŭdo	biŭdo
Son	sá-hw[1]shē (C) sawushe (P) (sa)wuce (G) voc. sáhw[1] (C)	Same as man uses	sa'o-shē voc. sa'wi-she sa'mot (obs.)	Same as man uses
Daughter	Same as for son ("child")	Same as man uses	sa'mak sa'o-shē	Same as man uses
Son's wife	Same as for brother's wife	Same as man uses	Same as for brother's wife	Same as man uses
Daughter's husband	Same as for sister's husband	Same as man uses	Same as for sister's husband	Same as man uses

English Term	1920–1925 Man Speaking	1920–1925 Woman Speaking	1947–1948 Man Speaking	1947–1948 Woman Speaking
Son's son	Same as for *father's and mother's father*	Same as for *father's and mother's father*	Same as for *father's and mother's father*	Same as for *father's and mother's father*
Daughter's son	Same as for *son's son*	Same as for *son's son*	Same as for *son's son*	Same as for *son's son*
Son's daughter·	Same as for *father's mother*	Same as for *father's mother*	sa'papa, sa'mak (*obs.*) voc. pa'pa	sa'ta-o voc. ta'o
Daughter's daughter	Same as for *son's daughter*	Same as for *son's daughter*	Same as for *son's daughter*	Same as for *son's daughter*
Father's brother's son	sá-tyúmshe (C) awa'wawa', tcutcumi, (s)anawa, (s)ana-wace, (sa)dyumice (G) wawa, chuchumi, sanawa, sad'umishe (P)	sá-mĕmĕ (C) nyenye, meme (G) voc. meme (C)	sa'na-washĕ voc. nawa ka'wawa (*obs. voc.*)	sa'nĕñĕ voc. nĕñĕ, ka'nĕñĕ
Mother's sister's son	Same as for *father's brother's son*	Same as for *father's brother's son*	sa'nĕñĕ, sa-tyum'shĕ, sa'na-washĕ voc. nĕñĕ, ka'nĕñĕ	sa'nĕñĕ, sa'mĕmĕ voc. nĕñĕ, ka'nĕñĕ
Father's brother's daughter	sa'mĕmĕ (C) yaya, meme (G) bro-sis terms (P) voc. meme (C)	sa-táo (C) yaya, (sa)wuce (G) ta'o, sooshe, da'ona (P) voc. saṭáo, ṭáo (C)	sa'nĕñĕ, sa'mĕmĕ voc. nĕñĕ, ka'nĕñĕ	sa'ta-o, sau'shĕ (when girl is older) voc. ta'o, ka'nĕñĕ
Mother's sister's daughter	sá-meme (C) mĕmĕ (G) br-sis terms (P) voc. mĕmĕ (C)	sa-táo (C) ta'o, (s)ooce, da'ona (G) ta'o, sooshe, da'ona (P) voc. sa-ṭáo, ṭáo (C)	Same as for *father's brother's daughter*	sa'ta-o voc. ta'o

Father's sister's son	(sa)dyumishe, tcutcumi (G) wawa, sanawa, sadᵞumishe, chuchumi (P)	nyenye (G) meme (G) (P)	sa'nawa, ka'wawa	sa'nēñē, papa
Mother's brother's son	Same as for *father's sister's son* (G) (P)	nyenye, meme (G) (P)	sa'wawa, momo	sa'nēñē, papa
Father's sister's daughter	nyenye, meme (G) (P)	ta'o, (s)ooce, da'ona (G) ta'o, sooshe (P)	ka'nēñē	ka'nēñē, sa'ta-o
Mother's brother's daughter	meme (G) (P)	ta'o, (s)ooce, da'ona (G) ta'o, sooshe (P)	sa'nēñē, papa	ta'o, sa'ta-o

Appendix 36

KINSHIP TERM VARIATIONS: 1951–1952*

English Term	Informant A (Man Speaking)	Informant A (Woman Speaking)	Informant B (Man Speaking)	Informant B (Woman Speaking)	Informant C (Man Speaking)	Informant C (Woman Speaking)
I (pronoun)	hin	hin	hin	hin	hin	hin
Great-grand-father			so'momo	sa'papa		
Great-grand-mother			sa'papa	ta'o		
Father's father			so'momo	sa'papa	momo	(sa) papa
Mother's father			so'momo voc. ko'momo	sa'papa	momo	(sa) papa
Father's mother			sa'papa	sa'ta-o	papa	da'o, sa'da-o
Mother's mother			sa'papa	ta'o, sa'ta-o	papa	da'o, sa'da-o
Father	o'mo	tata	o'mo	sa'nash-t¹⁰	u'mo	sa'nasht¹⁰ tata
Mother	ya'ya	ya'ya	ya'ya	ya'ya sa'nai-ya	ya'ya	ya'ya sa'nai-ya
Father's brother			so'momo	sa'papa	sa'na-washē an'a-wa	sa'nēñē, nēñē ka'nēñē

* These terms, collected from three adults, though primarily from Informant B, a middle-aged man, were gathered initially as a check on data in Appendix 35. The similarities and differences compared with those data were highly suggestive of the potential revelation of current terminology employed by various Cochití. It is hoped that future research will more fully exploit this point, hardly more than hinted at by the present data.

Mother's brother		o'mo	sa'nēñē	sa'nēñē, nēñē	sa'nēñē, nēñē ka'nēñē
Father's sister		sa'papa	ta'o	ya'ya (young) papa (older)	sa'da-o, da'o
Mother's sister		sa'nēñē	ya'ya, sa'nai-ya	ya'ya	ya'ya
Wife's father		o'mo		u'mo	
Husband's father			ta'ta		pa'pa
Spouse's mother	sa'treshē	ya'ya	ya'ya sa'nai-ya	ya'ya	da'o
Spouse	sıu'ko	sau'ko	sa'treshē	sau'ko	sa'trushē
Spouse's brother		sa'tyum-shē	sa'mēmē	sa'tyum-shē	ʒa'mēmē
Spouse's sister		sa'mēmē	sa'ta-o	sa'mēmē	sa'da-o da'ona
Brother		sa'tyum-shē	sa'mēmē	sa'tyum-shē	sa'mēmē
Sister		sa'mēmē	sa'ta-o	mēmē	sa'da-o, da'o
Brother's wife		pī'ʸᵃ	pī'ʸᵃ	pī'ᵀᵃ	pī'ᵀᵃ
Sister's husband		wa'ti	wa'ti	wa'ti	wa'ti
Widow		biuda	biuda	biuda	biuda
Widower		biudo	biudo	biudo	biudo
Son	sa'oshē	sa'oshē	sa'oshē	sa'oshē mo'tetze	sa'oshē sa'mot
Daughter	sa'oshē	sa'oshē	sa'oshē	sa'oshē ma'kutze	sa'oshē sa'mak

English Term	Informant A (Man Speaking)	Informant A (Woman Speaking)	Informant B (Man Speaking)	Informant B (Woman Speaking)	Informant C (Man Speaking)	Informant C (Woman Speaking)
Son's wife	pi^{ya}	pi^{ya}	p^{iya}	p^{iya}	pi^{ya}; *more respect,* sa'oshē	pi^{ya}; *more respect,* sa'oshē
Daughter's husband	wa'ti	wa'ti	wa'ti	wa'ti	wa'ti / sa'oshē	wa'ti / sa'oshē
Son's son	so'momo	sa'papa	so'momo	sa'papa	so'momo	sa'papa
Daughter's son	so'momo	sa'papa	so'momo	sa'papa	so'momo	sa'papa
Son's daughter	sa'papa	sa'ta-o	sa'papa	sa'ta-o	sa'papa papa	sa'da-o / da'o
Daughter's daughter	sa'papa	sa'ta-o	sa'papa	sa'ta-o	sa'papa papa	sa'da-o / da'o
Father's brother's son	u'mo	sa'nasht^{o}	sa'wawa	sa'nēñē	so'momo	sa'nēñē, nēñē, ka'nēñē
Mother's sister's son	u'mo	sa'nasht^{o}	sa'wawa	sa'nēñē	so'momo	sa'nēñē, nēñē, ka'nēñē
Father's brother's daughter	ya'ya / sa'nai-ya	sa'nai-ya	ka'nēñē	sa'ta-o	sa'papa	sa'da-o, da'o
Mother's sister's daughter	ya'ya / sa'nai-ya	sa'nai-ya	sa'nēñē	sa'ta-o	sa'papa papa	sa'da-o, da'o
Father's sister's son	u'mo	sa'nasht^{o}	ka'wawa	sa'nēñē	so'momo	sa'nēñē, nēñē, ka'nēñē

Mother's brother's son	u'mo	sa'nasht⁤ᵗo	sa'wawa	sa'nēñē	so'momo	sa'nēñē, nēñē ka'nēñē
Father's sister's daughter	ya'ya sa'nai-ya	sa'nai-ya	ka'nēñē	sa'ta-o	sa'papa papa	sa'da-o, da'o
Mother's brother's daughter	ya'ya sa'nai-ya	sa'nai-ya	sa'nēñē	sa'ta-o	sa'papa papa	sa'da-o, da'o

Appendix 37

MOIETY STRENGTH in 1948

Divisions	Total	Males	Females
Turquoise	204	99	105
Conservatives	176	88	88
Progressives	28	11	17
Pumpkin	219	118	101
Conservatives	113	64	49
Progressives	106	54	52
Total	423	217	206

Appendix 38

INTERMOIETY MARRIAGES in 1948

Men	*Women* Tur-quoise	Tur. Prog.	Pump-kin	Pump. Prog.	Alien Tur.	Alien Pump.	Alien Ind.	Alien A-Sp.	Total
Turquoise	22	0	9	0	3	0	1	1	36
Turqu. Prog.	0	1	0	1	0	0	0	1	3
Pumpkin	10	0	10	1	0	1	1	0	23
Pump. Prog.	0	3	0	4	0	0	3	6	16
Alien Turqu.	4	0	0	0	0	0	0	0	4
Alien Pump.	6	0	0	5	0	0	0	0	11
Alien Prog. Indians	6	0	0	5	0	0	0	0	11
Alien Prog. Anglo-Sp.	0	0	0	0	0	0	0	0	0
Total marriages (husband, or wife, or both, still living)									104

ALL-TIME INTERMOIETY MARRIAGES

Span	Turq. Man & Turquoise Wife	Pump. Man & Pumpkin Wife	Turq. Man & Pumpkin Wife	Pump. Man & Turquoise Wife
Pre-1874	0	4	1	2
1875–1899	9	7	10	8
1900–1924	13	18	19	12
1925–1948	17	11	5	13
Total	39	40	35	35

Appendix 39

CLAN STRENGTHS within MOIETIES in 1948

| | Turquoise Moiety | | | | Pumpkin Moiety | | | | |
| | Actives | | Progressives | | Actives | | Progressives | | |
Clan	Male	Female	Male	Female	Male	Female	Male	Female	Total
Antelope	1	0	0	0	0	0	0	0	1
Bear	1	0	0	0	0	0	0	0	1
Corn	0	2	3	5	1	0	4	2	17
Cottonwood	6	5	1	1	11	8	7	4	43
Coyote	9	14	0	0	4	6	0	0	33
Ivy	7	9	0	0	6	1	1	0	24
Oak	22	22	0	1	29	22	9	9	114
Pumpkin	4	2	1	0	4	1	1	0	13
Red Shell	1	0	0	0	0	0	0	0	1
Sage	12	6	3	5	6	4	8	15	59
Shipewe	9	11	1	0	2	2	4	4	33
Sun	0	0	0	0	0	0	0	0	0
Turquoise	9	8	0	0	0	0	0	5	22
Unknown	1	2	2	1	0	5	9	6	26
Water	6	7	0	1	1	0	5	0	20
Anglo-Spanish	0	0	0	3	0	0	6	7	16
Total	88	88	11	17	64	49	54	52	423

Appendix 40

COCHITI BIRTHS, Legitimate and Illegitimate, Single and Multiple, 1875–1947°

Year	Total	Annual Totals of All Births		Twins			Illegitimates		
		Males	Females	Total	Males	Females	Total	Males	Females
1947	11	7	4	0	0	0	2	1	1
1946	18	8	10	2	1	1	3	2	1
1945	13	5	8	2	1	1	5	2	3
1944	14	7	7	0	0	0	2	1	1
1943	6	4	2	0	0	0	1	0	1
1942	13	7	6	0	0	0	3	3	0
1941	9	5	4	0	0	0	1	1	0
1940	9	5	4	0	0	0	0	0	0
1939	17	8	9	2	0	2	1	1	0
1938	10	3	7	0	0	0	1	0	1
1937	12	7	5	0	0	0	3	1	2
1936	15	7	8	0	0	0	1	1	0
1935	13	8	5	0	0	0	1	1	0
1934	18	13	5	2	1	1	1	1	0
1933	11	5	6	0	0	0	0	0	0
1932	15	7	8	2	0	2	1	0	1
1931	17	5	12	0	0	0	1	0	1
1930	12	11	1	0	0	0	1	1	0
1929	12	5	7	0	0	0	0	0	0
1928	10	5	5	0	0	0	0	0	0
1927	16	10	6	0	0	0	4	3	1
1926	11	7	4	0	0	0	0	0	0
1925	11	3	8	0	0	0	2	1	1
1924	15	7	8	0	0	0	1	0	1
1923	15	3	12	0	0	0	1	1	0
1922	10	5	5	0	0	0	0	0	0
1921	9	5	4	0	0	0	0	0	0
1920	16	9	7	0	0	0	0	0	0
1919	7	5	2	0	0	0	0	0	0
1918	16	8	8	0	0	0	0	0	0
1917	11	3	8	2	0	2	0	0	0
1916	12	6	6	0	0	0	0	0	0
1915	18	9	9	0	0	0	2	1	1
1914	15	9	6	0	0	0	0	0	0
1913	14	7	7	0	0	0	1	0	1
1912	13	7	6	0	0	0	0	0	0
1911	16	7	9	2	1	1	1	1	0
1910	19	10	9	0	0	0	1	0	1

° Data based on the baptismal records of the Franciscan Fathers at Peña Blanca.

Year	Total	Annual Totals of All Births		Twins			Illegitimates		
		Males	Females	Total	Males	Females	Total	Males	Females
1909	14	5	9	0	0	0	0	0	0
1908	14	7	7	0	0	0	1	1	0
1907	9	4	5	0	0	0	0	0	0
1906	13	9	4	0	0	0	2	2	0
1905	14	5	9	0	0	0	2	1	1
1904	15	9	6	0	0	0	0	0	0
1903	13	6	7	4	2	2	0	0	0
1902	19	13	6	0	0	0	2	2	0
1901	7	3	4	0	0	0	1	1	0
1900	17	12	5	0	0	0	2	0	2
1899	14	8	6	2	0	2	1	1	0
1898	15	10	5	0	0	0	1	1	0
1897	20	10	10	2	0	2	2	1	1
1896	16	5	11	0	0	0	1	1	0
1895	19	9	10	0	0	0	1	0	1
1894	20	12	8	0	0	0	1	0	1
1893	25	15	10	0	0	0	2	1	1
1892	22	10	12	0	0	0	4	3	1
1891	18	11	7	0	0	0	5	3	2
1890	27	12	15	0	0	0	3	1	2
1889	18	7	11	0	0	0	4	2	2
1888	19	9	10	2	1	1	1	0	1
1887	22	10	12	0	0	0	5	1	4
1886	19	9	10	0	0	0	0	0	0
1885	14	9	5	0	0	0	1	1	0
1884	20	12	8	0	0	0	3	3	0
1883	20	11	9	0	0	0	3	1	2
1882	14	13	1	0	0	0	1	1	0
1881	19	14	5	0	0	0	0	0	0
1880	12	9	3	0	0	0	3	1	2
1879	15	9	6	0	0	0	0	0	0
1878	19	11	8	0	0	0	2	2	0
1877	14	8	6	0	0	0	0	0	0
1876	11	7	4	0	0	0	1	1	0
1875	22	9	13	0	0	0	1	0	1
Total	1,098	584	514	24	7	17	97	55	42

Appendix 41

DATES of MARRIAGES and FIRST BIRTHS[*]

Date of Marriage	First Birth	Age of Mother	Date of Marriage	First Birth	Age of Mother
12/26/47	7/16/47	21	2/13/30	5/20/30	19
12/26/47	5/9/48	19	12/6/29	3/17/30	25
6/13/47	10/19/47	20	9/6/29	1/14/30	20
5/6/46	5/5/47	19	8/10/29	6/20/30	20
5/5/46	7/8/45	19	3/9/29	9/19/29	24
2/21/46	11/4/46	24	1/22/27	12/19/27	19
11/24/45	10/4/46	26	8/30/26	8/6/27	16
4/27/45	6/18/45	21	6/3/26	3/15/27	34
6/11/44	2/18/47	27	9/6/24	1/30/29	21
3/10/44	4/5/46	23	7/14/24	8/5/24	19
9/21/42	5/11/43	22	3/3/24	4/6/25	29
4/18/41	6/4/41	37	3/3/24	5/30/24	20
4/14/41	3/20/42	----	11/1/23	5/11/25	19
8/10/37	10/29/38	36	4/13/23	2/12/24	26
12/23/36	1/5/38	27	1/22/22	2/2/23	29
11/28/36	4/16/37	30	8/1/19	12/10/19	26
11/12/36	5/15/37	25	8/17/18	4/17/19	20
5/12/35	4/25/36	20	11/3/17	5/31/18	17
4/28/35	5/3/37	25	1/20/17	9/5/18	23
1/14/34	5/16/48	32	6/12/16	12/20/16	37
12/29/33	2/17/34	26	2/9/16	12/15/16	21
12/24/33	2/22/35	30	4/28/15	10/6/16	22
9/24/33	2/17/34	20	7/14/13	8/27/14	20
9/24/33	7/30/36	34	6/28/13	12/6/17	27
7/14/33	6/18/34	23	9/10/12	5/8/15	29
5/8/33	11/8/33	24	4/15/12	11/23/12	21
1/22/33	10/5/34	29	2/5/12	12/17/12	19
1/22/33	4/5/34	24	4/7/10	5/23/10	17
12/25/32	9/13/33	19	4/7/10	11/25/10	18
12/13/32	6/24/33	18	4/7/10	2/24/10	17
10/9/32	4/11/31	18	2/7/10	2/15/14	25
7/14/32	8/14/32	16	2/7/10	11/2/10	18
6/21/32	5/31/32	24	5/4/08	4/4/10	21
4/13/32	6/1/32	17	4/27/08	11/30/08	24
1/30/32	3/16/34	----	4/27/08	6/11/09	----
8/2/31	11/19/31	18	3/2/08	4/5/09	15
1/15/31	10/1/31	19	1/8/08	3/25/08	18
10/4/30	7/3/32	19	11/11/07	8/14/08	18
4/28/30	9/16/31	18	8/2/07	1/3/09	20
4/26/30	6/22/31	22	6/20/06	5/7/09	19

[*] Data based on records of the Franciscan Fathers at Peña Blanca.

Date of Marriage	First Birth	Age of Mother	Date of Marriage	First Birth	Age of Mother
3/3/30	3/16/30	23	2/26/06	2/??/06	15
2/11/06	6/20/05	18	1/18/92	1/19/94	18
5/8/05	12/16/06	18	10/8/91	9/7/92	----
5/3/05	4/7/06	25	1/9/91	2/6/91	17
7/14/04	12/9/04	16	11/12/90	10/1/90	----
4/18/04	5/21/08	----	7/14/90	4/25/96	----
2/14/04	7/27/08	19	5/2/90	2/24/92	17
2/19/03	7/3/03	17	1/25/90	1/28/92	24
2/19/03	11/10/04	----	1/25/90	10/2/90	17
2/9/03	11/24/04	21	11/25/89	7/26/90	18
12/10/02	10/20/12	25	10/14/89	2/11/90	----
7/31/02	3/31/04	21	11/17/88	3/18/89	20
2/19/01	3/5/02	18	10/6/88	9/28/89	----
11/23/00	8/26/01	----	7/25/87	4/9/90	17
11/23/00	1/10/01	28	7/25/87	6/17/88	23
7/25/00	3/25/01	17	7/2/87	3/7/89	21
7/14/00	9/8/00	----	2/7/86	3/26/86	19
7/14/00	3/28/05	38	2/16/85	4/1/86	15
10/29/99	7/10/00	29	2/16/85	11/9/88	37
1/27/98	1/27/02	21	1/19/84	5/20/84	18
4/20/97	5/1/99	29	1/7/84	12/20/86	22
7/30/96	3/30/96	----	11/29/83	3/1/85	----
1/8/96	2/17/03	22	11/14/83	12/3/83	13
8/27/95	3/12/95	17	5/21/83	5/23/84	----
3/26/95	1/9/96	20	4/17/82	6/14/83	20
3/26/95	6/8/95	22	11/5/81	3/22/84	15
3/26/95	2/8/99	20	9/26/81	7/31/84	15
3/26/95	12/8/95	17	6/11/81	6/2/83	16
11/23/94	5/5/95	----	11/23/80	11/14/82	----
1/18/94	6/17/94	20	10/27/78	7/18/79	----
8/20/92	9/21/93	----	10/16/78	10/9/79	18
7/14/92	4/17/92	16	10/14/78	5/14/80	----
3/1/92	3/5/96	26	5/17/77	8/21/78	19
2/1/92	2/13/93	18	2/21/76	3/13/81	----
2/1/92	3/1/95	20	11/8/75	11/16/76	22
1/18/92	5/7/91	15			

Appendix 42

COCHITI DEATHS, 1878–1947*

Year	Total	Males	Females	Age by Months up to 2 Years**	Age by Years over 2 Years
1947	2	1	1	8	44†
1946	7	3	4	3, 5	22, 24, 70, 73, ?
1945	5	3	2	5, 7	25, 66, 70
1944	2	0	2		24, 70
1943	1	0	1		?
1942	4	0	4	3, 3, 8	?
1941	4	3	1		18, 20, 36, 75
1940	1	0	1		70
1939	4	3	1	3	32, 50, 68
1938	2	1	1	1	84
1937	4	1	3	9, 20	69, 70
1936	2	0	2		23, 29
1935	8	3	5	8, 21	21, 25, 33, 37, 52, 75
1934	3	0	3		30, 45, 68
1933	3	3	0	10	21, 58
1932	1	1	0		46
1931	4	3	1	4, 10	41, 53
1930	8	6	2	2d, 6d, 10, 11, 19	4, 39, 72
1929	7	0	7	13, 20	20, 21, 60, ?, ?
1928	12	7	5	1, 6, 10, 10, 16, 16, 22	3, 10, 11, 24, 35
1927	11	5	6	1d, 1, 8, 8, 9, 11, 16, 18	59, 74, ?
1926	7	3	4	1d, 3, 16, 21, 24	3, 60
1925	11	6	5	3, 3, 3, 18, 18, 23	21, 59, ?, ?, ?
1924	7	4	3	1, 2, 5, 11	19, 21, 34
1923	8	2	6	9, 10, 18, 23	5, 28, 30, 40
1922	3	1	2	12d, 8, 18	
1921	8	4	4	6, 10, 13, 21	2, 4, 42, 61
1920	8	5	3	6d, 7d, 15d, 14, 18	2, 33, 41
1919	10	7	3	4d, 11, 12, 13, 17, 23	3, 17, 55, ?
1918	11	4	7	6, 13, 15, 15, 20	3, 20, 23, 28, 80, ?
1917	8	4	4	1d, 1d, 1d, 12	29, 33, 50, 60
1916	15	9	6	1, 2, 4, 9, 12, 19, 20, 22, 24	3, 4, 8, 28, 45, 47

* Data based on the records of the Franciscan Fathers at Peña Blanca.
** A "d" following a number indicates days rather than months.
† Italicized numbers indicates males.

Year	Total	Males	Females	Age by Months up to 2 Years**	Age by Years over 2 Years
1915	14	7	7	2, 3, 5, 8, 9, 11, 19	3, 18, 22, 29, 35, 50, 50
1914	11	6	5	6d, 19d, 14, 14, 18	30, 31, 33, 50, 65, ?
1913	4	2	2	6	15, 19, 62
1912	15	7	8	1, 8, 9, 10, 10 12, 13, 22	4, 22, 36, 54, 60, 70, ?
1911	11	6	5	3, 12, 16	6, 27, 28, 30, 50, 55, 55, 60
1910	13	5	8	14d, 1, 2, 4, 8, 9, 18, 20	3, 22, 22, 24, 90
1909	9	3	6	10d, 6, 10, 13, 15, 16, 20	2, 70
1908	16	8	8	9, 15, 15, 16, 19, 20	2, 2, 2, 3, 35, 37, 55, ?, ?, ?
1907	6	5	1	5d, 7, 12	2, 3, 14
1906	7	3	4	11, 13, 17	6, 16, 31, 36
1905	4	3	1	11, 11, 15	43
1904	18	11	7	1, 3, 5, 6, 12, 14, 18, 20, 21, 24, 24, 24, 24	3, 11, 15, 27, 31
1903	9	4	5	1d, 3, 8, 13, 19	23, 49, 70, ?
1902	5	3	2	12	2, 26, ?, ?
1901	4	3	1		3, 10, 55, ?
1900	0	0	0		
1899	17	10	7	2, 4, 14, 21	3, 5, 6, 8, 25, 44, 50, 55, 60, 60, 65, ?, ?
1898	18	13	5	5, 9, 11, 11, 11, 13, 16, 24	3, 7, 16, 21, 22, 27, 33, 55, ?, ?
1897	4	4	0	1, 10, 13	55
1896	13	6	7	1d, 1d, 2, 2, 3, 8, 24	3, 4, 6, 20, 29, 80
1895	5	4	1		3, 4, 4, 40, ?
1894	29	18	11	3d, 3, 6, 7, 7, 9, 11, 11, 24, 24	19, 25, 27, 27, 28, 30, 34, 35, 36, 40, ?, ?, ?, ?, ?, ?, ?, ?, ?
1893	11	6	5	3d, 9d, 7, 12, 13, 17	15, 16, 30, 40, 50
1892	17	8	9	2d, 5d, 1, 2, 3, 12, 13, 18, 19, 23	12, 60, ?, ?, ?, ?, ?
1891	17	6	11	3, 6, 12, 14, 15, 17, 17, 19, 19	4, 8, 12, 38, 52, 60, 61, ?
1890	5	5	0	11	5, 11, ?, ?
1889	1	0	1	12	
1888	0	0	0		

Year	Total	Males	Females	Age by Months up to 2 Years°°	Age by Years over 2 Years
1887	1	0	1		11
1886	2	1	1		36, *50*
1885	3	2	1	9, 11	*3*
1884	8	3	5	2, 8, 12, 18, *24*, 24	*20*, ?
1883	2	2	0	*10, 17*	
1882	2	2	0	*24*	?
1881	1	0	1	4	
1880	0	0	0		
1879	2	2	0		*31,* ?
1878	1	1	0		*34*
Total	496	261	235		

Appendix 43

COCHITI CHOREOGRAPHIES AND SONGS

by Gertrude P. Kurath

Dance and song are indispensable forms of prayer at Cochití, as they are in other Keresan pueblos and are, indeed, in all pueblos. These two inseparable arts achieve their compulsive purpose by means both abstract and mimetic, both creative and traditional. The basic patterns of two types of dance ritual will illustrate the means. The writer co-ordinated the choreographies with songs by one of the eminent Cochití composers. In the course of a given performance, the basic patterns may be elaborated by various ingenious devices.

BUFFALO, OR GAME ANIMAL, DANCE

While *Tablita*, or Corn, dances are held on several occasions between January 1 and July 14, the animal dances take place only during the winter hunting season. They are regularly rotated in three-year cycles during the extended Christmas season. Thus, on January 6 (Kings' Day) the Cochití Turquoise Kiva in 1956 presented an Eagle Dance and the Pumpkin Kiva, an Elk Dance; in 1957, both kivas celebrated a Deer-Antelope Dance; and in 1958, both kivas gave a Buffalo Dance (see pp. 325–328).

During February each moiety, or kiva group, gives a dance of buffalo and game animals; in 1957, the Turquoise Kiva did so on February 9 and the Pumpkin Kiva, on February 17. There are also Buffalo dances for just two buffalo and one or two game mothers, and a Deer Dance with side lines and two pairs of deer men and deer women. The dance to be discussed here is the mixed dance, called Buffalo Dance (mo'sač u'cinʸi), but embellished by groups, or teams, of fours of deer, mountain sheep, antelope, and elk.

All Buffalo dances have an early-dawn prelude, when the mother lures the animals from the hills. The main dance in the plaza starts at 10:30 or 11:00 A.M. and continues through some eight appearances, with an intermission after the first four. Most songs are newly composed, and the dances are devised to fit them. Both follow precepts.

Tradition calls for three songs: one for a slow dance, one for a fast dance, and another for entrance and exit. This entrance-exit song may be a borrowing from an Oklahoma tribe or from the Apache. All the songs have nonsense syllables. The entire pattern follows.

NOTE.—The Wenner-Gren Foundation for Anthropological Research supported the field work in music and dance, and the American Philosophical Society Library aided by a commission for recordings and texts.

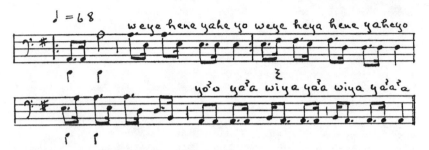

Fig. 1. Buffalo Dance entrance song.

Structure and Formation

1. Entrance from the Flint–Ku-sha'lī house to the plaza, to a slow song as in Figure 1 (Jicarilla Apache in this case)[1] in this order: drummers, two groups of singers, a standard-bearer (with jangling deer hooves on the standard) in war bonnet (present at dance on February 17, 1957, but not required in every dance); buffalo and buffalo women, led by the hunt chief; a pair of adult deer and several tiny deer, five years old; mountain sheep and other game animals. The game animals, leaning on sticks as forelegs, meander to the plaza; the others go straight.

2. Slow dance: chorus clustered in southeast of plaza, buffalo in center, animals meandering by pairs and crouching from time to time. The dance contains two parts (A. B., A' B' below), distinguished by varying drum beat; the same tune is repeated in each.

A. The song once through, to a drum tremolo. Dancers amble forward and back at right angles to their lineup (Fig. 4).

B. Same tune, with a quarter-note drum beat. Dancers prance forward for a section (Fig. 2, *x* to *z*), face about during *z*; back again for a section. Repeat.

A'. Hunt chief leads buffalo to reverse position, by sinister course so they face as in Figure 4 II' 2.

B'. Same as before in new position. Repeat.

During A' and B', the song shifts up one whole tone.

3. Fast dance: Buffalo group faces north; animals group in semicircle (as in Fig. 5).

A. Drum tremolo during Part *a* of song (Fig. 3). Buffalo group moves to original position.

B. Part *a*. Duple beat. Hunt priest and woman move left, buffalo right (Fig. 3), changing direction with each long phrase.

Parts *bcd*. Line moves north.

Parts *bcd*. Line returns.

[1] A cousin of one of the singers learned this song at the Jicarilla Apache festival, September 15, 1956.

A Word about the Figures

All song illustrations are from songs of the Turquoise Kiva. One Buffalo Dance diagram (Fig. 5) is from a Pumpkin Kiva performance. In *Tablita* dances the Pumpkin Kiva follows the same basic plan except that in dances on days other than July 14, the entrance is from the northwest corner of the plaza (the performers come directly from the Pumpkin community house). Ground plans are by Ellen Kurath; music copy by Gertrude Kurath.

For the key to dance symbols, see Bulletin 149 of the Bureau of American Ethnology, page 165. (The "L" symbol for the right foot is right of the center line; for the left foot, left of the line, with dots indicating direction of movement. Attached to the line, the symbol > and an inverted "L" represent forward knee flexion or raising.)

The stick figures at the top of Figure 7 indicate the arm positions of the singers; just underneath are graphs of the gesture levels during the first music phrase.

Texts with music have been held to a minimum. Where nonsense syllables are repeated for a recurrent musical theme, they are not written. For the meaningful words, the orthography omits phonemic ornaments. Full texts, including variants in musical repeats, appear with translations on pages 551–553.

Roman numerals (I, II) refer to appearances, I', II' to repeat in north half of plaza. The figures 1, 2, 3 refer to the three parts of each set or appearance. A and B identify the sections of the dances (1, 2, 3), A' and B' label the repeats in reversed formation within the dance; x, a, b, c, z mark musical introduction, phrases, and coda.

Fig. 2. Buffalo Slow Dance, with tramp step under *a'*.

Fig. 3. Buffalo Fast Dance, with basic steps and ground plan.

A'. Reverse position.

B'. Same as before, oriented south.

2'. Chorus in northeast of plaza; dancers reverse (Fig. 4, like II' 2). Whole dance repeated in reverse, oriented west.

3'. Dance repeated in reverse.

2. Sometimes repeated in original arrangement.

1. Exit in same order as entrance, to same song.

The entire form presents the mirror pattern of 1 2 2 3 3 2' 2' 3' 3' 2 2 1.

Rhythmic Patterns: Steps and Gestures

1. Game animals walk; other dancers and chorus walk.

2. Buffalo group trot, men lifting feet at each step, one step to a drum beat (Fig. 2, second line). During changing tempo (Part *b*), they tramp heavily on each beat. Progression forward, with occasional back step. Animals run and pose ad lib.

3. A. All amble.

   B. Buffalo paw ground (beat 1), raise knee (beat 2), right foot when moving right, left foot when moving left, forward when moving ahead as in Part *b*. Stamp and lean toward foot at end of each section (Fig. 3, first line, last note). During rhythmic changes:

Part *b*, measures 3 and 4, stamp three times, with strong accent on third beat, swinging bow to left with right hand;

Parts *b*, measures 6 and 7, and *c*, step back with slight right pivot; step forward with left pivot, swinging bow, raise knee; extra beat in measure 7 stamp in place.

Hunt chief and woman perform same steps without accents and gestures. Deer and other animals bounce in place, like *Tablita* Dance fast step (Fig. 3, Part *b*); mark rhythmic changes with step from foot to foot (Part *c*), or by two double bounces and knee-lift (Part *b*, meas. 6, 7 ff.). Buffalo raise their feet forward; other animals lift theirs back.

All gestures are rhythmic; none interpret texts, for there are no texts. The mimetic aspects take the form of impersonation—of lumbering like a buffalo, bounding and peering nervously from side to side like a deer. Toward the end of the day, when a dance is repeated in front of the Flint–Ku-sha'lĭ house, the animals are symbolically pursued, killed, carried to the Flint–Ku-sha'lĭ house, and treated ritualistically. A special group of youths portray the hunters.

On this basic pattern many formations and step combinations can be devised. For instance, in the February 17, 1957, ceremony, the buffalo circled the two women, in one dance by a simple circuit, in another with an extra twist (Fig. 5). Late in the day, the animals can line up in double

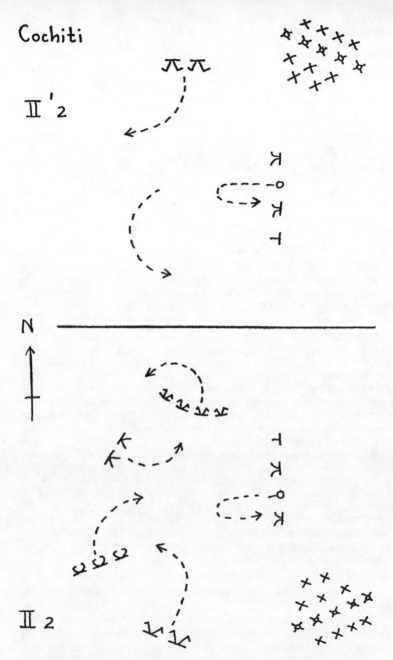

Fig. 4. Buffalo Slow Dance and repeat, typical ground plan (February 9, 1957). Buffalo group to right of animal groups; singers and drummers in southeast, then northeast, corners of plaza.

file while the buffalo trot past them and worry them with their bows. The rhythmic changes can be even more complex than in the examples. In fact, Keresan dancers and musicians are distinguished by the complexity of their inventions.

TABLITA, OR CORN DANCE

Each set or appearance contains two dances, a slow one and a fast one. During the slow dance, the chorus precedes the dance group from the kiva to the plaza; they progress slowly, moving straight ahead while the dancers trot in a counterclockwise circuit (Fig. 6). The dancers are aligned by twos or fours in couples, with the women to the left and back of the men. They follow the tempo of the drum beat with their step—the males with gourd rattles and the females with spruce sprigs (see pp. 322–323, 335–338, 341–353). The song has four major sections, each repeated: A A B B C C D D (Fig. 7). In accordance with these eight sections, the dancers and their banner-bearing leader (if any) proceed slightly zigzag, obliquely right, obliquely left with each musical change.

After this ten-minute entrance there is a pause during which the singers cluster into an arc focused on the drummer. At this time the dancers face each other in two lines, each headed by a male leader—the head of each line opposite the tail of the other (Fig. 6).

The second portion, a fast dance (Fig. 8), bears the name of the entire ceremony—a'yast^{y}ekuc—which refers to the follow-the-leader formation, the women following their partners. The song is in a rondo form: A A B B A A B B hapime C C B B hapime C C B B, plus a monotone introduction and coda. Part B, which is static choreographically, contains the most complex musical rhythms and melodic contour. Part C, with the most intricate formations, is melodically the clearest. During the introduction, conclusion, and hapime which announces the chorus—Part C—the dancers mark time. They continually pulsate in a step called k'a'yast^{y}ekuc. With each step they flex the supporting knee twice, to two drum beats (Fig. 8, Part A, meas. 1). The men bounce more emphatically than the women, and they raise the free knee higher.[2]

Sometimes, later in the day, yo'ran^{y}i replaces a'yast^{y}ekuc. This is in a slower, strongly accented beat, in circular formations, and with downward impulses of both arms from side to side.

The second dance takes about ten minutes. Then the performers reverse their positions and repeat the set at the other end of the plaza. After this forty-minute double set, they file out without music.

The following outline, which refers to Figures 7 and 8, associates the musical and choreographic components, which are interlocked.

[2] All details of step and gesture appear in "Labanotation" in Kurath 1957 and in manuscript notes.

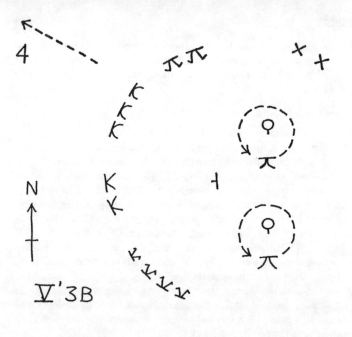

$\underline{V}'3B$

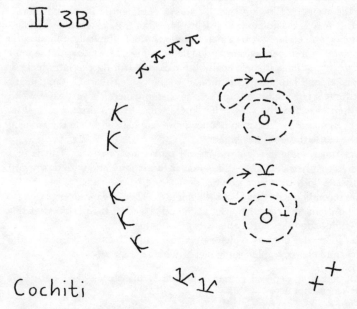

$\underline{II}\ 3B$

Cochiti

Fig. 5. Buffalo Fast Dance, second and fifth appearances, February 17, 1957.

Structure and Formation

1. Singers progress straight ahead. Dancers circuit against the sun (counterclockwise), with eight zigzags corresponding to eight musical sections (Fig. 7).

2. Singers in a group, dancers in two facing lines (Fig. 8).

A. During Part *y*, mark time. Then each man circles woman, three-quarters.

A'. During Part *y*, mark time. Then each man returns to place.[3]

B. Mark time, all facing leader.

B'. Mark time, all face to face.

A A' B B' hapime.[4]

C. Men cross over to other line. Women stationary or follow men.

C'. Reverse back to position.

B B' C C' B B' as before. In more elaborate dances, Part *C* may vary.

Tempo, Meter, Rhythm, and Step

1. Moderate trotting tempo, even drum beat (sometimes syncopating voice), a step to a beat. Metric units of one beat grouped into "measures," which affect dance step only in such cases as Part *D*, measure 6. Dancers pause on the drum pause. They also change tempo if the drum changes tempo. Singers shuffle.

2. Rapid tempo, to fit double knee-bounce with each step. Drum unit is double beat, with step pulsation. If unit is triple beat (as Part *x*), step has triple bounce (hapime). To phrases in slower tempo, dancers take single steps (Parts *A* and *B*, *y*). To a rhythmic break, they halt. Singers mark time with right heel, following changes in tempo and rhythm.

Melody and Gesture

Some gestures relate to the contour and phrasing of the melody, though not to its rhythmic figures. They always follow the drum beat, the men with the rattle in the right hand, the women and singers with the raising and lowering of the forearms in alternation. Singers may follow the rise and fall of the melody in two ways, mimetic and abstract, respectively. They interpret the song texts with symbolic gestures, usually a gesture to a word (which may occupy one or two musical measures). As they gesticulate in front of the body in various levels, and as the song melody is fitted to the conceptual levels in the text, they follow the melodic contour in a

---

[3] At each phrase-beginning and direction-change, the male dancers flourish their rattle in the right hand and the banner-bearer raises his banner.

[4] To the Cochití singer, "hapime" appears as an unexplained nonsense syllable with tonally indefinite chanting; it always introduces the "chorus." It is probably derived from the Tewa word for *song*, "xa·" (or "ha·"). Songs to traditional Tewa dances use a "hapembe" introduction and interlude as regular parts of the structure.

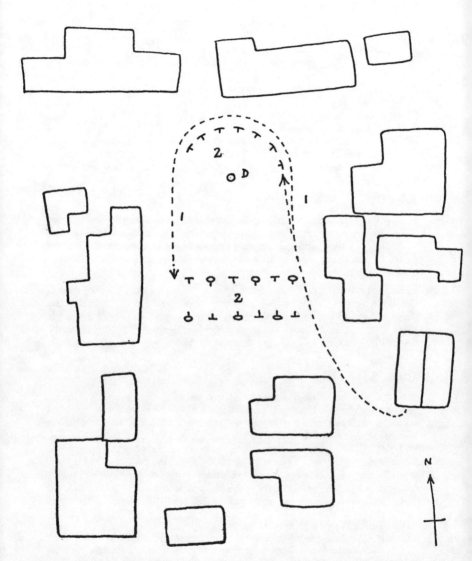

Fig. 6. *Tablita* Dance entrance (1) and line-up for Fast Dance (2). *D* indicates position of drummer.

general way. During passages of nonsense syllables, as "heheya" and "hineneya," many singers execute the fundamental forearm lowering and raising, in levels corresponding to the melodic contour. In "neutral" they pump at waist level; at the highest point they pump overhead. Mimetic gestures use four levels, corresponding to concepts as follows:

1. The highest level, overhead, is for the sky, the four directions—we'nima. The singer points literally to the direction mentioned in the text. If he is facing north but mentions the west, he points with his right hand across his face, or he turns to look west and point forward. To lure the rain gods and clouds, he beckons with a circling of the wrist. To invoke lightning, he zigzags downward.

2. The second highest level, the area in front of the face, is for the shi'-wana, the clouds and fog. For shi'wana, the palms are forward and sway to left and to right. For clouds, the hands mold the air. To express the speaking or singing of the shi'wana the right hand carries from the mouth horizontally forward.

3. The third level, from shoulder to waist, is for the people, the pueblo, and the sacred lake, respectively, downward and forward, with both palms. For ko'ʰname, the hands descend through this area, palms toward body, as this term for "beautiful" also implies "thanks."

4. At and below waist level are the horizontal fields, symbolized by a sweeping forward motion, and the ground and seeds. For growing crops, the right palm scoops upward to waist level, or higher.

The all-important rain falls through all areas—a vertical motion with lowered palms.

In place of the complexities of notation, the level and character of a few gestures are shown in the first line of Figure 7, by semistick figures and graph. A table can summarize a few of the most important gestures, which are associated with the appropriate words in the song.

Level	Concept	Design	Hands
1	Sky		
	Directions	Diagonal up	R index point
	Lightning	Zigzag down	R palm to L
2	Rain-bringers		
	Shi'wana	Lateral	R, L palms forward
	Shi'wana speaks	Forward, horizontal	R index lead
	Clouds, fog	Lateral arc	R, L palms in
3	People		
	Thanks	Vertical down	R, L palms up, then in
4	Ground		
	Fields	Forward, horizontal	R, L palms down
	Crops grow	Vertical up	R palm up
1–4	Rain falls	Vertical down	R, L palms in or down

Fig. 7. *Tablita* Dance Slow Entrance song, with texts. Some cadenzas are omitted.

Song Texts[5]

Slow dance:

A. me'šu ka'yu   we' nʸima ko'ʔowa te'rašu   ši'wana
   Early this morning from we'nima from a beautiful lake arise the shi'-
                                                              wana,

   si'wana   gʔa'naya   ša'tuwitʸa'nisa   heheya heheya
   shī'wana.   Their mother   is preparing   her offspring

   ko'tʸitʸi ko'meše   tu'we   ka'čanoma
   Cochití to visit; [she] lures [them] so it will rain.

   sko'wiyata'noma hi'na hi'na
   It is being prepared.

A'. (Repeat)

B. ya'ne ya'ne ya' heho' ha he'ya he'ya ya'we ʔa we'ʔawiyo'

C. tu'we   tʸ'itʸu   ši' wana   kʔo'ʰname   he'natʸe   tʸu'weša
   Called from north the shi'wana beautifully clouds are luring

   he'yawina winaya
   for the fields.

C'. tu'we pu'nʸi   ši'wana   kʔo'ʰname   he'yaši   tʸu'weša   he'yawina
    Called from west the shi'wana beautifully fog are luring for the fields.

D. he'yawina   haheya'ne   ha'heha'wi   he'yawi'na   he'ya   heya'
   ši'wana   kʰaca'noma
   The shi'wana are speaking.

D'. ši'wana   kʰuyu ta'noma
    The shi'wana are singing.

Fast dance:

A. y   he'hayi'ha' . . .
   ka'weštimayo'   ši'wana   he'natʸe   tʸu'weša   ha'hiya
   The northern   shi'wana   clouds   are luring;

A'. ci'pinayo'   ši'wana   he'yaši   tʸu'weša   ha'hiya
    The western   shī'wana fog   are luring.

B. o ho . . . ha . . . tʸi'tʸu   ši'wana   mo'moka'nʸite   ka'čanoma
   From the west shī'wana with thunder and lightning make rain.

B'. oho . . . ha . . . pu'nʸi   ši'wana   mo'moka'nʸite   ka'čanoma
    From the south shī'wana with thunder and lightning make rain.

[5] Dr. Hans Kurath worked out the phonemic system of Keresan in interviews.
In the text transcriptions, the orthography conforms to the system approved by
the American Folklore Society. Thus, š represents *sh;* č is *ch;* c denotes *ts,* and ʔ
is a glottal stop.

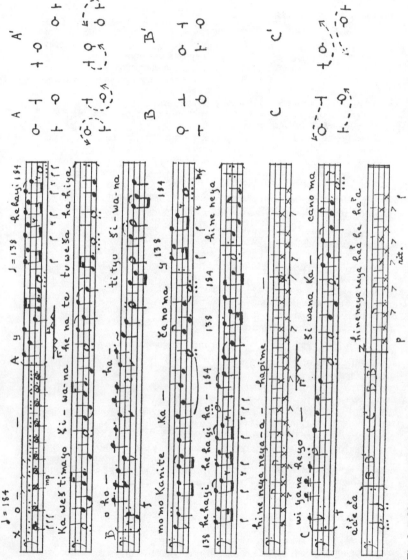

Fig. 8. *Tablita* Fast Dance, with texts, dancers' basic steps, and positions.

A. A'.

B. o ho ... ha ...   tʸi'tʸu   ši'wana   mo'moka'nʸite   ka'čanoma
From the south shi'wana are making raindrops so it will rain;

B'. oho ... ha ...   pu'nʸi   ši'wana   mo'moka'nʸite   ka'čanoma
from the east ...
y he'hayi'   he'hayi'ha   hi'nene'ya   hi'nene'ya   neya
ha'pime   hapi'me   hapime'   ha'pime   ha'pime

C. wiya'naheyo'   ši'wana   kʰaca'noma   a'a'e   a'a
The shī'wana are speaking.

C'. wiya'naheyo'   ši'wana   kʰuyuta'noma   a'a'e   a'a
The shī'wana are singing.

z. hi'nene'ya   ne'ya   ha'a   he ha'   a

In the course of an entire song the melody begins low, climbs to several peaks, is highest during nonsense syllables, and ends low. The levels of text and gesture follow a similar course, but they open and end on a middle level. Much of the meaning is implied rather than explicit. The four levels already mentioned call for the following set gestures:

(2) The singer addresses the shī'wana in we'nima.

(1) He calls clouds from the directions.

(2) He shapes clouds.

(1–4) Rain falls and beautifully covers the fields.

(3) The people receive the moisture and are thankful.

(2) The shī'wana are speaking and singing.

Singers can invent gestures for less codified expressions. Sacred clowns, if any, improvise frequently, though they sometimes use the set gestures. Sometimes the mimes move in unison, sometimes diversely.

PATTERN COMPARISONS

The Buffalo and *Tablita* dance types have several points in common. Both have a slow and a fast dance, with repetition of each section, and a complete, reversed repeat, thus a pervading pattern of duality.[6] The slow dance uses a trot; the fast dance, the same bouncing step for corn dancers and deer, though a distinctive prance for buffalo. Straight lines and sinister circuits carry through both types. Yet the structure, detail, and style differ. These are clearest in the music.

The Buffalo Dance differs from *Tablita* Dance in the division of each dance because of a tremolo A and a rhythmic B drum beat, with choreographic correspondence. Our Cochití singer claims provenience from the Comanche and Kiowa for this pattern and points out the analogous pat-

[6] This duality also pervades other aspects of the ceremonialism, as the moiety alternation (see above, pp. 193, 205, 305–313 *passim*, for instances).

Fig. 9. Weighted scales of songs.

terns of the Puebloan Comanche and Eagle Dances. Indeed, Great Plains songs and steps are sometimes featured in the Buffalo Dance. And, indeed, the binary structure of tremolo and beat is prominent in Central Plains Eagle,[7] Sun,[8] and other dances. Aboriginal Comanche song repertoires are almost extinct. Relationships by trade or raid with the Comanche are of long standing (Pueblos hunted buffalo in northern Texas) and continue by means of the powwow.

Despite the exotic structure, the Buffalo Dance has been thoroughly "pueblo-ized," as exemplified by the scales and melodic treatment of the songs (Fig. 9).

The Jicarilla song, Buffalo Dance, 1 (Fig. 1), contrasts with the *Tablita* Dance songs, especially with the first. The Buffalo song is pentatonic and repeats one simple rhythmic unit in descending trend. The *Tablita* Dance is tetratonic, with a semitone between tonic and second, but it accumulates additional notes in the course of shifts to two different "keys" in B and D (see inverted notes in Fig. 9).[9] The melody rises and falls in irregular, often rhapsodic phrases, in changing rhythms, and in varying dynamics. *Tablita* Dance, 2, has a hexatonic scale, four of the notes being basic; it has the same wide compass of thirteen tones and similar wide intervals, no tonal shift, but rhythmic shifts. Buffalo song 2 has a pentatonic scale with semitones between second and third, and between fifth and sixth; song 3 has a semitone between second and third in its pentatonic scale with twelve-tone compass. Both songs have bold cascades, rise and fall, ornaments, rhythmic shifts. All the songs are sung with a vibrant and exuberant voice.

The common elements and the mutations point to fundamental Pueblo characteristics. Line formation, tromp, pawing,[10] pyramidal song structure and contour, and rhythmic shifts find their prototypes in the sacred dances of the unmasked ka'tsīna. The *Tablita* Dance appears as an elaboration on the ancient style, especially in multiple formations of huge groups. In the course of centuries the two Buffalo dances and the structurally similar Eagle and Comanche dances have re-formed an exotic pattern into native style.

At all times, exultant creativity obeys basic patterns. Though Eagle and

[7] The Eagle-Calumet Dance complex and associated musical form, similar to the Buffalo fast dance structure, have been traced to the Pawnee and Omaha (Fenton and Kurath 1953). The Kiowa derive their Eagle Dance from the Omaha (Gamble 1952: 103).

[8] Parsons notes the prominence of the buffalo in the Great Plains Sun Dance (1939, II: 1037). Linton describes a Buffalo Dance in the Comanche Sun Dance (1935: 423). A Sioux Sun Dance song, recorded by Rhodes (Rec. 1420 B, 1), states the tune with drum tremolo, then repeats with rhythmic beat.

[9] For explanation of "weighted scales," see Kurath 1951: 135.

[10] The pawing is a mimetic variant of the typical Pueblo "foot-lifting" step, termed "antege" by the Tewa. It is the step of the Ka'tsīna dancers.

Comanche songs are traditional, Buffalo, *Tablita*, and many others are new for each occasion. But no improvisation is allowed. At the final performance, every note and every step show the careful rehearsal and painstaking co-operation of artists.

BIBLIOGRAPHY

Fenton, William N., and Gertrude P. Kurath
    1953. The Iroquois Eagle Dance. Bureau of American Ethnology, Bulletin 156. 324 pp.
Gamble, John
    1952. Changing Patterns in Kiowa Indian Dances. Acculturation in the Americas (29th International Congress of Americanists, Proceedings). University of Chicago Press. Pp. 94–104.
Kurath, Gertrude P.
    1951. Local Diversity in Iroquois Music and Dance. Part 6, Bureau of American Ethnology, Bulletin 149. Pp. 109–136.
    1957. Notation of a Pueblo Indian Corn Dance. Dance Notation Record: VIII, 4. Pp. 9–11.
Linton, Ralph
    1935. The Comanche Sun Dance. American Anthropologist 38: 420–428.
Parsons, Elsie Clews
    1939. Pueblo Indian Religion, I, II. University of Chicago Press. Pp. 1–549, 551–1275.
Rhodes, Willard
    n.d. Songs of the Sioux and Navaho. Ethnic Folkways Album 1401.

Appendix 44

A NOTE ON COCHITI LINGUISTICS
by J. R. Fox

Three languages are in constant use in Cochiti Pueblo: the indigenous Keresan, Spanish (introduced circa 1540), and English (from circa 1832). This note will first consider the range of use of each of these and then sketch briefly some features of the Cochiti dialect of Keresan.

As might be expected, the use of these languages is not random; each has its defined place, implicit or explicit, in the total linguistic usage of the village. There are roughly four major focuses of usage: age, sex, occasion, and faction.

AGE

If the population is divided roughly into four age groups (1–20, 20–40, 40–60, 80——), the ratio of each language spoken in each group will differ considerably. The oldest group speak largely Keresan and Spanish and use little English, some being almost totally ignorant of it. Their fluent Spanish (which they can neither read nor write) was learned from the children of Spanish-American residents in the pueblo (now few in number) with whom they played when young. Some members of this group, however, speak better English than do the younger people. These have usually worked for an extensive period outside the pueblo. Those who have rarely left the pueblo within their lifetime make up the core of the predominantly Spanish/Keresan speakers.

The 40–60 age group seem evenly divided between the three languages and are equally competent in all three.

The 20–40 group seem to have lost their fluency in Spanish while picking up a good deal of English. Two factors account for this: the relative absence of Spanish-speaking children during the socialization of this group, and wartime service, many of the group being veterans. Some even complain that they have "forgotten" Keresan, and indeed they are sometimes confused and embarrassed by this lack, though they seem competent enough in conversation. It may be that the Keresan they have forgotten is from the ceremonial variety (discussed below) rather than the colloquial.

The 1–20 age group know practically no Spanish, and are not yet fluent in Keresan. Some of them, it seems, never will be; parents complain that school makes the children forget their own language. High value is placed both on knowing the native tongue and on having a "modern" education.

NOTE.—The field work on which this appendix is based was made possible by the Social Science Research Council. I should like to thank Charles H. Lange, Evon Z. Vogt, Stanley Newman, Dell H. Hymes, and Irvine Davies for their help in this project. I also thank my wife for assistance in preparing the manuscript.

There is consequently a good deal of conflict in the school and in the home over the relative merits of English and Keresan, and the children, caught between two fires, turn out to be equally poor at both languages. Within the group, the most Keresan is probably spoken by the very youngest, who know little else. After about the age of eight, the influence of school, radio, records, and movies begins to tell, and English gains the upper hand, reaching its highest peak in the midteens. If the post-school adolescent returns to the pueblo to live, he may pick up more and better Keresan; if not, then his knowledge of it may dwindle to little more than a few conventional phrases. In any case, the linguistic standards of this young group are very low. No effort is made, for example, to produce some of the more difficult glottalized sounds.

The most potent influences in the change of the balance of languages over the eighty-year period under review have been the decrease in the number of Spanish residents in the pueblo, and the increase in educational opportunities, together with the influence of radio and television since the electrification of the pueblo.

SEX

In everyday dealings, the men use much more Spanish than do the women (neither use much English colloquially), the result of their contact with the local Spanish Americans as workers on farms nearby and in trade, etc. The women, being usually in the pueblo, have little need to use Spanish, and consequently are often better speakers of Keresan than the men, and chatter incessantly in it. The teaching of Keresan to the children is largely the woman's responsibility, and this maternal training is reflected in the fact that men now use a good many of the kinship terms that formerly were used exclusively by women. In cross-sex conversation, Keresan is used, but the men often speak Spanish with each other, particularly during card games at one of the two pueblo stores.

OCCASION

Ceremony. During ceremonies, whether in the kivas or at society meetings, Keresan is used exclusively. Moreover, it is very archaic, with a special lexicon and set of usages. The cardinal points, colors, and natural objects have their own ceremonial words. The kiva itself, colloquially referred to as čitya, is called on ceremonial occasions by its archaic name, šipapⁿ (the place of emergence in pueblo mythology). These usages are known to fewer and fewer men year by year. Women, though knowing some words, have little systematic knowledge of the ceremonial language.

Speeches. An archaic form of cadenced, repetitive Keresan prose is used in speeches. It is not a distinct subdialect like the ceremonial language but is rather comparable to our own rhetorical "public" style in oratory. We might call this "formal" Keresan, as contrasted with the ceremonial and colloquial. This mode is used for speeches in church by village officials, in marriage exhortations, and in council deliberations.

Conversation. Colloquial Keresan, English, and Spanish are all used in conversation, with the restrictions noted under age and sex above.

Relations with Outsiders. Spanish was a boon to interpueblo relations in that it provided a lingua franca for the diverse linguistic groups. It is still used for this purpose, but—perhaps as a result of the work of the Indian Service, which co-ordinates interpueblo activity—it is rapidly being replaced by English. Spanish is used exclusively in dealing wth local Spanish Americans, English in contacts with whites (which includes the local Catholic priests).

Songs. There are roughly three types of song: sacred, nonsacred, and popular. The sacred (corn-dance songs, katchina songs, grinding songs) are sung exclusively in archaic Keresan. The nonsacred songs (buffalo-dance, deer-dance—animal dances generally—travel songs, lullabies, occasional play songs) are sung largely in Keresan but can include odd choruses in Spanish, though these never amount to more than a few words; any extensive passages are sung in Keresan. If a song is borrowed from another pueblo, it is likely to be borrowed in its entirety, words and music. Hence Hopi and Zuni songs are sung in their native languages. A good many dance songs consist of conventional nonsense syllables and are valued for their tune rather than their words. Some old songs are unintelligible to anyone under sixty, for meanings and usages have changed over the years. Popular songs are the interpueblo "top forty," and often have verses in English and Spanish ("Oh, how I love you, honey! I don't care if you've been married sixteen times, I'll get you in the end.")

Greetings. Most greetings are in Keresan but some Spanish is used (the Spanish *bueno* is used alternately with the Keresan *rawa'e* as a reply). Owing to the in-marriage of Hopi girls, a few Hopi greetings are used, and a few Navaho words (*hakone* [good-by]) are used as humorous greetings by those who have been in Navaho country.

Baseball. At this important ceremonial event the linguistic pattern is well illustrated. On the field, English is the official language (it is also the language of abuse between the mothers of the competing teams). When Tewa-speaking teams play at Cochiti they are severely censured if they use anything but English on the field. It is considered unfair in the extreme to use "secret" instructions, i.e., those couched in Tewa. Off the field, however, the teams speak animatedly in their indigenous tongues, while the spectators alternate between calling out conventional baseball phrases in English ("Nobody walks," "your own time") and talking to each other in any of the languages. Spanish-American residents who come to watch join in vociferously in Spanish and are addressed in that tongue. Consultations between the teams—before, after, and midgame—are conducted in English and Spanish. The pueblo sense of the appropriate language for the appropriate occasion is thus clearly brought out at the ball game.

Faction

There is some overlap between the groupings by age and those by faction, but if one takes the factions as reference points there are some distinctions that are peculiar to this division. The ultranativists (the Conservatives) are the preservers of the linguistic, as well as the religious, ceremonial, and social, traditions. They therefore are the experts on ceremonial usage and place great emphasis on correctness in speech. Their standards of correctness are pedantic—hence they make excellent informants. At the other extreme the progressive element (the Progressives), which has usually had more education than its opponents, tends to use more English. The education of this group, however, has made its members sensitive to language and they often have very fine linguistic standards and are able to compare English intelligently with Keresan. The group of nativists who nevertheless support some progressive measures, such as electrification, and include a good many veterans, speak a good deal of English and correlate with the 20–40 age group by and large. Some make a concerted effort to learn and retain the ceremonial vocabulary; for others the effort is not worth the rewards. The moderates in the pueblo speak all three languages with some fluency, a fact which typifies their stand. They are drawn largely but by no means exclusively from the 40–60 group.

The rise and fall of factionalism, the presence and eventual decline of Spanish influence, the insistence on the use of English in schools, the intensification of government-sponsored interpueblo activity, the growth of interpueblo baseball, the tenacity of the traditional religious system— all these have contributed to the changes and shifts as well as to the constancies in the Cochiti linguistic scene.

One thing that has not happened and that one might expect would have happened is the blending of these languages into some composite, like Swahili among the diverse peoples of East Africa. This has never even been an issue on the Rio Grande, for several reasons. First, the pueblos do not see themselves as part of a merging and blending society. They have fought to maintain their integrity, and the language has been one of the diacritics of their "Indian" identification. Second, they found Spanish too useful as a lingua franca to want to contaminate it with the indigenous languages. Obviously its usefulness would have been seriously impaired if each pueblo had made up a mongrel version of its own. Third, the very structure of the Keresan language does not lend itself to extraneous additions. (This seems true for Tanoan also, to judge by the absence of extensive borrowing.) The total social setup—involving different pueblo groups, Spanish-American villages, English-speaking government, and tourists—has conspired to keep each language separate and assign it to its own sphere of influence.

Keresan is usually divided into two groups: The Western (Acoma and Laguna) and the Eastern, or Rio Grande (Cochiti, Santo Domingo, San Felipe, Santa Ana, and Zia, though Zia is sometimes classed as Western). The two dialects differ in some features of phonetics and lexicon, and while the grammatical structures are basically the same, enough differences of usage occur to cause difficulty in understanding between the two groups. Within the Eastern group there are many differences of pronunciation and usage. Thus one can easily identify a man's village by his speech; particularly noticeable is the "Italianate" pronunciation of the Santo Domingo, who "lean" on their vowels, giving them a sung quality. The Cochiti maintain that they are the only pueblo speaking the "straight" language. Their speech, it is true, has a flatter and more even sound than that of their immediate neighbors. Like the San Felipe, the Cochiti speak with fewer extremes of intonation than the Santo Domingo.

The relationship of Keresan to other Indian languages is uncertain. Sapir placed it in the Hokan-Siouan phylum but the accuracy of this has yet to be determined. Keresan studies are still in a tentative stage and careful surveys need to be made of all the dialects before any over-all patterns or reconstructions can be established with confidence. Previous studies have been carried out by Boas (1923, 1928) and Spencer (1946). Boas' work was largely on the Western dialect (Laguna) and though he worked on Cochiti, he published nothing on it. His account suffers from a failure to see certain basic similarities between categories which he insisted on separating. Spencer tries to give an over-all picture of the Keresan phonemic pattern which in some essentials does not seem to fit all the Cochiti data.

The following data on the Keresan language as spoken in Cochiti is essentially tentative and is intended as a first approximation which subsequent research will no doubt modify. Only a few features that may be of interest are presented here; I have tried to strike a balance between the interest of the specialist and the curiosity of the layman.

The Sounds of Keresan

Consonants[1]

	Bilabial	Alveolar	Retroflex	Alveopalatal	Velar	Glottal
Stops	p	t			k	'
Affricates		c		č		
Fricatives:						
slit						h
groove		s		š		
Nasal	m	n				
Semivowels	w				y	
Flap			r			

Features. Retroflexion (here symbolized by [.]) e.g., ha:č°cᵉ = man, ha:ç°cᵉ = rooster (male animal); Length: nasals; Aspiration (here symbolized by [°]: stops, affricates, and fricatives, e.g., č°.

Consonant Clusters

A common series of consonant clusters are the phonological "backbone" of the language. These consist of combinations of *p, t, k, c, č, s,* and *š,* followed by, or rather coarticulated with, *y,* ['],*y'*, and aspiration or *y°*. The series goes roughly as follows (only a few examples given):

k	k'	k°	ty	ty'	ty°
ky	ky'	ky°	s	s'	s°
t	t'	t°	sy	sy'	sy°

The glottal stop can appear with any of these consonants. As yet I have been unable to determine with certainty whether any of the above are separate phonemes and prefer to treat them as clusters, pending further evidence. Some of them are very rare and some never appear in the idiolects of young women or young people who learned more English than Keresan. Particularly prone to extinction are the retroflexed affricates and fricatives, and the glottalized consonants, which leads to some confusion (e.g., ka:š = knee, k'a:s = fish), but the difficulty of distinction is minimized by context and the general flexibility of the language situation.

The other most common series is the clustering of š with certain consonants: šk, šk', šty, šč, šp, škw, št, št'.

---

[1] To the reader unfamiliar with linguistic sound-charts, the following illustrations may help: c = *ts* as in *cats*; č = *ch* as in *church*; š = *sh* as in *shoe*; ' = breath catch. Others as in normal English equivalents.

Vowels[2]

	Front Rounded	Central Rounded	Back Unrounded	Back Rounded
High	i		ɯ	u
Higher mid	e			o
Higher low	ɛ			
Low		a		

Features. Length (e.g., t°ihya = dog, t°i:hya = far away); Labialization: the back unrounded vowels are often heavily labialized, sometimes to the extent of losing the actual sound early in the delivery and sounding like a protracted *w* (e.g., ta'ow = grandmother, old lady). Phonemically, labialization appears to be an allophone of the length phoneme appearing with the back rounded vowels. Tone and Stress: stress is used to make phonemic distinctions, but with some words a tone interval is used: šami (rising tone) = properly, šami (level tone) = already; t°ihya (level tone) = dog, t°ihya (falling tone) = born. Compare t°i:hya (level tone) = far away, where length rather than tone is the distinctive feature. Nasalization: cina = again, cina (with final vowel nasalized) = it's starting to get cloudy; ha:nu = female, ha:nu (with final vowel nasalized) = people. (c.f. ha:nuč = clan.)

THE STRUCTURE OF KERESAN WORDS

Syllables are commonly open (C + V), but can be closed (CVC), or be single phonemes. Combinations include the CV + CV + CV pattern: ku-na-tyu-mɛ (plentiful), and the CVC + CVC pattern: kač°-tat (it is raining.). European languages tend to have a large number of syllables which they combine in a number of ways. Keresan uses a relatively small number of syllables and distinguishes words on the basis of subtle re-positioning of the same elements. Take the word given above—ku-na-tyu-mɛ (plentiful): each of these syllables is a morphemic element in Keresan, but its meaning is derived from the context in which it occurs. Sometimes, as in the cited word, one cannot assign separate meanings to each morpheme but only to the whole sequence. In other contexts these morphemes might mean any of the following:

ku: (1) third person prefix of inflected words—ku-kač° (he is looking),

---

[2] Again, for those unfamiliar with linguistic sound-charts, the following illustrations may help: i = *i* as in the French word *si*; e = *e* as in the French *été*; ɛ = *e* as in *Betty*; a = *a* as in London English *father*; u = *oo* as in *cool*; o = *o* as in the French word *mot*; ɯ = *u* pronounced with lips flattened instead of rounded.

ku-kač°-nyi (they are looking); (2) *and,* when standing independently;
(3) an aspectual suffix; (4) the stem of the word "to be in a place"—kaku (he is [somewhere]), ša-ku—(you are [somewhere]).

na: indicator of non-singularity, suffix.

tyu: (1) stem "to hear"—s'owtyu (I heard it); (2) third person singular
dubitative mode—tyu-poca (he blew it), [when the action was not
witnessed by the speaker]).

mᵉ: (1) non-singular aspectual suffix—sa'wetyu-mᵉ (we heard it); (2)
together with *na* it indicates direction—pu-na-mᵉ (west). (Here *na*
appears again with changed meaning in a new context.)

Such examples could be multiplied to fill pages, for these are very common morphemes. To the nonpueblo listener this constant rearrangement of
elements gives the impression that the language is constantly repeating
the same sounds all the time (of course, it is), which makes learning it
very difficult. A further problem is the "whispering" effect, produced when
certain morpheme sequences are pronounced slowly, or alone, or at the
end of utterances. This effect does not occur in rapid speech. It seems to
result from a heavy aspiration of a consonant, which leaves the remaining
morphemes to be spoken "through" the aspiration and hence whispered.
As this does not make any phonemic difference in Keresan it is ignored
here, but is conventionally written with raised letters—sety°ᵉⁿʸⁱʷᵃ (I
laughed).

GRAMMAR

There are basically only two types of words in Keresan: those that are
inflected and those that are not. The inflected words are all inflected for
the same things, though the manner of inflection differs. To European
speakers there is something strange about a language that does not distinguish "noun" and "verb" and "adjective" and supply a separate paradigm for each, but Keresan ignores such distinctions and busies itself with
erecting other, equally valid, ones. This makes translation difficult. For
example, take -owanyi (hunt) and -owky'enyi (friend). Now in English
we can use "hunt" as noun or verb, but we would use a different paradigm for each. Similarly we can, with the addition of the prefix "be-," use
"friend" as a verb, but then it must follow the verb paradigm. In Cochiti
there is no such distinction. One paradigm is followed for both roots, and
the speaker uses this nominally or verbally, whichever is called for. Thus
s'owky'enyi may be translated "my friend," "I have a friend," "I am his
friend," or "we are friends"; and nowky'enyisi may be "I will befriend
him," "I am going to be his friend," "we are going to be friends." This
parallels s'owanyi, which may be "I hunted" (perfective), "my hunt" (one
that I organized), and nowanyisi, "I will hunt." The glosses are at best a

guide. The main point is that structurally all these words are equivalent. They are treated exactly alike. This will come out very clearly from one obvious example of what to us would be a nominal-verbal distinction:

> s'owtyu = I heard
> nowtyusi = I am going to hear
> atowtyu = did I hear?
> s'anaya = my mother
> nanayasi = I am going to be her [a] mother
> atanaya = is she my mother?

Inflected words are the major part of the language and form the basis of all utterances. They cover what would be nouns, verbs, and adjectives in English. If the reader finds this strange, let him imagine English with only the verbal paradigm. To the Cochiti, "there was a hunt" is equivalent to "they were hunting," and "I am going to be his friend" to "I will befriend him." Instead of two types of inflection they make one do, and possession is stated verbally—not "my head," but "I have a head" (sᵉ:naska).

What kind of work does the inflected word do? Within its structure are contained the following features:

Mood. There are altogether six moods: affirmative, dubitative, negative, imperative, negative imperative, and future imperative. The affirmative and dubitative make the distinction between facts that the speaker has personally experienced (affirmative), and those that he has not experienced, is surprised at, or questions. The negative mood differs only in some persons from the affirmative, and the negative imperative in only some persons from the imperative. The future imperative is infrequently used. The most common moods are the affirmative and dubitative and informants can give these with greater accuracy and completeness than the others.

Tense. There are only two tenses, future and non-future. Each word has only to specify whether or not the thing spoken of has yet to happen.

Number, Person, and Case. Singular, dual, or plural number is indicated, and subject and object are distinguished. First, second, and third person are distinguished in each category.

Aspect. There are a large number of aspectual suffixes that specify the nature of the action. The two most common are the perfective and the durative. The first states that the action ("having a head" is here treated as an action) has been or will be completed, the second that the action has been, is, or will be continued over a period of time. Other aspects such as iterative (over and over again), inchoative (about to be), and discontinuous (on and off over a period of time) are used. There are many more not yet identified. (See Whorf [1956] for a description of how a language can function without prime consideration of tense.)

Some meat will be put on these bones if we consider a few examples of all these features at work in the inflected word. The word for "hear," or "listen," has the root -*tyu*. To make the simple perfective, non-future affirmative, first-person singular of this word I add the prefix *s'ow*—*s'owtyu*— "I heard it." If I wish to retain all these elements (the aspect is here indicated by the absence of suffix) except the mood, i.e., change to dubitative, I change the *s'* to *t*—towtyu—"Did I hear it?" If I wish to make it future, I change it to the following: nowtyusi—"I am going to listen." If the future were dubitative, it would be nowtyuti. To put it into the durative, I add -*piča* to the stem-plus-pronoun (this would be "whispered" if the word was pronounced alone)—s'owtyu^piča. The paradigm for the non-future perfective and durative and the future perfective is given in Table 1. The reader can work out for himself what the various morphemes indicate. This is only one way of inflecting roots. Some words change the personal pronoun prefix to indicate number rather than adding affixes of number. Others do not change the prefix but alter the aspectual suffix by infixation to achieve the same result (e.g., "pull," first person singular = syunu^sita; first person plural = syunu^sitia; first person dual = syunustan^t'i [syu-nu-sita-na-t'i]—this latter, in fact, combines both principles, altering the suffix in the plural and adding more morphemes in the dual). Some roots always suffix the affixes (e.g., caca-se = I breathe, cu-nye-si = I will move; or are even more complicated, e.g., tuwne-si-cu-nye-si = I will come back [i.e., move toward someone again in the future]). "Adjectives" characteristically suffix elements: kɯ-kanyi = it is red (affirmative), kɯ-tanyi = red? (surprise).

TABLE 1

Inflection of -tyu ("hear," "listen")

NON-FUTURE

		Perfective	
		Affirmative	Dubitative
Singular	1	s'owtyu	towtyu
	2	šowtyu	čowtyu
	3	kowtyu	čowtyu
Plural	1	sa'wetyumɛ	ta'wetyumɛ
	2	ša'wetyumɛ	ča'wetyumɛ
	3	ka'wetyumɛ	ča'wetyumɛ
Dual	1	s'owtyumɛt'i	towtyumɛt'i
	2	šowtyumɛt'i	čowtyumɛt'i
	3	kowtyumɛt'i	čowtyumɛt'i
		Durative	
Singular	1	s'owtyupiča	towtyupiča
	2	šowtyupiča	čowtyupiča
	3	kowtyupiča	čowtyupiča

Plural	1	sawatyupiča	tawatyupiča
	2	šawatyupiča	čawatyupiča
	3	kawatyupiča	čawatyupiča
Dual	1	s'owtyupičanat'i	towtyupičanat'i
	2	šowtyupičanat'i	ȼowtyupičanat'i
	3	kowtyupičanat'i	čowtyupičanat'i
FUTURE			
Singular	1	nowtyusi	nowtyuti
	2	nowtyušu	nowtyuču
	3	nowtyuku	nowtyutyu
Plural	1	nowatyumɛsutrusa	nowatyumɛtutrusa
	2	nowatyumɛkutrusa	nowatyumɛtyutrusa
	3	nowatyumɛku'sa	nowatyumɛtyu'usa
Dual	1	nowtyumɛt'isu'ču	nowtyumɛt'ituču
	2	nowtyumɛt'iku'ču	nowtyumɛt'ityutru
	3	nowtyumɛt'iku	nowtyumɛt'ityu

The class of uninflected words includes independent personal pronouns, interrogatives, correlatives, locatives, numerals, and negatives. A number of substantives (e.g., parts of the body) have an independent form that can be used if the speaker does not want to introduce possession, aspect, etc. Some words can never be used without inflection—e.g., s'owky'enyi (my friend). To say "a friend," one would use the third person—kowky'enyi, "somebody's friend."

ONE TYPE OF TRANSITIVE INFLECTION

To give some idea of the internal complexity of the Keresan inflected word, we will here examine one type of inflection which is geared to making precise the subject-object distinction in a transitive word. Let us take the affirmative mood of the word "see" (-kač°).[3] Obviously one sees someone and therefore there is always an object, but this is not always specified. When such specification is absent, the paradigm employed is what we might call the simple paradigm—that in which the object is indefinite. This will be similar to that for the word "hear," given above. Table 2 shows this paradigm for the perfective and the future perfective. When we wish to specify the number of the object, however, another scheme is used. The scheme for the perfective non-future is given below.

[3] The following inflection of the root -kač° is used to describe seeing a person or persons. For seeing things or events another inflection is used, e.g., nya-wa-kač°-si = I am going to see (something).

TABLE 2

Non-future Perfective and Future, Affirmative Mood, of -kač° ("see ")

		Non-future perfective	Future
Singular	1	syukač°	nyukač°si
	2	šukač°	nyukač°su
	3	kukač°	nyukač°ku
Plural	1	syukač°nyi	nyukač°nyisutrusa
	2	šukač°nyi	nyukač°nyikutrusa
	3	kukač°nyi	nyukač°nyiku'usa
Dual	1	syukač°nyt'i	nyukač°nyt'isutru
	2	šukač°nyt'i	nyukač°nyt'ikutru
	3	kukač°nyt'i	nyukač°nyt'iku

Non-future perfective of "see"

	Object persons		
Subject persons	1	2	3
1	sow-kač°	šow-kač°	syu-kač°
2	ṭyu-kač°	čow-kač°	šu-kač°
3	šku-kač	kuču-kač°	ku-kač°

Here both subject and object are singular and are marked as such by zero morphemes (i.e., the absence of a morpheme is the indicator). The actual morpheme sequence goes:

1	2	3	4
syu-	φ	-kač°-	φ
persons are first subject and third object	object singular	action is seeing	subject singular

If the object were dual, then the morpheme -'u would be introduced—syu'ukač°:

1	2	3	4
syu-	-'u-	-kač°-	φ
as above	object dual	as above	as above

So syu'ukač° = I saw those two. If the object were plural, then the morpheme -'a- would be used: syu'akač° = I saw those many . . .

In the above examples the subject has been kept constant at singular. If we wish to make it plural, we introduce the plural perfective aspect number suffix for this paradigm which we have seen before:-nyi, or for a dual subject nyt'i. Thus šku'akač°nyt'i = those two saw all of us:

1	2	3	4	5
šku-	-'a-	-kačʰ°	ny-	t'i
persons are	object plural	action is	subject non-	subject dual
third-person		seeing	singular	
subject and				
first-person				
object				

šku'akač°nyᵗ'ⁱ ha:č°cᵉ su ruɯ'ma čitya = those two men saw all of us over by the kiva yesterday.

For purposes of comparison with the future scheme, Table 3 gives the whole scheme for first-to-third and third-to-first persons.

TABLE 3

First Person to Third Person and Third Person to First Person in Non-future, Affirmative Mood, of -kačʰ° ("see")

		Object persons	
	3 S.	3 P.	3 D.
Subject 1 S.	syu-kačʰ°	syu'a-kačʰ°	syu'u-kačʰ°
persons 1 P.	syu-kačʰ°-nyi	syu'a-kačʰ°-nyi	syu'u-kačʰ°-nyi
1 D.	syu-kačʰ°-nyt'i	syu'a-kačʰ°-nyt'i	syu'u-kačʰ°-nyt'i
	1 S.	1 P.	1 D.
Subject 3 S.	šku-kačʰ°	šku'a-kac°	sku'u-kačʰ°
persons 3 P.	šku-kačʰ°-nyi	šku'a-kac°-nyi	sku'u-kačʰ°-nyi
3 D.	šku-kačʰ°-nyt'i	šku'a-kac°-nyt'i	sku'u-kačʰ°-nyt'i

Future Perfective of "see"

I am less certain of the accuracy of this analysis, as many forms are rarely used and difficult to determine. Here again, however, there is a simple paradigm—the third-person indefinite (see Table 2); the pronouns are suffixed rather than prefixed as in the non-future. The most common future prefix is *n-* and replaces in this paradigm the first consonant of the word. Other paradigms differ in this according to the nature of the prefixes in the non-future. The change is easy to follow in this case:

Non-future	Future
syukačʰ° = I saw (somebody)	nyukačʰ°si = I am going to see (somebody)
Compare	
s'owky'enyi = my friend	nowky'enyisi = we are going to be friends.

The scheme for the subject-object relation, however, though using the same elements as in the non-future, differs from it. Thus syu'ukačʰ°nyi = we saw those two; nyukačʰ°nyisyu'uma = we two will see them all.

1	2	3	4	5	6
n(yu)-	-kač°-	-nyi-	-syu-	-'u-	-ma
time is	action is	object is	persons are	subject is	(mark of
future	seeing	plural	first subject,	dual	future
			third object		transitive)

Thus -nyi- and -'u- still indicate plural and dual, respectively, but in the future they change their reference to object-subject rather than subject-object.

The general scheme of suffixes for the future transitive definite is as follows:

	Object persons		
Subject persons	1	2	3
1	nowkač°-si	nyukač°-šowma	nyukač°-si
2	nyukač°-tyu'ma	nowkač°-šu	nyukač°-šu
3	nyukač°-šku'ma	nyukač°-kuču'ma	nyukač°-ku

In all forms except those of the third-person object, the morphemes -'a- and -'u- indicate plural and dual subject, and -nyi- and -nyt'i- plural and dual object.[4] In the forms involving a third-person object the number of the subject is indicated not by the above morphemes but by the special forms shown in the simple paradigm (Table 2). These forms parallel some characteristic non-future prefixes.

For comparison with the non-future, the scheme for first person to third person and third person to first person is given in Table 4. A comparison of Tables 3 and 4 should bring out the differences. This is a further

TABLE 4

First Person to Third Person and Third Person to First Person in Future, Affirmative Mood, of -kač° ("see")

		Object persons		
		3 S.	3 P.	3 D.
Subject	1 S.	nyu-kač°-si	nyu-kač°-nyi-si	nyu-kač°-nyt'i-si
persons	1 P.	nyu-kač°-sutrusa	nyu-kač°-nyi-sutrusa	nyu-kač°-nyt'i-sutrusa
	1 D.	nyu-kač°-sutru	nyu-kač°-nyi-sutru	nyu-kač°-nyt'i-sutru
		1 S.	1 P.	1 D.
Subject	3 S.	nyu-kač°-šku'ma	nyu-kač°-nyi-šku'ma	nyu-kač°-nyt'i-šku'ma
persons	3 P.	nyu-kač°-šku'ama	nyu-kač°-nyi-šku'ama	nyu-kač°-nyt'i-šku'ama
	3 D.	nyu-kač°-šku'uma	nyu-kač°-nyi-šku'uma	nyu-kač°-nyt'i-šku'uma

[4] In the non-future of some inflected words, when the aspect suffix does not change to indicate number of subject, -'u- and -'a- act as dual and plural subject indicators in the same pre-stem position which they occupy as object indicators for -kač°.

illustration of the importance of position and environment as they affect the meanings of Keresan morphemes.

As stressed before, this is only one type of inflection and only one possible analysis of it. More data may complicate or simplify the whole scheme. When it comes to actual usage there are further complications. For example, if one clearly states the number and nature of the objects of an action, then there is no need to state this in the transitive word itself: one uses the simple inflection:

hᵉ   tyu'me   nowanyi'isutrusa   Navaho = we are going to kill those
those   two   we will kill   Navaho   two Navaho

Here the object is clearly stated (hᵉ tyu'me . . . Navaho) and so "we will kill" uses the simple plural form. Had the statement been "we will kill those two" without the object's being stated independently, it would have been rendered

nowanyityit'isutrusa— n(ow)-   -anyi-   -tyit'i-   -sutrusa
                      future   kill   dual object   first plural subject.

The whole field of usage in this transitive area is loose, and some forms are, by pure convention, never used. Moreover, conventional misuse of some forms has been standardized in terms of common understanding— even though it violates the linguist's careful analysis.

EXAMPLES OF THE USE OF NON-FUTURE AND FUTURE

(1) I hit him because he hit me = syuk'ac kyᵉ'mᵉ škuk'ac
(2) I am going to help you because I like you = nyumacanyišoma kyᵉ'mᵉ šowcima
(3) I am going to be his friend because he helped you = nowky'-enyisi kyᵉ'mᵉ kučumaca

In (2) and (3), -nyi- occurs as the "stem classifier" and not a plural prefix as in the inflection we have analyzed. Another example of the morpheme-position-environment-meaning complex.

This analysis of the transitive word enables us to understand the nature of certain inflections commonly used with kinship terms. For example, the word for "father" would normally be construed as follows:[5]

1st person singular: s'anaštyu = my father (you are my father, I have a father, I am his father)
2nd person singular: kuɪ'č°naštyu = your father (he is your father, you have a father)

---

[5] Boas thought this was a separate type of "noun class" delineated by these prefixes.

3rd person singular: k'anaštyu = his father (he is his father, he has a
father)

The second person here, as the second of the glosses shows, is the third-
to-second pronoun prefix. Thus kɯ'č°naštyu t'i'ya kaku = here is your
father—he is your father [and] here he is. Remembering our "verbal"
approach to the inflected words, a better translation would be "he
fathered you" and for s'anaštyu, "you fathered me." This latter would
correctly be an instance of the second-to-first direct address, and the
reference would be: škanaštyu—"he fathered me," "the one who fathered
me." In fact either is used as a reference, the first being more common.
This is largely due to the use of another word—umu—as a term of address,
thus releasing s'anaštyu for referential purposes only. All this could be
pursued further, but this brief analysis will show how a study of language
can help the ethnographer in analyzing other aspects of culture which
bear linguistic labels.

CONCLUSION

The over-all impression of the Cochiti language is that of a series of
oppositions. Inflected versus not-inflected, future versus not-future,
singular versus not-singular, certain versus not-certain, completed versus
not-completed. The fact that what is and what has yet to be, and that
what is certain and what is uncertain are the basic distinctions in this
language makes conjecture on the psychology of the people tempting. But
that subject does not lie within the limits of this brief note.

BIBLIOGRAPHY

Boas, Franz
    1928. Keresan Texts. American Ethnological Society—Publication 8.
    1923. A Keresan Text. International Journal of American Linguistics 2. 171–
    80.
Spencer, R. F.
    1946. The Phonemes of Keresan. International Journal of American Linguis-
    tics 12, 4, 229–36.
Whorf, B. L.
    1956. Language, Thought, and Reality. The Technology Press, MIT.

BIBLIOGRAPHY AND INDEX

Bibliography

Abel, Annie H.
   1915. The Official Correspondence of James S. Calhoun while Indian
   Agent at Santa Fe and Superintendent of Indian Affairs in New
   Mexico. Office of Indian Affairs, Washington, D. C. 554 pp.

Aberle, Sophie D.
   1948. The Pueblo Indians of New Mexico: Their Land, Economy and
   Civil Organization. Memoirs of the American Anthropological Association 70. 93 pp.

Adair, John.
   1944. The Navajo and Pueblo Silversmiths. University of Oklahoma
   Press, Norman, Okla. 220 pp.

Adams, Eleanor B., and Fray Angelico Chavez.
   1956. The Missions of New Mexico, 1776: A Description by Fray
   Francisco Atanasio Domínguez; with other Contemporary Documents. University of New Mexico Press, Albuquerque, N. M.

Applegate, Frank G.
   1929. Indian Stories from the Pueblos. J. B. Lippincott Company, Philadelphia. 178 pp.

Bailey, Florence M.
   1928. Birds of New Mexico. Judd and Detweiler, Inc., Washington,
   D. C. 807 pp.

Bailey, R. W.
   1935. Epicycles of Erosion in the Valleys of the Colorado Plateau
   Province. Journal of Geology 43: 337–355.

Bailey, Vernon.
   1913. Life Zones and Crop Zones of New Mexico. Bureau of Biological
   Survey, North America Fauna 35. 100 pp.

Bancroft, Herbert H.
   1889. Arizona and New Mexico, 1530–1889. History of the Pacific
   States of North America XII. History Company, San Francisco. 829
   pp.

Bandelier, Adolph F.
   1880–92. Unpublished journals. Archives of the Museum of New Mexico, Santa Fe, N. M.
   1890–92. Final Report of Investigations among the Indians of the
   Southwestern United States, Carried on mainly in the years from

1880 to 1885, Parts I and II. Papers of the Archaeological Institute of America, American Series III and IV. 323 pp. and 591 pp.

1893. The Gilded Man (El Dorado) and Other Pictures of the Spanish Occupancy of America. D. Appleton & Company, Inc., New York. 302 pp.

1946. The Delight Makers. Dodd, Mead and Company, New York. (Earlier printings in 1890, 1916, 1918.) 490 pp.

Benedict, Ruth.
1931. Tales of the Cochiti Indians. Bureau of American Ethnology, Bulletin 98. 256 pp.

Benson, Lyman, and Robert A. Darrow.
1944. A Manual of Southwestern Desert Trees and Shrubs. University of Arizona, Biological Science Bulletin 6. 411 pp.

Biblioteca Nacional Archives.
V.d. *Legajo X*, Documents 30, 43, 59, 70, 74, 79, 80, 82.

Bloodgood, Dean W.
1930. The Ground Water of Middle Rio Grande Valley and Its Relation to Drainage. Agricultural Experiment Station of the New Mexico College of Agriculture and Mechanic Arts, Bulletin 184. 60 pp.

Bloom, Lansing B.
1913/14. New Mexico under Mexican Administration, 1821–1846. Old Santa Fe I: 3–49, 131–175, 235–287.
1928. Antonio Barreiro's *Ojeada Sobre Nuevo Mexico*. Publications in History V. Historical Society of New Mexico. 60 pp.
1935/36–38. Bourke on the Southwest. New Mexico Historical Review X: 271–322; XI: 217–282; XIII: 192–238.

Boas, Franz.
1921/22. Unpublished manuscripts and field notes. Library, American Philosophical Society, Philadelphia.

Bolton, Herbert E. (ed.).
1916. Spanish Explorations in the Southwest, 1542–1706. Charles Scribner's Sons, New York. 487 pp.

Bourke, John G.
1884. The Snake Dance of the Moquis of Arizona . . . with an account of the Tablet Dance of the Pueblo of Santo Domingo. Charles Scribner's Sons, New York. 371 pp.

Brand, Donald D.
1935. Prehistoric Trade in the Southwest. New Mexico Business Review 4: 202–209.
1938. Aboriginal Trade Routes for Sea Shells in the Southwest. Yearbook of the Association of Pacific Coast Geographers 4: 3–10.

1939. The Origin and Early Distribution of New World Cultivated Plants. Agricultural History 13: 109–117.

Brayer, Herbert O.
1939. Pueblo Indian Land Grants of the "Rio Abajo," New Mexico. Historical Series Bulletin I. University of New Mexico, Albuquerque, N. M. 135 pp.

Bryan, Kirk.
1925. Date of Channel Trenching (Arroyo Cutting) in the Arid Southwest. Science 62: 338–344.
1929. Flood-water Farming. Geographical Review XIX: 444–456.
1941. Pre-Columbian Agriculture in the Southwest, as Conditioned by Periods of Alluviation. Association of American Geographers, Annals 31: 219–242.

Bunzel, Ruth L.
1932. Zuñi Katcinas. Bureau of American Ethnology, Annual Report 47: 837–1086.

Castetter, Edward F.
1935. Uncultivated Native Plants Used as Sources of Food. Ethnobiological Studies in the American Southwest 1. University of New Mexico, Albuquerque, N. M. 62 pp.
1943. Early Tobacco Utilization and Cultivation in the American Southwest. American Anthropologist 45: 320–325.

———, and Willis H. Bell.
1942. Pima and Papago Indian Agriculture. Inter-Americana Studies I. University of New Mexico, Albuquerque, N. M. 245 pp.

Curtis, Edward S. (ed.).
1926. The North American Indian XVI. Plimpton Press, Norwood, Mass. 322 pp.

Cushing, Frank H.
1920. Zuñi Breadstuff. Museum of the American Indian, Heye Foundation, Indian Notes and Monographs VIII. 673 pp.

Dale, Edward Everett.
1951. The Indians of the Southwest. University of Oklahoma Press, Norman, Okla. 283 pp.

Densmore, Frances.
1938. Music of Santo Domingo Pueblo, New Mexico. Southwest Museum Papers 12. 186 pp.

Douglas, Frederic H.
1932. Modern Pueblo Indian Villages. Denver Art Museum Leaflets 45–46: 177–184.

1933. Modern Pueblo Pottery Types. Denver Art Museum Leaflets 53–54: 9–16.

1939. Weaving of the Keres Pueblos; Weaving of the Tiwa Pueblos and Jemez. Denver Art Museum Leaflets 91: 161–164.

Dumarest, Father Noël.
1919. Notes on Cochiti, New Mexico (ed. Elsie Clews Parsons). Memoirs of the American Anthropological Association VI: 139–236.

Dunn, Dorothy.
1952. The Art of Joe Herrera. El Palacio 59: 367–373.

Dutton, Bertha P.
1948. New Mexico Indians, Pocket Handbook. New Mexico Association of Indian Affairs, Santa Fe, N. M. 96 pp.

Eggan, Fred.
1950. Social Organization of the Western Pueblos. University of Chicago Press, Chicago. 373 pp.

Eickemeyer, Carl, and Lilian W. Eickemeyer.
1895. Among the Pueblo Indians. The Merriam Company, New York. 195 pp.

Ellis, Robert W.
1930. New Mexico Mineral Deposits Except Fuels. Geological Series Bulletin IV. University of New Mexico, Albuquerque, N. M. 148 pp.

Espinosa, J. Manuel.
1940. First Expedition of Vargas into New Mexico, 1692. University of New Mexico Press, Albuquerque, N. M. 319 pp.

Evans, Morris.
1945. New Mexico Dry-Farming Areas. Agricultural Experiment Station of the New Mexico College of Agriculture and Mechanic Arts, Bulletin 320. 34 pp.

Forde, C. Daryll.
1937. Habitat, Economy and Society. Harcourt, Brace and Company, New York. 500 pp.

Forrest, Earle R.
1929. Mission and Pueblos of the Old Southwest: Their Myths, Legends, Fiestas, and Ceremonies, with some accounts of the Indian tribes and their Dances; and of the Penitentes. The Arthur H. Clark Company, Cleveland. 386 pp.

Goldfrank, Esther S. (nee Esther Schiff).
1921. A Note on Twins. American Anthropologist 23: 387–388.
1927. The Social and Ceremonial Organization of Cochiti. Memoirs of the American Anthropological Association 33. 129 pp.

Hack, John T.
   1942. The Changing Physical Environment of the Hopi Indians of Arizona. Peabody Museum of American Archaeology and Ethnology Papers XXXV:1. Harvard University, Cambridge, Mass. 85 pp.

Hackett, Charles W. (ed.).
   1923–26–37. Historical Documents Relating to New Mexico, Nueva Vizcaya, and Approaches Thereto, to 1773, Collected by Adolph F. A. Bandelier and Fanny R. Bandelier. Carnegie Institution of Washington, Publication 330: I, II, III. 502 pp., 497 pp., 532 pp.
   1942. Revolt of the Pueblo Indians of New Mexico and Otermin's Attempted Reconquest, 1680–1682, Parts I and II. University of New Mexico Press, Albuquerque, N. M. ccx, 262 pp., 430 pp.

Hammond, George P., and Agapito Rey.
   1927. The Gallegos Relation of the Rodríguez Expedition to New Mexico. Publications in History IV. Historical Society of New Mexico. 69 pp.
   1929. Expedition into New Mexico made by Antonio de Espejo, 1582–1583, as Revealed in the Journal of Diego Pérez de Luxán, a Member of the Party. Quivira Society I. 143 pp.
   1938. New Mexico in 1602. Quivira Society VIII. 143 pp.

Harper, Allan G., Andrew R. Cordova, and Kalervo Oberg.
   1943. Man and Resources in the Middle Rio Grande Valley. Inter-Americana Studies II. University of New Mexico, Albuquerque, N. M. 156 pp.

Henderson, Junius, and John P. Harrington.
   1914. Ethnozoology of the Tewa Indians. Bureau of American Ethnology, Bulletin 56. 76 pp.

Hill, W. W.
   1938. The Agricultural and Hunting Methods of the Navaho Indians. Yale University Publications in Anthropology 18. 194 pp.
   1948. Navaho Trading and Trading Ritual: A Study in Cultural Dynamics. Southwestern Journal of Anthropology 4: 371–396.

Hodge, Frederick W. (ed.).
   1907–1910. Handbook of American Indians North of Mexico, Parts 1 and 2. Bureau of American Ethnology, Bulletin 30. 972 pp., 1,221 pp.

Hoebel, E. Adamson.
   1949. Man in the Primitive World. McGraw-Hill Book Company, New York. 543 pp.

Holmes, Jack D.
   1932. Carrying Water to the Indians. New Mexico Magazine 10: 22–23, 41.

Ickes, Anna W.
  1933. Mesa Land: The History and Romance of the American Southwest. Houghton Mifflin, Boston. 235 pp.

Jones, Volney H.
  1936. A Summary of Data on Aboriginal Cotton in the Southwest.
  Anthropological Series Bulletin I:5: 51–64. University of New Mexico,
  Albuquerque, N. M.

Kelly, Henry W.
  1940. Franciscan Missions of New Mexico, 1740–1760. New Mexico
  Historical Review XV: 345–368.

Kidder, Alfred V.
  1931–36. The Pottery of Pecos, I, II. Yale University Press, New Haven,
  Conn. 166 pp., 636 pp.

Kluckhohn, Clyde.
  1944. Navaho Witchcraft. Peabody Museum of American Archaeology
  and Ethnology Papers XXII:2. Harvard University, Cambridge, Mass.
  149 pp.

Kubler, George.
  1940. The Religious Architecture of New Mexico in the Colonial Period
  and Since the American Occupation. Contributions of the Taylor
  Museum. Colorado Springs, Colorado. 232 pp.

Lange, Charles H.
  1950. An Evaluation of Economic Factors in Cochiti Pueblo Culture
  Change. Unpublished dissertation, University of New Mexico Library. 522 pp.
  1950a. Notes on the Use of Turkeys by Pueblo Indians. El Palacio 57:
  204–209.
  1950b. Kings' Day Ceremonies at a Rio Grande Pueblo, January 6, 1940.
  El Palacio 58: 398–406.
  1952. The Feast Day Dance at Zia Pueblo, New Mexico, August 15,
  1951. Texas Journal of Science IV: 19–26.
  1952a. Problems in Acculturation at Cochiti Pueblo, New Mexico.
  Texas Journal of Science IV: 477–481.
  1952b. San Juan's Day at Cochiti Pueblo, New Mexico, 1894 and 1947.
  El Palacio 59: 175–182.
  1953. The Role of Economics in Cochiti Pueblo Culture Change. American Anthropologist 55: 674–694.
  1957. Tablita, or Corn, Dances of the Rio Grande Pueblo Indians.
  Texas Journal of Science IX: 59–74.
  1958. Recent Developments in Culture Change at Cochiti Pueblo, New
  Mexico. Texas Journal of Science X: 399–404.

Leonard, Irving A.
1932. The Mercurio Volante of Don Carlos de Sigüenza y Góngora, An Account of the First Expedition of Don Diego de Vargas into New Mexico in 1692. Quivira Society III. 136 pp.

Linney, Charles E., Fabian Garcia, and E. C. Hollinger.
1930. Climate as It Affects Crops and Ranges in New Mexico. Agricultural Experiment Station of the New Mexico College of Agriculture and Mechanic Arts, Bulletin 182. 84 pp.

Lowie, Robert H.
1940. An Introduction to Cultural Anthropology. 2d ed., Rinehart and Company, New York. 584 pp.

Lummis, Charles F.
1928. The Land of Poco Tiempo. Charles Scribner's Sons, New York. 310 pp.

Matthews, Washington.
1884. Navajo Weavers. Bureau of American Ethnology, Annual Report 3: 375–391.

Merriam, C. Hart.
1898. Life Zones and Crop Zones of the United States. Biological Survey, Bulletin 10. 79 pp.

Morgan, Lewis H.
1877. Ancient Society. Charles H. Kerr and Company, Chicago. 570 pp.

Myer, Dillon S.
1951. The Program of the Bureau of Indian Affairs. Journal of Negro Education XX: 346–353. (Reprinted by the United States Indian Service, August 15, 1951.)

Nations, Walter W.
1950. Annual Report of Division of Extension and Credit, January 1, 1950–December 31, 1950. United Pueblos Agency, Albuquerque, N. M. (Mimeographed.)

Northrup, Stuart A.
1944. Minerals of New Mexico. University of New Mexico Press, Albuquerque, N. M. 387 pp.

Parsons, Elsie Clews.
N.d. Notes and photographs, unpublished, Library, American Philosophical Society, Philadelphia.
1925. The Pueblo of Jemez. Yale University Press, New Haven, Conn. 144 pp.
1929. The Social Organization of the Tewa of New Mexico. Memoirs of the American Anthropological Association 36. 309 pp.

1932. The Kinship Nomenclature of the Pueblo Indians. American Anthropologist 34: 377–389.

1936. Taos Pueblo. General Series in Anthropology 2. 121 pp.

1939. Pueblo Indian Religion, I, II. University of Chicago Press, Chicago. Pp. 549, 551–1275.

Payne, Charles B.
1943–44–45–46. Annual Reports of Extension Work, United Pueblos Agency, Division of Extension and Industry. United Pueblos Agency, Albuquerque, N. M. (Mimeographed.)

Poore, Henry R.
1894. Condition of 16 New Mexico Indian Pueblos, 1890. Report on Indians Taxed and Indians Not Taxed in the United States (except Alaska) at the Eleventh Census: 1890. Department of the Interior, Census Office, 52d Cong., 1st sess., H. Misc. Doc. No. 340, Part 15: 424–440.

Reed, Erik K.
1951. Turkeys in Southwestern Archaeology. El Palacio 58: 195–205.

Robbins, Wilfred W., John P. Harrington, and Barbara Freire-Marreco.
1916. Ethnobotany of the Tewa Indians. Bureau of American Ethnology, Bulletin 55. 124 pp.

Roberts, Frank H. H., Jr.
1939. Archaeological Remains in the Whitewater District, Eastern Arizona, Part I, House Types. Bureau of American Ethnology, Bulletin 121. 276 pp.

Romer, Alfred S.
1941. Man and the Vertebrates. University of Chicago Press, Chicago. 437 pp.

Sanchez, Pedro.
1895. Report to Commissioner of Indian Affairs, Santa Fe, August 8, 1883, Pueblos in New Mexico. Report on Indians Taxed and Indians Not Taxed in the United States (except Alaska) at the Eleventh Census: 1890. Department of the Interior, Census Office, 52d Cong., 1st sess., Misc. Doc. of House, 1891–92, Vol. 50, Part 6: 414.

Schiff, Esther. See Goldfrank, Esther S.

Scholes, France V.
1929. Documents for the History of the New Mexican Missions in the Seventeenth Century. New Mexico Historical Review IV: 45–58.

1937. Church and State in New Mexico, 1610–1650. Historical Society of New Mexico, Publications in History VII. 206 pp.

1942. Troublous Times in New Mexico, 1659–1670. Historical Society of New Mexico, Publications in History XI. 276 pp.

———, and Lansing B. Bloom.
   1944/45. Friar Personnel and Mission Chronology, 1598–1629. New
   Mexico Historical Review XIX: 319–336; XX: 58–82.

Schulman, Edmund.
   1938. Nineteen Centuries of Rainfall History in the Southwest. American Meteorological Society, Bulletin 19: 211–215.

Shepard, Anna O.
   1936. The Technology of Pecos Pottery. Part II in Vol. II, The Pottery
   of Pecos, A. V. Kidder. Yale University Press, New Haven, Conn. Pp.
   389–587.

Spicer, Edward H.
   1940. Pascua: A Yaqui Village in Arizona. University of Chicago Press,
   Chicago. 319 pp.

Spier, Leslie.
   1924. Zuñi Weaving Technique. American Anthropologist 26: 64–85.
   1928. Havasupai Ethnography. American Museum of Natural History,
   Anthropological Papers XXIX: III: 83–392.
   1933. Yuman Tribes of the Gila River. University of Chicago Press,
   Chicago. 433 pp.

Starr, Frederick.
   1890–99. Scrapbook. University of Chicago Library, Archives.
   1897. New Mexico Trip, September, 1897. Manuscript diary in The
   Newberry Library, Chicago.
   1899. A Study of the Census of the Pueblo of Cochiti. Davenport Acad-
   emy of Sciences, Proceedings VII: 33–45.

Stephens, W. B.
   V.d. W. B. Stephens Collection, Folder 1904: Documents 2, 3. University of Texas Library, Archives.

Stevenson, James.
   1883. Illustrated Catalogue of the Collections Obtained from the Indians of New Mexico and Arizona in 1879. Bureau of American Ethnology, Annual Report 2: 307–422.

Stevenson, Matilda C.
   1894. The Sia. Bureau of American Ethnology, Annual Report 11: 3–
   157.

Stubbs, Stanley.
   1950. A Bird's-Eye View of the Pueblos. University of Oklahoma Press,
   Norman, Okla. 122 pp.

Sutherland, Mary.
   1947. Two Lives to Live. Family Circle, Inc., Newark, N. J. Family
   Circle 31: 30–31, 80–82.

Tanner, Clara Lee, and Anne Forbes.
  1948. Indian Arts Fund Collection of Paintings. El Palacio 55: 363–380.

Thomas, Alfred B. (ed.).
  1932. Forgotten Frontiers, A Study of the Spanish Indian Policy of Don Juan Bautista de Anza, Governor of New Mexico, 1777–1787. University of Oklahoma Press, Norman, Okla. 420 pp.
  1932a. Antonio de Bonilla and Spanish Plans for the Defense of New Mexico, 1772–1778. New Spain and the Anglo-American West I (historical contributions presented to Herbert Eugene Bolton). Los Angeles. Pp. 183–210.

Twitchell, Ralph E.
  1914. The Spanish Archives of New Mexico, I, II. The Torch Press, Cedar Rapids, Iowa. 525 pp., 683 pp.

United Pueblos Agency.
  1928–44. Annual Reports. Typewritten and mimeographed copies on file at United Pueblos Agency, Albuquerque, N. M.
  1939/40, 1940/41. United Pueblos Quarterly Bulletin, I, II. Mimeographed copies on file at United Pueblos Agency, Albuquerque, N. M.

United States Department of Agriculture.
  1938. Soils and Men. Yearbook of Agriculture, 1938. 1,232 pp.
  1941. Climate and Man. Yearbook of Agriculture, 1941. 1,248 pp.

United States Department of Commerce.
  1915. Indian Population in the United States and Alaska, 1910. Bureau of the Census. 285 pp.

Walpole, N. S.
  1899. Report of Agent for Pueblo Agency, Santa Fe, August 10, 1899. Department of the Interior, Annual Report 1899: 245–253.

White, Leslie A.
  1930. A Comparative Study of Keresan Medicine Societies. 23d International Congress of Americanists, Proceedings, 1928. New York. Pp. 604–619.
  1932. The Pueblo of San Felipe. Memoirs of the American Anthropological Association 38. 69 pp.
  1932a. The Acoma Indians. Bureau of American Ethnology, Annual Report 47: 17–192.
  1935. The Pueblo of Santo Domingo, New Mexico. Memoirs of the American Anthropological Association 43. 210 pp.
  1942. The Pueblo of Santa Ana, New Mexico. Memoirs of the American Anthropological Association 60. 360 pp.
  1943. Punche: Tobacco in New Mexico History. New Mexico Historical Review XVIII: 386–393.

1943a. New Material from Acoma. Bureau of American Ethnology, Bulletin 136: 305–359.

Whiting, Alfred F.
1939. Ethnobotany of the Hopi. Museum of Northern Arizona, Bulletin 15. 120 pp.

Whitman, William.
1940. The San Ildefonso of New Mexico. Acculturation in Seven American Indian Tribes, ed. Ralph Linton. D. Appleton-Century Company, New York. Pp. 390–462.
1947. The Pueblo Indians of San Ildefonso: A Changing Culture. Columbia University Press, New York. 164 pp.

Winship, George P.
1896. The Coronado Expedition, 1540–1542. Bureau of American Ethnology, Annual Report 14: 1: 329–598.

Wittfogel, Karl A., and Esther S. Goldfrank.
1943. Some Aspects of Pueblo Mythology and Society. Journal of American Folklore 56: 17–30.

Wooton, E. O., and P. C. Standley.
1915. Flora of New Mexico. Contributions from the United States National Herbarium 19. 794 pp.

Subject Index

Acoma Pueblo: cacique, 240; Catholic Church, ownership of, 61 n.; intermarriage with, 297, 377; ka'tsīna dances, 295; ka'tsīnas impersonated at Cochití, 297; kiva membership, 394; language, 297; pottery used at Cochití, 154; mentioned, 29
Adobe: 65, 68, 89, 144
Adolescence: 409–411
Adoption, clan: 214, 374, 382–385
Age groups: 394–396, 557–558
Agricultural implements, individually-owned: See Ax; Digging stick (dibble); Fork (wooden); Hoe; Plow; Saw; Scythe (reaping hook); Shovel; Sickle
Agricultural land holdings: 41–42, 440–443
—— ownership, community. See Cochití Pueblo; Community-owned property
——, individual: acquisition by—homesteading, 31, 38, 40, 221, 440; and inheritance, 40–41; and petition, 41; and trade or purchase, 40; attitudes toward, 36–37; land rights, legal aspects, 221–222; obligations of, 82–83; tracts preferred, 44; value of, 44
Agricultural machinery: 90–92. See Combine harvester; Hay (-baler); Threshing (machines); Tractor; Truck
—— produce: economic importance, 104, 189; ownership, 74, 369; statistics, 102–104, 437–438; statistics, Santa Ana, 103. See also Crops (aboriginal); Crops (European); Livestock
—— rites: cacique's fields, 83–85, 128, 207, 251, 331–333; decrease in, 332; Hopi, 332; irrigation ditches, 261, 330; March ceremonies, 329–333; October ceremonies, 362–363
—— techniques: See Crop rotation; Cultivated land; Dry farming; Fertilizers; Floodwater farming; Harvesting; Irrigation farming; Planting; Threshing

A'ha-ī-hī Ka'tsīna: 470, 507. See also Shrū'tzī Society head
Alfalfa: 99, 438, 440–443. See also Hay
Algodones: 80
Alguacilitos: canes, official, 204, 323; Council of Principales select, 192, 199, 210; qualifications, 199, 210; roster, 452–453; selection of, 192, 199, 210–211, 323
——, duties: announcements to tribe, 48, 84; assist war captains, 192, 199, 210–211; ceremonial retreats, 262–263, 270; communal herding, 107; communal hunts, 131–132; footraces, 211; gallo games, 211; grind gypsum for kiva plaster, 53, 211; guard ceremonies, 211, 260, 263, 330, 460; Ka'tsīna Cult, regarding, 199, 210–211, 287, 289; report to war captains, 211–212; serve ceremonial smokers, 211; witchcraft, guard against, 201, 211
All Saints' Day: 363
All Soul's Day: 363–364, 367
Almagre. See Ochre (red)
Almor (Almud): 364
Altars: bear effigies used, 256; cacique, installation of, 245; medicine society initiations, 258; solstice ceremonies, 262
Amole. See Yucca
Anega: 39. See also Fanega
Animal (hunting) dances: canes carried, 204, 210; Christmas season, 365–366, 539; fasting, 312; impersonators use Flint–Ku-sha'lī house, 265, 324–325, 540, 543; Kings' Day, 324–328, 539; occurrence, 324–329, 365–366, 539; taboos, sex, 312. See also Antelope; Buffalo; Deer; Eagle; Elk; Mountain sheep
Animal Ompī. See Warriors Society
Announcements, public: 48, 81–82, 84, 207, 209, 212
Antelope: Dance, 539, 540; disposition of carcass, 133, 443; hunting, 128, 130, 152; hunting tales, 443–445; ka'tsīna, 468–469, 483, 498–499;

274–275, 294, 302–303, 309, 325, 327–328, 330–331, 348, 416–417; goose, 294–295; hawk, sparrow, 139, 294–295, 308–309, 377; owl, 300, 302; parrot (macaw), 152, 275, 302, 327, 345, 348; stored, 139, 144, 174; turkey, 112–113, 235, 327. See various ka′tsīna descriptions in Appendix 26

Federal government: attitudes toward, 26, 224; census taken for, 368; educational facilities and program, 26–29, 36, 63, 65; elections, participation in, 32; extension services, 29–30; fencing project, 37; government "farmer," 29, 50, 56; health program and effects, 29, 319, 398–399; influence of, 13; land claims, 30, 218; liaison through governor, 29, 206; supervisory offices listed, 25–26; technical experts and services, 29–30, 45, 105; United Pueblos Agency, 25–26; Veterans insurance, 188; Veterans Training Program, 71, 174; welfare services, 29. See Factionalism; Military service

——, Indian agents: Sophie D. Aberle, 25–26; James S. Calhoun, 12, 110; Pedro Sánchez, 27; Walpole, 27, 80, 90–91; John Ward, 102; Major E. H. Wingfield, 12

Fence rider: 187, 218–219

Fences, Cochití Reservation: 37

Ferryboats: 60, 69, 182, 207, 362

Fertility: ceremonial emphasis on, 318–319, 330, 332, 335–336; Ku-sha′lī Society, 298; Kwe′rana Society, 308; Tablita dances, 323

Fertilizers: 84, 441–442

Fetishes: cacique makes, 223, 248; corn, 101, 247, 258–259, 328, 332, 363, 398, 399, 416–417; stone, 144, 241, 245, 247–248

Fire. See Clan names

Fire Society: 266–267

Fiscale and lieutenant fiscale: canes, 210, 294; Fiscale mayor, term used, 214; roster, 451–452; Santa Ana, Santo Domingo, 208; selection of, 195, 208, 272; Shī′kame head selects, 195–196, 208, 272

——, duties: announce church services, 209; Campo Santo, in charge of, 210;

civil community labor, 82, 182, 208; fiscalitos, supervision of, 208–209; physical structure of church, supervise care of, 63, 182, 207–208; resident priest, care for, 86, 182, 207–208; sermon after each Mass, 209

Fiscalitos: administer punishments, 225–226; announce activities to village, 48, 81–82, 207, 212; assist governors and sacristán, 212; assist fiscales, 63, 208–209, 212; canes, official, 212–213, 323; ceremonial smokers, serve, 212; dig graves, 418; impersonate "River Men," 338; peace officers, serve as, 212; qualifications, 212; retreats, guard society houses during, 262; roster, 454–455; selection of, 199, 212

Fish, Law of Abstinence concerning: 23

Fishing: 122, 140–141, 147–148, 207

Flagelantes. See Catholic Church (Penitentes)

Flint Society: assisted by Ku-sha′lī, 231, 262–263, 265, 300, 308, 355; cacique as member, 205, 237, 240, 259, 360; degrees within, 265–268, 272, 355; qualifications for membership, 264; roster, 457–458. See Flint Society (head)

——, duties: care for Ku-sha′lī, 264, 269–270, 420; combat witchcraft, 264; crises rites, 264; curing, 259–260, 264; formerly over Santa Clara Bear Society, 259; naming rites, 264; set fractures, 264; weather control, 264

——, head: cacique, 135, 195, 238–241, 252, 255, 264, 267, 287; cares for scalps, 239, 249–250, 283; ceremonial council, member of, 287; selects war captain and lieutenant, 194–196, 199, 220, 237, 252

——, house: animal dances, used during, 265, 324–325, 540, 543; cacique's "office," 135, 249, 265, 333; ownership, 55–56; shared with Ku-sha′lī, 55–56, 249, 265, 305; uses, 135–136, 210, 333, 363

Floodwater farming: 38, 44, 78–80

Food preparation: baking, 122; cooking under ramadas, 68, 102; commercial products, 102, 118–119; electricity used in, 105, 118, 435–436; fuel, 69,

tion, 247; water, medicine, sprinkled on seed corn by cacique, 332. *See also* Fire Society; Flint Society; Giant Society; Po'shai-añī Society; Shī'kame Society; Snake Society

——, headmen: anual selection of secular officers, 55, 192–196, 208, 220, 255–256, 261, 272; cacique installation, clothing worn for, 247; Flint headman (cacique) selects war captains, 194–196, 199, 220, 237, 252; Giant headman selects governors, 195–196, 204–205, 271; participate in installation of cacique, 245, 261; plant prayersticks before ditch opening, 261, 330; request for curing, 259; secular matters, influence upon, 192; Shī'kame headman selects *fiscales*, 195–196, 208, 272; social controls, 192

——, houses: built by community labor, 55, 181–182, 249; community-owned, 50, 55–56, 181–182, 249; electricity, 264; Flint house, 55–56; animal-dance impersonators use Flint–Ku-sha'lī house, 540, 543; Giant house, 55; retreats guarded, 210–211, 262; Shī'kame house, 55

——, retreats: general tribal purification, 262–263, 278, 285, 364; guarded by *alguacilitos*, 263; guarded by war captains, 200, 263; new members, 258; taboos, 262; mentioned, 203

Melon. *See* Clan names; Muskmelon; Watermelon

Mescalero. *See* Apache

Metates: bins, 42, 68, 116; chili, 68, 116, 144; corn, 68, 70, 116, 445; grades of, 116; single, 68; stone objects, 174–175; wheat, 68, 70

Middle Rio Grande Conservancy District. *See* Irrigation farming

Military Service: First World War, 187–188; Korean War, 188–189; Second World War, 188

Milpas: 39

Mineral pigments: 65, 144. *See also* Ochre (red)

Moieties (Pumpkin, Turquoise): clan strength within, 531; *see* Community houses; Conservatives, relation to, 530; defined, 389; endogamy, evi-

dence of former, 392–394; intermarriage, 392–394, 530; Keresan, 394; *see* Kiva; membership, 389–391; membership shifts, 390, 393; numerical division of, 391, 530; patrilineal, 367, 390; Progressives, relation to, 391–392, 530; values, characterized, 392

Mo'katch. *See* Mountain lion

Mo'katch (Mountain Lion) Ka'tsīna: 468, 482–483; was'tich, 468

Monogamy. *See* Marriage

Mo'ña-kai   Kē'awī-charla   (Black Speckled) Ka'tsīna Dance: 469, 502. *See also* Ku-sha'lī Society

Mo'ña-kai Shpū'la (Black Fawn) Ka'tsīna: 468, 483, 485

Montezuma: 228, 268, 337

Morada. See Catholic Church (*Penitentes*)

Mormonism: 20

Motor habits: 54, 369, 404–405

Motor vehicles: 74, 153

Mountain cottonwood: 146–147

Mountain goat. *See* Kash'ko Ka'tsīna

Mountain lion (cougar, Mo'katch): "brother" relationship of killers, 134–137, 275–277; ceremonial importance of, 234; Cougar Man, 129–130, 272; guardian spirit, 233–234; hunting, animal Ompī, 134, 275–277; hunting, ceremonial aspects, 135–137, 139, 275–276; hunting, decline in, 139; hunting, described, 128; Ka'tsīna, 468, 482–483; kiva firebox called Mo'katch, 54, 245; *Matalotes*, 277; meat not eaten, 136; medicine men, rituals, 135–137; occurrence, 6; skins buried as offerings, 136–137; skins not sold, 139; Stone Lion Shrines, 8 n. 3, 132. *See* Clan names

Mountain mahogany: 147, 166–167

Mountain sheep: 6, 128, 130, 539–540

Mules: 38, 107

Murals: church, 62; kiva, 51, 53–54

Muskmelons: 99, 101–102, 119–120, 169, 439, 442

Mythology: Creator (Cenquitye), 237; Frijoles Cañon, 7–8, 228; Ku-sha'lī, the first man, 299, 309; Ku-sha'lī, home of, 229, 299; Kwe'rana, home of, 229, 299; Montezuma tale, 228;

"Yerba de San Pedro": 151
Yucca: amole, referred to as, 148; gathered, 147–149; uses of—baskets, 142, 148, 163; and clan adoption rites, 385; and fibers, 148; and fish nets, 140, 147, 207; and food, 122–123, 148; and present-throwing, 148; and medicine, 148–149; and paint, 148; and paintbrush, 148, 291; and sandals, 163; and shampoo, 148

Zia Pueblo: Catholicism at, 20–21; cattle thievery, 224; feast day, 21, 202, 362; interpueblo marriage, 411; interpueblo relations, 238; Ka'tsīna Cult, 284; Keresan-speaking, 3; Ku-

sha'lī and Kwe'rana, curing, 298–299; pottery used at Cochití, 117, 154, 159; punishment at, 202, 254; *Tablitas*, 349; tale of Po'shaiyanne, 268; witchcraft, 254; mentioned, 23, 342

Zuñi Pueblo: attitude toward agricultural machinery, 91; floodwater farming, 78; food taboos, 271; ovens, 117; Pai'yat-yama, 349; pottery used at Cochití, 154; songs from Cochití, 351; songs to Cochití, 311, 559; suffix for personal names, 404; traders at Cochití, 155; transvestites, 415; water rights, 44; weaving, 165–166; mentioned, 110

Index of Sources Cited

Abel, Annie H.: 12, 110, 426
Aberle, Sophie D.: 25–26, 36, 38, 103, 191–192, 201 n.
Adair, John: 170–172
Adams, Eleanor B., and Fray Angelico Chavez: 11
Applegate, Frank G.: 328–329

Bailey, Florence M.: 5 n.4, 6 n.6
Bailey, R. W.: 6 n.5
Bailey, Vernon: 5, 6
Bancroft, Herbert H.: 10
Bandelier, Adolph F.: vii, 4–5, 8 n.3, 9, 12, 14–15, 18, 20, 22–24, 26–27, 30, 36 n.1, 37, 41–42, 44, 49–51, 57–58, 60, 66–69, 74–75, 78–82, 84–88, 90–91, 93–95, 97–99, 101, 106, 108, 111, 113–118, 120, 122–123, 125–126, 128, 132–133, 138–140, 143–149, 151–152, 158–159, 163–166, 168, 172, 178, 185, 193–194, 196–197, 203–204, 207–208, 210–211, 217, 220–225, 228–229, 237–243, 248–254, 257–258, 260–261, 263, 266–268, 270, 272–276, 279–281, 288, 291–292, 298–305, 308–309, 317–318, 322–323, 328, 331, 335–337, 342–343, 364–365, 367–368, 374–375, 380, 382, 388, 391–394, 399, 402, 406–407, 410–412, 415–417, 426, 439, 443, 462–463, 515

Benedict, Ruth: 7, 80, 228, 233, 349, 367
Benson, Lyman, and Robert A. Darrow: 6 n.6
Biblioteca Nacional Archives: 5 n.3, 11, 37–39, 46, 77–78, 80, 95, 164, 182, 344, 426
Bloodgood, Dean W.: 4
Bloom, Lansing B.: 12, 426. See Bourke, John G.
Boas, Franz: 54, 163, 233–236, 284, 286, 321, 384–385, 387, 403–404, 417, 561, 571 n.5
Bolton, Herbert E.: 9
Bourke, John G.: 167, 348; diary of, ed. by Lansing B. Bloom: 12–13, 46, 51, 70, 79, 88–89, 94, 105, 109–112, 115, 174, 375, 377, 515
Brand, Donald D.: 93–94, 154, 377
Brayer, Herbert O.: 36 n.1
Bryan, Kirk: 6, 78
Bunzel, Ruth L.: 349, 351

Castetter, Edward F.: 95–96, 149
——, and Willis H. Bell: 78, 87, 93–94
Chavez, Father Angelico: 23–24 n.10
Clabaugh, Stephen E.: 144 n.1
Cochití *Newsletter*: 338
Curtis, Edward S.: 126, 128–130, 152, 196, 199–200, 202–203, 214–215, 241, 257, 265–267, 269–272, 277,